NORTHROP FRYE

Selected Letters,
1934–1991

NORTHROP FRYE

Selected Letters,
1934–1991

Edited by ROBERT D. DENHAM

McFarland & Company, Inc., Publishers
Jefferson, North Carolina, and London

LIBRARY OF CONGRESS CATALOGUING-IN-PUBLICATION DATA

Frye, Northrop.
[Correspondence. Selections]
Northrop Frye : selected letters, 1934–1991 / edited by Robert D. Denham.
p.   cm.
Includes bibliographical references and index.

ISBN 978-0-7864-4362-8
softcover : 50# alkaline paper ∞

1. Frye, Northrop — Correspondence.   2. Critics — Canada — Correspondence.
I. Denham, Robert D.   II. Title.

PN75.F7A4 2009   801'.95092 — dc22 [B]   2009026660
British Library cataloguing data are available

On the cover: Barbara Braunohler. *Northrop Frye in His Role as
Victoria's Chancellor*, oil on canvas, 38" × 52", 1990-1991, Toronto, Ontario.

Manufactured in the United States of America

*McFarland & Company, Inc., Publishers
Box 611, Jefferson, North Carolina 28640
www.mcfarlandpub.com*

For Jean O'Grady and
Margaret Burgess

Acknowledgments

To the Frye Estate for permission to edit and publish selections from Frye's correspondence. To Victoria University for permission to publish Frye's letters from the Frye Fonds in the E.J. Pratt Library, Victoria University. To the University of British Columbia Library for copies of twenty-two of Frye's letters to Roy Daniells, which are in the Roy Daniells Fonds at the University of British Columbia Archives. To the Library and Archives of Canada for providing copies of Frye's correspondence with George Johnston and Miriam Waddington. To the Concordia University Library, Montreal, Canada, Special Collections for providing copies of Frye's letters to Irving Layton in the Layton Collection. To the Rare Book and Special Collections Division of McGill University for permission to publish Frye's letter to Lawrence M. Lande. To the Mills Memorial Library, McMaster University (William Ready Division of Archives and Research Collections) for permission to publish Frye's letters to John Gray and Frank Upjohn, which are in the Macmillan of Canada archives. To the Special Collections Library of the University of Michigan for permission to publish Frye's letter to Clarence D. Thorpe. To the Special Collections Library at Queen's University for permission to publish Frye's letters to Lorne Pierce. To the Harry Ransom Center of the University of Texas for providing copies of Frye's letters to Edith Sitwell. To the Thomas Fisher Rare Book Library of the University of Toronto Library for permission to publish Frye's letters to W.A. Deacon and Earle Birney, and to Madam Justice Wailan Low, literary executor for Earle Birney, for permission to reproduce Birney's holograph annotation to Frye's letter of 15 August 1947. To the United Church of Canada/Victoria University Archives, Toronto for permission to publish Frye's letters to Walter T. Brown and Edward W. Wallace. To Special Collections, University of Washington, for permission to publish Frye's letters to Robert B. Heilman. To the University Archives at Trent University for Frye's 1961 letter to A.J.M. Smith. To those who sent me copies of Frye's letters from their own correspondence files: Norman Friedman, William O. Fennell, Graham Forst, Hazard Adams, and Hugh Moorhouse.

Contents

Preface

Northrop Frye is one of the preeminent humanists of the last century. His reputation derives in large measure from *Anatomy of Criticism* (1957), which, twenty years after its publication, was the most frequently cited book in the arts and humanities by a writer born in the twentieth century. But Frye wrote some thirty books following the *Anatomy*, and The Collected Works of Northrop Frye (1996–2009, University of Toronto Press), which has republished his books in scholarly editions along with his previously uncollected essays, notebooks, diaries, and interviews, reveal that Frye's achievement is much larger than the formalist and structural principles on which his reputation was originally formed. Revisionary studies of his work have already begun to appear and will continue to do so as the large body of his previously unpublished work becomes more widely known. His correspondence is an important part of the expanding Frye canon. Along with the now published letters between him and his wife when they were young (Collected Works of Northrop Frye, vols. 1 and 2),[1] his letters represent a distinctive genre for those interested in Frye and his ideas, revealing features of his life and thought that are not available elsewhere.

Frye was a prodigious letter writer. The correspondence files in the Northrop Frye Fonds of the Victoria University Library, University of Toronto, contain more than eight-and-a-half meters of textual records. These are arranged in seven sub-series: general correspondence, family correspondence, correspondence with publishers, correspondence relating to translations of Frye's works, correspondence relating to speaking engagements, University of Toronto correspondence, and correspondence about media projects. The correspondence files in the Frye Fonds are estimated to contain some twenty thousand leaves, and although the total number of letters in these fonds has not been tallied, almost 5,200 written by Frye are in the general correspondence files. The majority of the letters in present selection, which contains 695 letters, are drawn from the general correspondence sub-series.

The general correspondence came to the Victoria University Library in five installments. Almost 3,500 letters by Frye and the accompanying letters and other materials from his correspondents were deposited in the library in 1988 when Frye's secretary, Jane Widdicombe, began to run out of file space in her Massey College office. Some 516 files, now archived in forty boxes, were then sent to the library. Another thirteen files (five boxes) were deposited in 1990. Following Frye's death in 1991, the remainder of the correspondence came to the Victoria University in three installments: 1991 (eighty-six files; thirteen boxes), 1992 (two files; one box), and 1993 (fifteen files; five boxes). A small number of letters that were in the possession of Jane Widdicombe were added to the collection in 2001.

These accessions contain a fairly complete record of Frye's correspondence from 1968 on, the year Jane Widdicombe became Frye's secretary and began keeping carbon typescripts of his letters.[2] Before this, the record is sketchy at best. *The Guide to the Northrop Frye*

1

Papers (Victoria University Library, 1993) lists seventeen repositories outside of Victoria University that contain Frye's letters (pp. 263–5), most of which are original holographs or typescripts. Carbon typescripts of the original letters in these repositories from 1968 and following are, as just said, in the Frye Fonds. The present selection includes some letters written before 1968 and housed in other repositories: letters to Roy Daniells, which are now in the archives at the University of British Columbia, correspondence with Edith Sitwell from the papers at the Harry Ransom Center at the University of Texas, letters to George Johnston housed in the Library and Archives Canada, several letters to administrators at Victoria University located in the papers of the United Church of Canada/Victoria University Archives, and correspondence with Miriam Waddington in the Library and Archives Canada. Other letters come from the special collections of the University of Washington, the Thomas Fisher Rare Book Collection at the University of Toronto, McGill University, McMaster University, the University of Michigan, Trent University, and Queen's University. A small number of additional letters written before 1968 have come from Frye's correspondents who responded to a call issued in the *Northrop Frye Newsletter* for readers to send me copies of Frye's letters to them.

I have selected for inclusion letters that reveal things about Frye's life and mind that seemed to me to be of interest and would provide still another window onto his personal, intellectual, and imaginative life. The letters contain what one might expect from a lifetime of letter writing by one who became a renowned international figure — requests for Frye to comment on manuscripts, to agree or disagree with various readings of his books, to offer an opinion on an issue, to give his imprimatur to diagrams of his categories, and the like. The letters also contain a great deal of personal or autobiographical information, which will be useful to Frye's next biographer: his response his financial woes, his request for promotion, and his experience as the Class of 1932 lecturer at Princeton (1954). In the earliest of his letters, he gives a detailed reaction to his first cousin, Donald Howard, of his time as a student preacher in a desolate Saskatchewan farming community (1934). The letters reveal Frye's attitudes toward scores of topics: the value of James Bond thrillers, the gap between faith and reason, surrealism, hippies, the Phil.M. degree, Milton's imagery, comparative literature, political hysteria in the U.S., the nature of the educated imagination, the fire stealing myth, anarchism, the teaching of religion in the university, the Proteus myth, the distinction between subjects and themes, the connection between Nietzsche and Yeats, the difference between cliché and aphorism, Dryden as a prose stylist, the relations between literature and religion, the honors curriculum at the University of Toronto, and science fiction. His speculations about numerous other topics can be tracked in the index. Frye makes judgments about other writers and critics (Irving Layton, J. Wilson Knight), expresses his feelings on the fussy rules of copy editors, gives his reasons for amalgamating the Ontario Curriculum Institute and the Ontario Institute for Studies in Education, and addresses scores of other issues.

Among the people to whom Frye wrote, almost always in reply, are those well known in literary studies and in the academic world generally. They include Edith Sitwell, Robert B. Heilman, Carolyn Kizer, A. Bartlett Giamatti, David Erdman, Hazard Adams, Dorothy Van Ghent, Jerome Brunner, Hans Jonas, Leon Edel, Howard Mumford Jones, Frank Kermode, Philip Wheelwright, F.R. Scott, Geoffrey Hartman, Harold Bloom, Roger Shattuck, Martin Amis, Angus Fletcher, Helen Vendler, William K. Wimsatt, Jr., Richard Kostelanetz, Germaine Breé, John Glassco, Wayne Booth, Tzvetan Todorov, Walter Ong, Paul Ricoeur, Herbert Lindenberger, Daryl Hine, Jaroslav Pelikan, James Reaney, Douglas LePan, Hugh Kenner, Joseph Campbell, Karl Polanyi, Ray Bradbury, Earle Birney, Margaret

Atwood, Paul Ricoeur, Al Purdy, M.H. Abrams, Jonathan Culler, Dennis Lee, and Pierre Trudeau. Countless other letters are to lesser-known people: academics, secondary school teachers, friends and relatives, colleagues, former students, readers of his books, and perfect strangers. Most of Frye's correspondents are in the U.S. and Canada, but his letters are posted to more than two dozen foreign countries. I have had to exclude a large body of specialized correspondence, for example, the sixty-nine letters in the Archives of the University of Western Ontario from Frye to Carl Klinck, most of which are related to the two editions of the *Literary History of Canada* in which Frye played a central role. Similarly, the present selection does not include samples of Frye's extensive correspondence with his publishers or letters related to speaking engagements, media projects, translations of his books, and faculty business.

For two of Frye's correspondents—his friends Roy Daniells and George Johnston—I have made a fairly generous selection: thirty-two letters to Daniells written over a forty-four year period and twenty-four to Johnston.

The letters are arranged chronologically, covering a fifty-seven year period from 1934 to 1991. The heading that accompanies each of the letters gives, in bold-face type, the name of the correspondent and the date the letter was written. The second line contains the location of the correspondent on the left, when this information is available, and for letters not written in Toronto, Frye's location on the right. Almost all of the letters were written in response to correspondence received. A brief headnote, intended to provide enough context for understanding Frye's response to his correspondents, accompanies most of the letters. The headnotes also list the location of Frye's letters that are not among his papers at the Victoria University Library or that were not sent by his correspondents to me. In the interest of saving space, I have excised Frye's complimentary closings (ordinarily "Yours sincerely"), his name, and his secretaries' initials. I have retained Frye's spellings, which often follow Canadian conventions. The endnotes explain things that might not be immediately obvious to some readers and provide other kinds of supplementary information.

All material in square brackets, including question marks for those few instances when I have not been able to decipher Frye's handwriting, is an editorial addition. The absence of a headnote means that the letter from Frye's correspondent is not extant; that Frye was not replying to a correspondent, having initiated the letter himself; or that the context of the letter is obvious from his reply.

I express my thanks to those who have answered my queries or provided other kinds of assistance: Germaine Warkentin, Jane Widdicombe, Hans Schwarz, Herbert Deinert, Janice Castro, Sheafe Satterthwaite, Kathryn L. Beam, Richard Workman, Jocelyn Godolphin, Sharon P. Larade, Anne Dondertman, Madame Justice Wailan Low, Chris Hives, Rick Stapleton, Nicholas Graham, Lisa Sherlock, Paul Gooch, Gillian Pearson, Gilles L. Durocher, Catherine Hobbs, Wendy Knechtel, Richard Virr, Bruce Whiteman, Margaret Burgess, Jodi Aoki, and Paul Banfield.

Abbreviations and Shortened Forms Used in the Headnotes and Endnotes

[Book titles are Frye's unless otherwise indicated]

AC *Anatomy of Criticism: Four Essays*. Princeton: Princeton University Press, 1957.

Ayre John Ayre, *Northrop Frye: A Biography*. Toronto: Random House, 1989.

BCM Northrop Frye and Jay Macpherson, *Biblical and Classical Myths: The Mythological Framework of Western Culture*. Toronto: University of Toronto Press, 2004.

BG *The Bush Garden: Essays on the Canadian Imagination*. Toronto: House of Anansi Press, 1971.

CP *The Critical Path: An Essay on the Social Context of Literary Criticism*. Bloomington: Indiana University Press, 1971.

DG *Divisions on a Ground: Essays on Canadian Culture*, ed. James Polk. Toronto: Anansi, 1982.

Diaries *The Diaries of Northrop Frye, 1942–1955*, ed. Robert D. Denham. Collected Works of Northrop Frye, vol. 8. Toronto: University of Toronto Press, 2001.

DV *The Double Vision: Language and Meaning in Religion*. Toronto: University of Toronto Press, 1991.

EAC *The Eternal Act of Creation: Essays, 1979–90*, ed. Robert D. Denham. Bloomington: Indiana University Press, 1993.

EI *The Educated Imagination*. Bloomington: Indiana University Press, 1964.

EIOW *"The Educated Imagination" and Other Writings on Critical Theory 1933–1963*, ed. Germaine Warkentin. Collected Works of Northrop Frye, vol. 21. Toronto: University of Toronto Press, 2006.

ENC *Northrop Frye's Writings on the Eighteenth and Nineteenth Centuries*, ed. Imre Salusinszky. Collected Works of Northrop Frye, vol. 17. Toronto: University of Toronto Press, 2005.

FI *Fables of Identity: Studies in Poetic Mythology*. New York: Harcourt, Brace & World, 1963.

FMW *Northrop Frye's Fiction and Miscellaneous Writings*, ed. Robert D. Denham and Michael Dolzani. Collected Works of Northrop Frye, vol. 25. Toronto: University of Toronto Press, 2007.

I *Interviews with Northrop Frye*, ed. Jean O'Grady. Collected Works of Northrop Frye, vol. 24. Toronto: University of Toronto Press, 2008.

LS *Northrop Frye on Literature and Society, 1936–1984: Unpublished Papers*, ed. Robert D. Denham. Collected Works of Northrop Frye, vol. 10. Toronto: University of Toronto Press, 2002.

MB *Northrop Frye on Milton and Blake*, ed. Angela Esterhammer. Collected Works of Northrop Frye, vol. 16. Toronto: University of Toronto Press, 2005.

MM *Myth and Metaphor: Selected Essays, 1974–1988*, ed. Robert D. Denham. Charlottesville: University Press of Virginia, 1990.

MythC *Mythologizing Canada: Essays on the Canadian Literary Imagination*, ed. Branko Gorjup. New York: Legas, 1997.

NFC *Northrop Frye in Conversation*, by David Cayley. Concord, ON: Anansi, 1992.

NFCanada *Northrop Frye on Canada*, ed. Jean O'Grady and David Staines. Collected Works of Northrop Frye, vol. 12. Toronto: University of Toronto Press, 2003.

NFCL *Northrop Frye on Culture and Literature: A Collection of Review Essays*, ed. Robert D. Denham. Chicago: University of Chicago Press, 1978.

NFF The Northrop Frye Fonds, Victoria University Library, University of Toronto.

NFHK *The Correspondence of Northrop Frye and Helen Kemp, 1932–1939*, ed. Robert D. Denham. 2 vols. Collected Works of Northrop Frye, vols. 1–2. Toronto: University of Toronto Press, 1996.

NFL Northrop Frye's library, now housed in the Victoria University Library, University of Toronto.

NFMC *Northrop Frye on Modern Culture*, ed. Jan Gorak. Collected Works of Northrop Frye, vol. 11. Toronto: University of Toronto Press, 2002.

NFR *Northrop Frye on Religion*, ed. Alvin A. Lee and Jean O'Grady. Collected Works of Northrop Frye, vol. 4. Toronto: University of Toronto Press, 2000.

OE *On Education*. Markham, ON: Fitzhenry & Whiteside, 1988.

RT *Northrop Frye's Notebooks and Lectures on the Bible and Other Religious Texts*, ed. Robert D. Denham. Collected Works of Northrop Frye, vol. 13. Toronto: University of Toronto Press, 2003.

RW *Reading the World: Selected Writings, 1935–1976*, ed. Robert D. Denham. New York: Peter Lang, 1990.

SE *Northrop Frye's Student Essays, 1932–1938*, ed. Robert D. Denham. Collected Works of Northrop Frye, vol. 3. Toronto: University of Toronto Press, 1997.

SER *A Study of English Romanticism*. New York: Random House, 1968.

SeS *The Secular Scripture: A Study of the Structure of Romance*. Cambridge, MA: Harvard University Press, 1976.

SM *Spiritus Mundi: Essays on Literature, Myth, and Society*. Bloomington: Indiana University Press, 1976.

StS *The Stubborn Structure: Essays on Criticism and Society*. Ithaca, NY: Cornell University Press, 1970.

TBN *The "Third Book" Notebooks of Northrop Frye, 1964–1972: The Critical Comedy*, ed. Michael Dolzani. Collected Works of Northrop Frye, vol. 9. Toronto: University of Toronto Press, 2001.

WE *Northrop Frye's Writings on Education*, ed. Goldwin French and Jean O'Grady. Collected Works of Northrop Frye, vol. 7. Toronto: University of Toronto Press, 2000.

WGS *A World in a Grain of Sand: Twenty-Two Interviews with Northrop Frye*, ed. Robert D. Denham. New York: Peter Lang, 1991.

WTC *The Well-Tempered Critic*. Bloomington: Indiana University Press, 1963.

THE CORRESPONDENCE

1930s

Donald Howard   **1 June 1934**
Craftsbury, VT   Stone, Saskatchewan

Donald Howard was Frye's first cousin, the son of his mother's brother John. A Methodist minister living at the time in Vermont, he held pastorates in New York and other at other churches in New England. Frye was serving a mission field in Stone, Saskatchewan, as a twenty-one-year-old student minister, following his first year at Emmanuel College.

Dear Cousin,

I am very much obliged to for your letter and your good wishes. By this time you will have heard of Uncle Rate's death, which removes perhaps the most prominent of the Howards.[3] He was a relative I would like to have known better than I did. When I saw him two years ago he had the look of a sick man who would never recover. It is quite a shock to Mother.

You can probably find Maple Creek on your map, and it is easier to locate me from there, as we are forty-five miles east of it, much farther from Swift Current. Stone, apart from the post-office, is not a place but a figure of speech. We are very isolated—the nearest village from anywhere on the field is about eighteen miles—and if your map had been constructed on medieval lines, we should probably be represented by an elephant or hippogriff. I am beginning to enjoy myself a bit better than I thought I would. Everything in the life is so utterly different from anything I have ever been used to that I was pretty homesick at first, and thought I was going to be hate everything in connection with my work. Even yet, I do not feel that I shall try a second field. I am naturally a bit shy, and every social contact I make is like a plunge into cold water, but less exhilarating. I am afraid I am a natural-born Cockney, preferring pavements to meadows. The simple joys of country life are lost on me, and I find them a bit exaggerated. The people are friendly enough, but my social status, on week-days, is largely that of a non-paying guest. I should greatly prefer a field here to one further east judging from all reports. The country is a high table-land, rolling and uneven, broken by very lovely valleys—it is a height of land and the source of rivers that find their outlets in the Hudson Bay, Atlantic Ocean, and the Gulf of Mexico. So it isn't altogether the bare flat prairie, but I miss the trees—I mean trees, not hedges, or a constipated-looking bush with a few dozen poplars in it. God seems to me a bit impersonal on the prairie. It's been a hopelessly dry and windy spring, and the grasshoppers, which flew in last year, are settling in in good earnest this summer, and all probabilities point to a crop failure—the first, if it comes, that this district will have had.

If you want Blake's poems, may I suggest *The Poetry and Prose of William Blake*, edited by Geoffrey Keynes, published by the Nonesuch Press, London. It is the only edition available at a moderate price which contains more than a small portion of his work, and it has everything he ever wrote. There are several reasons for my interest in him. No great poet, with the very doubtful exception of Shakespeare, has, since the rise of Christianity, been able to write without the inspiration of the Christian religion behind him, and consequently he is forced to give expression to the deepest religious impulses of his age. Hence in every period there is one supreme poet who expresses the very essence of that period's attitude to Christianity. In English literature such were Chaucer, Spenser, Milton, Dryden, and Blake to their various times. But Blake is peculiarly interesting because he lived in the time when the French and Industrial Revolutions, and all that they signified, were shattering the unity of Christian civilization, and he, and Goethe, are the two great artist intellects who represent the final and culminating effort of Western culture to express that unity. (I am getting a bit obscure, but I am writing this and trying to listen — or rather trying not to listen — to my hostess as she reads extracts of a letter to me.) Blake was one of the world's greatest painters, as well as a poet, and that makes him doubly interesting. Middleton Murry has a fairly good book out on him.[4] I have read a bit of Edwin Markham, but not in any detail. I know the Man with a Hoe, of course. I like the way he handles blank verse. The connection between Chaucer and Blake goes deeper than one might suspect. I think Blake regarded him as the greatest of English poets. He wrote one of the best criticisms of Chaucer in existence, and some of Chaucer's characters — the Plowman, the Miller, and the Monk — reappear as symbols in Blake's later work. Blake disapproved of Wordsworth on philosophical grounds, but recognized him as the greatest of his contemporaries. I know little of the Lollard movement, but have always been fascinated by Wyclif's prose, and I want his Bible as soon as I can afford it.

The work in the field is interesting in its way, though it has its own difficulties. The great weakness of Protestantism is that it has little if any conception of the authority of the Church, with the result that the congregation or communities can impose their own home-grown standards of morals upon the minister, and force him tacitly to acquiesce in them, even when he thinks them false and pernicious. It is a special application of the weakness of democracy generally. The Methodist prejudices I encounter on the subject of smoking, dancing, playing cards, etc. I regard as the most superstitious of fetishes, and merely a way of avoiding the real problems of religion. That is the most obvious of rural deficiencies — making piety consist of taboos — and yet what gets me is not any lack of intelligence, of courtesy, of moral sense — there is plenty of all three — but I think the religious problem is bound up with the cultural deadness. What these poor people use for literature, art and music is to me the source of the whole evil that makes them regard religion as a social convention rather than an experience. I admire and respect the people in themselves, for the cheerful and uncomplaining way they get through their daily routine. But they work too hard, and get too little out of their work.

The province is excited over politics. The Conservatives are in power — they correspond, as no doubt you know, to Republicanism in the States. The Liberals are more like your left-wing or progressive Republicans — they do not represent a genuinely different political idea. A new party, called the Canadian Cooperative Federation or C.C.F., is getting surprisingly strong.[5] And most of the seats here have a triangular contest. It is really the party of Canadian liberalism, like your Democrats, but much more avowedly socialistic. Conservatism is in disrepute all over the country — we made a ghastly mistake when we committed ourselves to Conservative policies at the beginning of the depression, as it meant the rule of big business and the consequent starvation of John Canuck.[6] Bennett,[7] our premier, swept the West in 1930, but now a "Bennett buggy" is a car with no engine, "Bennett underwear" is gunny sacking, and "Bennett coffee" is a filthy concoction made from wheat. The province goes to the polls June 19. I rather expect the Liberals to carry it, and the federal election too.[8]

I think this summer will set me up physically, and if so I may be able to face my work in the fall with a bit more equanimity. Lecturing one hour a week to freshmen, taking graduate work in English and second year Theology, is no joke, just by itself. I had a pretty good time with my kids in St. Andrews Sunday-School, and they all spoke as though they would like to continue it next year, so I'll be around, I expect. I am sorry you didn't come to Emmanuel—I think the United Church represents a purely Canadian religious idea, and it is a favorite theory of mine that there should be a definitely established national church to represent the nation's religious genius before there can be a coherent religious consciousness in that country. The Anglicans in England, the Presbyterians in Scotland, the Lutherans in Germany, the Catholics in Latin countries, represent a central focal point of intellectual, social and artistic activity, and I think the United States will always be a good deal of chaos, and a "melting pot," till it moves toward greater unity.

I apologize for my seedy-looking stationery. They don't pay my board here—they shove me around from place to place every week, and my belongings keep bumping against my horse's side, to their great disadvantage. My regards to the wife and family,

Roy Daniells   [14 July 1935]
Victoria College, Toronto, ON

This holograph letter, written on Frye's birthday, is in the Roy Daniells Fonds at the University of British Columbia, box 2, file 5. Frye has completed his second year at Emmanuel College. In his journals Daniells, a junior instructor in English at Victoria College, indicates that he and Frye began to see each other fairly regularly from late September 1934 on, having tea, going for walks, and seeing movies together. On 23 February 1935, Daniells wrote his parents: "This afternoon I went on a walk with Frye down the Rosedale ravine to the zoo and we had tea on the way back. It did us both good. Frye is about the best example of pure unadulterated intelligence I have ever met (small, thin, bent, spectacled, with no physique to mention, but with a brain like a glass cutter). It's good to have him round the place. Though I admit one couldn't live in a society composed of nothing else but Fryes" (Roy Daniells Fonds, box 40, file 7). Daniells returned to London in April 1935 to continue his studies, and Frye stayed in Daniells's room for the summer. His girlfriend Helen Kemp had been in London since September 1934, studying art at the Courtauld Institute. Daniells sent Kemp a note shortly after arriving, and they had tea together on several occasions. The Daniells-Frye-Kemp relationship during this time can be traced by following the index entries for "Daniells" in NFHK. A note and a letter from Kemp to Daniells, written during June and July 1935, are in the Roy Daniells Fonds, box 2, file 6 and file 7.

My Dear Roy:

Now some people might begin this letter by saying, "I should have written you long before, but you know how it is, one so seldom gets around to these things; I've thought of you so much and intended to write and well anyway here's the letter." All I propose to say is, "Between the potency, And the spasm, Falls the shadow."[9] Speaking of Eliot, I'd like to see *Murder in the Cathedral* sometime—I hear it's pretty fine. For my entertainment I've had to get along on summer shows. Which are mostly lousy. They did Becky Sharp in color, but shouldn't have.[10]

Jerry[11] is back, of course, and at present busy with his girl friend who is down marking papers. Today I have completed my twenty-third year, and they came around this morning and presented me with a toy glider (which doesn't work; at least I can't make it work) and took me to church (not bad; T.R. Glover, a genial S.C.M.er) and to dinner afterwards.[12] A twenty-third birthday, of course, calls for a sonnet:

> Milton considered his declining spring
> And realized the possibility
> That while he mused on Horton scenery
> Genius might join his youth in taking wing;
> Yet thought this not too serious a thing
> Because of God's well-known propensity
> To take and re-absorb inscrutably
> The lives of men, whatever gifts they bring.
> Of course I have a different heritage;
> I've worked hard not to be young at all,
> With fair results; at least my blood is cooled,
> And I am safe in saying, at Milton's age,
> That if Time pays me an informal call
> And tries to steal my youth, Time will get fooled.

which is horrible doggerel, like all my alleged poetry. I have a few jobs. For one thing, I was engaged shortly after you left to help with the notes for *Representative Poetry*.[13] So I worked with Davis[14] on Milton, Pope, Swift, Addison, etc., and did the Blake myself. I think perhaps another week with Endicott will be in order before long.[15] I got fifty bucks for the work I have already done. And MacGillivray[16] waylaid me and asked me to mark some of his teachers' essays for him. So the Extension Department hired me — one hundred and fifty bucks. If this keeps up I'll be able to pay off some of my debts and get domesticated. Now I know Helen is coming back,[17] things are going more smoothly. I never realized how much I wanted her back until I realized that I didn't have to resign myself to the fact that she wasn't (God knows where my syntax has got to, but you get the idea). Thanks a lot for looking after the girl; I think your casual contacts have meant quite a bit to her. And the next time a reasonably attractive young lady proposes a cycling trip to Vienna, how about accepting and taking a chance on the Victoria College staff's not finding it out?[18]

The work is going as well as can be expected, which is perhaps the best phrase to use when one is giving birth to something. The Blake thing is going to be a minor masterpiece, I think. I've given it absolutely everything I possess, and if it's no good, I'm no good. The first hundred and fifty pages or so will go down to Davis this week or next, I hope.[19] I've been bothered a lot with my eyes, but apart from that keep going. It's desperately hot, sticky, muggy and moist: I have to bury myself in the lowest bowels of the stacks to get any work done. My Ph.D. thesis, I have definitely decided, is going to be Blake and his relation to rococo on the one hand and romanticism on the other. Only I won't tell them that yet, or give it that name. And I think the freshmen will be better informed about English literature by me next year than last. I think the new second year pass is a big improvement.[20]

I come up blushing shyly to confess that I am taking advantage of my unaccustomed freedom to start working a bit on a novel. It provisional title is *Quiet Consummation*. It's not much of a novel, but I want to get it out of my system. No plot or theme or thesis or anything, just yet. It's laid out in sonata form. Amusing, I think, if it comes off at all.[21] I am beginning to realize that, while I may and probably will turn out some fairly decent things on Blake and Shakespeare and Augustine and the rest critically, the larger problem they refer back to, the relation of religion and art in symbolism, will require fictional and dramatic treatment. I have drawn up prospectuses of a magnum opus on purely specula-tive lines, but, while I could write it, it wouldn't carry conviction to anybody. You can't talk about symbols in those terms. (This, by the way, is a secret, except for H. [Helen]).

I am beginning to know Arnold[22] a bit better, as he's had me up a good deal, and we've talked over various things. He has a violent prejudice against Christianity, of course, and is teaching me German. Or at least he's given me books to read in German. Peggy,[23] of course, is trying to teach me Anglo-Saxon, but I haven't started yet, as the thesis keeps my head pretty well in a whirl. The girls[24] are well, in general; Mary went to Boston a little while ago and they have been away at various times. I spent a week up north with Roy Kemp, at the Kemp cottage in Muskoka.[25] It rained every day, and we — or at least I — had forgot-ten to bring any money up, so we lived off porridge and eggs and coffee.[26]

The slightly disordered appearance of this page, if I send it, is owing to a moth which lit on it and got hit with the first thing I reached for, which turned out to be a very wet bathing cap. I spend a good deal of time under the shower.

Langford, the Emmanuel registrar that is, told me that the Council wanted to give me a first and Johnston[27] held out against it. So he said to send him a note saying I wasn't going to attend any lectures next year, and then the eructations of friend Johnston could pass unnoticed.

Cragg[28] writes from the mission field saying he's lonesome but doing quite a bit of work. I'm going up to his girl friend's place tomorrow for a few days.[29] Just got the invitation. Would prefer to get out of it, but I think my hostess has an ulterior motive.

I trust your thesis is progressing. I think the best test to see whether you have thor-oughly mastered the subject or not is to try to read *Hydriotaphia*[30] in a subway.

Look here, I had intended to write you a much longer letter, but this invitation drop-ping down on me in the course of writing it means that I have to get busy and clean a few things up and get out of here. So I'll have to restrain my exuberance until the next letter — in the meantime you can get details from Helen, which aren't frightfully important. The gist of my life is that it's quiet. I'm having a good time, getting my work done, and spend a lot of time basking in this room and thinking how lucky I am.

Roy Daniells   Oct. 6 [1936]
Victoria College, Toronto, ON   London, England

On 4 September 1936 Frye had sailed from Montreal for England to begin his first year at Merton College, Oxford. He arrived in Plymouth on 10 September, and spent almost a month in London before going up to Oxford. Frye's account of his early London experiences in this letter might be compared to his similar but more detailed accounts in his letters to Helen Kemp (NFHK, 2: 560–92). This holograph letter is in the Roy Daniells Fonds, University of British Columbia, box 2, file 12.

My dear Roy:

The scene is London, and the curtain and the hero go up to Oxford in three days. At present I am buying assorted crockery, cutlery and bedding, getting my trunk packed, and generally preparing for leaving — I feel as though I were accompanying myself on a honey-moon. My life has been uneventful enough during the last two months — August, of course, I spent in Moncton with my parents, working the streets with the fugitive glance of one who knows that he is constantly ignoring people he went to school with. The crossing was a good one, or what is known as a good one — ten days on a small Cunarder breeds a stifling sense of claustrophobia, however, and I discovered that there were a good many ways of being heartily sick of the sea without being sea-sick.[31] I met one man on the boat who used to be a professor of architecture at McGill[32]: then he took up floriculture (he calls it that) and is going to England to run a pipe underground, heat up the soil, raise red, white and blue asters months before anyone else can, and clean up money at the Coronation. Then I struck this country where the subtlest colors are all blended together in everything you see, where everything is so close to the ground and so closely packed in, where the trains give a sort of hysterical giggle and sidle up apologetically through one Constable landscape after another. London is warm (I mean aesthetically rather than physically) richly varied, and somehow accessible — there is nothing of the huge impersonality of a city like Chicago, with its immense streets and buildings and distances. I had expected something twice as large as Chicago and was agreeably surprised to find the city so manageable. And why didn't someone tell me about the Belisha beacons,[33] that make the town look as though it were holding a continuous carnival?

I got hold of the boarding house where Helen was last year — it's in Bloomsbury just off Russell Square.[34] Bloomsbury and the part around the British Museum is a mysterious place — people in various colors walk around in native costumes mainly Hindu, and the bookstores advertise the most exotic kinds of literature — theosophy, Rudolf Steiner, Swedenborg meet you on every corner and almost every other time you go out, you run into someone you know, as though you had caught a dose of cosmic consciousness on your own account. I have met two recent graduates of Emmanuel that way,[35] and a shipboard acquaintance.[36]

I don't feel as though I'd seen anything in London — the museums are as depressingly large as the city is invitingly small. At the moment, I think I prefer walking and riding buses around the city. The result is that so far I know practically nothing about the major museums and very little about the major art galleries. I shall be back here at Christmas time, and will try to make up for things then, after I have been mentally stimulated by Oxford, let us say, and am more used to the country. At the moment I'm traveling. Travel gratifies an appetite: the appetite of curiosity, and when an appetite is being gratified one hesitates to put forth any display energy. I'm being fed with new sights and sounds, till I feel replete, lazy and disorganized. I can't eat what this country calls food, so I have to subsist on sandwiches and scenery. My mind is passive and uncritical, taking in impressions. Anything in the nature of brilliant generalization would have been brewed in Ontario before I left. It's a good job I'm not in Russia, as my letters from there would be the last word in bourgeois escapism.

I haven't been up to Oxford yet — the only place I've been is Cheltenham, where I went to see Wilson Knight's brother. I read part of Wilson Knight's novel while I was there — it looks quite bad. Knight (Jackson Knight I think his name is) is very kind and hospitable, and much more capable of small talk and personalities than his brother.[37] But he speaks the same language, having the same interest in symbolic patterns — he's proofing a book now on labyrinths and mazes,[38] and is a professor of classics in Exeter University. A far more genuine scholar than his brother, I am inclined to think. I opened up to him as I've never opened up to anyone before, sat and drank gallons of cider and talked and listened to him talk, for most of two days. Cheltenham is a health resort, full of retired colonels and other unhealthy people, and of private hotels of devastating respectability. Knight's own set-up reflects that: more Fascist than Communist, a believer in Oxford Groups, and full of a mystical devotion to the army. Somehow that doesn't seem to matter when we talk the same language. He introduced a poet to me — Francis Berry — only a boy, but a genuine poet — he read us some of his stuff, and it's all right. He's got a sort of D.H. Lawrence nature mysticism in which Nature huge boiling *pot au feu* and he likes being part of it. I don't like that sort of poetry, but he can write it.[39]

In this boarding house there is a man called Dickinson, a student or attaché of some kind at the British ~~Museum~~ (what's the matter with me?) Consulate at Beirut, Syria. He's working at Arabic and Russian — got a nervous breakdown as soon as he connected with the Russian and came home — being a completely phlegmatic Englishman, he makes the least convincing neurotic I've ever seen. I've got quite friendly with him, and, as he knows something about clothes, he took me downtown yesterday and, after bullying half a dozen stores, eventually got me encased in a brown imitation Harris tweed jacket, grey flannel trousers and a lemon yellow pullover. He has a friend[40] with some good phonograph records, and as they have Communist connections, though they are wild enough Tories themselves, took me out to a kind of concert in which the proceeds were to go the Spanish government. Two plays, one by Ernest Toller, all about Communists being steadfast under torture in various Fascist countries.[41] It was impressive enough, but somehow I suspect the word masochism of being derived from mass schism. Then there's a girl named Veronica Wedgwood, a friend of Barbara's,[42] who writes seventeenth century history. I had lunch with her and dinner with her and her father.[43] The latter was the first occasion on which I have seen the entire process in operation of chauffeur calling with car, butler serving dinner, and the rest of it, and was quite amused.

I have been to three Queen's Hall proms, don't think I shall get to Murder in the Cathedral after all, have looked up and run into a few Canadians, and in general continue to produce the impression of being extremely busy and treat practically all my time as though it were hardly-won leisure. This is a vacant sort of letter and I hope my next will display more of the intellectual acumen expected from Oxford.

Pelham Edgar   **28 December 1936**
Victoria College, Toronto, ON   London, England
   This letter constituted Frye's half-yearly report to Pelham Edgar, the Canadian supervisor for his Royal Society Fellowship to study Blake's prophecies during his first year at Oxford. The holograph letter is in the Pelham Edgar Fonds, box 2, 12.5 a–b, Victoria University Library, Toronto.

Dear Dr. Edgar:
   I had intended to write you about the progress of my work towards the end of January, but as I had not been informed that I had a Canadian as well as an English supervisor,[44] I did not know that this would be an official report. I shall write you again at the end of January, as I can give you at present only a tentative survey.

   I am reading Schools[45] here, of course, and like it very well: it suits me much better than a B.Litt. from every point of view. During this past term I have covered Chaucer, Langland, the fifteenth century, and have started Anglo-Saxon, which means that I have had to concentrate on my courses, much of those periods being entirely new to me. Actually, the fact that I read theology rather than graduate English at Toronto during the last three years makes it necessary for me now to spend some time getting a firm grasp of English literature, which I really know very little about. I can say very little definitely about my progress as an Oxford student beyond the fact that nothing seems to be wrong. Mr. Blunden[46] is quite satisfied with my work, or so he said when he reported on me at the end of the term. I am spending the present vacation in London, and hope to put a bit of time in at the British Museum during the next two weeks.

The Blake thesis is gradually separating into two parts. The first is a general guide to the Prophecies, based on the four-chapter scheme submitted to you earlier, written in fairly popular style, and running to perhaps 80,000 words. The first chapter of this works out the thesis that the Prophecies are based on a philosophy which includes an aesthetic theory and a religious belief, the former dictating the form and the latter the content of the Prophecies as well as the other poems. The second chapter applies this principle to Blake as far as *The Marriage of Heaven and Hell*; the third takes it to *The Four Zoas*; and the fourth completes it. I shall forward the first half of this in about three weeks: the rest I should have ready before the end of the Hilary Term. I think you will agree with me when you see this work that it is totally different from anything else on Blake in both its method of approach and its general critical attitude.

As a sequel to this I shall work out a detailed study of Blake's own reading, his debt to it as recorded in the Prophecies, and the way in which his thought was influenced by others. I have collected some of the important material for this: I think I can handle Blake's relation to English philosophy and literature fairly well, and this is the butt of it. Swedenborg I have gone over pretty thoroughly, including his big book on the *True Christian Religion* which Blake seems to have read, in Latin, very carefully, and which Foster Damon seems to have overlooked.[47] The chief thing that remains is a study of the books of Blake's own time which helped organize the symbolism of the Prophecies. Blake seems to have real a good deal of contemporary works on Anglo-Saxon, Celtic, and Norse literature: there are also a large number of works on free masonry and [?] brands of occultism which I have to look at, though I am quite sure Blake did not: and there are all the books published by Blake's friend Johnson[48] some of which Blake certainly read. This second piece of work will take me at least all of my second year here, though when I write my final report I can send enough of it to give you an idea of what I shall be doing.

I had a quiet Christmas, and am trying to get letters off to Roy [Daniells], Ned [Pratt] and Mr. [Herbert] Davis within the next week. My regards to Mrs. Edgar: I have met a friend of hers since coming to Oxford — Elizabeth Fraser.[49] I send vicarious greetings to your son as well.

Walter T. Brown   **2 April [1937]**
Victoria College, Toronto, ON   Florence, Italy

   Walter T. Brown was president of Victoria College. In March 1937 Roy Daniells, Frye's friend who was teaching at Victoria, wrote to Frye at Oxford, urging him to write to Brown and inform him of his plans for the following year (NFHK, 2:711). On 18 March Frye set off with his Oxford friend Mike Joseph for a tour of Italy. Two weeks later he wrote to Brown from Florence. This holograph letter, along with Brown's reply to Frye, is in the United Church of Canada/Victoria University Archives, 87.067V, box 3, file 3, pt. 2.

Dear Dr. Brown:
   I have put in two terms and a vacation in England, and have come to Italy during the Easter vacation for a change. It isn't so much of a change in one way, as it has poured rain in every town I have been in, but the language is different. I have been working at Oxford I should think fairly well — at least my tutor Mr. [Edmund] Blunden[50] has given me quite good term reports and seems to be interested in me, so I should like very much to be able to complete the course next year. At the same time I have been trying to get enough of my Blake thesis in shape to be able to submit it to a publisher here. Work on this has not been going as well as I should like, as it is so hard to give both my course and the thesis the amount

of work they deserve. But I think I should have enough in shape in the next two weeks to give a publisher some idea of whether he would want it or not, and Mr. Blunden has promised to give me an introduction to Blake's editor Geoffrey Keynes, whom he knows slightly.

For my next year in Oxford I assume I should need about the same amount of money I needed this year — $1500. I am rather out of touch with Canadian scholarships, but I should think an I.O.D.E. would be the only possibility,[51] and that is not awarded until about Christmas. I am very anxious to come back to Victoria College after I get through here — I can't say that I'm exactly homesick, but I am anxious to come back afterwards all the same — and if the chances of my doing so are strong enough to provide security for a loan, I should be very grateful if I could borrow that sum, as a maximum, from Victoria College.

The logical time for me to complete the Blake thesis for publication is this summer,[52] as to take too much time during the term would make my chances for a decent mark on my exams next year rather faint. It would be much better for me to stay in London this summer if I did that, I should [need] immediate assistance as soon as the term closed on June 22, or at any rate very soon afterwards. Or, I could return to Canada — I have an invitation to Muskoka for the summer[53] — and put my Oxford work in shape then enough to do the Blake next year. The former seems to me somewhat the better plan, but I should be very glad if you would be kind enough to give me an opinion on this.[54]

Walter T. Brown   [April 1937]
Victoria College, Toronto, ON   Merton College, Oxford

Frye's letter is undated, but it was written shortly after he returned from Italy to Oxford in late April 1937. He indicates to Principal Brown that he may stay in England. Whether he was serious about this, which would have meant applying for the I.O.D.E. fellowship mentioned in the previous letter, is uncertain. He made no effort to apply for it during the year, and he waited until late April to ask Helen Kemp to make an inquiry. In fact, Kemp ended up filing a late application on Frye's behalf, and Brown wrote to support it (see his letter of 1 June 1937 (United Church of Canada/Victoria University Archives, 87.067V, box 3, file 3, pt. 2). Nothing came of the application. Frye, however, did believe that Brown had promised him financial assistant for the second year. See his letter to Kemp of 18 May 1937 in NFHK, 2:750. In this letter we also learn that Brown wrote to Frye, in a letter that is not extant, that Victoria might be able to give him a teaching job and then offer him a leave of absence. The present letter is in the United Church of Canada/Victoria University Archives, 87.067V, box 3, file 3, pt. 2

Dear Dr. Brown:

I have since learned that I will be able to stay with friends in Muskoka[55] if I return to Canada, and as I have no resources for staying in England, I think that may be the best move after all. England is a brutally expensive country, and while I might make my fortune in London this summer by writing, the chances of my doing so are so enormous that I hesitate to take them. Besides, I have been disagreeing with the English climate ever since I caught the flu last Christmas, and I think a bit of Canadian sunshine would improve my health.

With regard to next year, if I am awarded Professor Currelly's scholarship, I shall get through it somehow. There are not many scholarships here for undergraduates, but there is a small one I might pick up by writing a set of exams for it, and Mr. Blunden tells me he can probably arrange a small bursary for me.

I am sorry I shall not be here when you are in Oxford, but I hope you will not miss seeing Merton College, if it is not closed for repairs. It isn't as sumptuous as Christ Church or Magdelan, but is, I think, more charming than either.

Pelham Edgar   June 10, 1937
Victoria College, Toronto, ON   Merton College, Oxford

Frye wrote this letter in response to Helen Kemp's scolding him for not keeping in touch with Edgar and others at Victoria College. She had received word from Principal Walter T. Brown that Edgar had been hurt by Frye's silence. See her letter to Frye of 29 May 1937 (NFHK, 2:757–8). The present holograph letter is in the Pelham Edgar Fonds, Victoria University Library.

Dear Dr. Edgar:

I am sending under separate cover the first chapter of the Blake, expanded into six because of the number of footnotes. You are familiar with the general outline, but I have added a great deal of new material, and, though I have rewritten it several times, I think I have it right now. Mr. Blunden has high hopes for its publication and suggests Faber & Faber as a first venture. I don't really think that it will finally not be accepted. Should it be published, I should of course want to dedicate it to you; and as soon as a publisher accepts it, I shall write you again asking for your permission to do so.

I shall be returning to Canada on June 24, and will be in Muskoka, during the summer, so that I may be able to get your suggestions at first hand. Of course I already have your approval of my general line of approach, and that has not been essentially changed; I feel fairly sure of my facts as well, and I even hope that your opinion of its style (not my best) will not be too unfavourable. But I shall want to make sure of your approval before I publish anything.

This has been an addled, scrambled, lunatic sort of year, in which I have tried to do the work of three men with the health of considerably less than one. I am sorry I could not keep up the schedule I outlined in my Christmas letter: that was impossible; and I felt ashamed to write without having something definite to show for my year's work. My strength is, however, coming back with the spring; and I hope before long to produce more tangible evidence of that fact.

Roy Daniells   [June 1937]
Victoria College, Toronto, ON   Oxford, England

This letter is in the Roy Daniells Fonds, University of British Columbia, box 3, file 2.

Dear Roy,

At the end of a year at the above location [Merton College] I came out of a trance to discover that the year was over, and there was I with a book written, and I had been intolerably rude to my friends. The trance seemed genuine enough while it lasted, but it may not have been so. If I thought an apology was possible I would offer it: I have no idea what is possible.

Whatever the status of the trance, I think the book itself is genuine enough. Nothing more than an explanation of Blake's thought and a commentary on the prophecies: it's been a great relief to me to discover that I had made a book, and that the research I had been doing outside Blake was a separate issue altogether. At Blunden's suggestion, I am leaving half of it with Faber & Faber as a first venture. If I don't see my way to getting it off my hands before Christmas, Blake will have been responsible for still more lunacy. I finished up what I intended to send Faber and Faber on the last day of term, seized a boat within twenty-four hours, and am now coming across to Canada.[56] I am going to Gordon Bay[57] with Helen and want to flatten out there for three months. If I am to make a decent job of schools at Oxford next year I shall need that, as my health is definitely not good. Bad, too, in a curious way I can't define. I should imagine that last year for me resembled in some way your own period or readjustment after the collapse of your apocalyptic Calvinism. My ideas haven't changed except to consolidate, but that has been rather disturbing. Blake is finally coming out straight: he's a bigger man than I thought; he leads straight into the fourteenth century, and I'm going to write a tetralogy of four novels.[58] That's part of the consolidation. I arrived at it partly by writing five and six thousand words a week for Blunden, who got very tired.

I am very glad — have been ever since I heard the news — about your Cleveland job, and I hope you will quash all hideous rumours about your leaving Toronto.[59] That's a monstrous idea: Davis was quite enough to lose.[60] In any case, I hope I can see you this summer. I'd like you to look at the Blake. Blunden is so much like God — very inspiring to talk to as long as you do the talking.

My mind goes blank at this point: it always does. I don't know whether I like Oxford or not: I've hardly been conscious of Oxford. I got the final push toward writing that I had been waiting for, but I wish it hadn't been quite so ingrown an affair — it was the cracking of my health that did that. The Blake finally came out right — at least I think it did — but it was always just around the corner, week after week.

Will you let me off a newsy letter, at this impossible date? I'll see you this summer and can talk to you then. Nothing external has happened to me, and the internal things terminate in temporary exhaustion. I shall do some work at Gordon Bay, I think — it's the only place where I have ever succeeded in reading Swedenborg. But not until Canadian air, a lake, and Helen have begun to fit my pieces together.

I should think Cleveland was one of the few highly civilized cities left in the world. If you have to move from Toronto, Cleveland would be the best move, I should think. I am becoming sensitive to American civilization in Europe.

Edward W. Wallace   **15 July 1937**
Victoria College, Toronto, ON   Gordon Bay, Ontario

Edward W. Wallace, president and chancellor of Victoria University, had written Frye about a possible job at Victoria College for the 1937–38 academic year. A position had come available because of Roy Daniells's resignation to accept a job at the University of Manitoba. Wallace asked whether Frye might not be able to come to his summer cottage at Go Home Bay to discuss the possibilities. In addition to the present letter, Frye also wired Wallace on 15 July, saying that he would like to meet at the proposed time. After meeting Wallace, Frye was offered a one-year appointment as a special lecturer at a salary of $1520 (Ayre, 143).

Dear Dr. Wallace:

Thank you for your letter, and your invitation. I have been canvassing the possibilities of getting to Go Home Bay; but as neither Helen nor I are sufficiently experienced with a canoe,[61] it would perhaps be simpler if I went to Toronto. If Thursday, the 22[d], say at eleven o'clock in the morning, would be convenient for you, I should like it very much if I could see you then.

I am very glad to be back in Canada, as its climate and its atmosphere are quite unapproachable in England, at any rate for a summer holiday. Studying seems more painless in consequence. I should like to be remembered to Mrs. Wallace, and to your son if he is with you.

Roy Daniells   [late July 1937]
Cleveland, OH   Gordon Bay, ON
    This letter is in reply to Daniells's letter of 14 July. Typescript: Roy Daniells Fonds, University of British Columbia, box 3, file 2. The final paragraph is a holograph addition.

My dear Roy:
    This is in the nature of an emergency letter. Your going to Manitoba, for which I suppose congratulations are in order, alters the shape of my existence slightly. You left at least three large gaps in the Department of English, to wit, first year honour, sixteenth-century course, third year honour, Milton, fourth year honour, nineteenth century thought. They seem to want me to do (this typewriter sticks)[62] something about it. As I'm broke it seems a good enough idea. I've just seen our (pardon me, my) ethereally-minded Chancellor, who wanted to know if I'd been in Oxford or London, how I would take to lecturing, which was new to me, and whether I were sure if reading frantically all summer long would put me one jump ahead of my pupils or not. Obviously [Walter] Brown and [Pelham] Edgar had the idea, at least among the brass hats. I'm getting married the last week in August, when my sister will be in Toronto, and I hope I can see you about that time. The Chancellor was distressed at the idea of marriage — seemed to think the College could exploit me with less strain on its Nonconformist conscience if I remained single.[63]
    Apparently John and Sally [Sallee][64] have got something in a small Vermont college — I explained to the Chancellor that Helen wouldn't need to give up her job at the Art Gallery as there wasn't the same prejudice against married women there that there was elsewhere, and he winced slightly. As they have no intention of getting anyone for her [Sallee Creighton's] place, it looks as though I shall have enough group work to do. What I want to know chiefly about these three courses is the arrangement and proportion of material. In the Milton course, for example, do you put Milton first or in the middle, and how much time does he get? If I had a general layout of your courses I could go ahead with comparative serenity. Roy Kemp says he has a fairly complete set of Woodhouses (please insert apostrophe) notes, which should prove useful. Also, it occurred to me that Cousland's method of organizing his Church History course might be a good one to adopt for the sixteenth-century course.[65] He used to have a mimeographed sheet for each lecture with the points summarized, with a little bibliographical list at the bottom. Do you think this a good idea, or how easy is it to get the Office to mimeograph anything, in case I typed the stencil? It seemed to me that a large, complicated and difficult course like that for first year shouldn't leave too much to their powers of note-taking. That, of course, is known among the superior English-trained as Spoon Feeding. And it is. I shall spoon-feed those children till they retch.
    There will be a lot more to consult you on later, of course: I should think that getting Woodside[66] to do the Latin poems and giving them a copy of Woodhouse's bibliography are two precedents I might well follow, if they worked all right for you. I suppose the nineteenth-century stuff means that one of them writes a paper for each group. I can draft a list of papers all right, I expect, though you'd better give me yours if you have it. And with the first year, do you run the poetry and prose concurrently or take first one and then the other? I can't remember.
    No news otherwise. I'm glad of that Helen has two brothers here,[67] one a violinist and

the other a 'cellist, and the three have played half a dozen Haydn trios. The Blake grinds slowly and small. Faber and Faber said no: Cambridge Press has it now. I type better than this when I don't have to push the carriage after every stroke or so. The novels won't be tautological: the characters in them will be. This is the bottom.[68] All the best.

You aren't jealous of me: if you were you'd belittle my abilities instead of exaggerating them. I don't see how anyone can be really envious of another and still regard death, where other people don't matter, as having a positive relation to life.[69]

Roy Daniells   [late July 1937]
University of Manitoba, Winnipeg, MB   Gordon Bay, ON
Immediately after arriving in Toronto from England on 1 July, Frye went to the cottage of Helen Kemp's parents in Gordon Bay. Three weeks later he took the train to Toronto to negotiate the terms of his contract for the next academic year with Chancellor Edward Wallace, who recommended a salary of $1500, and told Frye he could not become a permanent member of the staff until he had completed a second year at Oxford. Daniells had just accepted a position at the University of Manitoba, so Frye, as he explains in his next letter, inherits Daniells's course in Milton, and he is assigned to teach as well the first-year course in the sixteenth century (English 1c) and the fourth-year course in nineteenth-century thought (English 4d). This letter is in the Roy Daniells Fonds, University of British Columbia, box 3, file 2. Beside the address at the top of the first page, Frye wrote, jestingly, "I never date letters."

Dear Roy,

Thanks very much for your letter. I shall probably be in Toronto from Aug. 21 on, and will look ~~up~~ you up ~~again~~.* The summer remains restful. A girl I met in Oxford,[70] who has been acting as my secretary with the Blake, says she thinks we'd better wait until autumn before sending it to Cambridge, which is next on my list, so no news from that quarter. I think I'll start 3d[71] with the metaphysical poets, go from there to Milton, and lead from Milton's prose into the other prose. The thing worrying me about the prose is the lack of a prescribed anthology — I know there are good ones, however — I don't like to talk about Burton and just make a vague gesture in the direction of the Anatomy.[72] But I can thrash all this out when I see you. I merely made the remark to fill up space. I feel vague. It is about to rain. The best.
*Please refrain from psychoanalyzing this one.

Roy Daniells   [Autumn 1937]
University of Manitoba, Winnipeg, MB
This letter is almost certainly written close to the beginning of the 1937 academic term. Daniells had just left Victoria College, where he had taught the course in sixteenth-century literature. Frye had sent Daniells outlines for the courses he is teaching, asking for Daniells's approval. Typescript is in the Roy Daniells Fonds, University of British Columbia, box 3, file 3.

Dear Roy:

Thanks very much. Glad you approve of the outlines — I tried hard to get that sixteenth-century course arranged so that they would be told everything twice. Term will be a week late in opening, so I shall certainly have to take three hours a week for a while, perhaps in the third year class too.

Miss Ray[73] was in yesterday with Helen. She went to South America this summer on a freighter loaded with dynamite, nitroglycerine, and neurotics. The second mate nearly drank himself to death for love of her. Or in order to love her — she wasn't too clear.

Helen is both well and ambitious, trying to get the Art Gallery publicized in periodicals like the Christian Science Monitor.[74] We had dinner with the Riddells[75] the other night. Marriage makes Jerry feel protective — me too, doubtless. My brains are addled, for reasons which you will understand anagogically from the next page.[76]

Roy Daniells   [**September 1937**]
University of Manitoba, Winnipeg, MB
    Typescript is in the Roy Daniells Fonds, University of British Columbia, box 3, file 2.

My dear Roy:
    I'm starting away down, as I can't stay long.[77] The Blake is done and off. It's been frightfully high-pressured, and contains some of my very worst writing. One rewriting and it'll be good. Ernie Gould, Sid's younger and much more attractive brother,[78] gets Pickersgill's job in Wesley College,[79] so you might run into him. Art Cragg[80] leaves for Cambridge with $750, less return ticket, in his pocket and not yet definitely accepted by his college. I'm worried about him. Last night Helen picked up Arnold[81] on the street and waltzed him in here. He complained that the ceiling was too low, and then glowered at me and announced that he would go into the whole matter of his views on the subject of marriage at some later date — alone.[82] I told him that when he thought of me as a married man he should make the following set of associations: Christianity; proletarian religion; slave psychology; a preference for easy yokes and light burdens. Also the Magian world-as-cavern, for the crick in his neck. We have an enormous wedding-cake in a plaster cast we haven't touched. I'm going to decoy Arnold in here and make him devour large chunks of it, the while pressing the ceiling on his head and holding forth on the subject of sacramental meals. Woodside congratulated Jerry[83] on getting an M.A. B.Litt. from Oxford and said he was proud to know a man who could pay for two Oxford degrees at once. Marriage, says the prayer-book, is a state instituted by God in the time of man's innocence.

Roy Daniells   [**November 1937**]
University of Manitoba, Winnipeg, MB
    This typed letter was written to Daniells at the University of Manitoba, where he had recently gone as a replacement for E.K. Brown, who had accepted an appointment at University College. Frye, who had married in August 1937, was living in the University Apartments at 6 St. Thomas St., not far from the Victoria College campus. This letter is in the Roy Daniells Fonds, University of British Columbia, box 3, file 3.

Dear Roy:
    If you read Gilbert on *Ulysses*,[84] he will tell you that as a work of art is a microcosm of universal experience, a knowledge of the elementary principles of the universe will be a valuable preparation in the understanding of *Ulysses*. And if you talk to Principal [Walter] Brown, he will tell you that the conflict in philosophy today is between a realism, or sometimes an idealism, founded on mathematics and recognizing universal law, and a philosophy founded on biology recognizing development and change — change anyway — which ranges from a materialism to a kind of idealism. We have biological novels, said Brown with a gesture; why aren't there any novels that show characters under the reign of universal law? I told him to read William Dean Howells.

    I was bobbed by Pacey,[85] I understand, not well, except for a huge yellow wig. I am thinking of splitting first year honour in two for a third hour, between myself and Peggy Roseborough.[86] Doug LePan,[87] who was at Merton with me last year and is now doing some lecturing in U.C., dropped in to see me. Speaking of Merton reminds me that this is essentially a begging letter. Can you lend me seventy dollars ($70.00)? The Bursar of Merton wants to be paid twenty-five pounds for last term. I've got it, as far as salary goes, but not now; I can pay you back in two months. I wrote that bastard explaining that I had been recently married and would like to be let off battels[88] until next year, when I returned to Oxford. He said he had every sympathy with married couples, but that a year after marriage events frequently transpired which proved even more expensive, so I'd have to pay up. I hate Oxford, but, like war, one has to be in it to realize how awful it is.

There isn't a great deal of news that would interest you, and in any case I should require a fresh sheet and another post to give you what news there is. Pelham [Edgar] said he gave you my term papers for Blunden; do you think the Wyatt one is publishable?[89]

Roy Daniells   20 July 1938
University of Manitoba, Winnipeg, MB

Frye is completing his first year of teaching at Victoria College, the year between his two stints at Oxford. Daniells had left in 1937 to take an appointment at the University of Manitoba. This holograph is in the Roy Daniells Fonds, University of British Columbia, box 3, file 8.

Dear Roy,

I daresay this letter will find you, as it leaves me, teaching summer school. I'm now doing third year pass—19th c. poetry and prose. Norman has the second year and Smith the first.[90] My students are earnest, much older than I,[91] and, I think, fairly intelligent, but this Christmas-goose method of stuffing them makes it difficult for me to organize much discussion. One of them was a junior when I was a freshman — he failed his second year once and his third year twice, and is now trying his B.A. from another angle. Not dumbness, just criminal negligence.

Helen and I spent June at my father-in-law's cottage in Muskoka,[92] and built up what we've been running on since. Then we invited Peggy Roseborough, Bill Stobie, and Bill Stobie's car up for the next weekend. We came back with a square foot of sunburn apiece. Helen has been a bit sun-touched ever since. She says she's all right: just feels soggy and stupid. At the moment she's curing herself on the homeopathic principle by reading a book on Dutch painting.

The summer course takes all my time. The Blake is in good shape, except for the recasting of some of the work on the major prophecies. I couldn't have picked up a subject calling for more exacting writing and arrangement of material. It takes its own time.

The year itself was fairly successful, I think. Best of all was my music group in the Women's Lit. [Women's Literary Society]: mixed, and mostly my first year honour people. I really did something there, even if I did get the whole Conservatory of Music sore at me, as my youngsters coolly informed me. They seem to have quoted me rather often. I haven't met Maclean yet, the new man. Joe seems to think it'll be a fairly congenial staff.

What with you and Davis both away it's been a small town. The Fairleys were the bright spot. Barker organized a forum of people interested in art, at which Helen gave a talk on the W.P.A. and I one on surrealism.[93] Magda Arnold and her youngsters are in the cottage next to ours in Muskoka and we took Bert up with us for that weekend. Magda has the most masculine brain of any woman I've ever met, I think. I rather expect she'll do something big.

My letters are depressing documents. All I want to do is register my continuing existence and affection. Helen sends regards and says she'll miss you next year. She donning again for Jessie Macpherson.[94]

Edward W. Wallace

Victoria College, Toronto, ON

23 August 1938

Gordon Bay, ON

Frye has just completed his first year of teaching at Victoria College and has gone to the Kemp's cottage at Gordon Bay before sailing to England for his second year at Merton College. This holograph letter is in the United Church of Canada / Victoria University Archives, 89.130V, box 26, file 281.

Dear Chancellor Wallace:

At the moment I am resting from the summer school, escaping the worst of the heat, and feeling generally rather prised and hovering, with all my possessions packed away and ready to take off for England as soon as my boat sails on the 24th of September. I am feeling a bit let down without anyone to teach here in Muskoka; the woodpeckers and blue jays catch a didactic glint in my eye and uneasily get out of the way.

Back in January I received a note from your office to the effect that members of the teaching profession on sabbatical leave, certified by the institution they teach in, would be granted a 20% reduction in steamship rates. I don't know whether this applies to me, or could be made to apply to me, but as I received a copy of the notice I thought I might inquire about it.

Helen joins me in sending regards to Mrs. Wallace, Ed,[95] and yourself. I'm very glad Ed got a good standing.

Roy Daniells

University of Manitoba, Winnipeg, MB

[September 1938]

Aboard the *Empress of Britain*

This brief letter was written sometime during the week following Frye's departure for his second year at Oxford— aboard the Empress of Britain *sailing from Montreal— on 24 September 1938. The surrealist show Frye mentions was an exhibition of surrealist art held at the Canadian National Exhibition 1938. Roland Penrose was the moving force behind the exhibition, which was earlier shown at the New Burlington Galleries in London. He was assisted by Herbert Read, Henry Moore, Paul Nash, and others. The foreword for the C.N.E. catalogue was by Read. Frye reviewed the show for the* Canadian Forum, *apparently having written the review before leaving for England: "Men as Trees Walking,"* Canadian Forum, *18 (October 1938): 208–10; rpt. in RW, 35–9, and in NFMC, 92–5. The Canadian National Exhibition was familiarly known as "the Ex"; during the 1930s it was the world's largest annual exhibition, held on Toronto's lake front for two weeks in late August and early September. Many students, including Helen Kemp, worked at the C.N.E. to earn money for the coming academic year. The letter is in the Roy Daniells Fonds, University of British Columbia, box 43, file 9.*

Dear Roy:

I don't know if you came Saturday morning or not: the sur-realist show turned out to be more important than I thought, and as it was the last day of the Ex, I decided to go back and have another look. Two Picassos, two Klees, two Dalis, two Chiricos, two Paul Nashes, and a lot of very good Englishmen I'd never heard of before. Surrealism is damned important, I think.

The Empress is rather dull, with restricted deck space.

Walter T. Brown   **6 January 1939**
Victoria College, Toronto, ON   Paris, France
This holograph letter is in the United Church of Canada / Victoria University Archives,
87.067V, box 3, file 3, pt. 2.

Dear Dr. Brown:

I have finished a term in Oxford and practically all of my first vacation in Paris.[96] I don't know whether it's the way the terms are arranged or the monotony of the rainy climate, but the time goes with incredible speed here: in another month half my time will be gone. Six weeks of winter in Paris are, however, considerably cheaper than six weeks of winter in London, and infinitely more cheerful. The English have a genius for unrelieved grimness which fits the climate well, and is probably due to it, but which is a little oppressive to an exotic. The French are very like the Americans superficially: they have the same buoyancy and the same liking for both ceremonial politeness and jovial rudeness.

European dictators are always at their most bellicose during the more comfortable weather, so there is a lull in war-scares. Mussolini wants Tunis, but the Paris press doesn't seem to take that as a serious threat: so far I've seen little but ridicule, although the newsreels put out propaganda films, very realistic ones explaining quite unemotionally that Mussolini must not have Tunis because too much French capital is invested there. It doesn't sound as though he would get far, but he may.

I wanted an easy-going holiday rooted in one spot, with time both for work and for unhurried sightseeing, so I haven't seen much of the provinces, beyond taking short trips to the cathedral towns, Rouen, Chartres and Amiens.[97] But I like this country: it seems so balanced and sensible I understand from people who were here that they took the crisis much more calmly than the English, and even now I've seen very little of the curiously bitter unhappiness one finds everywhere in England. That's probably an impression derived from my indifferent command of French, however.

When I got back to Oxford I found Blunden quite firm: I must give up the Blake publication scheme until my exams are over. That's because all his overseas students got seconds and thirds last year, and he want me to get a first. That prospect bores me to death: I've been working fairly steadily, but I find that the goal I'm working towards is not exams, but lecturing. I've lost interest in one, and am increasing my interest in the other.[98] I found last year that by a curious coincidence all my dull lectures were dull because I didn't know enough about the subject. I think they'll brighten up a bit now.

Helen writes that she and Henry Noyes are consoling each other for the lack of partners.[99] Otherwise, I don't know much about how the Department of English is making out, although Joe Fisher has promised to write.[100] I think Helen must be doing quite a lot of work in residence, to judge by her letters.[101] I myself am having a very good year: my health is all right, most of my Oxford friends are still up, and I'm more used to England. But I left a lot of roots in Canada, and there are times I catch myself counting up the number of weeks to go.

Edward W. Wallace   **13 January 1939**
Victoria College, Toronto, ON   Merton College, Oxford
This holograph letter is in United Church of Canada / Victoria University Archives,
89.130V, box 26, file 291. Chancellor Wallace's reply of 31 January 1939 is in the same file.

Dear Dr. Wallace:

I intended to write you at Christmastime, but the terms are so curiously arranged in

Oxford that nothing happens to one before then except a term's work. And the terms go very quickly in Oxford, once they start. I can hardly realize that my trunk is unpacked, yet in two or three weeks half the year will be gone.

I have just finished my Christmas vacation, spending most of my time in Paris. France is incredibly cheap and seems to bear its political humiliations with far less bitterness than England. Reserved as the English generally are, this time they seem to be unhappy and cynical as well. The French are at least superficially cheerful, perhaps because, in spite of not being on an island, they feel less responsible for events outside their country than the English are able to do.

Paris was my headquarters, but I made side trips to Chartres, Rouen and Amiens— the cathedral towns. It was the first time I had really studied at first hand the big encyclopaedic Gothic cathedral, and, although a terrific cold snap at Chartres started me thinking more about my toes than about the medieval soul, it opened a whole dimension of experience. There is something about the enormous completeness and relevance of the medieval achievement that is overpowering when one sees it in the plastic arts, however little one may be affected by its philosophy or literature. The Protestant is, I suppose, committed to iconoclasm, but when he sees the icon in front of him in all its splendour he can realize the sacrifice he has made.

When I came to Oxford Blunden was quite determined, for so mild a man, that I should postpone trying to get the Blake published and concentrate on my exams. All his overseas students turned up with seconds and thirds last year, so he's backing me this year. I think I may say, after deliberate and mature reflection, that I do not care two hoots on a penny whistle whether I get a first or not: yet I worked fairly hard last term. The sort of glib precocity one needs for examinations does not appeal to me much as a goal; but now that I have discovered that I can make a fairly good teacher I have something tangible to work for. I not only have a vocation: I am beginning to find out what the word "vocation" means.

So it's a good year, but no matter what sort of year it was I should still be lonesome for Helen and anxious to get back home.

Roy Daniells **8 February 1939**
University of Manitoba, Winnipeg, MB Merton College, Oxford
The letter is in the Roy Daniells Fonds, University of British Columbia, box 43, file 11.

Dear Roy:
This leaves me in the middle of an English winter, learning some things rather meaningless about the Middle English diphthongs, bored with exam cramming, and waiting for the year to end. I think last year was on the whole the best year I ever had, and I am anxious for more of it.

Blunden wants me to chuck the Blake until after schools, the point being that I'm a possible first and his students haven't done so well of late years.[102] I suppose I could get it ready for Cape in the three weeks or so before the viva. That's if Helen doesn't come over. She wants to come but I don't know how possible it is. She seems to be very busy this year to judge from the infrequency of her letters, and is doing things like broadcasting as well as haranguing old ladies on art and donning in Wymilwood.

I spent the vac. [vacation] in Paris, as I think I told you, with a very steady New Zealander who drinks like a tank.[103] On the last night I got very drunk and maudlin and begged him to stay with me indefinitely in Paris, but I came back to my Nonconformist self and returned.

England is an unhappy and depressed country, ever since Munich. A sort of dementia praecox seems to have got hold of the country with every prospect of continuing. France is more cheerful, perhaps because it's better fed.

Edward W. Wallace   **22 July [1939]**
Victoria College, Toronto, ON   Paris, France
   This holograph letter is in the United Church of Canada / Victoria University Archives, 89.130V, box 26, file 297.

Dear Chancellor Wallace:
   I received your letter appointing me to the permanent staff of Victoria College when I was in London. I have been associated with the College too long now to make it necessary to say that I shall look forward to going home in the autumn: I have always enjoyed teaching at Victoria: I know the staff, I know what sort of students go there, I know something of the religious and historical traditions of the College, and would rather work there than anywhere else.
   I have just finished my oral exam at Oxford,[104] and Helen and I and a fellow student from New Zealand[105] are planning a two-weeks trip through North Italy. I am sailing from Southampton on August 12, and will be home in plenty of time to get my courses organized. Helen and I had not done any traveling since we were married, and are having the time of our lives. She was over five years ago studying art in London, but impressions of buildings and pictures get a little blurred in that time.
   Helen sends her best regards with mine to Mrs. Wallace and Ed. We are of course looking forward to seeing you in September.

1940s

Roy Daniells   15 May 1940
University of Manitoba, Winnipeg, MB
This letter is in the Roy Daniells Fonds, University of British Columbia, box 3, file 16.

Dear Roy:

I have just finished marking a huge pile of Milton papers, which were dull apart from a tendency to confuse "circumscribe" with "circumcise." Plans for publishing the Blake in England have, of course, been badly bogged down, as England has run out of paper. It really doesn't do to keep anything nine years: it's developed from a complicated puzzle figured out by the brightest little boy that ever was around here into a work of what I hope is some maturity. In the course of which development I have acquired more subsidiary ideas than are good for me.

Helen and I have got to know the Cassidys quite well, and they're charming.[106] I think his photographs are, some of them, quite amazing: they have everything the best abstract painting has and often a good deal more. I suppose the main difference between photography and painting is that painting is less epigrammatic, which gives the photographs greater pungency.

Joe, as you doubtless know, signed up at the beginning of the war. Archie Hare is the one who hears from him: he seems quite cheerful, obviously loves the army, and has acquired a serenity in it he could never find in teaching English.[107] His honour 18th-century course was bequeathed to me, which about doubled my work. Next year the curriculum is being all revised again, and most of the new courses happen to be mine: it's a good thing I like teaching.

I was very pleased about Henry[108]: that makes quite a colony of our friends in Missouri, what with the Stobies[109] and a Rhodes Scholar I lived with at Oxford.[110] I shouldn't have thought the climate good for Gertrude [Noyes], but Mrs. Noyes Sr. says it is.

There seems to be some centrifugal force in Toronto that keeps sending all our friends away: Helen has lost the three best people the Art Gallery, and for me, Davis,[111] you, Henry, and now Mary Winspear is going to Columbia to do a thesis on a tenth-rate eighteenth-century occultist.[112] Is that progress? Maybe this town will have another cycle of life, but I'm not too hopeful. I like Victoria and like it thoroughly but it gives me exactly what Oxford gave me in a different way, a sense of the connotations of the word "retreat."

I'm told on all sides that your radio talks are admirable[113]: we haven't a radio or we'd have heard them. The rest of the space on this page is reserved for shrewd and penetrating comments on the political and economic situation of the world. All the best.

Roy Daniells   [ca. August 1940]
University of Manitoba, Winnipeg, MB   Moncton, NB
   This letter is in the Roy Daniells Fonds, University of British Columbia, box 3, file 17.

My dear Roy:
   I find that what I was determined to treat as an undergraduate's excuse, war jitters,
really does interfere with my serious duties, hence the postponing of letters to inexcusably
late dates (the plural is truthful as well as polite)[114] and hence the abandonment of Montaigne for Wilkie Collins. England can't lose. England can't lose. England can't lose. Smug,
rich, moral, perfidious Albion has played Moby Dick to a long string of exasperated Continental Ahabs, and what's Hitler got that Philip II and Louis XIV and Napoleon and the
Kaiser didn't have? England can't lose...
   I'm home at Moncton, trying to persuade my parents that I must get back to work. I
have finally arrived at academic middle age — I know so much that I can't remember it all —
and am planning a card catalogue of notes. Mother is seventy and rather feeble: I keep trying to insist on a doctor, but, like many old people, she thinks all doctors are charlatans
and blackguards. Dad is the same age but looks like her son, and keeps tearing all over the
Maritimes in an ancient Dodge selling hardware and paint. I've been here since July 1—
Helen was with me during July but has gone back to the Gallery. I look forward to a fall of
hacked salaries, worried students and the most frightful hell yet in Europe.
   I've just been to see an old friend of mine who lives next door. He's French-Canadian,
and a brakeman-conductor now, I believe — on the train.[115] Brought up as a Catholic, he's
broken with the Church in his own way: collected the biggest library I've even seen of
books proving that Jesus was a mythical figure. Naturally he's delighted to have a theologian to take apart — I keep feebly trying to tell him I've read The Golden Bough and a few
more of his classics, but he won't listen. His great hero is J.M. Robertson, the man [Doug-
las] Bush calls the "veteran disintegrator."[116] He's reading Chaucer now, and is going from
there to Rabelais and Apuleius.
   I'm a little frightened about next year's courses: what with Woodhouse on one side
and Endicott on the other,[117] our prescribed texts are in danger of expanding into a mere
reading list. There's a vast Renaissance survey course, 1500 to 1660, and I'm expected to
include Machiavelli, Castiglione, Montaigne and Erasmus in it. My policy in lecturing, so
far, is to include everything on the course: I'm sure the students feel a lot better if something is said about everything — it gives them more impetus to keep up. But that's evidently not U.C. [University College] policy. Last year I did far too much straight talking —
partly because the courses were mainly new ones, and I had to talk fast to persuade myself
I knew my way along. I don't know about undergraduate seminars. I put in a year getting
my brats to read papers on Milton and 19th c. thought. They got their work done on time,
that's one thing. But they all read as though they were praying from a rosary, the other kids
couldn't hear them, couldn't follow them, and there wasn't so much time to do anything
afterwards. I'll have to work out some scheme of short papers introducing a subject, I think.
A good paper is too much for mediocre students to follow — they haven't the background —
and a mediocre paper hasn't anything in it anyway. Maybe they could be broken in in first
year.
   My father has a car this summer and I've made several trips to the Maritimes.[118] The
history of the Maritimes has been an oscillation between New England and New France,
with economic facts pointing one way and political expediency the other. Maritime popu-
lation is stationary, its industry at a standstill, its debts mounting, and its spirit despon-

dent. It's been that way ever since its only real market — Boston — was closed off by protective tariff, and it will be that way until Boston is accessible again.

I don't think Cassidy's expenses are unreasonable, granted that he wants to establish himself in business and has to borrow money to do it.[119] It's only in nursery rhymes that one can put a wife and family into a shoe or a pumpkin shell, and he can't carry photographic equipment on a street car. But I quite see your point, and I think your gradual repayment scheme about the best thing you can do.

I suppose this war will end with the total destruction of Germany. The feeling that there may be one of a long series of similar annihilations is what gives me futurist nightmares. I wish Spengler had gone in for collecting butterflies.[120]

A.J.M. Smith   **[early 1940s]**
English Department, Michigan State University, East Lansing, MI

A.J.M. Smith was a Canadian poet and critic who produced a number of important anthologies of Canadian poetry and prose. He left Canada in 1936 to teach at the Michigan State University, where he remained until his retirement in 1972. Because of Frye's reference to Ernest Sirluck's service in the Canadian Army, this undated letter was written sometime between 1942 and 1945.

Dear Art:

Thanks very much for the two Quarterly articles, both of which I have read with interest. The one on 19th c. poetry I want to go over again with the stuff itself when I have time. I am pondering a series of articles under the general heading of "The Problem of a Canadian Culture," though I haven't time for it now, but hope to put part of the summer on it. The trouble is that the stuff itself bores me so.

Eleanor[121] says she'd like some more poetry, please. Meanwhile, unsolicited stuff keeps pouring into the Forum office, some of it fair: Margaret Avison, James Wreford, Irving Layton have been getting started with us.[122]

All the best, and hope of course to see you whenever you return to Toronto. Earle and Sirluck[123] seem to be thriving in the army, though I trust Earle won't get weaned so far from his earlier prejudices as to forget that he wrote one hell of a lousy poem on going to the wars.

A.J.M. Smith   **[Summer 1942]**

This undated letter was written during the summer of 1942, which is when E.J. Pratt read his poem The Truant *to a group of friends at the apartment of Earle Birney — an occasion mentioned by Frye in the second paragraph. Frye was literary editor of the* Canadian Forum *at the time.*

Dear Art:

Eleanor[124] spoke to me about getting some poems out of Margaret Avison, but as she forwarded a letter from you suggesting that you might get her for November or December, I've said nothing to Margaret, so as not to get our wires crossed. The general run of poems Alan Creighton[125] has been sending up is gloomy: we live in the age of the statue's feet, of iron mixed with miry clay and a certain amount of horseshit. To crown that, they send me two volumes of "Poets of the Month," the monthly discharge of the New Directions people.[126] Why should poetry have a direction?

Ned has just read us his best poem yet, I think, called "The Truant." It's Blake's conflict of Orc and Urizen, the Prometheus-Jesus agent of humanity revolting against the God of universal machinery. It's the subtlest and maturest piece of symbolism he's done, and he always has been a symbolic poet rather than a chronicler or ballad-spinner. Furthermore, it's the keystone of all his earlier symbolism, and it's the target the earlier best things were pointing to. I hope you can clean out a place for it in the anthology[127]: it would be a calamity not to have it in, I think.[128]

All the best: hope to see you before too long. Earle [Birney] seems to take to the army like a duck to the Dead Sea. I mean, he floats all right, but it isn't quite his element.

Miriam Waddington [mid–1940s]

This undated letter posted to Miriam Waddington at some unknown address is in response to Waddington's having sent Frye a copy of her story that was rejected by Alan Creighton, managing editor of the Canadian Forum. *Frye was literary editor of the* Forum *from 1942 to 1948, when he became managing editor, so the letter almost certainly was written during that period. Waddington (1917–2004), a poet, translator, short story writer, dramatist, editor, and social worker, was at the time a member of a Montreal circle of writers that included Irving Layton and Louis Dudek. The letter is in the Miriam Waddington Papers of the Library and Archives Canada.*

Dear Mrs. Waddington:

Thank you for sending me your story, which I was glad to get and interested to read. I hadn't seen it before, but I assume Mr. Creighton just sent it back automatically because of its length: the Forum has so little room for fiction and what it takes are sketches and vignettes rather than stories.

It's a pretty story, and very well written. I suppose that for publication purposes it would have to be more sharply pointed: there's a certain amount of advertising in all published work, and so much of the meaning of this story depends on the irony of the title and on one or two passing remarks like "an artificial claim which she wished didn't exist." Also, it isn't quite clear whether the camp itself is Jewish or Gentile, which is rather an important point. Still, I liked it, though I know it would have to be cut a good deal, perhaps in the section dealing with the youngsters, before Mr. Creighton would consider it. What this country needs is a good five-cent fiction magazine.

Hugh E. Moorhouse 14 November [late 1940s]

Hugh Moorhouse does not recall the year this letter was written, but he believes it was before 1950— at the time he "was between Heim and Barth."[129] Moorhouse was a classmate of Frye's and lived next door to him during their Emmanuel College days, 1933–36. He returned to Emmanuel for an M.A. in philosophy and theology in 1950.

Hugh:

I imagine that the reason why there is a gap between faith and reason, of the sort you felt some years ago, is that reason deals with certain mental categories and, not being able to go beyond them, is perpetually calling them ultimates, whereas revelation is constantly insisting on the limitations of the human mind. The two most pervasive reasonable categories that exist are time and space, and our conception of both of these is probably all wrong, as you say, or quote Heim as saying, both are indefinite, which means that they are part of Mystery, not of revelation. Revelation encourages us to think in terms of infinity and eternity, not in the mathematical sense, in which they are identical with the indefinite, but in the religious sense. As we experience time, the present, the only part of it that we do experience, never quite exists. As we experience space, the centre, or the here, never quite exists either — everything we perceive in space is "there." Under the impact of reve-lation the whole fallen world turns inside out, into an eternal now and an infinite here. In terms of the Kantian distinction between the thing perceived and the thing in itself, we never see the thing in itself because we are the thing in itself. Reality is the immediate data of ordinary experience universalized — that is why it is revealed to the childlike rather than the sophisticated in us. The beginning of the vision of eternity is the child's realization that his own home is the circumference of the universe as far as he is concerned. The end of it is the regenerate Christian's realization that the universe is a city of God, the home of the soul, and the body of Jesus.

Man is always trying to find security in a temporal continuum, either with the past (the Pharisaic approach to the law, repeated in Roman Catholic ideas of apostolic succes-sion) or the future (the humanitarian idealistic approach to social reform). And if, as Heim says, the idea of heaven as the world's attic is gone, the association of God with the mys-tery and remoteness of nature is not.[130] Hence the total form of human reason, of the sort that denies God, in other words the body of fallen man, is this temporal and spatial con-tinuum which stretches out to indefiniteness. Does this make sense? Is it what the Preacher means when he says (Eccl. vi, 10): "That which hath been is named already, and it is known that it is man: neither may he contend with him that is mightier than he"?

Roy Daniells   **23 March 1945**
University of Manitoba, Winnipeg, MB
    This letter is in the Roy Daniells Fonds, University of British Columbia, box 4, file 16.

Dear Roy:
    Thanks very much for the divine revelations concerning the doings of George and Margaret Vance in Krasnovodsk, Turkmen S.S.R.[131] It's a charming thing, quite as good as most of the Gnostic systems, and more readable. There's a good deal of theological acumen in it too, as when he says that God is omniscient, at least as far as He knows. He's a kindly soul, and I can easily believe that God signified his approval by miraculous changes on the sound tracks of motion pictures.
    I hear your broadcasts irregularly, but like what I have heard.[132] Canadian literature has, for the time being, lost its sense of direction, if it ever had any, but in the meantime is exploring some interesting possibilities. Unit of 5 seems to me to have some good stuff in it,[133] and more things should be coming. You may have become conscious of a great pub-lic desire for better literature increasing on all sides — I suspect its existence, though I haven't directly met it.

Roy Daniells   **30 May 1946**
University of Manitoba, Winnipeg, MB
    This letter is in the Roy Daniells Fonds, University of British Columbia, box 5, file 4.

Dear Roy:
    I went to see Robins and told him about our luncheon date; Robins went to see Brown,[134] and Brown went to see the Board of Regents, which met yesterday, luckily for me. They raised me to Associate Professor and jumped my salary to the point it would nor-mally have been at in about three years. Brown made me a charming speech in which he said I wasn't to think I'd blackmailed him into this, but that I had given him an opportu-nity to do something he was glad of the excuse to do. So your kind intentions regarding me met with complete fulfilment, and I have a great deal to thank you for in consequence.

Earle Birney   **15 March 1947**
Department of English, University of British Columbia, Vancouver, BC
Birney, who had been asked by William Arthur Deacon to become editor of the Canadian
Poetry Magazine, *ran the magazine from Vancouver, where he had accepted a teaching posi-*
tion in 1946 at the University of British Columbia. He had apparently written Frye to see if
the Canadian Forum *was going to review three recent issues. Frye's letter is in the Thomas Fisher*
Rare Book Library of the University of Toronto Library.

Dear Earle:
    Thank you for your letter. Yes, Eleanor[135] dropped out of the Forum some time ago,
and had rather lost interest in it long before that. In the new setup Grube[136] is Editor-in-
Chief and I'm Literary Editor. Alan[137] is Assistant Editor, which means in practice that he
is Secretary of the Board, and handles all the correspondence. I haven't time to do much
more than direct the policy, and even if I had Alan is in the office and has all the information about amount of space, overmatter, proportioning of material and so on in his head.
He is also the only other member of the Editorial Board who can tell a poem from any other
piece of staggered type.
    The September issue of the Canadian Poetry Magazine must have come in before I took
over — I certainly don't remember any number coming into the office for review. If you'll
send me the three issues you mention I'll have a notice of them put in. Like you, we have
legacies, A.J.M. Smith in the role of High Pontiff of Canadian letters being our chief one,
as you have doubtless noticed.
    All the best to Esther and yourself; U.B.C. sounds as though you were living in quite
a stimulating environment. Best of luck with the magazine; I'm pleased but not surprised
to hear that the circulation has doubled since you took over.

William Arthur Deacon   **19 May 1947**
Toronto, ON
    Deacon — writer, critic, essayist, and syndicated book reviewer — had reviewed Frye's
Fearful Symmetry *for the Toronto* Globe and Mail: *"Masterly Interpretation of William Blake's*
Poems," 17 May 1947, p. 12. He called the book "a notable achievement," a book that "has
enriched the whole literary world by rescuing the major works of a great poet from misunder-
standing and obscurity."

Dear Mr. Deacon:
    Just a note to thank you most sincerely for exactly the kind of review an author most
appreciates getting — one that praises his book for what he thinks are the right reasons.
If the book is as good as you say and I hope it is, you have done a considerable service
not only to me but to the man you so aptly refer to as "the least read favorite poet of all
time."

Roy Daniells   **10 August 1947**
University of British Columbia, Vancouver, BC
    Daniells had written to Frye (26 July 1947) about the publication of Fearful Symmetry.
Frye's letter is in the Roy Daniells Fonds, University of British Columbia, box 6, file 6.

Dear Roy:
    Thank you very much for your note. As one interested in the sale of the book, I'm not
sure that I approve of all this promiscuous lending around,[138] but as one interested, like
Paul, in continuing to persecute Blake by spreading his gospel, I find it highly gratifying.

It's curious how one talks (and to some extent feels) about a published book as though it were a badly ulcerated tooth: Well, it's out at last; it's been bothering me a long time and should have been out long ago. I guess the reproductive and excretory functions must be associated on the mental plane as well. However, mothers don't talk that way about their children, but then Nature keeps more accurate schedules than publishers. Besides, children grow, and although my friends have rallied nobly and the Canadian reviews[139] have been very good—too kind, as Florence Nightingale would say[140]—the only review in the States I've seen four months after publication is a dull and uncomprehending piece of foolishness in the Saturday Review.[141] But I suppose all publishing of MSS is only a slightly improved form of corking them in bottles and tossing them into the drink.

I met Sedgwick [Sedgewick][142] when he was in Toronto recently, and grew promptly as fond of him as I gather everyone else does. You must have a very lively and keen department, and visiting B.C. is still one of my chief ambitions.

All the best from me and Helen.

The photograph *doesn't* do me justice: the photographer knew what I wanted a picture for and aimed deliberately at that expression of fatuous self-satisfaction.[143]

Earle Birney   **15 August 1947**
Department of English, University of British Columbia, Vancouver, BC

In response to Birney's having sent Frye some poems for the Canadian Forum, *for which Frye was literary editor at the time. Birney's holograph note on the letter indicates that Frye had rejected "some of the best of my poetry," which later appeared in* The Strait of Anian *(1948). Frye's letter is in the Thomas Fisher Rare Book Library of the University of Toronto Library.*

Dear Earle:

Thanks very much for the letter and for the poems, although I doubt if it's practical to use them. They've kept squeezing our poems out of so many issues that we now have a large backlog of accepted stuff, and we'd have to hold yours at least till fall, when you say your book will be out. I am very keen to see the book, as I liked the specimens you sent, and will try to get it reviewed promptly. As you are probably in a better position to realize than anyone else, a lot of Canadians write poetry.

Yes, I'm very glad to see the book [*Fearful Symmetry*] out at last, and I think Princeton made a very attractive job of it. They have an excellent art department there and gave it the works in type & paper & binding. The reviews, apart from the Canadian ones, are slow in coming out—I suspect that the book is too academic in subject for the large-circulation magazines and too popular in style for the *Wissenschaft* journals.

Sedgwick [Sedgewick][144] was in Toronto this spring and I met him then for the first time and liked him very much. Jack Grant[145] I believe has just left here. You must have a wonderful department there and a lively and go-ahead spirit in the university as a whole. I was a little startled at the G. Andrew appointment, as I didn't know English was his line.[146] All the best to Esther & you from Helen & me.

Edith Sitwell   **7 January 1948**
Renishaw Hall, Renishaw, North Sheffield, Derbyshire, England

This letter is in the Sitwell Papers at the Harry Ransom Humanities Research Center, University of Texas, Austin, TX.

Dear Miss Sitwell:

Ever since I read your review of *Fearful Symmetry* in the Spectator[147] I have been wanting to write you and wondering what to say. I have finally decided that the best thing to say is thank you.

Walter T. Brown   February 1948
Victoria College, Toronto, ON

In response to this request for promotion, President Walter T. Brown wrote to Frye on 18 March 1948 confirming that the Board of Regents had approved of his promotion to professor of English, with a salary of $5000. This typed letter is in the United Church of Canada / Victoria University Archives: 89.130V, Frye file. Brown's reply is in the same file.

Dear Dr Brown:

After carefully thinking over your suggestion, I have come to the conclusion that I should ask for the full professorship for next year. My decision is based on the following considerations:

1) If I went up now the promotion could be presented as a quite impersonal matter, as recognition of a major publication and an offer from another university. It appears to me that to postpone it for a year would be more likely to suggest irrelevant considerations of personal merit.

2) This applies particularly to colleagues within the department. I have thought over my personal relationships with the others, and am convinced that they would realize that when it comes to promotion I am a rather special category.

3) There is not and cannot be any question of fair dealing at issue: the College has treated me very well, and my refusal of the Wisconsin offer is pretty tangible evidence that I realize that fact. I do have to consider the question of how far I can afford to keep on refusing offers for promotion and greatly increased salary. The Wisconsin one is the fourth full professorship I have been offered in the past eighteen months: I have no reason to suppose that such offers will cease coming, and I should be greatly fortified in my desire to refuse them by possessing the rank which they offer.

4) The Wisconsin offer in particular was a very great honor to a man of my age, and my friends there would be certain to notice it if I kept on here as associate. They would, I think, interpret the situation as evidence either that I thought there was something wrong with their university, or that I lacked enterprise.

5) In the interests of the College as a whole, and for the sake in particular of younger men who will be joining the English staff, I should like to see the precedent established of immediate recognition of major publications.

Accordingly, after trying to be as objective about my own interests as it is in nature to be, my opinion is that I should take the promotion in rank now. The decision to implement this is after all in your hands, and my conviction of your personal concern for my welfare has always been an essential factor in my desire to remain at Victoria College.

Edith Sitwell   12 April 1948
Renishaw Hall, Renishaw, North Sheffield, Derbyshire, England

In reply to Sitwell's having sent Frye a copy of her The Shadow of Cain. *On 7 January 1948 Frye had written Sitwell a note thanking her for her review of* Fearful Symmetry *and enclosing a copy of his essay, "Yeats and the Language of Symbolism." Sitwell's reply to the present letter has been published in* Selected Letters of Edith Sitwell, *ed. Richard Greene (London: Virago Books, 1997), 294. Frye's letter is in the Sitwell Papers at the Harry Ransom Humanities Research Center, University of Texas, Austin, TX.*

Dear Miss Sitwell:

Thank you very much for *The Shadow of Cain*, a very lovely, haunting, and almost unbelievably suggestive poem. The apparently effortless way in which a contemporary situation expands, by way of certain human archetypes, into its ultimate values of primeval cold and unquenchable life, makes the poem a kind of miniature epic.[148] I know by this time what to look for in major poetry, and I always find it. Reversing the axiom, when I find what satisfies me in a poem I know that it is major, and *The Shadow of Cain* belongs to the restricted canon of major poetry. The close connection between your mind and Blake's, which has become so striking in recent years, is an additional and personal reason for my liking it, not because I want all poetry to be "Blakean," but because you are one of the few poets who confirm the authenticity of the experience I went through in submitting myself to Blake's influence.

Thank you very much too for your letter and its warm appreciation of my book. I am glad to hear what is slowly being confirmed by personal letters that it is gradually finding its way to the people for whom it is intended. I know Messrs. Tchelitchew and Bowra only by reputation,[149] but that is considerable enough to make me pleased with the success I have had in helping modern readers to know Blake. I have written my publisher about having the book published in England, but he says that the shortage of paper in England makes it inadvisable, and that the best thing to do is to sustain pressure on Oxford, who distribute the book in England, to keep advertising it until the ban is lifted. Meanwhile, of course, copies can be ordered from Princeton. That's the official communiqué: actually, I don't think any pressure is being put on Oxford or that Oxford is responding if it is. However, that's his [Bowra's] decision. I'm sorry the book should be short when you and Mr. Keynes and the T.L.S. reviewer have been so good to it,[150] and I can only hope that eventually the people who want it will get it. I am much obliged to you for the name of your agent, which will sooner or later be of great help to me.

I am pleased to see in a publisher's announcement you are editing a selection of Blake for the Chiltern Library, which is building up one of the best reprint collections available.[151] Your remarks about Blake (e.g. in *The Pleasures of Poetry*) constitute a part of my own enlightenment on that subject, and I am eager to see more of them.

The academic term here, with the registration three times what it was two years ago, and which has kept me effectively snowed under all winter, is gradually relaxing, and I am looking round for more jobs to do. I want to move back into the sixteenth century and write about *The Faerie Queene* and Shakespeare's comedies and Rabelais. Once a critic learns his job, criticism ought to come very easily, for if he is writing about a greater man than himself (the normal procedure), he has that man's power available and ready to be tapped, if he will only realize that it is greater, and puncture the hole in the dam of his own ego. The arrogance and self-sufficiency I find in so much contemporary criticism, especially in America, bewilders me, as it seems to make things needlessly difficult. Once again, thanks very much for your kindness to me, which, coming as it does from a famous poet to an unknown critic, has given me an idea of what is meant by the phrase "republic of letters."[152]

Pelham Edgar   9 August 1948
Toronto, ON

When Pelham Edgar, one of Frye's Victoria College teachers, was preparing an essay on "Creative Criticism in Canada," he wrote to Frye (2 August 1948), asking him to send an account of "what led you in the Blake direction." Frye obliged, and Edgar included almost all of Frye's response in his biography, Across My Path (Toronto: Ryerson Press, 1952), which Frye himself edited. The two letters differ, however, in some details, and these are recorded in the notes below. Frye introduced the changes in the process of editing the book. The typescript is in the Pelham Edgar Fonds, Victoria University Library.

Dear Pelham:

I was very sorry to hear about the thrombosis: the only glint of silver lining is that apparently nature makes her own adjustments in time. But it can't be any fun waiting for that to happen. It's a shame to have your summer interfered with in such a way, and I hope the fall will find you active again.[153]

Your letter started me thinking about the length of time I had grown up with Blake, waiting to get enough maturity and authority[154] to write about him. I was startled to realize how far back he goes in my life. I remember looking into the Yeats Modern Library volume of Blake in the Moncton Public Library at the age of fifteen: I was interested, but at that age I was considerably more interested in Bernard Shaw.[155] I came to Victoria at seventeen, did the first year pass, and for the summer Barber got me (pure kindness on his part) a small job[156] in the Toronto Public Library, pasting labels into new books. I remember Saurat's Blake and Modern Thought was one of them, and I have no idea why it fascinated me so, or why I used to come to work half an hour early to read it. Next year you made a remark about Blake in the Shakespeare course[157] that kept him in my mind, and that summer, when I went home, I took some of the long prophecies with me, and used to take them out and stare at them and think how nice it would be if I could read them. The third year came your eighteenth century,[158] and I signed up for a paper on Blake. From then on I was hooked. You may remember the paper. In my fourth year I could hardly talk about anything but Blake, and Helen gave me the one-volume Keynes Poetry and Prose for my graduation present. Next year was theology, and I snatched[159] at a graduate course on Blake that H.J. Davis was giving. That year I read all the secondary sources on Blake, and Davis assigned me[160] a paper on *Milton*. I sat down to write it, as was my regular bad habit in those days, the night before, and around about two in the morning some very curious things began happening in my mind. I began to see glimpses of something bigger and more exciting than I had ever before realized existed in the world of the mind, and when I went out for breakfast at five-thirty on a bitterly cold winter morning, I was committed to a book on Blake.

Soon after that I discovered what is still my opening lead — the connection of Blake with Berkeley — and began an M.A. thesis on Blake. I never finished it, but I did hardly anything else in theology, I regret to say, except read The Golden Bough. I spent most of my time in arts reading Spengler, and so I had three big pieces of pattern, which I had a hunch fitted together, though it took me many years to discover how. Then came the Royal Society award and[161] a year at Oxford with Blunden, who listened patiently and wisely to my burblings for a good many tutorial hours. I came back to Canada with a "book," as I imagined it to be, on Blake over half done, got married and stayed home to teach for a year, spending my honeymoon typing the last half. That manuscript went to Faber and Cambridge,[162] was promptly rejected by both, and when I got it back I decided I still had a lot of growing to do. I finished Oxford next year and came back on the permanent staff here in 1939, but I didn't seriously start writing again until the spring of 1942.

Before the term started in September of that year I had done about half the book, and the second half nagged me all winter long, so in spring I started on the second half. The only trouble with that was that I had to tear up and rewrite the first half first. Again September came with me stuck in the middle of The Four Zoas, but I made a strenuous effort and got it done, in a kind of way, in February of 1944. I sent it to Random House, and they took until November to say no,[163] but I had lost interest in their report long before it came, as I had been spending the whole summer tearing it up and rewriting it. *That* version got done in February of 1945, and, missing a nervous collapse by inches, I sent it to Princeton University Press. They put a reader on it who read it very carefully, very accurately and very sympathetically, and he turned in a report saying he didn't think it ought to be published in its present version (a MS[164] of 658 pages), as it was too long, difficult and confusing, but it had some good stuff in it. His report enabled me to get an objective view of the book at a time when I was long past the ability to get one on myself. In summer of 1945 I rewrote it again, cutting 170 pages out of the manuscript, and that time, fall 1945, they accepted it.

I don't know if this account of my labor pains is of any use: after all, I'm an exceptional case. Very few people are ill-advised enough to pick one of the hardest and most complicated jobs in English literature for their first effort. At the same time I consider myself extraordinarily lucky. Victoria is an amazingly tolerant place: nobody once hinted that I ought to publish something to "make good." I had plenty of time to do the job in my own way. Also it was a considerable privilege to discover Blake and grow up inside his mind, as it were: I don't see how I could have got a better education.

All my best,

I notice that I haven't said anything about the actual process of writing. That was a matter of waiting for things to crystallize. Toronto is an excellent town to mind one's own business in, and a lot of the writing and drafting was done in its restaurants, pubs and street corners as well as in my office. Some sentences even go back to a Saskatchewan field,[165] with the Keynes one-volume tossing in a saddle bag. The conception of how Orc, the underground Titan who bursts into bloom every spring, could be both Adonis and Prometheus came to me in the corner of a store where Helen was shopping for dress material.[166] I remember being in a pub and staring with some distaste at an early version of the last chapter, and a drunk across the table saying very wisely: "That's somebody else's stuff you're reading. I can always tell. When people read their own stuff they look pleased."

Lorne Pierce   **9 November 1949**
Ryerson Press, Toronto, ON

Pierce (1890–1961), an ordained minister, founding member of the Canadian Authors Association, and for forty years the editor of Ryerson Press, contributed substantially to the development of Canadian literature. He had asked Frye to edit the memoirs of Pelham Edgar, Frye's teacher and later his colleague at Victoria College. Edgar had been at work on his memoirs at the time of his sudden death in 1948. After much discussion back and forth of Frye's several proposals in the present letter, the book eventually took shape as a three-part volume ("A Memoir," "The Canadian Scene," and "The Literary Horizon"), edited by Frye and published as Across My Path *(Toronto: Ryerson Press, 1952). Frye's letter is in the Queen's University Archives, Kingston, Ontario.*

Dear Dr. Pierce:

I have been thinking a good deal lately about Pelham's memoirs. My present feeling about them is that the MS I have does not constitute a book and cannot be published in its present form. It begins with a beautifully written and well-organized account of his early days in Toronto, and of the Edgar family. That part is excellent memoir material. But after his Johns Hopkins days, at the latest, there is simply no connecting thread to hold the book together. I know that he changed his intentions in the course of writing it, and was planning to do a series of vignettes, half-personal and half-critical, on the people he had known and met. Some of these are well done; others, such as the story of the Arnold Bennett incident, are quite pointless unless directly related to a central narrative, which is not there. The same is true of several disjointed anecdotes, such as the encounter with Ezra Pound, the dinner with the drunken cook, the meeting with Meredith, and the story of Bell and the lectern, which are very good memoir material, but only if the memoir is there. And it isn't there. Anyone sufficiently interested in Pelham to want to read the book would feel badly cheated by not finding many things there that he would expect to find. Thus:

1) There is no connected account of his work as a teacher in Victoria College, and no reference to any of his colleagues there except Ned [Pratt] and myself. Nor are there any personal details about his later life, or any mention of Dona and Jane,[167] his life in the censorship department at Ottawa, and so on.

2) Of the Canadian poets he knew, [D.C.] Scott and Pratt are the only ones dealt with in detail. His readers would expect some treatment of [Charles G.D.] Roberts and [Bliss] Carman at least. He knew a great deal about both that no one else knew, and his lecture at Victoria a few years ago had some fascinating reminiscences of Carman.

3) The encouragement and help he gave to younger writers is not mentioned even to the extent that I think he would have been willing to mention it. There is nothing about Marjorie Pickthall, Raymond Knister, Audrey A. Brown or Dorothy Livesay, to mention a few obvious ones at random. Nor Earle Birney, Louis Mackay or A.J.M. Smith, with all of whom he was in close touch.

4) There is nothing about his work as a scholar: no reference either to Henry James or to his book on him, only a brief and rather cryptic reference to his Art of the Novel, and nothing about any of his numerous critical articles, some of which were of considerable historical importance. And although he has a charming passage on his discovery of Shelley and an account of his graduate work at Johns Hopkins, he does not say that his doctoral dissertation was on Shelley's imagery, which is the link the reader would need — this last, of course, could be fixed up by an editor.

5) I know that he intended to add Douglas Bush and E.K. Brown to his chapter on criticism. Their omission is not fatal, but the fact that two of his disciples are not there while [Charles] Cochrane and [Barker] Fairley, who had only the slenderest personal connection with him, are there, makes the chapter seem like a somewhat arbitrary choice of names for a memoir.

6) Several of the existing fragments, such as the Macphail paper, have no narrative connection with anything else in the book, and in several cases I am quite unable to supply any editorial connective tissue. This is true of the account of the Egyptian expedition with [Charles] Currelly, for example, and of the fragmentary remarks about his connection with the Canadian Authors' Association, the P.E.N. Guild, and other societies.

This list of omissions is not exhaustive, but long enough to show that anything like an adequate memoir of Pelham does not exist among the fragments he left, interesting as those fragments often are in themselves. To print a chaotic and disjointed sequence of anecdotes and articles with an apologetic note at the beginning explaining that the book would not be such a hodge-podge if the author had lived to finish it seems to me out of the question. At first I thought, and I daresay you thought too, that skilful and patient editing might make a plausibly connected narrative out of what is here. But the list I have just given shows that the omissions of essential material go far beyond any editorial patching-up. I should have to write myself a good two-thirds of the book that ought to be there, which, even if I were qualified to do it, wouldn't make it much of a memoir.

What I have to propose as alternatives is as follows:

1) I have looked through Victoria's collection of letters as well as the memoir. There is nothing there that would improve the continuity of the memoir by being inserted into it. But the memoir and the letters together form the basis of one of the best biographical studies available in Canadian literature. In fact, I don't think Canadian literature could get along without a good biography of Pelham. The board of regents here recently commissioned Sissons to write a history of Victoria College, and I think it might well commission somebody to write Pelham's biography. I couldn't do it myself: I don't know enough and couldn't get to know enough without taking two or three years at least out of a writing career that is irrevocably dedicated to other writers. Other names occur to me: Mrs. D.C. Scott, Margaret Ray, you, Dorothy Livesay, or even a graduate student who was good enough. But it seems to me that the real and obvious destiny of the present memoir is to be incorporated into a biography.

2) A collection of Pelham's essays and papers under some such title as "Portraits and Personalities." These would include such material from the memoir as:

   i) The Edgar family (some of the present first chapter and the passages on his ancestors).

   ii) The Macphail article.

   iii) The Leacock article.

   iv) The chapter on Ned Pratt.

   v) The material on D.C. Scott.

   vi) The sketch of Mrs. Humphrey Ward.

   vii) Perhaps the Egyptian chapter from the memoir, but I think a recent article on Currelly in the UTQ [*University of Toronto Quarterly*] would fit better.

   viii) I hesitate to add the section on myself from the memoir, but as a matter of fact it is one of the most finished parts of the book

There might be, in addition, a few of his more important critical essays as a second part of the book.

3) A memorial volume of essays like the one you have just done for Davidson. There would be an introductory memoir of Pelham, perhaps by Ned or me. I suggest as contributors the six people whom Pelham often spoke of, in conversation, as the centre of a sort of Canadian renaissance: Pratt, Cochrane, Fairley, Bush, E.K. Brown and myself. The presence of two well-known American scholars in the book[168] would help to get it well received across the line. Cochrane is dead, but we could reprint the fine essay on "The Mind of Edward Gibbon" which appeared some years ago in the UTQ.[169]

Project No. 1 ought to be done no matter what else is done. Nos. 2 and 3 are no doubt mutually exclusive, and in any case all decision here rests with you.

Thanks you for your patience in reading all this.

1950s

Robert Heilman   **29 October [1951]**
English Department, University of Washington, Seattle, WA

Robert Heilman was chair of the English department at the University of Washington. At Heilman's invitation, Frye had taught a course on the Romantics at the University of Washington during the summer of 1951. The typescript is in the Robert B. Heilman Papers, University of Washington Library, Manuscript Collection (accession number Acc 1000-031). The attachment that Frye mentions in his first sentence is not in the Heilman Papers.

Dear Robert:

Attached is the best I could do: I trust Sewanee isn't in financial straits. That's why I dragged in my Canadianism at the end — I've noticed that American foundations with dough are more responsive to good-neighbour stimuli.

I am very deeply obliged to you for being responsible for my having a wonderful summer. I have seldom enjoyed a summer so much. We topped it off with ten days in San Francisco and two weeks in New York — one at the English institute, which turned out to be a very good one. I got Marshall McLuhan down to give a paper.[170]

If Ruth is still interested in burgers, a friend of mine reports a Crescent-of-the-Moon-Burger from Washington (D.C.).

Robert Heilman   **12 November [1951]**
English Department, University of Washington, Seattle, WA

The typescript for this letter is in the Robert B. Heilman Papers, University of Washington Library, Manuscript Collection (accession number Acc 1000-031). Heilman's letter is not extant, but he had obviously written Frye to recommend someone for his teaching staff, and he had extended a feeler about Frye's possible interest in a job at the University of Washington.

Dear Robert:

Thanks very much for your letter. If there weren't a catch, I could recommend the best teacher of Middle English that you or any other English department is ever likely to get. She's a wonderful girl named Margaret Stobie,[171] now at Winnipeg, Manitoba, Ph.D., author of a Middle English grammar and of several articles ranging from scholarly notes in PMLA to studies in the metre of Hopkins. Excellent teacher. It's no doubt irrelevant to add that she's a great pleasure to look at. The catch is her husband Bill, a most agreeable and likeable chap, will get along in any society, probably do a good teaching job with elementary composition classes, but no scholarship and little promise of any. The conventions of modern society don't permit the woman to do the job and the man to wash the dishes, which is what's appropriate here: Bill would make an excellent faculty wife. They've had a lot of jobs because people hire Bill to get Peg, and then a new administration comes in that fires

41

all married women, which is why she's unemployed now. Dearly as I love Bill, I don't think it's a good team; but there at any rate is my recommendation.

It was very good of you to inquire about the state of my permanent affections.[172] It's difficult for me to say, and I don't suppose there's any hurry about having to say it. But, as your own letter implies, my difficulties are connected with leaving Toronto and not with going to Seattle. I look around at my desk and see it piled high with Royal Commission reports on Canadian culture, Canadian magazines and books, letters about jobs in Canada, Royal Society and Canadian Humanities Research bulletins, and I realize how deeply intertwined I am with this community. I think I should be unlikely to move except to a job that could absorb my teaching and writing interests completely — that's the nearest I can get to indicating a state of mind at present.

George Johnston   8 December 1952
Carleton College, Ottawa, ON

Johnston, poet and professor of Old Norse and Anglo-Saxon, had begun teaching at Carleton College (later, University) in 1950. He encouraged Jay Macpherson to begin graduate study with Frye at Toronto. Following his service in World War II Johnston had done graduate study himself at Toronto, where Frye directed his M.A. thesis on Blake's poetry. After another year of graduate work, he taught at Mt. Allison University, and returned to Toronto for further study before going to Carleton, where Frye had helped secure him a teaching position and where Frye's classmate Monroe Beattie was chair of the English department. Frye and Johnston remained lifelong friends. Frye's letter is in the George Johnston Papers in the Library and Archives Canada.

Dear George:

Thank you for your letter and for Miss Macpherson's poems. I suppose I shall be reviewing them in the Quarterly in any case,[173] I am very pleased that you are writing the article on Colville and Brittain[174] and both Helen and I would like very much to have it in the Forum. You are perfectly right when you say I'm very busy, though most of my work right now is getting papers written. I don't take kindly to rule, and so far the department doesn't seem to be suffering.[175]

All best wishes to all of you, whether five or six, from both of us,[176]

George Johnston   20 February [1953]
Carleton College, Ottawa, ON

This letter is in the George Johnston Papers in the Library and Archives Canada.

Dear George:

Thanks very much for your letter and article: the latter looks fine, and I am sending it along to the Forum. I'd be very glad to see the Macpherson girl at any time.[177]

I'm interested to see that you keep coming back to Blake as a subject.[178] There is certainly no doubt that he's solidly rooted in the later eighteenth century, and all the connections haven't yet been traced by any means. But the primary ones, I think, are with Ossian, Cowper, Chatterton, the cult of fancy and sensibility, the Methodist movement — that sort of thing, and the connections with Neo-Classicism, which certainly exist, go on from there.

This has been a hell of a year: one begins to hate it, in that irrational way one looks at a year as a contained "thing." I think if possible it's been even tougher on Ned — John after all was his contemporary.[179] Our love to Jean [Jeanne], and kiss Cathleen[180] for us.

George Johnston   [1953]
Carleton College, Ottawa, ON
This letter is in the George Johnston Papers in the Library and Archives Canada.

Dear George:

I thought your Jay Macpherson was a completely charming youngster, and I was delighted to meet her.[181] Only I feel a bit embarrassed about her wanting to study with me next year — I've told her I'm going to Princeton in February — it's a new lectureship they're inaugurating, and it's quite a break for me.[182] I hope they don't think I'm Christopher Fry: Eisenhower, it is said, got to be President of Columbia because someone wanted his brother, who's President of Pennsylvania. She says she'll follow me to Princeton — but, dammit, that's a men's college. Rather ironic in view of her background.[183]

Look me up in July — I'll be here teaching summer school. I'll be in Ottawa Aug. 24, speaking to librarians and full of hay fever, quite a miserable sight in fact.

I thought the Forum article was very good, and I'm much obliged to you for it. Delighted to hear about the Spectator.[184]

All the best to all of you.

Norman Friedman   11 November 1953
Queen's College, City University of New York, New York, NY
In reply to Friedman's having sent Frye a copy of his article, "Imagery: From Sensation to Symbol" (Journal of Aesthetics and Art Criticism 12, no. 1 [September, 1953]: 25–37).

Dear M. Friedman:

Thank you very much for your fine article, which I have, of course, read with the greatest interest, especially as I am myself in the middle of the job of sorting out my own notions of what such words as symbol and metaphor and archetype mean. Your exhaustive footnotes provide a useful bibliography in themselves. The final reference to me is the most satisfying form of evidence that what I am trying to say makes sense to the people best able to judge of such matters.[185]

I am rereading *The Egotist* now, for the first time in many years, and am astonished by how extraordinarily well organized its imagery is. Even the curious image of feet-on-breast you found in the poetry turns up, in the right place.[186]

I have a review of the new translation of Jung coming out in the next Hudson Review.[187] I suggests, though much less concisely than you do, something of the integrity of the quest theme in its Frazerian anthropological and its Jungian psychological aspects, although I was compelled to talk more about alchemy than I wanted to.

Please give my best to Charles Owen,[188] as well as accepting my sincerest wishes for yourself and for many more articles of similar caliber.

George Johnston   30 November 1953
Carleton College, Ottawa, ON   Princeton, NJ
This letter is in the George Johnston Papers in the Library and Archives Canada.

Dear George:

I've just heard from Jack Harris about your accident, and am sending this home in the hope that they've let you out on parole at least. The sincerest condolences from both of us, and I hope it doesn't turn out to be a long-term affair. If what I hear is true, that both elbows are fractured, the only bit of silver lining I can see is the character-building resulting from the unaccustomed sobriety. But you've probably had that joke ad nauseam already. Another advantage is that you can't write back, and are in the position I'm in when my dentist, who is a one-man splinter from C.C.F. [Cooperative Commonwealth Federation], starts arguing politics with me when I can make only a gargle in reply.

Today is a horrible gloomy day, with people arriving at the house at the crack of dawn to tear off the front porch, a job promised for last summer, and somebody coming up to fix the fence, a job promised for last year. I fled in terror and left Helen to give the orders, which fortunately she takes to doing. The day was very like the day we moved into the place in 1945, also a pouring rain, with only two things left in the house, Reid MacCallum and the cat.[189] Reid had a watermelon grin on his face, because he loves moving; the cat didn't, and glowered at me like a reincarnation of Heathcliff, which from what I've heard of her she could be. I think she put a spell on me in all matters connected with household management.

Jay [Macpherson] is doing very well here, attending all my lectures, which I find a little disturbing, and sitting as far as possible from the other students, which I find considerably more disturbing. But there's no doubt the poor youngster does have a problem trying to find where she can fit in. Graves, from what she tells me,[190] tended to dramatize her as a little girl and a symbolic child, which presumably helped to give her all those Betty-Boop mannerisms, and yet her precocity removes her from her own age group. She'll just have to find her own specific gravity, whatever it is.

Jack [Harris] said something about your interest in a magazine. I hope you lose the interest, but fast, and decide in favor of a wiser and more placid life. Sure, there's place for a good new magazine in Canada—I wish I had a dollar for every time that's been said to me. Economically, there's no place for a good new magazine anywhere, unless heavily subsidized by a private income. A magazine that could pay its own way would have to be a magazine you'd have no interest in running. The Forum [*Canadian Forum*] setup, which has no parallel anywhere, is an exception that goes a long way to prove the rule. The good, solid, interesting, worthwhile magazine with a large and regular body of readers is a nineteenth-century fact and a twentieth-century mirage. Unquote.

Well, I'm getting fairly close to the Princeton deadline—close enough to think it's time I started writing my four public lectures.[191] Meanwhile I'm trying to talk fast in order to finish up my lecture courses.

All the best to Jeanne and the kids. And I do hope you're not too badly crocked. And, to quote my bank manager after I had my accident in New Jersey[192]: "Trusting your arm is knitting properly."

Gordon Wood   **12 March 1954**
Carleton College, Ottawa, ON   Princeton, NJ

Frye is writing to Gordon Wood from Princeton where he was serving as the Princeton Class of 1932 lecturer, the first holder of the lectureship. He offered one seminar and delivered four public lectures. Wood was a 1943 graduate of Victoria College who returned to Victoria in 1946 and enrolled in Frye's Blake and Milton courses. He received his M.A in 1947 and began his teaching career at Carleton College (Ottawa) in 1951.

Dear Gordon:

Yesterday was the last of my four public lectures—five to six, after which I went off to a restaurant, sank a dinner and two martinis, went home, lost the dinner, and collapsed into bed. So now I can turn to more pleasant duties. The lectures were unexpectedly tough to do, for some reason, and even though I knew I had to do them for months I needed to come and look over the possible audience first. Well, anyway. Hall seating two hundred filled every time, mostly undergraduates, big ovation at the end, everything declared to be unprecedented in the recent history of Princeton, so I feel very relaxed about it. Actually it was a wonderful audience.

Helen and I were very distressed to hear about the bad time you've had: it must have been about as tough on the morale as anything could have been, and I very much hope you extract a good long resting period from Carleton. I suppose it's partly a nervous condition that's been building up since the war.[193] Anyway, medical people feed me the bromide occasionally that the more acute the suffering, the less likely it is to be a long-term thing. ( ). That space is for silent sympathy and the general sense that there is nothing to say except we hope very much you're better and damn the goddam disease.[194]

We've rented an apartment-house arrangement in a block of flats owned and operated by the University! Very convenient: they do the upkeep, pay for the heating, mow the lawn if any, and the like. But from the outside the appearance is very unpretentious, to the point of being unimpressive, which is amusing because it's at the end of Prospect Avenue, a street that runs straight out from the university campus and has the undergraduate eating clubs at the other end. They're Princeton's substitute for frats, and the smallest one (there are about a dozen) would be at least as large as Victoria's old Wymilwood.[195] So walking from the library down to home past all these lush and pompous palaces to our own slave quarters gives one a sense of the social setup. They have a strict admissions committee with orders not to let anyone but sterling upper-middle class types in. I have twelve boys, highly intelligent, vociferously articulate (the teaching staff here knocks itself out to make them so: they have "preceptorials" where professors have to attend their colleagues' lectures and then discuss them with small groups, Woodrow Wilson's idea, so one Assistant Professor my own age is now, after about ten years on the staff, giving a lecture course of his own for the first time). A remark Yeats makes in his autobiography about meeting a man in America who combined the American passion for ideas with the American intellectual indolence keeps haunting me.[196]

The owner of our house is a man named Baumol,[197] a mathematical economist, which is a very wonderful and desirable thing to be. So Princeton is very apprehensive he'll stay at California, where he's gone for this term, and makes him all sorts of concessions. His demands are peculiar. He's a quite clever painter, with Chagall, Klee and perhaps Tamayo derivations. He likes backgrounds. Living room has two walls a green-gray, two an electric blue. Dining room, two green gray, two brilliant cerise. Hall cerise, kitchen yellow. Bedrooms, two pale blue, two brilliant mauve. The two smaller bedrooms he wanted spattered, one blue on white, the other red on white. Princeton's painters watched him in horror while he demonstrated what he wanted, then they packed their apparatus and walked off home in high dudgeon. (I've never seen anybody in low dudgeon, but I gather they were high anyway.) After all, they had just convinced somebody else that they really didn't want pink in their bedroom, just a nice pleasant cream. So Baumol phoned the superintendent, the superintendent phoned the painters and said this man's a mathematical economist; he does what he likes; do like the gentleman says. So they came back with a foot ruler, dipped it in paint, and proceeded to do the most unconvincing spattering job I've ever seen. Like an old maid on a boy's bike, as we used to say in Moncton. The kitchen has an automatic dishwasher, a washing machine, and a clothes dryer — to get them in Baumol knocked out two walls with a sledge-hammer — only if you run any two of them at once you blow a fuse. Television, record player and radio. Practically nothing in the damn house to sit on. If you were here we'd have to keep you in bed.

Social engagements have piled up very rapidly, of course, and for two normally rather introverted people they're a good deal of a strain. Tonight, dinner with an archaeologist (Dorothy Thompson, Homer Thompson's wife — he's in Greece and they're both at the institute here),[198] tomorrow, dinner with an undertaker (an old friend of a Victoria classmate of ours). Next day, tea with the English department, next day cocktails to be met at, and so it goes. Most alcoholic bloody university I've ever seen. Helen says if anyone would ask her in for a saucer of milk she'd jump at it. But I don't have to attend any committee meetings.

Well, I must stop this drivel — I hope I can get some work done on the book now. The press here has suggested I publish the four lectures as they are, which might be a possibility if the book isn't done for another couple of years.[199] Meanwhile they've effectively absorbed my time. Do take care of yourself, and give our best to our friends — I expect to be writing George[200] right away.

With the most affectionate (but slightly concerned) greetings from both of us,

George Johnston   **18 June 1954**
Carleton College, Ottawa, ON   Princeton, NJ
This letter is in the George Johnston Papers in the Library and Archives Canada.

Dear George:

I was most pleased to get your letter so soon after my arrival here, where we've had a wonderful and fantastically busy time. I had only one day's teaching, to twelve students,[201] but it's in my nature to find social obligations far more taxing than academic ones. So, although we both needed this kind of change, and are all the better for it, we're really quite exhausted, and more than ready for a further change. Next Thursday we fly to London, and will be in Europe until the middle of September.[202] During that time I hope to read nothing but time tables. We think of a possible trip through the Scandinavian countries in late August, when it gets hot. I've never seen Scandinavia, but it gives me the feeling of something cool, comfortable, clean, middle-class, and not too damn educational.

Princeton is a very curious place in a very curious country. One out of three applicants to come to Princeton is picked by an admissions committee which has no academic representation on it. The students spend most of their time in fourth year writing a thesis, which has to be, I think, thirty thousand words long. The staff knocks itself out fussing over its students, worrying about their little blocks and the like, and, apart from that, they have a preceptorial system, inaugurated by Woodrow Wilson. Like our pass groups, but far more expansive, and frequently involves attendance at colleagues' lectures. The result is that the students are intensively trained to be articulate. The morale in the humanities is exceedingly high — no notion of leaving literature and such to the women, as there aren't any women. Graduates are fanatically loyal to Princeton — out of 28,000 they get approximately a quarter out to the annual reunion, which was last week. We watched the parade, which went on for over an hour. The twenty-fifth year out, which this year of course was 1929, gets the place of honor in the parade — over three hundred in that class. Then they go chronologically, starting with 1885 — there is an older one, but he can't walk. The younger years go in for sandwich boards and hangover humor. Three-day festival, with tents and free beer.

Meanwhile, of course, we got the full treatment, and have drunk so much alcohol that none of our clothes fit any more. We've made a lot of good friends, and listen sympathetically to all the tensions and antagonisms, of which there are the usual number. It's a very small town really, and, as in Harvard, we find that the normal tendency is to gossip. Toronto is much more stimulating intellectually than either place, as far as staff is concerned. Students are another matter. One young mother reported to us that her little girl had come home from kindergarten with an A plus in Facing Reality. American students go on from there. The little girls grow up to be beautiful big girls of the kind my students go with and have been bringing lately to show me. One of them got Helen into the women's washroom and asked her what it was like being married to a real intellectual type, and did she try to read everything I read?

I'll be glad to get out of this country, although I think that fundamentally it's trustworthy enough. That is, when American democracy decides, in its confused, lumbering, dithering way that it really can't get along any further with Senator McCarthy, it sticks him into a damn soap opera,[203] and lets the housewives decide whether he's hero or villain. I can see the logic as well as the humor of that, but both are on a deep level of unconsciousness at which this country appears largely to function. It makes me nervous, watching this inspired somnambulism — if it *is* that — they did the same kind of thing with MacArthur the last time we were here.

Our love to Jeanne and the kids.

Earle Birney   [August 1954]

English Department, University of   17, Falkland House,
British Columbia, Vancouver, BC   Marloes Rd., W.8. [London]

In response to Birney's objection to the notice of his anthology in Frye's annual review of poetry for the University of Toronto Quarterly. *Frye had written: "Two anthologies appeared last year:* Canadian Poems 1850–1952 *([Toronto:] Contact Press), by Dudek and Layton, and* Twentieth-Century Canadian Poetry *([Toronto:] Ryerson), by Earle Birney. Both, with their explanatory notes and their cautious introductions, seem to be aimed at the high school trade. The former is the better book: the editors have obviously tried to avoid the hackneyed and yet to include nothing that they did not themselves believe to be reputable poetry. The result is a collection representing fresh insights and discoveries, well worth examining. The Birney anthology also has its virtues, but it seems deliberately over-simplified: it contains a number of poems that the editor could not possibly have believed to be very good, and must therefore have included because he thought his readers would think they were good"* (University of Toronto Quarterly, 23 *[April 1954]; rpt. in* NFCanada, 123). *Frye's letter is in the Thomas Fisher Rare Book Library of the University of Toronto Library.*

Dear Earle:

I am sorry that you take such exception to my UTQ notice of your anthology. I have no wish to argue about the merits of my opinion: no critic is infallible, and so he always has to take his chance of being wrong. I can only say that what I said was said in perfect good faith: what prejudices I have would naturally work strongly in your favor rather than against you: if I am right in my opinion my opinion will do you little if any harm, and if I am wrong I shall do harm only to myself.

Lawrence M. Lande   30 September [1954?]

In response to Lande's having sent Frye a copy of his book, Toward the Quiet Mind: A Guide to Self-discovery through the Study of the Book of Job *(Toronto: McClelland & Stewart, 1954). Frye's letter is in the Department of Rare Books and Special Collections, McGill University, Montreal, QC.*

Dear Mr. Lande:

I have once more to thank you for a copy of your fine and unique production of the Book of Job, and for the kind letter which accompanies it. The blue is very attractive, though perhaps not so suggestive of sackcloth as its predecessor[204]; the title is a great improvement, and you were certainly right in including the entire set of Blake's plates. They form, as you realize, a profound and subtle criticism of the poem by themselves.

I think one main difficulty with the popular reading of Job is its presence in the Bible: people think of it as part of the vast elaborated texture of Judaism and Christianity rather than as a work of art in itself. Your presentation does a great deal to isolate it for specific study. Thank you very much again.

Norman Friedman   26 November 1954

Queen's University, City University of New York, New York, NY

In reply to Friedman's letter, which is not extant, but in which he obviously asked Frye about some of his central terms and principles. The article that Friedman enclosed was "Versions of Form in Fiction: Great Expectations *and* The Great Gatsby," *Accent 14 (Autumn 1954): 246–63.*

Dear Mr. Friedman:

Thank you for your article. For me, an archetype is a typical or recurring image in literature; identifying archetypes is entirely a matter of studying, first, conventions, and then genres. I have no interest whatsoever in speculating about any "primordial necessity of the human mind," or about any collective or racial consciousness or unconscious or quasi-memory. Criticism must be in part a morphological study of the structural principles of literature, because the formal principles of literature come only out of literature. Things like the whale journey in Jonah and Pinocchio you mention and the "who are the parents?" problem in Great Expectations that goes, as a convention, back through Menander and Euripides into myth, are all part of the principle that poetry can only be made out of other poems, novels out of other novels. In form, that is, not content: the forms of literature can no more exist outside literature than the sonata and fugue can exist outside music. I don't feel that Crane has grasped this principle of convention and genre very clearly: he talks about it, but doesn't actually get much further than the isolated individual as poem, or whatever it is.[205] And the Jungians don't seem to me to get to any *literary* principles at all, partly because they're still rooted in personal psychology, and the only psychological question that's relevant to criticism is not what's buried in the poet, but what's revealed in his work to his audience. If Oedipus Rex owes part of its power to dramatizing the Oedipus complex, that has nothing to do with the personal life of Sophocles.

Your comparative study of Great Expectations and The Great Gatsby is interesting, and sound enough: the word "great" common to their titles indicates irony, an irony which leans to comedy in Dickens and to tragedy in Fitzgerald. These three words, tragedy, comedy, irony, occupy the middle area in criticism between pure archetype and pure genre, and show how the connection is to be made between them.

George and Jeanne Johnston   [January 1955]

Ottawa, ON

This letter is in the George Johnston Papers in the Library and Archives Canada. The poem Johnston enclosed with his letter, apparently a Christmas verse, is uncertain.

Dear George and Jeanne:

Thanks so much for your metrical remembrance. We had a quiet Christmas with my father & sister over from Chicago. (He's living with her now.) We had also a very pleasant New Year's Eve party with Gordon Wood present — I was delighted to see how fully his spirits had recovered from what must have been a pretty rough time.[206] Jay Macpherson dropped in, with a young poet Darryl [Daryl] Hine, who's attending McGill. Jay is doing very well here, both academically and socially. Our best love to you both.

I'm not a poet, as you know, but I agree with your sentiments:

> In the frenzied arsy-versy
> Of Jesus' coming-to-earth day,
> Let us thank his tender mercy
> For having only one birthday.

George Johnston   21 January 1955
Carleton College, Ottawa, ON
This letter is in the George Johnston Papers in the Library and Archives Canada.

Dear George:

Thanks so much for your letter and the offprint of the delightful Schaefer article, which seems to me an admirable balancing of personal and critical elements.[207] I first heard about it, I think, from Carl himself: he was very anxious, with good reason, that people interested in him shouldn't miss it.

I'm sorry, but not altogether surprised, at your remarks about Gordon [Wood]. The root of his trouble is, I expect, his thesis, which is manoeuvring him into a position in which he can neither finish it nor abandon it, and will consequently block the way of any later writing he might want to do. I'm not sure that a change of environment would make much difference.[208] Certainly I'm no disciplinarian, but I already have two similar problems on my own staff.

My affection for Jay, like yours, grows with my growing sense of her solid qualities. [Daryl] Hine is all set for a quite remarkable career if his precocity doesn't trip him up. We've spoken of Jay's having been too much with older people, and I get some amusement, I think and hope unmalicious, out of seeing her with an attractive younger boy in tow, and in a position to be slightly protective and maternal.

Everybody seemed to like the TV program except Helen and the girl who reviewed it in Varsity.[209] Helen said I'd used the pictures as cafe music. The idea was to have poems read and pictures connected with the theme to be run for the visual side. Thus The Tiger had the plate of the poem itself first, then a series of Satan pictures ending with Nebuchadnezzar going on all fours. The commentary had previously explained the symbolic set-up. It asked a certain amount from the viewer, or whatever the hell the victim of a TV set is called; and I learned a good deal about the limitations of the medium. You can't see pictures properly unless the photography is a hell of a lot better than anything Canadian TV can produce.

Love to Jeanne and the best to yourself.

Norman Friedman   2 May 1955
Queen's College, City University of New York, New York, NY
In reply to Friedman's letter, which is not extant, but in which he has apparently asked Frye about certain features of his theory of literature and how they relate to R.S. Crane's idea on inductive and deductive critical methods.

Dear Mr. Friedman:

I am sorry to have unloaded on you, some months ago,[210] the undigested mass of a large and complicated thesis I have been working frantically to unravel all year. I doubt that I can really give any satisfactory answer to your questions until my book [*Anatomy of Criticism*] is completed, which I sincerely hope will be soon. I am probably just repeating what I said then, but the general idea is something like this: in painting there are structural and representational elements, the former seen most clearly in abstract painting, the latter in realism. Abstraction gives simply the conventions of painting found only in pictures, not bothering to adapt itself to representation. Music is dominated by abstraction of this sort; that's why its theory is in far better shape. In both literature and painting the main emphasis in criticism has fallen on the representational end. We pick up a novel and instantly start trying to compare it with "life."

Now, literature too has its structural principles, and they are seen most clearly in abstract literature — that is, myths, where the characters do whatever they like, which in practice means whatever the storyteller likes, and where what happens is the kind of thing that happens only in stories. Realism in literature consists of mythical patterns displaced in the direction of plausibility. Critical technique should be neither naively inductive, as Crane suggests, nor naively deductive, as he says other critics are. It should be based on structural analyses of particular works which lead to the building up of general principles of literary structure. The existence of convention and genre indicate that such general principles exist. I do hope this makes sense, but if it doesn't maybe my book will.

Irving Layton   **18 November 1955**
Montreal, QC
   Frye's letter is in the Irving Layton Papers, Special Collections, Concordia University Library, Ottawa.

Dear Mr. Layton:
   I am afraid that this is a very belated acknowledgement of your kindness in sending me a copy of THE COLD GREEN ELEMENT. It arrived when other books were arriving from the Press, and I did not notice for some time that I had in fact two copies of your book, and one a presentation copy by the author. That one, naturally, I shall keep, and give the other to someone else who ought to be reading it. I shouldn't have far to look.[211]

Irving Layton   **20 February 1956**
Montreal, QC
   Frye's letter is in the Irving Layton Papers, Special Collections, Concordia University Library, Ottawa.

Dear Mr. Layton:
   Thank you very much for the copy of The Blue Propeller, which arrived just in time. The UTQ [*University of Toronto Quarterly*] survey had to be considerably hurried up this year, as we have a new and less casual editor. Thank you also for the copies of *Origin*: it's impossible for me to keep up with everything, and I'm very dependent on such courtesies as well as grateful for them.
   I would never, of course, claim that my criticism of your poetry is correct or adequate, only that it is honest in intention.[212]

Irving Layton   **18 May 1956**
Montreal, QC
   Frye's letter is in the Irving Layton Papers, Special Collections, Concordia University Library, Ottawa.

Dear Mr. Layton:

I note resignedly once again I have delayed writing to thank you for the two copies of *The Bull Calf*, which I was delighted to receive. I'm at Victoria, but the other one came all right, and I've been lending it out. The latest comment I got was "Boy, can he write!"

I was very interested to learn that W.C. Williams is to do an introduction to your selected poems, and considerably more interested to learn that there is to be a volume of selected poems.[213] I hope it will give me the opportunity to write a little more coherently about your achievement thus far.

Miriam Waddington   9 August 1956
                                                         Bloomington, IN

Waddington had written to compliment Frye on the paper he had given at the annual meeting of the Royal Society of Canada in Montreal, May 1956 — "Preface to an Uncollected Anthology." Frye is replying from Indiana University, where he was teaching a course in Blake during the summer session. The letter is in the Miriam Waddington Papers of the Library and Archives Canada.

Dear Miriam:

Excuse the informality, but I have met you more than once — chiefly at the Birneys. Thanks so much for your very kind note. I was extremely grateful to have others in the audience besides section II of the Royal Society, not all of whom were particularly sensitive to what I was talking about.[214]

I think Canada, jumping in a generation or two, as you say, from one civilization into a totally different one, is faced with a unique problem of articulation. We missed out on the whole phase of community development that comes between pioneering and urban conditions. That means that our poets and novelists are faced with unusual technical difficulties, and the way they solve them will be of unusual interest, or should be.

Irving Layton   1 December 1956
Montreal, QC

Frye's letter is in the Irving Layton Papers, Special Collections, Concordia University Library, Ottawa.

Dear Mr. Layton:

Thanks so much for the Selected Poems. There are a few I was a little disappointed not to see, such as "Me, the P.M. and the Stars," which I catch myself muttering at times in the intervals of insomnia, as well as a few early ones, like "Lady Enfield," that one remembers — but of course in every selection one instantly complains about omissions. Meanwhile, it's a most attractive book.

Clarence D. Thorpe   21 January 1957
Department of English, University if Michigan, Ann Arbor, MI

In reply to Thorpe's invitation for Frye to serve with James V. Logan of Ohio State University and John E. Jordan of the University of California, Berkeley, as an editor of a volume of essays on the British Romantics, Reappraisal of the Romantic Writers. *Thorpe was chair of the Committee on Research Projects, Group IX, of the Modern Language Association. Frye had recently contributed as essay on Blake to another volume sponsored by the Committee on Research Projects. The* Reappraisal *was eventually published as* Some British Romantics: A Collection of Essays *([Columbus]: Ohio State University Press, 1966). In addition to co-edit-*

ing the volume Frye wrote an essay for it on Blake, "The Keys to the Gates." Frye's postcard reply to Thorpe is in the Special Collections Library of the University of Michigan.

Thank you for a most kindly and thoughtful letter. I don't think the job's too good for me[215]; I just want to make sure it's a strong book with an individual point. Perhaps what's really bothering me is the feeling that I'd be more useful as a contributor than as an editor. But I'm quite willing to serve as editor; only Messrs. Jordan and Logan and I ought to get together, if possible physically, to do some careful planning before issuing invitations. If they both are going to be at the MLA in September, everything will be very simple.

  With all best wishes (I do my own typing)

Roy Daniells   **15 April 1957**
University of British Columbia, Vancouver, BC Apt. 8, 473 Beacon St., Boston, MA
  Frye was teaching at Harvard during the spring term of 1957. This letter is in the Roy Daniells Fonds, University of British Columbia, box 7, file 11.

Dear Roy:
  All right, I'll do the paper for June 16, but I'd like to know in more detail just what sort of thing you would consider thematically appropriate — it looks as though you had a definite occasion in mind, in which case it shouldn't be left to me altogether.[216] Perhaps the sort of thing I'd have done at the Kingston Conference if Douglas Grant hadn't done it instead?

  Things continue to go well here, but are winding up very quickly; five more lectures apiece. My students are certainly bright, and are certified Grade A by all the aptitude tests in the country; but there's something about the terrific indoctrinating in the American system of education that blinkers the mind. It's not quite like teaching Marxists, but not unlike. It would take me ten or fifteen years to figure out what the assumptions all are and how they condition the reception of knowledge, and by that time I'd be wearing the same blinders. But there is a difference.

  I turned down all my offers; Rochester would have paid me anything I asked for and would have appointed any colleagues I liked, and so on; but the job entailed reconciling feuds, and would have given me stomach ulcers in no time.

  I was delighted that you took Hopwood[217]; you won't regret it.

  Love to Laurenda from us both, and looking forward eagerly to seeing you,

George Johnston   **15 November 1957**
Carleton University, Ottawa, ON
  This letter is in the George Johnston Papers in the Library and Archives Canada.

Dear George:
  I was delighted to hear from you and get the poems. I should say that not commenting on poems is a deliberate policy of mine — unless I'm definitely asked to comment, which I do with great reluctance. The reason is that if it's a serious poet, their proper context is the book he's building up, and anything short of that book is to some extent quoted out of context. Once I'm sure of a large enough context, I can go ahead and say something; otherwise it's extremely easy to make random and misleading comments, which is disastrous where my opinion has any weight. For instance, I never comment on the poems Jay hands me, unless she teases, which now she seldom does. So all I can say is that I like these poems very much, especially the river poem — the white goddess in Sunday-school clothes is a twist Graves is too corny to think of.[218]

I've just been falling in and out of planes, lecturing on Blake in Montreal (Thomas More Institute, adult education, Catholic, very good), Cincinnati (two lectures) and Skidmore College (Saratoga Springs, N. Y., a second-rate girls' college with for some reason a first-rate reputation. Well, actually, I discovered the reason; it's got on the grape-vine that girls who go there have more dates than they can handle.) As I remarked to Jay [Macpherson] recently, being a sixty-year-old smiling public man[219] at forty-five is a little disturbing, but in the age of sputniks one's evidently expected to travel and in the age of Eisenhower one's quite obviously expected to smile. Speaking of Jay, she gave a reading of her poetry at a series Ray Souster is arranging — [Irving] Layton was the first, and I gather had a much smaller audience. Jay kept them on hard uncomfortable chairs for over an hour reading one poem after another in a flat monotone (or so I thought: Helen thought better of her reading), without a syllable of explanation or comment, and apparently they loved it. They asked her questions like do-you-really-hate-the-world-Miss-Macpherson, which she answered very well. You're certainly right in thinking that my conception of popular poetry fits Jay but not [Louis] Dudek — Dudek, and until recently [Raymond] Souster, keep trying to compete with some other form of statement that's not poetry, and on its ground.[220]

I hope Gordon [Wood] is feeling a bit more cheerful — I have a notion he still didn't get much done on his thesis this last summer, and he gave me the impression of feeling that his friends, at any rate the Fryes, were losing interest in him. Munro [Beattie], on the other hand, is as imperturbable as ever.[221] I came through Chicago on one of my recent jaunts and saw Dad again — eighty-seven, and tottery, but still with his mind perfectly clear and his morale very good.[222]

All the best, and love to Jeanne,

Miriam Waddington   17 January 1958

In reply to Waddington's having sent Frye a copy of a review of a book by Irving Layton. The letter is in the Miriam Waddington Papers of the Library and Archives Canada.

Dear Miriam:

Thanks very much for your letter and the review of Layton, which I read with great interest. I feel that there are and always have been two poets in Layton, one a person of greet sensitivity of feeling and exuberance of expression, the other much more stereotyped, at times almost a caricature of the genuine poet. It's been a problem for me as a critic to keep the two disentangled. I'd never thought of him as particularly a Jewish poet, in the way that Klein is, nor, I note, do you. I think we perhaps agree very closely, while emphasizing different aspects of the same thing.

The ideas about popular poetry I'm now working out are new to me as well, and are still tentative, only I think the fundamental hunch is sound.

John Gray   9 February 1958

Macmillan Company of Canada, Toronto, ON

In reply to the telephone invitation of John Gray, president of Macmillan of Canada, to edit a collection of E.J. (Ned) Pratt's poetry. The project proceeded with considerable dispatch, Frye's edition of The Collected Poems of E.J. Pratt *appearing in late autumn 1958. Gray also asked Frye if he would be interested in editing and writing an introduction for Joseph Conrad's* Victory *for a Macmillan series. Frye's letter is in the records of the Macmillan Company of Canada in the Mills Memorial Library, McMaster University (William Ready Division of Archives and Research Collections).*

Dear John:

On thinking over your phone call, I feel that I am extremely interested in the idea of editing a new collected edition of Ned, with an introduction by me. The new edition should, in my opinion, present his work in chronological order, the different books properly separated in the table of contents and dated. Perhaps a short bibliographical index at the end would indicate to the reader just what wasn't, at the author's own request, being reprinted.[223] I think the order, or disorder, in the present 1944 edition makes a confusing and shapeless book—I know it was probably Ned's own choice, but it doesn't do a thing for him, or for the reader either.

I repeat that an introduction by me isn't necessary, but it could be damn useful to most of the people who would actually use the book, assuming that there's be nothing about it that would try to patronize Ned or otherwise get in the reader's way. And I think I can guarantee that.

As for the Conrad *Victory* job, I think I'd better bow out of that. I have so many commitments now that another one would be rash to take on, unless it's right in the middle of my own immediate interests, as the Pratt job is.

P.S. Philip Child, if he didn't want to do it himself, would be supervising students now working on Conrad.[224] Henry Kreisel, of Alberta, is a possibility, and so is A.E. Sawyer, of British Columbia.[225]

P.P.S. I hope you will get somebody to design the new collected poems so it will look like what it is, one of the essential books of Canadian literature and a definitive collection of Canada's biggest poet, and not like a rebound copy of the Ford Salesman's Handbook.

George Johnston   **5 September 1958**
Carleton University, Ottawa, ON

In reply to Johnston's letter about the death of Peter Fisher, Frye's former student and friend, who had drowned in a sailing accident on 2 September. In the 1940s and early 1950s Frye and Fisher often met to drink beer and talk about literature, philosophy, and religion, and Frye frequently records the essence of their conversations in his Diaries, *especially in his 1949 diary.*[226] *Fisher had done a Ph.D. thesis under Frye's supervision on Blake, and for almost a decade had been teaching at the Royal Military College in Kingston, Ontario. Frye's letter is in the George Johnston Papers in the Library and Archives Canada.*

Dear George:

Thanks very much for writing: I've been too stunned to react. I keep dreaming he's still alive, the way I did for some months after Jerry Riddell went.[227] I was content enough to see him three or four times a year, but those three or four times were damn important. He was one of the few people I could talk to, and in a good many areas he was the only one. One doesn't feel sorry for the person who's gone, only for the survivors, including oneself. It's true what you say about the reckless squandering extravagance of nature or fate or whatever the hell it is, yet Peter was one of the few people I knew who seemed to have something in him to respond to that rhythm. He can make sense of it if anybody can.

I'm glad you liked the review of Jay: it was tough to write, at first, until I reminded myself that my personal fondness for Ned Pratt was equally public and equally involved with my critical views.[228] I thought I'd keep clear of entanglements by refusing to write poetry myself, but I haven't altogether. So far I've escaped being very fond of a very bad poet, and I saw no reason for leaning over backwards about Jay. At least two reviewers, Norman Endicott and Kildare Dobbs, referred pointedly to me as some kind of influence on her, which as far as her actual writing goes is clearly nonsense, but that was what made me self-conscious.

Summer school at Columbia in New York this summer[229]: not hot by New York standards, but hot by mine. Noise hazards too; left me with a profound disinclination to live in New York, not that I ever had any. North Carolina next week — some damn Comparative Literature conference I got talked into reading a paper at.[230] I'd like to get a chance to see you if I get to Ottawa this October. Love to Jeanne, and all your swimming family.

Frank Upjohn   15 September 1958
Macmillan Company of Canada, Toronto

Upjohn, vice-president and manager of the trade department of Macmillan of Canada, had sent Frye the page proofs of the edition of E.J. Pratt's poems that Frye had edited (see letter to John Gray, 9 February 1958). Frye complains about the design of the book. He did not prevail in his objection to the narrow columns used for both his introduction to Pratt's poems and for the text of the poems: the book was published with three-inch columns. Frye's letter is in the records of the Macmillan Company of Canada in the Mills Memorial Library, McMaster University (William Ready Division of Archives and Research Collections).

Dear Mr. Upjohn:

What on earth is your layout man thinking of? This is no way to set PROSE: prose is supposed to go into sentences that can be taken in by the eye in two or three lines. If one is writing for a poverty-stricken magazine like The Canadian Forum, one expects to have one's stuff distorted by being squeezed into narrow columns (though the columns in the Forum [*Canadian Forum*] are slightly wider than this) but even the most grinding poverty cannot excuse a bungle of this kind. All the internal organs of a prose sentence get pushed out of alignment in a corset of this kind. To take a sentence at random: I wrote: "In Methodism at that time the battle of 'higher criticism' had been won, Biblical archaeology (see 'The Epigrapher') was opening up, there was general enthusiasm for such new world-pictures as 'evolution,' *Angst* and *Existenz* were unheard of, and there was no difficulty — certainly the poet has never found any — in being Christian and liberal at the same time." Now that, I concede, is a longish sentence, but in anything like proper typography it's quite easy to follow. Here the eye has to trip and stumble over nine lines, including two hyphenated words, lose its way in the syntax, and get confused by the allusions. Quotations too get distorted:

> But what made our feet miss the road that
> brought
> The world to such a golden trove...

What *is* the point of such a broken-up setting? I'd much rather not see my introduction appear at all than have it appear is so preposterously unreadable a form,

> where it looks like a po-
> em of Mr. Arthur Bourinot
> 's.[231]

Yours sincere-
ly,

Frank Upjohn   25 September 1958
Macmillan Company of Canada, Toronto, ON

Upjohn had replied to Frye's previous letter (15 September 1958) explaining the reasons for the typographical and design decisions for Pratt's poems. This is Frye's response.

Dear Mr. Upjohn:

Thank you very much for your most full and careful explanation, the thanks being of course also addressed to Mr. Davies.[232] As Mr. Davies says, if he had had my introduction at the beginning, he would have seen, from the way the quotations got squeezed together, that a wider setting would have been advisable. But he didn't, and this is Ned's book, not my book. I have no interest in it that isn't directly connected with making it useful and readable to readers of Pratt, and I don't feel I can hold you up on an issue affecting only myself. The text itself is admirable — it's hardly in the same world as the first edition[233] — and that's all that matters. Only I cannot forbear adding that the expansion of my introduction from the twelve-page maximum you expected to sixteen pages has a lot more to do with your typography than with my verbosity.

I shall look forward to Mr. Davies article when it appears in Tamarack.[234]

George Johnston   28 October 1958

Carleton University, Ottawa, ON

This letter is in the George Johnston Papers in the Library and Archives Canada.

Dear George:

I feel even more embarrassed at the way my alleged Ottawa visit turned out: my one effort to phone you was unsuccessful and there wasn't even time for another. I arrived at 11:30 P.M., got up to breakfast and a morning session that adjourned for lunch at 1:45, and got away from lunch table only in time to catch the 3:30 out. This kind of thing ought to exhilarate me, but it doesn't. Still, Claude's inaugural party was a big success, including even the inaugural lectures.[235] All three were shutouts, and my own at Hart House Theatre, besides admitting 150 more than fire regulations permitted (on Claude's personal order), turned away at least 500.

I love multiple Bridget,[236] and am delighted at the prospect of having your poems in a decent format, that being one of the advantages of Oxford. (I'm editing the second collected of Ned's for Macmillan, and have lost several arguments with the styler, who's writing an article for Tamarack to prove how right he was. He wasn't.)[237] When your book comes out Canadian lyricism will be firmly established, even though all it can say as yet is Auk and Ark.[238]

Love to Jeanne from us both,

Irving Layton   6 January 1959

Montreal, QC

Frye's letter is in the Irving Layton Papers, Special Collections, Concordia University Library, Ottawa.

Dear Irving Layton:

I was delighted that you liked the Arts in Canada article,[239] more especially as I wrote it a year ago under great editorial pressure and unwillingness, and for a year had about it only a gloomy conviction that it was both dull and pointless. Such a reaction as yours can be quite as encouraging to a critic as any critic can be to a poet.

Lorne Pierce   9 February 1959

Ryerson Press, Toronto, ON

Frye's letter is in the Queen's University Archives, Kingston, Ontario.

Dear Lorne Pierce:

Thank you very much for a most gracious letter. Ryerson Press without you will be bound to seem for a long time, whoever succeeds you, like *Hamlet* with only Gertrude and Polonius and a couple of lords in waiting to patch up the story.[240] But I shall certainly be interested in continuing to work for the Press—I assume I shall continue, and that the four Ryerson books I have helped to make possible are not the end of my connexion with it.[241]

I am still a little apprehensive at finding myself in an administrative job,[242] but I am hopeful it will prove a logical evolution of my quarter-century of devotion to the college.

George Johnston   **18 November 1959**
Carleton University, Ottawa, ON

In reply to Johnston's letter of 25 October 1959. Frye's letter is in the George Johnston Papers in the Library and Archives Canada.

Dear George:

I was delighted to get your letter, which I'm rather a long time answering. I find myself still subject to mental dizzy spells—I do my best to make out lists of Things To Do the night before, but the versatility of action that's required takes a bit of getting on to. A university community doesn't want a leader, in the sense of a strong man—even Claude[243] hardly has that job. What it does seem to want is a kind of focus of articulateness and it seems almost pathetically grateful to have anyone try to be that. But I rather miss the freedom with which I could drop everything and hike out along Bloor Street trying to solve *ambulando* some problem about prose form or verse rhythm.

That was a most pleasant evening when you dropped in,[244] disconcerting as it was to see Jay's [Jay Macpherson's] gentle face with her schoolgirl overbite suddenly transformed into a femme fatale, with a couple of drinks lighting her up behind the eyes. I find cocktail parties disastrous: I'm usually hysterically tired by the time I arrive at one, which is no condition to start drinking heavily in, although the impulse to drink heavily in such a state is almost irresistible. The usual result is that I go home to beat my head on the wall and wonder if what I said sounded as remorselessly idiotic to everyone else as it does in retrospect to me. Good theme for one of your more sardonic poems.

Of course I'd like an autographed copy of your QQ [*Queen's Quarterly*] set of poems, which, like [Irving] Layton, though probably for different reasons, I liked very much. I like the way your characters epiphanize from time to time out of a fog, and I hope you don't try to round them out fictionally, the way that radio programme of yours was starting to do. Cuts them down to the wrong size, I think.

The installation[245] was all right—surprisingly festive considering the sacrificial nature of the symbolism. Now I'm joining committees at the average rate of one a day, and am getting the illusion of making policy while learning about the relative merits of travertine and terrazzo tile, statistical predictions of staff-student ratios in 1968, property values on Bloor Street, and the proper number of formal parties to allow the residences. One banks one's fires, and hopes that one is also adding more fuel, in some mysterious way.

All the best to Jeanne, and kiss Nora for me.

David Erdman   **[ca. 1959]**

This letter is in reply to Erdman's having sent Frye a manuscript on Coleridge for his critique. Erdman's book was never published.

Dear David:

The book you have now in hand could take either of two forms: (A) a biographical study of Coleridge by Erdman, adding in an appendix only the essential documents, which

I suppose would be the reviews never before published but here claimed as Coleridge's or (B) a collection of Coleridge's reviews with an introductory essay, with appendices of doubtful ones and of reviews of Coleridge. The latter would make a useful handbook for Romantic specialists, the former a contribution to Romantic criticism for anybody seriously interested in English literature. My recommendation, after pointing out first that I don't think you can combine the two ideas, as the present MS tries to do to some extent, is that you junk (B) and concentrate on (A). A would be more fun for you, more readable, more significant, and a job that only you can do, whereas it would be easy to include a description of what should be in B in A, whereupon anybody else could assemble B under your directions. Or, if anyone threatens a complete Coleridge, they could co-opt you later for a book of reviews. If you stick to A, you have, I think, potentially as important a study of Coleridge as any on the market. But at present you're somewhat in danger of making the importance of your book depend on the number of new reviews that you can claim for Coleridge, and your thesis has an importance quite independent of that.

Well, if you do a full-length book of your own on the reviewing aspect of Coleridge, I suppose a good deal of your Morning Post and Courier work could go into it. I don't know about that. Your present introduction is extremely parenthetical and allusive, and you assume that you're writing only for Romantic specialists who'll be roughly familiar with everything that isn't absolutely new material. The reason for such a style, I take it, is the physical pressure of all the texts still to come — you have to compress to the limit, which is fine, but you don't want too cold a compress. If you think of the whole book as yours, you can expand. You'll be able to bring out, perhaps in an expanded preface, such important things, alluded to here only in passing, as the distinction between a magazine and a review (p. 152); the complicated moral questions posed by the reviewers' anonymity (p. 118); the fact that real money was involved, and so on. And, of course, you'll be able to tell a chronological story properly, and be able to sell your book to Miss Jennifer Jones, Assistant Professor of Speech Arts, Podunk Teachers' College, who won't know balls, all about John Scott's duel, or even that Jeffrey and Judge[246] Jeffrey were two different people. My opinion, for what it's worth, is that a straight biographical and chronological arrangement would be much easier to follow than a series of chapters following one review after another, in which the chronology continually overlaps with others.

The central thesis of A, I take it, is that Coleridge revolved around the conception of the ideal review all his life, and made some of his greatest work, including the Biographia and the Friend, incarnations of it. The nineteenth-century review sprang into being because nineteenth-century England was a country of powerful politico-cultural pressure groups. Nothing is more culturally significant about the twentieth century than the almost total collapse of this type of review in Anglo-Saxon countries. In the U.S.A., with its department-store parties, I can think of no such review today: the reviews there are are mostly disembodied intellectuals' journals, and, much more significantly, aren't popular or geared to anything organized in society, which is why they have to be heavily subsidized if they pay for contributions. Coleridge was so fascinated with the review because his own Romantic and genetic type of criticism is dialectic in shape: at one end there's a huge sunken body of metaphysical assumptions he was forever trying to dredge up; at the other there's a total conception of values, in the light of which all discussions of poets become impersonally personal. I see no difference *in tone* between his criticism of Wordsworth and his criticism of Shakespeare or Virgil. Everything leads up to a kind of ideal critical Last Judgement, and such things as The Friend are comparable to Blake's efforts to get independent of publishers by illuminating his own poems.

You all know this, and say most of it; but I think if you felt you had more room you'd say it more clearly. If you did, the biographical aspect of the book would come clear. The biographical picture of Coleridge you build up in tracing out all his weaseling and wuffling is very close to that of Wilson's attack — it's a clever and plausible caricature rather than a genuine biographical study in line with others. But if you treat all his manoeuvres in the light of an attempt to adjust himself and his apocalyptic ideal review to actual reviews, rising to a climax in the Maga self-parody business,[247] you'd have a real critical biography in the book instead of just a piece of literary detection.

So I'd be in favor of cutting down the review texts as far as possible. It's extraordinary what murder reviewers could get away with then, collecting their ten guineas a sheet with yards and yards of straight quotation. But if you make a feature of reprinted reviews, I'd suggest more explanatory footnotes, less preoccupied with the question of the Coleridgian authorship. You have a few of these already. You could use your knowledge of the anti-slavery agitation for the Kotzebue and the Clarkson book; you could explain who Paisiello was; you could write a lively note on the reference to the Hottentot Venus. (In the Musée de l'Homme, Paris, they have a wax model of the creature, along with a print depicting her reception in England, with a typical French stage Englishman, all front teeth and eyeglass, contemplating her awe-inspiring steatopygia with the comment: "Oh goddam quel rosbif.") Probably the anti-odontalgic teeth of St. Apollonia would be amusing too— Coleridge's humor is pachydermatous, but he had an eye for a good story. If you want a pure crystal-gazing psychic reaction, the Udolpho review sounds to me very Coleridgean, the Olmutz one not Coleridgean at all.

Thanks for letting me see this: I shouldn't be surprised if it were an early version of a Coleridge study as important as the Blake one.[248]

Best to Virgie and yourself from us both.

1960s

Lorne Pierce   **4 January 1960**
Ryerson Press, Toronto
Frye's letter is in the Queen's University Archives, Kingston, Ontario.

Dear Lorne Pierce:

Thanks you very much for your Christmas card with its valedictory message.[249] This is just to wish you a long and busy life in retirement. I first heard the name of Lorne Pierce in childhood, when my mother used to read me your writings in what I think was then the New Outlook,[250] and I have grown up to think of you as something like Confederation, one of the permanent factors in one's environment that one is grateful for. You have done more for Canadian literature, especially poetry, than any other single Canadian, and there cannot be anyone who knows you who is not eager to see the results of the "number of ventures" you speak of.

George Johnston   **14 January 1960**
Carleton University, Ottawa
This letter is in the George Johnston Papers in the Library and Archives Canada.

Dear George:

Thank you very much for the inscribed copy of the QQ [*Queen's Quarterly*] collection. I like your poems very much, and I think Layton may have been right in a way. They show a command of a longer and more flexible rhythm, with more variety of cadence, than *The Cruising Auk* in itself gives much hint of.[251] Maybe you're unduly suspicious of this less epigrammatic side of yourself.

All the best to Jeanne and the family,

Garrick I. Clarke   **18 January 1960**
Clarke Irwin & Co., Toronto, ON
In response to the publication of Frye's installation address, "By Liberal Things," which was initially published by Clarke Irwin in paper wrappers and then in a case-bound edition.

Dear Mr. Clarke:

Thank you very much for the letter from Miss MacNaughton. I remember her very well, and I was delighted to have this message from her. I shall be writing to her without delay.

Naturally I am most pleased and flattered not only by your interest in my address and the beautiful job you have made of printing it, but for your continuing interest in it. I have given it the title, for your hard-cover edition, of "By Liberal Things," which is a quotation from Isaiah, although the passage is not referred to in the address. But I always have trouble with titles.

Mother Mary Christopher Pecheux, O.S.U.   **25 January 1960**
College of New Rochelle, New Rochelle, NY
The letter from Mother Mary Pecheux to which Frye is responding is not extant, but it appears to relate to her remarks about footnote 41 to chapter 10 of Fearful Symmetry. *She may also have been referring to Frye's account of the Virgin Birth and Immaculate Conception in chapter 11 of* Fearful Symmetry *(393).*

Dear Mother Mary,

Thank you very much for your letter. I much appreciate the interest you have taken in the matter. I think I am fairly clear on the distinction between the Virgin Birth, which of course Milton would have accepted, and the Immaculate Conception, which I think lies outside the orbit of his theology. The purpose of the footnote was to attempt to indicate something of this distinction. However, the Immaculate Conception was not a particularly lively issue for Milton, and for that reason the note is probably unnecessary, and, if it causes misunderstanding among students, inadvisable. I shall therefore recommend to the publishers that they delete the note in the next edition.[252]

George Johnston   **28 January 1960**
Carleton University, Ottawa, ON
In response to Johnston's having sent Frye a copy of his poems Beside the Sea, *which had been published in* Queen's Quarterly, *and* Multitude. *Both poems were included in Johnston's second collection,* Home Free *(1966). Frye's letter is in the George Johnston Papers in the Library and Archives Canada.*

Dear George:

Thanks very much for your letter and the report on the pullulation of Sadie.[253] What I liked about your QQ poem was chiefly, I think, its suggestion of growth. The poems in *The Cruising Auk* are perfection in their way, and for that very reason there's a limit to what you can go on doing in that form. Beside the Sea[254] is an imperfect poem that seems to me to show a direction of development, towards a less externalized kind of vision. It has no resemblance whatever to Layton.[255] It's pure Johnston, but of a kind that adumbrates another collection shaping up — to be called, possibly, The Oozing Crock.

Don't worry about being called vitriolic: you won't communicate with the sort of people who would really find you so. Mithridates, he died old.[256]

Hazard Adams   **11 February 1960**
Department of English, Michigan State University, East Lansing, MI
In reply to Adams's asking Frye's advice about a conference on twentieth-century literature. The conference was in fact held on May 4–6 the next year, and the proceedings were published as Approaches to the Study of Twentieth-Century Literature: Proceedings of the Conference in the Study of Twentieth Century Literature, First Session *(East Lansing: Michigan State University), 1961.*

Dear Hazard:

Thank you very much for your prospectus. I am startled to learn even at a groundswell, that twentieth-century scholars lack an adequate scholarly morale. I sometimes get the impression that there is nobody but twentieth-century scholars in the United States. I am afraid that my suggestions at the moment are somewhat vague. I feel that all commentary on Joyce, Eliot, and Yeats at least ought to be suspended for a little while — say about five hundred years. Likewise Dylan Thomas, Faulkner, Kafka, and about fifty others you will find no difficulty in naming yourself.

What I feel such a conference might do is to try to arrive at some conception of a pattern or a structure of twentieth-century thought, so far as that can be approached through literature. I am somewhat disturbed by the fact that all our political philosophies to-day are entirely nineteenth-century growths, and it seems to me that certain distinctive twentieth-century developments, particularly in the area of symbolism, might be looked at in a more comprehensive way. The chief trouble with critical study of one's own century is the trouble of the fly on the fresco trying to see the picture. A systematic effort at contemporary perspective would interest me a good deal: the general pattern of ordinary twentieth-century literary criticism does not.[257]

I trust this will confuse you completely.

Hugh Kenner   22 February 1960
University of California, Santa Barbara, CA
In reply to Kenner's inquiry about a teaching position in Canada.

Dear Hugh,

Thank you for your letter. I was most interested to learn that you would like to come back to Canada.[258] I don't know what to suggest in Canada at the moment. Someone of your ability would need a university with a fully developed graduate school, and Toronto is the only one in Canada. And even Toronto doesn't make graduate appointments as such. Woodhouse controls that situation, which is also the University College situation.

For other universities, I don't know what is available at anything like your level. I remember a somewhat wry comment from a woman who was an associate professor in the west, and whom I was trying to move east, that her offence was rank. And she certainly had nothing like your abilities or publication record.[259] Adam Smith remarked that of all objects of transportation the most difficult is the human body, and that seems to be still true.

I should have thought that a university in the United States which is busy trying to build up a good graduate school and combine it with undergraduate teaching would be in a position to make you a better proposal than any Canadian university could do at present, as well as giving you more scope and making you feel less like a scene out of Modern Times. You must get such offers very frequently, and some of them would be well worth investigating. Canada is certainly expanding, but its academic pace, even of expansion, is still leisurely.

Nevertheless I shall be making further inquiries, as it would certainly be wonderful to have you back in Canada.

With all best wishes.

Malcolm Ross   24 February 1960
Department of English, Queen's University, Kingston, ON
At the time Ross was the only university representative on the committee of the Ontario Board of Education charged with determining matriculation standards for grade XIII students.

Dear Mac:

I have been wondering for some time how the new arrangement with regard to the Grade XIII Prescription Committee is working out. In addition to my wonderings, the department here has taken a very dim view of the reduction of university representation on this committee, in view of the fact that Grade XIII is supposed to be university work under university control, as far as curriculum is concerned. I am sure that the Department of Education's intentions were not sinister at all, and that they merely wished to get a less cumbersome committee. But I do wonder if the university representation on it shouldn't be increased to at least three members. In any case the Department has made me chairman of a committee to look into the matter and I turn to you as the only person who would know anything about it.

Before I call my committee I should like to know, first, what you think of the new arrangement, and secondly, whether you think the university representation should be increased, and thirdly, whether the department here, if so, would be justified in raising a squawk, and fourthly to whom the squawk should be addressed. I'd be grateful for any help you could give me.

Leeds Barroll   7 March 1960
Department of English, University of Texas, Austin, TX
In reply, apparently, to a request by Barroll for Frye's advice about accepting a position at the University of Cincinnati. Barroll's letter is not extant.

Dear Leeds:

My only knowledge of Cincinnati is derived from having spent two or three days there in the course of delivering two lectures. There are also two Canadians on the English staff, Hugh Maclean and George Ford, both of whom have left or are leaving, Ford to Rochester and Maclean to York University here. It seemed to me a pleasant community and the people I met were thoroughly likeable. On the other hand, I should not have said that it was the first-rate university with which you say you would like to be finally associated. I should have thought that Texas was closer to being that. So you would probably need to think in terms of a relatively short stay there. And as the examples of Ford and Maclean indicate, it is not too difficult a place to get away from, being in the more populous area and within easy reach of most of the learned conferences. Cincinnati itself struck me as a somewhat demoralized town, but my first impressions of such things are likely to be unreliable. And I think too that there are some tensions in the relation between the university and the city, but others could tell you more about that.

On the whole my instinct would be to use the Cincinnati offer, if it comes, for all it's worth in Texas, and stay there if Texas comes up with anything comparable. If not, I should think you would still have quite a pleasant sojourn at Cincinnati, even if it doesn't take a sudden turn for the better, as second-rank institutions quite often do these days.[260]

Milton Wilson   26 July 1960
Department of English, Trinity College, University of Toronto
Wilson had assumed responsibility for the annual poetry review ("Letters in Canada"), which Frye had written for the previous ten years, for the University of Toronto Quarterly. *The books Frye sends along with this letter are to be reviewed by Wilson in next annual survey.*

Dear Milton:

I send along the bits and pieces of things that came to me before you took over. There isn't much there. There is also, as I understand, a privately printed booklet called "Acis in Oxford" by Robert Finch. The Outram booklet[261] was sent to me for review last year, and through some accident it got mixed up in my papers and for that reason was not included in my review. As you will see, it seems to have been sent to me personally, and it was for that reason that I mislaid it. You can use your own judgment about reviewing it.

It seems very ungracious of me to return Margaret Avison's book.[262] I know that I ought to be reviewing it, but for this summer I have eight articles to write, two books to edit, at least five theses to read so far, and the result is that I'm beginning to feel a little desperate about my schedule. In any case, I'd be afraid of putting the review off so long that it wouldn't be fair either to Margaret or to the Forum. I should think Eli Mandel would make an admirable reviewer.

As I am still a member of the Governor General's Awards Committee, I'd be extremely grateful if you could keep me posted on anything in poetry that seems worth serious consideration. My guess is that Margaret [Atwood] and Eli [Mandel] (if Eli's book comes out this year)[263] would be the only possibilities,[264] but if anything else comes up I might just possibly not see it. The possibility is the kind of thing I get nightmares about.

I am delighted that you are doing the UTQ review, and it couldn't be left in better hands. I know you know I think this, but you may as well have it in writing.

Harold Bloom   21 September 1960
Department of English, Yale University, New Haven, CT

Dear Mr. Bloom:

I was very sorry not to be able to get to the English Institute this year to hear your paper. It was quite impossible for me to get there, and I rather got the impression that my presence there would have instituted an unwarranted interference with freedom of speech.

I am writing you at the moment to inform you that I am nominating you, without your consent, for a Hodder Fellowship at Princeton. This Fellowship is worth 6500 tax free dollars, and a year without any prescribed duties.

Should you be able to accept this nomination, would you please write to Professor Arthur Szathmary of the Department of Philosophy at Princeton, sending him a vita, and an account of the work you would do. This would be of course for the year 1961–62. I am sorry that circumstances beyond my control have made this so hurried.[265]

Herbert M. Schueller   1 November 1960
Department of English, Wayne State University, Detroit, MI

The letter to which this is a response is not extant, but apparently Schueller had asked Frye's opinion of the journal Criticism, *which Schueller edited from 1969 to 1972.*

Dear Professor Schueller:

Thank you very much for the copies of *Criticism*. I have been following the progress of the magazine with the greatest interest. I feel that in some ways it still lacks a clear focus, as it seems to alternate between critical articles on the various arts and more specialized articles far within the individual disciplines. I should think that some of the trouble lies in the fact that critical theory is not sufficiently developed for a magazine of the scope of this one. At times the critical language seems to collapse into the sort of unmeaning babble that arises from the pages of *Essays in Criticism* and similar dimwitted screeds.

I wonder whether *Criticism* shouldn't unify itself around a more contemporary centre: that is, devote its main efforts to developments in critical theory and aesthetics that are in the intellectual news. In general, I should be against such a policy, but it seems to me that it might be justifiable in these rather exceptional circumstances.

Harold Bloom   5 January 1961
Department of English, Yale University, New Haven, CT

Dear Mr. Bloom:

Thank you very much for your letter. I am very interested in what you tell me of your approaching books, as I wasn't aware that you were being quite so prolific. Naturally I am greatly looking forward to seeing them both. I'm attaching an offprint of the Stevens article,[266] as requested. As you will note, it doesn't deal with the posthumous material, but I don't think there is anything in that to change the argument.

With best personal wishes to your wife and yourself as always,

Dorothy Van Ghent   **5 January 1961**
Pacifica, CA
In reply to Van Ghent's request for a Guggenheim fellowship recommendation.

Dear Miss Ghent:

Thank you for your letter and for the very gracious acknowledgement. I'm glad that *Nostromo* did get published after all[267]; when publishers pretend to be gentlemen it is often a slow business.

If you send the first hundred pages of your Keats book, I will certainly glance through it sufficiently to be able to write a letter to the Guggenheim people about it. I'm not sure at the moment that I can promise anything much more thoroughgoing than that, in view of the number of manuscripts and theses I have now. It will be a little easier when the *Anatomy* generation gets installed in the senior posts because so many of them at present are graduate students struggling with recalcitrant supervisors and as a result send what they've written to me.

With all best wishes and wishing you the best of success,

Jerome S. Bruner   **11 January 1961**
Department of Psychology, Harvard University, Cambridge, MA
Bruner was a well-known cognitive psychologist and philosopher of education.

Dear Professor Bruner:

Just a note a say how delighted I am that you are to be coming to Toronto to help us with our new educational venture.[268] I was so impressed with your cogent remarks at the Myth Conference of last spring[269] that I warmly supported the proposal mooted here of asking you to come. Everyone here is filled with the greatest enthusiasm for "The Process of Education," and we are all convinced that your work at Woods Hole has the greatest relevance to what we are trying to do here.[270]

Looking forward greatly to seeing and hearing you,

Sidney Feshbach   **21 April 1961**
Florence, Italy
In reply to letter from Feshbach that has not survived.

Dear Mr. Feshbach:

Thank you very much for your letter: it was a great pleasure to hear from you again. Your Master's thesis sounds extremely interesting and very central to its subject. If your present plan is to write a longer work on Joyce which might serve either as a book or a doctoral thesis, I should be glad to look at it, as a whole or in pieces, and be of whatever help I can. I would certainly feel that the points you have made about metamorphosis and about the Platonic references to Daedalus are themes which run all through Joyce, and should make a fuller study of him along such lines one of unusual interest.

I wish you the best of luck in your graduate work and expect that you will be enjoying Firenze as it should be enjoyed in the spring.

A.J.M. Smith　　　　　　　　　　　　　　　　　　　　　　　　**12 May 1961**
Michigan State University, East Lansing, MI
On 2–4 May 1961 Frye had attended a conference on twentieth-century literature, held at Michigan State University, where A.J.M. Smith taught. Frye's letter is in the University Archives at Trent University.

Dear Art:

I got back to pick up the aftermath of the Canadian Conference of the Arts,[271] which apparently turned out to be quite a big affair. Irving Layton informed the waiting public that tycoons weren't a threat to poets anymore; that there was only one real enemy left in Canada, and that was Northrop Frye. Maybe that's because you're living in the States.

One disagreeable bit of news; Anne Wilkinson died of cancer last Wednesday — she'd been ill a long time, but seemed to have recovered entirely.[272]

Love to Jeanie: it was wonderful seeing you.

Frederick Morgan　　　　　　　　　　　　　　　　　　**18 September 1961**
The Hudson Review, New York, NY

Dear Mr. Morgan:

I am very sorry that I seem to have lost touch with the Hudson Review during the summer. I was extremely busy getting a commissioned book on Eliot done and finishing up various odds and ends. My major creative effort at the moment is writing a citation for the Prime Minister, who gets an honorary degree here.[273] But I should be glad to review Kenneth Burke's book,[274] though I'm not sure I could promise the October 20th deadline.[275] I have a copy of the book, and will get the review done as soon as possible.

D.J. Barr　　　　　　　　　　　　　　　　　　　　　　　　**4 January 1962**
Toronto, ON
In reply to Barr's inquiry, which has not survived, about a line in Blake: "Truly My Satan thou art but a Dunce."

Dear Mr. Barr:

In the line from Blake to which you refer I think there is an allusion to the passage in Bunyan's *Pilgrim's Progress*, where Christian falls asleep under the hill Difficulty and loses his roll. In more general terms, Satan is the spirit of superstition and terror which would be the only thing left to contemplate if one had had no moment of vision in life. As you know, the poem from which this line comes is the epilogue to *The Gates of Paradise* which depicts in its last three plates the traveller entering a subterranean door and going into the world of death. Because an instant of vision has preceded this the traveller is not "lost."

Belinda Humfrey　　　　　　　　　　　　　　　　　　　**26 February 1962**
St. Hugh's College, Oxford, England
In reply to an inquiry, which has not survived, about alchemy in Spenser.

Dear Miss Humfrey:

The obvious alchemical link for Spenser is the hermaphroditic Venus of book four, canto ten, which is the alchemical *res bina*. Then, of course, the elaborate red and white symbolism in the first book, and its quest theme leading up to the wedding of the king and queen, would have suggested alchemy to a contemporary reader familiar with that language. The point is that philosophical alchemy is really a form of biblical typology and

Renaissance poets using either would be involved in both. I had a graduate student who started out on this topic, but got side-tracked on Yeats instead.

Karl Hill   9 March 1962
Beacon Press, Boston, MA

In reply to an inquiry about whether Beacon Press should publish books by Leslie Fiedler and György Lukács. Beacon Press chose not issue a second Fiedler title but it did publish Lukács's The Historical Novel, *with a preface by Irving Howe, in 1963.*

Dear Mr. Hill:

I find it very difficult to make a judgment on the two books you mention, because I find it hard to assess the American temper from this slightly cooler region. Ordinarily, I should have said it was very curious that a publishing house dedicated to liberalism should hesitate to publish a book on the ground that it was Marxist, and be favorably disposed to publishing Fiedler, who seems to me to be climbing on a somewhat disreputable band-wagon. However, Fiedler undoubtedly sells well, and on purely literary matters he often has very astute insights. I think in your place I should be guided by the sales of *An End to Innocence.*[276]

As for the Lukacs book, it is true that it might be described as out of date. It seems to me that being kept in ignorance of Marxist criticism is a curious way of preparing American students for life in the 1960s, and my own feeling is that the book is significant enough to be brought into print, especially if Irving Howe writes an introduction to it. It's true that it would not be "adopted" in a great many institutions, but it might be recommended even in some of them. On the other hand, my own very amateur guess at the prospect of sales would be on the low side.

George Johnston   26 March 1962
Carleton University, Ottawa, ON

In reply to Johnston's letter of 23 February 1962, with its enclosed poems. Frye's letter is in the George Johnston Papers in the Library and Archives Canada.

Dear George:

Thanks very much for your letter and the poems. I had read the nitro-glycerine story a long time ago, but for some reason hadn't disgorged it from my other papers. Jay [Macpherson] has it now.[277] I thought it was a quite successful treatment of a very difficult genre — except for one or two self-conscious phrases like "I'm gruntled all right," the balance of tone seems admirable. I like the poems too, which are as beautifully written as ever. They continue with the same dramatis personae — Daisy has her sisters in the Auk,[278] but I'm relieved to see that Mr. Murple and the rest are not taking on independent existence.[279] They'd become oppressive to you if they did that.

I've had an unreasonably busy year, and have provided myself with a donkey's carrot of a sabbatical in another year or two. That is to say, I dream of having a year off, but the chances of my getting one may not be so bright. What tires one is the variety of hands clutching and grabbing, and the dialectics of decision. Some of the things suggested to me are crude temptations, like being President of Mount Allison; others are insidious temptations, like becoming general editor for a publisher of an unending series of books; others are chances to produce things in me I ought to be producing, and should be accepted. But most, of course, are straight routine — speaking to high schools, attending committees, advising students, and so on. Virtue goes out of one quickly when one has so little of it.

Too bad the Friends didn't work out as a community for you, but probably the really important things about them can't be adapted to a social organization.[280] They have a dreary compromise called "pastoral Quakerism," which is just one more colorless church. I imagine Bob[281], being young, has an accurate instinct for finding the right social organization.

I'm somewhat taken aback by Jack Harris' desire to go into metamorphosis—it was difficult to write to the Canada Council about him when I've seen so little of his work. It would be like writing for you on the strength of Annabel.[282] I hope he lands on his feet.

Once again, thanks very much for the letters and poems, and my best to Jeanne and the family. Next week I start on a series of seven lectures over the following month — Haverford, Brown, Harvard, Nebraska, Rochester, Toronto (over 3000 psychiatrists in Convocation Hall)[283] and Mount Allison.

Clarence Tracy   6 April 1962
Department of English, University of Saskatchewan, Saskatoon, SK
In reply to Tracy's having sent Frye and offprint of his "The Unity of Gulliver's Travels," Queen's Quarterly 68 *(1962): 597–609.*

Dear Professor Tracy:

Thank you very much for the Swift offprint. Having recently struggled through that absurd book of Dobrée,[284] and learning from that that it is possible to read Gulliver's Travels and misinterpret its meaning on every point, it was a great relief to turn to your incisive study instead.

Hans Jonas   26 April 1962
New School for Social Research, New York, NY
In reply to Jonas's having sent Frye an offprint of his "Immortality and the Modern Temper: The Ingersoll Lecture, 1961," Harvard Theological Review 55, no. 1 *(January 1962): 1–20.*

Dear Mr. Jonas:

Thank you very much for the offprint of your article on *Immortality*. I am greatly impressed with both the eloquence and the cogency of the writing. You realize clearly that Immortality, whether the arguments for or against it have any weight or not, is a subject in which a great deal of human dignity is bound up. I was also very interested, and a little surprised, to find that the myth you propose is a pure incarnation myth — pretty well what the third book of Paradise Lost would be if Milton's idiotic grinning father were removed from it.

With all best wishes to you both,

Roy Daniells   11 May 1962
University of British Columbia, Vancouver, BC
In response to Daniells's request for an assessment of Irving Layton as a possible appointment at the University of British Columbia. Frye's letter is in the Roy Daniells Fonds, University of British Columbia, box 7, file 18b.

Dear Roy:

It's not easy to know what to say about Layton, and perhaps I'd better write you the kind of letter you could summarize for rather than show your Dean. I've talked to at least two people in authority at George Williams, and they agree with enthusiasm that Layton is a most valuable asset as a teacher and influence on students. He doesn't teach at the university level, but that wouldn't matter. He's extremely interested in teaching, and in students likely to become writers. His weakness would be, I should guess, that the students he would be interested in would be disciples, though possibly he might be more tolerant in practice than in theory. He's apt to identify his own rigorous and rigid literary convention with the state of creative freedom, largely because of its subject-matter, but then many young people would respond to that. As a writer himself, he seems to me to have defined himself in his Robert Creeley-Jonathan Williams-Jargon-Black Mountain group, and will show little real development from now on, despite his statements.

As a colleague, he's an egomaniac, like many writers. You don't say whether appointing him to U.B.C. is partly Layton's idea: if it were I should recommend him more strongly. Otherwise, I'd be doubtful if he'd want to leave Montreal or could function well out of it, but that's his business. His anti-academic pronouncements are of course without significance — that party line would be ignored or changed overnight. But I'd be less keen about seeing him at U.B.C. than at some other places. He knows where his bread is buttered, and would choose his partisanships accordingly, but in a large department like U.B.C. he might be confused about where his partisanships should be. He might, for example, want to take over either Prism or Can. Lit. or both, or he might prefer to attack them.[285]

He's now making what seems to me a rather difficult adjustment to middle age, moving from angry young man to lion-roaring institution. He hasn't made this adjustment yet, and his psychological state will be clearer, I should imagine, in two or three years' time. So while this may be a rather fence-sitting letter, I feel that at the moment Layton is too unpredictable to make a clear judgement on. Perhaps you should examine his letter in the current Canadian Forum and then decide on the basis of your knowledge of U.B.C. and of similar temperaments in your department.

George Johnston 26 June 1962
Carleton University, Ottawa, ON

In reply to Johnston's letter (19 June 1962), recommending one of his students for graduate study at Toronto and asking if there might be a position for her as a don in one of the women's residences.

Dear George,

Thank you very much for your letter. I was very pleased to hear about Janet O'Brien, and will be looking forward to seeing her. What she should do is apply immediately to Jessie Macpherson[286] for a Donship in residence. Jessie is up North on Georgian Bay, but a letter sent to the college will be forwarded. I think there may be a place or two available, but normally Jessie doesn't give donships to people who were undergraduates the year before. But a good deal would depend on a personal interview.

I'm very sorry to hear about Gordon Wood,[287] but given a general history of his health up 'til now, I can't say I'm really surprised. About all one can say is that one is thankful it's no worse.

Our love to you both.

Leon Edel 20 September 1962
New York, NY

In response to Edel's request to reprint Pelham Edgar's "Henry James: The Essential Novelist" in an anthology of James criticism he was editing — Henry James: A Collection of Critical Essays (Twentieth Century Views Series), published the following year.

Dear Leon:

Kathleen Coburn has turned over your letter about Pelham Edgar's book to me. I think

I may assume to myself the position of Pelham's literary executor, and give permission to reprint accordingly, as I did once before. If there is any fee available, as clearly there should be, it should go to Mrs. Pelham Edgar, who is now living in Cyprus. Her mailing address is: The Canada Trust Company, c/o O.H. Firth, London, ON.

As you have probably heard by now, I read your admirable paper on Faulkner at Edinburgh. It provoked quite a lively discussion, but not all of it was relevant to the subject. I think that this was because they felt in a holiday mood because the author of the paper was not present.

J.A. Gonsalves   20 October 1962
Supervisor of Publications, Canadian Broadcasting Corporation, Toronto, ON
In reply to Gonslaves's letter about Frye's Massey Lectures, published the following year as The Educated Imagination *by CBC Publications and by Indiana University Press. Frye made a number of additions to the transcripts of the oral lectures.*

Dear Mr. Gonsalves:

Thank you for your letter of October 18th and its clarification of the copyright situation. The terms you set out are quite satisfactory to me. I don't think that the scripts as submitted are quite in shape for publication, in view of the numerous cuts and minor corrections that have had to be made on them. I shall prepare a manuscript for you from the scripts at my earliest opportunity, and when I have done that, the book will require an absolute minimum of editing. The lectures have been written in a deliberately conversational style, and the printed version will be very carefully edited by me, and not by anyone else, to conform faithfully to the rhythm of the spoken word. I shall also require a set of galley proofs for proof-reading, and page proofs if possible.

M.W. Duckworth   7 December 1962
Department of Extension, Mount Allison University, Sackville, NB
Duckworth's letter to Frye, which described a summer institute he was planning and requested possible speakers, is not extant.

Dear Mr. Duckworth:

Thank you very much for your letter of November 27th and for the program of last year's summer institute. I think that discussions on Christianity are rather tricky to manage. And the suggestion in your letter of beginning with an anti–Christian and answering him with a defender of the faith would look as though you were rigging the discussion in advance. I wonder whether it would not be better to define in each of the points you mention, such as the condition of the working classes, the forces that seem to be anti–Christian in tendency. For example, to what extent do the working classes regard Christianity as merely a shop-front for the middle classes? Or, similarly, to what extent does Christianity merely symbolize colonialism to, for example, an African nationalist? The theoretical debate between the Christian and anti–Christian is unanswerable in any case, because religion is not proved by arguments.

I think President Moore[288] would be a better person than myself to suggest speakers for your institute. One obvious name that strikes me is that of Ernest Long, the Secretary at the United Church building here, whose views on the world situation today are unusually penetrating and sensitive. I don't know whether you would want Paul Blanshard, who has written so much about the political opinion of Roman Catholicism, to deal with the theme of the Church in a political context. There are people here, such as Charles Hendry,

Director of the School of Social Work, who could discuss very sympathetically the relation of the Church to such problems as juvenile delinquency.

James R. Squire   14 January 1963
National Council of Teachers of English, Champaign, IL

Squires's letter to Frye, which is not extant, solicited his reaction to a proposal for a conference on language teaching that was being planned by the National Council of Teachers of English, and he invited Frye's attendance at the conference.

Dear Mr. Squire:

Thank you very much for your letter of December 18th and its accompanying prospectus about your experimental program. This is naturally something that interests me a good deal, and the quality of people you have lined up on your advisory committees and as attendants at the conference is extremely impressive. I can say little about my possible attendance at such a conference until I know the date. I don't know that I have any comments on the prospectus itself, except that I thoroughly approve of your resistance to the superstitions about keeping a child's vocabulary limited. In regard to paragraph four of pages four and five, my own view is that the teaching of grammar is bound to fail if it is conceived as a means of building up a child's powers of articulation from word to phrase, phrase to sentence, sentence to paragraph, and so on. Children tend to speak in an unbroken play of monologue, and it seems to me that grammar and punctuation should be taught as a means of breaking into this flow and transforming it from monologue into something addressed to other people.

G.O. Dale   18 February 1963
Scarborough, ON

In reply to Dale's inquiry, which is not extant, about certain passages of Scripture, which appear to be from the Sermon on the Mount, more particularly Matthew 6:25–27.

Dear Mr. Dale:

I am not quite certain what your difficulty with these passages is, but certainly it is central to Christianity that the conditions of life are to be taken as given, and the religious value of one's life depends on the intensity of response within those conditions. It is a fact of experience that one cannot increase one's height by efforts of will, and that verse [Matthew 6:27] is a rhetorical question giving a restriction or analogy to the general principle that there is no use quarrelling with the postulates of one's own existence.[289] Again, planning for the future is as unproductive from the religious point of view as brooding on the past, because life in time is discontinuous, and by the time one reaches the future one has planned for one is a different person and the whole operation of planning has become futile.[290] Several contemporary writers have taken up Zen Buddhism because they have found the same doctrine there, but it is equally central to Christianity. In all great religions the field of reality is the present moment.

Harold Bloom   8 April 1963
Yale University, New Haven, CT

Bloom's letter, which was apparently enclosed with a copy of his Blake's Apocalypse, *is not extant.*

Dear Mr. Bloom:

Thank you very much for your letter. As you already have a copy of *The Well-Tempered Critic*, I am sending the only other one I have available at the moment, an essay I did for Nebraska. I think — I'm not sure — that it represents a comment on what seems to be a difficulty you have with Blake: his identification of art and apocalypse.[291]

I have enjoyed reading your Blake book[292] very much, and feel that it is exactly the kind of book that needed to be written and which I hoped someone — preferably you — would soon write. I am particularly impressed, as always, by your handling of *The Four Zoas*. For some reason or other, possibly because I am waiting for a new text, I have never given this poem a great deal of attention since I finished my own book. Your book stimulates me to read it again.

With all best wishes to you both, and with great pleasure about your promotion.

Winthrop Tilley   8 April 1963
Castleton State College, Castleton, VT

In reply to Tilley's query about inductive and deductive critical approaches in teaching, apparently triggered by what Frye says about induction and deduction in Anatomy of Criticism, *p. 22. Tilley's letter is not extant.*

Dear Professor Tilley:

Thank you for your letter of April 1st. The answer that occurs to me is that there is no real difference between a deductive procedure and a pseudo-inductive one. They differ in the rhetorical forms of their presentation, but not in their logic as methods. I would agree that no subject should be presented deductively to any student, and that every opportunity should be given to him to feel that he is discovering things empirically for himself. At the same time there does have to be a deductive plan in the teacher's mind, and this is all that I am pleading for.

R.M. Wiles   2 May 1963
Department of English, McMaster University, Hamilton, ON

In reply to an inquiry about the Ontario matriculation examinations and the preparation of secondary school students for university study. Wiles's letter is not extant.

Dear Roy:

I'm afraid I have little concrete to suggest beyond general approval of what you are doing. I think that one thing that badly needs overhauling is the representation of universities on the grade 13 prescriptions committee. This has been cut to a single person for all the universities in Ontario and makes a farce out of the claim that the matriculation examinations are set by the university. The publication of Design for Learning,[293] again, is leading to the setting up of an Ontario Curriculum Institute, which ought to act as a kind of clearing-house for the sort of problem that you are dealing with. Certainly there is no substitute for direct action with the department and the minister. It is a waste of time trying to fiddle around with remedial courses in universities, as you and everyone connected with the university knows.

J.R. Bilder   15 July 1963
Department of English, Georgetown University, Washington, DC

In reply to Bilder's request (11 July 1963) for permission to use portions of Frye's critique of an article Bilder submitted to PMLA. *He also asks Frye to expand on the points he made about the novel of ideas.*

Dear Professor Bilder:

Thank you for your letter. I am afraid that I have completely forgotten what I said in my report on your article, and while I certainly have no objection to your making whatever use of it you please, I am not sure that my expansion of the point I made will be very helpful.

It seems to me that a novelist, if he knows his job, is concerned not to express ideas but to set up a human situation that contains ideas by implication. Everything conceptual in a novel should be digested into human relationships, and presented in this oblique and implied way. With the novel, as we have it in Jane Austen, or Henry James, this is obvious enough. With the other tradition which runs through Peacock and Huxley, the same rule holds good, even though the material used is more conceptual than situational. I take it that this is what you are saying too. One great weakness of the latter type of writing is its tendency to incorporate the novelist with his notebook as one of the characters, and such a character, whether Philip Quarles in *Point Counterpoint* or Pursewarden in Durrell,[294] always sounds like a fraud.

With best wishes and good luck,

Karl Polanyi   **25 July 1963**
Pickering, ON

In response to Polanyi's letter Frye (21 July 1963) regarding a proposed quarterly journal to be called Co-existence. *Polanyi, who was seeking Frye's endorsement of the venture, enclosed copies of letters from European scholars interested in the proposal. Polanyi was a distinguished economic historian, best known for his book* The Great Transformation.

Dear Mr. Polanyi:

Thank you very much for the documents you have sent me in connection with *Co-Existence*. The journal seems to me a distinctive and thoroughly worthy object, badly needed and well timed for its appearance. I am not sure how active a role you want me to take, and certainly economics is not a field in which I have any competence. But I am certainly willing to give the "moral and intellectual support" that one of your letters speaks of.

May I say also how delighted I am to receive a copy of *The Plow and the Pen*.[295] Naturally I was particularly interested in the poetry at the end, some of which is quite obviously poetry of major importance.

With best wishes to you both,

Joseph Campbell   **12 August 1963**
New York NY

Campbell's letter is not extant.

Dear Mr. Campbell:

Thank you very much for your letter: it was most pleasant to hear from you again, and I feel greatly interested in your wife's play[296] and in the prospect of its coming here.

This University is not set up in a way that would make such visits very easy — it would take a bulky dossier to explain why — but I am turning your letter and the reviews over to a colleague in close touch with dramatic activities here, and if anything can be set in motion, he will be able to do it.

I am off for Ireland tomorrow, and I note that this play is one of the things I might be able to take in during my vacation. I hope so, at any rate.

With best personal wishes to you both.

Lewis Leary   **24 December 1963**
Department of English, Columbia University, New York, NY
In reply to Leary's offer (9 December 1963) for Frye to become a visiting professor at Columbia University for the following year. Frye had just returned from giving the Bampton Lectures at Columbia the month before: the lectures were published as A Natural Perspective: The Development of Shakespearean Comedy and Romance *(1965).*

Dear Lewis,

I was just on the point of writing you to thank you for that most pleasant party and the chance to meet the Taylors. I was especially pleased when Mrs. Taylor turned out to be a student of Blake. Fred Johnston of course is a very old and close friend.[297]

It would be very pleasant to teach at Columbia next year, but I have to be rather ruthless about deciding that if I do succeed in getting off next year, which is by no means a certainty,[298] I should devote my energies to reading and resting. I have not had a year off since 1950, and consequently, no real intake of literature since that time. I am beginning to feel like a spider trying to spin a web in the desert.

I am very appreciative of your comments on my lectures and of Columbia's response collectively. I could not have asked for a better audience.

The best of the season to you both.

Helen D. Willard   **28 December 1965**
Curator, Harvard College Library, Theatre Collection, Cambridge, MA
In reply to a request for Frye to supply a draft of one of his books for the Harvard College Library.

Dear Helen:

Thank you very much for your letter: we were delighted to hear from you. We were also glad to be reminded of Narcissa Williamson.[299] I am afraid that my instinct is to burn every sheet of working material as soon as a book is published, but of course I could make an exception for some future book. My general practice is to write in long-hand, until the revisions and corrections begin to look unintelligible even to me. Then I type it out, and continue revising and retyping for about five drafts, after which it begins to look somewhat like what it is going to be. I don't know what stage of this gestation would be most appropriate for the Library.

Albert Trueman   **7 February 1964**
Director, Canada Council, Ottawa, ON

Dear Dr. Trueman:

I should like to apply to the Canada Council through you for some assistance in the furtherance of my scholarly work. I have been trying, with a good deal of difficulty, to arrange things so as to be given leave of absence during the academic year 1964-1965, and I am now in a position to say that I have succeeded.[300] The normal arrangement is that I should be on half salary for that year from Victoria College. My present salary is $19,000.

I have not had a year off since 1950, when, on a Guggenheim Fellowship, I spent a year at Harvard drafting out the plans of what eventually became the *Anatomy of Criticism*, published in 1957. This book is now regarded, I think I can say, as one of the most authoritative works of criticism in our time, and although it still meets with fierce resistance here and there, as a controversial book should, it has in general established its authority. This was my second major scholarly enterprise, the first being a commentary on the symbolism of William Blake, *Fearful Symmetry*, 1947, which is still in use as a standard work in its field. I have written a good many articles, series of lectures, and short books since the *Anatomy*: details are on the attached bibliography. But I should like now to plan a third major book, one that deals primarily with the *external* relations of literary criticism: the difference that a properly organized theory of literature would make in our present comprehension of religion, psychology, philosophy and anthropology — all the subjects where, as in literary criticism, the conception "myth" is of functional importance.[301] The educational role of literature, from Kindergarten to graduate school, is also involved in the argument. A great deal of hard reading in several languages lies ahead of me, and it is difficult to do this systematically during the few intervals of an administrative job.

I am leaving the category of application, the amount of financial assistance, and parallel matters to the Canada Council for its decision. As for the place where such study would be carried on, I have at the moment no settled convictions. Anywhere within reach of a good academic library would be satisfactory to me, and for much of the year it would be simplest merely to stay where I am in Toronto, though doubtless this will not prove to be a practicable idea, in view of the invention of the telephone. I am committed to a six-week visit to universities in England during that year,[302] and may stay there longer. I have received several invitations from British and American universities to visit them on a teaching basis, but have refused them, on the ground that I should want to keep the year free of teaching commitments.

I enclose a *curriculum vitae* and a bibliography, and am prepared to supply as many copies of both as you will need.

With profound thanks for your courtesy in considering this application.

Bettie M. Wellons   13 February 1964

Managing Editor, *The Hudson Review*, New York NY

The Hudson Review had asked Frye to review volume 3 of Paul Tillich's Systematic Theology *and had offered to send him volumes 1 and 2. He wrote the review, but it was not published at the time. It has since appeared in* FMW, *363–8.*

Dear Miss Wellons:

I should dearly love to have the first two volumes of Tillich's *Systematic Theology*. I don't possess them, and it would be very inconvenient to have only library copies to refer to.

Victor Lange   25 February 1964

Department of German, Princeton University, Princeton, NJ

In reply to Lang's inquiry about candidates for honorary fellows in the Modern Language Association. As it turned out, Alain Robbe-Grillet was elected as a fellow for 1965.

Dear Victor:

Thank you for your letter. I would go along with [André] Breton and [Mikhail] Sholokhov for two of our three names, if you think three is the right number. I don't at all like the idea of [Ernst] Jünger. Of [Henri] Peyre's suggestions I should prefer [Louis] Aragon to any of the others, including [Jean] Anouilh. I should support [Mario] Paz, [Robert] Graves, with some reservation, and so far I feel luke-warm about your three German candidates, though I shall do some more research on them. I wonder whether it is really our job to recommend American writers who would be academic members of the M.L.A. in any case. I don't think it is a mistake to feature English, Continental or Latin American writers. [Alberto] Moravia was suggested by this committee some years ago, and turned down by the Executive Council when I was on it.

Kingsley Joblin   14 April 1964
Claremont, CA

Kingsley Joblin, Frye's long-time friend, had agreed to serve as principal of Victoria College while Frye was on sabbatical for the 1965-66 academic year. Joblin had graduated from Victoria College a year before Frye, and they were both 1936 graduates of Emmanuel College.

Dear King,

Thank you for your letter. I am, of course, extremely grateful to you for agreeing to take this job on: my letter to the President said you were doing it in the name of old friendship, and I can add nothing to that.

I am drawing up a list of the standard things to do. You will find them surprisingly light: it isn't being Principal that keeps me busy, it's being Northrop Frye. The main thing is the Freshman Week-end (which won't be a week-end this autumn but a Wednesday and Thursday), where you make a twenty-minute speech of welcome. Then there is a First Class Honour Dinner in January, where I have been getting a speaker from outside the University and paying him one hundred dollars of my entertainment fund. You may want to alter this procedure. At Convocation you read out half the names of the Victoria graduates from the General Course, the Registrar doing the other half, and give another First Class Honour Dinner, to which the fifty and sixty year graduates are also invited. There are the two prize-giving evenings at Charter Day and in the spring, where you say as little as possible and give the time to the Registrar. You turn up regularly to the Council of the Faculty of Arts and Science at which you are the main Victoria spokesman though I don't imagine there will be much to say. At the University Senate it is mainly the President who speaks for the College and is on the committees. You're *ex-officio* on a number of Faculty Council committees: Applications and Memorials, Undergraduate Studies, Examinations, and others: you will get notices of them. You will preside over the Victoria Council each month, and over the Victoria Senate when the President is absent.

But your main job is dealing with the six Departmental Heads, who will consult you on appointments and promotions. You are the Faculty Advisor of the V.C.U. [Victoria College Union], but I have never worked much at being that. You collect the President, Associate President and Social Directress, in your office, along with the Senior Tutor, Dean of Women and President Moore to get the Social Slate approved. The V.C.U. President is Gary Kelly, the Associate President is Cathy Rank and the Social Directress is Nancy Caldecott. I think they are in English, Moderns, and History respectively. All very fine kids.

I hope to get the office space nuisance out of the way before I leave. I expect to be around for a great part of the year, with an unlisted phone number which you will have. You will not have Judy[303] next year, as she is going to New York: but somebody else should be trained into the routines before you begin.

There is a fair amount of social standing up to do, much of which I have dodged by accepting lecturing engagements in Nebraska. There are about seven Burwash formals, the women's formal, the Victoria formal and the Annesley and Burwash Christmas dinners. There are the Board of Regents meetings, but they don't involve you in much work. On the other hand, you will be on a number of the Board's committees: Residences and Services, Planning (a new building for class-rooms and offices will take up some time) and one or two others. As you see, you will have an abundance of time for concentrating on Tantric formulas for achieving Samadhi.

The personalities involved among departments are best not put in a letter. The Chairmen of the two big departments, Ken MacLean and Hilliard Tretheway are admirable in every respect.[304] Some of the others require more qualification.

This is all I can think of for now: but I will be sending more bulletins out. I shall be around most of the summer in any case.

Once again I am very grateful to you for helping me to get my first year off in fourteen years, and my second year off ever.

Love to you both.

James R. Squire   8 June 1964
Executive Secretary, National Council of Teachers of English, Champaign, IL
Squire's letter of invitation for Frye to join the Commission on Literature of the National Council of Teachers of English is not extant.

Dear Mr. Squire:

Thank you very much for your letter with its invitation to join a Commission on Literature. I have one problem from my end. I have just succeeded, with some difficulty, in getting next year off, and am still not sure where I shall be at any point next year. Beyond the fact that I know I shall be in Great Britain for the most of the fall. Accordingly, I am wondering whether it would be possible to have my membership on the Commission postponed for a year. It is probably better to drop me entirely, but the work of this Commission is so closely in line with what my nonconformist conscience tells me is my duty that I hesitate to refuse.[305]

James Rogers   29 July 1964
First Unitarian Congregation of Toronto, Toronto, ON
In reply to Rogers's invitation for Frye to participate in some unknown program or event having to do, apparently, with the theme of dehumanization. Rogers's letter is not extant.

Dear Mr. Rogers:

Thank you very much for your letter and for the copy of your address, which I have read with interest. I am very sorry that a commitment of several years will take me to Great Britain to speak at British universities this fall, and so at the time that you suggest I shall be in London. I wish very much that I could give a more cooperative answer, but you see my position.

In connection with literature and dehumanization, I think it is important to distinguish the imaginative portrayal of dehumanization from falling into a state of dehumanization oneself. Contemporary literature is full of the problem of dehumanization, with its scenes in slums, concentration camps, and other crisis situations of the sort. But most of this literature is written by people who are by no means dehumanized themselves and are not appealing to that instinct in their readers but to the opposite of it. The people who want to be dehumanized invariably regard this kind of writing as "depressing." There is, of course, a type of dehumanized literature, such as the brutal thriller of the Mickey Spillaine variety, but even that is held by its fictional form in the area of something which is not quite a disintegration of personality that you were talking about. The former kind, the real literature, is a branch of irony, and irony has always been one of the central modes of literary experience.

A.J.M. Smith   30 July 1964
Department of English, Michigan State University, East Lansing, MI
In response to Smith's review of The Well-Tempered Critic: *"The Critic's Task: Frye's Latest Work." Canadian Literature 20 (Spring 1964): 6–14.*

Dear Art,

I can hardly say how overwhelmed I was to read your extraordinarily generous review of my book in *Canadian Literature*. I am delighted that you were so pleased with the book, and, of course, so sympathetic a response does a great deal to restore one's belief in the power of communication.[306]

The very best to you both, and once again my gratitude and thanks.

John Sweeney   31 July 1964
Department of English, Harvard University, Cambridge, MA

John L. Sweeney, critic, teacher, and closet poet, was curator of the Woodberry Poetry Room in the Lamont Library at Harvard.

Dear Jack,

I don't know where you will be when this letter reaches you, and there is no immediate hurry about answering, but we are planning to open a poetry room here at Victoria College in memory of the Canadian poet, E.J. Pratt, who was a professor of our English Department through all his productive career and died a few months ago. I was thinking of a small seminar room with a collection of modern poetry, records, and provision of tea for visiting poets and lecturers. Any advice you could give me about what might be done with such a room, either as opportunities to exploit, or as pitfalls to avoid would be greatly appreciated.[307]

The very best to Moira and yourself.

Clifford Leech   7 November 1964
English Department, University College,
University of Toronto   49 Gordon Sq, W.C. 1 [London]

In reply to Leech's invitation for Frye to deliver the prestigious Alexander Lectures.

Dear Clifford Leech:

Thank you very much for the great honour of being asked to give the Alexander Lectures. I am deeply touched by the invitation, will accept, and do my best.[308]

My first reaction was to say that despite the honour I didn't see how I could manage it, as I have another series to do in May.[309] But half an hour after reading your letter I saw Woodhouse's obituary in the Times,[310] and that decided me, as I should very much want to have a book that I could associate with his memory.

Please convey to Douglas, Claude[311] and the U.C. [University College] Department my great sense of obligation to them.

Irving Layton   8 February 1965
Frye's letter is in the Irving Layton Papers, Special Collections, Concordia University Library, Ottawa.

Dear Irving Layton:

Thank you for your very kind note at Christmas: the delay in answering has been partly flu and partly lack of knowledge of your address, which Robert Weaver finally supplied. I have never worried much about your comments on me,[312] because I have never felt there was anything personal in them. Personally and impersonally, I remain the admirer of your best work that I have always been, and as anxious as ever to do what I can to help it reach its proper audience.

E.B.O. Borgerhoff   27 April 1965
Princeton University, Princeton, NJ

Borgerhoff, whom Frye had known from his earlier stint at Princeton, was professor of Romance Languages and Literatures. His letter, which contained an invitation for Frye to lecture at Princeton, is not extant.

Dear Borge:

Thanks very much for your letter and invitation. I am sorry to have delayed answering, but I have been absent for two weeks in California, visiting a sick sister.[313]

I love Princeton very dearly, and it is most unwelcome to me to have to refuse so pleasant an invitation. But I have to take back my administrative job after a year's leave of absence, and I do not see the physical possibility of being able to take off any such period as six weeks. I shall have to keep my nose firmly on the grindstone, apart from being already heavily committed for other visits and two complete series of lectures in the spring. I wish I could divide myself into several parts like Gaul, to do all the things that it would interest me to do, but that seems to be a prerogative of what we call lower forms of life.

I feel very depressed by Dick Blackmur's death.[314] He was one of the people that one wanted to be always there. I was recently in Princeton for a day and tried hard to get in touch with him, but without success.

Love to Mimi from us both.

A.A. Ansari   29 April 1965
Muslim University, Aligarh, India

In reply to Ansari's request (29 March 1965) for Frye to write a foreword to his book on Blake.

Dear Mr. Ansari:

Thank you very much for your letter. I am looking forward to seeing your book when it appears, and I wish very much that I could undertake to introduce it. The trouble is that my desk is piled high with previous commitments, including two complete series of public lectures for next year, and it would be a little short of suicidal for me to undertake anything further at this time, even something that would interest me so much as this.

I am delighted if my own work was of any help to you, and I wish you all success.

Howard Mumford Jones   30 April 1965
President, Modern Language Association of America, New York, NY

In reply to Jones memorandum about possible changes in the structure of the Modern Language Association.

Dear Professor Jones:

I have read your memo with the greatest interest, and I am not sure that I have anything very helpful to suggest or add. History has produced two anomalies in the organization. One is the attachment of English to the modern languages, as though the affinities of English were closer to Russian than to Philosophy or Classics. The other is the growth of the numerous huckster organizations, in your word, which exist primarily to purchase text books and junior lecturers. Both of these are, in my opinion, immovable. The MLA is in a period of political influence which it could not exercise if it did not have so large a registration, although in the nature of things that registration cannot consist exclusively of scholars.

For this reason I am inclined to support your proposals for more frequent meetings of the Council, for relieving the work load on the Secretary at the present time, and for creating an Academic Senate to initiate academic policies. At one time, there was an attempt to keep the Secretary from being the Editor of *PMLA*, and I do not know why this was given up. It seems to me a very logical division of labour.

As for choosing the Senate from the existing groups, I have no better suggestion to add, but I should hate to see the same completely automatic procedure employed that is now used in electing the Chairman and Secretary of the group. I think the regional presidents might be made members of such a Senate: I cannot see what earthly use they are on the Council.

As for lengthening the term of the President, I quite see the argument in favour of it. But if this were to be done, the rotation among fields would have to be given up. Academic statesmen seem to be, e.g., in short supply among the Germanists, and I should not want to be restricted to Germanists if I were going to be stuck with the incumbent for four years. The principal of rotation could be confined to the present scheme of two Vice-Presidents not eligible for immediate promotion.

If they were eligible, it would give them a very long term at this kind of work, especially if they have previously been members of the Council.

I am not sure that the pattern of meetings should be drastically changed: the meetings are essentially an intellectual circus, with a midway where one can meet the kind of colleague one is satisfied to see once a year. It seems to me that genuine conferences would have to be held in some kind of secession from the MLA, such as the English Institute attempted twenty years ago.

I hope this doesn't sound cynical, as I don't mean it to be: I am simply drawing on my own experience, which has found MLA meetings extremely pleasant but seldom intellectually stimulating.

I hope these random comments are of some use: whether they or not, I am extremely grateful to you for having formulated so lucidly and systematically so many of my own perplexities, and for having suggested a way out of them.

A.A. Ansari   **18 August 1965**
Muslim University, Aligarh, India
In response to Ansari's having sent Frye a copy of his book on Blake.

Dear Mr. Ansari:

Thank you very much for your book on Blake,[315] which I have been reading with great interest. It seems to me a comprehensive and very central study of Blake's Myth. Such things as Blake's conception of imagination, the attack on Locke, the realization that Locke, Newton, and Bacon are "states" rather than individuals, the fact that Blake is both revolting against and attached to his own time, are all essential to the understanding of Blake, and all of them are dealt with here with great lucidity. I like the chapter on Wordsworth and Coleridge, which deals very well with the tricky problem of cultural analogy when there is no question of direct influence. You show a very unusual grasp of the three long poems, which most commentators on Blake skip over or avoid. Your book is a genuine contribution to the scholarship not merely of Blake but of the whole Romantic period.

With best wishes and renewed thanks,

William Arthur Deacon   **18 August 1965**
Toronto, ON
Deacon was a writer, critic, essayist, and syndicated columnist for the Toronto Globe and

Mail *(1938–60) and literary editor of* Saturday Night *(1922–28). Deacon had applied for a grant to write a history of Canada after Confederation.*

Dear Mr. Deacon:

When I wrote my letter of recommendation I suggested that you might be willing to change the dates of your history to the straight Centennial dates 1867–1967. I did this because I thought that it would be easier to justify your application to the people in charge of the Centennial awards. I do hope that this was not a mistake and that it will help the application. I think of the change of dates as adding approximately one paragraph to the beginning of your book — general background about the new nationalist feeling between 1867 and the appearance of *Orion* in 1880.[316] As for the period 1960–1967, you say that you are going to refer to books written after 1960 anyway, and nobody would expect an exhaustive treatment of that period. I am very interested in the idea of such a history written by you, and I am anxious to see it properly supported.

Henry A. Barton   8 November 1965
Harvard University, Graduate School of Education, Cambridge, MA

In reply to Barton's request (5 November 1965) for information about any accounts of the teaching of literature based on Frye's "rationale and method." Barton later wrote a dissertation at Harvard entitled "A Study of the Interrelations among Criticism, Literature, and Literary Education in the Thought of Northrop Frye" (1972).

Dear Mr. Barton:

I am not in a very good position to answer your question, as I seem to be about the last person to hear about curricula designed on a basis of my writings. People are continually telling me that they are doing this, but the information is so meagre and so casually delivered that I can keep no record on it. I have been told, for example, that a high school in California has based a curriculum on the *Anatomy*, but I have still to receive specific information about this. I have also been asked to serve as an advisor on extensive curriculum studies, sponsored — in one case at least — by Harcourt Brace, who want to design new textbooks.

I naturally believe in the principles that I have set out in the works you mention, but if they are practicable their application to the classroom could be made by others, and I should much prefer to have them made by people who have more experience in elementary and secondary teaching. I imagine that the projects coming out of NDEA's summer schools next year would reflect some of my influence, as I have been asked to speak at least nine of them. But so far, the most tangible evidence of my influence has been in university textbooks.[317]

Arlin Turner   22 November 1965
Duke University, Durham, NC

Frye had been appointed as a member of the Commission on Literature of the National Council of Teachers of English. Turner's letter is not extant, but he appears to have solicited Frye's reactions to the first meeting of the Commission.

Dear Arlin:

I came away from the New York meeting feeling rather disappointed and bewildered by what seemed to me a quite disproportionate emphasis on the preparing of theoretical statements addressed to some hypothetical public. I had thought that the context of the Commission was the NCTE, a group of people who had already devoted their lives to the study and teaching of literature, and who therefore might be assumed to understand its importance. I had expected rather more concrete and specific issues connected with the reshaping of the curriculum of literary studies at all educational levels. Am I entirely wrong about this?

This letter will not get to you until after the Boston meeting, so my reflections may be out-of-date by then.

James V. Logan   24 November 1965
Department of English, Ohio State University, Columbus, OH

In response to Logan's having sent Frye (18 November 1965) the page proofs for his essay, "The Keys to the Gates." The essay was later published in Some British Romantics: A Collection of Critical Essays, *ed. Northrop Frye, James V. Logan, and John E. Jordan (Columbus: Ohio State University Press, 1966), 3–40, reprinted in* StS, *175–99, and in* MB, *337–59.*

Dear Mr. Logan,

You were right: Joyce's spelling is "Isreal," and his pun is completely lost unless we change it back.[318] The quotations seem to be all right, apart from the typos I've caught. I'm sorry that the OSU styler goes in for that fussy and niggling punctuation that ruins the rhythm and blurs the sense: I always have to fight for my own proper punctuation, and I've taken these damned commas out. I don't have a copy of my original MS, and so have asked you to check two places where the copy is obviously wrong.

Richard Schoeck   24 November 1965
Department of English, St. Michael's College, University of Toronto

Frye's letter inquires about the contents of a projected anthology of myth criticism. The collection was to be part of the Gemini Series, Patterns in Literary Criticism, *published by the University of Chicago Press and under the general editorship of Schoeck, Marshall McLuhan, and Ernest Sirluck. Frye wrote a preface for the proposed collection, but the project was for some reason aborted. Frye's preface was published forty years later in* FMW, *326–8.*

Dear Dick:

You may know that Marshall and Ernest have asked me to do a collection of comments on myth and criticism as one of the Gemini books. I gather that their original idea was to collect contemporary essays on the subject, but I thought it might be more interesting and useful to go back into the history of the tendency. Things like Raleigh's History, the opening of Purchas, Camden, Reynolds' *Mythomystes,* Bacon's *Wisdom of the Ancients,* Sandys' Ovid, from that period; some of the "Druid" stuff from around Blake's time; some of the material used by Shelley and Keats, and so on down to Ruskin's *Queen of the Air,* but without incorporating anything much later than *The Golden Bough* and the turn of the century. An introductory essay would of course indicate the relevance of this to what came after Frazer.[319] I've spoken about this to Marshall [McLuhan] and he suggested that I might consult the other editors. Jay Macpherson, my research associate, has done a good deal of work on collecting and excerpting from these materials, but I don't want to go any further unless you think the whole idea is acceptable.

H. Pullen   21 February 1966
Chairman, Board of Governors, Ontario Curriculum Institute, Toronto, ON

In response to Pullen's letter (11 February 1966), explaining the care that was taken in reaching the decision to amalgamate the Ontario Curriculum Institute (OCI) and the Ontario Institute for Studies in Education, a decision to which Frye was opposed. The OCI had been established in November 1962 through the efforts of the joint committee of the University of Toronto and the Toronto Board of Education. Frye was a member of the Board of Governors of the institute and served on its program committee. Because the institute lacked funds, its work came to little. As early as 1964 the William Davis government, committed to a program of educational expansion, suggested that the institute form part of a proposed Ontario Institute for Studies in Education (OISE); in April 1965 the OCI endorsed the idea in principle, and shortly thereafter began to wind down its affairs. Frye's address to the first annual meeting of the OCI was published as "We Are Trying to Teach a Vision of Society," published in the Educational Courier *34 (January-February 1964): 21–3; reprinted in OE, 187–91.*

Dear Mr. Pullen:

Thank you very much for your letter about the recent decision of the Curriculum Institute. As you may perhaps realize, my reason for joining the deputation was my strong belief that an academic body not concerned with the implementing of its own research was essential, and that this was the reason for the loyalty the Curriculum Institute attracted from all types of teachers. I had been led to feel this as a result of listening to people whose opinions I greatly respect saying so continually, in both public and private, including Roy Sharp, Arch Morgan, Nora Hodgins, and Bob Jackson.[320] Once my loyalties are set, it is difficult for me to change instantly to another party line. But I certainly do not question the care and the sense of responsibility with which the decision was reached. The issue is one on which I would much rather be wrong than right.

With renewed thanks for the courtesy of your letter.

Sheila McDonough   **24 February 1966**
Department of Religion, Sir George Williams University, Montreal, QC

In reply to McDonough's undated request welcoming Frye's suggestions for forming a society to promote the study of religion in Canada. McDonough proposed a founding meeting at the meetings of the Learned Societies at the Université de Sherbrooke in June 1966.

Dear Dr. McDonough:

Thank you for your letter about the possibility or organizing a Learned Society in the field of Religion. If I possibly can, I shall try to be at Sherbrooke during at least part of the meetings there, and would certainly like to be included in this meeting if possible. My own interest in Religion is somewhat peripheral, but as a literary critic I have scholarly interests in imagery, symbolism and typology which give me some connection with the field.

Julia Osborne   **5 April 1966**
The Canada Council, Ottawa, ON

Osborne's letter is not extant.

Dear Miss Osborne:

Thank you very much for your letter of April 4. It was also a surprise to me to learn that I had got through last year with only the first half of my Canada Council grant. Now that I am back to work on full salary, only able to work at my writing in odd moments, I should like, if I may, to postpone claiming the other half until I am in a position to be writing for most if not all of my time.

During my year off I planned, drafted and read for my proposed book on the external relations of literary criticism. Even though its scope has been reduced to nearly half of the original project, it is still a huge conception, at least as big a one as the *Anatomy of Criticism*. I have been asked to do a number of special lectures, each of them to be published in their own right. I am making these to a large extent preliminary studies for the book as a whole. This means that my next four books, of which I hope the fourth will be the work itself, will be indebted to the Canada Council's help and will say so in the preface.

I have come to the conclusion that I cannot carry on my writing programme on a full scale and still retain this administrative job, which I am therefore giving up at the end of the year, although this arrangement is confidential at the moment. This is why I speak of expecting soon to be in a situation where I can devote my main energies to writing.

James Thorpe III   27 May 1966
New Haven, CT

In reply to Thorpe's inquiry (22 May 1966) about whether Frye did in fact remark, as reported by John Hollander, that he read Wittgenstein's Philosophical Investigations *only after he has finished* Anatomy of Criticism *and then thinking that he was reading a mirror image. Thorpe is proposing to write on the similarities between Frye's work and that of Wittgenstein and Stevens.*

Dear Mr. Thorpe:

Thank you for your letter. It is quite true that I did make that remark to John Hollander, though perhaps I had already been conditioned in such a direction by the *Tractatus,* which I had read earlier. As for Stevens I hesitated a long time before writing anything on him, because of the number of people who say that I am a deductive critic reading my own system into everybody whether it is there or not. So I didn't do any systematic work on Stevens until the *Anatomy* was in proof.

Munro Beattie   13 October 1966
Department of English, Carleton University, Ottawa, ON

In reply to Beattie's request (10 October 1966) for a recommendation from Frye in support of an application for a Canada Council senior fellowship. Beattie was proposing to resume his study of Henry James, and he asked Frye to comment on his chapters in the Literary History of Canada, *which some reviewers had treated negatively. Beattie and Frye had been classmates at Victoria College.*

Dear Munro:

Thank you for your letter. I should be delighted to write for you to the Canada Council, as I am quite sure that your sabbatical is overdue, and I should very much like to see you carry on with your Henry James memoirs.

The trouble with reviews of the *Literary History* was that practically everybody competent to review it was engaged in writing it. Not all the reviews were careless, however: there was a brief note by the man who runs the *Canadian Poetry* magazine who obviously thought that your contribution was the only thing worth reading.

The very best to you both.

François Jost   18 April 1967
Program in Comparative Literature, University of Illinois, Urbana, IL

In reply to Jost's letter (4 April 1967), soliciting an opinion from Frye about the value of the journal Comparative Literature Studies.

Dear Professor Jost:

Thank you for your letter about Professor Aldridge.[321] It seems to me that *Comparative Literature Studies* is about as useful a periodical in this field as I know. It is less conventional than the one published in Oregon,[322] but seems to me to be presenting compar-ative literature on its proper basis, as a study of literature which recognizes that the differ-ences among languages should not be allowed to determine literary study beyond a certain point. A great many people in Comparative Literature seem to have a mentality rather like that of Swiss hotel keepers: that is, because they know several languages, they assume that Comparative Literature is a matter of mixing languages rather than of unifying literature. This periodical gets well away from that, and such things as its recent symposium on lit-erature and religion present the subject in broad and comprehensive terms. I should hope very much to see it expand and develop as it deserves.

Sister Bettina   25 April 1967
Newman, Christ the Teacher Chapel and Student Center, De Kalb, IL
In response to Sister Bettina's question (18 April 1967) about the influence of John Stuart Mill on Frye's thought.

Dear Sister Bettina:
    Thank you for your letter. For a Professor of English who teaches a wide variety of texts, it is not always easy to say what the decisive influences have been. But it is true that a course in 19th century thought was one of my first and longest continued teaching assign-ments, and Mill was certainly the person who interested me most in that group.[323] I am not sure whether it was the Wordsworth business in the *Autobiography* that struck me most, because the lopsidedness of Mill's education up to that time was so obvious. I think the main influence has been rather in following Mill's conception of liberalism into education and society. You may know an article of mine on the problem of spiritual authority in the 19th century, and I think that expresses what my real debt to Mill has been.[324]
    I greatly appreciate your interest.

Joan Baum   4 May 1967
Kew Gardens, NY
In reply to Baum's questions (1 May 1967) about Blake's intentions with his Edward III *fragment and his interest in drama.*

Dear Miss Baum:
    I am not sure that I can be of much help to you, because the amount of evidence is very small and equally available to both of us. In my opinion the two prologues certainly, and *Edward III* probably, were not intended to be in any sense stage plays. The strong emphasis on a certain political attitude suggests to my mind a reader rather than an audi-ence. In short, these early exercises seem to me to be imitative reactions to Shakespeare's histories, but no more intended as plays than the "Imitation of Spenser" was intended to grow into an epic. The situation seems to me to be a little different with the *Ghost of Abel*, where some kind of Yeatsian intimate theatre may have been in Blake's mind.
    I don't remember much about drama in Blake's critical views, apart from a comment on *Macbeth* in the *Descriptive Catalogue*.
    I hope this is of some help but I quite realize that probably it is not.

Angus MacQueen   16 May 1967
St. George's United Church, Toronto, ON
In reply to MacQueen's letter (11 May 1967), thanking Frye for his baccalaureate ser-mon, which MacQueen had read in Victoria Reports *17 (April 1967): 3–10. Frye delivered the*

sermon to the graduating classes of 1967 at Victoria and Emmanuel Colleges, in the Victoria College Chapel. It was later reprinted in RW, *243–50, and in* NFR, *280–6.*

Dear Dr. MacQueen:

Thank you very much for your gracious and kindly note. I was extremely grateful to receive it, because sermons are one form of expression in which I have very little trust in my own professional competence. Never having had a charge, I have never learned this branch of rhetoric thoroughly, and I was rather surprised that my Baccalaureate effort was so well received.

Rose M. Harkness   29 May 1967
Corner Brook, NL

In reply to Harkness's reaction (21 May 1967) to Frye's baccalaureate sermon, which she had read in Victoria Reports: *"As I read your sermon I wept tears of joy, first for myself, for the words fell like rain on arid land, and secondly for the graduating class of '67 who were given such a wise and true address." See headnote to previous letter. Harkness (née Kant) was a 1957 graduate of Victoria College.*

Dear Mrs. Harkness:

Thank you very much for your most kindly letter about my Baccalaureate sermon. Naturally I was extremely touched by your reaction to it, and I am delighted if it succeeded in finding an audience beyond its immediate one. I am an amateur when it comes to sermons, and consequently am all the more pleased if they make their point to former as well as contemporary students.

Thank you very much again, and best wishes,

Berton E. Robinson   29 May 1967
Halifax, NS

In reply to Robinson's request (19 May 1967) for a copy of Frye's "The Baccalaureate Sermon," which Berton had read in Victoria Reports *17 (April 1967): 3–10, and which he described as a fine and impressive piece of work. Robinson was secretary of the University Grants Committee of the Province of Nova Scotia. Frye's sermon was reprinted in* RW, *243–50, and in* NFR, *280–6.*

Dear Mr. Robinson:

Thank you very much for your most kindly letter. The very generous reception of my sermon has pleased me, though I still find it puzzling. I never preach sermons, and only preached this one because I thought it was part of my job as Acting President.[325] Evidently religious thought has reached the kind of stage where an amateur voice can be helpful.

Thank you again, and best wishes.

George Johnston   9 June 1967
Carleton University, Ottawa, ON

In reply to Johnston's having sent Frye a copy of his second collection of poems, Home Free *(Toronto: Oxford University Press, 1966). Frye's letter is in the George Johnston Papers in the Library and Archives Canada.*

Dear George:

I have been an interminable time thanking you for the inscribed copy of *Home Free.* Nobody is too busy to answer such things, but some people get schizophrenic when they are busy. Especially me and especially now. As far as a desk job is concerned I've had it, and resistances toward it build up in me at compound interest all the time. So this year I get to be both Principal and Acting President until Jan. 1, thereafter Acting President only until April. Sometimes I think I'm one of nature's predestined sacrificial victims.

But of course I do admire the book immensely: less variety in tone than the Auk,[326] but what there is tightened up and with the two long poems[327] giving it tremendous cumulative power. The more whimsical tone of the earlier book was a tone of transition, and I'm glad to see it entering on a new phase, continuous with it, but involving you as a person more.

Thank you again, and the very best to Jean and all the family.

Sidney Feshbach   18 July 1967
State University of New York at Stony Brook, Long Island, NY

In reply to Feshbach's letter (12 July 1967), inquiring about an essay, "Aristotle or Else" that he was told Frye authored, asking about guidance for a curriculum restructuring, and offering to resend an essay on Joyce he had mailed two years earlier and about which he had received no reply. On Aristotle, Feshbach apparently had mistaken Frye for W.K. Wimsatt, Jr., who used to give a lecture entitled "Aristotle or Else," referring to the Aristotelian scholar Gerald Else.

Dear Professor Feshbach:

I am sorry to write a rather negative response to your enquiries, but the article on Aristotle and Else was not written by be. Nor have I much that would be useful to you in planning a sequential programme in a university. My writings on the subject, including my *PMLA* essay, my *College English* essay, and my Introduction to *Design for Learning*,[328] are concerned mainly with pre-university levels. The great difference in admission standards between Canadian and American universities has rather discouraged me from writing much along university curriculum lines.

I did read your essay on the *Portrait*, and thought it both fascinating and lucid, as it brought out a central structural principle with great simplicity and related it to what everyone should realize would be Joyce's sources. I thought I had acknowledged it earlier, but as books and articles and offprints arrive at the rate of several a day, I sometimes slip up.

H.G. Thode   2 August 1967
President and Vice-Chancellor, McMaster University, Hamilton, ON

In reply to Thode's request, which is not extant, for recommendations for an administrative appointment.

Dear President Thode:

Thank you very much for your letter. I do not know whether my suggestions are very appropriate or not, but the post you describe seems to me a very difficult one to find the right man for. If the whole of the Humanities is to comprise one-third of one-third of the prospective set-up, you will need a very strong man, but a person interested in administration might find such a minority role a bit confining.

At the University of Washington, in Seattle, there is an excellent scholar named Albert Hamilton. He came originally from Manitoba, was trained here and at Cambridge, and is a scholar of distinction in the field of the English Renaissance. I know that he would like to return to Canada and that he would be interested in an administrative job, as he has a good deal of administrative experience. My understanding is that he is going to Queen's next year, but that he might be pried loose from there after a year. Much the same remarks would apply to Hugh Maclean, at present with the Department of English at the University of New York at Albany. Hugh is also a Renaissance scholar, trained in Toronto, who has been at R.M.C. [Royal Military College] and at York. I don't know how strong the pull back to Canada would be for him.

A much more famous name than either is Arthur Barker of the University of Illinois, an extremely well-known Milton scholar who was at Trinity College here for many years. He has not said so to me, but my understanding is that he would be glad to return to Canada, and he would certainly impart the very highest distinction both to McMaster University and to his administrative appointment.

You don't say whether you would consider a man on your own staff, but if you would, I think you might give consideration to the name of Alvin Lee, in your Department of English. Lee seems to me a person with great objectivity and fairness of judgment, and I think he would have all the advantages of a neutral candidate along with the strength and firmness of a positive one.[329]

These are of course extremely tentative suggestions, and taken from English, which is the field I know best. I can probably be more helpful in commenting on other people that I have failed to think of but that you are considering.

Kelly Crichton   4 August 1967
Public Affairs Department, CFIO-TV, Toronto, ON

Crichton had gotten in touch with Frye's secretary, Pam Hillier, on 2 August 1967, saying that she would like to consult with Frye for a fall television program on hippies. See also letter to John Garabedian of 12 September 1967, below.

Dear Miss Crichton:

My only connection with hippies is that *Time* magazine quoted a passage from an article of mine, the relevance of which to the subject is not as clear to me as it apparently was to them. They also asked one of their reporters to interview me, and I did my best to answer her questions, as I should do my best to answer yours if you also thought an interview worthwhile. But I am emphatically not an authority on the subject, and I certainly do not wish to be included in any programme about them. They don't want to talk to me, and still less would they want to listen to me.

Jack Finegan   4 August 1967
Dean, Graduate Theological Union, Berkeley, CA

In response to an invitation to teach a summer course at the Graduate Theological Union in Berkeley, CA. Finegan's letter is not extant.

Dear Dean Finegan:

Thank you very much for your letter and invitation. I am afraid that the summer of 1968 is completely filled up, but it so happens that I have been invited as a Visiting Professor to Berkeley in the Spring Term of 1969. So while I cannot commit myself at this stage, I should be interested in knowing what sort of thing you would want me to teach. Looking through your catalogue, I see one course on Theology and Literature that I imagine I could do. It also seems to me at the moment that I could only manage one of your three week periods, probably the early one, rather than the whole summer session.

I am much honoured by your interest in me.

W.L. Morton   **21 August 1967**
Champlain College, Trent University, Petersborough, ON
   In reply to Morton's request (16 August 1967) for Frye to join a committee in support of the Hon. Duff Roblin, a candidate for the leadership of the Conservative Party of Canada. Morton was master of Chamberlain College at Trent University.

Dear Mr. Morton:
   Thank you very much for your letter of August 16th. I have thought about it very carefully, and have reluctantly come to the conclusion that it would be better for me not to join your committee of support. I understand very well that the issue is one of having a sufficiently good man at the head of a major party, and has nothing to do with coming out myself in support of the Conservatives. But I doubt whether the public would make this distinction. I also have some reservations about the tendency in Canada, which seems to me too strong already, to follow the Americans in emphasizing the personal qualities of the leader rather than the principles of his party. I do feel that Mr. Roblin[330] is the best candidate in the field for his party, but I feel that I don't have the right to take sides in the strategy of a party to which I am not myself committed. I am sure you will understand my reasons, whether you would agree with them or not.
   With best personal wishes,

John Garabedian   **12 September 1967**
The New York Post, New York, NY
   In reply to an letter by Garabedian (1 September 1967), a feature writer for the New York Post, *wanting Frye to expand on a comment quoted in an article in* Time *magazine that hippies were inheritors of the "outlawed and furtive social ideal known as the 'Land of Cockaigne.'" The* Time *article also referred to Frye as a disciple of McLuhan.*

Dear Mr. Garabedian:
   Thank you for your letter. I am not sure that I can be of much help to you, as I did not have hippies in mind when I spoke of the Land of Cockaigne as one form of Utopia. The association was due to the *Time* writer, and I doubt very much that the Land of Cockaigne is really what the hippies are talking about. Neither was it correct to describe me as a disciple of McLuhan, although he is a colleague and a good personal friend.
   The only thing that I have said about hippies is that they seem to me to represent an unconscious effort to define a proletariat in Freudian rather than in Marxist terms. I should connect them also with the tradition of anarchism, which for centuries has always had two aspects, one peaceful and pastoral, the other violent and terroristic. In the West the Amsterdam provos represent the revolutionary movement most clearly. The Red Guard in China seems to be mostly on the terroristic side, and perhaps the stilyagls in Russia represent the anarchist goals, of the withering away of the state and the like, which Marxism accepts in theory but does not pursue in practice.

Frank Kermode   **11 October 1967**
University College, University of London, London, England
   In response to Kermode's review of Fools of Time, *which had appeared as "Reading Shakespeare's Mind,"* New York Review of Books 9 *(12 October 1967): 14–17.*

Dear Mr. Kermode:
   This is just to thank you very sincerely for your most generous review of *Fools of Time*, which has certainly done a lot for my morale.

I was interested in your word "mnemotechnical," because it has occurred to me that my overall critical structure is in many respects very like a classical memory theatre.[331] I imagine you and I would draw different inferences from that principle, if it is a principle.

Paul Smith   **24 October 1967**

Trinity College, Hartford, CT

In reply to Paul Smith's having sent Frye the diagram below of the four mythoi, drawn by one of the students, Lionel Tardif, in his course based on Frye's four narrative patterns. Smith had proposed to Ron Campbell of Harcourt Brace Jovanovich that the diagram be used as a frontispiece to the anthology he and Robert Foulke were editing, An Anatomy of Literature, *organized on the basis of the four* mythoi. *Campbell rejected the suggestion, but the diagram was used on the cover of the instructor's manual when the anthology was published five years later (New York: Harcourt Brace Jovanovich, 1972).*

Dear Mr. Smith:

Thank you very much for the diagram which I have posted up over the door of my office. It is considerably more lighthearted than most of the ones I receive. Generally I get something looking like a cross between a protein graphic formula and a psychedelic dream with an earnest request accompanying it to ask me if this does not represent my essential intentions. I always reply that I don't have that kind of ingenuity. But I do wish that Mr. Tardif had got a B+.[332]

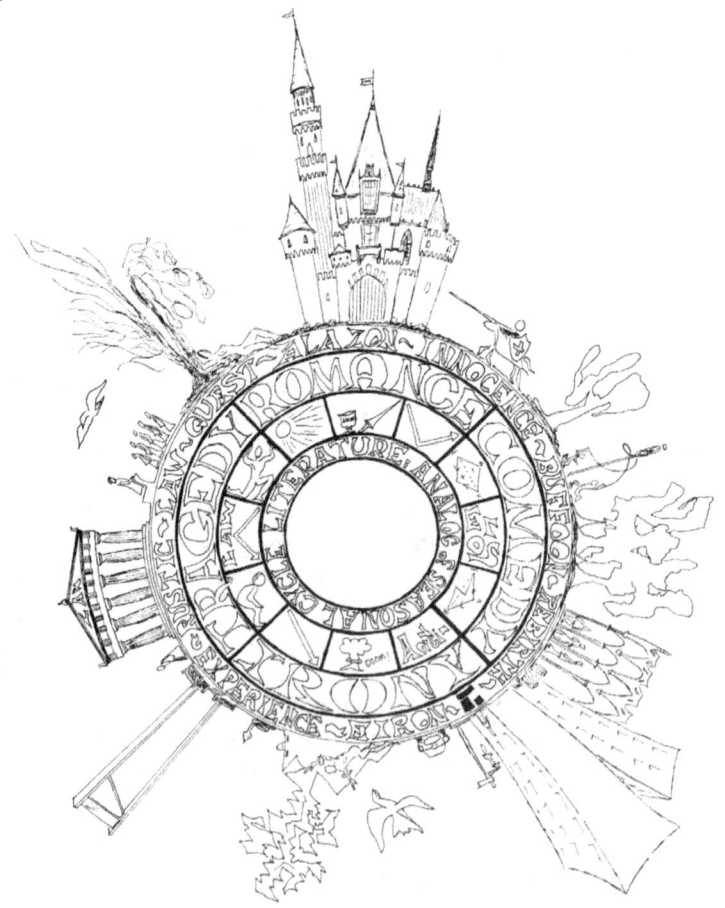

Doug Spettigue   **31 October 1967**
Department of English, Queen's University, Kingston, ON
In reply to Spettigue's request (27 October 1967) for Frye to clarify what he meant by once saying to Spettigue that Frederick Philip Grove was "a pathological liar."

Dear Mr. Spettigue:

Thank you for your letter. I am afraid that my comment was not very polite, but I think I made it at a time when Pacey was accepting Grove's *Search for America* as an auto-biography. As nobody accepts this now, perhaps my comment is out of date. I suspect that *In Search of Myself* is equally unreliable, however, but I don't actually know any more than that.[333] You might drop a line to Ronald Bates at Western,[334] who I think actually did look into the matter of Grove's earlier life when he was in Sweden.

The very best to you both.

John Van Domelen   **6 November 1967**
Department of English, University of Northern Iowa, Cedar Falls, IA
In response to Van Domelen's request (20 October 1967) for information about G. Wilson Knight, who was at the University of Toronto from 1931 to 1940. Van Domelen, who was writing a critical biography of Knight, asked specifically whether Frye saw any indications of Knight's preoccupation with spiritualism during those years.

Dear Mr. Van Domelen:

Thank you for your letter. I got to know Wilson Knight quite well when he was here, and I had many long talks with him. At that time he was a person totally without small talk, and for practical purposes unable to converse on any subject whatever except Shakespeare. There was a kind of innocence and utter guilelessness about him that made him extremely attractive. He was a person entirely without resentments, and was never afraid of admitting his own ignorance of scholarly problems that did not interest him, even though he wrote many of his most influential books at a time when he literally did not know the difference between a folio and a quarto text. The kind of unconscious courage this took made him a very healthy influence. I discussed some of my embryonic views of Shakespearean comedy with him, getting little response except an exhortation to get busy and write a book about it. When he talked to me it was very largely a monologue, which naturally I was at an age to benefit from a good deal. I also remember an evening at which both of us were present and at which the subject of spiritualism did come up, but so far as I remember he made no comment. My impression is that this interest developed later, after the death of his mother.

M.M. Tolnai   **9 November 1967**
Department of Political Economy, University of Toronto
Frye had requested of Tolnai, administrative assistant in the department of political economy at Toronto, a translation of the Hungarian review of the German translation of Anatomy of Criticism *by Barlay Laszlo in* Helikon 4 (1966).

Dear Mrs. Tolnai:

It was extremely kind of you to provide me with such a full and faithful translation of the Hungarian review. It is very frustrating to be staring at a review of oneself that one cannot read. Certain forms of Marxist criticism remind me of a squid shooting ink at random at anything that annoys it, but this, for all its jargon, is trying to work out some kind of consistent point of view.[335] I am extremely glad to have it, and most grateful for your help.

Hamilton B. Timothy   **13 November 1967**

Department of Classics, University of Western Ontario, London, ON

In reply to Timothy's letter (7 November 1967), asking if Frye could elaborate on a point he heard in one of Frye's lectures about spiritual ascent from the demonic world. Timothy, who was planning to write a paper on deification in a Platonic sense in Clement of Alexandria, wonders whether Frye had written elsewhere about the ascent of the soul.

Dear Professor Timothy:

Thank you very much for a most interesting letter. I don't know that I have much to say of any direct usefulness to you, but of course Milton is using the same images to describe the ascent of the soul towards God that have been used since Plato. These images include the "medicine" which turns up in *Comus* and elsewhere as a magic herb. Milton is very careful to keep his ascent within a Christian framework: the soul goes *towards* God, but can't go beyond a certain point without the process reversing itself and divine grace taking the initiative. Hence the last two lines of *Comus*. The same thing is true of Dante, where, after Virgil leaves him his own Pope and Emperor, Dante is then passed on to Beatrice and becomes a child again. Clement of Alexandria is much bolder, and of course much closer to the real Platonic tradition.

I should be very glad to see what you do in this area, which is one of great interest to me, although of course I am working on poetic images rather than philosophical concepts.

J.H. Wheatley   **29 November 1967**

S. Glastonbury, CT

In reply to Wheatley's having sent Frye (22 November 1967) copies of two talks he had recently given to a conference of high school teachers and asking for Frye's response. Wheatley taught at Trinity College in Hartford, CT.

Dear Mr. Wheatley:

Thank you very much for your letter and for the historical account of your Institute, which is a very lively piece of writing and which I greatly enjoyed reading. I am particularly glad that you stressed how much I have left still to be done in the field of critical theory. Far too many people discuss me as though I regarded myself as having said everything essential, and would expect only footnotes to follow. I hope very much that your Institute continues to flourish and stimulate further work in the theory of criticism. Many people have suggested that Chomsky, Burke, and others including myself do come together to make a pattern, but you seem to be working on the problem with unusual energy.

George Grella   **11 December 1967**

Department of English, University of Rochester, Rochester, NY

In response to Grella's having sent Frye (4 December 1967) an offprint of an article on James Bond, which "was written under the influence of Anatomy of Criticism.*"*

Dear Mr. Grella:

Thank you very much for your letter and for the offprint of the article on James Bond,[336] which I greatly enjoyed reading. I was amused at your comment about Bond's stupidity. In another book I remarked that when the hero of a thriller miraculously gets out of his scrapes, that is convention; but if he had to be extremely stupid in order to have got into the scrape in the first place, we are apt to get impatient with the convention.[337] I was thinking of James Bond when I wrote this, and trying to account for the fact that I never succeeded in finishing any book in which he figured. You have clearly done much better.

I am delighted if my own work has been of use to you. With best wishes,

Barry Butson   **13 December 1967**
St. Catharines, ON

In response to the letter from Butson (8 December), a reporter for the St. Catharines Standard, *who wants to become a university teacher. His letter was spurred by Frye's remark in a speech at Brock University about the bottleneck that prevents graduate students from entering into the teaching profession easily. Butson indicates that he doesn't "especially long for a Ph.D."*

Dear Mr. Butson:

Thank you for your letter. When I spoke of the bottleneck in graduate studies I was thinking of the infuriating slowness with which the university processes your instructors. I am afraid however that the utopian scheme that I sketched out is not going to be adopted in the near future. The University of Toronto has introduced an interim degree, called a Phil. M., which in theory enables people to teach in a university without writing a research thesis. But Toronto is in the curious position of selling a degree they certainly won't buy themselves. Nobody is likely to be appointed to the Toronto staff without the Graduate Department in mind, which means that the appointee will have to be geared toward graduate work, and hence a Ph.D.

I think if you were to enquire of the Secretary of the Graduate Department, Professor Hugh MacCallum, you could get specific and authoritative information from him. As for the money problem, a great many of our graduate students are married, and subsist, at least, on Ontario Government scholarships.[338]

Mrs. Lawren (Bess) Harris   **5 January 1968**
Vancouver, BC

In reply to Harris's account (20 December 1967) of her husband's reaction to Frye's introduction to Lawren Harris, *ed. Bess Harris and R.G.P. Colgrove (Toronto: Macmillan, 1969), ix–xii. "When Pete [R.P.G. Colgrove] sent me a copy of your introduction to Lawren's book, I was deeply moved and touched by what you had written. I read it aloud to Lawren. When I had finished Lawren said, 'It's weird.' My reply was — 'Weird — is that the right word?' Lawren said, 'Well, it may not be, but it will do. It is weird to have someone see right through you.' He took the typewritten sheets and carefully read them. Then he said, 'I can take that. It is good for me.' Lawren tends to draw away from praise or acclaim but he welcomed your understanding and perception." Frye's introduction was reprinted in* BG, 181–97, *and in* NFCanada, 398–402.

Dear Mrs. Harris:

Thank you very much for your most kind and gracious letter. Naturally I am delighted if my introduction does what I had hoped it might do, and I hope very much that it will do something to the appeal of the book itself, which, of course, carries its own message.

With all best wishes to you both.

Theodore Philias Soucy   **30 January 1968**
St. Leonard, NB

In reply to Soucy's request (2 January 1968) for Frye to return the collection of poems he had sent for review and comment in October 1967.

Dear Mr. Soucy:

Thank you for your letter and for your poems. I am sorry that you feel I have been neglecting you, but it always takes a long time to process anything across my desk, especially with so many long visits to make to other universities.

There are two kinds of poetic value. It is always a good thing for people with sincere and deeply felt emotions to express them, whether in verse or in any other medium. By that standard, there is certainly no question about the genuineness of your feelings. The other is an objective standard relating to the publishability of poetry. Your poems are acceptable as essentially private communications, expressing the attitude of a cultivated person to the problems of life and war and the beauty of nature. They are not publishable, as other standards come into play here. Apart from such things as grammar and spelling, which could always be corrected, such a metaphor as "renches from the bile" is so mixed as to seem grotesque to a reader, and the rhythm of free verse would be a distinctively poetic rhythm and not simply regular prose in irregular lines, but these are observations which are perhaps less relative.

Mary Campbell   1 February 1968
Board of Education for the City of Toronto, Toronto, ON
In reply to Campbell's having sent Frye (30 January 1968) an anthology of children's poems produced as part of the Canadian Centennial project.

Dear Mary:

Thank you very much for the collection of children's poems. This is quite extraordinary stuff: I am quite sure it would have been impossible to get this sort of thing out of students even ten years ago. I wonder whether the courses in mythology are making some of the differences, along with the publicity of folk singers and people like Dylan. Would it be possible for me to have two or three extra copies? I would like to spread them around among people in the States who would be interested.

John E. Grant   6 February 1968
Department of English, University of Iowa, Iowa City, IA
In reply to Grant's having sent (30 January 1968) Frye an offprint of an article on Blake. Grant remarks that Frye's The Modern Century *"contains a fine blueprint for civilization."*

Dear Jack,

Thank you very much for your letter and offprint,[339] which I have read with great interest. It seems to me that you follow a very subtle and elusive text with remarkable accuracy. I am also delighted about your fellowship, and hope that the Young project will go ahead without hitches.[340]

My book[341] was, among other things, an attempt to show how the arts today, and criticism with them, are involved in a militant and crusading moral struggle and will have to carry on that struggle without compromising with the value-judgement shell game. Your own disputes are over questions of fact, not value, at least as far as Blake is concerned. It is of course quite true that my paper said nothing I haven't already said, and I greatly resented having agreed to write it.[342] But I had not read Murray's paper beforehand, and didn't mean to skewer him in the way that some people thought I had done.[343]

Philip Wheelwright   6 February 1968
University of California at Santa Barbara, Santa Barbara, CA
In response to Wheelwright's having sent Frye a copy of his essay "On the Meaning of 'You,'" Proceedings and Addresses of the American Philosophical Association *40 (1966-67): 35–48. The essay was Wheelwright's presidential address at the fortieth annual meeting of the Pacific Division of the American Philosophical Association.*

Dear Philip,

Thanks very much for the offprint on You, which I enjoyed reading. Speaking off the top of my literary bump, it seems to me that the tendency of so many languages to avoid a second person singular and develop another out of plural or third person forms, has a good deal of relevance to your investigation.

Best wishes to you both,

G. Sabri-Tabrizi   10 May 1968
Department of Persian, University of Edinburgh, Edinburgh, United Kingdom
In reply to Sabri-Tabrizi's letter (2 May 1968) outlining his interest in Blake's The Marriage of Heaven and Hell *and wondering whether the name "Rintrah" in that work might be a combination of "wrath" and "Indra."*

Dear Mr. Tabrizi,

Thank you for your letter. I see no reason why Rintrah should not echo some phrase as "the wrath of Indra," if the possibility of Blake's having seen the Jones translation of *Sakuntala* in time is possible.[344] I think the M.H.H. [*Marriage of Heaven and Hell*] reference to Rintrah is the earliest one, and it was probably written in 1790. The connexion, if it exists, would help to explain the association of Rintrah with India in The Song of Los. I looked for a Hebrew source of the word once, but found nothing tangible.

I am a little surprised by what you tell me about the indifference to and suspicion of Blake at Edinburgh.[345] On this side of the Atlantic the situation is very different, perhaps partly through my own influence. But it is generally recognized now by American scholars that some understanding of him is the key to the whole Romantic movement.

With best wishes for good success in your work.

G. Sabri-Tabrizi   23 May 1968
Department of Persian, University of Edinburgh, Edinburgh, United Kingdom
In response to Frye's letter of 10 May 1968, Sabri-Tabrizi wrote (17 May 1968) to ask for clarification of Frye's comment that Blake's Rintrah might well derive from a combination of "wrath" and "Indra." Wrath, writes Sabri-Tabrizi, would be peculiar to the Reprobate and Indra peculiar to Urizen.

Dear Mr. Tabrizi:

Thank you for your letter. All I was suggesting was the possibility that "wrath" and "Indra" might both be echoed in the name Rintrah. As you know, Rintrah in his regenerate state is the isolated prophet or voice crying in the wilderness, exemplified by John the Baptist, Elijah, and Blake himself. In his perverted state he would be a projected angry god like Indra. But, of course, there could be a regenerate or prophetic Indra just as there could be a perverted Rintrah.

Sheafe Satterthwaite   27 May 1968
Center for Environmental Studies, Williams College, Williamstown, MA
In reply to Satterthwaite's request, which is not extant, for Frye's reaction to a proposed Countryside Institute. The institute never came to fruition (Sheafe Satterthwaite to Robert Denham, letter of 26 February 2008).

Dear Mr. Satterthwaite:

Thank you for your letter and very interesting project. I should think a summer institute on the countryside would be a sufficiently fresh and original idea to be quite a smash hit. I suppose your normal line would be to set up a counter-environment to the centrifugal and cancerous advance of the big city, as it lays waste first the suburbs, then the market garden area, then the more rural areas (as New York is now doing to so much of New England), and finally the parks and natural beauty spots. I should think one would start with the parks and the reasons why it is essential to preserve them. The reasons given would apply, with proportionally greater chances, to all the other areas up to the metropolis itself. I should think the European experience, especially the Scandinavian, would be relevant. The Communist Manifesto makes quite a point of uniting the country to the city, but that process has been carried so far that it would be worth trying to reverse the process. I notice that today education in Marxist countries does a good deal of transplanting of students from city to country and back again: this may be for political reasons, but I think its educational aspect is a genuine one.

William Sacksteder   28 May 1968
Department of Philosophy, University of Colorado, Boulder, CO

In reply to Sacksteder's having sent Frye an offprint of an article of his which he says Frye "might find amusing," adding, "I am technically in Philosophy, but I indulge inter-disciplinary dabbling, in the course of which I have become quite an admirer of the Anatomy, *which I am occasionally able to use in off-beat courses and for my own enlightenment." Sacksteder's article was "Looking Glass: A Treatise on Logic,"* Philosophy and Phenomenological Research *27, no. 3 (March, 1967): 338–55.*

Dear Mr. Sacksteder,

Thank you very much for your offprint which I was very glad to get, and which I read with great interest and pleasure. I don't know what branch of logic deals with the problem of identity, but it seems to me that that is the central question on which all the jokes and paradoxes of the looking-glass book converge on. Your article is a most helpful effort to disch-cover the riddle.

D.C. Boothroyd   4 July 1968
United Church of Canada, Chignecto Presbytery, Moncton, NB

In reply to Boothroyd's letter (26 June 1968) informing Frye that he should make application each year to the Chignecto presbytery "to be left without appointment to a pastoral charge."

Dear Mr. Boothroyd:

Thank you very much for your letter. As I understand it, the appropriate committee brought into the Maritime Conference some years ago a recommendation that members permanently on leave should be placed in a special category and would not need to make annual application for leaves of absence. For this reason I have not been making such applications. You say that failing such annual applications, my name would go on a special list at the General Council Office. In view of the fact that I am likely to be anywhere at this time of year (specifically, at Berkeley next year and Oxford the year following), it might be more sensible for me to have my name on that list anyway. I should be reluctant to drop my connexion with the Maritime Conference, but it is true that it becomes increasingly difficult for me to maintain a vital connexion with it. I should greatly appreciate it if you could find time to drop me a line giving me your advice in the matter.

Jack Ludwig   **4 July 1968**
London, England

In response to Ludwig's letter (14 June 1968), offering to make accommodations for Frye in London, inquiring about the status of his daughter Susan's application to the university, and recounting the difficulty he had had with U.S. officials concerning his passport because he had visited a Communist country. Ludwig, Canadian novelist and short story writer, had been teaching at the State University of New York at Stony Brook since 1961.

Dear Jack,

As soon as I got your second latter I went around to the Registrar's Office and enquired about Susan. There was no response for some time, but apparently all the pointless obstacles have finally been recognised to be pointless and she has been admitted. I am greatly looking forward to seeing her.

I am sorry, but I am afraid not surprised, to hear about your passport difficulties. Even for American citizens, the passport appears to be thought of as a privilege given by the government, instead of, as in British countries, the right of the citizen. There are rumours here that some very distinguished Americans may be moving to Toronto because they can no longer stand the hysteria and confusion of their own country.

I hope all goes well with you, and we look forward to seeing you, either in the fall or sooner. Our plans beyond Ireland are not clear as yet.

The very best to you both,

Virginia V. Hlavsa   **2 August 1968**
Bayside, NY

In response to Hlavsa's having sent Frye (2 April 1968) a copy of a twelve-page paper she had written on Frye's theories, which included two charts.

Dear Miss Hlavsa,

I am so sorry to have left this so long, and a postal strike doesn't help. I was most pleased to hear from you and read your paper, although I find it extremely difficult to comment with any sort of adequacy on papers dealing with me. For example, if the points made on page 2 and 3 are criticisms of my argument, most of them have been answered, whether rightly or wrongly, in the text itself. The fact that Chaucer was master of every mode is one I have noted, and I tried to distinguish Elizabethan high mimetic comedy, not only Shakespeare's, from later comedy. Like you, too, I don't understand the objection that we don't think in terms of a cycle of nature any more: we still do Christmas shopping, surely.

What I most appreciated was your comment on page 10, that I work from the centre outward which is certainly something I always try to do. For that reason, however, I couldn't say much about your two tables, or at least the first one, before seeing how they would work out in practice. I can see the connexion between medicine and the comic, but surely science as a whole would have aspects of law, philosophy and even, as in geology, history. The value of all such constructs is in their practical application and when people propose to me that they would like to modify or expand my categories I can only wish them good luck and say that if their constructs explain more literary facts than mine do they are better constructs.

Once again, I greatly appreciated hearing from you.

Helen Nason   **16 September 1968**
Statesville, NC

In reply to Nason's inquiry (5 September 1968) about the disposition of the opening of an epic she had sent to Frye, along with a paper, based on Anatomy of Criticism, *that she and*

Peter Van Wagingnen had written. The paper included a section entitled "Extension of the Ironic," which Nason wonders whether Frye found to be of any value.

Dear Mrs. Nason,

Thank you for your letter of September 5. I wrote to Mr. Van Wagingnen in August, returning all the materials to him, and I assumed that he would be getting in touch with you and letting you have my comments. My reason for using the terms irony and satire rather than realism and naturalism was that realism and naturalism seem to me to be techniques of displacement within a mode rather than actual modes. As I see it, irony begins in a slightly more realistic version of low mimetic, shades through naturalism, and then begins, around 1900, to become increasingly mythical and fantastic. It is the quality of fantasy which is so prominent in twentieth-century irony, which makes it difficult for me to think of naturalism as anything more than a temporary and intermediate phase. In music, there seems to me to be nothing directly comparable with an ironic mode, but the use of new schemes, such as the twelve-tone scale, have some analogy to [the] return to myth.

In regard to your poems, I am afraid that I cannot be of much help. You are quite right when you say that every writer has his own personal rhythm, and the finding of that rhythm is something that there are no rules for. In this case I think that a more tightly controlled rhythm, and the avoiding of such phrases as "heady dome," would make a long poem easier for the general reader.

I feel very much complimented by the interest you have shown in my work.

Andrew H. Davis   **20 September 1968**
Canford School, Wimborne, Dorset, England

In reply to Davis's proposal (3 September 1968) regarding Frye's statement in Anatomy of Criticism *that "there is no cycle of air." Davis suggests that such a cycle may exist, its four phases being:*

1. whirlwind [dust-devils & preliminary eddies]: Jehovah speaking from the whirlwind.

2. the roaring mighty wind ["Aeolian visitations" etc.]

3. storm. Christ on Galilee

4. still calm. Christ on Galilee. cf. "Resolution and Independence"

"Desert people & sea-faring people," writes Davis, "would all be aware of the distinguishable phases of developing winds through to hurricanes, and I wonder whether there aren't enough symbols clustered around them for you to add an eighth category."

Dear Mr. Davis:

Thank you very much for your letter. I shall certainly rethink the question of a cycle of air. I have been somewhat confused by another category, the one that Yeats calls the gyre, or spiral, to which whirlwinds belong. But you are quite right about there being a possibility of such a cycle.

I did hear Maynard Mack's lectures at Toronto,[346] and am greatly looking forward to seeing them in print.

I am most grateful to you for your interest and help.

Gabrielle Lamport Nohrnberg   **20 September 1968**
New Haven, CT

In response to the announcement from James Nohrnberg, one of Frye's former students, and his wife that they were the parents of a daughter, Gabrielle.

Dear Gabrielle,

Take that silver spoon out of your mouth and pay attention. This is just a note to welcome you to a very confused world. If your parents should happen to see this, please give them my congratulations and best wishes.

Geoffrey Hartman   24 September 1968
Department of English, Yale University, New Haven, CT

Dear Geoffrey:

Thank you very much for the two offprints,[347] which have just arrived, and which I am greatly looking forward to reading. I have to leave at the moment for the Maritimes to engage in public service, like Cromwell deserting his bergamot.[348]

Violet Pratt   30 September 1968
Toronto, ON

A note to the widow of E.J. Pratt about the Johns Robins scholarship fund. Robins was one of Frye's admired teachers and later his colleague.

Dear Vi,

Just a note to clarify the situation about the Robins Scholarship before your reunion. I had, as I told you, instituted an open scholarship annually of $200 until a capital fund was built up. I was waiting for a clear moment in my schedule before approaching the people who I thought would support such a fund, and in the meantime the College took over the annual payment. Nobody so far has paid into the capital fund except Leila,[349] though of course I should be willing to make a sizable donation myself. But if the class of 1913 is willing to accept the conditions of an open scholarship in the first year, there will be no obstacle to establish a scholarship in the name of that class. I suppose there would be no real difficulty anyway, but certainly not in that case.

My reason for choosing the incoming first year was that is a time of great financial difficulty for students, and making it an open scholarship, without tying it to a course makes it very much easier for the Registrar to award it. It also seemed to me in keeping with John's very open-minded attitude to education.

The very best to Claire and yourself,

Margaret Atwood   8 October 1968
Department of English, University of Alberta, Edmonton, AB

In response to Atwood's having sent Frye a copy of her first book from a commercial publisher (Boston: Little, Brown, 1968). The Canadian edition appeared the following year.

Dear Peggy,

I have been reading *The Animals in that Country* with great pleasure, and a sort of tickling of the engrams. You are developing a quite extraordinary immediacy of statement, giving your reader a feeling that he must have written the poem himself in a previous existence and is only now just recognizing it.

The very best to you both.

J. Bascom St. John   8 October 1968
Toronto, ON

In reply to St. John's letter (28 September 1968) which expressed appreciation and enthusiasm for Frye's The Modern Century. St. John, an editorial writer for the Globe and Mail, wrote a daily column, "The World of Learning," from 1958 to 1964.

Dear Mr. St. John,

It was a great boost to my morale to get your letter, and I am deeply grateful for it. Writing is in some ways one of the loneliest of occupations: I have felt about everything I have written that it was really a message in a floating bottle that might or might not get picked up. Such a letter as yours makes one realize the community one is in, and such a realization is more important than I know how to say it is.

Jean H. Hagstrum   28 October 1968
Northwestern University, Evanston, IL

In response to Hagstrum's sending Frye a copy of A Community of Scholars, *a report that came from a faculty committee he chaired. The report recommended a number of changes in the educational environment and eventually resulted in the establishment of residential colleges at Northwestern.*

Dear Jean,

Thank you very much for *A Community of Scholars*, which has just arrived. I am delighted that somebody still believes in the community of scholars. We are going in the opposite direction here, trying to transform a very fine university into another big academic packaging plant. I shall read you carefully for ammunition.

Ian Brown   29 October 1968
Willowdale, ON

Brown reports (21 October 1968) that he has been studying The Educated Imagination *in a special course at Newtonbrook Secondary School, but that his teachers have not helped him understand the book. He therefore asks, "What do you mean by 'Educated Imagination'? Who has it? What are some of its qualities? What are the advantages of having it?"*

Dear Mr. Brown:

Your questions are extremely difficult to answer because the book itself is an attempt to answer them. Most people think of the progress and advance in any subject of education as connected only with reason. Consequently they feel that only mathematics and the sciences, or factual disciplines like history, can be systematically learned. They feel that a subject based on the imagination, like literature and the arts, could only be a matter of experience, and that there is no such thing as learning about it, educating the imagination and the emotions as systematically as science educates the reason. My book is an attempt to show something of the kind of structure that the student of literature enters into, and thereby to show also that those who have been trained, or have done systematic and progressive reading, in literature have educated imaginations.

It is particularly the last lecture that attempts to explain what the advantages are of having it. We participate in society mainly through our imaginations, and not through our reason, and hence those with educated imaginations are the ones who have the best chance of developing the tolerant and flexible minds needed by responsible citizens in a democracy.

Robert F. Sayre   2 January 1969
Department of English, University of Iowa, Iowa City, IA

In reply to Sayre's letter (27 December 1968) which encloses a research application that draws on Frye's Modern Century *and his essays "The Knowledge of Good and Evil" and "Varieties of Literary Utopias."*

Dear Professor Sayre,

Thank you very much for the copy of the application, which I have read with the greatest interest. I am delighted if my own work is of any help to you. I have recently been interested in a conception which I call the "educational contract," trying to see myths of Utopia and of the social contract as essential projections, into the future and past respectively, of a theory of education. This has been forced on me by all the demands made on academics these days to talk about the cause of student unrest and the like.

Very best wishes for the continued success of your work.

A. Bartlett Giamatti   8 January 1969

Department of English, Yale University, New Haven, CT

In reply to Giamatti's note of 19 December 1968: "I hope you won't mind if a stranger foists upon you a small essay. It is the only way one can repay teachers from whom one has learned much but never met."

Dear Professor Giamatti,

Thank you very much for your article *Proteus*,[350] which I have read with fascination. I expect to be not only rereading it, but using it. My particular interest is in the connexion between the cluster of images in Virgil's fourth *Georgic*, the descent to the submarine cave, the list of rivers, and the encounter with Proteus, with their development in the third book of *The Faerie Queene*. But of course there are many other things in your paper, which brings out the conceptual elements in the Proteus myth as well.

Harold Bloom   23 January 1969

Cornell University, Ithaca, NY

Bloom's letter, which is not extant, had apparently included an inquiry about Frye's recent writings, along with an account of Bloom's own developing theory about the "anxiety of influence."

Dear Harold:

Thank you for your letter. I am afraid I have written rather little of any permanent interest since that Cornell paper last spring.[351] There was a Yeats paper which I read in the summertime,[352] but I have not got around to writing that out yet, and all fall I was being harried and bedevilled by different requests to make oracular pronouncements on student unrest. I am sending one such paper along with this,[353] because it mentions the myth of concern in passing, and I doubt that it will be of any help to you and you need only glance at it.

You don't say much about the general direction or scope of your book. If you mean influence in the more literal sense of the transmission of thought and imagery and the like from earlier poet to later one, I should think that this was simply something that happens, and might be a source either of anxiety or of release from it, depending on circumstances and temperament. But of course it is true that a great poet's maturity brings with it a growing sense of isolation, of the kind one feels in Yeats' *Last Poems*, Stevens' *The Rock*, and perhaps even Blake's *Job* series. I should very much like to hear more about the book and about your progress with it.[354]

M.H. Abrams   29 January 1969

Department of English, Cornell University, Ithaca, NY

In reply to Abrams's letter of 25 January 1969, asking Frye to identify the source of a German author who described "the moment of epiphany as an intersection of eternity in time."

Dear Mike:

Thanks for your letter, but the reference is not mine, and I can't place it, though I should dearly love to know where it is from. There are phrases like this in Rilke's letters, which I have been looking through, but without success. I shall continue looking, and asking my colleagues, but I think it more likely that Harold Bloom or Geoffrey Hartman was the one who referred to it. Sorry not to be more helpful at the moment.[355]

The very best to you both.

G. Sabri-Tabrizi   29 January 1969
Department of Persian, University of Edinburgh, Scotland

In reply to Sabri-Tabrizi's having sent Frye on 23 January 1969 a copy of his article on Rintrah in Blake's The Marriage of Heaven and Hell *and asking Frye his opinion of it. See previous correspondence with Sabri-Tabrizi of 10 May and 23 May 1968. Sabri-Tabrizi later published a book on Blake's satire,* The "Heaven" and "Hell" of William Blake (*London: Lawrence & Wishart, 1973*).

Dear Mr. Tabrizi:

I think that the *Argument* to *The Marriage of Heaven and Hell* describes the kind of historical circle which occurred at the Exodus, at the time of Christ, and in Blake's own time. Rintrah is the prophet in the wilderness, incarnate in Elijah, John the Baptist, and Blake himself, who announces the coming of a new age. His motto, which Blake adopts, is "the voice of one crying in the wilderness." In this time and context, therefore, Rintrah is not in his perverted state but his genuinely prophetic one, and is present in the spirit of the just man raging in the wilds.

The association of Rintrah with Indra is quite possible, but if the only source is *Sakuntala* it is difficult to understand the association with the "abstract philosophy" of India made in The Song of Los.

In the second line of the *Argument* the word is "swag," not "sway."

Walter Miale   18 February 1969
Venice, CA

In reply to Miale's question about a passage in the Tentative Conclusion of Anatomy of Criticism *having to do with the relation of literary criticism with other fields of study.*

Dear Mr. Miale:

Thank you for your card. I assume that you are referring to a passage near the end of my *Anatomy of Criticism*. You may notice that the phrase "confused swirl" is a part of the sentence you refer to.[356] I was trying to describe a general ferment of ideas, as they were developing around 1954, which was about when the sentence was written. At that time, Cassirer, whose major works were just coming out in translation, was obviously a central figure in my field. Korzybsky was, because of his anti-literary bias, a person I was bound to have reservations about, but there was still the possibility that he might be, like Marshall McLuhan today, probing and prodding in directions that might turn out to be useful.

Harold Bloom   19 February 1969
Cornell University, Ithaca, NY

In reply to Bloom's letter of 27 January 1969, in which he enclosed a copy of his talk on poetic influence that he gave at Cornell. Bloom asked Frye about a further exposition of "the myth of concern."

Dear Harold:

Thank you very much for your letter, and for the copy of your Cornell lecture. I have read the latter with the greatest interest and think it quite one of the best things you have done. A very personal statement of the kind you make all too rarely.

A large and complicated design for a successor to the *Anatomy* is gradually taking me over. The myth of concern is certainly a central part of it, but at present it looks like being the end of it, so it will probably take me a fair time to get there. There may, of course, be various mirages along the way. If one of them should materialize, in however a ghostly a form, I shall remember your interest.

Nobuaki Kozaki   12 March 1969

Kumamoto-ken, Kyushu, Japan

In reply to Kozaki's question (2 March 1969) about using John Dryden as a model for developing a prose style. This is one of many letters that Kozaki wrote to Frye over the course of a decade about English prose style. See, for example, Frye's replies of 27 August 1974 and 22 December 1975.

Dear Mr. Kozaki,

Thank you very much for your letter. It seems to me that one can interpret the word "model" in two ways. One may train oneself to write by close imitation of a specific writer, or one may simply use a great writer as a model in a much less direct way, as a writer who suggests the qualities of clarity, rhythm, and the like which one wants to attain in a different way for oneself. It is quite true that Dryden is still about the finest prose writer that English literature has ever produced. It is also true that his sentence structure and word order are substantially those of contemporary English. At the same time, the changes in vocabulary and in the nuances of expression would make it necessary to be aware of twentieth-century English prose, and of using that as the more direct and specific model. But I am delighted that you have discovered Dryden, and enthusiastically recommend that you continue your daily reading of him. If I may say so, I think that your own handling of English, as evidenced by your letter, is remarkably good.

Ray Bradbury   31 March 1969

Los Angeles, CA

Frye and Bradbury had been seated together at some unidentified faculty dinner. Bradbury asked Frye for two of his books, which Frye mailed to him. Bradbury wrote on 16 March 1969, thanking Frye for the books and saying that he hoped they could "meet again some day under quieter auspices, and not have to discuss the pros and cons of such 1968 vaudeville miseries as HAIR." With his letter, Bradbury sent Frye several of his own books,[357] prompting the present reply.

Dear Mr. Bradbury,

I am just taking off for your part of the world again, but your books have just arrived and I did want to thank you for them. I am quite familiar enough with your work to know that the statement quoted from Isherwood in one of the introductions, that yours is a very great and unusual talent, is a simple factual statement.[358]

Patrick J. Keane   9 May 1969

New York, NY

In reply to Keane's query (17 April 1969) about whether a study of the influence of Nietzsche on Yeats would be a worthwhile topic for a thesis.

Dear Mr. Keane:

Thank you for your letter. Of course a thesis on the influence of Nietzsche on Yeats would be an extremely valuable study to have. It would be valuable even if it had to be based on pure analogy, with no specific influence from Nietzsche to draw on. As it is, I think the connexions are startlingly close between Nietzsche and Yeats's *Vision*, some of it perhaps secondhand through Spengler or Ossendowski, and thorough investigation of the relationship could become a study of considerable cultural importance. Naturally, one would have to allow for the bad translations and misleading contexts available to Yeats, but that might be an asset in bringing out the extraordinarily penetrating quality of Yeats's insight. I should greatly look forward to seeing what you do on this line.

Geoffrey Hartman   18 June 1969
Yale University, New Haven, CT

In reply to Hartman's request (1 May 1969) for Frye's ideas about a literature major for undergraduates, presently under discussion at Yale.

Dear Geoffrey:

Thank you very much for your admirable article,[359] which I have read with the greatest interest. The combination of precision and comprehensiveness in it is extraordinary. I only wish you had contrasted the phoenix of Raphael with the peacock of Michael, with its image of the closing eyes. I suppose the image of "balmy sweat" connects with Yeats's *Vacillation* as well as with Joyce.

I am not sure just what you mean by a Literature major for undergraduates. We used to have an honours course in English Language and Literature, which in the course of four years gave the student everything from *Beowulf* to *Finnegans Wake*. This has now been thrown out, on the usual reformation principle of getting rid of babies as well as bath water. In its day it was, I think the best undergraduate training available on the continent. It is still theoretically possible to get the same training, but only in theory.

In my opinion one of the most effective forms of education is the grouping of related subjects around a historical period. That is, if the student takes the literature of the Renaissance, and a course in philosophy or history or art or music of the Renaissance at the same time, he gets a kind of stereoscopic training that he simply cannot get from a single department. I had this kind of course as an undergraduate myself, largely by accident, and it would still be my chief constructive principle if I were free to design a curriculum.

Sister Margaret Cantwell   14 July 1969
University of Alaska, College, AK

In reply to Sister Cantwell's question (4 July 1969) about whether Frye has changed any of his views since Anatomy of Criticism *and whether he has "any comment on Hopkins that [she] could use." She was writing an M.A. thesis on "The Poetry of Gerard Manley Hopkins according to the Critical Theories of Northrop Frye."*

Dear Sister:

Thank you very much for your letter. I am afraid it takes me so long to write a book that when I finally get it into print it represents a position that I am unlikely to change. I cannot think of any position involving Hopkins which I took up in the *Anatomy* that needs any revision now, as far as my own attitudes are concerned.

For some reason I have not said much about Hopkins in my critical writings, beyond an occasional quotation here and there, but if your library possesses a copy of *The Well-Tempered Critic*, there are some remarks about Hopkins there that you may find useful.[360]

Neil Tracy   **15 July 1969**
Lennoxville, QC

In reply to Tracy's letter (5 July 1969), indicating that in a Sherbrooke newspaper from the 1850's he has come upon a scandal involving a Dr. Ryerson that might be a source for the dilemma of Dr. Walker in Anthony Trollope's The Last Chronicle. *Tracy also says that he remembers Frye's parents from their Sherbrooke days and that both the house his father built and his hardware store are still standing.*

Dear Mr. Tracy:

Thank you very much for your letter. The link between Ryerson and Trollope would be certainly fascinating if one could establish it. If this was a source for Trollope, he certainly reworked it before writing his novel, as there could hardly be a greater contrast in character between the successful and perhaps rather pompous Ryerson and Trollope's tough and gritty little curate.

I have of course been familiar with your name for many years but didn't realize that you knew my parents. Some years ago, when I was a guest of Mr. Gray's at Bishop's, I had a brief look around Sherbrooke, and thought I had located the house where I was born, although the street numbers have been changed. But did not realize that the Hardware Store would be still there, and when I return to Sherbrooke I shall make another pilgrimage. I suppose you may also have known my brother Howard, who was killed in the First World War, and my sister Vera, who died in Los Angeles three years ago.

William G. Davis   **24 July 1969**
Toronto, ON

In response to Davis's letter (13 May 1969) asking for Frye's response to an enclosed report of the Committee on Religious Education in the Public Schools of Ontario.

Dear Mr. Davis:

This is to thank you for the copy of the report of the Mackay Committee on Religious Education.[361] It seems to me that the Committee did an extraordinarily good job, considering the great difficulties of their task. In my opinion religion, both as an academic subject and as a subject of concern, is of central importance in all education, but because of the number and variety of social anxieties going on within it, it seems impossible to introduce it into any curriculum below that of the university. I have taught a course on the English Bible myself for over twenty years in the university, and the students ranged from Greek Orthodox ordinands to Maoists. But I quite see that at younger age levels such teaching is impracticable.

Sister Elaine Jahner   **25 August 1969**
Mary College, Bismarck, North Dakota

In reply to Sister Elaine, who encloses an intricate diagram with her letter (15 August 1969) and reports that she has used the diagram, based on Frye's Anatomy of Criticism, *as a way of helping teachers in an in-service training program to see the literature curriculum as a whole. She asks Frye to respond if he feels her diagram has misrepresented anything.*

Dear Sister Elaine,

Thank you very much for your letter and for the copy of your diagram. The latter seems to be quite full and accurate, and I certainly see nothing that would give students a misleading impression on my book. I find that a good many people who use my book do reduce it to diagrammatic form, and that the diagrams they send me are usually much more ingenious than I could ever be. I foresaw that this would be true, and for that reason I made no attempt to supply diagrams myself.[362]

Naturally, I am delighted if my book is of any use to you in your work. It seems to be the general experience that it is useful for teachers with your specific problem of retraining their teachers [sic].

Charles E. Hendry   7 October 1969
Toronto, ON

In reply to Hendry's letter (14 September 1969) expressing his "sheer joy" over Frye's piece "Utopia on the Campus," which appeared in the Toronto *Globe and Mail Magazine, 13 September 1969, pp. 5–8, an abridged form of Frye's "The University and the Personal Life: Student Anarchism and the Educational Contract," published originally in* Higher Education: Demand and Response, *ed. W.R. Niblett (London: Tavistock Publications, 1969), 35–59. Frye and Hendry, who had been chair of the graduate department of social work, School of Social Work, University of Toronto, had been long-time friends.*

Dear Chick,

Thank you very much for your note: it was extremely decent of you to write me. I am delighted to know that your retirement has been largely a fictitious one, as I had rather expected it would be. I am just back myself from a Comparative Literature Conference in Pakistan.[363] West Pakistan speaks Urdu and East Pakistan speaks Bengali; Bengali is their native language, but West Pakistan says that their desire to speak it is nothing but propaganda and they can speak Urdu if they want to. From somebody brought up in English-speaking Canada it all sounds horridly familiar.

The very best to you. I shall look up the Kurt Lewin book right away.[364]

L. Allan Bell   8 October 1969
Mississauga, ON

In reply to Bell's question (1 September 1969) about Frye's statement, in the context of boundaries and peripheries which circumscribe subjects and themes, that it is better to study a subject than a theme. The remark had come from an interview with Bruce Mickelburgh, "The Only Genuine Revolution," Monday Morning, *February 1969, 20–6.*

Dear Mr. Bell,

Thank you for your letter. One has to remember that all talk on boundaries and peripheries is metaphorical only. The reason why subject is preferable to theme is that subject really exists and a theme is only an allegorical shadow of something that exists. Every subject is inexhaustible, and it is only the most superficial approach to it which becomes conscious of boundaries. In real study, things are attracted by the centripetal force of the student, and relate to the subject. In short, the difference between subject and theme is simply the difference between genuine study and teaching and a kind of secularized sermon-preaching.

F.R. Scott   15 October 1969
French Canada Studies Programme, McGill University, Montreal, QC

In response to Scott's request (30 September 1969) for recommendations of satirical prose extracts to be included in an anthology, The Ruddy Maple, *that he and A.J.M. Smith were proposing to publish. The book was to be a companion volume to their* The Blasted Pine: An Anthology of Satire, Invective and Disrespectful Verse Chiefly by Canadian Writers *(Toronto: Macmillan, 1957).* The Ruddy Maple *was never published.*

Dear Frank,

Thank you very much for your letter about your new anthology. What you plan to do sounds fascinating, and I wish I could think of something appropriate off the bat. As it is, I shall have to think about possibilities. I am glad you are including that Leacock story,[365] which is one of my favourites, and perhaps that poem of Pamela Vining Yule, which Art Smith put into the first edition of his anthology, is also possible.[366] Bennett's remark[367] is almost conservative compared to some of the things said in Alberta during the early Aberhart campaigns,[368] but you would know about that. I remember in particular a radio talk asserting that the second syllable of the Biblical name Isaac was the root of the word Saxon.

Roy C. Flannagan   5 November 1969
Milton Newsletter, Ohio University, Athens, OH

In reply to Flannagan's inquiry about making the Milton Newsletter *into a quarterly. Flannagan had begun the* Newsletter *in 1966; after three volumes it became the* Milton Quarterly.

Dear Professor Flannagan:

Thank you for your letter about the *Milton Newsletter*. It seems quite reasonable to raise the subscription rate, and of course expansion is inevitable. There are certainly enough Milton scholars around to expand it into a quarterly, and it seems to me that regular periodicals are much easier to read than newsletters.

I hope it will not seem ungracious if I ask to be left off the Board of Advisory Readers. I am on several such boards now, and it is getting so that it takes a long time to pick up and process anything that lands on my desk. I am now in the position of a camel who gets his exercise from trying to duck out from under the last straw.

Jelte Kuipers   5 November 1969
Editor, "Ti Estin," McMaster University, Hamilton, ON

In reply to Kuiper's letter (20 October 1969), which enclosed a critique of Frye's article in the Toronto Globe and Mail, *"Utopia on the Campus," which was an abridged version of "The University and Personal Life: Student Anarchism and the Educational Contract," in* Higher Education: Demand and Response *(The Quail Roost Seminar), ed. W.R. Niblett (London: Tavistock Publications, 1969), 35–59. Both Frye's and Kuipers's articles had been circulated to the Senate Committee on Undergraduate Education at McMaster University. Kuipers is interested in whether or not Frye might like to make any supplementary remarks for the faculty and students at McMaster. For Kuipers' critique, see his "Pro and Contra Frye," Collage, 3 October 1969: 5–8.*

Dear Mr. Kuipers,

Thank you very much for your letter and for the article which I have read with great interest. I am particularly grateful for your defence of the essential good faith of my own article against the gentleman in the TLS.

I didn't see the Globe and Mail version of my article, which appeared when I was out of the country, so I don't know whether it was cut, or, consequently, whether you had the full text of it. In the full text I did not identify anarchism as a purely left-wing movement, but spoke of its ambivalence, and the fact that some anarchist movements of today seem to be heading in a neo-fascist direction. Neither did I speak of it as a purely negative move-ment. I said that there had always been two tendencies in it, one a terroristic tendency which had never got anywhere, the other a decentralizing tendency which was very deeply embedded in the revolutionary democratic tradition in America.

On minor points, I think there is really no disagreement about the dialogue in Plato: I was using the term in what you call its depraved modern sense. In that sense, Plato moves away from dialogue towards what you call symmetry and what I should call dia-lectic, the attempt to understand something by a process which includes defining its opposite.

My article also spoke of the uneasy and inconsistent alliance between political democ-racy and economic oligarchy in the United States. Because of this, it is quite possible that America will "abolish capitalism," but if that version is to mean anything it must mean developing a new economy and that new economy could hardly be very similar to any at present in the world: the Marxist countries, for instance, seem to be incapable of develop-ing from the industrial to the electronic stage.

The original paper was delivered to a group of educators who were deeply concerned about student opinion, not to the Globe and Mail public. They were people who believe that they and the students are fundamentally on the same side, and that the attempt to define university teachers and administrators as attached to a hostile "establishment" is com-pletely mistaken. In this context, my closing remark would have a very different set of reverberations.

I hope this is of some use to you, and thank you again for your lively and candid article.

David Armstrong   **14 November 1969**
Arion, University of Texas, Austin, Texas
In reply to a questionnaire on Horace from the editors of Arion, *who had sent to a num-ber of literary figures a list of seven questions regarding their attitude to Horace, suggesting that "you may answer any, or all, of the questions, or simply describe in your own terms what-ever encounters you have had with Horace." Except in the last paragraph, Frye chose the lat-ter approach. Frye's response was published in* Arion 9, nos. 2 and 3 (Summer and Autumn 1970), 132.

Dear Mr. Armstrong,
I am glad you are doing something about Horace, who in spite of the interest in him seems a somewhat neglected poet. When I was seventeen I was compelled to slog my way through the Odes and ever since I have realized that education has a great deal to do with compulsion and doing things that at the time one thinks one doesn't want to do. Horace has always seemed to me to represent the authority of the humanist tradition, the incor-porating of all its values into a life style. His chief virtue is the virtue of urbanity, which means primarily the virtue of being able to live in a civilization. This means that he has limitations as a poet both on the personal side as compared with Catullus or Propertius, and on the philosophical side as compared with Virgil and Ovid. But the point is that his limitations are his strength.

Of your questions, the answer to the sixth one[369] is that Marvell and Pope not only limited Horace but transmitted him, so that any course which teaches them and ignores Horace operates like a dentist who extracts a tooth and leaves the root sticking in the jaw.

Charlie Bruce   **21 November 1969**
Toronto, ON

In response to Bruce's having sent Frye a photocopy of two pages from John Lehman's A Nest of Tigers, which includes Edith Sitwell's comments on Fearful Symmetry — "a really wonderful new book on Blake." Sitwell also mentioned that she had heard from a lecturer at Strasbourg University who had written a long book on Blake.

Dear Charlie:

Thank you very much for the extract from Lehman. It was extremely good of you to send it to me.

I have a suspicion that the man from Strasbourg was somebody named Jacques Roos, who published, some years after mine, a thick book on Blake and Swedenborg,[370] full of the most elementary boners that one would pluck a freshman for. If so, the increase in interest in Blake which I think my book helped to cause, really got him his own way, even without Edith.

Carolyn Kizer   **1 December 1969**
Washington, DC

In reply to Kizer's having sent Frye (22 November 1969) a copy of the journal which she kept in Pakistan, where she and Frye attended the Eleventh Triennial Congress of the Fédération Internationale des Langues et Littératures Modernes, Islamabad, Pakistan, September 1969. Kizer, the American poet, had worked for the State Department in Pakistan, and became the first director for literature of the National Endowment for the Arts (1966–1970). In her Carrying Over: Poems from the Chinese, Urdu, Macedonian, Yiddish, and French African (Port Townsend, WA: Copper Canyon Press, 1985) she translates verse from several languages and juxtaposes works by known and less familiar writers with journals she kept while living in Pakistan.

Dear Miss Kizer,

Thank you very much for the xerox of your Pakistan Journal which brought the whole experience back to me very vividly. Your remarks about me are very kind, and certainly your quotations are quite accurate.[371] I remember that I was very impressed with your talk and with the conception of translation implied in it. I looked around for afterwards to tell you so, but apparently you had already left for Swat.

The Pakistan visit was a particularly rewarding one for a Canadian, I should think, because it gave me some perspective of what a country gets out of separatism and a cornball ideology, which seems to be damn little.

Everett C. Frost   **3 December 1969**
Department of English, Fresno State College, Fresno, CA

Dear Mr. Frost:

Thank you very much for your letter and for the diagram, which I have been studying with great interest and profit. It is perfectly true that I think schematically, because I think poetry does. But I don't include diagrams in my works, partly because I have very little ingenuity in such matters, and partly because there are readers who have considerably more, including yourself, and I feel that they can get much more out of my books if they make their own spatial renditions. Your diagram is remarkable evidence of that fact. I know that my six phases of four mythoi all belong in a co-ordinating spatial scheme, but I have to learn from such readers as yourself how that is true.[372]

Stephen R. Graubard   **10 December 1969**
Editor, *Daedalus*, Harvard University, Cambridge, MA
In reply to receiving the proofs for "The Critical Path: An Essay on the Social Context of Literary Criticism," which appeared Dædalus *99 (Spring 1970): 268–342.*

Dear Mr. Graubard:

I have sent the galley proofs of my article back, and like them very much. This is the first set of proofs I have had where some styler didn't make a lot of extra notes to correct by trying to improve me. So there was nothing to correct except actual misprints.

At the very end of the article, and at the end of the note where I say that two other papers have been absorbed in the *Daedalus* one, I wonder if it would be possible to add the sentence: "I am grateful to Indiana Press and Tavistock Publications for their courtesy in allowing me to use this material."[373] The reason why I didn't make the correction on the galleys is that I have just had the notice from Indiana about publishing the article in their Yearbook: I did not realize they were going to do this. Apologies and best wishes.

Gordon Albright   **13 December 1969**
York University, Faculty of Arts & Science, Downsview, ON
In reply to Albright's lengthy (seven-page) letter, offering several answers to questions about fire-stealing myths Frye had raised in a lecture on 11 November 1969. Albright also remarks that in the East children's imaginations are nurtured and developed, whereas in the West they are taught that the only thing real is the outer world.

Dear Gordon:

I had intended to thank you earlier for your very full and thoughtful letter, but have been absent in Ottawa on a Government Commission. I think your psychological explanation of the fire-stealing myth is probably the best one psychologically and, as I think I mentioned to you, Jung's explanation is not dissimilar. I was hoping for some answer within the structure of myth itself, but of course there may not be one, and the psychological reduction may be the only possibility. I was particularly struck by your contrast between the pastoral myth of order and the revolutionary myth of sex and fire, which incidentally anticipates a great deal that I have still to say in this graduate course.

The bias in Western education towards the outer world is certainly there, but it seems to me a somewhat new development in the West itself, and to be spreading in a very rapid and sinister way to the East. When I was recently in Pakistan I was made aware of how vital the oral tradition still is in the East, and the revival of oral poetry in the West seems to me a hopeful sign.

As for the worshipping of Prometheus, I was thinking of the parallel with Christianity, which not only got over the hurdle of the martyrdom of a god who was a son rather than a parental figure, but made it the corner stone of other religion [sic]. Perhaps my question is really why didn't the Greeks invent Christianity?

Daniel C. Noel   **16 December 1969**
Branford, CT
After having heard Frye speak at Yale University on 4 December 1969 on "Pure and Applied Imagination," Noel sought Frye's response (5 December 1969) to a series of ideas on the relation between theology and literature.

Dear Mr. Noel,

Thank you very much for your letter and for the material you sent along.[374] The importance for religion of my own work is getting clearer to me all the time, and I feel that I am steadily moving in the direction of some kind of book on the typology of the Bible. My present thinking about it is included in a very long essay which is to be appearing in a forthcoming issue of *Daedalus*. The subject of the issue is the role of theory in the humanities: my own essay is called *The Critical Path*.

Like you, I have been considerably put off by Bultmann's insensitivity to literature, and at one time felt that the general trend of theological criticism in our day was going in the opposite direction from everything I was interested in. I no longer feel this, but I do feel that some training in literary criticism is badly needed for writers on religion. So far, there has been little work done to connect the two: most people with both interests, like Amos Wilder, are interested mainly in the religious content of literature. But I think this whole field may clear up quite quickly in the next few years.

1970s

John Dancy   **14 January 1970**
The Master, Marlborough College, Wiltshire, England
In reply to Dancy's request (8 January 1970) for a bibliography of literary-critical approaches to the Bible, the beginnings of which Frye mentions in Anatomy of Criticism. *Dancy sees the Book of Tobit as a high-mimetic work and the Book of Judith as a naïve romance, and he asks Frye to comment on this classification.*

Dear Mr. Dancy:

Thank you very much for your letter, which I greatly appreciated. It seems to me that the best way to arrive at the question of the mode of such works as Judith and Tobit would be to lay Hebrew literature out along a historical sequence and see where things fall. My own feeling, as expressed in the *Anatomy*, is that Hebrew literature never got far enough away from romance formulas to develop a definitely mimetic form. Hence it would be quite feasible, I should think, to say that Judith was a romance trying to develop high mimetic characteristics and Tobit a romance with some low mimetic ones. Assigning them to these categories would depend partly on the amount of sophistication you would find in Judith — it seems to me quite as much a folk tale as Tobit in its underlying structure — and the extent of comic elements in Tobit. I know Tobit only in the standard versions, including the Charles edition, so I cannot express an opinion on the text you are using.

My remark about the beginnings of a literary approach to the Bible was somewhat optimistic. I had thought that the form critics like Dibelius and Bultmann would take was in the direction of a genuinely literary criticism. But this does not seem to have happened, partly because Bultmann appears to have no literary sense whatever. I have been teaching a course on the typology of the Bible for many years, largely because I cannot do anything else for my students, and some day I shall write out my lecture notes.[375]

I am interested in the question of the relation of the New to the Old Testament, and I agree that that there are many tricky pitfalls in relating them. But the way in which the form of the collection of proverbs or maxims handed on down to the next generation develops into the post–Pauline epistles seems to me a possible line of investigation, and of course there is the whole apocalyptic development that except for Daniel got mostly squeezed out of the Old Testament. If one only had world enough and time, to say nothing of erudition, to write the history of literary forms!

Stephen R. Graubard   **14 January 1970**
Editor, *Dædalus*, Harvard University, Cambridge, MA
Graubard wrote on 12 January 1970, thanking Frye for two articles he had written about the New Left protests, "Anarchism and the Universities" and "The Educational Contract" in

New Society 14 *(13 November 1969): 769–71 and (20 November 1969): 811–14. In response Frye sent Graubard another article, which was almost certainly "The Ethics of Change: The Role of the University," in* A Symposium: The Ethics of Change *(Toronto: Canadian Broadcasting Corp., 1969), 44–55. The article was reprinted in DG, 156–66, and in WE, 345–59.*

Dear Mr. Graubard:

Thank you very much for your most gracious letter. I am taking the liberty of inflicting another piece on you, which is shorter than the other two. This is about all I have said so far about the Children's Crusade,[376] and I very much hope I shall not have to return to the subject, as it is clearly running out of gas. The process of thinking about the restructuring of the University is of course another matter.

Patrick O'Reilly   4 February 1970
Windsor, ON

In reply to O'Reilly's request (8 December 1969) for Frye to comment on his understanding of Yeats's A Vision *and on a number of patterns he has deduced from it.*

Dear Mr. O'Reilly,

I am very sorry to have left your letter for so long, but I have been somewhat taken over by a book recently and so the processing of letters has taken me even longer than usual.

It seems to me that you are at a point at which quite a number of patterns are swirling around in your mind, and at which an almost infinite number of combinations seems possible. This is not an uncommon state of mind, and it may recur several times. It would be a great mistake for me to try to say which connexions were rewarding and which ones unrewarding, let alone which ones are "right," and which "wrong." All you can do really is to go on to the next stage, when you will find in your own writing and practice that certain ones hold up and others do not. Some of the insights that have come to you, such as the distinction between humility and obsequiousness, are capable of generating a great number of similar and parallel distinctions, as a great many conceptions have their true and false aspects. Similarly with the theme of the male and female principles within the human being, where there are so many literary ramifications, as well as the psychological ones in Jung and elsewhere.

Walter Miale   25 February 1970
New York, NY

In reply to Miale's letter (14 February 1970), which concluded with this question: "Ought not the critical faculties be applied to the historical question of the relation of (ritual) origin to (dramatic) form? (Cf. Anatomy of Criticism, *pp. 108–109)."*

Dear Mr. Miale:

Thank you for your letter. In the passage in the *Anatomy* which you refer to I was trying to distinguish the critical from the historical problems about the relation of ritual to drama, because of the way in which the subject had been confused. Cornford, for example, had assigned many things in Aristophanes to a ritual origin in the past which were not necessarily that at all, and he had been attacked by such scholars as Pickard-Cambridge, who in their turn were critically illiterate: that is, they made some assumption that a ritual feature must survive unchanged in a drama, and that if the dramatist modifies it its ritual origin is thereby disproved. I did not want to rule out the importance of the historical question, merely to separate the two problems.

David Anderson   **27 February 1970**
University College, Michigan State University, East Lansing, MI
In reply to Anderson's having sent Frye (12 February 1970) a copy of his article on "The Mushaira." Frye and Anderson had met at the FILLM conference in Pakistan in September 1969.

Dear Dave:

Thank you very much for the article on the Mushaira. It occurred to me at the one [conference paper] that I heard that Pakistan was going to have quite a struggle to prevent Bengali from taking over the whole country. As I didn't know a syllable of either language, I could concentrate on the rhythm, and Bengali was obviously so much richer and more supple a language than Urdu that there isn't any question which a poet would prefer if he had both.

The very best to you both, also to Messrs. Buddha and company,[377] whom I hope to have the pleasure of greeting again. I am sorry we didn't manage Denver,[378] but it was just too much, and having done a great many jobs for MLA I feel that I can be less conscientious now.

A.E. Parr   **9 March 1970**
Hamden, CT
Parr was a marine biologist and museum director.

Dear Dr. Parr,

Thank you very much for the offprints, which I have read with great attention.[379] You raise the kind of issues that I have been trying to think about without getting very far. I was particularly interested in the article on the problems of reason, feeling and habitat. I have been living in Toronto for forty years, have seen it change from a quite habitable town to the usual wilderness of freeways and highrise apartment buildings, and consequently I have experienced something of what you call the realities of sentiment and nostalgia. I am quite convinced that space and shape pollution is quite as important a social problem as noise and dirt.

Sergio Peretti   **22 July 1970**
Milan, Italy
In reply to Peretti's questions (4 July 1970) about Frye's influences and sources, his inheritance from Aristotle, and his understanding of rhetoric. Peretti, a fourth-year undergraduate at the University of Milan, was writing his thesis on Frye's theory of literature.

Dear Mr. Peretti,

Thank you for your letter. It is difficult for me to list my sources and influences, because such things tend to get very mixed up in my own mind. My original interest in myth and archetype was derived from my study of Blake. I then read extensively in Frazer, Freud and Jung, and later in Whitehead, Cassirer and Mrs. Langer. I am not sure how much I am indebted to these latter writers because my own views had been pretty well established by then. At the same time, I began to understand something of the great interest in critical theory that was developing, particularly in the United States. As this interest seemed to centre so much on Aristotle, I read the *Poetics* with the greatest care, and felt that from that and from other works of Aristotle I acquired a kind of skeleton of critical terms to articulate my own approach. I think I have set this out more clearly in the *Anatomy of Criticism* than I can explain it here. My conception of rhetoric is also Aristotelian, and embraces two aspects in particular: the persuasive powers of the orator and the figuration of nature. Both of these senses are traditional in the history of rhetoric.

Joanne Witke   26 August 1970
Berkeley, CA
In reply to a Witke's sending Frye an offprint of her article on Blake's Jerusalem, *enclosed with her letter of 19 August 1970.*

Dear Miss Witke,

Thank you very much for the offprint on *Jerusalem* which I am very glad to have.[380] The traditional material about the gospels is particularly interesting. Two things occur to me: one is a remark of Blake's, in the marginalia to Bishop Watson, that Matthew is the earliest gospel, which of course is not surprising, but is additional documentation. The other is the fact that the episode of the woman taken in adultery, which is so crucial to Blake's conception of the historical Jesus, is peculiar to John, and almost didn't get in there. The episode of Joseph and Mary in *Jerusalem* is also an insertion, in the third part, it is true, but as an anticipation of the final message to the Christians.

Theodore A. Webb   16 September 1970
Winchester, MA
In reply to a letter from Webb (11 April 1970) in which he compliments Frye for his essay "The Search for Acceptable Words" and encloses one of his sermons.

Dear Reverend Webb,

I am very sorry to have been so long in replying to your letter: I have been at Oxford for the last six months, and a good deal of my mail was not forwarded. I have read your sermon with great interest and like its historical sense. I suppose the God who is dead (not that he was ever alive) is the creator and sustainer of the order of nature. The importing of this essentially Greek god into Christianity was, I suppose, a necessary stage in its history, but it's gone now. I think Christianity will now have to go back to its original primitive emphasis on God as suffering and enduring man.

I was very interested to hear of your connexion with North Hatley[381]: I was born in Sherbrooke, and that part of the world still exerts a great fascination on me.

Sandra Djwa   25 September 1970
Department of English, University of Alberta, Edmonton, AB
In reply to Djwa's questions about E.J. Pratt's relation to C.G.D. Roberts and his views of Christianity.

Dear Dr. Djwa:

Thank you very much for your letter and the most interesting account of your research. The influence of Roberts on Pratt is something that would not normally have occurred to me, as I knew Pratt's connexion with Roberts only from their later days, when Roberts had acquired a knighthood and was getting a bit soft in the head. But once you say it, it looks like a very logical and obvious source, and I should think that this would be well worth following up, whether with a computer or not.

In connexion with your reference to Wundt, the late Professor [John] Irving at Victoria told me that Pratt had absorbed the central idea of Wundt's theory of perception and had made it to the basis of most of his important poems. Unfortunately he died before he could explain more fully to me what he meant, but here too there seems to be a lead well worth following up.

As for Pratt's view of Christianity, it is important to get that clear, because a great deal of ignorant nonsense has been written about it. In the first place, Pratt never repudiated his theological training or his ordination. He simply decided, as I was to decide myself some years later, that his vocation was for university teaching and not for parish work. When you talk about "doubts" and about the impact of evolution, you are talking about a mental climate of about fifty years earlier, one which affected, say, James Thomson and in a different way Thomas Hardy but which was not at all the mental climate of Pratt at Victoria College. Those were the days when the theologians at Victoria were fascinated by the new horizons opened up in science. For example, the head of the head of the theological school urged the younger man to learn Greek and become a Professor of the New Testament. When he protested that his training up to that point had been mainly in geology, he was told that that was exactly the kind of training that the Church wanted. Of course there was the emotional impact of natural situation [selection?], cruelty and ferocity of nature, the endless eons of existence without mind, and the source of ruthlessness and competition. But Pratt had gone on to the next stage, the twentieth-century stage: for him, the creator of the order of nature which Christianity had imported from Greek philosophy was no longer to retain his [its?] old principles. But that particular fact had thrown all the more emphasis on the original focus of Christianity: its identification of divinity with the suffering humanity of Jesus. This leads to the sense of the existential contrast between humour and physical nature which I suppose all serious modern poets have. It is this view of Christianity that organizes all of Pratt's poetry, and makes sense of such poems as "The Highway" and "The Truant."

Morton D. Paley   **30 September 1970**
Department of English, University of California at Berkeley, Berkeley, CA
In response to Paley's having sent Frye a copy of his Energy and the Imagination: A Study of the Development of Blake's Thought *(Oxford: Clarendon Press, 1970).*

Dear Morton,

I suppose you will have returned from your year off now and will be back in the paradisal atmosphere of the academic world, with its mixture of tear gas and smog. I was thinking of you when a student came into my office with a proposal to take a year off studying Blake in England. He is actually a student of architecture and Blake is an acquired interest; consequently he doesn't know what people in England to look up. And in spite of having spent the last four or five months in Oxford, neither do I. The people I did know there — [Sir Geoffrey] Keynes, [Vivian de Sola] Pinto, [Herschel M.] Margoliouth, [Joseph] Wicksteed, [William] Vaughan — are all dead, retired, or otherwise advanced in age,[382] and it occurred to me that you would probably know more than I do about who the younger people are who are coming along to replace them. At any rate, you are certainly in a uniquely well placed position to know.

All of which is by way of prelude to something that should have come first. That is to say that I am delighted that your book has appeared, delighted to have a copy, and above all delighted to read it. It is an essay in the very centre of Blake's own vision and structure of values, which is something I cannot say of a great deal of recent Blake scholarship. For that reason alone I should be extremely grateful for the appearance of a book which puts Blake back on the rails again and links him, as you do so unobtrusively, with the twentieth century.

The very best to you both.

Leonard Isaacs   **2 October 1970**
Director, School of Music, University of Manitoba, Winnipeg, MB

*In reply to Isaacs who reports (24 September 1970) that he is using Frye's third, fourth, and fifth Massey lectures (*The Educated Imagination*) as a way of helping his students understand musical meaning and make musical judgments.*

Dear Mr. Isaacs:

Thank you very much for your kind letter, which I was naturally delighted to receive. I have been very impressed by the number of musicians who have been concerned with the problem of meaning in music, and I have talked to some who have become interested in the applications to music of my own theories. One reason why this interests me is that I think my tastes in music were established in my own life even earlier than my literary tastes, and I occasionally have the feeling that I am really writing about music rather than literature. In my bigger and more complex book, *Anatomy of Criticism*, I even make the suggestion that I am trying to produce a grammar of rudiments for literature corresponding to those already available in music.[383] The question of the social significance in music is a much more elusive one, and I have only been able to get hints here and there of what it might be. I should be extremely interested in any conclusions that you came to.

Sandra Djwa   **19 October 1970**
Department of English, University of Alberta, Edmonton, AB

In reply to Djwa's query about her approach to E.J. Pratt's religious views.

Dear Dr. Djwa:

Thank you very much for your letter. Your general approach seems to me to be safe enough: I am not trying to defend Pratt's orthodoxy, only to point out that the heavy-handed melodrama between an orthodox dragon and a secularist St. George is not good enough for him, but you are unlikely to caricature the situation in this way. As for Wundt, I think Irving had in mind something more in the field specifically of his theory of perception,[384] but I don't know, and you certainly seem to have looked into the matter.

With all best wishes, and looking forward to your publication.

Lawrence J. Clipper   **21 October 1970**
Indiana University, South Bend, IN

In response to Clipper's inquiry (14 October 1970) about whether Frye knew of courses based on Anatomy of Criticism. *Clipper anticipated using the* Anatomy *as the basis for a course for secondary-school teachers.*

Dear Professor Clipper:

Thank you very much for your letter. I am deeply grateful for what you say of my work and am delighted if it is of any use to you. The *Anatomy* has actually been used a good deal as the basis for courses, particularly in Graduate School. I found this out by casual contacts rather than by correspondence and in many cases I have forgotten the names of people who have been trying to base a teaching course on the book. But I do know that such courses have been given at Cornell, at Nebraska, at Trinity College, Hartford, at Illinois, and at several of the summer NDEA courses. There have also been quite a number of books containing anthologies of the four major mythoi. If you write to Mr. Ronald Campbell, c/o Harcourt, Brace and Jovanovich, Third Avenue, New York, he could supply you with the names of some text books based on this principle.

Once again, may I express the great pleasure that your letter has given me.

Elizabeth L. Wood   **29 October 1970**
Elmira, ON
   In reply to Wood's query (25 October 1970) "whether or not the boy 'Simon' in Golding's Lord of the Flies *is a Christ symbol."*

Dear Mrs. Wood,
   I think I should hesitate to call any character a "Christ figure," unless the story in which such a figure appears shows a running parallel with the New Testament story and characters, or is an allegorical transcription from the gospel model. The *Lord of the Flies* is not that, but of course it does have religious references and dimensions. Simon's solitary trips up the mountain, and his scapegoat and sacrificial role are certainly borrowed from the story of Christ, but that in itself is not enough to make him a Christ figure: it simply indicates the larger resonance of the story.

Paul Ricoeur   **2 November 1970**
Université de Montréal, Montréal, QC
   In reply to Ricoeur's letter of 27 October 1970, expressing regret that during his recent visit to Toronto he was unable to meet Frye.

Dear Professor Ricoeur,
   Thank you very much for your note. I was very greatly disappointed to have to be absent for your lecture, as I had read *The Symbolism of Evil* with the greatest admiration and was much looking forward to hearing you speak. I understand however that the lecture is available in French, and if so I shall ask Mr. Mueller to look it up for me.
   I hope I shall be less delinquent when you come to visit us again. Meanwhile, may I thank you very sincerely for coming to us and for delivering a lecture of which I have heard the very highest praise.

Fanny Campbell   **3 November 1970**
New York City, NY
   In response to Campbell's letter (22 October 1970), addressed to "Helen and Norrie" and enclosing Charles Reich's long article "The Greening of America," which appeared in the New Yorker, *26 September 1970.*

Dear Fanny:
   Thank you very much for your note and for the copy of the *New Yorker* article which I read with interest. I think his discussion of the corporate state and all the conflicts of what he calls Consciousness I and Consciousness II were very good.[385] So good, in fact, that I was very disappointed when Consciousness III turned into simple-minded cooings about nice kids in bell-bottomed trousers.[386] The nice kids are there, and I hope they are as important as he says. But a lot of other things are there too.
   You asked about my sermon in the Merton College Chapel, and I am sending you a copy. I have no wish to conceal this side of my activities: I just find it unusually difficult to talk about.
   The best to you both.

Ralph Cohen   **16 November 1970**
Editor, *New Literary History*, University of Virginia, Charlottesville, VA
   In response to Cohen's request (9 November 1970) for permission to publish Frye's talk,

"Mythology and Revelation," presented as one of the "Seven Lectures on Hermeneutics" at the University of Toronto.

Dear Mr. Cohen,

Thank you very much for your letter. It catches me in my usual flounder: I gave my lecture from headings only, without any manuscript, and I am not sure that I can find time to write it out during this term. What I had planned to do was to use it as a starting point for a series of three lectures that I have to give at McGill next year at a special foundation. I am sorry about this: all I can say is that my approach to the subject of hermeneutics is such a very free-wheeling one that it perhaps would not fit very well into your special issue in any case.

John MacQueen   23 November 1970
School of Scottish Studies, University of Edinburgh, Edinburgh, Scotland

In reply to MacQueen's request (6 November 1970) for Frye to recommend candidates for the Regis Professor of English Literature at the University of Edinburgh, the oldest chair of English in the world.

Dear Professor MacQueen,

Thank you for your letter. One difficulty about suggesting names is that of age. The Edinburgh Chair is a very distinguished one, and most of the people whom one would think of immediately—such people as Clifford Leech or Kathleen Coburn here, [Alfred] Harbage or [Harry] Levin in Harvard, [Cleanth] Brooks or [William K.] Wimsatt at Yale, [Lionel] Trilling at Columbia, and the like—are of an age which would bring you back to the same problem of choosing a successor in another two or three years. There is also the point that the more senior the scholar is, the less movable he normally is.

At a slightly younger level there is Geoffrey Hartman at Yale, and Maynard Mack. Hartman has still to find himself, but I think he is potentially a scholar of very great distinction. Hillis Miller of Johns Hopkins also has a very fine record of production, but I should not place him on quite the same level. In Canada about the only person I could think of would be Balachandra Rajan, now at the University of Western Ontario. In his more recent work on Milton and Yeats, there is a quality of insight, even of wisdom, that I find very impressive.

I don't know whether this kind of random suggestion is of any use to you or not. As for my own candidacy, it would of course be a very great honour to be considered for such a Chair, but you are perhaps right in feeling that I have really committed myself to the Canadian environment.

It was very pleasant to have seen you in Pakistan,[387] and I hope you will be at Istanbul next summer,[388] where I plan to be myself.

Peter Dwyer   24 November 1970
The Canada Council, Ottawa, ON

The matter raised in Frye's letter was resolved. Dyer wrote on 29 December 1970 that monies not used reverted to the general fund but that if Frye had a plan of research the Canada Council would be pleased to extract the funds again and make them available to him. Alternatively, Frye could apply for another full $8,000 award. On 4 January 1971 Frye wrote to Dwyer, "Thank you very much for your most friendly letter and helpful answer to my question, which lays a somewhat disturbing ghost to rest. As always, I am greatly impressed by the Council's generosity and goodwill."

Dear Peter:

Seeing you the other day reminded me that I am in a rather silly position in regard to the Canada Council and would like to ask your advice about it.

Seven years ago, in 1964, I applied for a Senior Fellowship to the Canada Council, as part of the financing for getting a year off. I got the Fellowship and the year off, and there are something like five books as a result which express thanks to the Canada Council in their prefaces, at least three of them published. During the year, I stayed at home, working in my own study, and never realized until some time later that I had actually collected only half of the money I was awarded. As soon as I realized this, I wrote to suggest postponing the rest of the award until the next time I could get leave of absence. But now that I have been set up as a University Professor, with a secretary and a research associate, there is really little point in my taking a year off. Do you think I should continue doing nothing at all about this situation, or that I should embark on a more energetic plan of campaign?

Geoffrey H. Hartman   1 December 1970

Department of English, Yale University, New Haven, CT

In response to Hartman's having sent Frye a copy of Beyond Formalism: Literary Essays 1958–1970 *(New Haven: Yale University Press, 1970).*

Dear Geoffrey:

I was delighted to get the copy of *Beyond Formalism,* which I am busy reading now. Not unnaturally, I read with greatest relaxation the essays which are not about me.[389] I am also reading some of them with the pleasure of recognition. My only disappointment is that the lecture on *Endymion,* given here, about which I heard so many good things, is apparently not included. But there will always be another book.

With all best wishes.

Hugo McPherson   7 December 1970

Montreal, QC

After a teaching at McGill, Manitoba, British Columbia, Toronto, Yale and Western Ontario, McPherson joined the National Film Board of Canada in 1967 as Film Commissioner. He had recently resigned (1970) to direct the Graduate Program in Communications at McGill University.

Dear Hugo,

Thank you very much for your letter. Of course I should be delighted to see you when you are in Toronto: perhaps we could have lunch together some day after Christmas, as you will be near the College.

Apart from how pleasant it would be to have you here, I feel that you are probably right in committing yourself to McGill. It seems on the whole the most logical place for you at the moment, what with Grierson[390] being there and other NFB [National Film Board] connections. My own feeling is that the separatist movement in Quebec has to some extent passed its meridian, and that the automatic economic connections with the rest of Canada will be taking over, much as the British connections took over in Ireland.

The very best to Louise and yourself.

D.W. McGibbon   8 December 1970

Toronto, ON

In reply to McGibbon's having sent Frye (22 December 1970) a copy of Alex Comfort's review of Kathleen Raine's William Blake, *which had appeared in* The Guardian Weekly.

Dear Don,

Thank you very much for the review of Kathleen Raine's book, which I had not seen. I read her book years ago for a publisher and made some fairly destructive criticisms: it is a lot better since she has rewritten it, but I still think it's full of baloney. However, reviewers don't know the difference, especially British reviewers.

Love to Pauline and yourself from us both.[391]

Peter Van Toorn   18 December 1970
Montreal, QC

In reply to Van Toorn's request (30 November 1970) for Frye to read and comment on his poetry.

Dear Mr. Van Toorn,

Thank you very much for *Leeway Grass*,[392] which I have read with interest and enjoyment. I think I prefer the longer and more cerebral poems, like "Swinburne's Garden," best, as you have more room to expand there. I am also very pleased at your interest in Tibullus, who is a greatly neglected poet, even Ezra Pound not being much interested in him.

I also liked *The Derelict Room*, for the same reasons, that gave you room to expand and develop your ideas. As compared to the other poems in the published volume, the rhythm at times gets a trifle facile, though that is very difficult to avoid in this type of free verse structure. But when it tightens up it becomes very eloquent.

I am sorry to have taken so long to reply, but such a mass of material comes across my desk these days that it is usually many months before I can pick any of it up.

Susan Glicksohn   21 December 1970
Toronto, ON

In reply to Glicksohn's inquiry (15 December 1970) about Frye's interest in science fiction. She encloses a copy of a science-fiction magazine, Energumen, *edited by her and her husband Mike, and she wonders whether it might be possible to institute a college course in science fiction. Glicksohn was a Ph.D. student at the University of Toronto.* Energumen *was nominated for a Hugo Award in 1971.*

Dear Mrs. Glicksohn,

Thank you for your letter and for the copy of your magazine, which I have read with interest. My interest in science fiction is of a fairly casual type, as I have very little time to read much of it. I am interested in all forms of literature that seem to show clear connexions with mythology, and twenty years ago science fiction seemed to be about the liveliest and most interesting literary genre from this point of view. It has not, so far as I can see, really fulfilled its promise, but one has hopes.

I have several colleagues who are interested in science fiction, in much the same rather relaxed way that I am. At Victoria I think particularly of David Knight, who has written a very good science fiction novel that I hope will be soon published. I should think that the only way of getting a science fiction course into the curriculum would be for a member of the Department to offer one of the new courses that are open to students of all Colleges, and usually reflect a special interest on the part of the person giving it. These are called 370 and 470 courses at present. Innis College is also experimenting with courses of film and other subjects which are not featured in the regular curriculum.

Mrs. D. Lawrence   **7 January 1971**
Willowdale, ON

In response to Lawrence's request (4 January 1971) for assistance in writing a paper on Twelfth Night *based on Frye's definition of comedy: "A comedy is not a play which ends happily, it is a play in which a certain structure is present, whether we or the cast or the author feel happy about it or not." Lawrence said she was confused by what Frye meant by "author."*

Dear Mrs. Lawrence,

When I speak of comedy as a play with a certain structure rather than a certain mood, I am referring to the fact that some plays may be extremely light-hearted or festive in tone, others dark, sardonic or bitter, and yet both may be comedies. When I speak of an author, I mean primarily the kind of author whose attitude to his plays is easy to see. This is particularly true of, for example, Aristophanes, whose comedies sometimes depict the triumph of things we know he was plugging for, and sometimes the triumph of what he clearly regarded as absurd. Similarly with Bernard Shaw, who calls one group of his comedies "unpleasant" and another group "pleasant." We also know about Shaw's attitude from his prefaces. We know nothing directly about Shakespeare's attitudes, but the difference in tone and mood between *All's Well That Ends Well* and *A Midsummer Night's Dream* is clear enough. *Twelfth Night* is a very good example of the way in which we have to go by structure rather than mood. Most people say that it is a light-hearted and good humoured comedy, but I have seen it done at Stratford as a very dark and bitter comedy, and it seemed to be equally convincing. It is quite possible to regard Sir Toby Belch either as a jovial companion or as a slob. What Shakespeare thought we don't know, probably both things at once.

Bruce Rusk   **8 January 1971**
Ontario Institute for Studies in Education, Toronto, ON

In reply to Rusk's having sent Frye his ideas for a curriculum center.

Dear Mr. Rusk.

Thank you for the proposal for a new centre for Urban Alternatives in Education, which I have read with interest. As you know, I was a charter member of the Ontario Curriculum Institute, which was set up, first to examine the rationale of curriculum in various subjects, and intended to go on from there to a much broader study of educational alternatives. When OISE was founded, the executive of the OCI decided to vote for their own absorption into it. Robin Harris, Roy Sharp and myself protested against this, on the ground that the OCI was doing the kind of job that the OISE could not really replace. We were regarded at the time as somewhat offensive nuts. Naturally I am very interested in the feeling that there could be a new centre established, and I should be delighted to see you director of it. May I suggest that you call it The Ontario Curriculum Institute.

Martin Wolfson   **18 January 1971**
Brooklyn, NY

In reply to a series of questions by Wolfson (7 January 1971) about Frye's The Modern Century. *He found the book to be "superb," but asked why Frye did not have sections devoted to philosophical revolutions, mathematical logic, logical empiricism, logical analysis, linguistic analysis, philosophy of science, philosophy of art, and the mind-body-consciousness-language issue. He adds, incidentally, "I know when I pick up a book by Northrop Frye I am guaranteed masterliness and masterfulness."*

Dear Mr. Wolfson,

Thank you very much for your note. The main reason for the omission of the topics you list is my own ignorance of them. There is also another reason: the fact that a small book containing three public lectures has to unify itself around a relatively restricted area if it is to be intelligible to either the oral or the reading audience. This is not to deny the relevance of the subjects you mention to the theme of the book.

Lucas Longo   **24 February 1971**
Brooklyn, NY

In reply to Longo's offer to send Frye a copy of his first novel, The Family on Vendetta Street *(New York: Doubleday, 1968; paperback ed., 1971).*

Dear Mr. Longo,

Thank you for your letter. I should be pleased to receive your novel, though it is only fair to say that so much material comes into my office that I cannot do any sort of critical justice to more than a small fraction of it. This is not laziness, stupidity or lack of interest on my part, but simply the tremendous improvement in the efficiency of communications, along with the tremendous extension of verbalizing.

Lucas Longo   **5 March 1971**
Brooklyn, NY

In reply to Longo's letter responding to Frye's previous letter (24 February 1971). Longo insists that he had written an important novel, and says he is aware his letter may have been in poor taste or an invasion of privacy.

Dear Mr. Longo,

There is no question about any invasion of privacy or poor taste. It is simply that the number of critical judgments I have to make, divided by the amount of time that I have for them, is so large that I no longer have any confidence in my own ability to respond adequately to a great deal of what comes to me. What I get is not junk by any means; it consists mainly of poetry, fiction, and critical monographs from friends, former students and writers who have simply heard of me, and which I get in all stages from original manuscripts to books from publishers who would like publishable comments. I am saying only that my ability to respond adequately as a critic very frequently has no relation to the value or merit of what is sent me, and that this is true for reasons beyond my direct control.

Pauline McGibbon   **30 March 1971**
Toronto, ON

In reply to McGibbon's letter of 4 March 1971 saying that she and her husband will not be in Ottawa to see Frye receive the Molson Award and reminding him of the earlier fuss at Victoria College about liquor ands brewery stocks. McGibbon, like Frye, was a 1933 graduate of Victoria. In 1974 she became Ontario's first woman lieutenant governor. The Molson prize was awarded by the Canada Council for the Arts from funds provided by the Molson Foundation for outstanding contributions to the arts, humanities, social sciences, or national unity.

Dear Pauline,

I understand from Jay [Macpherson] that you are back from your vacation now, so I wanted to thank you for your very kind note. Yes, it is a big relief not to have to worry about repercussions over Brewery stocks any more. I hope that my thirty years of unflinching vice may have done something to alter the mood at Victoria.

Apparently Anansi did not have the loss it thought it had at first: the books were in big cartons, and the water damage extended only a little way.[393] In any case my own book was not in stock at the time. I was just about to write Dennis a sympathetic note when he turned up with a presentation copy.[394]

The very best to you and Don[395] from us both.

Viola Pratt   **30 March 1971**

Toronto, ON

In reply to Viola (Mrs. E.J.) Pratt's congratulating Frye for having received the Molson Prize.

Dear Vi,

Thank you very much for your most kind letter. Yes, I think Ned would have been pleased, and also by no means unwilling to have a Brewery the source of the money. He is as much alive to me as he ever was, and always will be.

I was delighted to see how much success Claire's work has had, and what a very large and loyal turn-out there was that Sunday afternoon.[396]

With love to you both from us both.

Brian Coates   **31 March 1971**

Eastbourne, Sussex, England

In reply to Coates's undated letter asking whether Frye had had time to review some of his research, which he had mailed in November 1970. Coates was teaching at the Eastbourne College of Education, Sussex, England.

Dear Mr. Coates:

Thank you for your letter. I did receive your papers on [Joyce's] Bloom, on the Demonic Vision, and on the introduction to your research, and have read them with interest. Of course I have no difficulty with this way of thinking, so perhaps I am not the most valuable critic.

I think one should keep in mind, when dealing with modern literature, that the mythical map of the universe is much more ambiguous than it was before the Romantic period. For Dante, heaven was up there, hell down there, and consequently all myths of descent were likely to have a sinister or demonic implication. In modern times, the poles of the mythical universe are not heaven and hell, nor are the poles consistently associated with certain spatial projections. The two poles are alienation and identity. In some writers, including Blake and Shelley, the pole of alienation is associated with the sky, and the pole of identity with a submerged world like Atlantis. It is quite possible to have a demonic descent theme, as the one in *Heart of Darkness* or the *Waste Land*. But it is equally possible to have a journey to the deep interior in search of identity. It is only in this latter case that the theme of rebirth is really built into the mythical structure. The theme of rebirth may of course also be expressed by the theme of eternal recurrence, as it is in Yeats and in *Finnegans Wake*. And of course recurrence may be looked at in two ways: as an ironic unending cycle or as an image of recreation and the making of all things new. In *Finnegans Wake* it is unmistakably both; Yeats warbles on the point, partly because he was trying to listen to "instructors" who didn't know what they were talking about.

I hope this may be helpful as a guideline. In any case you seem to know very well what you are about, and all I have to say is good luck with the rest of the voyage.

I am returning your papers, along with a letter addressed to you, which I am sorry to have kept for so long. Naturally the postal strike is also responsible for the delay.

Andrew Brink 1 April 1971

Greensville, ON

In reply to Brink's letter (27 March 1971), thanking Frye for his address at McMaster University on 24 March on "Motives for Metaphors" Brink remarks that he "was sorry not to be able to say more about [his] venture with F. Crews' essay on psychoanalysis and literature which is to appear as a review in the Queen's Quarterly.*" Brink was a member of the English Department at McMaster.*

Dear Andrew:

Thank you very much for your most thoughtful letter. I should be glad to see your review of Crews when it appears, and I am anxious naturally to be impartial. So far, I am deeply suspicious of all attempts to explain kinks in writing by kinks in writers. My own approach has always been what is now being called phenomenological. That is, I am concerned not with intention but with intentionality. I would take a lot of convincing before I could believe that what a work of literature reveals about its writer can then be thrown back to reveal still more about the work of literature, but I don't have a closed mind on the subject. It's as only that Crews' articles failed to open it.[397]

The very best to you both.

Hugo McPherson 1 April 1971

Montreal, QC

In reply to McPherson's congratulating Frye for having received the Canada Council's Molson Prize. McPherson, who had recently resigned from the National Film Board to direct the Graduate Program in Communications at McGill University, had been appointed to the Governor General's Literary Awards committee, administered by the Canada Council.

Dear Hugo,

Thank you very much for your letter and your congratulations. Having once been on the Governor General's Committee, I can understand the difficulties in arriving at a reasonable award in the non-fiction category. During the time I was on it, there was usually only one rather pedestrian academic book to be considered in either language. This was apart from the fact that I had to strike off four or five books of my own as ineligible. Speaking purely on the question of procedure, I am not very keen on dropping a book for consideration on a rumor that the author is getting something else: this kind of saw-off is rather below the dignity of a Governor General's Committee. But the Committee has a very difficult and thankless job, as I found to my cost.

The very best to Louise and yourself.

Edward F. Sheffield 1 April 1971

Higher Education Group, University of Toronto

In reply to Sheffield's note of congratulations (29 March 1971) on Frye's having received one of the Molson prizes, awards for outstanding contributions to the arts, humanities, social sciences, or national unity.

Dear Ted,

Thank you very much for your most kind note. I was naturally very pleased to get the award, especially at it came at the same time as the government turned one of their taxation thugs loose on me in order to squeeze another $2,000 out of me. Private business giveth, and government taketh away: blessed be private business!

Allton Dryden   **8 April 1971**
Bible Hill, NS

In reply to Dryden, an elementary school classmate of Frye's in Moncton, NB. After having seen a news story in Maclean's *about Frye, Dryden had written (2 April 1971) to congratulate him and reestablish contact.*

Dear Allton:

Thank you very much for your letter: I was delighted to hear from you and to get the news of you. I am sorry we didn't meet when I was at Acadia, but that was a somewhat hectic time.[398] I was teaching at Berkeley in California, and not only had to cross the continent to get the degree from Acadia but I also had to cope with an Air Canada strike, so I was fairly groggy by the time I got there.

I don't often get to the Maritimes these days: both of my parents have been dead for a long time and there is nothing of a personal nature to bring me down. On the Acadia visit I saw James Davidson, and on a recent visit to Moncton, in connexion with the CRTC [Canadian Radio-Television Commission], which I am now attached to, I phoned Jack Grainger. Otherwise, I have not kept up with my Maritime friends as well as I should like to, though occasionally I get letters like yours that remind me very pleasantly of earlier days.

The very best to you, and I trust that your heart condition is not too confining a one. I know the name of Professor Dryden at Buffalo but have not met him personally,[399] so I am not sure what his background is. Dryden is of course a very famous name in English literature.

Bert O. States   **15 April 1971**
Department of English, Cornell University, Ithaca, NY

In reply to States's having sent Frye a copy of his Irony and Drama *(Ithaca: Cornell University Press, 1971).*

Dear Professor States,

Thank you very much for the book: it was most thoughtful of you to send it to me and I am greatly looking forward to reading it. Meanwhile, I am delighted to see that it is a book growing essentially out of Kenneth Burke. I had been worried for a long time because Burke did not seem to me to be a kind of influence that he ought to be, and I am delighted to see that you are an exception.

With best wishes.

John Frye Bourne   **3 May 1971**
Rose Hill, Sidbury, Sidmouth, Devon, England

In reply to Bourne's request (17 January 1971) for information about the Frye genealogy. Bourne's letter was sent to Frye in care of Methuen and Company, publishers of the British edition of The Stubborn Structure. *Bourne had run across Frye's name in a review of that book in a London newspaper.*

Dear Mr. Bourne:

Thank you very much for your letter. I really know very little about my family, but I have always understood that a Puritan preacher named John Frye left Andover Hampshire, somewhere around 1630 and founded Andover, Massachusetts. There were Fryes on both sides of the Revolutionary War, but most of the family remained in New England. The town of Fryeburg in Maine is named after them. I have always understood that this Puritan family was quite distinct from the Quaker Fry family around Bristol, who produced not only chocolate but Elizabeth Fry, Roger Fry and Christopher Fry.

OXFAM Canada   June 1971

In reply to a request (18 June 1971) by Emilio del Junco, a Toronto architect, for Frye to write a letter appealing for funds for Pakistani relief. Frye's letter was mailed to OXFAM Canada, Toronto, for distribution to people in the art community.

This letter is written on behalf of OXFAM Canada, and is an appeal to you for funds to help the refugees in East Pakistan. It is earnestly hoped that you will make whatever contribution you can, however small or large, to mitigate, so far as you can, one of the most appalling situations of human agony in the world.

This is an appeal made purely on the basis of human compassion and has no political significance whatever. It is merely assumed that you, who have committed your life to what is creative in humanity, will have an especial concern for whatever destroys that creativity and the happiness that results from it.

Janice Castro   18 June 1971

Life, Time & Life Building, Rockefeller Center, NY

Castro had been a student of Frye's when he was teaching at the University of California, Berkeley, during the time of the violent student protests in 1968. She served as his teaching assistant, organizing discussion groups and the like. After graduating, Castro worked for Time-Life in New York City and went on to have a distinguished career in journalism. She and Frye kept in touch by correspondence until 1977.

Dear Janice,

Thanks very much for your letters: as always, I am delighted to hear from you. I shudder somewhat to think of you on a bicycle going through Manhattan, but if it is part of a trend perhaps you will be reasonably safe. In my opinion the bicycle represents the point at which the Industrial Revolution should have stopped, and it looks as though other people were coming around to the same point of view. I shall be most interested to know how your literary studies continue, and the Chaucer course sounds like an admirable one to be taking. I don't know if I told you of my own experience in trying to teach Milton at Columbia during the summer. As nothing is air conditioned in Columbia, and as it was as hot as the inner lid of hell, I had to open all the windows, which let in riveting machines, construction machines, carpenters' hammers, low flying planes, and, to top it off, hysterical birds, of a kind that only New York can produce. What I discovered was that a shouted lecture used up far more material than a spoken one, because every sentence had to be an epigram.

Love from us both and from Jane.[400]

Albert C. Labriola   6 July 1971

Department of English, Duquesne University, Pittsburgh, PA

In reply to Labriola's having sent Frye (29 June 1971) an offprint of his article on Samson Agonistes, *motivated by Frye's discussion of Samson in* Anatomy of Criticism *and "The Typology of* Paradise Regained.*" The article, "Divine Urgency as a Motive for Conduct in* Samson Agonistes,*" appeared in* Philological Quarterly *50 (January 1971): 99–107.*

Dear Professor Labriola,

Thank you very much for your letter and for the offprint, which I have read with great interest. It seems to me that the word "dispensation" is the word which connects Samson's marriage to the woman from Timnah and his decision to go to a heathen temple to take part in its rites.[401] Dispensation of this sort is the nearest, for Milton, that a man under the law can get to experiencing the freedom of the gospel. As for the marriage to Dalilah, I imagine Milton would have had in his mind the parallel with Hosea.

It was most pleasant to hear from you. I am not sure when I shall be in the Pittsburgh area again, as I have been there twice, once to the University and once to Carnegie Tech.

Al Purdy   7 July 1971
Ameliasburgh, ON

In response to Purdy's having asked Frye, somewhat apologetically, for a letter of recommendation. Purdy indicated he enjoyed Frye's The Bush Garden *but thought the title no longer as applicable as it once was. Purdy was a popular and important poet, referred to by some as "the unofficial poet laureate" of Canada.*

Dear Al Purdy,

Thank you very much for your letter: it was most pleasant running into you in Ottawa.[402] The books are sent back with this.[403] I think "The Bush Garden" is perhaps more suitable to a book of essays that date mostly from the 40's and 50's, when Canadian literature was beginning to get out of the bush. Also it's more suitable to the strongly historical tone of some of the longer articles. If the book were more contemporary I certainly would have looked for a different title.

Naturally I'd be glad to recommend you whenever you like. I think, as a result of serving on some Canada Council Committees, that letters of reference are genuinely helpful: they mean that the committee is not depending wholly on personal knowledge, and consequently on personal predilection. I agree that it is a nuisance for applicants to be constantly asking for letters, but we have to think of all the young people in Ottawa who would die of frustration if they didn't have letters on file.

Floss Pratt   19 July 1971
The Agnes Pratt Home, St. John's, NL

In reply to an undated letter from Floss (Florence) Pratt, E.J. (Ned) Pratt's sister and the last surviving of the eight Pratt siblings. She sends news of her relatives and reports on having dizzy spells.

Dear Floss,

I was very pleased to hear from you, only sorry that you're not feeling better. I know what a misery dizziness can be, because Helen has had a good deal of trouble with her middle ear, and some time ago fell down the attic steps and knocked herself out. It was a bit embarrassing having to take her to a University convocation with a black eye.

I don't have much news of the University at the moment. There has been quite a to-do over some temporary camps for wandering youth on the campus. What with the Board of Governors on the way out, the President retired and replaced by an acting President, and it being the middle of the summer vacation, things can get quite confusing. I spend quite a bit of time these days running up to Ottawa to attend meetings of the Canadian Radio Television Commission. The Newfoundland representative is Dr. Gordon Thomas, who is connected with the Grenfell Mission in the north. He sometimes comes to meetings and has to fly back for an operation.[404] The Commission has just issued a rather important statement on cable policy that I hope will mean improved service in more isolated parts of the country.

We are going to stay here for the summer and then go to Istanbul for a conference.[405] We shall be away about three weeks. Love from us both.

Margaret Avison   9 August 1971
Toronto, ON

Avison's letter to Frye is not extant — or perhaps Frye's response followed a personal request. His letter makes clear that she wanted him to review a student paper and the grade it was given.

Dear Margaret,

I have looked at Anne MacKay's analysis of the Lowell poem with great interest. In the series of numbered comments I recognize the familiar symptoms of an unusually good and interested student. This is what I have come to call the "kaleidoscope" phase, when a wide variety of reading produces a sense of a great many patterns just on the point of coming together. Whenever I find a student in this situation, I tell him or her to keep going until things begin to come into a sharper and clearer focus. It seems to me that this is a keen and profoundly interesting student who should be encouraged if at all possible to keep going.

She was asked, of course, to do a close reading of a single poem, and such reading is simply not in her mental horizon at present. For this reason the mark given her is technically quite justifiable. At the same time one has to realize that good students cannot always do well what they are assigned to do, because of other forces working in their minds. For this reason the mark given her is not in my opinion an index of her actual abilities.

Robert M. Jordan   August 9, 1971
Department of English, University of British Columbia, Vancouver, BC

In response to Jordan's request that Frye recommend a speaker for an educational conference.

Dear Professor Jordan,

Thank you for your letter. I gather that your immediate problem is that of a keynote speaker rather than of the concluding summarizing speaker. The keynote speech seems to me a trifle over Collie's head,[406] and I should think that Claude Bissell might be a real possibility. He is moving in the opposite direction from [Ernest] Sirluck, and may feel that his new freedom from administration will enable him to think more continuously about theoretical problems. Another possibility is Douglas LePan, who has also retired from administrative problems, is also in English, and has taken an active role in many educational conferences. Another possibility would be Murdo MacKinnon of Guelph, who is always a good lively speaker. Millar MacLure seems to me a good suggestion for the concluding paper.[407]

It seems to me one major problem is the breakdown of the old *Wissenschaft* conception of humanistic studies, which was founded on a false analogy with science. The scientist works a great deal with offprints and abstracts; the humanist tends to wait for the book. The implication is that in the humanities problems get stuck together. This is the major difficulty, of course, with the Ph.D. thesis, which in the humanities can hardly be prevented from becoming a full-scale book. Some of the old compartmentalized research projects can be taken care of by technological developments. For example, with computers, a concordance to a minor poet is no longer a lifetime commitment.

I understand from some scientists I have talked to that science itself is moving out of its compartmentalized period and is now turning increasingly to books and broader summary approaches. It would be interesting if Preston could deal with this from his point of view.

William V. Spanos   10 August 1971
State University of New York, Binghamton, NY

In reply to the letter by Spanos and Robert Kroetsch (30 July 1971), asking if Frye might contribute to their new journal boundary 2 *and requesting possible topics for the journal and possible contributors.*

Dear Mr. Spanos

Thank you very much for your letter. What you are doing in your new Journal seems to me very well worth doing, and I shall watch its development with interest. I entirely agree that the period since 1950 has been the beginning of an entirely new cultural age, and that such a journal could be of immense benefit to writers and critics anxious to get their bearings. I wish I could be equally positive about my own capacity to contribute to it, but I am deeply absorbed at the moment by several projects, which will take all my time for the foreseeable future. Anything else I can do is invariably on commission, and getting out of the commitments I have already accepted will in itself take me quite a while.

As for suggestions, it seems to me that your letter is full of them, and very good ones. It seems to me that science fiction is a rather significant field to explore, as much for its obvious weaknesses as for its strengths. Science fiction in the Western world is very largely a matter of missed opportunities: in the Soviet Union it seems to have a more genuine relation to their cultural developments, as it certainly ought to have in these days of space flights and moon landings. As for other countries, the one I know best is Canada, and there is a good deal of very lively writing, mainly in fiction, done by the younger people, and published by the younger publishers, especially Oberon, Anansi, and the New Press. I should also like to see some attention devoted to the topic of Marxism as a means of renewing traditional imagery and symbolism, as it operates in, for example, [Ferenc] Juhasz in Hungary. Then there is the emergence of what might be called guerrilla poetry, in [Daniel] Berrigan and others.

Gordon V. Boudreau   13 October 1971
Le Moyne College, Le Moyne Heights, Syracuse, NY

In reply to Boudreau's inquiry (13 October 1973) about possible readers for his manuscript on Thoreau, which has not received a sympathetic reading from editors.

Dear Mr. Boudreau:

Thank you very much for your letter. I am very sorry that your Thoreau manuscript has had a discouraging response, but it is always difficult for a new writer to get established, especially if he has anything original to say. So don't take the one refusal as final, but keep on sending the manuscript out until it finally hits the right reader. I should suggest the University Presses, because they are most likely to send the manuscript to readers who will have at least some kind of knowledge of the subject. It is true that there is probably a greater concentration of stupidity among Americanists than elsewhere in English literature, partly I suppose, because the approach is so sociological that they don't really read their texts, but use them as documents illustrating something else. I should say at once that I could not read the manuscript myself: it takes several months before I can pick up anything from my desk, and that would be a disheartening wait for you. If you want to send it to the Toronto Press, the man here who would probably read it is Lynen.

Hans Hauge   **13 October 1971**
Aaarhus C., Denmark

In reply to Hauge's query (1 October 1971) whether there is a connection between what Frye calls the two levels of nature, the Lutheran doctrine of two realms (the temporal and the spiritual), and the Marxist notion of two spheres (the economic and the natural).

Dear Mr. Hauge:

Thank you for your letter. My conception of two levels of nature has to do with the Medieval and Renaissance conception that man was placed in an upper level of nature (the Garden of Eden) which is still his natural home, and that he is now born into a lower nature which is "fallen." The question is what the means are that will help to raise man from one state to the other. There is general agreement that obedience to law, the sacraments of the church, the practice of moral virtue, are genuinely educational in this sense. There was less general agreement that the arts, including literature, are educational in this way. Sidney, Spenser, and Milton all maintained that they were. Coming the other way, this would mean that culture could be one of the means by which God reaches man. Even Luther himself seems almost to concede this as regards music.

It seems to me too that in the Hebrew and Christian tradition there is a strong emphasis on receiving the Word through the ear, in marked contrast to the emphasis of visual symbols that we find in paganism. The consequence of this is that the vision incorporated in the Word has to be internalized. This in turn means that culture is something to be created out of man rather than imitated from an external world. This is ultimately what Aristotle's "imitation" amounts to. And I think the Marxists are right on that point, their position being that of a Judeo-Christian heresy.

Sister Ruth Ellen   **19 October 1971**
St. Catherine's Training College, Maseru, Lesotho, Southern Africa

In reply to Sister Ruth Ellen's letter (17 September 1971), asking Frye whether there has been a book written on the topic of Christ as an archetype. Sister Ruth Ellen (Ruth Siddall) had been a graduate student of Frye's when she was at the University of Toronto from 1947 to 1949, and she had visited with Frye in 1965 at Victoria College.

Dear Ruth,

It was most pleasant to hear from you and to learn where you are and what you are doing. I am afraid however that I cannot be of very much concrete help about your problem. Of course I don't know the field well at first hand, but my impression is that there is no book on the subject of Christ as an existential archetype. That's why I have finally decided to write a book myself on the relation of the Bible to literary criticism. I have just come from McGill, where I gave three lectures on the subject to the Divinity School. I may say that I consulted some of them about your problem and got an equally negative response from them.

The very best to you in your work, and I hope some day you will be able to repeat the visit you made me sometime ago. I have never been in Africa, but it would be pleasant to go if anything could take me there.[408] At the moment I am pretty preoccupied with my teaching and with the state of communications in Canada, as I have just been made a member of the Canadian Radio Television Commission, which takes up a disconcerting amount of time and energy. I never knew there was so much paper in the world, even in Canada.

Stephen R. Graubard   **25 October 1971**

Editor, *Dædalus*, Harvard University, Cambridge, MA

    In response to Graubard's request (18 October 1971) for Frye to contribute an article to Dædalus *on the adequacy of institutional support for research.*

Dear Stephen:

    I have thought very carefully about your most kind letter, and it doesn't really seem to me that this is quite my cup of tea. Apart from all the people who say that I am not a scholar at all, I think I am one of the last survivors of an earlier age. I am not the kind of scholar that uses a big research library, nor am I well acquainted with anything more than the most obvious sources of support. In the course of a teaching career of about thirty-five years, I have had one full year off, on a Guggenheim, and another year partly off on a Canada Council [grant]. I have never worked at the big libraries, the Folger or the Huntington, and have got to the stage in my own work where I work best at home, with my own books about me, with a secretary to take care of all the load of correspondence. In short, a scholar who works with a pencil, a piece of paper, and a nervous twitch in the right wrist is not the right person to "reflect on the adequacy of the institutional supports that presently exist for research." As for my nationality, which you mention, I think there are certain social factors in Canada with predispose Canadian scholars to try to insert their view of their subject into their view of the universe. But I am not sure that this would be a subject of much value to the members of the conference. If you want a Canadian, I would suggest someone with a background of administrative experience, such as Claude Bissell here, or Ernest Sirluck of Manitoba, or John Deutsch of Queens.

    With apologies, genuine regrets, and best wishes.

Robert J. Heaman   **31 October 1971**

Department of English, Wilkes College, Wilkes Barre, PA

    In reply to Heaman's letter (2 October 1971) which asks Frye to explain what he meant in a paragraph of his essay, "The Keys to the Gates." He also requests some insight into how he might arrive at the apocalyptic vision that he finds in Frye, Shelley, Yeats, and Marvell.

Dear Mr. Heaman,

    Thank you for your letter. I don't have the Bloom book by me,[409] but the fourth paragraph from the end of my own essay is the one beginning "Los is not single creative power." This is a summary of the conception of Los as I outlined it in the eighth chapter (I think) of *Fearful Symmetry*. Our normal experience of time is that it annihilates everything: this is the experience that Blake calls the Spectre of Urthona. At the same time every consistent and contiguous creative life, whether it is creating in the arts or simply in ordinary social relations, has for its assumption, whether the person realizes it or not, the principle that a creative life in time is helping to build up something which is above time and does not go away. This assumption may come to the consciousness in the form of a specific experience, as it evidently did to Proust. But for the most part it is not a matter of knowing what other people don't know. It is rather a matter of being able and willing to do things that most people are not able or willing to do, or don't see the importance of doing.

Roger Shattuck   **2 November 1971**

Lincoln via Bristol, Vermont

    In reply to Shattuck's request that Frye read and comment on the draft of an essay on "The Humanities in Higher Education."

Dear Mr. Shattuck:

Thank you very much for your paper which I have read with great interest and general agreement. I suppose some of the bewilderment in modern humanities comes from the false analogies to business which are made at one end of the university, and the false analogies to democracy at the other. The former fallacy assumes that the university, instead of being a process which is, in Newman's phrase, its own end, must be a process with a product, like all other assembly lines. The product is assumed to be either the works of "productive scholarship," or students in the form of "trained minds." The conception of a university which is not essentially committed either to offprints or offspring is a difficult one to take in, as your paper says.

I think your paper, with some pulling together, is quite an impressive piece of writing, and I hope that you will not let it go stale, as your headnote suggests you may do.[410]

Where we met was in the Twentieth Century Conference at Michigan State University in, I think, 1963, or somewhere around there.[411] I had been an admirer of your *Banquet Years*[412] ever since it appeared.

Martin Amis   23 November 1971
Lemmons, Hadley Common, Barnet, Hertfordshire, England

In reply to Amis's inquiry (13 November 1971) about the possibility of doing graduate study at Toronto. Amis had graduated from Exeter College, Oxford, during the summer of 1970, and had heard Frye lecture at Oxford during his second year (1969–70).

Dear Mr. Amis:

Thank you very much for your letter. I am most pleased to hear that you would like to come to Toronto. I have applied for a sabbatical for next year (1972/73), so I shall not be available for that year. But after that I shall be back at work again. This is my first full sabbatical in twenty years, so it is a rather important matter for me.

I am sorry to have to tell you that you have missed the Canada Council deadline, but you could still write to the Admissions Office of the School of Graduate Studies in the University of Toronto. Ask them to send application forms and explain what kind of thing you are looking for. These have to be in by February 1. There are also teaching fellowships available, but for these you would need to apply to the chairmen of the undergraduate departments. These are: for University College, Professor Hugh MacCallum; for Victoria College (the college I am attached to), Professor David Hoeniger; for Trinity College, Professor Milton Wilson, for St. Michael's College, Professor D.J. Dooley. There are other colleges but two of them are in the sticks—that is to say, the suburbs—and one should avoid them if possible.[413]

You might also apply to "Admissions," Massey College, 4 Devonshire Place, Toronto 5, for a junior fellowship, if you are interested and unmarried.[414] The fees for this would be $1,200 for the year, but this would be probably much less than you would need to support yourself outside, and the conditions of life in the college are extremely pleasant. I am sending you a brochure.

With best wishes, and looking forward to seeing you.

Usher Caplan   24 November 1971
State University of New York at Stony Brook, Long Island, NY

In reply to Caplan's undated letter, asking what Frye meant in the Anatomy *by saying that the notion of fiction as falsehood is of no use to the literary critic. He also inquires about the place of Wayne Booth in Frye's critical scheme.*

Dear Mr. Caplan:

Thank you for your letter. The remark you refer to has to be taken in its context. The mere instinctive association of fiction with not telling the truth is of no use as a basis for the classification of prose forms. I was not intending to raise in that passage the nature of poetic truth. The latter would be related to the Aristotelian conception of form and content, according to which "truth" may be an attribute of content. The form which organizes it is neither true nor false in itself, but simply a mode of presentation.

It looks as though your question about Wayne Booth were concerned with his conception of the unreliable narrator is fiction. To me this device is an element in the ironic perspective, and raising it is a way of complicating the irony. *The Turn of the Screw* would be a straightforward ghost story if we could believe the governess: our difficulty in believing her is what creates the ironic tone. I much appreciate your interest.

Lydia Bodnar   25 November 1971
Toronto, ON

In reply to Bodnar's request (30 June 1970) for her poetry to be "evaluated by some recognized person."

Dear Miss Bodnar:

I am very sorry to have taken so long with your poems, but, apart from the fact that they arrived when I was in Oxford, I have such a heavy moving belt of reading to do that it takes many months before I can pick anything up off my desk. And even as it is I doubt that I have much to say that you don't already realize yourself. The poems are sensitive and highly intelligent, and almost any short passage, by itself, has a genuine feeling in it. Taken as a whole, the rhythm gets somewhat monotonous, giving the effect of prose sentences being cut up into free-verse strips. This is the kind of feature that eventually disappears with incessant practice. The Mother Goose poem seems to me to be the most completely realized in theme. It is also less dependent on conceptual argument, and points forward to a more complete realization through imagery.

Henry Weinfield   21 December 1971
New York, NY

Dear Mr. Weinfield,

Thank you very much for your letter, for the poem, and for the great honour of dedicating the poem to me.[415] I don't find it ironical that criticism should influence poetry, because a fair number of poets have spoken to me about being substantially helped in their creative work by my criticism. Some other poets have attacked me in tones which suggest some influence there too, even though a negative one.

I was most interested in your remark about a cycle of return to the confines of poetry. I have felt for a long time that what a great deal of the agitation in contemporary universities and elsewhere is all about is really a movement back from specialization and the intellectual division of labour towards a new period of enlarged perspectives and the building of mental bridges.

Johan Aitken   22 December 1971
Department of English, College of Education, Toronto, ON

In reply to Aitkens's having sent Frye copies of Wavelengths *(Dent, 1970), a series of textbooks based on Frye's literary modes for students in the elementary grades.*

Dear Johan,

Thank you very much for the copies of *Wavelengths*, which I have been reading with great interest. It took me a while to get on to the fact that they were not readers but writing manuals, and now that I have grasped this, I can appreciate very much better the ingenuity of your devices and the variety of things you refer to. I hope you don't mind if I send copies to the American publisher I spoke of, who is bringing out a series of text books, from Grade 7 to 12, based on the Frye cartwheel.[416] Naturally he would be interested in parallel ventures.

It has been a great encouragement to me to see how much genuine material gets into school readers now. A generation ago they were unbelievably prissy, and I think the resentment of young people in the last few years reflects the fact.

The very best to you both.

P.S. I still have the manuscript you sent me and if you would like it returned please let me know.

Robert Fulford   17 January 1972

Saturday Night Publications, Toronto, ON

In response to Fulford's review of The Critical Path — "It's Enormously Liberating to Read Our Leading Essayist," *Toronto Star 24 December 1971: 33.*

Dear Robert,

I am rather late in thanking you for your extremely generous review of *The Critical Path* in *The Star*, which I did not see until quite recently. I was very pleased and grateful to have a review which was based on a careful reading of the book: there are still people who think I am only making jokes when I say that much of our behavior consists in acting out certain literary stereotypes.

There doesn't need to be any secret about what I am doing for the CRTC [Canadian Radio-Television Commission]. Apart from listening to the hearings, and taking what part I can in the in camera discussions, I am supposed to be working out questions in the theory of communication with the CRTC's Research Department. This means a certain amount of monitoring of programmes, and some effort to see how my own conceptions of criticism can be adapted to the electronic media.[417]

With best wishes and renewed thanks.

René Wellek   21 January 1972

Department of Slavic Studies, Yale University, New Haven, CT

In reply to Wellek's having sent Frye a copy of his "American Criticism of the Last Ten Years," Yearbook of Comparative and General Literature *20 (1971): 5–14.*

Dear René:

Thank you very much for the offprint on American criticism, which naturally I have read with the greatest interest.

Incidentally, the church I am attached to is called the United Church of Canada* a much less ambitious title than the one you assign to it. I wish I did belong to the United Church of Christ, but I am afraid that is never likely to come into existence, at least as an organization.

*part of the point being that like I.A. Richards I am not American

Kenneth W. Graham   27 January 1972

Department of English, University of Guelph, Guelph, ON

In response to Graham's request (25 January 1972) for Frye, as general editor of the

College Classics series published by Macmillan, to consider his editing William Beckford's Vathek *for the series.*

Dear Professor Graham,

Thank you for your letter. Unfortunately the Macmillan series has gone down the usual spout. It was bought up by Odyssey Press, who sold it again to Bobbs-Merrill. I don't even know whether I am considered to be still General Editor of the series or not. I certainly don't want to be: I took on the job to encourage young Canadian scholars, and have no interest in its present development.

Bob Bossin   2 February 1972

Advisory Bureau, University of Toronto

In response to Bossin's undated note suggesting that Frye might be interested in attending a conference on madness hosted at the University of Toronto by the Students' Administrative Council. Bossin, who had attended the University of Toronto, receiving his Ph.D. from Rochdale College, was a consultant for the Council.

Dear Bob:

Thank you very much for the note on the madness conference. I am sorry that I have to be in the Maritimes while it is going on, as I should like very much to come and consult with all the other lunatics. I am afraid that I have to have the role of the Mad Hatter, sneaking out of the proceedings before the evidence is all in.

Ronald Bates   9 February 1972

Department of English, University of Western Ontario, London, ON

In response to Bates's having sent Frye a copy of his Northrop Frye *(Toronto: McClelland and Stewart, 1971).*

Dear Ronald:

I have not been able to thank you before for your book on me, because it has only just arrived. It is a very complete and concise job of summary, which gets the essence of what I have tried to say into a very brief compass. I only wish your publisher had seen fit to make a slightly better production job of it: compression is a virtue, but typographical compression added to it is not. I say this because I think the modest appearance of the book hardly impresses the casual reader with a sense of the amount of work and organization that has gone into it. I expect that the book will be used a good deal by students, and hence may be reprinted. If so, I suggest putting a note in telling the uninstructed reader where the chapter titles come from.[418]

I think you are the first person to write about me at any length who has been a student of mine, and that makes a good deal of difference to me, as people who have never studied with me are apt to get very curious notions about me as a kind of computer that, like the one in the *New Yorker* cartoon, disgorges "I think, therefore, I am" at the end of an immensely complicated process.

Thank you very much again, and the very best to Kirstie — or should I say the very best Kirstille?[419]

S.A. Ashraf   11 February 1972

Department of English, University of Karachi, Karachi, West Pakistan

Frye had met Ashraf in Pakistan at the FILLM Conference (September 1969) and later at the IAUPE Conference in Istanbul (August 1971). Ashraf, from Bangladesh, was head of the

English department at the University of Karachi but was finding it increasingly dangerous to be there because of the political turmoil between East Pakistan (Bangladesh) and West Pakistan. He therefore was seeking a temporary appointment outside the country. Frye proposed that four universities (Toronto, McGill, Queen's, and Saskatchewan) submit a joint proposal to the Canada Council to bring Ashraf to Canada for a year, so that he could spend several months at each institution. Frye also wrote to Dalhousie University and the University of New Brunswick on Ashraf's behalf.

Dear Ali Ashraf,

Thank you very much for *The New Harmony*,[420] which I have been reading with great interest. It seems to me that the book represents not so much a phenomenon of language as a culture: that is, many of the contributors seem to me to be, like Joseph Conrad, not so much non–English writers writing in English as writers in English literature domiciled in a different environment. I hope very much that Pakistan doesn't give up its connection with English, which would immensely deepen the range and significance of its literary imagination.

I don't know whether Doug Cherry[421] has come through with anything or not: in any case we both wish you the maximum of peace and quiet for the future.

Malcolm Ross   11 February 1972
Department of English, Dalhousie University, Halifax, NS

In response to Ross's having sent Frye a copy of his review of The Stubborn Structure, *which appeared in the* University of Toronto Quarterly *41 (Winter 1972), 170–3.*

Dear Mac,

The copy of the *Quarterly* has just come, with your extremely generous review in it, and I write to express my thanks and gratitude. You are very charitable about some features in me which are, as you recognize, not so much inconsistencies as unresolved tensions. Some of those perhaps will get added up in my next phase, wherever it takes me. Incidentally, Blake believed very deeply in original sin, and the salvationism I derive from him is not of the Shelleyan perfectibility type.

I managed to get down to Acadia last week, but Canadian travel in mid-winter is a bit of a fag.

The very best to you both, and thanks again.

Robert Denham   14 February 1972
Chicago, IL

In reply to Denham's queries about a number of details for a bibliography of Frye's writings he was compiling, including the reason one of Frye's stories was published in the Canadian Forum *under the pseudonym of Richard Poor. The ellipsis signals the omission of information Frye provided about several dozen particular items in the bibliography. Denham's list was published as* Northrop Frye: An Enumerative Bibliography *(Metuchen, NJ: Scarecrow Press, 1974).*

Dear Mr. Denham,

It was a great pleasure for me to receive your letter and bibliography, and I am naturally delighted and very grateful that you are doing this work. During the last few years I have become rather negligent about my bibliography, but you seem to have caught practically everything published. In fact, you reproduce a great many titles of things that I had forgotten having written, and a few that I wish I could forget.

Re Richard Poor: I submitted one or two "fables" to the Canadian Forum around 1940: one of them appeared in the same issue as a signed review of mine, and consequently the editor, who at that time was a girl of nineteen,[422] decided that my fable should go under the pseudonym of Richard Poor, which she invented. Nobody knew anything about this except the editor, the author, and the bibliographical detective squad of the Canadian Library Association. The result was that I got listed with this wretched pseudonym for years, and all because of a single skit three hundred words long....

I never know how exhaustive a bibliography should be, especially with the development of that snake in the grass the tape recorder. With me, the difference between writing and speaking from notes is a chalk-and-cheese difference, and when I'm asked to speak I often make it a condition that I am not to produce a manuscript. But of course when I turn up either a tape recorder is revolving somewhere or the CBC has gone into action, and *they* produce what purports to be a manuscript. Thus there now exists a speech of mine printed in the *Educational Courier*, Nov.-Dec. 1968, Vol. xxxix, No. 2, (listed as) "The Social Importance of Literature," pp. 19–23. The same magazine printed a speech in another issue which I am sending you: use your own judgement. Similarly with campus magazines. I recently wrote out a speech for the local alumni called "The Quality of Life in the Seventies," which was printed in the *University of Toronto Graduate*, Spring 1971, Vol. III, No. 5, pp. 38–48. But to this was added a speech called "Education and the Rejection of Reality," pp. 49–55, which, as the editor says, "consists of Dr. Frye's words as they came off the tape." This is one I know about, but I quite often hear about recorded speeches of mine that I haven't even seen, and didn't until then know existed. I think this is probably illegal, but the copyright law is in such a chaos that nobody really knows what is legal.

Well: if it would help you, I could make an exhaustive investigation into my files and turn up with whatever's there, such as Forum editorials and speeches of this half-written half-spoken kind. But I'll wait for a directive from you about what you want.

The same offer applies to the shipload of students' texts that have cut steaks out of the *Anatomy*: such things seem to me to be non-books, and I don't keep any record of them, but of course they keep coming across my desk, and I have to stow them somewhere, while looking for some unhappy university in an under-developed country I could bestow them on.

Once again, my thanks and gratitude.

Roy Daniells   **23 February 1972**
University of British Columbia, Vancouver, BC
    In reply to Daniells's letter (16 February 1972) asking for Frye's opinion of Morse Peckham's criticism. In his Man's Rage for Chaos *Peckham had criticized at some length Daniells's book* Milton, Mannerism and Baroque *(Toronto: University of Toronto Press, 1963).*

Dear Roy,
    Thank you for your note. Morse Peckham is, I think, at the University of Pennsylvania, and has written mainly on the Romantic poets. I came across him when I was writing my history of Blake scholarship,[423] but left him out because I didn't think his article on Blake really made its point. After that he worked out a conception of Romanticism in which he practically identified it with "Enlightenment." If you have handy the book on Romanticism that I edited for the English Institute, *A Reconsideration of Romanticism*, you will find some rather detached, not to say contemptuous, comments in Wellek's essay.[424] It would be harsh to say that Peckham is a phony, but I do think he makes rather a point of taking

up extreme or paradoxical positions. I haven't yet got hold of his new book which you mention [*Man's Rage for Chaos*], but I'll try to do so before I see you here. Which, needless to say, I am very much looking forward to doing.

Love to Laurenda from us both.

John Neubauer   24 February 1972
Case Western Reserve University, Cleveland, OH
In response to Neubauer's request for Frye to contribute a paper on Romanticism and science to a session at the Modern Language Association's 1971 meeting.

Dear Professor Neubauer:

Thank you very much for your letter and invitation. I have been tending to avoid the MLA ever since I got off the Executive Council, and the bigger and more political it gets the less inclined I am to revisit it.[425] For this reason I am afraid I cannot say that I am very likely to be there this coming Christmas. This is not any lack of interest in your topic, which seems to me a very interesting one, but part of a planned campaign to save my energies.

Robert Denham   9 March 1972
Chicago, IL
In reply to Denham's questions about unsigned editorials Frye had written for the Canadian Forum, *and other bibliographic matters. Denham had also asked Frye about possible publishers for his bibliography. The first ellipsis signals the omission of information Frye supplied about an early article in* Here and Now. *The second ellipsis is Frye's.*

Dear Mr. Denham,

It will take me a little while to go through my files and extract the other stuff, perhaps a couple of months, as I have to be away for most of April. But I gather there's no particular hurry at your end. The Ezra Pound editorial,[426] alas, is mine: I regret having written it, but we all make mistakes. The Dylan Thomas I'm pretty sure is not, but will check it. I also remember one on the death of H. G. Wells, which included a comment on Shaw....[427]

You say you are not sure how useful it is to list the original appearances of articles now readily accessible. But apart from usefulness and accessibility, it is surely of some importance to note when things first appeared. The fact that my discovery of the "anatomy" form is recorded in an article dated 1942 is of some interest. The reverse is also true. When Crews wrote those curious articles in the *New York Review of Books*,[428] he gave the date of the *Anatomy* as 1964, that being evidently the date of the reprint he was working with. It would have been better scholarly procedure to have given the correct date, even at the risk of having his reader infer that I had got rid of that book some time ago and might have got interested in other things since.

The *Anatomy* reprintings are quite a problem. I constantly get a permission form in the mail from Princeton, attached to a note saying that such things are wonderful to help advertise the book. There's a strong implication that they'd give permission even if I refused it. Some are collections of critical texts like those of Jack Bate or Hazard Adams[429]: they're serious books, and my inclusion there is of genuine significance in marking the absorption of the *Anatomy* into ordinary academic procedure. (A third collection of the same type, by Lipking and Litz of Princeton, is even more enterprising in its treatment of me, but avoids the *Anatomy*, they being the first, apparently, to discover that the *Anatomy* doesn't lend itself to anthologizing.)[430] On the other hand ... well, some years ago Oscar Williams was getting up an anthology, the gimmick of which was to print a well-known poem with a critical commentary on that poem attached. He wrote to me and said he had about three poems left, and would I do a commentary on Burns's *A Man's a Man For A' That*. I said no. Williams died (no connection), somebody else took the book over, and it appeared with Blake's *Mental Traveller*, followed by some remarks from the *Anatomy* which referred to the poem but weren't in any sense a commentary on it. Any unprejudiced person, reading that extract as my commentary on Blake's poem, would think I was in the last stages of schizophrenia. This permission was not referred to me at all: the permissions editor left shortly after, no doubt for good reasons, and I had only her successor to complain to. But I'm not sure that I'd have realized what was going on even if I had seen the permission. It's impossible to guard against such things unless one controls one's own publisher, like Eliot, but, as you can imagine, I'm not too keen on having that venture listed in my bibliography.

David Erdman's NYPL Bulletin would be a good bet, I should think; there are several Canadian publishers that run series of things on Canadian authors that might be interested. McClelland & Stewart has just issued a tiny booklet on me by Ronald Bates—the series was I think supposed to be partly bibliographical, though this one isn't particularly.[431] A leaflet came in the mail from another publisher I've forgotten promising a book on me: I hope the person assigned the job can spell my name better than they did. But I should think Gage as a good prospect as any. By the time you're ready to send it somewhere the situation should have cleared a bit. As for the other bibliography of writings about me, I have a notion that the real spate of that is just beginning, and that you will need a very firm cut-off date if you're to avoid distraction.

Kalipada Chakrabarti   15 March 1972
Midnapur, West Bengal, India

In response to several questions posed by Chakrabarti (4 March 1972): What does Keats mean by "fine excess"? What is meant by "Romantic exaggeration"? What does "reptilian classification" (Frye's phrase) mean? And what is the subject matter of The Return of Eden? *Chakrabarti was a post-graduate student at the University of Calcutta.*

Dear Mr. Chakrabarti,

Thank you for your letter. I think the remark of Keats means first of all, that great poetry impresses us as something beyond our own powers to create, hence "excess." Secondly, while the curious, the odd, the unusual, are features of minor art, in the very greatest poetry there must be some quality of recognition, some sense that this is the way things really are, however far out of our normal range of experience as such works as *King Lear* or *Paradise Lost* may be. I imagine that the remark about "exaggeration" refers to the same passage.

My remark about Classicism and Romanticism was really a joke: an ironic reference to the over-simplified teaching of this conception in our universities. That is, oversimplified teaching makes the Classicism cold and dry and intellectual, and the Romantic passionate and emotional, so I used two figures of the reptile and the mammal to describe this.[432]

The Return to [of] Eden published by the University of Toronto Press in 1965 is a book on Milton. There are five essays, four on *Paradise Lost* and one on *Paradise Regained*.

Myrna Gregson   5 April 1972
Barbados, West Indies

In response to Gregson's request (22 March 1972) for Frye to comment on an essay she had written on Heart of Darkness, *which one of her instructors said might be publishable.*

Dear Miss Gregson,

Quite an interesting paper: if you want to make it into an article, it should be a short article, designed for something like *Modern Language Notes*. The main theme should be the contrast between the black woman of Kurtz's present and the white woman of his future, his "intended." The former symbolizes what Kurtz has actually done in Africa; the latter the illusions about what he was doing it for. For the Intended the only possibility of communication was through a lie: she belongs to the women who are out of it: the black woman obviously isn't out of anything. Around this come the women who get the action going: first the plotting and scheming female relatives, then the knitting women who seem like the Fates: a memory of one of them does recur near the end of the story, by the way. I think your noting of the role of the woman whose intrigues get Marlow his appointment is particularly distinctive.

Hugo McPherson   11 April 1972
Montreal, QC

In reply to McPherson's letter (23 March 1972), complaining that Frye's The Bush Garden *and* The Critical Path, *both nominated for the Governor General's Award, were rejected in favor of Pierre Berton's* The Last Spike.

Dear Hugo,

Thank you very much for your letter. I am sorry that you were disappointed in the awards, and I can well understand why. One thing in particular I hope you will include in your recommendations to Naim Kattan. When Douglas Grant and Guy Sylvestre and Roger Duhamel and I set up the first committee, it was a primary axiom with us that all English members were supposed to be interested in the French awards, and vice versa, and that everybody should vote on all awards. I remember once when the English subcommittee was deadlocked on the fiction award and we broke the deadlock as a result of a very helpful and enlightening consultation with the French members. Surely one of the things that a Governor General's Committee should do is to try to promote the image of a united and cooperating country. This is in reference to your remark that a French judge was told that he had no right to express an opinion on an English book. It seems to me that this kind of thing is much more important than simply the question of who gets the awards in what year: there will always be room for disagreement over that.

I am very glad that the degrees in communications have gone through,[433] and I wish you the very best of luck with the working out of the programme. By the end of the programme you may have decided that the bureaucracy in Quebec is no worse than the developing bureaucracy in Ontario.

Love to Louise from us both.

Susan Newcomer   2 May 1972
New Brunswick, NJ

In reply to Newcomer's query about feminism and Blake.

Dear Miss Newcomer,

Thank you for your letter. I think the important thing to get clear in connexion with feminism in relation to such people as Blake is the distinction between actual sex and symbol based on sex. In traditional Christian symbolism Christ is symbolically the only male: all Christians, men as well as women, make up the female body of the Church. In Blake's symbolism, all human beings, women as well as men, are symbolically male, and what is symbolically female is nature, which humanity struggles to transform into a human shape. When humanity succeeds, nature becomes a female "emanation"; when humanity fails, nature becomes a remote and tantalizing "female will." The tendency of this symbolism is to put men and women on the same level except when the sexes dramatize the relationship of man and nature, as is done, for instance, in Courtly Love poetry.

I think that this is also the real basis of the relation of men and women in Milton; that is, that the sexual relation symbolizes the relation of creation and creature. But of course Milton mixes it up much more with the relation of the sexes, because he felt that the authority of the Bible compelled him to do so.

Duane Jones   4 May 1972
Pittsburgh, PA
In reply to Jones's queries (25 April 1972) about the meaning of (1) the tent image in Blake and (2) Blake's four states of being.

Dear Mr. Jones:

Thank you for your letter. The meaning of the "tent" image in Blake depends on the context. Usually it refers to man in a state of wandering in exile, like the Israelites in the desert. It also refers to military operations, and more particularly to the murder of Sisera by Jael in the Book of Judges. Your other questions relate to the four states of being in Blake. Eden, the world of the "four-fold" vision, is the full paradise which man could live in; Beulah is the lower paradise of love, dreaming and childhood; Generation is the original world that we all normally live in, and Ulro is the world we live in distorted by cruelty and terror into a hell.

My book is in print and in paperback, but if it is unavailable, there is also the Modern Library edition of Blake, with an introduction by me.

Elizabeth Skelton   4 May 1972
McGill Information Office, McGill University, Montreal, QC
This letter regards the talk — "Pistis and Mythos" — that Frye was to give at McGill University in June to the Canadian Society for the Study of Religion. "Pistis and Mythos" was published in NFR, 3–9.

Dear Miss Skelton,

Thank you for your letter. I will send an advance text, or more probably, an abstract if I can possibly get one drafted before I arrive in Montreal.

I have something of a psychological block about languages, which I find humiliating, but at this stage unremovable. I am therefore forced to consider myself unilingual for the duration of the conference.

W.J. Keith   15 May 1972
Department of English, New College, University of Toronto
In reply to Keith's report (10 May 1972) that the first issue of the Journal of Canadian Fiction, *of which Frye was a member of the editorial board, contained "a vulgar and silly attack" on Keith by Robin Mathews. Keith suggests that Mathews' "outbursts" are not the kind of thing that is "worthy of support."*

Dear Bill:

Thank you for your letter. It is, as you know, a custom for a new magazine to get lists of well-known people for their advisory board, and such people are deadheads as far as the editorial policies are concerned. I should imagine that most such people, certainly including myself, would make this deadhead rule mandatory before consenting to have their name listed. Usually it is a harmless enough way of indicating that certain people are interested in the field which the new journal covers.

I am sorry that the editors fell into the usual trap represented by the word "controversial," and published this Mathews article in their first issue.[434] I can hardly withdraw my name because of its appearance, however, in view of the fact that he has also attacked me at greater length and frequency, and at least equal personal virulence. I have also accepted an invitation to speak at ACUTE in Montreal,[435] and I note to my chagrin that Mathews is also on the programme there. I can only hope that having got Mathews out of the way the editors will settle down and try to do a more honest job.

Ted Scott   **26 May 1972**
Toronto, ON
In reply to a protest, which is not extant, about a failing grade received by Scott's son.

Dear Mr. Scott:
I am sending with this your son's essay, along with his test. As you will see, the decision about his mark, while it may been right or wrong, was not whimsically or arbitrarily arrived at. Also, a total of four people were involved in the marking, and Miss [Jay] Macpherson's mark was based on their consensus. The total mark is arrived at by taking the mathematical average of tutorial, essay, and two tests. When there is a failure on both the essay and one test, it is almost impossible for the student to pass the course.

One is never sure of the justness of any failing mark. Anybody who has done any teaching knows how many errors of decision can creep in. There is also the fact that in other departments instructors do not have the staff to do the careful research that was done in the case of this essay, and sometimes students get false ideas about how well they are doing, through no fault of theirs. I can only say that, to my personal knowledge, nobody feels anything but regret at your son's failing grade. I may add that students were expected to pick up their essays and tests from Miss Macpherson, so that there is no breach of confidence in sending you this.

Michael Atkinson   **7 June 1972**
University of Cincinnati, Cincinnati, OH
In response to Atkinson's having sent Frye (31 May 1972) an article on phenomenology that Frye had asked to see when he was visiting the University of Cincinnati. He had lectured there on "The Rivers of Eden" during the second week of May 1972.

Dear Michael,
The article on phenomenology and the Robbe-Grillet chapter arrived safely, and I am looking forward very much to reading them both. My difficulty with Husserl is that I can follow every sentence consecutively, but can't seem to put it together into a structure with any great relevance to literary criticism. That is where I am sure you can be of some help.

Once again, I had a most pleasant time at Cincinnati, and am well aware how much you and Larry Coffin did to make it so pleasant. I still find the Serpent Mound curiously haunting,[436] as though it represented the Kundalini which the Hindus say is inside me.

The very best to you both, and thanks again.

Margaret Eno   12 June 1972
Brookings, SD
    In response to Eno's series of questions (7 June 1972) about her difficulties with Frye's view of tragedy. Eno was writing a thesis, and her advisor indicated that if she were going to use Frye's ideas she would have to use his process as well. She had written an earlier letter (18 May 1972) indicating she was doing her master's thesis on archetypal patterns in Shakespearean comedy and asking whether the comedies could be regarded as representations of Frye's theory of anagogy.

Dear Mrs. Eno,
    Put tragedy wherever you like by all means. What matters is what you get out of the identification, not where it belongs in somebody else's schema.

Bert Hansen   27 June 1972
Council of Ontario Universities, Toronto, ON
    "The Ten O'Clock Scholar? What a Professor Does for His Pay" was a widely circulated study undertaken by the University of Toronto in 1967 and later published (Canadian University Association of Teachers Bulletin 21 [1973]: 4–10). Hansen was one of the three authors of the study, which revealed that during the 1966-67 academic year the average professor's work load exceeded fifty hours per week, while over a twelve-month period the average work week was forty hours.

Dear Mr. Hansen:
    Thank you very much for the copy of *The Ten O'Clock Scholar*, which I have read with interest. Of course it makes its point, but that unfortunately will not stop newspapers from writing silly editorials on the subject. I imagine that from the public point of view, the focus of attack should be on the popular myth that a professor has four months in the summer with nothing to do. Naturally this is taken care of in your brief, but it doesn't seem to have penetrated the consciousness of the general public.

Roy Daniells   17 July 1972
    This letter is in the Roy Daniells Fonds, University of British Columbia, box 8, file 7.

Dear Roy:
    Thanks very much for a most kindly note. Naturally I am very pleased at the appointment,[437] though I don't know at the moment whether the holders of it constitute an actual group that meets together or not.
    Last Friday, July 14, a group of local students who call themselves Maoists met on the campus to declare their undying opposition to that apostle of fascism and clerical obscurantism Northrop Frye.[438] They didn't know it was my sixtieth birthday, but the coincidence made me feel that even the ironies of survival have their pleasant aspects.
    Love to Laurenda from us both,

John B. Vickery   5 August 1972
Department of English, University of California, Riverside, CA
    In reply to Vickery's having sent Frye a copy of his Robert Graves and the White Goddess *(Lincoln: University of Nebraska Press, 1972).*

Dear Jack,
    Thank you very much for the book on Robert Graves which I shall be reading with great interest. I periodically get very impatient with Graves, because of the rather silly tee-

hee side to him: he seems to juxtapose serious ideas and leg-pulls, though not as readably as Samuel Butler does, who I understand is a major influence on him. I hope to learn from your book which is which.

Clara Thomas   8 August 1972
York University, Downsview, ON

Clara Thomas, professor of English at York University and president of the Association of Canadian Teachers of English, had written Frye, Margaret Laurence, Hugh McLennan, Dorothy Livesay, and Rudy Wiebe on 28 June 1972 complaining that the CBC had made no previous arrangements to tape and then air on its Ideas program the talks given by each of the addressees on a panel of ACUTE at McGill University. Thomas was distressed that none of the participants had been contacted about permission or about a fee.

Dear Clara,

Thank you very much for your letter. I am very pleased that you are taking the position you are, as it is a professional position and badly needs to be taken. Perhaps I can give you another example. Last October, I was asked to deliver three lectures at McGill to the Divinity School.[439] Because of my heavy commitments at the time, I stipulated that they would have to be informal lectures not intended for publication, intended for an audience of clergymen, theological students, and whatever arts students wanted to listen. I spoke from headings and had directed the lectures towards a discussion period afterwards. When I got there, I found that the CBC had already wired me up and were prepared to transmit the lectures, I think on their Overseas Service. I said, well, you certainly haven't cleared it with me: have you cleared it with my host, Professor Johnston, the Dean of the Divinity School? No, they had not, but they had cleared it with the Public Relations Department at McGill. In other words, Andrew Allan, who's a very fine person, but in my opinion, doesn't have the authority to give this kind of permission. Being weak minded, I let them go ahead with working their apparatus, but I don't imagine they got anything they could use, whereas, if I had formally given permission beforehand, I should at least have taken account of a different audience before delivering the lectures. I know that there is a budget freeze on the CBC, but a letter, even at the present postal rates, would not strain their budget, and might even save them some money.

Lawrence P. Rapp   9 August 1972
Department of English, University of Louisville, Louisville, KY

In reply to Rapp's letter (29 June 1972), asking Frye for clarifications of his use of the word "myth." Rapp was writing a dissertation on myth criticism at the University of Louisville.

Dear Mr. Rapp,

Thank you for your letter. I think all my definitions of myth derived out of my conception of it as a certain kind of story, that is, a story about divine beings which imposes no obligations on the teller to be plausibly realistic. These obligations produce what I call displacements, and that's what produces the series of modes. The definition in the glossary [of *Anatomy of Criticism*] reinforces this. I have recently expanded this definition, in a book called *The Critical Path*, where I say that in primitive verbal culture myths have a distinctive social function, but don't differ structurally from other stories contemporary with them, such as legends and folk tales. I am not sure what you mean by the word "monistical," but I certainly think of myth-making as an autonomous activity. Man makes myths because he makes myths, and no deterministic explanation will work for all myths.

I haven't read very much on Jungian myth criticism, but what I have read suggests an obsessive adherence to Jung's doctrines and a very undeveloped sense of literature. In general, I think of the connexion of literature with myth as one of a great many facts that the critic should keep in mind. I don't see that there is such a thing as myth criticism, which insists on going in this direction rather than that direction. Critics who ignore the relation of literature to mythology and critics who ignore anything else are being equally silly.

Angus Fletcher   **17 August 1972**
Paris, France

Fletcher had written Frye (4 August 1972) about a forthcoming meeting for a project they were engaged in, the editing of a Harcourt Brace Jovanovich anthology entitled The Survey of British Literature, *for which Frye had been appointed general editor. Other editors for the project — John Leyerle, Paul Fussell, Geoffrey Hartman, and J. Hillis Miller — were to prepare introductions for the various periods of English literature and to write separate author introductions. Planning for the project began in the mid–1960s, with an expected publication date of 1969. Although all of the editors completed a substantial amount of work of the project, which was to supersede the* Major British Writers *anthology published by Harcourt Brace Jovanovich, the* Survey *never came to fruition, even though the editors continued working on it in the early 1970s. After Oxford University Press published its two-volume* Anthology of English Literature, *Harcourt let its own project linger, and for various reasons it eventually faded away. Fletcher was working on his assignment in Paris, where he reports he had met Jacques Derrida and had reviewed a book by Paul de Man. He also indicates that his cousin Ian Fletcher is interested in leaving England for a university position, and he hopes his cousin might be able to meet Frye on a visit to Toronto.*

Dear Angus,

Thank you very much for your letter, which I was delighted to have. I am vary much looking forward to seeing you in September, if the meeting comes off, and I hope we can get these tedious introductions[440] wound up shortly. I am on sabbatical now, as you doubtless know, trying to work on an almost insanely complicated book on the Bible, and this hangover from an earlier and more indiscreet life keeps turning up as punctually and neurotically as a ghost.

I am very glad that you are getting interested in the phenomenological people, whom I don't know personally, apart from Paul de Man, whose views seem to me to be mostly warmed-over Mallarmé. Todorov published a translation of an article of mine in *Poetique*,[441] but I have had no other connexion with the group.

I should be delighted to see Ian Fletcher at any time. He was here a couple of years ago, giving two lectures on Yeats, and I went to a party for him. He would make a very distinguished addition to any Canadian department, and I should be delighted if he could stay here, though I understand the difficulties, especially at this time.

The very best from us both.

David J. Jehn and Stephen O. Ellis   **1 August 1972**
Dayton, OH

In reply to an overview of the correspondents' project to develop a college preparatory English curriculum based on Frye's principles. Jehn had written Frye earlier (18 January 1972) asking whether there were any secondary schools that based their English curricula on Frye's principles.

Dear Mr. Jehn and Mr. Ellis,

Thank you very much for the project, which I have been reading with interest. If I may make one suggestion, which may not be a correct one at all: I wonder whether "Myth" can really be treated as a category like the others. In my own scheme, a myth is rather an informing principle, a narrative movement which enters into all forms of literature in varying degrees of what I call displacement. Myths, so far as they are verbal, cannot exist outside incorporation in such verbal form, but I doubt that there is a verbal form that one can point to and say "This is a myth." In other words, I think you will have a great deal of difficulty in establishing myth as a literary genre. That is merely a suggestion based on my own experience, and you may well feel that your approach is a different one.

Jorge Melo   21 August 1972
Lisbon, Portugal

In reply to a twenty-three-year-old Portuguese student who thanks Frye effusively for having written A Natural Perspective. *He outlines at length his 400-page thesis on comedy, wonders whether Frye might have time to critique an abstract of it, and asks about the possibility of coming to Canada to study with Frye.*

Dear Mr. Melo:

It was of course a great pleasure to receive your letter, which I have read several times with the keenest interest. What you are doing seems to me very promising, as mistaken identities constitute a very large and central area of comic structure. The way you are setting up your scheme seems to me very sound, as it keeps its eye on the question of structure from the beginning. I am sending you an essay on *The Tempest* and another essay on Dickens.[442] I don't know how familiar you are with Dickens, but his treatment of the symbolism of the family might be of some interest to you. As for *The Tempest*, I think it perhaps illustrates the movement of comedy from *Pistis* to *Gnosis*, from illusion to reality, more clearly than any other play I know.

I am sorry not to be able to read anything at the moment, as my desk is piled high with other manuscripts, and as soon as I have cleared them off I shall be going on sabbatical for the year, and my whereabouts will be uncertain. If you find it possible to come here as a graduate student, I should look forward to seeing you. Thesis topics of the breadth of yours are not unusual here, nor particularly difficult to accommodate. In any case, I should be most interested to hear how you get along with and develop your present project, even if you decide to make it a book rather than a thesis, as you may be well advised to do. There must be a good deal in Vicente and others in your own literary tradition which would round out your examples.

William V. Spanos   30 August 1972
English Department, State University of New York, Binghamton, NY

Dear Mr. Spanos:

Thank you very much for the copy of *Boundary 2*, which I have been reading with interest. It seems to me a journal of the most variety of content, with something for every type of interest. I am particularly pleased to see that it continues to be concerned with the modern world, and doesn't attempt the neoteric hysterical suggested by the word "postmodern."

Herbert Lindenberger   **22 September 1972**
Department of Comparative Literature, Stanford University, Stanford, CA

Dear Herbert,

Thank you very much for the offprint,[443] which I have read with great interest. The older I get, the less I seem able to take in other approaches, and the more I feel that the best I can do is to continue with my own assumptions and techniques. This means that I am dependent on such critics as yourself to tell me what else is going on and what my relation to it is.

Martin Kessler   **27 September 1972**
Department of Social Sciences, Clarkson College of Technology, Potsdam, NY

In reply to Kessler's request (22 September 1972) for Frye to review a draft of his proposal to the National Endowment for the Humanities.

Dear Mr. Kessler:

Thank you for your letter. I wish that your prospectus could state clearly, and as its main point, the fact that in all areas of critical analysis there are two perspectives, which complement one another. One is the genetic problem: how did the text get into its present form? The other is the teleological problem: what is the meaning of the text in the form in which we have it? In the criticism of Shakespeare, for instance, it is quite obvious that we need a study of the textual sources, analytical bibliography, the use made of earlier plays and other sources, and entries in the Stationers' Register and the like. The actual criticism of what the play means as it stands is something else again, but is never thought of as contradicting the former type of study. In biblical criticism an extraordinary lop-sided situation has arisen whereby all criticism is assumed to be genetic and historical, and the study of the text as it stands is assumed to be, if anything, a matter of exegesis or preaching, and not really a genuine critical issue at all. As the two forms of criticism fertilized one another, it follows that biblical criticism is stuck like the Ancient Mariner. It doesn't know any more about historical sources than it did a hundred years ago, no matter how much Ugaritic may have been learned in the meantime. As a result we can only get more and more guesswork on the thinnest possible structure of established facts. If I read you correctly, you want to find out, in the case of Jeremiah at least, why the book that we have is the way we have it. This requires critical methods which are elementary to literary critics but are not employed by biblical critics because they don't know enough.

What you have is all right, only I think if you emphasize what I have said above a bit more, you wouldn't need to worry the committee at this point with talk about mythological cycles, which might frighten them off. The specifically archetypal approach perhaps comes into play more when you are considering Jeremiah in his general biblical context.

Sidney Feshbach   **3 October 1972**
Department of English, City University of New York, New York, NY

In reply to Feshbach's invitation (25 September 1972) for Frye to attend the literary criticism session of the Northeast Modern Language Association, meeting in Boston, 6–7 April 1973. Feshbach also announced his intention to begin a journal called Metacriticism *that will "be directed primarily at an intense inquiry into the* Anatomy, *to reveal as clearly as possible its strengths and weaknesses, to test its arguments and its validity, and to suggest places where it might be improved."*

Dear Mr. Feshbach:

Thank you very much for your letter. The first thing I have to say is that I am afraid I shall not be able to attend the meeting in Boston. This is my first sabbatical year in twenty years, and I am keeping the year rigidly free of commitments, as what I have tackled — a large-scale book on the Bible and English literature — is so demanding and exhausting that any other engagement gives me claustrophobia. I should certainly be more cooperative if I could.

I have no immediate plans for revising the *Anatomy*, and for three reasons. First, the economics of book publishing make revisions of this kind more difficult than they were a generation or two ago. Second, I have other books I want to write, and new things to say would be continually fighting against efforts to rephrase what I have already said. Third, I feel that every book is a product of its time and that in a time so different as ours is to that of the mid-fifties, there are new problems to face and there should be new books to face them with. But this would not, of course, preclude a future revision of the *Anatomy* if your efforts should make it clear that there are specific ways in which the book could be made more useful to the present generation. And, of course, I could not undertake any kind of revision without the help of such discussions as might emerge from your efforts.

With best wishes, and with the deepest gratitude for your interest.

Margaret Atwood   14 November 1972
Writer in Residence, Massey College

Dear Peggy,

Thank you very much for the copy of *Survival*, which I am delighted to have. I am even more delighted to have been included in the dedication. It is very brightly and incisively written, with an immense amount of helpful information in it as well as a broad and consistent point of view, and I hope it will sell us well as it deserves to do, as I am sure it will.

Charles F. Altieri   14 December 1972
Department of English, State University of New York at Buffalo, Buffalo, NY

In response to Alteiri's having sent Frye a copy of his essay "Northrop Frye and the Problem of Spiritual Authority," PMLA 87 (October 1972): 964–75.

Dear Mr. Altieri:

I don't know what the etiquette is about writing to one's critics, but I did want you to know how deeply I appreciated the article on me in the October issue of *PMLA*. I find that as I get more absorbed in my own work it is increasingly difficult, in fact impossible, both to do that work and to figure out where I am in relation to contemporaries engaged in parallel activities. As I am constantly being asked what my position is in relation to Barthes, Levi-Strauss, Burke, Ricoeur, and others, I am not only deeply grateful for but utterly dependent on the kind of assistance given by your admirably lucid article.

Lawrence Lipking   14 December 1972
The Center for the Humanities, Wesleyan University, Middletown, CT

In response to Lipking's invitation (4 December 1972) for Frye to present a paper at a session on "New Approaches to the Eighteenth Century" at the 1973 meeting of the English Institute. Lipking also asked whether Frye had seen the section devoted to his work in the anthology of criticism he and A. Walton Litz had edited, Modern Literary Criticism, 1900–1970 *(New York: Atheneum, 1972).*

Dear Professor Lipking,

Thank you very much for your letter. It was very remiss of me not to have acknowledged the receiving of *Modern Literary Criticism*, as I was sure I had done. It seems to me an admirably arranged and laid out text, and naturally I am very pleased with the selections from me, which are pretty well the sort of thing I should have selected for myself. I think the other three critics in the first section,[444] too, have been extremely well represented, as a result of a very fresh and first hand investigation of their work.

You ask for corrections: in reprinting the "Nature and Homer" article, you give a footnote reference to *Fables of Identity*, but apparently you took the text from the original *Texas Quarterly* version. This would normally have been the correct scholarly procedure, except that I never saw a proof of that article, and as a result the text is unreliable. It seems, for example, to have fallen into the hands of someone who knew more about popular books on yoga than about literary criticism, hence the word "tapas" for "topos" on page 229.

In regard to your invitation: it seems very ungracious to have to refuse, especially when I have a very bad conscience about the English Institute, of which I am a Trustee, and which I never seem to get to. (Part of the reason for this is personal: it comes at the height of the hay fever season.) The trouble is that I am on sabbatical this year, and have been working very hard over some very long and complicated writing projects. They have filled my horizon to such an extent that I find myself getting claustrophobia at the thought of other commitments, at least until the whistle blows on my first full sabbatical in twenty years and sends me back to the academic soup line. I am very sorry about this, as normally nothing would give me greater pleasure than to try to reconsider some critical problems of the eighteenth century.

With best wishes, renewed thanks, and genuine regrets.

T.J. Ray   28 December 1972
University of Mississippi, College of Liberal Arts, University, MS
In reply to a request from Ray (15 December 1972) for suggestions Frye might have for a doctoral student preparing to write a thesis on Blake's syntax, with particular attention to ambiguity.

Dear Professor Ray:

Thank you for your letter about Mrs. Janis Scott. I don't know that there is anything I can helpfully say on this point as I do not have very much to go on in regard to her particular approach. Blake doesn't strike me as a poet particularly given to ambiguity in the way that, for example, the metaphysical poets are, but I have no doubt that a fruitful thesis could be worked out on his use of language. I know of very little criticism on this point: perhaps an essay by Josephine Miles in an English Institute Annual for (I think) 1953 might be of some use.[445] Naturally she will understand the importance of working from reproductions of the original plates, in the case of the engraved poems, paying particular attention to Blake's distinctive but very sparse punctuation. Modernized and over-punctuated texts like those of Keynes can be very misleading.

Martha W. England   5 February 1973
Queens College of the City University of New York, Flushing, NY
In reply to England's letter (28 January 1973), giving an account of her battles against the laissez-faire state of things at Queen's College and remarking on her teaching The Winter's Tale, *which she says she prefers to Frye's favorite,* The Tempest. *England had met Frye at one of the meetings of the English Institute.*

Dear Martha England,

Thank you for a delightful letter, which I am naturally most pleased to have. We have had an experience somewhat similar to yours at Toronto recently. Starting out with an honour course which gave what I thought was the best undergraduate training on the Continent, we are now stuck in the morass of free electives.

I'm not sure that I prefer *The Tempest* to *The Winter's Tale*; I merely find *The Tempest* a little easier to talk about. I am coming more and more in my final period to return to the subject of Romance, and to see what it is trying to say through all its variants and displacements. At the moment, however, I have to struggle with a large book on the Bible and English Literature.

Florence R. Sandler   7 March 1973
Department of English, University of Puget Sound, Tacoma, WA
In reply to Sandler's having sent Frye (18 January 1973) an article on Blake and Milton and asking for his critique.

Dear Professor Sandler,

Thank you very much for the offprint of your article on Blake, which I have read with great interest. I don't feel that you are on the wrong track or that you have misunderstood either *Milton* or Blake's attitude in general. If you go further with this, however, I think you might perhaps look into the question of why Blake regards Deism and rationalism as essentially the consolidation of everything that he dislikes about orthodox Christianity. His reason is that his attitude to religion is existential, as we now call it, regarding systematic reasoning as a structure erected by an ascendant class to safeguard its own interests. In Christian times this structure was concealed by religious anxieties: from the eighteenth century on its function was to rationalize exploitation and continuing war, or what Blake calls religion hid in war. You know this, of course, but it might be worth working it out in more detail, looking at such later exponents of the same view as Kierkegaard. I suggest this only because I should like to see other articles from you.

Jon Pearce   12 March 1973
Preparatory School, Upper Canada College, Toronto, ON

Dear Mr. Pearce,

Thank you very much for your copy of *Marked by the Wild*[446]: it was extremely kind of you to send it to me. It comes of course on the heels of Margaret Atwood's *Survival*, which in itself I find a rather over-simplified and somewhat derivative thesis. Your book confines itself to the area of Canadian Literature to which her conception of "survival" really does apply, and consequently it is a well unified and distinctive collection.

Desmond Pacey   20 March 1973
Academic Vice-President, University of New Brunswick, Fredericton, NB
In reply to Pacey's having sent Frye a copy of his article "The Study of Canadian Literature," Journal of Canadian Fiction 2, no.2 (Spring 1973): 67–72.

Dear Des,

Thanks very much for the article. I am sorry if your illness deflected you from the presidency, but as long as the open season for presidents lasts it will probably be a lot more comfortable being a vice-president.

I have read the article with great interest. I think Victoria has had a rather unusual interest in the subject of Canadian Literature, although the federation system and the honour course meant that it couldn't be put in the curriculum. But of course Pelham was writing articles on Canadian Literature around the turn of the century, was founding societies to help writers before the Canada Council, and continually used to refer to Canadian writers in his innumerable and interminable digressions. John Robins too, as soon as he became Chairman of the Department, organized several series of lectures in Canadian Literature, most of them given by members of the Victoria staff. They were quite well attended, but then as now students were apt not to listen unless they got academic credit for doing so.

Walter J. Ong, S.J.   28 March 1973
Department of English, St. Louis University, St. Louis, MO
Ong's letter to Frye is not extant.

Dear Walter,

Thank you very much for the offprints, which I have read with great interest. You certainly are exploring on a variety of fronts and the psychiatry report was particularly interesting to me. I think I was particularly interested in your comments on Tolkien, not because I am all that fascinated by Tolkien, but because I am beginning to get interested in Greek Romances of the Daphnis and Chloe type, which also focus on a latency period. The way their formulas reappear in Scott and later romancers will probably by a theme I shall be exploring for Harvard, where I am to be Professor of Poetry for 1974/5.

The very best for the Stanford venture, and hoping to run across you again before very long. I saw Marshall [McLuhan] the other day at a meeting on Canadian Studies, where we were discussing the question of how difficult it is for students in this bilingual country to acquire a second language when they don't possess a first one.

Helen Vendler   9 April 1973
Department of English, Boston University, Boston, MA
In reply to Vendler's letter (9 March 1973), saying what "a beautiful series of pages" she found in Frye's "The Search for Acceptable Words," Dædalus 102 (Spring 1973): 11–26; reprinted in SM, 3–26.

Dear Helen,

I think Jay Macpherson, when she met you in Montreal, told you something of how much your letter meant to me. It was the most personal article I have ever written, and I felt so naked and exposed after I had written it that I urged Stephen Graubard[447] to withdraw it. However, I forgot I had friends.

Love and best wishes from us both.

Margaret Stobie   24 April 1973
Department of English, University of Manitoba, St. John's College, Winnipeg, MB
In reply to Stobie's having sent Frye a copy of her book, A Critical Study of Frederick Philip Grove *(NY: Twayne, 1973). Stobie had been a member, along with Frye, of Herbert Davis's Blake seminar at Toronto in 1934–35.*

Dear Peg,

Thanks very much for the Grove book, which Helen and I are both reading with great interest. It's a very solid piece of work, combining the biographical with the critical in a way that isn't usually done, and you make a good deal of personal connexion with your subject. I always found Grove personally something of a bore, as he always reminded me of the man in Dickens who was constantly composing eulogistic epitaphs for himself, but you make him much more believable as a human being than he tended to make himself. I only wish I could say something in favour of the physical appearance of the book, but Twayne's designer appears to have learned his trade in the penitentiary.

The very best to Bill and yourself.

Wendy J. Keitner   2 May 1973
Kingston, ON

In reply to Keitner's query (28 April 1973) about the significance of Ralph Gustafson's Anthology of Canadian Poetry *(1942) in comparison to Arthur Smith's* Book of Canadian Poetry *(1943)*

Dear Mrs. Keitner:

I should agree that Gustafson's anthology had an importance equal to Smith's in popularizing Canadian poetry throughout English-speaking world. There is also a remarkable coincidence of taste between the two anthologists, so that one reinforces the influence of the other. What was so important to me about Smith's book[448] was his critical introduction, his elaborate head notes, and the fact that his poems appeared in the context of an articulated critical attitude. At this distance I don't remember whether Smith discusses Gustafson or not in his article on Canadian anthologies.

M.H. Abrams   3 May 1973
Department of English, Cornell University, Ithaca, NY

In response to Abrams's having sent Frye an offprint of his "Coleridge's 'A Light in Sound': Science, Metascience, and the Poetic Imagination," Proceedings of the American Philosophical Society *16, no. 6 (21 December 1972): 458–76.*

Dear Mike:

Thank you very much for the erudite and comprehensive offprint, which is a most valuable acquisition. It's extraordinary how you keep finding new things in the Romantics: I should have thought your last book[449] would have exhausted you for years, as it would have done anyone else. It's nice too to find myself in the direct line of descent from Schelling, who has always attracted me in spite of the number of silly things he says.[450]

The very best to Ruth and yourself.

Eveline Bates Doob   7 May 1973
Woodbridge, CT

In reply to Doob's lengthy letter (1 April 1973) recording the "thunderous impact" Frye's books were having on her, and describing a Blakean epiphany she had in 1947 that she has since been trying to capture in poetry.

Dear Mrs. Bates:

I was very pleased and felt very privileged to get your letter, with an eloquent and impressive poem attached. The experience you speak of is, I think, one of the central intuitions of poetry, and I try to treat it in that way in the *Anatomy of Criticism*. I quote, for example, Rilke's letter to Ellen Delph, where he speaks of feeling an identity with an angel on the circumference of time and space, blind and looking into himself.[451] Any experience such as yours would naturally be likely to commit you to writing, though whether it was fiction or poetry would depend on personal rhythms that can only be reached by instinct.

Once again, many thanks for your letter: I know that what I am trying to do is a considerable help to poets, or should be. I get two kinds of letters from poets: those that tell me that I am helping them and those that tell me I am hindering them. I much prefer your kind, mainly because I think the others were talking about something else.

I shall look forward to seeing your piece in the *Chicago Review*.[452]

G. Milburn   24 May 1973

Department of History, University of Western Ontario, London, ON

In reply to Milburn's request (9 May 1973) for Frye to comment on Don Gutteridge's article, "Teaching Canadian Literature: Notes toward a New Curriculum," which is to be part of a special issue of Curriculum Theory Network.

Dear Professor Milburn:

Thank you for your letter and for Professor Gutteridge's article. It is a very good article, which speaks for itself quite adequately, and I don't know that I have any particular criticism to make. All that occurs to me as a comment is that when it comes to the setting of a novel, all settings are strange to their reader, and if they aren't they ought to be made so. Hardy is no easier for British readers than he is for Canadians, unless the British reader happens to come from Dorset, and certainly Joseph Conrad would be equally strange to both. Similarly with Canadian fiction: not only are some very good novels, like those of David Knight and Margaret Laurence, set in Africa, but, of those with Canadian settings Buckler would be strange to a Westerner, Sinclair Ross to a Maritimer, and the Ontario of Robertson Davies and the Quebec of Ringuet are as far apart as the earth and the moon. It is possible to catch a student's interest by telling him that the book he is about to read is the work of a fellow countryman. But even if it is set in the very same milieu as the student himself grew up in, the effort in teaching ought to be towards making the description of that setting as strange and remote as possible, so that the student will be able to see his own culture objectively. Naturally this applies to time as well as to space: all novels, including contemporary ones, ought to be read by the historical imagination.

I suppose this is really said, certainly implied, in the article itself. But not all teachers clearly realize that their function, in teaching Canadian literature, is not to say, "This is about you," but "You too are a subject of study."

John Celli   7 June 1973

Boston, MA

In reply to five questions posed by Celli (28 May 1973) in connection with his dissertation, an effort to identify and define the various uses of the work "archetype"

Dear Mr. Celli:

In your first thesis, "The size of an archetype is variable," your interpretation seems to me to be correct. In practice it is the smaller units, or images, that are called archetypes, because of the confusion of calling everything an archetype that recurs.

On the second point, identical doesn't mean exactly similar; it expresses a relationship of an individual to its class. When I say that that individual brown and green object outside my window belongs to the class "tree," I identify it, although it is not just like any other tree, even of its own species.

Third, I don't see the point of pushing the question of the origin of archetypes any further than language. Behind the individual languages of English, French, and so on, there is a general language potential which embodies itself in the actual languages, and archetypes belong to that common potential language.

Fourth, I am not sure that there is a hierarchy of archetypes, or rather, there could be any number of hierarchies, depending on what one was interested in. There are certain ones which are universal in the sense that they are potentially comprehensible by everyone, such as food and drink. This doesn't make them more important; it just makes them more easily communicable. Such figures as Adonis or Hamlet grew up in a specific cultural environment, and with some effort they can be made comprehensible to anyone who understands what literature is at all. The fact that literature is a technique of communication makes me feel very hesitant to say that certain archetypes "are common only to certain groups of people," even if they begin in a limited area.

There are many philosophical implications in the anagogic phase, which will doubtless not concern you. So far as I know, there is no critical technique particularly appropriate to it. But archetypal criticism, which supplies the context for a poem, may make one feel that one is getting close to the centre of one's whole literary experience in a poem that particularly interests him. It is a considerable danger to think that there is a specific objective centre of literary experience. This is why one has to make the final decentralizing effort, and realize that you are always in the centre whatever you are reading.

Richard P. Adams   25 June 1973
Department of English, Tulane University, New Orleans, LA

Dear Professor Adams,

Thank you very much for the two Wallace Stevens papers,[453] which I have read with great interest. Stevens seems to me to have an extraordinary philosophical sense, whatever the degree of his technical knowledge of the subject, and to see very clearly what the diagrammatic basis of the philosophy is. The two articles together sound as though you were working on something more extended on Stevens, as I hope you will be.

John Ross Baker   25 June 1973
Bethlehem, PA

In reply to Baker's having sent Frye (18 June 1973) "an offprint of a brief piece of mine that mentions your work."

Dear Professor Baker,

Thank you very much for the offprint[454] and your letter, which I have read with interest. I don't know what Crews is talking about, and I doubt very much if he does either, but he certainly thinks that he is talking about me: he published two long articles in the *New York Review of Books* attacking the *Anatomy of Criticism*, which were later published somewhere else.[455] If his own critical career had stopped with *The Pooh Perplex*, it would have been less ironic.

Naomi Lowinsky   9 August 1973
Theatre of Man, San Francisco, CA

In reply to Lowinsky's questions (3 August 1973) about Blake's access "to the occult in general and the Tarot in particular." The Theatre of Man, a small experimental company with which Lowinsky had a connection, was planning to produce a "ritual theatre piece" on Blake's Illustrations to the Book of Job.

Dear Ms. Lowinsky,

Thank you for your letter. It is very difficult to say what Blake might have used as a source, because of his professional connexion with publishers and his very desultory habits of reading. There were eighteenth-century sources for the Tarot cards, of the sort listed, in A.E. Waite's book,[456] but I am very doubtful about the one-to-one correspondence between the Job engravings and the Tarot trumps that Damon works out.[457] I think it more likely that Blake knew, possibly through Swedenborg, of certain speculations in cabbalism connected with the twenty-two letters of the Hebrew alphabet. If one used seven as the symbolic number of historical time, as Blake does, the obvious number for a circumferential or cyclical vision, corresponding to our pi, would be between twenty-one and twenty-two, which can be symbolized by a sequence of twenty-one, with a twenty-second left unnumbered. Thus, although the division of biblical books into chapters is late, has no ancient authority, and often seems to be done purely at random, the twenty-two chapters of the Book of Revelation probably have some significance.

My own remark was simply to the effect that certain types of visionary poetry are most economically and efficiently expressed in the kind of sequence that I call an "alphabet of forms." If Blake had been using the Tarot sequence for Job, and found any difficulty in the order, he would certainly have altered the order for his own convenience. There are also features in the Tarot deck, such as the use of the four natural virtues, which he would have disliked, and which almost certainly indicate a late corruption in the Tarot symbolism. Accordingly, I should think your best bet would be to see the series as a cycle going down to the low point of Plates 11 to 13, corresponding to the Hanged Man-Death-Devil sequence, and then coming up again to the final apocalyptic vision.

I greatly appreciate the final paragraph of your letter.[458]

Janet L. Smarr   **9 August 1973**

Department of Comparative Literature, Princeton University, Princeton, NJ

In reply to the comments of Smarr's letter of 5 August 1973, which questions Frye's view about the relation between morality and literature set down in The Educated Imagination. *Smarr, a graduate student at Princeton, also remarks on Frye's position that artists are akin to neurotics in their dissatisfaction with present society, maintaining that that was not always the case.*

Dear Ms. Smarr,

Thank you for your letter. The passage you refer to[459] is part of a general attack on censorship, which is based on the conception of a passive reader being magically or automatically affected by what he reads, just as an eater of mushrooms might be poisoned by eating one that was full of cyanide. In my opinion this is a preposterous analogy, as the moral basis of literature has to be the activity of the reader's mind. Every book is its reader's opportunity. A reader passively stimulated to virtue by a book is just as delinquent as a reader passively stimulated to vice. Of course there are books which convey morally bad visions of the world: but there is no possibility of any sane system of censorship which assumes that these qualities are inherent in the book itself, and operate independently of the reader.

I think my analogy between the artist and the neurotic[460] was intended only as an analogy. The analogy is a significant one, in my opinion, not because the neurotic *qua* neurotic has anything on the ball, but because society is also neurotic. What is sane and normal represents a basically social judgement, and such judgements always have an element of something wrong and inadequate. I am afraid I don't agree with you that there ever was a time when the artist was a healthy craftsman. Some artists may have been; it would depend on their art and on historical accidents.

I much appreciate your interest.

Robert D. Denham   **7 September 1973**
Department of English, Emory & Henry College, Emory, Virginia
In reply to Denham's having sent Frye news about his book, Northrop Frye and Critical
Method, *along with some bibliographic information on a Maoist attack on Frye,* Northrop
Frye: The High Priest of Clerical Obscurantism, *written under the pseudonym of Pauline
Kogan and published in Montreal by Progressive Books in 1969.*

Dear Mr. Denham,

Thank you very much for your letter. I am most pleased to hear how well the study is
proceeding, and as always deeply grateful to you for undertaking it. You are to take this
letter as a blanket permission to quote whatever you like from me, so far as my permission
legally extends.

Thanks for the note about the Maoist article: I had assumed that the original screed
which came out of Dublin was different from Pauline Kogan's pamphlet, of which I have
a copy (paying 75¢ to the local student representative: they don't give anything free to the
bourgeoisie). But I did not read either carefully enough to identify them.[461]

Roy Daniells   **12 September 1973**
University of British Columbia, Vancouver, BC
*In reply to Daniells's undated letter in which he remarks, "I notice your reference to the
fact that few theologians now regard the loss of the word 'God' from their vocabulary a seri-
ous moral or doctrinal deprivation. I think I know what you mean." Daniells also asked Frye
how he manages to retain a sense of the spiritual life in the face of the fact that the text of the
Gospels cannot be taken literally. Frye's letter is in the Roy Daniells Fonds, University of British
Columbia, box 8, file 10.*

Dear Roy:

Sorry about the ribs[462]: I hope the effects are less painful by now.

I think you must be speaking of my remark in *The Stubborn Structure* that theologians
would mostly consider the statement "there is a God" one of very little significance.[463] What
makes it insignificant is the indefinite article: "a" God is only a vague notion of Something
Upstairs. Christianity, which unites the conception of God to a specific man whose characteristics and attitudes are described, is more concrete than this. If you say, as I should be
inclined to say, that a man's religion consists or whatever he is trying to identify himself
with, this does at least provide some standard of acceptance or rejection, whatever one
decides for.

We tend to think of "truth" as truth of correspondence, when a pattern of words cor-
responds sufficiently well to a body of facts or ideas. So we say that the stories in the Gospels
are "true" only if they are historically true, and correspond to facts as experienced two
thousand years ago and ten thousand miles away. But long before we had this notion of
truth, which is a by-product of the art of writing, we had stories (mythoi), which appeal
to a sense of imaginative truth, and this kind of truth is the only kind appropriate to a religion, where the source of truth is a person and not a proposition or even a historical event.
Religion must use the language of myth and metaphor because that language is the language of the present tense, the only language that expresses what happens, not what may
have happened.

In a later book, *The Critical Path*, I say that the "fundamentalist" notion is that if we
had been present at, say, the last moments of Elijah on earth, we should have seen precisely
what the Book of Kings says Elisha saw. I consider that this greatly over-rates my own capac-

ity for spiritual vision. As I say there, if I had been on the hills of Bethlehem at the time of the birth of Christ, I don't think I'd have heard any angels singing, because I don't hear them now, and there's no reason to suppose that they've stopped. Similarly, I think if I'd been present on Resurrection morning I might have seen nothing but an empty tomb. I think Sir Thomas Browne's "I thank God that I never saw Christ or his disciples" a very shrewd remark.[464] The Gospels make it clear that the disciples themselves didn't know what the hell was going on even when they were in the middle of it. Such things can only be conveyed mythically. As for atonement, that has always meant to me literally at-one-ment, unity in what Blake calls the Divine Humanity, not Anselrn's absurd argument that it was an ingenious way of cheating the devil out of our souls. Theologians are always trying to translate metaphors into propositions, but they'd do better if they left them as metaphors, as some of them are beginning to realize.

All the best: I'm also extremely pleased about the Order of Canada,[465] and I wish it were more of an actual society, like the Royal Society, so that one could meet the other members more often.

Love to Laurenda and the girls,

George Johnston   17 September 1973
Carleton University, Ottawa, ON

Johnston — poet, translator, teacher, and Frye's long time friend — expected to be granted a sabbatical for 1974–75 and had asked Frye to write a letter on his behalf (letter of 11 September 1973). He anticipated applying for a leave grant or a senior creative grant from the Canada Council.

Dear George,

Thanks very much for your letter: I was very interested to hear of your plans, and of course would be delighted to write for you. As a snap judgment, it seems to me that the senior creative fellowship grant from the Canada Council would be simpler and more lucrative than a leave grant, but you will know more about this than I.

I don't know whether you were at the conference in Iceland that I understand took place this summer. Helen and I got so fed up with the heat and humidity in Toronto that we went to Reykjavik for two weeks, staying in the airline hotel and taking bus trips out. I love the country, with its quiet unpretentiousness, and read half a dozen of the Sagas in translation on the spot — not your Gisli one,[466] of course, which I already knew and possessed.

The very best to the family.

Patricia Clarke   24 September 1973
Associate Editor, *United Church Observer*, Toronto, ON

In reply to Clarke's request (19 September 1973) for suggestions about how to honour the fiftieth anniversary of the United Church of Canada.

Dear Mrs. Clarke,

Thank you for your letter about the approaching fiftieth anniversary of the United Church. Being an academic, I naturally think in terms of books, and I should like to see a group of interested people produce a volume of essays on the general subject of "Union after Fifty Years." There could be essays on the changes in the theological situation, on the present prospects for further union, and on the elements favouring and obstructing the ecumenical movement generally. I think a practising clergyman would be better qualified to advise about celebrations within the churches themselves.

Fred Grossberg   **9 October 1973**
Cambridge, MA

In reply to Grossberg's inquiry (28 September 1973) about his proposed dissertation topic, "The Revelation of Reality in Wallace Stevens and Northrop Frye." In particular, Grossberg asks Frye if he could send suggestions for further reading about the principle of identity. Grossberg had been a member of Frye's 1970 seminar at Oxford and had visited him in Toronto the following year.

Dear Mr. Grossberg:

Thank you for your letter: of course I remember you very well, and I remember how much you contributed to my Oxford seminar. I am very interested that you are working on Wallace Stevens, but the particular problem that you are concerned with is not one that I have many concrete suggestions about. The whole question of identity belongs to that area of theoretical problems which I have to work out myself in my own terms, and other discussions of it I don't find very helpful. I understand that my theory of identity in comedy runs parallel with some other investigations of Caesar [Cesar] Barber at Amherst, who has also written on comedy from the same point of view.[467] I also have a second essay on Stevens himself, in a *festschrift* for Bill Wimsatt called *Literary Theory and Structure: Essays in Honour of William K. Wimsatt*.[468] I don't know that the article will be much use to you, but I felt I needed to write a second article[469] trying to evaluate not only the *Opus Posthumous* but the Letters, which I find very baffling. Perhaps you would have more specific questions as you went on.

Daphne Rogers   **12 October 1973**
Peterboro, ON

In response to Rogers's letter (25 September 1873), asking what the phrase "moral imagination" means.

Dear Miss Rogers,

Thank you for your letter. It seems to me that one uses the term "moral" in two senses, one much broader than the other. You want to credit Darwin, quite rightly as I think, with a moral imagination in the broad sense. That is, he is a scientist with a great enough mind to see beyond his scientific project into the human context of scientific discovery. He understood and was sensitive to a kind of impact on human life that a major scientific discovery would make. You are also, I think, trying to avoid using "moral" in the more restricted sense of conforming to some kind of accepted code behaviour, according to which certain things are good because they are socially accepted or bad because they are not. In the latter sense of the word there would be no such thing as a moral imagination, as such an attitude to life is essentially unimaginative. But in the broader and more appropriate sense of the word, you are certainly right in applying the phrase to Darwin.

Edward Jayne   **18 October 1973**
Freiburg, West Germany

Along with his letter (2 October 1973) Jayne sent Frye a Marxist critique of The Critical Path, *recommending that he look into "responsible leftist books" by Baran and Sweezy, Harrington, Galbraith, and others. Jayne's review, which was published in* Kritikon Litterarum, *1 (1972): 316–20, argued that* The Critical Path *was a conservatively oriented form of archetypal criticism and a reactionary work — "a defense of Burkean conservatism in [its] asking for the preservation of existing institutions to protect the freedom of both the artist and critic."*

Dear Mr. Jayne,

Thank you for your review and your letter. One never knows enough, but I think I have sufficient acquaintance with Harrington, Marcuse, and Adorno (I don't know the book on *Monopoly Capital*) to realize that my book doesn't meet them on their level. This is because I was concerned with a different and much more primitive aspect of Marxism, the question of what Marxist bureaucracies do to literature. There are also Christian writers whom I consider prudent and intellectually honest, but it doesn't follow that I want to see Christianity put into a social position where it can control literature according to its own anxieties as happened in, say, Ireland until very recently.

Incidentally, I wasn't really trying to be definitive in the book, which is very much of a transitional book, written mainly for the purpose of getting my own mind clear, or at least clearer, in a somewhat cloudy social situation. I felt I had to write the book before I could write anything else, and many of its characteristics derived from the very specific time of its writing.

Gordon Patterson   18 October 1973
Murnau, Germany

In response to Patterson's letter (3 October 1973), outlining his Ph.D. work on Egon Friedell and asking whether or not he could do postdoctoral work under Frye tutelage.

Dear Mr. Patterson,

Thank you for your letter. I imagine that there would be fellowships and financial aid possible at Toronto for the work you propose, but as the situation keeps changing very rapidly, mainly as a result of the unstable position of universities financially, I think it would be better for you to write directly to the School of Graduate Studies at the University of Toronto to see what is available and to see what you would be eligible for. A much more serious matter is that I am promised to Harvard for the year 1974/75, as the Charles Eliot Norton Professor of Poetry.

I was delighted to hear of your interest in Friedell. He was a very early enthusiasm of mine, as I encountered him as an undergraduate, about the time that his books were first appearing in translation.[470] Since then I have hardly seen any references to him, although I think his history was in many respects a very remarkable achievement. At least, my hazy recollection of my youthful enthusiasm registers that. The other works I don't know, but I'd be very interested to hear about them.

Donald Unruh   October 18, 1973
Department of English, University of Colorado, Boulder, CO

In response to Unruh's request (26 September 1973) for Frye to comment on his essay on Blake's The Marriage of Heaven and Hell —*an essay that had been returned to him from several journals without comment.*

Dear Mr. Unruh,

Thanks you for your letter and article. I think that articles dedicated to finding conflicts in a poet are rather hard to bring off, because poets are professionally concerned with constructing larger and inclusive patterns. It seems to me that *The Marriage of Heaven and Hell* is quite explicitly a "Devil's" manifesto, and to that extent a satire. As a deliberate exaggeration it comments on a contemporary revolutionary situation, rather than necessarily conflicting with a much larger structure. I think too you should be careful to distinguish Milton's Satan, the Satan of the Book of Job, Blake's own Satan, and the "Devil" of

The Marriage of Heaven and Hell, before saying (page 18) that Blake identifies Jesus with Satan.

George Johnston   22 October 1973
Carleton University, Ottawa, ON

In response to Johnston's sending Frye the forms for a Canada Council grant for his sabbatical, 1974–75. Johnston intended to work on another collection of his poetry and enclosed with his letter (5 October 1973) several poems copied in his exceptional calligraphic hand.

Dear George,

Thank you for your letter: naturally I have sent off the recommendation and wish you the very best of luck.

It was extremely good of you to write out the copy of the new poems, which will be a cherished possession of ours. I like the poems very much, as always, and there is something about your handwriting that seems appropriate to them: I think you should consider putting out a calligraphic edition of your works some time.[471]

The very best to all of you from us both.

John E. Grant   19 November 1973
Department of English, University of Iowa, Iowa City, IA

In reply to Grant's announcement (28 October 1973) that he and Mary Lynn Johnson will be married in 1974, along with a request for "summaries, diagrams, or fugitive publications" by Frye that might be useful for a course on Frye's criticism he intends to teach.

Dear Jack,

First of all, my heartiest congratulations. I hope to meet both you and Mary Lynn before very long. Of course you were right in using my name as a reference, although Boston has not yet written me. If you would prefer to have me write them directly I would be glad to do so.

A lot of other people have constructed diagrams of my schematisms, but I have never done so myself, because of a disinclination to make any one such diagram definitive. The same thing is true of fugitive pieces: all my writing is definitely commissioned these days, and I can produce nothing that is not instantly swallowed up in somebody's linotype.

Peter Schneider   4 December 1973
English Department, Clark University, Worcester, MA

In reply to Schneider's letter (20 November 1973) in which he asks Frye to respond to a critique of the theory of tragedy in Anatomy of Criticism *that he had presented in a graduate seminar at Clark University.*

Dear Mr. Schneider,

Thank you for your letter. I much appreciate your interest in my work, but it really is not possible to read "The Mythos of Tragedy" in the way that you appear to have read it. I call the story of Adam the archetype of tragedy because it sets out explicitly what is implicit in the general tragic pattern, of a fall from a higher destiny into a state of law which usually involves the hero's death as well. There is no one-to-one relationship between the Adam story and any other tragedy, of the type you suggest. There is no question of Hamlet's ever having been "innocent," nor of his having descended from or returning to another paradisal or timeless state.

If you still have any interest in my views on Shakespeare tragedy, there is a small book called *Fools of Time*, three lectures on the shape of Shakespeare's tragedies.

Tom Brown   **17 December 1973**

CBC Learning Systems, Toronto, ON

In response to Brown's letter (10 December 1973) saying that CBC Publications owes Frye more than $5000 in back royalties. "I can find no evidence," writes Brown, "that you have asked for payment over the years, which suggests to me that you were not aware of your rights — or have been remarkably patient!"

Dear Mr. Brown:

Thank you very much for your letter with its welcome news. I know that I should examine my contracts more closely, but when one has fourteen publishers in addition to a full time job one tends to leave most of the initiative to them. I suppose too that I have subconsciously been assuming that anything done for education, religion, the glory of God or the benefit of man gets very low royalties.

Roy Daniells   **20 December 1973**

University of British Columbia, Vancouver, BC

Daniells had written Frye on 6 November 1973, asking him if he would be "willing to look at a brief statement of some theological difficulties" and make some comments in the margin. Frye obliged, Daniells replied, and Frye then followed up that response with this letter.

Dear Roy,

Following our marginal notes on the first five of your ninety-five theses:

1. It seems to me that there are two mental processes which are quite distinct, both called belief. One is the existence of evidence which seems conclusive, as when I believe that the earth goes round the sun and not vice versa. The other is a belief derived not from evidence, but from imaginative vision. A belief of this kind is an axiom of one's conduct: what a man believes in this sense is only what his actions show that he believes. Such beliefs represent a voluntary choice from an infinite number of imaginative possibilities. The gospels present their story as a myth, an imaginative vision. They are remarkably careless about collecting or appealing to evidence in the form of testimony or reason. The account of the resurrection is designed to elicit the response "I can believe in a conquest over death achieved by human, backed by divine, power," or something like that. I don't think they are trying to elicit the response "I find that these things happened exactly as described, because I believe that the writers are trustworthy historians." They are not trustworthy historians: they tell four different stories. But they are all agreed that resurrection is an important subject to decide on for belief, one way or the other. From this point of view, it is not necessarily a misleading myth to say "in Adam all die," which simply means that everybody dies.

2. I agree about the habitual dishonesty of theologians, but of course they are just as confused as everyone else about the distinction between the two kinds of belief. As long as they could they tried to insist that belief in Christ was the same kind of belief as belief in the global shape of the earth. Forced out of that position, they find themselves with no standards for any other kind of belief. Very few theologians know or care much about literature or about the mental processes it calls for. So they cannot understand that the gospel writers wrote in mythical rather than historical language because they felt that what they had to say was too important to be trusted to factual language.

3. I don't know Julian Huxley, but of course Blake also says "God only acts and is, in existing beings or men."[472]

4. My only difficulty with this is that I don t see any basis for a Jesus behind the gospels. From the very first moment that we see him, Jesus is imprisoned within the gospels, pre-

sented within a framework of assumptions derived from the early church. But as to the betrayal of a prophet by his followers, that of course always happens.

5. Certainly the tradition of Christianity has been overwhelmingly in favour of persecution: how much of this derives from the personality of Paul I am not sure. I'd be inclined to start the really vicious period of Christianity with Constantine. The Church developed a power structure parallel to that of the Empire, so it could go underground when persecuted, and emerge to administer things in the old imperial way when times changed. It's the old story of revolution coming to power.

Incidentally, have you seen a novel called *The Master and Margarita*, by Mikhail Bulgakov? Bulgakov was a much persecuted writer in Soviet Russia who produced this extraordinary story a year or two before he died. It's about a man who is writing a book on Pontius Pilate.

Jean Hagstrum   **20 December 1973**
Department of English, Northwestern University, Evanston, IL

Dear Jean:

Thank you very much for the Blake articles,[473] which I have read with great interest and approval. It is very important to insist on Blake's power as a love poet: something a distressing number of critics seem either not to see or deliberately to ignore.

David W. Ehrenfeld   **15 January 1974**
Department of Biological Sciences, Barnard College, Columbia University, NY

In reply to Ehrenfeld's query (28 December 1973): why is Spengler not juxtaposed more often in the critical literature with Roderick Seidenberg? Ehrenfeld reports that he had just read Frye's essay on Spengler, "The Decline of the West by Oswald Spengler" (Dædalus 103 [Winter 1974]: 1–13), which he found to be reminiscent of Orwell's critical style.

Dear Mr. Ehrenfeld:

Thank you very much for your letter. I am glad if I was like Orwell, who seems to me an admirable stylist, but he is impossible to imitate, because his lucidity is a direct product of his moral integrity.

I cannot say that I know Seidenberg's book[474] well enough to answer your questions properly. From what I can gather of him, I should say that you have answered them yourself pretty accurately.[475] I don't know why he isn't mentioned more often: I suppose one thing is the difference in date. Seidenberg seems to me to be predominantly a writer reflecting the age of science fiction as an extremely important and central cultural development. But the kind of questioning of cultural values which he embodies seems very like the kind of thing one keeps running into in Clarke, Bradbury, Ballard, and others. In general, I am inclined to feel that Seidenberg's thesis is really a more superficial and simplified version of Spengler's, as you yourself strongly hint.

I wish you the best of luck in your own reflections on the subject.

Janice Castro   **18 January 1974**
New York, NY
See headnote to letter of 18 June 1971.

Dear Janice,

I was delighted to get your letter, and naturally fascinated to learn of your discovery of Blake. Blake is the kind of writer who ought to come as a discovery, otherwise he doesn't make his full impact. That is why I am content to have him regarded by most academics as a minor writer, so he won't be assumed to be part of a cultural establishment.

You certainly seem to be God's gift to *Time*, and I am most pleased that you had a Canadian story to deal with. It's extraordinary how the nationalist mood in Canada has intensified within the last few years: English Canada seems to be discovering itself as an entity, partly in reaction to all the French-Canadian turmoil of a few years ago. If I had emigrated to the United States ten years ago, there would have been nostalgic sighs of regret; today there would be howls of outrage. And, of course, we are just beginning to realize what it feels like to be sitting on a hell of a lot of oil — the tar sands of Alberta have enough for the whole world if we could figure a way to get it out. As I expect I told you, I am attached to the Canadian Radio-Television Commission, roughly the equivalent of the F.C.C. in the United States, though with considerably more direct authority. It gives me a fascinating perspective of the country that I couldn't get otherwise, and has taught me one elementary but essential fact: that the most important communications medium is money.

The very best from us both, and from Jane.

Roy Daniells   **18 January 1974**
University of British Columbia, Vancouver, BC

On 2 January 1974 Daniells wrote Frye a brief note, thanking him for his letter 20 December 1973. But the letter to which the present response is a reply has apparently not survived.

Dear Roy,

Of course nobody can defend the historical record of Christianity, beyond remarking that it proves one of Christianity's central doctrines, the doctrine of original sin. But I doubt if it's any worse than, say, the record of law, which has been largely a record of vicious cruelty and oppression. And yet we may still feel that we ought to live within a framework of law, while trying to make it less ghastly.

Sorry to hear about Lionel Stevenson[476]: I think my last talk with him was at the English Institute in New York, where I gave a paper on Dickens.[477]

The very best to you both for the New Year.

Owen L. Dickman   **18 January 1974**
Institute for Communications Studies, Toronto, ON

In reply to Dickman's request (14 January 1974) for Frye's comments on a position paper, enclosed with his letter, about the lack of effectiveness in personal and corporate communications and the potential of "behavioural communications" to solve the problem.

Dear Mr. Dickman:

Thank you for your letter and for the position paper, which I have read with interest. Two things occur to me in particular. One is, that of all communications media, the most important is money. I have become aware of this through my connection with the Canadian Radio-Television Commission, where the most glowing promises about improvement in programming invariably get bogged down in a commercial routine. This means that the economic context of communications is so important that I doubt whether communication itself can be realistically isolated as a subject of study.

My other reflection also relates to context. In the theory of communication there is something called a noise factor which intervenes between sender and receiver. This is a mechanical problem, to be solved in a mechanical way. But it seems to me that there are emotional noise factors, connected mainly with anxiety, which are even more important.

They include the anxieties of broadcasters and newspaper owners about sponsorship and advertising, and the growing panic of many viewers of T.V. sets at being shown in an increasingly passive role. This suggests that the psychological and cultural context of communications is as important as the economic one. For these reasons, I have reservations about the possibility of making the study of communications a "behavioral" one.

Dominick Yezzo   24 January 1974
Flushing, NY

In reply to Yezzo's request (26 November 1973) for Frye to help him understand the secrets of Blake's imaginative vision. Yezzo, from a working class background, had begun his study of literature at Queen's College, New York, after having served in Vietnam. He had been teaching Blake's The Marriage of Heaven and Hell *since 1980.*

Dear Mr. Yezzo,

It is a little difficult to know how to answer your letter, because when you speak of Blake's "secrets," you seem to be implying that there are certain procedures, almost certain gimmicks, available for imitating his intensity of vision. So far as I know there are no procedures in the West, though of course the Indian students of yoga have an oral tradition of such things. Blake himself had great creative powers in poetry and painting, and he developed his visionary intensity by concentrating on the craftsmanship of those two arts. I think he would perhaps say that everybody has something in him which is creative, and that concentrating on that is the way to raise one's perception into a freer world. Your general intuitions about Blake's attitudes are sound enough, though what he ultimately saw was not so much a vision of God as a vision of the Creation as divine. That is, he thought of God as the perceiver within himself, not as anything objective or out there. But you do go on to say that, and perhaps the most helpful thing I can say is that if you continue trying to release your own imagination you will set going a process that will not let you down.

Robert D. Denham   12 March 1974
Department of English, Emory & Henry College, Emory, Virginia

In response to Denham's having sent Frye a copy of his Northrop Frye: An Enumerative Bibliography *(Metuchen, NJ: Scarecrow Press, 1974).*

Dear Mr. Denham,

The bibliography is a most impressive achievement: your introduction in particular, which I had not seen before, seems to me an excellent and very judicious one. Reading through Section 3, I am astonished at the number of people who seem to have rushed into print with the notion that my view of literature is preposterous. Something tells me that the twenty-first century will have a good deal of difficulty in understanding what all the fuss was about.

I need not labour again what I have said many times, that I am profoundly grateful and deeply appreciative of your work. I hope there will be rewards in it for you as there certainly will be for me.

Betty Cole   17 April 1974
Toronto, ON

In reply to Cole's inquiry (8 April 1974) about what Frye meant by saying that every society is geared to certain prejudices, some good and some bad.

Dear Miss Cole:

Thank you for your letter. I was using the term prejudice in the sense used by Edmund

Burke, where he speaks of prejudice as the kind of deductive principle that one adopts for practical reasons, in an area where in general only inductive and pragmatic standards are operative. It seems to me that where such prejudices are good or bad is in the area of ultimate choices. I think there has to be some assumption that life is better than death, freedom better than slavery, happiness better than misery, equality better than exploitation, for all men everywhere without exception. I would even say that this choice was bound up with the indivisible nature of God that you refer to.

I much appreciate your interest.

Thomas D. Thibeault   17 April 1974
Bishop's University, Lennoxville, QC

In reply to Thibeault's request (7 April 1974) for Frye to send him "a reading list of the twenty most important books" that would lead him to appreciate and understand literature.

Dear Mr. Thibeault,

Thank you for your letter. For the life of me I don't see what benefit it would be to you to give you a list of twenty books or so to read, when all the rest of your letter says very clearly that it is not what you have read but how you have read that makes you dissatisfied. There is no magic concealed in any book that you have not yet read, whatever it may be. In the course of your very extensive reading there must have been things which struck you more than others. Perhaps the first thing to do is to reread what has struck you most forcibly and see if it can make an impact at a deeper level. You say that you have read a good deal of Conrad, and that what you got out of him was the storyteller rather than the artist. Conrad's artistry is inseparable from his storytelling, and if you reread any book of his that struck you with particular force I think you will see this.

I suggest beginning with rereading some of the things you have read, for two reasons. One is, that if you reread Shakespeare, for instance, you will be reading some plays that would certainly be on anybody's list of twenty books. Reading them when you are older, and have more experience to bring to them, would transform their effect on you. Second, reading is a leisurely occupation: it is not self-indulgent, but it has to be done without panic, without thinking of how much there is still to read. Neither you nor anyone else can possibly make much of a dent in everything there is to read.

I feel quite sure that if you follow your own tastes you will come much more quickly than in any other way to the source of what you must need to read. Every reader has his own structure, founded on his own particular characteristics as a person, and the foundations have to be laid accordingly.

J.M. Godfrey   18 April 1974
The Senate, Ottawa, ON

In reply to Godfrey's letter (11 April 1974) relating his encounter in Cairo with Dr. Magdi Waba, who insisted that the first book his students read is Frye's Anatomy of Criticism. *"As far as he is concerned, you are Canada's most famous citizen." Godfrey was a Senator, a member of the Liberal Party of Canada, and the driving force of its National Finance and Treasury Committee from 1968 to 1974.*

Dear Mr. Godfrey,

Thank you very much for your note, which it was most thoughtful of you to send. I am somewhat dimly aware of the extent to which I am being used in other countries, and am largely dependent on the kindness of people like yourself for my knowledge of it.

With thanks and best wishes.

Martin Wolfson   10 May 1974
Woodridge, NY

Wolfson has effusive praise for Frye, calling him erudite, lucid, enlightening, illuminating, provocative, subtle, and relevant. But he asks (letter of 26 April 1974) why Frye does not tantalize him like Wittgenstein, Popper, Strawson, Quine, and Geach do, providing "intellectual sweat," and he begs Frye to write an article on Wittgenstein.

Dear Mr. Wolfson,

Thank you for your letter. It looks as though the articles that you find particularly challenging are those written by philosophers, and I do not consider myself a technically competent philosopher, only a literary critic interested in philosophy. Wittgenstein is certainly a subject that would interest me, but as I have no commission to write on him it will probably be some time before I can. There is also the possibility that the lucidity in my writing, which you mention, is deceptive.

Donald Greene   28 May 1974
Department of English, University of Southern California, Los Angeles, CA

In reply to Green's having written Frye (20 May 1974) a note of congratulations on his having won an election for office in the Modern Language Association, meaning that he would assume the presidency of that organization in 1976.

Dear Don,

Thanks very much for your note. I have just attended a meeting in New York, and I really feel more pleased than I thought I would at returning to that group, different as the personnel is. I also feel somewhat amused at the fact that I am likely to be giving the presidential address in 1976, and so taking part in the celebration of 1776, the year made immortal by the publication of Adam Smith's *Wealth of Nations*.

William Harmon   29 July 1974
Department of English, University of North Carolina, Chapel Hill, NC

In reply to Harmon's request (8 July 1974) for the source of Joyce's referring to Eliot as "the Bishop of Hippo," which Frye quotes in his book on Eliot (pp. 67–8). Harmon replied with a note of thanks, which prompted Frye to write again (13 August 1974) to say "Marshall McLuhan was present when this tag from Joyce was quoted, and his memory of it may be more accurate than mine."

Dear Mr. Harmon:

I am afraid that my reference was a somewhat irresponsible one, having been quoted orally from someone who had been working in the Joyce papers at Buffalo. I ought to resist the temptation to introduce such things when I haven't checked them myself. But this one seemed too good to pass up.

With best wishes and useless apologies.

Morris E. Eaves   29 July 1974
Blake Newsletter, University of New Mexico, Albuquerque, NM

Dear Mr. Eaves:

I have been subscribing to, and regularly reading the *Blake Newsletter*, and I hope very much that it will be put on a permanent basis. A great variety of such newsletters come into my office, but this one stands out among them all, both in the variety of its contents and in the quality of its layout and reproductions. It seems to me that scholarship is moving into a period where so much is being done that journals of this sort are become increasingly indispensable as a scholarly tool. A journal like this, which not only tells us what is being done on Blake, but prints a great deal of it too, brings together an amount of work that saves everyone in the field months of searching through other journals, besides, of course, saving months, or even years, for Blake scholars who would otherwise have to find less likely places for publication, or wait until their research had swelled into something else. I am no longer very active as a Blake scholar, but even so I would not like to be without the newsletter, and if I were I should feel quite crippled without it.

Gordon Fellman   11 August 1974
Department of Sociology, Brandeis University, Waltham, MA

In 1973 Frye was asked by The Franklin Mint to become a member of the advisory panel that would select one hundred great books. He consented and was sent a checklist with certain titles already on the list and with instructions that it was possible to add alternate titles. Frye duly constructed his list, taking his assignment seriously, as can be seen from the list he compiled, which is included in a note to this letter. He was paid $1000 for agreeing to participate in the venture. Shortly after the Franklin Mint made its list of titles available, Frye began receiving mail, such as Fellman's letter, criticizing him for lending his name to such a cheap commercial enterprise and noting that the gimmicky advertising brochure of the Franklin Mint did not indicate the titles selected or the editions used. Frye received a similar protest from Anthony Wolf and John McAleer, to whom he responded on 22 May 1974: "My connection with the Franklin Library scheme was confined to agreeing to serve as an 'advisor' for their list of titles. They sent their list of titles to me; I sent them back my own notion of what a hundred "great books" might be, and they went ahead with their original selection. In other words, consulting me was pure ritual. If you were to say that I should have known in advance that this was the case, you would doubtless be right."

Dear Mr. Fellman:

Thank you for your letter. You were quite right about the participation: I should never have lent myself to such a business, and much regret having done so. I am not at my most perceptive on the end of a long distance telephone, and the proposal to ask for my advice in selecting a list of books, accompanied with various distinguished names who are friends of mine,[478] looked at the time more innocent than it is, and than I should have known it would be.

Herbert F. Ostrach   13 August 1974
Boston College, Chestnut Hill, MA

In response to Ostrach's letter (22 July 1974), asking for a commentary on his theory of the Western movie, which he develops in some detail.

Dear Mr. Ostrach,

Thank you very much for a most thoughtful letter. I suspect that you have very largely clarified the problem in your mind by writing to me, but one or two observations may be helpful. They are not, however, made of any extensive or even adequate knowledge of Westerns.

I am not sure that I follow your distinction between displaced myth and what you call "myth itself." It seems to me that some displacing is already inherent in the mere structure of narrative presentation itself. The nearest one could get to "myth itself" would probably be some kind of concrete poem, in which there was no narrative progression at all but only a set of interlocking metaphors.

The Westerner as you describe him surely has his roots very deep in American literature. He develops out of such figures as the Hawkeye in Cooper, who goes back into the woods at the end of *The Last of the Mohicans*, a similar figure I've forgotten in *The Deerslayer*, and so on. Fiedler, as you know, has written about this, and talked about the American hero without a bride.

The Western has always seemed to me a pastoral form, and in American culture it seems to me to express something of the pastoral feeling that all social ideals, however Utopian, are tentative and transitional, and that behind them there is still the reconciliation of man with the nature which he has conquered and violated. The symbol for this is the withdrawal from the social group of a figure who is not an idyllic or innocent figure, but a figure of weary experience who points to something that the conclusion of comic pastoral has yet to do. An example in the mainstream of literature would be the withdrawal of the melancholy Jaques from all the marriages in *As You Like It*.

Dorothy Bartram   14 August 1974
Toronto, ON

Dear Mrs. Bartram,

Robin Harris[479] sent to me some time ago your essay on the idea of the University, and I have read it with fascinated appreciation. Your study is extremely valuable to me, not only for recalling many articles that I had totally forgotten having written, but for documenting so fully what I already knew, that almost everything I have written is connected with my conception of the university and its social role.

Best wishes and renewed thanks.

Margaret Stobie   15 August 1974
Department of English, University of Manitoba, Winnipeg, MB

In reply to Stobie's letter of 11 August 1974, saying that she was just back from England, congratulating Frye for his appointment as the Norton Lecturer at Harvard, and announcing that she, like Frye before her, had resigned from an unidentified humanist consulting committee, adding that she was opposed to the movement afoot by the government to split the Canada Council.

Dear Peg,

Thanks very much for your letter: I have just got back myself from a month at Merton College, where I was working on the Norton lectures. It was a relief to hear that you had resigned from that infernal committee too, as I don't have guilt feelings any more about deserting you. It was clear that neither of us could stop that mindless machine from rolling down hill. I entirely agree about the Canada Council business, and hope the move can be stopped in time.[480]

Love to yourself and Bill from us both.

Nobuaki Kozaki   27 August 1974
Kumamotoshi, Japan

In response to Kozaki's request (19 August 1974) for assistance in developing practical expository prose "without fully absorbing the language of poetry and literary prose."

Dear Mr. Kozaki,

Thank you for your letter. I think it should be possible to get a good grasp of practical English and expository prose, though I should think that a teaching course in such a subject would be more useful if you could obtain such a thing at a university or technical college near you. It is quite possible to get a practical working knowledge of a language without studying its literature in depth, but there are many nuances of expression that make it difficult for anyone working on his own. To give you an example: your letter says "I am learning English mostly from written matters": normal English usage would say "materials" rather than "matters." The authors that you mention[481] are very good ones, and I think that my own book exists not only in a Japanese translation, but in an English version edited for Japanese students.[482] In this latter form it is one of a series in which there are many other useful books, such as one by Lionel Trilling. My own book, incidentally, is not a safe guide for your purposes, because it is written in a deliberately colloquial style.

Kenneth J. Weber   30 August 1974
Faculty of Education, University of Toronto

In reply to Weber's letter (26 August 1974), announcing that he is sending Frye a copy of his forthcoming book and apologizing for the printer's failure to include a reference to one of Frye's articles.

Dear Mr. Weber,

Thank you very much for your book,[483] which has just arrived and which I am greatly looking forward to reading. It looks at first glance to be a more practical and constructive book than another book which for all its limitations I found a genuinely moving book: *English for the Rejected*.[484] Don't worry about the footnote reference: there are many people who have based their entire careers on my work without acknowledgment.

Best wishes and renewed thanks.

Sidney Feshbach   13 September 1974
Department of English, City College, City University of New York, New York, NY

During 1973 Feshbach wrote several letters to Frye (15 March, 13 May, 5 October) indicating his intention to begin a journal, Mamalujo, *devoted to* Anatomy of Criticism. *As Frye was on sabbatical, the present letter in reply was not sent until about a year later.*

Dear Mr. Feshbach:

I have not been communicating with you about Mamalujo, because my role in it seems to me a very difficult one for me to define. I think it's admirable to have critical discussion of me, as part of a continuing dialogue on criticism generally. After prolonged reflection, however, it seems to me that the less I have to do with this dialogue the better. I find that critical discussion on my work often finds contradictions in it which exist for the writer but nor for me, and that the assumptions are too remote from mine for me to deal with them. That is, while I highly approve of criticism of my work, I don't seem to be temperamentally capable of using it to revise the *Anatomy* or any other work of mine. I simply have to go my own way, and leave it to others to make what sense they can of it. The *Anatomy* does not seem to me to be a revisable book, even though the criticism of the next generation will certainly include a great deal of revision of it by other people.

What I have still to write are large-scale studies of the Bible, of the general shape of the mythological universe (which my Norton lectures at Harvard this year will partly deal with), with conceptual myth, and other things. The *Anatomy* already seems to be very much a product of its time, the mid-fifties; in a sense the man who wrote it is dead, and the person continuous with him is going on to other things.

I know that this is a most unsatisfactory letter: I have merely tried to make it an honest one.

Ian Montagnes   30 December 1974
General Editor, University of Toronto Press, Toronto

Dear Ian,

I am sorry to have been so long in considering your letter about taking part in the projected work on contemporary Canadian art. At the moment I am so immersed in finishing the Norton lectures for Harvard—Harvard having left me no time to do anything of the sort while there—that I can hardly take in anything else. I still feel that I am not very useful to you in this project, and that my background is too literary and verbalized for me to contribute much about the more abstract developments. What interests me mainly about post–Group-of-Seven painting in Canada is a somewhat extended form of what's sometimes called magic realism. This would include not only Colville and Kurelek and Hughes and Blackwood,[485] but, first, Eskimo spirit paintings and the like; second, a great deal of primitive painting and painting that uses primitive motifs, such as Lamieux[486]; third, nostalgic-and-searching-eye painting of the Albert Franck[487] type, and fourth, the ghosts of landscape in Riopelle[488] and others. I also feel that the *refus global* manifesto was pretty significant historically, whatever it may have been intrinsically.[489]

Ivan-Constantin Hekimian   30 January 1975
Cairo, Egypt

In reply to Hekimian's query (26 November 1974), "How can I acquire your vision and insight?" Hekimian, now twenty, reports that he has been searching for the past nine years and has come "to see what an insignificant straw" his ignorance has left him.

Dear Mr. Hekimian,

Thank you for your letter. There is really no way of acquiring whatever glimpses of vision and insight one has: they are given, not acquired. All that one can do, in order to have them given, is what you tell me you have been doing: making a constant and recurring discovery of one's own total ignorance. Knowledge is acquired: wisdom begins when we have realized that we know nothing and that nothing is really acquired.

Roy Daniells   19 March 1975
Via della Maratona, Rome, Italy   Cambridge, MA

In reply to Daniells's letter (24 February 1975) in which he outlines his religious anxieties and wonders if Frye can tell him how he worked through his own beliefs about hell, the Assumption of the Virgin, betrayal by the Church, and the like. This letter is in the Roy Daniells Fonds, University of British Columbia, box 8, file 13.

Dear Roy:

Thank you for your letter: I hope your year in Italy is as productive and pleasant as it should be. I have been having an exhilarating but very exhausting time here, teaching a course in Biblical typology to four hundred students and trying to get my Norton lectures ready for April. Working without a secretary is also confusing, as I tend to revert to my usual schizoid habits, picking up pieces of paper and forgetting where I set them down. I don't have to teach, but the fine print in my contract says they want me to be "available" to students, and I thought I'd prefer to be available through the normal channels.

Aristotle says that history is a primary verbal imitation of action, states particular facts, and is judged by truth of correspondence between the words and the facts they describe. Poetry is a secondary verbal imitation of action, states universal truths, and is judged by truth of its inner coherence. To me, poetry and myth are interchangeable. Some clunkheads talk about trying to "demythologize" the Gospels or the Bible, subtract everything that seems incredible and keep a historical residue. If you tried that with the Gospels, all you'd have would be something like "Jesus wept." Not until EVERY GODDAM SYLLABLE of the Bible has been translated into myth does it even pretend to make any sense. Historical meaning: the Jews and Romans crucified Christ. So what? Mythical meaning: you and I crucified Christ. That at least makes sense in its own terms, whether one accepts it as faith or not: the essential thing is to get rid of it as fact. Historical meaning: in the beginning God made heaven and earth. Interesting primitive hypothesis long ago superseded by a coherent biological and geological science. Mythical meaning: let's assume that reality has an original identity connected with an infinitely higher power and intelligence than ours. Again, that makes sense in its own terms. Or: we're told that Adam was kicked out of Eden into a wilderness but will eventually get back his lost trees and rivers. That's pure myth. Israel descended into Egypt, the furnace of iron, and made its way back to its Promised Land. That's historical reminiscence of some kind; we don't know what kind. The Jews went into exile in Babylon and returned to build the temple. That's roughly historical, plus a good deal of didactic manipulation. The point is that all these up-and-down-and-up movements are all equally mythical. If anything that's historically true is in the Bible, it's there by accident and because it fits the myth.

What fills me with horror and terror, to use your words, is the mystery of the corrupted human will. That is never more corrupt than when it gets to work in the religious area, in obedience to Swift's principle that we use religion to hate each other and not for love.[490] The desire to persecute is never founded on "believe in God," but always on "believe in what I mean by God"—all persecution and inquisition have been products of man's deifying of his own understanding. That and the lust for political power. In the Apocalypse of Peter, one of the earliest NT pseudepigrapha, Peter is shown hell, given a strong hint that the sufferings there may not be everlasting after all, and then cautioned not to say this to anyone when he gets back, because people won't behave properly unless they're threatened with this kind of bogie.[491] That's the way social institutions operate, and they operate in the same way even in Marxist countries where there's no religious basis as such. They all try to paralyze man with fear.

Christianity makes a good deal of sense to me because its myth does. It identifies man and God in a way that doesn't cripple our critical faculties, and the kind of man it sees as divine is a man who cared enough about what was happening to other men to go through a pretty grim death. I know that the Christian myth has been treated as fact but the people who did that were repeating the crucifixion when they made martyrs of people like Bruno and Servetus.

Love to Laurenda from us both.

Herbert Ostrach   **31 March 1975**
Boston College, Chestnut Hill, MA

In reply to Ostrach's second letter about his theory of the Western movie. See Frye's responses of 13 August 1974 to an earlier letter.

Dear Mr. Ostrach,

Thank you for your letter. It seems to me that you have your categories set up in a way that makes sense to you, and that I should only be a hindrance if I were to attempt to redefine or refine my own distinctions. I am quite willing to accept Westerns as sacred history in your sense. I have more difficulty with them as being myths in the sense of being extensively used for non-literary social purposes, as the archaic myths are. The few Westerns I have seen seem to me to be literary in the sense in which you use it. But if you can make your case, I should infinitely prefer to have you make it than have you feel that I was running interference with you.

Patrick Cheney   1 April 1975

Department of English, Victoria College

In reply to Cheney's letter (20 February 1975), asking whether two character types he has found in Renaissance literature — the amphibian figure and the hermaphrodite figure — are related to the Eros-Narcissus distinction Frye makes in A Natural Perspective. *Cheney was a teaching assistant at Victoria College, working on a Ph.D. thesis on Spenser.*

Dear Mr. Cheney:

Thank you for your letter. I only wish I could reply to it more satisfactorily. It seems to me that your "amphibian" figure would have a natural connexion with Narcissus, because of the reflecting-figure-in-water theme, and many agents of love are detached from sex, though as a rule by having no sex than by having both. If you heard me last year on Shakespeare's *Phoenix and the Turtle,* you may remember the two attendant birds, the surpliced swan (asexual) and the crow that changes its sex every time it breathes. It seems to me also that Narcissus themes are themes of descending into a state of greater restriction, and Eros figures themes of escaping out of it. It is possible that you are trying to categorize too quickly, and should simply note the occurrences and overlappings of your different figures until some pattern emerges. I don't think Cupid or Eros is very frequently what you call amphibian: it's his victims that would suffer rather than himself. The prototype of the latter is the Psyche of Apuleius. If I could see your paper on *The Roaring Girl*, I could perhaps get a clearer notion of what your problems are, though I couldn't promise to look at it before May.[492]

Roy Daniells   1 April 1975

Rome, Italy

Written as a follow-up of Frye's letter of 19 March 1975. Daniells wrote to Frye on 29 April 1975, thanking him for his "most useful and thoughtful letters."

Dear Roy,

I wrote you recently from Harvard, but am not sure that I said very much helpful to you in that letter. Nor am I sure that I can now. In early adolescence I suddenly realized, with an utter and complete conviction of which I have never lost one iota since, that the whole apparatus of afterlife in heaven and hell, unpardonable sins, and the like was a lot of junk. There remained, of course, the influence of my mother, and the fact that I had already agreed to go on to college as a church student. My mental processes were pretty confused, but restructuring them by hindsight I think they were something like this: if I go through the whole business of revolting against this, I shall be making a long and pointless detour back to where I shall probably come out anyway, and will probably have acquired a neurosis besides. I think I decided very early, without realizing it at the time, that I was going to accept out of religion only what made sense to me as a human being. I was not going to worship a god whose actions, judged by human standards, were contemptible. That was where Blake helped me so much: he taught me that the lugubrious old stinker in the sky that I had heard so much about existed all right, but that his name was Satan, that his function was to promote tyranny in society and repression in the mind. This meant that the Methodist church down at the corner was consecrated mainly to devil-worship, but, because it did not know that, it would tolerate something better without knowing what that was either.

I learned nothing from the people at Victoria or Emmanuel: [Edward W.] Wallace, coming from his missionary compound, was only what the Irish call a spoiled priest; [Walter T.] Brown was only rhetorically a Christian, actually a Platonist who thought Christianity was the best way of indoctrinating middle-class supremacy, and the Emmanuel people were dazed professionals, spokesmen of what Kierkegaard calls, with such contempt, "Christendom." I realized very early that the New Testament was full of pious frauds, like the Second Epistle of Peter, and that there was not one trustworthy word about a historical Jesus anywhere in the New Testament. I never felt outraged or betrayed by this particularly: I always knew that Christianity was a revolutionary movement, like Marxism, and that it cared only about *its* truth, not for truth as such.

What struck me in the Gospels was the extraordinary thoroughness with which it obliterated any credible or historically conceived Jesus. This suggests, of course, a double fraud: the New Testament writers deliberately concocting a myth and the church deliberately perverting the myth into an alleged historical fact. The perversion was something I had to accept, as a fact about history and human nature, as far as the church was concerned. The Gospel writers were different: they seemed to be so *damned* clever in the completeness with which they transformed the something historical, assuming it was there, into myth. And yet they didn't seem to be such clever men. I began to see that myth was the opposite of history, in a sense: that what it describes is essentially what is supposed to start happening in the reader's mind while he reads. This is what Milton calls the Word of God in the heart[493] and ultimately gives the highest authority to. So the whole drama of the human movement, which was also a divine movement, incarnating itself in the world and pulling the world up with it at the Resurrection, seemed to me to make sense. In this process everything demonic gets left behind. Hell and torture and punishment and revenge and unpardonable sins all vanish into nothingness in that upward movement. So the Gospel writers weren't really liars, any more than poets are. The difference between them and poets is that the structure they give the reader is existential, something he can take as a basis for action.

I am attaching a few pages from a recent book of mine that you may not have seen yet which comments on the whole operation.[494]

Love to Laurenda from us both.

Goldwin French   **1 April 1975**
President, Victoria University
In reply to French's letter (17 February 1975), following up on their discussion about Frye's becoming the general editor of a cultural history of Ontario.

Dear Goldwin:

I have been thinking very deeply about the possibility of becoming Chief Editor, and it is with a great deal of regret that I have to say that it doesn't seem to me to be a physical possibility. I won't bore you with all the details, but they include a long book on the

Bible and literature which I am frantically anxious to get at, the preparing for publication of the Norton lectures, which are also part of a long and complex book, three or four commitments in the fall, the Presidency of the MLA, which comes up next year, and various sleeping dogs likely to wake up and bite me in the rear at any moment. This last includes Carl Klink's project, the *Literary History of Canada* which is now being updated from 1960, and will consequently need a new conclusion to be written by Canada's official concluder.

I am genuinely sorry about this, but you can see what the situation is like. I can hardly expect my typewriter to stop clicking at all next year.

With genuine regrets and best wishes.

Kirpal Singh   1 April 1975
Department of English, University of Singapore, Singapore
In response to Singh's letter (10 March 1975) asking Frye for further illumination of his ideas in The Educated Imagination *about belief, self-expression, and the moral qualities of literature, among other things.*

Dear Mr. Singh,

Thank you for your letter. I quite agree with you about the necessity of belief: belief as such is really a desire to attach oneself to a specific community, and of course we all have to belong to communities. We belong to something before we are born. The differences among beliefs reflect the differences among communities: what is genuine about them is universal, but one can hardly reach the universal directly.

It is difficult for me to comment on your remarks about *The Educated Imagination*, not because I have any dislike of having my statements queried, but because I am not ruling out such things as self-expression or moral quality: I am merely trying to arrange things in forms that make more sense, as I see it, in making a systematic study of literature.

It is somewhat late for birthday greetings but I wish you all the best in any case.[495]

Eugene (Bud) Korkowski   14 May 1975
Department of English, Texas Tech University, Lubbock, TX
In reply to Korkowski's letter (6 May 1975) which complains that Frye's anatomy as a form of prose fiction is just another name for the Menippean satire. Korkowski encloses an offprint of one of his articles.

Dear Mr. Korkowski,

Thank you for your letter and article.[496] I am sorry that you found my conception of the anatomy an obstacle in your work, but the Menippean satire is a very specific tradition, and there ought to be another word to describe a technique of fiction-writing which includes the Menippean satire but also extends to many writers that are not primarily interested in that tradition, such as Sterne and Melville. I think the chief tendency of my work has been to make people much more aware of the Menippean satire than they were before, and consequently more receptive, among other things, to your article. When I started writing on such subjects there was not one in a thousand University English teachers of *Gulliver's Travels* who knew what Menippean satire was: now there must be two or three.

John E. Grant   20 May 1975
Department of English, University of Iowa, Iowa City, IA
In reply to Grant's request (9 May 1975) for a bibliographic update in connection with his teaching a course devoted to Frye's work at Emory University during the summer term. Grant

remarks that Harold Bloom's A Map of Misreading *has convinced him that Bloom's "revisionistic anxieties will never be allayed." He enclosed a copy of his article on Blake's* Sun Flower.

Dear Jack,

Thank you very much for your letter. As you may know, I spent last year at Harvard as the Norton Professor of Poetry. That meant six lectures to be published by the Harvard Press. They have the manuscript, but I haven't had a deadline on publication as yet. My secretary is including a list of publications since Denham's bibliography.[497] I expect that most of these articles will go into a new collection of my essays, probably to be done by Indiana, but I still have to work that out.[498]

I am disappointed with Harold's book: it seems to me such a perverse application of a quite sound critical principle. You are quite right in using the word "anxieties" about him: I'm afraid they're almost on the point of taking him over.

Thanks very much for the "Sun Flower" article, which I am delighted to have.[499]

Earle Labor   20 May 1975
Department of English, Centenary College of Louisiana, Shreveport, LA

In reply to Labor's inquiry (4 April 1975) about the reversal of the archetypes for spring and summer in Anatomy of Criticism *from what they had been in "The Archetypes of Literature," romance having been changed from the spring to the summer seasonal analogue. Labor was revising the entry on the "mythological approach" in the* Handbook of Critical Approaches to Literature, *which he and others had written.*

Dear Mr. Labor,

Thank you for your letter. I am sorry I have taken so long in answering it, but I have been in transition from Harvard back to Toronto.

I have, as you can probably imagine, had a good deal of embarrassment about the discrepancy between my two seasonal categories. When the essays for my *Fables of Identity* were complete, my publisher insisted on including the very early *Kenyon Review* article. I let it go because the association of the four *mythoi* with the four seasons was not intended as a statement of fact, but was purely symbolic and mnemonic. The *Anatomy* version is much easier for the people who have read that book and have followed my later work. The reason why I made the change was that it was easier to work with as my conceptions grew more elaborate and complex. I very much dislike rereading my works once published, and this is the chief example so far of the way that this morbidity in me catches up with me.

I am afraid this is not a very helpful letter, but it is not a subject I can easily be helpful about. If you prefer to quote the earlier version, it might be helpful to have a footnote explaining that there is a later and different version.

W.K. Wimsatt   29 May 1975
Yale University, New Haven, CT

In reply to Wimsatt's letter (23 May 1975), which announces that he is planning a new collection of essays, one of which will be his critique of Frye, "Criticism as Myth." Wimsatt wonders whether Frye will be offended by the reprinting of his polemical attack.

Dear Bill,

Thank you very much for your letter: I am very glad that a new collection of your essays is to come out.[500] Certainly you should include your piece on me: as regards prose style alone, it's as bright and lively a piece as you have ever done.

Marian Trites Davis   **2 June 1975**
Fredericton, NB

In reply to a childhood next-door neighbor in Moncton, NB, who offers to return a set of book-ends, given to her by Frye's father, that she thinks Frye may have made in a manual training class.

Dear Marian:

Thank you very much for your letter: it was most pleasant to hear from you, and if you come to Toronto, I should like to get the news about you and about Vaughan and Lois. If the book-ends look like book-ends, they are unlikely to be mine. If they look like something that a gorilla would have torn out of a tree, they may be mine. In either case you are very welcome to them.

Fred Grossberg   **2 June 1975**
Fairfax, VA

In reply to Grossberg's request for a meeting with Frye to discuss a book on Wallace Stevens. Grossberg had completed a Ph.D. dissertation on Stevens at Harvard: "Wallace Stevens: The Structure of His Thought and Imagery" (1975).

Dear Fred,

Sorry to be so long answering your letter: I gave the six Norton lectures in April, and getting through them and out of Harvard was quite an engrossing job. I don't know how helpful I can be about a book on Wallace Stevens, and it is so long before I can pick up any manuscript from my desk that the delay would be unproductive for you. One advantage about the Humanities is that studies of important writers are inexhaustible: nobody with something of his own to say needs to worry about its having been said before. There has been a great deal done on Stevens recently, but in a sense that's an advantage: publishers are likely to be more receptive to trends than to new discoveries. If I were you, too, I think I should finish the book first, if you really want to write it, and try out publishers afterwards. You will get a much more specific response if you say, "Will you publish *this* book on Wallace Stevens?" instead of "*a* book on Wallace Stevens."

Marketing conditions for academic books are of course very bad, but such a phrase as "something that might never see the light" is over-despondent. Everything goes in cycles, even bourgeois economics.

Roy Daniells   **18 July 1975**
Via della Maratona, Rome, Italy

In reply to Daniells's letter (25 June 1975) in which he asked Frye about the relation of the literal and the figurative in the gospels and about the foundation of the assurances in the New Testament. He enclosed two poems he had written in Rome.

Dear Roy,

Thanks for your letter and the poems, which I liked very much: clearly Rome is having a very many-sided effect on you.

The relation of myth and truth goes back to the fact that man lives in two worlds: the physical environment he is actually in ("nature"), history, in time, and the world of culture and civilization he is trying to build out of that environment ("art"). In the first world what is true is what can be verified; in the second world the question is not so much what is true as what can be made true. The myth in the Gospels is certainly a perversion of the truth in the sense of historical fact. If we had been there, we should have seen nothing of any profound spiritual significance, and it seems clear that the twelve disciples themselves hadn't a clue that was going on. The myth that is not a perversion of the truth is an activity that starts with the reader, or what Milton calls the Word of God in the Heart. Human nature being what it is, man pretends as long as he can that his own mythical universe is really the scientifically verifiable one; similarly, he thinks of spiritual reality as objective fact, revealed from some external supernatural source. What Paul is really saying about the Resurrection, I think, in the Corinthians passage at least, is: "I know the Resurrection happened because it happened to me." I think that faith, in the New Testament, consistently means one's own capacity for understanding the spiritual meaning of what one is experiencing: hence, as in Hebrews, the substance of the hoped for, the evidence of the unseen.

Incidentally, I don't accept Gilbert Murray's antithesis.[501] I think Athene and the other Olympians always have a power of veto over the Furies, but the whole automatic nemesis process represented by the Furies still goes on. They're different but simultaneous levels, like Paul's levels of law and freedom.

It was a shock to me to hear of Des Pacey's death, as I hadn't realized that things were so bad with him.[502] At least the family is large enough for Mary not to be too isolated. I have suggested to Carl [Klinck] that the supplementary volume of the *Literary History* be dedicated to him by the other editors, along with a memorial written by one of us: I suggested Alf Bailey.[503]

Love to Laurenda from us both.

S. Vasudeva   25 July 1975
Birla Institute of Technology & Science, Pilani-Rajasthan, India

In reply to Vasudeva's request (6 March 1975) for copies of Frye's "Blake's Treatment of the Archetype" and "Literary Criticism" and for an explanation of what he meant by "a system of verbal relationships" and how that system contained life and reality.

Dear Mrs. Vasudeva,

I am sending you photocopies or offprints of the two articles you requested.

It is very difficult for me to answer your question about the system of verbal relationships more clearly than I tried to put it in the book itself.[504] The general Aristotelian view of imitation is that in literature the imitation of nature doesn't mean the copying of an external model, but the shaping of material from nature into a form. That is, imitation is not the copying of a natural object, but an internal relation of content and form. The essence of content is to be contained. Thus in the work of art, the nature that is being imitated is content, surrounded by, enveloped in, the container of form. As the container must be bigger than the thing contained, the form is bigger than the content. Extending this principle to the world of literature, one sees that as long as we are dealing with literature, we have to think of everything it uses for material as inside it, and no longer outside.

Herbert F. Ostrach   29 July 1975
Boston College, Chestnut Hill, MA

In reply to Ostrach's third letter (3 June 1975) about his theory of the Western movie. See Frye's responses of 13 August 1974 and 31 March 1975 to the earlier letters. Ostrach accompanies his letter with a draft of his present thinking about myth, Frye's theory of modes, and related issues.

Dear Mr. Ostrach,

Thank you for your letter of June. I am sorry for the delay in answering it, but I came back to a very heavy logjam of Ph.D. theses, previously committed articles, and all the rest of it.

I don't quite know how to comment on your letter except to say that I really have no difficulty at all with your thesis in the form in which you now put it. What worried me before was the "either/or" aspect of it, but that has been taken care of now. When I wrote about the modes, back in the fifties, it had actually occurred to me what we were probably in for was a kind of democratizing of the modes, in which the mythical figures would also be popular conceptions, and hence could be treated in any or all of the five modes without any difficulty in interpretation. I couldn't work this out at the time, because, for one thing, I didn't have any notion then how far television would change the picture, and all my notions of the subject had been derived from film, and, to a much lesser degree, radio. I feel now that the cultural situation in regard to mythical creations is very much as you have stated it.

Richard J. Preston   1 August 1975
Department of Anthropology, McMaster University, Hamilton, ON
In reply to Preston's request (4 February 1975) for further comments Frye might have on Edward Sapir, whom Frye had referred to in The Bush Garden *(p. 10) as one of the most important Canadian thinkers.*

Dear Dr. Preston:

I am very sorry for what seems a considerable discourtesy in not replying to your letter of February about Sapir. I was visiting Harvard last year, as the Norton Professor of Poetry, and some of my correspondence, without a secretary to take care of me, got buried under the usual piles of paper.

I suppose Sapir is only incidentally a Canadian, as he was born in Europe and spent most of his professional life in the United States.[505] The reason why he came to mind was that he seemed to me to represent the kind of thing that [Harold] Innis also represented, the sense of the unity of all media of communication, verbal and non-verbal alike. And within the verbal area, his scope and range is almost breath-taking. There are not many people who can write about both the Nootaka Indians and the poetry of Hopkins, or about linguists and Jungian typology.

F.G.B. Maskell   8 September 1975
Ottawa, ON
In reply to Maskell's letter of 31 August 1975 saying that Frye, as a member of the Canadian Radio-Television Commission, had neglected the distinction between writing for money, which should be regulated by the government, and writing to exercise freedom of expression. Maskell's letter was motivated by his reading press accounts of a CRTC seminar.

Dear Mr. Maskell,

Thank you for your letter. The reason for my opposition to censorship is that [it] seems to me to be bad tactics. As I said, it is easy to pass regulations, but even easier to evade them. My point of view was twofold: first, to realize that violent television programmes are not a cause of violence in society, but a symptom of it, and that consequently direct efforts at banning such programmes would do no good; secondly, that the only way to deal with such programmes ultimately is to mobilize and inform and arouse public opinion. The analogy that comes to my mind is that of the manufacturers of passenger cars which are death traps. Legislation requiring safety measures in cars now has enough public opinion behind it to force manufacturers to comply.

Margaret Peacock								**26 September 1975**
Wellcroft End, Berks, England

In reply to Peacock's complaint (13 September 1975) that Frye has not acknowledged receipt of a book— Vercours' Cahiers du Silence *—she had mailed him several years ago, given in appreciation for his having sent her a copy of* Fearful Symmetry. *She asks that the book be returned so that she may give it to her son.*

Dear Mrs. Peacock,

Your letter was a surprise to me, and very puzzling. Your book must have come at a time when I was away—-there have been several protracted absences from Toronto in the last few years— and if my secretary sent a routine acknowledgment saying that I would write later she was only doing what was required. As an average of eight to ten books, not periodicals and offprints, come over my desk every week, and as this piles up immensely during my absences, some things undoubtedly do get overlooked and not acknowledged, although I hope, and think, that this does not happen very often. What I find confusing is that I cannot find the book, nor, in the files, your letters of inquiry or any copy of my secretary's acknowledgment. Needless to say, we are both searching hard for the book, and as soon as it turns up will send it to you.

Claudia Wolfe								**29 September 1975**
Willowdale, ON

Wolfe, a grade thirteen student at Georges Vanier Secondary School, wrote Frye on 23 September 1975, saying that her teacher told her Frye was an authority on metaphor. Thus, she asks, "If it is convenient I am hoping you can send me your definition of metaphor."

Dear Claudia,

Most words, especially nouns and verbs, present what we call images. If you are reading a poem in English, but don't know English, you have to look up words in the dictionary. That means that you're relating the images separately to the outside world. If you see the word "cat" on a page, you associate it with a certain kind of animal. That's language used for descriptive purposes, putting a structure of words up against a structure of things. But you're also putting the images together, relating them to each other, to make sense out of what you are reading. If you're looking at the relation of two or more images, you're looking at their metaphorical relation. There is a poem by Carl Sandburg that begins:

> The fog comes
> On little cat feet.

Here you're not going to learn anything about fogs or cats' feet: the sense of something silent and furry is describing the fog. The statement is really "The fog is silent and furry like a cat's feet." Take the word "like" out of that sentence and you have a metaphor. With the word "like" in it's a simile.

Rick Goranowski								**9 December 1975**
London, United Kingdom

In reply to Goranowski's claim (1 October 1975) that there is a close connection between Frye's theory of modes in Anatomy of Criticism *and Peacock's "The Four Ages of Poetry." Goranowski had pointed out "this unfortunate oversight" to Princeton University Press, which suggested he get in touch with Frye directly.*

Dear Mr. Goranowski,

Thank you for your letter. It is quite true that there is a close connexion between Peacock's essay and my "Theory of Modes": I have repeatedly and insistently called the attention of my readers to Peacock's essay.[506]

Nobuaki Kozaki   22 December 1975
Kumamotoshi, Japan

In reply to Kozaki's query (8 December 1975) about the rise of modern English prose style. In particular, Kozaki wants to know whether Frye endorses Morris W. Croll's view that such anti–Ciceronian writers as Bacon, Hall, Wotton, and Jonson are the founders of modern English prose, or the view of others who regard Dryden are the originator.

Dear Mr. Kozaki,

I think for your purpose you should regard Dryden as the source of modern English prose style. The people referred to by Croll and Williamson are said to have belonged to a "Senecan" movement in prose designed to loosen up and make more informal the prevailing humanist conventions.[507] But this is a very complex question, and even the existence of the Senecan movement has been disputed recently. The oscillation between formal and informal prose is something that keeps acting and reacting all through English literature. You have, for example, Hooker (formal) and Burton (informal) around 1600; there is Gibbon (formal) and Fielding (informal) in the eighteenth century; Macaulay (formal) and Dickens (informal) in the nineteenth, and so on.

Allan Megill   5 January 1976
University of Iowa, Department of History, Iowa City, IA

In reply to Megill's request (26 December 1975) for Frye's advice on how to correct his unjust treatment as a Canadian citizen in a U.S. university. Although he was the top candidate from among 150 applicants, the Bureau of Labor refused to grant him "alien employment certification" because there were U.S. citizens who satisfied the minimum requirements for the job.

Dear Mr. Megill:

Thank you for your letter. I quite agree that the situation is an absurd injustice. But I really have no suggestions to make about what one can do about it. The practice is very deeply entrenched in American law, and the only people I know who have beaten the system have been able to apply political pull and pressures from very high up. One Canadian at Harvard managed to get his contract renewed through the intervention of Senator Kennedy, but that is the only kind of thing that seems to me likely to work. There is no point in insisting on your merits, because they don't come into the picture for those bureaucrats. With apologies for not being more helpful.

Richard Kostelanetz   7 January 1976
New York, NY

In response to Kostelanetz's having sent Frye (12 December 1975) a draft of a portrait he had written and which was later published as "The Literature Professors' Literature Professor," Michigan Quarterly Review *17 (Fall 1978): 425–42.*

Dear Mr. Kostelanetz,

Thanks very much for the profile: it is true that I an apt to get panicky when addressed in a foreign language.[508] I told my French-Canadian publisher that what I needed was not a crash course in French, but a psychiatrist. He laughed until he nearly fell off his chair, because he had heard the same thing from so many English and French Canadians.

Please don't make me an enemy of Marshall McLuhan: I am personally very fond of him, and think the campus would be a much duller place without him. I don't always agree with him, but he doesn't always agree with himself.[509]

The statement of Colombo's on page 16 strikes me as curious, but it's your article.[510]

Kirpal Singh   7 January 1976
Department of English, University of Singapore, Singapore
In response to Singh's letter (12 December 1975) asking about the function of criticism and the relation of science fiction to romance.

Dear Mr. Singh,

Thank you for your letter. I think the answers to your questions are set out, so far as I can deal with them, in the opening pages of *Anatomy of Criticism*. The artist today doesn't approach his public any more directly than he did in Old Testament times, and the critic is far more essential now than he ever was. As for the future of literature in an age of technology, either our civilization will survive or it won't. If it does, it will survive by virtue of its standards, including its literature: if it goes to smash, everything will smash.

I have a good deal of interest in science fiction, which I regard as a very lively and creative development in literature, though I don't get as much time to read it as I should like to do. The book that Harry Levin referred to is my lectures at Harvard which I gave as Norton Professor of Poetry there: *The Secular Scripture: A Study of the Structure of Romance.* I am now engaged in a book on the Bible which will naturally deal with the book of Job.[511]

Germaine Brée   19 January 1976
Wake Forest University, Winston-Salem, NC
In reply to the Brée's letter (1 January 1975), indicating some of the issues with the staff of the Modern Language Association and with its policies that Frye, the incoming president, will have to face. Brée was outgoing president of the MLA.

Dear Germaine:

Thank you for your very helpful and thoughtful letter, which will be of the greatest benefit to me. As you know, we are losing Elizabeth,[512] so the situation is serious enough. It was also a somewhat ironic confirmation of your views that within a day or so of getting your letter I got one from Bill[513] asking the Council to overrule its decision and let him do as he liked. I suppose it's natural for someone in his position to feel that he could do things more efficiently on his own.

I haven't heard anything further about the letter-signing assignment,[514] but hope to see you before long.

Best wishes and renewed thanks.

Kalliopi Alkmini Danikas Brander   3 February 1976
University of Hartford, West Hartford, CT
In reply to Brander's letter (5 December 1975), written to thank Frye for his books and his ideas and for wanting "to help others in their search in life."

Dear Kalliopi:

Not knowing which of your names would be most appropriate I am selecting the one most familiar and traditional. It was extremely kind of you to write me, and such things do a great deal to counteract the sense of loneliness and alienation that one feels in writing, especially in the critical area, where it is so often assumed that the motive for writing is some sort of ego trip.

With all best wishes and renewed thanks.

Antonio Franceschetti   18 February 1976
Division of Humanities, Scarborough College, University of Toronto

In reply to a request (4 February 1976) for Frye to review the way Franceschetti had applied Frye's theories in an article on Orlando Furioso.

Dear Mr. Franceschetti,

Thank you very much for the offprint of your article on Ariosto, which I have read with great interest. It seems to me that there are two aspects to Ariosto's relation to Boiardo. In the first place the *Furioso* is a unity in its own right, with the conventional characteristics that you have attributed to it, and the beginning and the end of the poem indicate a relationship to Virgil which shows how aware Ariosto was of the underlying epic-romance form. On the other hand, Homeric poems grew out of a vast corpus of epics (*ta epe*, the Greeks called it), and the fact that Ariosto, so to speak, cuts into and drops out of a much larger body of romance, whether written or only implied, seems to me important too.

Eli Mandel   26 February 1976
Department of English, York University, Downsview, ON

Dear Eli,

I have just had a letter from my bibliographer Robert Denham, of Emory & Henry College, asking me if I have any idea of the date of the interview that you did with me for the CBC.[515] As you doubtless know, the CBC's own files are utterly hopeless, and all they know is that it was done before 1969. I think it was also done before my present secretary took over and I moved to Massey College.[516]

Sorry to bother you about this: my bibliographer has a much greater passion for completeness in such matters than I have myself. I have just been talking to Jay, who had a very pleasant visit with you recently.[517]

W.A.C.H. Dobson   27 February 1976
Queen's Park Crescent, University of Toronto

In reply to Dobson's having forwarded to Frye a copy of a letter from Sidney Feshbach (see following letter) announcing that he is "beginning a new journal this spring based on the work of Frye and Kenneth Burke." Dobson was chair of the department of East Asian Studies at the University of Toronto.

Dear Bill:

It was most kind of you to send the letter from Feshbach, and to be reminded of the time that we had talked together about modal categories. I had rather lost touch with Feshbach after he proposed that I should revise the *Anatomy*, a notion which drove me up the wall as I had so many other things to do. I remember that at one time you thought that my categories were useful to you: I trust they still are.

Sidney Feshbach   27 February 1976
Department of English, City University of New York, New York, NY

Dear Mr. Feshbach:

Bill Dobson has sent me a copy of your letter to him about the possible influence of the *Anatomy* on his own work. I was very pleased to get this, not only because of the fact that Bill I had talked about such matters, but because I now learned that your journal is established. I was rather afraid that my letter to you last year had been a trifle ungracious, because I was so absorbed in major projects, including a very long and complex book on the Bible, that the notion of revising the Anatomy threw me into a panic.

My impression is that Bill Dobson did think at one time, at least, that there was a very considerable correlation with what he was doing with the Chinese lyric and the categories in the *Anatomy*, but naturally he will know about that.

David Holmes   23 March 1976
Université de Dakar, Senegal, West Africa

In reply to Holmes letter (4 March 1975) informing Frye that his preface to The Bush Garden *was being used as required reading in his course in Canadian civilization. He registers his disappointment with Louis Dudek's historical survey in a centennial volume entitled* The Canadians: 1867–1967 *(Toronto: Macmillan, 1976).*

Dear Mr. Holmes:

Thank you very much for your letter: I am naturally delighted that you find my work useful for your Canadian Civilization course. Canadian literature is becoming a heavy industry in its own country at the moment: the growth of nationalism in French Canada seems to have sparked a corresponding movement in English Canada.

Louis Dudek is a member of the Department of English at McGill, a poet of some interest, and a very pleasant person, but unfortunately not much of a critic.

David Olson   23 March 1976
Ontario Institute for Studies in Education, Toronto, ON

Enclosed with an undated letter, Olson sent Frye a copy of Eric Havelock's The Origins of Western Literacy *(Toronto: OISE, 1976), and a copy of his paper on the relation between oral and written language, "From Utterance to Text."*

Dear Mr. Olson:

Thank you very much for the copy of Havelock's book, and for the article, both of which I have read with interest. I remember the lectures very well, and am extremely pleased to have them in book form. I suppose the real danger in our cultural assumptions about the supreme importance of literacy is the political fact that the primary reason for teaching people to read is to make them docile and predictable citizens. Of course ultimately the process is a liberating one, or should be, but the foundation is things like traffic signs and advertising. The more you read, the more you depend on implicit acceptances. That is what is so refreshing about the peasant who had never been to Pinsk: it wasn't that he couldn't draw the conclusion, but that he saw no reason for accepting the premises.

Roy Kemp   5 April 1976
New York, NY

In reply to Kemp's letter (1 April 1976), which enclosed an invoice for several photographs of Frye he had taken. Kemp was the younger brother of Frye's wife Helen.

Dear Roy:

Thank you very much for your letter and the enclosed bill, which I am returning herewith.

I don't know if you guessed when you phoned that Helen is not at her best right now.

She has had a good deal of trouble with insomnia, dizziness, and nervous tension, has been sent by her regular doctor to a specialist in middle ear troubles, and is finally referring her to a psychiatrist. I don't think it's a very imaginative gesture on his part: Helen said she had claustrophobia and I suppose his mind still automatically said "shrink," but I'm trying to convince her that a psychiatrist is just one more doctor.

I don't know what to say about the colour prints: perhaps you could send them along to the office at Massey College.[518]

I am delighted that Vincent is sending a cassette of the programme along.[519] By sheer accident I got involved in a second television programme the same week, so I shall be considerably overexposed, and will have to avoid the subways for a while.

Andrew Foley   20 April 1976
Brookline, MA

In response to Foley's having sent Frye a photocopy of James E. O'Mahony's book The Desire of God in the Philosophy of St. Thomas Aquinas *(Cork: Purcell, 1928). Foley asked whether Frye might send him any notes he had made for the CBC television program,* Journey without Arrival: A Personal Point of View from Northrop Frye, *which had recently been released. Foley mentioned that he had been immersed in trying to define what was important in the work of Marshall McLuhan.*

Dear Mr. Foley:

Thank you very much for sending me the *Desire of God,* which I am very glad to have, and look forward to reading. I am asking my producer at the CBC, Vincent Towell, whether transcripts of the script of my television programme would be available or not. The script was not actually written by me, but of course contained material based on interviews with me.

I think psychologists are now moving away from the Freudian metaphors about an unconsciousness buried below a conscious mind, and are thinking more in terms of the division in the brain between the hemisphere controlling a linear and verbal activity and the one that is more spatially oriented. It seems to me that the most important aspect of McLuhan is his role in the development of this conception.

Earl E. Steeves   20 April 1976
Moncton, NB

In response to Steeves' having sent Frye news of people in his hometown. The Frye correspondence fonds contain another letter (undated) in which Steeves, apparently in reply to the present letter, provides three typed pages of additional news from Moncton.

Dear Earl,

I was delighted to get your letter and to hear of the Moncton news. Needless to say, since my parents died (and my sister about ten years ago) my contacts with Moncton have been pretty sporadic. I was at a CRTC hearing there some years ago, and ran into Stu Gillis and Jack Grainger, and I hear occasionally from Evelyn Rogers (Love)[520] and Marion Trites, our next door neighbour now living in Fredericton. I was also most pleased to hear that a high school has been named after Bernice McNaughton ("chiselhead," as I remember) and I did meet Muriel Steeves at a Mount Allison Convocation many years ago. I think Dorothy Allen took her to it. I also ran into Jim Davidson when I visited Acadia as he has a post there now. One of the few Moncton people I see frequently is Armand Cormier, who is the New Brunswick representative at the CRTC, which takes quite a bit of my time these days.

Once again, it was very good of you to give me the news about the Bullens, Jack and

Jennie Triees, your sister Margaret, Paul Kingston, and others whom I remember so vividly. I was very pleased to see, when I was back there, that the centre of the city had really changed very little. The centre of Toronto has turned into something quite unrecognizable and I find that disturbing.

With best wishes to you both, to Margaret and her husband. I am very sorry about your stroke, and I certainly hope you will recover the use of your arm. Recoveries of that kind are very common, or so I understand.

Daniel Pagnucco   21 April 1976
Toronto, ON

In reply to a desperate and passionate appeal (27 January 1976) from a former student who is suffering from a severe psychological disorder and who pleads with Frye to assist him in getting a university assistantship or a job in publishing.

Dear Mr. Pagnucco,

Thank you for your letter: I was glad to hear from you, despite the very bad news of yourself. It is extremely difficult to find positions for anyone now, in fact quite disheartening. I keep writing letters of recommendation to no effect.

I get the impression, in any case, that perhaps some further treatment and consultation might be of more benefit to you at this point, something that would not be white-coated doctors jabbing needles into you, and not the interminable conversations with a psychiatrist, but something which would be both humane and effective. There is a place in the primal therapy known as the Centre for the Whole Person on College Street, and two therapists named David and Evelyn Scott are connected with it. I don't know them, but my colleague Jay Macpherson does. I have noted what you say about your straightened financial circumstances but perhaps that will not be an insoluble problem if you were interested in this as a lead.

Incidentally, your letter was dated January 27 and I received it only in mid–April, so the delay was in either the sending or the delivery of the letter.

Roy Faibish   29 April 1976
Ottawa, ON

In reply to Faibish's letter of 26 April 1976, providing a commentary on Frye's reference in The Secular Scripture *to Plato's doctrine of anamnesis or recollection (p. 175) and relating it to similar ideas in Dom Gregory Dix, David Jones, Wilhelm Dilthey, and Charles Collingwood. Faibish's career took him from politics to the CBC to the Canadian Radio-television and Telecommunications Commission (to which he was appointed in 1976) and back to broadcasting. In 1978 he moved to London, England.*

Dear Roy:

Thank you very much for your letter. One book which has been a seminal influence on me is Kierkegaard's *Repetition*, where he distinguishes two kinds of repetition: the neurotic attempt to return to something in the past, and the creative repetition that follows the New Testament promise about making all things new. Kierkegaard says that this is the Christian principle that polarizes Plato's recollection. Perhaps it does, but, as you indicated, the two conceptions may be really very close together.

Jeffrey Antman   10 May 1976
English Department, Clark University, Worcester, MA

In reply to Antman's request (27 April 1976) for Frye's opinion of a projected undergrad-

uate thesis on visionary criticism from an ontological perspective. Antman also asks whether or not Frye is familiar with the works of G.I. Gurdjieff and Colin Wilson.

Dear Mr. Antman,

Thank you very much for your letter. I don't think I should worry about the "formalist" considerations: certainly there are ontological realities about literature, and they are certainly worth writing a thesis about. You may find it rather tough reading, but Heidegger's later works on language would bear very centrally on your thesis.

I don't find Gurdjieff's own books so rewarding as the people who have written about him, including Ouspensky and that man who did the book on his teachers.[521] He was obviously a very remarkable man, but a prolix and, I think, a deliberately misleading writer. Colin Wilson's *Mind Parasites* had interesting things in it, notably the account of the hero's near-breakdown, but I think it got rather silly towards the end.

Pierre van Rutten   10 May 1976

French Department, Carleton University, Ottawa, ON

In response to van Rutten's having sent Frye a copy of his essay, which was eventually published as "Northrop Frye et la littérature," in Etudes Canadiennes / Studies in Canada 6 *(1979), and reprinted in* Zagadnienia Rodzajów Literackich 24, no. 2 (1981): 61–80.

Dear Mr. van Rutten,

Thank you very much for your letter and for the essay on me. Naturally I am delighted if you find my work of value to your teaching, and you are interested in people that I should like very much to write about myself if the demands of other works were not more pressing. It is particularly with Rimbaud that I find both a challenge to my own synthesizing work (because of the lack of homogeneity in the imagery which you mention) and at the same time, and largely for that reason, a most rewarding person to study. Your essay on me seems to go to the centre of my own vision of literature, or what I call the anagogic perspective.

Roy Daniells   1 June 1976

University of British Columbia, Vancouver, BC

Dear Roy,

I am very sorry to have missed your dinner[522]: I had it on my agenda to send a congratulatory telegram, but the occasion found me moving from an MLA council meeting in New York to an honorary degree convocation in Iowa,[523] and the complications were too much for my dithery mind.

I was very interested in the article indicating that the image of god in kabalism was a machine: theologians have always known that God can be disassembled (or is it "dissembled"?) and put together again, but it's nice to have the evidence.

Florence Cragg   21 June 1976

Sudbury, ON

In reply to Cragg's letter (13 June 1976), saying that she had seen Journey without Arrival: A Personal Point of View from Northrop Frye *on television. Florence Clare Cragg and her husband Art, as well as the people mentioned in paragraph 3, were members of Frye's class of 1933 at Victoria College.*

Dear Florence,

Thank you very much for your letter about my programme, which it was very kind of you to write. I was also interested to see the stationary of the hotel in Lahore where we stayed some years ago.

Last year I was resting up after an exhilarating but somewhat exhausting year at Harvard as the Norton Professor of Poetry. It involved six public lectures and, although there was no requirement to teach, I did offer a course in the typology of the Bible and drew 420 students. You can see what I mean by exhausting.

The year has scattered a good deal, but some of us keep in touch. There seems to be a regular series of gatherings of the Romans, the Chittendens, Laure Riese, the McGibbons, the Fryes, the Bates, the Wyatts (Marjorie Laing's third husband), and the Gregorys. Last weekend Jean Elder drove us to see Elizabeth Eedy who is living in a wonderful old Victorian house near Simcoe.[524]

I am very sorry that Arthur is not well, and please give him our love and best hopes for a speedy recovery. Your trip sounds wonderful,[525] but such things do take a considerable physical effort.

All the best from us both.

John Glassco   23 June 1976
Foster, QC

In reply to Glassco's request (21 June 1976) for the source Frye's reference in The Educated Imagination *to D.H. Lawrence's notion that "it's a good thing for servants to be flogged because that restores the precious current of blood-reciprocity between servant and master." Glassco wants to know "how Lawrence arrived at this odd conclusion" because it relates to something he is treating in an early chapter of his present novel. He also congratulates Frye on having such a fine translator for the French edition of* The Educated Imagination *—Jean Simard. Glassco had helped Simard translate of some of the poems.*

Dear Mr. Glassco,

The allusion to D.H. Lawrence was a rather casual one, but it comes, as I remember, from his *Studies in Classical [Classic] American Literature*, and the essay on Dana, or possibly Marryat—I don't have the book with me.[526]

I was very interested to hear of your part in the Simard translation of the book.

Stephen R. Graubard   24 June 1976
Editor, *Dædalus*, Harvard University, Cambridge, MA

In reply to Graubard's request (10 June 1976) for Frye to contribute to a special issue of Dædalus *devoted to celebrating contemporary scholarship.*

Dear Stephen:

I have been thinking long and hard about your letter, and have very reluctantly come to the conclusion that it would be quixotic for me to attempt to contribute to your Contemporary Scholarship issue.

I am devoting this summer to a very hard slugging effort to break the back of the long and complicated book on the Bible which has been on my mind for many years. I don't know how much of that will actually get done before the term starts again in the fall, but in any case I have the MLA to preside over and the Presidential Address to make at Christmas. For all these reasons it seems to me entirely out of the question that I could do the kind of job required by next January, much as I should welcome the possibility of trying under ordinary circumstances.

In any case I should think that a younger person, perhaps Hillis Miller or Geoffrey

Hartman, might find it a little easier to deal with contemporary developments in literary and critical scholarship. My Bible book in itself will eventually take me through all the structuralist people, like Derrida and Saussure and all the other people who are revolutionizing critical techniques today. But I still have that ahead of me, and I could not guarantee that I would have anything like a stranglehold on the subject by the end of the year. I am very sorry about this, but I am getting to the age in life where I have to be rather strict about my priorities.

Peter C. Roberts   29 June 1976
Islesboro, Maine

In response to Roberts's inquiry (20 June 1976), asking for clarification of Blake's view of men and women and whether or not people living in a state of nature can be assimilated to Blake's view of humanity.

Dear Mr. Roberts,

Thank you for your letter. I think the main trouble that you have with Blake's sexual symbolism is really linguistic: English doesn't have words like the Chinese Yang and Yin, which express things that the relation of the sexes symbolize without getting fouled up in the relations of actual man and woman. We instinctively think of nature as female, because nature is the body that receives the seed of the human imagination. Christianity thinks of God as a father, because the parent is the handiest symbol for the fact that the identity we are given at birth is not our whole identity. Of the two parents, the mother won't do for this purpose, because the mother is the parent we have to break away from to get born. For Blake all creative human imaginations, whether of men or of women, are symbolically male, just as in traditional Christianity everybody except Christ is symbolically female.

I have read about the *Tasaday*,[527] but Blake is an eighteenth-century poet, seeing that the notion of a delimited Utopia can no longer exist and that man has to work out some kind of global existence. Out of every hundred primitive societies ninety-nine would be pretty dismal to live in: if the hundredth is an exception, it's still not a possible goal for modern humanity.

For Blake, man simply has to take his humanity as far as he can, and unite his own essence with God's. It is quite possible that we are surrounded by superior beings all the time, but that we cannot see or comprehend them, just as a dog may enter a library without being able to read the books in it.

With best wishes to you and your fiancée.

George Johnston   18 August 1976
Atheistan, QC

In reply to Johnston's inviting Frye to attend a dinner for his Victoria College classmate Munro Beattie in April 1978. Beattie taught with Johnston at Carleton University.

Dear George,

Thank you very much for your letter and invitation. I should love to attend such a dinner for Munro, and my only hesitation is about the possibility that April 24th may find me in Japan. The Japanese Consulate here has apparently offered me a grant to spend some time in Japan, and according to their own account I have to leave before April 1.[528] If I cannot make it, I shall certainly want to let Munro know that I am thinking of him and wish very much I could be there. Munro was a classmate of mine, and I remember how difficult it was for Pelham Edgar to start his lectures until he had located first him and then me in the class.

All the best to Jeanne and yourself from us both.

Mrs. D. O. Robson   **10 September 1976**
Toronto, ON
A note of sympathy to the wife of Donald O. Robson, who graduated from Victoria College in 1928, taught at the University of Western Ontario from 1930 to 1947, and returned to Victoria in 1947 as professor of Latin.

Dear Rhena,

Donald was the last of my teachers, and I shall always think of him in connection with my earlier memories of the College. When I was Principal and he used to come in to see me, I felt that he was a connecting link with the standards and the kind of ethos that the College used to maintain and stand for, and which it has been rapidly losing in the last few years. But he fought for these standards steadily all his life, and is a very important reason why Victoria is a place of great traditions.

With love and sympathy from us both.

Bill Adair   **28 September 1976**
Seattle, WA
In reply to Adair's letter of 21 September 1976, requesting that Frye examine the diagrams Adair had made of the four mythoi. *He also mentions that he has had an article on Hemingway published in the* Journal of Narrative Technique, *and he wonders if Frye, a member of the editorial board of the journal, had read it.*

Dear Mr. Adair:

Thank you for your letter. I think your diagrams are all right, including the ironic one. In my most recent book, *The Secular Scripture*, the Norton lectures I gave at Harvard, I talk about romance and realism, and draw a distinction between stories that end and stories that simply stop. That's more or less what ironic stories do.

I try to look through every periodical that comes across my desk, but they run to several dozen a week and I often miss things.

Alida Greydanus   **28 September 1976**
St. Hilda's College, Oxford, England
In reply to Greydanus's question (12 August 1976), "Which passage of Swedenborg's is it that is 'frequently referred to by Yeats' and which you mention on p. 265 of The Stubborn Structure?" *Frye had written: "The capacity for such complete union is ascribed to the angels by Swedenborg, in a passage frequently referred to by Yeats" (StS, 264–5).*

Dear Ms. Greydanus,

I suppose my reference was a somewhat careless one, as I was really dealing with Yeats' habit of referring to the same thing over and over again.* I should imagine that the reference is to the *Spiritual Diary*.

Best wishes.

*Without separate references

Juliet McMaster   **29 September 1976**
Department of English, University of Alberta, Edmonton, AB
In response to McMaster's request (23 September 1976) for Frye to provide her with the

source of a quotation from Milton in The Critical Path, *which she wants to use in a program for a literacy conference.*

Dear Juliet,

Thank you for your letter. The quotation is from the eighth of the Familiar Letters, to Benedetto Bonmattei. I followed the Masson translation.[529]

I am glad you are having a conference on literacy. The educators in this part of the world, whenever there's a public protest about their incompetence, instantly start to howl that we're going to destroy creativity. That's like the argument that if you feed a child you'll destroy its power of metabolism.

The very best to you both,[530] and with best wishes for the conference.

Russell A. Fraser   30 September 1976
Department of English, University of Michigan, Ann Arbor, MI

In reply to Fraser's request (8 September 1976) for any information Frye might want to provide about Richard Blackmur for a biography and personal memoir Fraser is writing.

Dear Russell Fraser:

Thank you for your letter. I assume you know the reference to Richard in *The Secular Scripture*,[531] and that that was what prompted your letter to me. I wanted to record that anecdote because it seemed to me to crystalize everything that I knew and felt about Richard: his extraordinary friendliness and kindliness, his exquisite sensitivity, and his ability to unite the academic and personal aspects of literature. Apart from that, I don't know that I have very many clearly rounded off anecdotes, or what Joyce would call epiphanies. There was a deep insecurity in him, of course, and I was always deeply touched by the fact that he never tried to conceal this, but made it an integral part of his relationship. He was a curious contrast to Perry Miller, who had the same kind of insecurity but was much more defensive about it.

I am delighted that you are doing a book on him, and I wish you every success.[532]

Margaret Atwood   1 October 1976
Alliston, ON

Dear Peggy,

Thank you very much for the copy of *Lady Oracle* which I am reading with immense pleasure and admiration. The level of wit is extraordinary, but it never takes over, and the more serious levels of meaning show through very clearly. You seem to be very fond of the imagery of food in your fiction, and I look forward to another novel reflecting the influence of David's lobsters.

In reverse, I wish I'd been able to read this book before I wrote the Norton lectures, as it has a good many fascinating patterns that I suppose came partly from your work with Jerry Buckley.

Kiss the baby for me: I don't even know what her name is yet.[533]

Love from our house to your house.

Roy Daniells   1 October 1976
University of British Columbia, Vancouver, BC

Dear Roy,

Thank you very much for the Interdepartmental Memorandum[534] which I am delighted to have. Like you, I haven't a great deal of personal news, but lack your gift for saying so. I spent the summer in retreat, trying to get this book on the Bible written. There was an immense amount of trouble trying to get the material distributed, so I don't have a great deal to show for the summer's work. But at least I do know what is to go where.

The voice in the burning bush certainly has a lot to answer for: he started a sequence of four revolutionary religions, Judaism, Christianity, Islam and Marxism, and with the same revolutionary characteristics of heresy-hunting, persecution, dogmatism, and wildly unfair arguing. But there are other things too, less depressing than, say, the Buddhist notion that one's highest aim should be to keep reincarnating for a billion years until the last individual has staggered across the finishing line into Nirvana.

Kirpal Singh   1 October 1976
Department of English, University of Adelaide, Adelaide, South Australia
In reply to Singh's letter of 11 August 1976, indicating that he had moved from Singapore to Australia and asking for advice about a project on Aldous Huxley he was undertaking. Singh also asked Frye about his relationship to F.R. Leavis and Matthew Arnold.

Dear Mr. Singh,

Thank you for your letter. I was very interested to hear that you are visiting Australia. I think Aldous Huxley is certainly very well worth working on. He seems to me to be primarily an essayist, and much of his fiction, especially his later works, seem to me too didactic and theoretically manipulated to be in the top rank of works of fiction. But as a prophet of a great deal in contemporary culture, such as the vogue for occultism, he seems to be a very significant figure. Thank you very much for the issues of *Commentary*, which I was very glad to get and read through.[535] I shall suggest to my publishers (Harvard University Press) to send you a copy of *The Secular Scripture*. The references to science fiction in the book are very slight, as I was compelled to devote nearly all of my attention to rather different aspects of romance.

I can hardly make much of a comment on my relationship to Leavis. He seems to me to be a kind of lay preacher, using texts from literature rather than religion. One admires his moral energy, his abhorrence of heresy, his sense of the extreme urgency of maintaining standards, and yet it seems to me that, like other volumes of sermons, his work stands outside the really serious and constructive work that other critics are doing. He does seem to represent the confusion in Arnold between literary and religious standards. I think Arnold's notion of poetry replacing religion is an extremely bad metaphor: the existential cannot be replaced by the hypothetical; the two things have quite different jobs to do, and two contexts that would debase literature and religion alike.

A.M. Gibbs   27 October 1976
Macquarrie University, New South Wales, Australia
In reply to Gibbs's having sent Frye (21 October 1976) a copy of his article on Shaw's Man and Superman, *which, he says, draws heavily of the discussion of comedy in* Anatomy of Criticism.

Dear Mr. Gibbs,

Thank you very much for the offprint of the Shaw article,[536] which I have read with great interest. I am of course delighted that you find my own work useful. I read in my teens everything that Shaw had written at that time, and I suppose his comic structure sank deeply in my mind at a very impressionable age. *Man and Superman* was always a favourite play of mine, and I think that you have integrated the fourth act into the comic structure much better than I have seen it done elsewhere.

Robert Denham   4 November 1976
Department of English, Emory & Henry College, Emory, VA

In response to Denham's proposal to edit a collection of Frye's review-essays, which was eventually published as Northrop Frye on Culture and Literature *(Chicago: University of Chicago Press, 1978). Denham enclosed, in addition to a proposed table of contents, one of the continuing updates of the Frye bibliography.*

Dear Mr. Denham,

Thank you very much for your letter: I think the Table of Contents is fine, and I hope the book will do well. I find as I get older that I have to go in for more and more self-plagiarism, and for that reason I pilfered a good deal from my *Forum* Toynbee and Spengler article[537] to make the Spengler essay in *Daedalus*.[538] I should like to see the *Griffin* review[539] included because it does say things that I haven't said elsewhere, so far as I remember. The only thing is that the Dobrée book was pretty bad, and the man on the *Griffin* staff who sent it to me, and had chosen it, was in danger of getting fired for his bad judgement. So I had to pretend that the book was a lot better than it actually was.

The bibliography is extraordinarily complete, as always. On page 5, all three of the items have now been published.

Herbert F. Ostrach   5 November 1976
Boston College, Chestnut Hill, MA

In reply to Ostrach's letter of 7 July 1976, the fourth in a series of inquiries in which Ostrach formulates a number of hypotheses springing from Frye's Anatomy of Criticism. *See Frye's earlier responses of 13 August 1974, 31 March 1975, and 29 July 1975.*

Dear Mr. Ostrach,

I am sorry to have left your letter of last July for so long, but my schedule really leaves me no choice in the matter. I am quite interested in what you say about movies, though I feel that you have rather painted yourself into a corner on the diachronic-synchronic distinction. You say that you want to contrast them for the sake of simplicity, and you say at the same time that they cannot be isolated from each other.

Regarding page 3: I don't think the genesis of literature is irrelevant to the study of literature. I merely say that it is totally out of reach because nobody was around when literature originated. The only way to talk about its genesis is to adopt the rhetorical fallacy of determinism, which I will not do. Still less would I assume any great improvement of value in literature (page 4), along the lines of a totally false analogy to biological evolution. I don't deny that some works of literature are "better" than others: what I do say is that there can be no theoretical formulation of value, and that even if there were, no genuine criticism can be founded on a basis of value judgements. Some people interpret this as meaning that I am contradicting myself whenever I say that Shakespeare is a great poet, but I don't think I am.

Neither do I think that I am taking a different line with thematic modes from my treatment of fictional modes. What historicists leave out of their historical purview, when they deal with literature, is precisely the history of literature. Greek drama developed out of religious ritual by means of the structural laws of literature itself, and consequently it cannot be looked at as vestigial ritual. We cannot look at the history of literature merely as part of history, and treat literary works as historical documents. What we have to see, in conventions and genres, is a series of internal transformations. In literature, diachronic and synchronic are different aspects of the same thing and cannot be separated for any purpose. I find much less difficulty with your more practical treatment of movies, despite my own lack of expertise in this field.

Robert Hain   **22 November 1976**
Merton College, Oxford, England
  In reply to Hain's letter (14 November 1976) about his interest in social anthropology, the issues of which parallel those, he says, in Frye's The Secular Scripture.

Dear Mr. Hain:
  I was delighted to hear from you, and very interested to hear about your whereabouts and ancestry. I don't know whether I met you at the recent party for your grandfather at Eaton Memorial Church or not, as we came late and contacts were a bit confused.[540]
  I taught for a term at Oxford in 1970 and had an office in Fellows Quad, and was later there in the summer of 1974.[541] It is not always easy to get over, but I am certainly delighted with my connexion with Merton, which goes back to my student days in 1936.
  I am aware of the rapidly growing connexions between literary criticism and social anthropology, and I keep reading some of the structural anthropologists, but I don't find their interest in literature always very specific and have had to supply most of that myself so far.

Roy Daniells   **3 December 1976**
University of British Columbia, Vancouver, BC.
  In reply to Daniells's having sent Frye a poem and a comment he had received from a friend in Rome about the new officer for cultural affairs at the Canadian Embassy, Amleto Lorenzini.

Dear Roy,
  Thanks very much for the verse.[542] The Amleto Lorenzini whom you referred to earlier is a man of boundless energy. He had a job with the Ontario government but has been actively cultivating various hobbies, including photography (two books of photographs of sculptures in the British Museum), Joyce's *Finnegans Wake*, and translating me into Italian. Thanks to him, I am practically complete in Italian now. When the original translation of the *Anatomy* came in,[543] I felt that I had something better to do than read myself in Italian, and put the book aside. But Lorenzini read it and blew his top: he said that I was being grossly misunderstood in Italy because of the badness of the translation, and he insisted on the publishers' revising it.[544] Now he is in Rome, and I think is darkly cooking up some scheme for me going to Italy to talk about Castiglione and Vico.[545]

William Park   **3 December 1976**
Sarah Lawrence College, Bronxville, NY
  In response to Park's letter of 23 November 1976, asking for comments Frye might want to make on two articles he enclosed, along with a portion of a "confession" which treats his understanding of the powers and limitations of Frye's literary theory.

Dear Mr. Park,
  Thank you very much for the letter and the offprints. I hardly know what to say to the paper on my criticism, as I find it difficult to recognize myself in it. It is true that I don't

think that literature and belief operate in the same area, and that to base a belief on literature would be a betrayal of both. I don't think that the whole effort of literature "saves" man any more than a single poem would. Romanticism to me is not something I "believe" in more than pre–Romantic literature: it is simply a different structure of metaphors. It can lead to aberrations like the Nazi movement, but the earlier structures produced things like the Spanish Inquisition. It would be nonsense to denounce it *en bloc*, as it includes the Blake I learned everything from and the Methodist movement in which I was brought up.

I do have my own beliefs and values, and it seems to me that they are written all over my work with no attempt to hide them or tease the reader. I don't think that man is God: I think that man is redeemable. The Romantic movement was primarily a historical event, something that happened, and its conception of the relation between the divine and the human as one of participating process is the one that seems to be appropriate to our own time. It is not the final truth, but it appears to be the present vehicle of understanding. If my book on Eliot is "uncharitable" it is because of what seems to me the quixotic in it, the attempts to pretend that the last three centuries shouldn't have happened. I have no quarrel with his religious views, only with the social and political inferences that he seems to draw from them.

Jonathan Culler   12 January 1977
Department of English, Yale University, New Haven, CT
In reply to Culler's sending regrets (25 December 1976) that because he will be getting married on 27 December he will not be able to attend the reception of 28 December hosted by Frye at the annual meeting of the Modern Language Association. Frye was president of the MLA for 1976.

Dear Mr. Culler:

Thank you very much for your note: I was sorry to miss you at the party, but I can certainly understand that you would be otherwise engaged, and may I offer my congratulations and best wishes. I just wanted to say that "Structural Poetics" was the original title of a book which later became known as *Anatomy of Criticism*.[546]

Margot Rabiner   20 January 1977
PMLA, Modern Language Association of America, New York, NY
A response to the copy-edited version of Frye's "Presidential Address 1976," published in PMLA 92 (May 1977): 385–91, and reprinted in WE, 483–93. A slightly abridged and edited version is reprinted as "Teaching the Humanities Today" in DG, 91–101.

Dear Ms. Rabiner,

Thank you for the copyedited manuscript, which I see has acquired the usual stylistic eczema. The changes for the most part are fussy, pedantic and unnecessary: they do not clarify the meaning and they play hell with the rhythm. I took endless pains to make sure that the spoken rhythm of every sentence was just right.

Page 2. The efforts to improve the tense appear to me to be ill-advised.

Page 3. I see no difficulty in what I wrote, and I wish you would leave it.

Page 4. The reference to Ophelia should be left without quotations and the following sentence would not be improved by the suggested changes. "Its creed" of the first line could be altered to "This creed." I'd prefer what I wrote, but if you want to change "whatever" to "much of what" I have no great objection.

Page 5. The passage seems to me clearer at it stands.

Page 8. If you insist on printing this gabble I should like the footnote to add the words "as edited by PMLA." Third line from the bottom: Being Canadian, I think of there being more than one society nearer home.

Page 12. I don't think much has been improved by cutting out the word principle, but you can have your more academic version.

Page 14. I don't greatly object to the change here.

Page 15. The phrase in the middle is as clear as I can make it.

Page 16. I am saying that wisdom and prophecy start from opposite ends and meet in the middle. There is no inconsistency in saying that wisdom becomes more discontinuous.

I don't mean to be waspish, but there is a difference between rhetorical prose written for a public performance and an academic article intended to be read. In my writing the two things are as different as chalk and cheese, and that is why I resist so strongly to making changes that only injure it as rhetorical prose and don't really transform it into prose to be read. I have a certain confidence in my ability to write rhetorical prose, supported by the fact that the audience who heard the address seemed to have no difficulty with it.

Margot Rabiner   8 February 1977
PMLA, Modern Language Association of America, New York, NY

In reply to Rabiner's letter of 24 January 1977 and in connection with Frye's letter of 8 February 1977, which was a response to the editing of his Modern Language Association "Presidential Address." Rabiner wrote, 'I am sorry that you found our suggestions heavy-handed," and she agreed to restore Frye's "original wording in those places you request us to."

Dear Ms. Rabiner,

I am sending the galleys back with this. I have not tried to deal with all the marginal questions, as I think the proof reading is perhaps self-explanatory.

I *am* sorry to have written such a nasty letter, and I really do understand the problems of a styler in trying to straighten out articles for a reader. But when it's a speech as official as this, and when I agonized over the writing as long as I did, I am unusually reluctant to take responsibility for anything I have not written. I am sure that you understand my difficulties too.

Best wishes and renewed thanks.

Eugene Hollahan   18 February 1977
Department of English, Georgia State University, Atlanta, GA

In reply to Hollahan's letter (13 January 1977), with a chapbook of his poems enclosed, along with a footnote in which he explains the distinction between the private and the secret as he has found it in Fanny Burney's Evelina. *Hollahan notes that the distinction also appears* Anatomy of Criticism *(p. 27) and he asks Frye if there are other places in his work where he discusses it.*

Dear Mr. Hollahan,

Thank you very much for your letter and for the chapbook, which I have read with interest and admiration. I think you have interpreted me quite correctly in your footnote: the experience of literature contains a number of irreducibly subjective impressions, whereas criticism is establishing a focus for a community. In a book of mine, *The Well-Tempered Critic*, I describe the exaggerated effect made on me by finding the phrase "golden rain" in a very mediocre poem, because of an ecstatic (and obviously Freudian) experience with fireworks in my childhood.[547] Recognizing this subjective experience was quite easily distinguishable from my critical view of the poem.

Brian Parker   14 March 1977
Department of English, Trinity College, University of Toronto
In reply to Parker's request (11 March 1977) that Frye sign a petition against the changes in policy of the Canadian Broadcasting Company.

Dear Brian,

Normally I'd have no difficulty with the petition, but I rather think that my position as a member of the CRTC [Canadian Radio-Television Commission] makes it very inadvisable to go on public record one way or the other. True, I am going off the CRTC in April, but there's this business of the enquiry into balanced programming, where I shall probably have an advisory role of some kind. It is not my own caution, but merely a disinclination to give your committee something that could be discounted or used to your disadvantage.

Robin Harris   30 March 1977
Higher Education Group, University of Toronto.
In reply to Harris's having sent Frye on 28 March 1977 an unidentified article, which apparently refers to David G. Pitt's biography of E.J. Pratt.

Dear Robin,

Thanks very much for your note and for the periodical. I wish Pitt would get his book out instead of talking about it.[548] I never had a high view of Floss Pratt's intelligence, and the fact that she burned all Ned's letters doesn't surprise me.[549]

Pat Parker   25 May 1977
Department of English, University of Toronto
In reply to a query from his colleague Patricia Parker about the significance of Rahab in the Old and New Testaments.

Dear Pat:

I am sorry to have been so long getting down to your last note, but you understand the reasons. I do not see that there can even be a distinction between Rahab who is a figura of the church, and Rahab the harlot of Jericho: from the beginning they have always been explicitly the same person. In seventeenth-century Protestantism, notably in Milton, there is a strong tendency to dissociate the church from the metaphor of "mother," as in Catholicism, and to replace it with that of the bride. As the Protestant view is that the church is capable of error, this bride figure can merge with the archetype of the forgiven harlot, of which the Old Testament prototype is Rahab and the New Testament one Mary Magdalen. The Hebrew word Rahab appears to mean something like wide or broad (perhaps in the sense in which "broad" is still a vulgar term for a woman), and this is of course the basis for the "dilation" metaphor.[550]

J. R. (Tim) Struthers   30 May 1977
Department of English, University of Western Ontario, London, ON
In reply to Struthers's inquiry (18 May 1977) about the influence of Blake on E.J. Pratt and Pratt's views on Newfoundland's entering into Confederation. Struthers is also interested in Frye's reaction to the thesis that Pratt's Toward the Last Spike *is "forward-looking" rather than "historical."*

Dear Mr. Struthers,

Thank you very much for your letter and enquiry. I wish I could be more helpful about the subject of your paper, but the fact is that Ned Pratt was simply not a person responsive to influences. I think he was very fond of me, and was personally delighted when I gave him a copy of *Fearful Symmetry*, but I should be extremely surprised if he had read it. I don't think either that Blake was a formative influence on him. What parallels there are between Pratt's outlook in that poem and Blake's conception of "mental fight" are in my opinion analogues only.

I remember very little that Pratt said about Newfoundland and Confederation. He himself had already confederated, and never understood what the fuss was about.

I think your conception of *Towards the Last Spike* as a poem looking to the future rather than the past is an excellent one, and thoroughly in harmony with both the spirit of the poem and of Pratt's habitual attitude. At the same time he was very conscientious about the sources for his poems themselves, and tried hard to give a historically authentic picture. But he got his larger outlook, as so many poets do, by trying not to think explicitly about it.

I think Pratt's "The Truant" was an important influence on my own book on Blake, but our respective ages made influences in the other direction impossible. During the war, Pratt was very much excited by the heroism of the people of the Soviet Union, with the result that he had to spend a great deal of time and energy in fighting off the local Communists, who were determined to kidnap him. As a result I think something of the Marxist future–oriented vision of the rebuilding of society does get into the poem, though in a way that Marxists would hardly endorse.

I am sorry if this letter is too late to be of any help, but I received it only this morning (May 30).[551]

Helen Vendler   18 August 1977
Department of English, Boston University, Boston, MA

In reply to Vendler's letter (15 July 1977), praising Frye's 1976 Modern Language Association presidential address: "it was more like a poem than an essay — or rather it was more like a work of art than a work of exposition." The talk was published as "Presidential Address 1976," PMLA 92 (May 1977): 385–91, and reprinted in a slightly abridged version as "Teaching the Humanities Today" in DG, 91–101. The complete talk was subsequently reprinted in WE, 483–93.

Dear Helen,

Your letter meant a great deal to me, not only because of what it was in itself but because I had taken the most fanatical pains with that address. I don't quite know why, except that it seemed appropriate. Nobody else, except twenty-five years ago, a young student who has become a close personal friend, has commented on the releasing quality that I sometimes manage to communicate, and as that is what I always aim at it's immensely helpful to hear that I managed it.

Dennis Lee   26 October 1977
Toronto, ON

Dear Dennis,

Thanks very much for the copy of *Savage Fields*,[552] which I have been reading with great interest. I am particularly interested in your growing interest in Heidegger, which I am gradually beginning to share, after a somewhat discouraging encounter with *Sein und Zeit*.

John Moss   16 November 1977
Department of English, University of British Columbia, Vancouver, BC

Dear John Moss,

Thank you very much for the copy of *Sex and Violence in the Canadian Novel*, which I am looking forward to reading. On a hasty glance through, it seems to be very comprehensive, though there are some people, such as Marika Robert,[553] who illustrate unusual aspects of the subject. But I suppose if one were to be really comprehensive one would have to write a book on dullness and pedestrianism in the Canadian novel.

Tzvetan Todorov   16 November 1977
Paris, France

Dear Mr. Todorov,

Thank you very much for the copy of *The Poetics of Prose*, which I shall be reading with great interest. Naturally, I regret that the only reference to me, in Jonathan Culler's introduction, is a totally erroneous one: my archetypes not at all being Jungian.[554] But that should not detract from the excellence of the book itself: I am sufficiently familiar with your work to look forward to reading it.

Penelope Tzougros   8 December 1977
Boston, MA

In response to Tzougros's letter of 29 November 1977, asking Frye to write letters on her behalf for teaching positions at Northeastern University and Boston College. Tzougros had been a student of Frye, who directed her 1977 Ph.D. dissertation, Hopkins and Blake: A New Heaven and a New Earth. *She eventually left academe to become a financial consultant.*

Dear Penelope,

Your chrysanthemums turned that foreign holiday into a very real occasion for us. They are still with us, though they have modulated from the floor to the table.

Penelope, my dear, please don't think of your oral defense as any kind of failure, as you seem to be doing. I know that Martin Nurmi was quite impressed with the thesis, and everyone thought that you defended yourself very ably. True, David Shaw and Cyrus Hamlin complained when you were out that you didn't seem to know what they were talking about, and in fact asked me to pass the complaint on to you. So I have just done it. When we were leaving, Brian asked me to go out with Martin Nurmi and point him in the direction of his hotel. When we were going downstairs, Martin said: "You know, I cannot figure out what those guys were talking about."

I have written letters to Boston College, Northeastern and the Dossier Service, and needless to say wish you the very best of luck.

Brayton Polka   20 December 1977
Toronto, ON

In reply to Polka's request (20 September 1977) for Frye's reaction to the first volume of a three-volume work on the theory and practice of interpretation. Polka was associate professor of humanities at York University, Downsview, ON.

Dear Mr. Polka:

I am sorry to have put off replying to your letter for so long: I have been in labour myself with an extremely complicated book, and phasing out of my various commitments on the eve of retirement is a very preoccupying activity. I have read your statement with very considerable interest, and would certainly look forward to seeing how you work it out. About the central hermeneutic thesis, I have little trouble. The historical part, with the assumption of a split between the Greek tradition and the modern one that starts with Kant, I find a bit more worrying. When I read Kierkegaard on moving into the area of ethical freedom, I am soon back to Kant's distinction between pure and practical reason. That in turn sends me back to Milton's "reason is but choosing," and that in turn sends me back to the medieval tradition deriving from Aristotle. The Christian development of Aristotle made a great deal of the element of *telos* in him, and this represents so close an assimilation to the later Kantian and Hegelian developments that I can't help wondering whether Aristotle himself will really fall into this "dualistic" category. However, you must have taken account of such criticisms in your full-length treatment of Aristotle.

I wonder whether you have got in touch with such people as Cyrus Hamlin in this University, who are also interested in such things as hermeneutics and history.

Fr. Walter Ong   22 December 1977
Department of English, St. Louis University, St. Louis, MO
    Ong's message, apparently a Christmas card, is not extant.

Dear Walter,

Thanks very much for your card.

I suppose by the time this letter reaches you you will be It, MLA-wise.[555] I am avoiding the MLA this year because we go to Guyana in the week of January 1st, and I have to stay home and pack.

The Bible book goes very slowly: it seems to take its own time. I have been soaking myself in Hegel's Phenomenology to try to work out some kind of modern statement of the four levels of meaning. Then there is the whole Logos business and its relation to all the socio-linguistic people, so many of whom, in contrast to yourself and a few others (Ricoeur), seem bent on avoiding it. Meanwhile, I have reached sixty-five and have gone on a three-year extension.

I saw something of your student Patrick Hogan this year, but he left early. I don't know whether he was disappointed in what we did or didn't do for him. He was very keen, and one of his proposals was that he and Marshall [McLuhan] and I should form a seminar to discuss *Finnegans Wake*, which hardly fitted my working schedule or, I should imagine, Marshall's.[556]

Robin Graham   17 January 1978
Department of English, University of Rhodesia, Salisbury, Rhodesia
    In reply to Graham's noting (15 December 1977) that Frye's remark in The Secular Scripture *that in detective fiction "law is not justice" is borne out by the conclusion of Raymond Chandler's* Farewell, My Lovely.

Dear Professor Graham,

Thank you very much for your letter. I went through quite a spell of reading Chandler about twenty-five years ago, because I was attracted by his very concrete style and sense of rhythm. I don't remember the stories very clearly now, and was very pleased to have your reminder.

Morton D. Paley   17 January 1978
Department of English, University of California, Berkeley, CA

Dear Morton,

Thanks very much for the offprint of your review of Harold Bloom. I hope it isn't too arrogant for me to think that I represent Bloom's chief anxiety of influence; in any case he seems to me to be increasingly isolating himself from the general critical tradition, and I find his books progressively less rewarding.

Howard Norman   18 January 1978
Toronto, ON

In reply to Norman's letter of 31 December 1977 about the influence of Christianity in Japan, the history of which he and his wife were presently writing. He indicates his argument against the view of a Japanologist, Ivan Morris, that the influence of Christianity in Japan has been nugatory. Noman, the son of missionaries to Japan, spent a number of years himself as a missionary to that country. He was a graduate of Victoria and Emmanuel Colleges.

Dear Howard,

Thank you very much for your letter. I once preached a sermon on the passage from Acts you refer to, and attempted my own translation of the AV's "What would this babbler say?"[557] My rendering was "I wonder what this bird has picked up."

When I was in Japan last spring I got the impression that the Christian influence was considerably stronger than the number of professing Christians in the country. The history of Christianity in the Tokugawa period is a terrible story, but apparently Christianity was never quite wiped out in the country. Certainly a man like Kagawa didn't spring out of nothing. And my visit to Doshisha, in particular, indicated something to me of the reality of the Christian faith there.

Roy Daniells   19 January 1978
University of British Columbia, Vancouver, BC

In reply to Daniells's having sent Frye (1 January 1978) four poems: 10 Thousand Angels, Their Net Brake, Lot's Wife, *and* O How Comely It Is and How Reviving.

Dear Roy,

I was delighted with the poems, which cheered up the end of my holiday considerably. I spent a week in Guyana[558] where they have just passed a law forbidding the importing of books, and now I am back to the meat grinder. If you publish a collection of your verse, as I very much hope you will, I'd suggest expanding the title of "Lot's Wife" to "Remembering Lot's Wife" (Luke 17:32).

With thanks for your Christmas message and love to Laurenda and yourself from us both.

John Wortley   20 January 1978
Editor, *Mosaic*, University of Manitoba, Winnipeg MB

In reply to Wortley's request for Frye's opinion about a special issue of Mosaic.

Dear Mr. Wortley,

Thank you for your letter. My general reaction to a special issue of liturgy and literature is that it is, in that form, a somewhat hampering topic.[559] I doubt if you would get a great variety of articles on such a theme that would be of genuine usefulness. I should recommend expanding the topic to the general question of myth and ritual, or even, perhaps, to the question of the relationship of myth to social and individual activities. That would take in the whole question of the relation of belief to myth and vision, and would also enable you to run articles on, say, the rituals of primitive societies. There is a new magazine called *Parabola*, which deals with this and related topics: it might be useful to see from it where you could go.

Martha Del Grande   30 January 1978
Toronto, ON

In reply to Del Grande's query (23 January 1978) whether Frye believed that Christ was really the Son of God, really lived, and really died on the Cross for us. After saying that she had the impression from her friend Bob Sandler, the producer of several films on Frye, that Frye believed Christ was only a symbol or myth, she gives a lengthy account of how she became a Christian.

Dear Mrs. Del Grande:

Thank you very much for your letter. For some years now I have been interested in such questions as why the phrase "Word of God" should be applied both to the Bible and to the person of Christ, why the historical evidence for the existence of Christ should be sealed inside a book, and other problems of that kind. I do not question for an instant the reality of what has become real to you, and I am very glad to have your account of it. But when you begin to imply that what has become real to you is really real, and other things, equally real to me, are unreal or half real or have only a secondary or shadow reality, then I recognize the attitude as a very familiar one which I have long since learned that I must not have anything to do with. In other words I have learned not to oversimplify the question of what is real in such matters.

Martin Amis   1 February 1978
New Statesman, London, England

In reply to a request from Amis (16 January 1978) for Frye to submit "up to 250 works of comment, assessment, personal recollection, or whatever" about F.R. Leavis. A dozen or so other writers and critics were asked to do the same, in lieu of a conventional obituary. In a postscript Amis asked if Frye's essay reprinted in the New Statesman *had come to his attention.*

Dear Mr. Amis:

Thank you very much for your letter. I am afraid that there is not very much that I can do to be helpful about the Leavis obituary. I have never met Leavis, but I have met enough of his students to know that he looks like a completely different person to them from the way he looks to the general public. My own feelings about him are a bundle of inconsistencies: I read him with enthusiasm when I feel that he really likes what he is writing about, such as George Eliot or D.H Lawrence. When writing about somebody he doesn't like, including the people whom he thinks of as enemies, I feel him quite unrewarding. This would make for a somewhat incoherent contribution, and I can't think of any way of tightening it up.

I was delighted to see my essay reprinted in the *New Statesman*, and thought it held up reasonably well, considering that it was written specifically for the period of student unrest ten years ago.[560]

George Haessler   **13 March 1978**
Detroit, MI
In reply to Haessler's query (22 February 1978), "Will civilization, as we know it, survive the century?"

Dear Mr. Haessler,

Thank you very much for your letter. Nobody can foretell the future with any certainty, but I should have thought that the probabilities of man's continuing to survive were rather better now than they were in the earlier part of this century. Man certainly has a capacity to destroy his civilization, but I think there is some unidentified force preventing him from doing so. As for the phrase "civilization as we know it," the whole of human history has been fairly consistent in its behaviour patterns, and so I think that if civilization does survive it will be recognizably continuous with what has preceded it.

Robert Denham   **22 March 1978**
Department of English, Emory & Henry College, Emory, VA
In response to receiving a copy of Northrop Frye on Culture and Literature: A Collection of Review Essays, *ed. Robert D. Denham (Chicago: University of Chicago Press, 1978).*

Dear Mr. Denham,

Thank you very much for the copy of the book. Now that I have seen it, I am very pleased to see that it is in print, as I worked quite hard over those reviews and feel that they were an organic part of my writing at the time, as you say. I am correspondingly grateful for your efforts and diligence. My one reservation has nothing to do with you, but concerns the idiotic notions of the Chicago Press about where to put commas. There appear to be only two places to put commas, the right place, which was where I put them, and the wrong place, which was where Chicago put them.

The spring of '79 should be all right: perhaps my secretary could work out a more precise date with you.[561] She is also sending you a copy of the summary of the "Options" conference.[562]

The Bible book will be quite a book if I can bring it off, but that in turn is quite an if. Best wishes and renewed gratitude.

John Fraser   **7 April 1978**
The Globe and Mail, Peking Bureau, Peking, People's Republic of China
In reply to Fraser's letter (26 March 1978) which records his reactions to a news story in which Frye was portrayed as aloof, austere, and generally unsociable.

Dear John Fraser:

I was delighted to get your letter and very touched by the effort you made to write it. I was a little disconcerted by the account of me in Charles Taylor's article,[563] but assumed that it arose from the paradox of a comparative stranger having to write an article in which he has to let his readers assume that they are getting on the inside track.

The television series is developing rapidly, and I view it with mixed feelings of excitement and apprehension. Your tip about seeing Jock Wilson is an excellent one,[564] and I shall act on it directly: he's the only Canadian precedent.

I read your dispatches in the *Globe and Mail* with great pleasure and profit: I think that you are doing an extraordinary job, and certainly I am learning a great deal about China from them, not that I had much in the way of previous knowledge.[565]

Don Thompson and Jim Hanley   3 May 1978
Toronto, ON

The context for Frye's letter was a proposed series of television programs featuring Frye to be called "The Story about Us." Thompson and Hanley were the producers. TVOntario was to produce the first episode with the hope "that either the CBC or National Film Board would pick up part of the tab for the remaining programs" (Ayre, 365). Within six months Frye had dissociated himself from the project.

Dear Don and Jim,

I have got to a point where I am feeling very unhappy about the way the television series is developing and I think I have to get something relatively clear before we can proceed.

I agreed to the series with a good deal of trepidation, because it is in a series which has included Sir Kenneth Clark, Bronowski, and Galbraith. These have been widely publicized, but I think the critical reaction after the Galbraith series is of a type that would come very heavily on me if anything went wrong. While watching the Galbraith series, I felt that everything he had to do with, his material, his idiom, his presence, was more or less all right. The general background for him was more or less all wrong. I have felt, and I have been warned by a number of other people with extensive knowledge in the area, that critics will simply be waiting to pounce if anything goes wrong with the present series. If I make a fool of myself on an international scale I want it to be my fault entirely.

Accordingly, I am in a position now where I feel that the series simply must not be taken out of my hands. The fact that the decision is to whether the programmes are to be an hour or half an hour in length is regarded as out of my hands is deeply disturbing to me because half hour programmes would in my opinion dissolve the whole series into nothing. Then again, I asked for Bob Sandler to produce the scripts: he knows my work well; he discusses everything carefully and repeatedly with me to make sure it is what I want; he is associate producer, and in general I think that we should not go on with this without involving him at every possible stage in the discussions, and making the whole procedure a cooperative effort.

I think that perhaps I was being unduly malleable when I told Don I could work with the version of the first programme that he produced. But in any case the difficulty is not so much with that programme as with the prospect of seeing the series as a whole being designed in a way that does not fit me. I think there will be a tendency to develop a talking-down approach which is all wrong for me and for my reputation as a teacher, and the best way to avoid that is to keep the discussion as open as possible and the script as close as possible to what Bob and I have worked out.

I am sorry to be obstructive, but if I don't say what I think at this point things will become much worse later on. I am concerned with an area for which I am in the long run solely responsible and that is an area in which I must guard my own interests.

H.G. Emmet   9 May 1978
Kings Langley, Herts., England.

In response to Emmet's query (2 May 1978), "if you were setting a series of essays for your students on Blake, what would be your subject matter?" Emmet, the head of a literary group in the diocese of St. Alban's, confesses to the influence that Fearful Symmetry *has had on him.*

Dear Rev. Emmet,

Thank you very much for your letter. It is a long time since I taught a course on Blake, but I think my instinct would be to give my students a number of representative poems and ask then to comment on them. Among them would be the "Introduction" to the *Songs of Experience*, the "Preludium" to *Europe*, "The Mental Traveller," and various poems from the Rossetti manuscript, such as the one on the myrtle tree. Other possibilities would be to discuss Blake's attitude towards the American Revolution, the French Revolution, the Pitt Government and its policy; or the relation of poetry to design in the engraved poems and what the respective arts do; or the conception of human mental states, Orc, Urizen, and the like, which turn into "gods" when they are projected, and what Blake meant by them. There is really no end to the number of questions that could be legitimately asked about Blake.

Richard L. Conville   11 May 1978
Department of Speech and Theatre, University of Tennessee, Knoxville, TN
In response to Conville's letter (2 May 1978), thanking Frye's for his lecture at the University of Tennessee. Frye's talk — "Comparative Literature: What Gets Compared?"— was presented on 28 April.

Dear Professor Conville,

Thank you very much for your letter and the offprints. You did send me the article on me before,[566] and I was very interested to get the more recent one. I think my remark about Levi-Strauss referred primarily to his mythical synthesis, *The Raw and the Cooked* and *From Honey to Ashes*. I had expected great things of these books and felt curiously baffled by them. It's different with his work on structural anthropology which I do find useful as well as provocative.[567]

I am trying to work on something parallel to your "helix" image in the Bible book, as I find that Hegel provides the basis for a restatement of the old medieval theory by levels of meaning. Only in Hegel you go up through negating a previous stage, as with your security and alienation argument.

Ron Keast   16 May 1978
Ontario Educational Communications Authority, Toronto, ON
See headnote to letter of 3 May 1978 to Don Thompson and Jim Hanley.

Dear Ron,

This letter is to say that after careful consideration I have decided that the television series proposed for me is an impossible project, and that I am compelled to break off procedures, before we get into a new contract and a point of no return.

It represents for me a tremendous effort of time and energy, at this time in my life, to add a television series to my other activities. I could afford that effort only if I felt that I was communicating at my own top level. My consultations with Don [Thompson] and Jim [Hanley], and my examination of the first script, have made it clear to me that I shall be fitted into a format which is not mine, feels alien to me, and has me communicating in what to me is a social and personal vacuum. Twenty years ago, I should gladly have fitted into such a format in order to gain experience of the medium and a wider audience. Today, when I neither need nor want that kind of experience or exposure, it would be an intolerable nightmare to undertake a heavy course of work to produce something that I cannot believe in or would be interested in.

This is not the result of any disagreement with Don and Jim, or any sense that I feel I might do better with other people. True, they seem rather inflexible about the kind of thing they want to produce, and a series of consultations where I would be constantly overruled by their superior knowledge of the medium is also something I can't face. But I have never doubted for an instant that they would do the very best they could for me, and I am quite prepared to believe that the best they could do is the best that can be done with me and my material in the television medium. If so, television is simply not my medium, not at my age at any rate.

Marjory A. Bancroft   **19 May 1978**
Bonn, West Germany

In reply to Bancroft's proposal (8 May 1978) to establish an interdisciplinary research institute in the humanities and her request for the names of authorities in the field of criticism who might be interested in participating in such an institute.

Dear Ms. Bancroft:

Thank you for your letter. Of course there is no question of my interest in and wish to support such a project as you outline, from the point of view of a concern for the humanities. There is a very lively group now in the United States concerned with the reframing of the whole approach to the humanities, especially at Yale and Johns Hopkins. I might mention Geoffrey Hartman, Hillis Miller, Richard Macksey, Paul de Man, and Fredric Jameson, who is at the San Diego branch of the University of California. Jacques Derrida is at present, I believe, in residence at Yale. Father Walter Ong, at Washington University of St. Louis, has a special interest in psychiatry as well as literature.

The people I have mentioned are all well aware of the extent to which literary studies are beginning to merge with conceptions and methods derived from the social sciences. They are all well established figures, so I am not sure about their availability, but they would all have younger students and followers who might get more directly involved.

Crerar Douglas   **25 May 1978**
Camarillo, CA

In reply to Douglas's having sent Frye (29 April 1978) the table of contents and the first chapter of a manuscript entitled Northrop Frye as Calvinist Comedian *and asking for comment.*

Dear Mr. Douglas:

Thank you very much for your letter and for the news of the proposed book. In the circumstances, I cannot offer much more than general encouragement, but it is a most fresh and attractive study. I speak as one who very seldom enjoys reading about himself. In the Blake book I speak of people in the sixteenth century who envisioned a greater and more radical reform of the church than either Reformation or Counter-Reformation achieved, thinking of such people as Erasmus, Ficino, Pico, Bruno, Rabelais and Reuchlin — perhaps Melanchthon too. I like to think of myself as descended from that tradition.

I suppose Tillich's role as a German-American bridge is not so really unusual,[568] in view of the tremendous influence that the pre–Kaiser Germany had on New England culture. In any case, in working on the Bible book, where there is a presence concealed and disguised in the Old Testament who was eventually revealed in the Gospels and takes over the whole show in Revelation, I find myself rediscovering the scheme of the Odyssey at every point.

Your reference to Calvin as a "Senecan humanist"[569] is perhaps a bit over-compressed: not many people will know what Calvin's first work was.[570]

Roy and Laurenda Daniells   7 June 1978

Vancouver, BC

This letter is in the Roy Daniells Fonds, University of British Columbia, box 8, file 20.

Dear Roy and Laurenda,

Thanks so much for your telegram and congratulations[571]: getting such awards is a somewhat numbing experience, and the good will of one's friends takes on more reality in consequence. Certainly the price of wisdom is above silver and gold, but, as with the musical banks in *Erewhon*, it's pleasant to have it incarnated in a more physical form.[572]

I like very much the rewritten conclusion to the *Pilgrim's Progress*.[573]

Dorothy Swartz   7 June 1978

Lexington, MA

In reply to Swartz's letter of 25 May 1978, containing the news of the death of James Craig La Drière, professor of comparative literature at Harvard from 1965 until his retirement in 1976. Frye apparently came to know both La Drière and Swartz when he was Norton Professor at Harvard during 1974–75.

Dear Dorothy Swartz,

It was extremely kind of you to write and tell me about Craig La Drière. I had not heard of it before, and one always wants to know such things. Helen and I were both extremely fond of him, and we shall miss him a great deal. He was always rather wryly amused by my compulsive busyness and once sent Helen a clipping of newspaper headline reading "Northrop in a Hundred Projects." The reference was to the Northrop Aircraft Company, but it had its allegorical point.

It was very interesting to hear that you are working on Walter Map,[574] who was one of my favourites in my student days when I was reading in that period more than I have been able to do since.

Hazel Merrett   21 August 1978

Senneville, QC

In reply to Merrett's letter of 7 June 1978, congratulating Frye for having received the Royal Bank Award. Merrett was Frye's first cousin on his mother's side, the daughter of E. Edwin and Evelyn Howard. She was the wife of the well-known architect, John Campbell Merrett.

Dear Hazel,

Thank you very much for your letter, which I am delighted to get. I have recently had a most pleasant letter from Alma,[575] to whom I also wrote after getting her address from Olive.[576]

Helen and I have just come back from a trip to New Zealand, where I was visiting the six universities and giving lectures. We are still a bit dizzy from the plane, but will be back in circulation shortly. I have just been made Chancellor of Victoria and expect a busy year.

No, the music seems to be entirely from mother's side of the family.[577] She taught me the piano when I was about three years old, but so far as I remember none of my father's family had much interest in music. I keep reading my fairly large collection of keyboard music and find it a tremendous relaxation.

The very best to you both, also to Tim and Brian,[578] though I don't think I have met Brian. It is now about fifteen years since we met your sister in New Brunswick: such meetings are all the more important for being so infrequent.

Ruth El Saffar   **24 August 1978**

River Forest, IL

El Saffar, a distinguished Hispanist and Cervantes scholar and professor of Romance Language at the University of Illinois, Chicago, had sent (13 July 1978) Frye a copy of her essay on Cervantes's Persiles. *El Saffar, who had served with Frye on the executive council of the Modern Language Association, saw connections between Frye's work and her own writings on Cervantes.*

Dear Ruth:

Thank you very much for your letter and for the article. I had noticed myself the way in which heroes of quests, whether drunk or sober, sane or insane, tend to leave all their women folk behind, and going in search of something that doesn't exist, while frequently there is a sequel in which women are more clearly featured, as in the second part of Bunyan's *Pilgrim's Progress,* and I was interested to see you find this true of *Don Quixote* as well. I don't know the *Persiles,* but you make it sound fascinating. I suppose what the wife and mother represent in such constructs is not only the unconscious but a taking root in actual society. In the Christian myth, for example, Christ is symbolically the only male, and the body of society that he rescues is symbolically female.

It is a great honour for me to have you taking part in the MLA seminar, and I shall look forward to seeing you there.[579]

All the best from Jane, Helen and myself.

George Johnston   **24 August 1978**

Athelstan, QC

In reply to Johnston's letter (20 August 1978), indicating that he and his wife Jeanne had accepted the invitation to attend the ceremonies for the Royal Bank Award, 18 September 1978.

Dear George,

I was delighted to get your letter and come up to date on the news. I was particularly pleased that you and Jeanne are making the effort to come to the dinner, which is a great honour to me. My only regret is that that stuffy idiot who is in charge of the invitations insisted on putting "black tie" on them: needless to say I would infinitely have preferred to have no such thing at all.[580]

Helen and I have just got back from a two months tour of the South Pacific, six weeks of which were spent in New Zealand visiting its six universities, with a week in Tahiti going and a week in Fiji coming. It was a very pleasant trip all round, largely because there were so many old friends and former students to be met. One of them, a man named Forrest Scott (I think), at Auckland, is an Icelandic scholar who knows of you and of your work.[581]

Love to Jeanne from us both.

John Truax   **24 August 1978**

Buffalo, NY

In reply to an inquiry (6 June 1978) about Frye's regard for Jacques Maritain and Paul Claudel. Truax, was a graduate student at the University of Buffalo, writing a dissertation on the relationship between Maritain and both Claudel and Georges Roualt.

Dear Mr. Truax,

Thank you for your letter. I wish I could be a bit more helpful about your scholarly concerns, but the fact is that Maritain is somebody I read a long time ago, and although he is on my list to reread, especially *The Degrees of Knowledge,* I haven't yet done so. He was at St. Michael's College here at the time that I was trying to work out my notions of centripetal and centrifugal reading, and about the possibility of words conveying knowledge through their inner coherence rather than though their reflexion of an outside world. I used to attend Maritain's lectures, and no doubt he played a part in shaping my thinking at the time, but I have not yet brought him up to date in my own mind.

Claudel I do have a high regard for, as a poet and dramatist, and he interests me mainly because, apart from his own merits as a poet, he is one of the few modern writers to have taught himself Biblical typology. This is a subject I have been teaching and studying for some time, and consequently such things as Claudel's Annunciation play have a particular relevance to my own interests.

I am sorry not to be able to be more helpful and specific.

John Grube   **28 September 1978**
Toronto, ON M

In reply to Grube's having sent Frye (17 August 1978) a copy of his story "Southern Exposure," published in Gut *4, no. 1 (August–September 1978) 13–17. Grube asked for his comments and added, "While attempting the standard Quebec novel expected of all Canadian authors, it gradually dawned on me that there were certain forces at work there, rarely mentioned in the press, that will replace the melodramatic scenarios so favored by novelists with the usual dull Canadian compromise." Grube, the son of the classical scholar G.M.A. Grube, earned his M.A. from the University of Toronto and was teaching at the Ontario College of Art.*

Dear John,

Thank you very much for your latter and for the copy of the story. It is vary pleasing to see someone tackling the Quebec situation with the assumption that people there have actually heard of such things as Vatican II, and that there is more going on besides Maria Chapdelaine overlaid by the quiet revolution. I think there is perhaps more than one chapter in the theme.

Pierre Elliott Trudeau   **1 November 1978**
Prime Minister of Canada, Ottawa, ON

In response to Trudeau's message, dated only 1978: "I am pleased that the Honourable John Roberts has agreed to convey my warmest greetings to all those attending the ceremony in honour of Northrop Frye as he is named Chancellor of Victoria College. On behalf of all Canadians, I wish to pay a special tribute to you, Northrop Frye. More than a distinguished scholar, renowned critic and great thinker, you embody within yourself and through your writings a cultural vision for Canadians: a belief that 'a sense of unity is the opposite of a sense of uniformity.' On this memorable occasion, I express to you my sincere admiration for the devotion you give to your work and to the mission it has come to represent. Your love for teaching makes you a most appropriate and welcome Chancellor and I know that your influence will continue to be felt in the generations of Canadians to come."

Dear Mr. Trudeau,

Just a note to express my very deep appreciation for your kindness in writing to me on the occasion of my Installation as Chancellor of Victoria University.

William Toye   **11 December 1978**
Oxford University Press, Don Mills, ON

In reply to a request for Frye's advice about a new edition of the Oxford Companion to Canadian History and Literature.

Dear Bill,

Thank you for your letter. It seems to me that if Norah Story's book[582] were carefully and fully revised, it would not only serve a useful purpose but would have a very steady sale. It seems to me that the various Colombo confections[583] are selling well, and they are much less generally useful. I should agree about cutting out the bibliographies, and whoever did the revising should adopt more flexible categories for inclusion. For example, it was nonsense to leave Barker Fairley out of her book merely because his major publications were in German literature.

It seems to me that the French supplement was an admirable public service, and the stupidity and narrow-mindedness of French reviewers never ceases to amaze me. I still remain of the opinion that in the present feeling for cultural nationalism there is a genuine market for such books as the *Companion*. I have been quite mystified by the way in which my own *Bush Garden* has sold, and can only put it down to receptiveness for Canadian information.

Ron Keast   21 December 1978
Ontario Educational Communications Authority, Toronto, ON

Dear Ron Keast:

I have been looking at the contract of June 16, 1976, between the Ontario Educational Communications Authority and myself. It mentions a series of television programmes connected with the book of the Bible which is now in progress. The original idea of basing a series on the Bible book has obviously been dropped. Just to keep things clear, I should like to say that I consider this material free for me to use in any other way that seems appropriate, on the assumption that OECA is no longer interested in it. If there is any misunderstanding on my part, please let me know as soon as possible.

Roy Daniells   9 January 1979
University of British Columbia, Vancouver, BC

In reply to Daniells's letter (18 December 1978) asking Frye how he "would tackle the RSC's [Royal Society of Canada's] contribution to our intellectual life." Daniells had been asked to write an article for Canadian Literature *on the Royal Society's contribution.*

Dear Roy,

Your letter did get rather lost in the Christmas mail after all, and I am sorry that this is the first time I have been able to answer it. It seems to me that you have pretty well the essential things about the Royal Society[584]: it is trying to be a national academy, and it is frustrated by lack of funds. Although I am very far from being bilingual myself, I have always been furious that the first two sections were split along language lines rather than along lines of discipline. I know that the French don't want their cosy little gentlemen's club broken by the invasion of Anglophones, but the present division has greatly weakened the Royal Society's efforts to speak for the Humanities and Social Sciences.

It seems to me that the various symposia that the Royal Society has attempted represent its most successful efforts to become something of an academic Senate. Sometimes these are held outside the regular Royal Society meetings, like the Copernicus one of a few years ago.[585] The difficulty is to find enough subjects on which scholars of different disciplines can unite. These are nearly always political, because their common concern as citizens of the country is the main thing that unites scholars in their pluralistic disciplines. The great disadvantage, of course, is the same difficulty that Canada itself finds in becoming articulate as a whole, and from sea to sea.

I am aware that there is nothing here that you don't know and haven't said, but I think what is true about the Royal Society is the obvious. As I have pointed out at such tedious length, culture tends to decentralize[,] and [a] cultural organization which is mainly scientific and is bound by its charter to be federal is handicapped in its publicity before it can say anything. Considering what the Royal Society was when I joined it in 1951, it seems to me that its efforts have been pretty impressive, even heroic.

Ruth El Saffar   24 January 1979
River Forest, IL

In reply to El Saffar's undated letter, written before the session devoted to Frye at the convention of the Modern Language Association (see letter to El Saffar, 24 August 1978, above) but not received by Frye until after returning from the convention. El Saffar expresses her awareness of the affinities between her own work and Frye's: "What I like, aside from the humor, is the clarity, the breadth of vision, and the sense that all this concern with literature is part of a much larger concern of our whole beingness here on earth."

Dear Ruth:

As I said, I had not had your letter before I returned home so it was all the more pleasant to have it when I got home. It was extremely helpful to me, because Denham's book on me[586] is just out, and it reminds me that almost everybody seems to be preoccupied with my charts and diagrams and with the question of whether they are logically airtight or not, instead of reading me as you do for what incidental help I may give to them in their own work.

Mr. Fernandez sent a snapshot of me autographing books which included a picture of you, and which I am very glad to have.

Blessings and love from Jane and myself (I am dictating this so that Jane can be included.)

Robert Denham   2 February 1979
Emory & Henry College, Emory, VA

In response to receiving a copy of Denham's Northrop Frye and Critical Method *(University Park: Pennsylvania State University Press, 1978).*

Dear Mr. Denham,

The book has just come in, and I have been looking through it. It is, as you know, extremely hard for me to comment on anything that concerns me so closely, but it looks as though the high praise given it by Wayne Booth and others is well deserved. I cannot help feeling a bit depressed, certainly not by you, but by the babble of voices toward the end of people who can see nothing but the schematic constructs of the *Anatomy*, and are concerned only with whether they are logically airtight or taxonomically exhaustive or whatnot. I wish people who care about literature would read me because I do, and go on from there. I'd like to see a book on me sometime that never mentioned the *Anatomy*. This is of course without prejudice to the very great debt I owe to you.

Ruth El Saffar   19 February 1979
River Forest, IL

In reply to El Saffar's letter of 7 February 1979, which solicits Frye's opinion of Derrida and other poststructuralist thinkers.

Dear Ruth:

Thank you very much for your kindly and thoughtful letter. I am delighted to have a copy of your paper on Cervantes and Calderon,[587] which will help to do something about my total ignorance of Spanish literature. I was particularly interested, naturally, in what you say about *Life Is a Dream*.

As for my problems in reading Derrida and the rest, my primary motive in consulting them is a somewhat paranoid one of looking in them to see if they have said anything that I haven't said myself rather better. So far, I have found them of rather limited value: they write about literature but not from within literature, and their eyes always seem to be scanning the horizon in quest of more promising material. But I can't ignore the fact that people are profoundly influenced by the question of who's in the cultural news: people will quote things from Lacan, who is fashionable, and be quite literally unable to see that the same point might be in Jung, who is not. And my own age makes me vulnerable: I know that may people are anxious to find me out of style, and I want to show them, not that I still feel young, but that I sympathize to some degree with their attitude. In your position, I should simply go ahead with your work on Spanish literature. But in mine, I have to deal with the Bible in relation to contemporary problems of critical theory, so I can't get out of acquiring some familiarity with tertiary criticism.

The very best from us both, and from Jane.

Father Eric O'Connor   5 March 1979

Thomas More Institute for Adult Education, Montreal, QC

In reply to Father O'Connor's letter (25 February 1979), telling Frye that he was "still under the spell of The Secular Scripture" *and enclosing a copy of Paul Ricoeur's "Que signifie 'humanisme'?"*

Dear Father Eric,

Thank you very much for your note and for the offprint of Ricoeur's article. The University of Toronto has set up a Northrop Frye chair that the first person to occupy it will be Paul Ricoeur. I can't think of anyone in the world I would rather have associated with me in that context.

Maureen Hall   26 March 1979

Secretary, Toronto Area Presbytery, Toronto, ON

Dear Mrs. Hall,

I have just been informed that at their meeting on March 21st, the Chignecto Presbytery approved my request to be Left Without Pastoral Charge and to be transferred from their Presbytery to the Toronto Area Presbytery. I should now be most grateful if you could please advise me of the steps to be taken to be attached to your Presbytery.

Bernard S. Adams   18 April 1979

President Ripon College, Ripon, WI

Dear President Adams,

Thank you very much for your letter and invitation. It would be a great honour to receive an honorary degree from Ripon College, but the trouble is that I expect to be in Italy on a lecture tour at the time of your commencement. I am very sorry about this, and would certainly be more cooperative if I could.[588]

George Johnston   30 April 1979

Naxos, Greece

In response to Johnston's letter from the Ariadne Hotel on the island of Naxos, Greece (12 April 1979). Johnston and his wife Jeanne had been travelling in Europe since January.

Dear George,

I was delighted to get your letter from Naxos, and I know that the article for Elizabeth Cowan's magazine will be fine.[589] I am still preoccupied at the moment trying to clear off my desk before a three-week trip through Italy, lecturing at five or six universities. After that I hope to dig myself into the attic here and try to struggle with that biblical leviathan that has been haunting me for so long.

I don't know if you knew that I had just been made Chancellor at Victoria, which is an honorary job without too much to do, beyond presiding at Convocations and chairing the Senate. In any case I assume it means that I shall be in active teaching for a while yet. I have taken on an extra teaching course, an undergraduate one in Shakespeare, and am very pleased to feel that I can still teach.

I am delighted about the degree from Carleton, which is certainly well deserved.[590] A much less welcome piece of news is that Roy Daniells has gone,[591] though apparently well and active until the last moment.

David Knight   10 May 1979
Department of English, Victoria College

In response to Knight's having sent Frye a copy of his novel, asking for reactions. If Knight's manuscript was accompanied by a letter, it is not extant.

Dear David:

I have read this book with a great deal of interest: the style, despite its somewhat unvarying *martellato* rhythm, kept pulling me on, and the last part I read with total involvement. Most of what follows is there only in the hope that it may be of some use in getting a detached view, which I understood was what was important to you.

I can understand that for a Canadian publisher, at least, and perhaps others as well, the David Crombie tie-up would be pretty off-putting, but that's incidental. What bothered me more, especially in Parts Two and Three, which I thought the weakest, was the constant feeling that the book was so busy nailing down every observation and emotional nuance that everything else seemed to disappear. I had to keep looking back to see who all these Jerrys and Barrys were, there being very little character differentiation. The characters all speak in much the same rhythm and idiom, and are characterized only in the most abstract way, like their tendency to moral judgement and the like. The women are even harder to distinguish: the most memorable, by far, is the helpless girl who keeps asking the narrator's wife how to cook. I know female undergraduates often seem as though they were constructed of interchangeable parts, especially in the dark, but that's not how they see or would like to see themselves, and there's little attempt to study them from the inside. The relations of the narrator and his wife form one of the most consistently attractive parts of the book, providing a sort of moral norm for the rest, but, again, they're not characterized relationships.

I understood and appreciated the way that so many symbolic images from the earlier part of the book — the scythe, the Bradford riot, and the like — were picked up and made to form part of a gradually unifying design. I could also see that this was a justification for the great length of the book: the difficulty is to persuade any large number of readers that there was anything going on except accumulation of observed detail. I found the masturbation and sexual-scuffling episodes particularly dull, as such things are purely generic, and bring no vision of human life into being. The use of a first-person narrative is, I think, somewhat unfortunate, because nothing seems to go on outside his mind. This gives the impression of a self-indulgent first novel, where the writer is still fascinated by the way that he can record all his observations in writing, but hasn't yet learned that they gain no significance from being so recorded. They gain significance only from a context which makes them more than the small experiences of small people.

Because the use of a first-person narrator makes the book so much of a transcribed Dear Diary, the flashback technique doesn't acquire the advantages it ought to have, of presenting the growing-up process beside the matured individuals. In the sixth part, where I was absorbed in the story, I found the flashbacks damn irritating. In that last part, I found the technique of maintaining and gradually increasing the suspense admirable and brilliant, and the political scenes I thought were very well done too. A whole novel written on this level would have been an incredible *tour de force*. The reason for the superiority of the concluding parts, I think, is not that the events were more sensational, but that the author became primarily interested in the story, and, because he was interested in that, the characters began to clear up and look different from each other. This sense of objective significance was what *Farquharson's Physique*[592] had.

Many of these strictures would be far less important, in fact they might not even be true, if prose fiction were more fashionable than it is and more in the centre of the cultural scene. But when publishers are so panicky and anxious to cut back, especially on long novels, and when the market has to compete with so many other media, the situation is different. If I were a writer of prose fiction, I'd be haunted by the feeling that there was a vast chorus of people saying "so what?" at every sentence. Fiction based on standard commercial formulas would not be affected by this, but more serious fiction is, and it seems to me that only a powerfully objective vision, possessed with the significance of what it has to say to the point of attending much less to the subtlety or even the accuracy with which it is said, can overcome the contemporary handicaps.

M.K. Joseph   **11 June 1979**
Department of English, University of Auckland, Auckland, New Zealand

In reply to Joseph's letter (29 May 1979), which reports that John Ayre has solicited information about Frye's Oxford years for his biography of Frye. (Joseph and Frye were classmates at Oxford; they became lifelong friends). Joseph wants Frye's approval before replying. His letter also contains news about an automobile accident, and he mentions Frye's 1979 Italian tour and the recent Canadian election.

Dear Mike:

I was delighted to get your letter, which came just after I had come back from Italy. Yes, it was a marvelous and exhilarating trip, though exhausting. Six places, seven lectures, half a dozen newspaper and television and radio interviews, including a full television programme called "Northrop Frye in Florence," besides all the social life, all in three weeks. At Rome we were entertained by the Canadian Ambassador and his cultural attache. The latter, a man named David Anido, started his career in New Zealand as a student of Jack Garrett's, and he knows you, or at least about you.[593]

Regarding John Ayre: he seems to have devoted himself to the idea of writing a biography on me, and he seems to me an extremely responsible and intelligent person, originally a student of mine at Victoria. I hate the thought of a biography being written about me, but not to the extent of trying to cramp his style.

We were very distressed to hear of your accident, though immensely relieved at the outcome. Some old friends of ours we met in Rome, Fred Sternfield and his wife — he's a Professor of Music at Oxford — were less fortunate. They were also hit by a drunk, but were both rather seriously injured. I am beginning to think maybe the devils invented automobiles along with gun powder.

The Canadian election didn't surprise me,[594] and apparently the new lot seem to have some sense of responsibility. I went though the Italian election there, and noticed that theirs was also a conservative shift, though a less decisive one. I am beginning to suspect that the Pope's visit to Poland may turn out to be one of the decisive historical events of our time.[595]

Helen is well, and stood the Italy trip very well, I think. It was boiling hot weather most of the time. We both send our love to Molly[596] and yourself.

Crawford Kilian   11 June 1979
North Vancouver, BC

Killian was a novelist who was teaching at Capilano College at the time. He sent Frye a copy of his book Do Some Great Thing: The Black Pioneers of British Columbia *(1978) and two of his science fiction novels,* The Empire of Time *(1978) and* Icequake *(1979). One of the characters in* Icebreak *is named Herman Northrop. See Frye's comment on* The Empire to Time *in his letter to Alex Comfort of 27 April 1982, below.*

Dear Mr. Kilian,

Thank you very much for the three books, which I am delighted to have. I have started reading the science fiction ones, which are written with extraordinary professional competence. I like science fiction, especially when it does tricks with time, and it's pleasant to see all the familiar Blake names turning up in such a context.[597]

Nobuaki Kozaki   22 June 1979
Kumamotoshi, Japan

Dear Mr. Kozaki,

Thank you for your letter. It raises some interesting issues, and I cannot claim any finality in attempting to deal with them. I think what I said about prose as ordinary speech on its best behaviour is true, but in the last hundred years the conception of standard prose has moved from the formal very considerably in the direction of the informal. No contemporary writer writing for the general public would adopt a style as formal as, say, Macaulay or Darwin in the nineteenth century. The great mass of academic articles are still written in a rather formal style, but they are seldom regarded as models of prose.

I think that the model for writers of non–English background to aim at in writing English is a relatively informal one, such as one encounters in, as a random example, the essays of E.B. White. One should be careful of using colloquial idioms, however, as it takes years of exposure to a language to get a feeling for these.

Anjan K. Nath   9 July 1979
Nongthymmai, Shillong, India

In reply to Nath's request for information about studies, bibliographic and otherwise, of Frye's work.

Dear Mr. Nath,

Thank you for your letter and your interest. I think the best thing for you to do would be to get hold of a copy of Robert Denham's book *Northrop Frye and Critical Method*, published by the Pennsylvania State Press in 1978. This is a full-length study of my work which also contains the kind of bibliographic information that you would need.

George Johnston   5 September 1979
Athelstan, QC

In reply to Johnston's letter of 27 August 1979, with which he enclosed a copy of his most recent collection of poems.

Dear George,

Thanks very much for the copy of *Taking a Grip*,[598] which I am delighted to have. There is far too little occasional poetry produced in this country, or in general, and I am very glad that you are not overlooking that kind of writing.[599]

I am very pleased that Nora[600] is coming to Victoria: if you are in touch with her tell her not to hesitate coming in to see me. Young people tend to duck out of duty visits, even when they would like to make them. And I suppose congratulations are really in order, as you undoubtedly have a busy and active retirement. You seem to be very well known in Old Norse circles: I met a man in New Zealand who was very familiar with your name.[601]

I had a quiet summer working on the Bible book. I cannot seem to feel a great deal of affection for that book, though I don't quite know why. I suppose, being the Bible, it stirs up too many things: parental injunctions and the like. Also I had to work unusually hard to prevent it from becoming a rewritten version of things I had already done. If I had any sense I would retire and devote myself to it, but I am really having a much better time teaching and being on campus.

Love to Jeanne and yourself.

R.D. Sparham   12 September 1979

Further Education Study, Government of the Northwest Territories, NT

Sparham was Head, Research and Planning Section, Research and Development Division of the Northwest Terrotories' Department of Education.

Dear Mr. Sparham,

Thank you very much for the copy of your report,[602] which I have read with interest. There is certainly nothing wrong with your main thesis: the difficulty is to align the kind of interest in the north and in indigenous peoples which any cultivated or concerned Canadian ought to have with the highly specialized sub-divisions within Canadian universities. This is without prejudice to the report itself, of course, which is very lucid and straightforward.

D.C. Williams   18 September 1979

Commission on Freedom of Information and Individual Privacy, Toronto, ON

In reply to Williams's request (16 August 1979) for Frye's ideas about the major problems in Canadian society and in the university — and what they might do mutually to solve them — that might help him as he prepares a lecture for the Council of University Presidents. D. Carlton Williams was president of the University of Western Ontario.

Dear Carl,

I don't know whether I have much to say that will really be useful to you, but what preoccupies me at present is still the rather paradoxical movement I have been talking about for some years. This is the fact that as a society matures, its culture tends to decentralize and regionalize while its political and economic systems, especially the economic, tend to centralize and build up bigger units.

This produces two faults or perverted forms of activity (as I consider them). One is the attempt to make a political or economic movement out of cultural regionalizing. This produces the various forms of separatism all over the world, and the connexion of separatism with violence and terrorism indicates that there is something wrong with it: you as a psychologist would know more about that than I. It is really an anarchist movement, and from the beginning the anarchists have tended to the two extremes of pacifism and terrorism. The other is the attempt to make economic centralization a cultural movement as well. This produces various forms of cultural imperialism, such as we had formerly in the democratic world and still have in the two big Marxist empires. This produces a pompous and hollow cultural development which pretends to be realistic but is actually the idealist in a bad sense, trying to glamourize the social establishment.

The regionalizing of culture does not mean drawing away from international standards: it means the opposite, growing into them and absorbing them. I have said elsewhere that standards cannot be made but only established: that is, no healthy culture can think of its standards as external to itself. That is one of the forms of a provincial culture, which means that it is a form of imperialism. There is a kind of international style in literature and the arts, and as Canadian culture matures it enters into that international style in its own specific way.

It is obvious that the universities have a very strategic place in this kind of double movement, as education is a provincial matter in Canada, universities are or should be closely related to their immediate communities, and yet they exist to transmit the international standards and perspectives of contemporary culture.

This separation of the culture from the economy is by itself very simplistic. One obvious question is the role of the mass media. My own feeling is that radio and television should be under federal control, as they are, because of the danger of being used as propaganda media by the provinces, but that the federal controlling body should be sensitive to cultural regional needs, as, I think, the CRTC has consistently tried to be. When, for example, Peter Lougheed in Alberta refuses to support the University there on the ground that it is much cheaper to import a few American experts, he is selling out to a kind of imperialism.

I don't think these reflexions are of much value, but while I do try to do a certain amount of thinking I don't always move very fast.

Dennis Kennedy   24 October 1979
Crawfordsville, IN

In reply to an undated request by Kennedy, a student a Wabash College, for advice about pursuing his interest in literature at the graduate level.

Dear Dennis Kennedy,

Thank you very much for your letter. I visited Wabash a good many years ago, and Crawfordsville more recently, when I taught for a summer session at Bloomington, where there were friends of mine at the time in Wabash. I am naturally very interested in what you tell me about your growing interest in Blake and Yeats, but I should be dishonest if I did not say first of all that the job market is at a depression level and that I don't expect things to improve very quickly. Consequently for practical and economic reasons I cannot conscientiously recommend graduate study in English at all. If that is not a problem of major importance for you, it doesn't matter too much where you go, as long as the place is large enough and good enough to enable you to pursue your own interests. Toronto would be all right, although I myself am too close to retirement myself to want to take on graduate students, as it is no help to them to have to abandon them in midstream. Your own state university in Bloomington would also be excellent, and one could easily name the obvious ones in New England and California, except that many of them, in deference to the job situation, have strictly limited the number of graduate students they will accept.

This sounds like a rather confused and floundering letter, but the combination of academic and economic complications makes it very difficult to give straightforward advice.

Margaret Atwood   6 November 1979
Alliston, ON

Dear Peggy,

I have two reasons for writing, both extremely obvious. One is to say what a very good time I had with *Life Before Man*, and how much I appreciated having a copy. The other is to thank you for the piece on me in the *CEA Critic*.[603] I think your remarks about Maritimers in particular were extraordinarily perceptive. It is quite an achievement to throw a new light on me to me.

Love to the three of you.

Robert Denham   6 November 1979
Department of English, Emory & Henry College, Emory, VA

Dear Mr. Denham,

This is just to say how very pleased and honoured I was on reading your piece on me in the *CEA Critic*. I am particularly glad that you spent so much time on *The Critical Path*: nobody seems to know what the hell that book is about, or, except you, much care. My indebtedness to you is piling up like the Tower of Babel, though I trust with less confusion of speech.

Jean O'Connor Perrault   6 November 1979
Saskatchewan Drive, Edmonton, AB

In reply to Perrault's undated letter enclosing an article from The Compass *that Perrault saw as indebted to Frye without acknowledging it. The article assumed, according to Perrault, that "the adjective 'Canadian' may be inappropriate to the study of our literature."*

Dear Ms. Perrault,

Thank you very much for your letter and the article. I dare say the indebtedness to me is an unconscious one, and, as I have never written on Kroetsch, though I know him, there was no occasion to mention me.

I don't really think that there is a clash or inconsistency between the existence of a distinctive Canadian literature and the existence of a kind of international set of styles and conventions which Canadian writers, like all other writers, have to adopt. Naturally with some types of writing, notably fantasy, the sense of the immediate physical environment is somewhat blurred, but it's still there, and the literary work is still growing out of it.

Donald Riccomini   6 November 1979
Department of English, University of Wisconsin, Madison, WI

Dear Professor Riccomini:

Just a note to thank you for your thoughtful and most welcome article on me in the recent *UTQ*.[604] It sounds ungracious to ask for more, but if you do complete the article on Derrida that you speak of, I'd love to have an offprint of it.

Rev. Howard Norman   28 November 1979
Toronto, ON

In reply to Norman's letter of 17 November 1979, asking whether Frye might not undertake the writing of a book on Richard Roberts (1894–1945), well-known preacher, theologian, and sixth moderator of the United Church of Canada. He had been the minister at the Sher-

bourne United Church during the student days of Frye and Helen Kemp and a part-time lec-
turer at Emmanuel College in 1933-34. On Norman, see headnote to letter of 18 January 1978.

Dear Howard,

Thank you very much for your letter. There certainly should be a book on Richard Roberts. I can't do much myself, as I am giving every moment of time and energy I have to completing my own writing projects, which at my age is not all that easy. But it seems to me that Gwen's material ought to be publishable.[605] I never heard of a biography being turned down because it was too personal. Ryerson Press was already pretty hopeless even before it collapsed. Perhaps the present McGraw-Hill management is more enlightened about such things. In any case, with the great spate of Canadiana coming out these days there should be, I should think, no insuperable difficulty about a book on Roberts, especially one that included some of his own writings.

We'd be delighted to see you. We know the Whitlas well, and of course Earle.[606] My wife Helen remembers Richard Roberts with immense pleasure: he picked us up when we were forlornly gazing at an art show at Eaton's College Street and took us into tea in the Round Room. A great moment in both our lives.

Rev. Lois Wilson   28 November 1979
Chalmers United Church, Kingston, ON

In response to Wilson's letter (23 November 1979), in which was enclosed a transcript of her recent dialogue with Margaret Laurence. It was published as "Margaret Laurence's Faith, Hope and Love," Kingston Whig-Standard 15 October 1979: 5.

Dear Ms. Wilson,

Thank you very much for your kindly letter and for the very interesting dialogue. It is a great encouragement to hear of clergymen who are making such serious efforts to naturalize our good writers in the communities they are addressing. The interest of the dialogue was very evenly divided between Margaret Laurence and yourself: I was fascinated by the lucidity of your efforts to get people away from the usual reviving-corpse notions of the Resurrection.

H. Keith Monroe   11 December 1979
Greensboro, NC

In response to Monroe's proposal (27 November 1979) to do a book-length interview with Frye. Because of Frye's busy schedule, John Ayre's fears that Monroe's project would scoop his biography of Frye, and Monroe's involvement with other obligations, the project never came to fruition.

Dear Mr. Monroe,

Thank you very much for your kindly enquiring letter. The relevant situation in relation to me appears to be this. First, a former student of mine who is primarily a journalist, has undertaken to write a biography of me, no doubt in response to the very ill-advised remark I once made that no biographer could possibly take the slightest interest in me. He has got a grant from the Canada Council to work on this, and seems to be collecting my skeletons, or bones of them at least.

Second, there was some talk of my doing a series of television programs, based on a book on the Bible that I am now working on, which would be along the lines of the Kenneth Clark and Bronowski series, at least as regards format. It was the provincial television authority that proposed this, and they got it as far as a pilot script, but it was obviously not anything they needed me for, so I backed out of it.[607] Meanwhile a former student[608] with some experience in television has been taping my lectures on biblical typology and Shakespeare with a view to planning such a series on his own.

I do not know of any other projects in relation to me that seem close to yours, and if you do not think these two impinge on what you want to do, the field seems to be open for you. Naturally, of course, I have to budget and watch my time schedule very sharply, and would greatly prefer to have as specific an estimate as possible of the amount of time and energy your project would take.

1980s

Elizabeth Sturges   17 January 1980
Billingslay, Bridgnorth, Shropshire, England

In reply to Sturges's letter of December 1979, bringing Frye news of life in Shropshire, where she and her husband Simon had moved in 1978. Sturges had been a reader for the Macmillan Company of Canada, assessing manuscripts for publication.

Dear Elizabeth,

We were delighted to get your letter to Helen and be brought up to date with your news. Any kind of life associated with fauna intimidates me. As I remember, Kay Coburn had a farm near here which kept her very busy around lambing time, and I was malicious enough to invent a story that a scholar came to stay with her expecting a conference on Charles Lamb and found himself snatching real lambs out of real ewes.

I hope Caroline[609] will like the Oxford Polytechnic: we have rather bad memories of it, as it was close to the very inadequate quarters we had during the term that I taught at Oxford and occasionally the students would fill up the noon hours with hideous recorded noises that there was no getting away from.

I passed on your message to Jay.[610] She is very busy and happy, but is running into difficulties about getting her book published, because the publishing situation has become so desperate: you can't even approach a publisher unless you can guarantee that your manuscript is full of either pornography or scandal.

I have just been made Chancellor of Victoria, which thank goodness is largely an honorary post, and am on a three-year extension after retirement, half way through the second year.

Love to Simon and yourself from us both.

George Johnston   24 January 1980
Athelstan, QC

Dear George,

I was really quite overwhelmed with your contributions to the *CEA Critic* issue on me[611]: it was surely beyond the call of duty for you to write so very careful and full an article. But it was packed with very pleasant memories for me, and it was a great joy to read and reread it.

Love to Jeanne and yourself from us both.

H. Keith Monroe   4 February 1980
Greensboro, NC

See letter of 11 December 1979.

221

Dear Mr. Monroe,

This is in response to your letter of January 3, and my secretary's subsequent telephone conversation with you. After consultation with my biographer regarding his schedule and checking my own, I find it will not now be possible to grant your interviews in the fall. He will need approximately the same number of interview hours as you and will be asking the same kind of questions, probably in the fall if not earlier. So will the other man that I mentioned who is planning to work out a series of programmes which will also have a personal basis. This would make impossible demands on my time and energy if you were to conduct your interviews at the same time, and if you could postpone your interviews until around this time next year, I should be most grateful, and my own schedule should be a little less hectic then also. I am very sorry for any inconvenience I may have caused you.

Hamish Guthrie   13 February 1980
Oakville, ON

In reply to Guthrie's letter of appreciation (3 February 1980) for "Creation and Recreation," the Larkin-Stuart Lectures Frye gave at Trinity College, University of Toronto, 30 January–1 February 1980. Guthrie remarks that he had difficulty with Frye's point that human beings are happiest when they are transforming their natural surroundings into artifacts, and he gives Thoreau as an example of someone who was interested not in transforming nature but in being transformed by it. Guthrie taught high school English and drama in Oakville, Ontario.

Dear Hamish,

Thank you very much for your extremely kindly and gracious letter, which I was naturally delighted to receive. Certainly I would never deny that there are writers who expose themselves very directly to the impact of nature, and that Thoreau was one of them. In fact I did cut out a reference, not to him, but to Hopkins: "Long live the weeds and the wilderness yet." But my point was rather that while nature is an inexhaustible field for observation, the sources of teaching have to come from something more structured within human life itself. This is true even for people temperamentally closer to oriental than to biblical attitudes, as I think perhaps Thoreau was.

The very best to you both.

Alvin Lee   14 February 1980
Stormont, West Flamborough, ON

Lee had been a student of Frye's. He taught English at McMaster University, where he also served as dean. After retirement, he became the general editor of the Collected Works of Northrop Frye.

Dear Al,

I gathered from what you said the other night that you had more or less decided to accept the Presidency of McMaster, but I have just heard the news publicized. This is merely to offer congratulations and best wishes. What I said about the importance of a university having a president who can speak for it with full academic weight is very central in my own mind, and for that reason I am very glad for McMaster as well. I hope it will not take too much time from your scholarship, but I think real scholarship is more of a synthesis of experience than of knowledge, and a wider range of experience will perhaps do it no harm.

Anja Gallus   **27 February 1980**
Willowdale, ON

In response to Gallus's thanking Frye for his Larkin-Stuart Lectures at Trinity College, University of Toronto, 30 January–1 February 1980 and then asking two questions: what did you mean in your lecture by saying "History started to wither away when Christianity emerged"; and what did you mean in The Educated Imagination *by saying that "the creative and the neurotic minds have a lot in common."*

Dear Ms. Gallus,

Thank you very much for your letter. I was perhaps talking too fast at the point you mention. What I was saying was that Christianity was in danger of losing the sense of urgency of its message as the centuries passed and "History, like the state in Marxist thought, failed to wither away."

The other point I don't know how to answer: I have rather a bad habit of announcing that I will deal with the subject later and then not doing it.[612] The creative and the neurotic attitudes have in common a sense of immense and portentous significance; where they differ is that the neurotic cannot get out of the prison of his own ego, although a number of genuinely creative people have been neurotic.

Murray MacQuarrie   **28 April 1980**
International Affairs Research Center, Genoa, Italy

In reply to a former student's having sent Frye a copy of a review from an Italian newspaper. MacQuarrie had formerly taught at the University of Waterloo. He was presently working as a translator and editor in Genoa.

Dear Murray MacQuarrie:

I was delighted to hear from you and discover where you were. I seem to remember that you were extremely interested in such things as film courses,[613] and I hope your work in Genoa is equally congenial. I was in Italy last year about this time. I was visiting seven universities, and had an exhausting but exhilarating time.[614] I was lucky enough to miss both the muggers in Rome and the terrorism squad in Padua.

I have reached retiring age, but am on a three-year extension and my [sic] consequently as busy as ever. I gave up the Principalship some years ago to become something called a "University Professor," and am now serving a term as Chancellor of Victoria, which keeps me busy attending meetings, though it is largely a ceremonial position.

I don't see Jim Carscallen[615] very often at the moment, because he has the term off, but when I do I shall certainly pass on your message.

William Fennell   **14 May 1980**
Principal, Emmanuel College, University of Toronto

In reply to an inquiry about Norma Arnett, who had graduated from Victoria College in 1949. She makes a number of appearances in Frye's Diaries. *On 12 May 1980 Fennell had written Frye about a letter and manuscript he had received from Arnett, the latter of which he sent on for Frye's assessment.*

Dear Bill,

The situation about myself and Norma is this. Shortly after she was graduated she started writing to me, and she averaged a letter a day, very frequently two letters, for about ten years. The letters contained nothing by psychotic blither, and were very frequently abusive. The reason for the abuse was mainly that I didn't undertake her [sic] full time support for her writing. But what very little writing she submitted was also psychotic blither. Finally, she ran out of money and appealed to me by telephone. I sent her a cheque, but made the stipulation that the cataract of letters was to stop. I have stopped reading most of them by that time in any case. She continued to send them at intervals, but my secretary had instructions to return them unopened. I felt that there was absolutely nothing else to do.

Naturally I am delighted if she has emerged from this sufficiently to write something that impressed you, but you will perhaps understand something of my reluctance to go back into this vortex again, as it seems clear that she is still in a quite disturbed state, even though what she has produced is infinitely more coherent that I could ever have hoped for.

You can tell her if you wish that I have looked at the manuscript, and that the poetry in particular I find impressive. But how much further I can go I am not sure. I may add that she has written to a number of other people, from Claude Bissell to her classmates of 1949, telling them that I have stolen all my ideas from her. I say this not to prejudice you against her, but merely to try to explain my own rather painful and embarrassing position in regard to her.

George Johnston   6 June 1980
Athelstan, QC

Dear George,

The variety and extraordinary competence of your efforts for me would almost embarrass me if I didn't feel so close to you. This is merely to repeat what you know already: that the poem you wrote is a great honour for me to have associated with me, a well a great pleasure to possess.[616]

Blessings to you both.

Robert J. Heaman   21 October 1980
Department of English, Wilkes College, Wilkes-Barre, PA

In reply to Heaman's note (4 October 1980) reminding Frye of his letter of 1971 and remarking, "I guess you know the impact you have had upon this generation of the Lord's people, but in the event that you yourself might sometimes become unsure, I for one can assure that you have opened up a dimension of literature and vision that is immeasurably important."

Dear Professor Heaman,

Thanks you for your most friendly and gracious note. Writing is a much lonelier occupation than most realize, and so such notes as yours mean a great deal.

Edward Quinn   22 October 1980
Department of English, City University of New York, NY

In reply to Quinn's recommendation (14 September 1980) that the published version of Frye's Shakespeare lectures, which Bob Sandler was editing, include the questions asked by students: "The loss in continuity is more than made up for by the insights into teaching that emerge from your handling of the questions."

Dear Mr. Quinn:

Thank you very much for your most friendly letter. I was delighted to hear from someone whom I have heard so much about, as Bob is a very genuine admirer of yours. I am naturally delighted that you like the Shakespeare lectures, and I would certainly want to include questions if I can. I used to feel that I was particularly good at handling questions from class, but with growing deafness I find that that is an increasingly hazardous business.

William A. Johnsen   9 December 1980
Department of English, Michigan State University, East Lansing, MI

In reply to Johnsen's having sent Frye a copy of his article, "The Sparagmos of Myth Is the Naked Lunch of Mode: Modern Literature as the Age of Frye and Borges," boundary 2 8 (Winter 1980): 297–311.

Dear Professor Johnsen,

Thank you very much for the offprint of your article, which I have read with great interest. I find myself increasingly unable to cope with the general scrimmage of ideas in critical theory today, at least so far as to determine my own place in it, and consequently I am heavily dependent on such people as yourself, as well as of course grateful to them, for saying things about me much more clearly than I could say them myself.

Penelope Tzougros   14 January 1981
Boston, MA

See headnote to letter of 8 December 1977.

Dear Penelope,

As always, Helen and I were delighted to hear from you, and the chrysanthemums are blooming gaily on our hearth rug. They almost make one reconciled to this hideous winter, which is about the coldest in living memory.

Things go along much as always here. A few days ago Pat Parker on the staff here came into my office and asked me if I would go over to Victoria College to meet a German scholar named Frau von Schriften from East Germany. When I got there I found Chaviva [Hošek], and Eleanor Cook, and Jay [Macpherson] and Julian Patrick giving me the horse laugh, because it was a committee meeting to consult me on a festschrift for me. That is one of the more cheerful things of advancing years. A less cheerful one was Marshall McLuhan's death on New Year's Eve: there were something like six groups of interviewers and photographers in my front parlour. I continue on a full time teaching session, recently extended for one more year.

Much love from us both and from Jane.

J. G. Patriquin   16 January 1981
Lennoxville, QC

In response to an appeal by Patriquin (7 January 1981) for details of Frye's early life in Lennoxville, Quebec, which might be used by the Historical Society in Lennoxville for a history of the town it hoped to publish. He had asked Chris Love, a former colleague at Bishop's College School and presently a colleague of Frye's at Victoria College, to forward the letter.

Dear Mr. Patriquin,

Thank you very much for your letter, which I received by way of Chris Love. I was born in Sherbrooke, and spent the first five years of my life there, but then two disasters happened at once: my father's hardware business failed and my brother was killed in the Battle of Amiens. So life was rather unsettled for the next three years, and most of those years I spent in Lennoxville.

We lived with my aunt, Mrs. Harriet Layhew, who had a farm not far from the St. Francis River, and we rented two houses. One was owned by a family named Reid, and was very close to the railway line; the other was occupied by Mrs. Burge. On a visit to Bishop's University some years ago, I failed to find the Reid house, though my sister, now deceased, had located it on an earlier trip. The Burge house, which was on the main street, had been replaced by a gas station. I also noticed that a grocery store bearing the name Craddock, or possibly Chaddock, was still in operation at the time. I also remember many rides on the streetcar line from Sherbrooke, the walk to Sherbrooke by way of Belvedere Street, and various names of people in the Lennoxville area. I don't know how much or what kind of reminiscence you want, but this gives the general idea of it.

Jack G. Oughton   19 January 1981
Saint John, NB

In reply to Oughton's letter of 4 January 1980. Oughton was a friend from the Fryes' student days. He lived around the corner from Helen Kemp at 882 Carlaw Street. An assistant in biology at the University of Toronto, 1933-34, he became an associate in zoology at the Royal Ontario Museum, later taught at the Ontario Agricultural College and at Guelph University, and worked for twenty years for the World Health Organization at the United Nations.

Dear Jack,

Helen and I were delighted to hear from you: it was clear that you were no longer at Guelph and we had wondered where you were. Some time in March I expect to be in St. John briefly to give a lecture, but the transportation arrangements are out of my hands and I would have to go directly on to Sackville.[617] But there should be time for a phone call, and I will try to get Helen to go with me. I haven't been in St. John since war time, when the Deichmanns and Jack Humphreys were there.

I am still on active service here, and have been made Chancellor of Victoria University, which fortunately is an honorary post. Helen's family is all gone now: Marian died in Rhodesia some years ago. She's had a rather hectic and unhappy life there with three marriages, and a son from her last marriage was killed in an accident before she died, when she was separated from her third husband. Roy died a year or two later in New York, and of course his wife Mary had gone some years before. But his two children are very much alive and apparently very successful in their careers.[618] Helen herself is very well.

We seldom visit the Danforth now, because, like you, we find it a bit depressing in some respects. Helen's mother sold the house on Fulton to Italians,[619] who seemed to be hard working and industrious, but certainly create a different kind of neighbourhood following.

Love and best wishes to you both from both of us.

Charles Hollander   30 January 1981
Baltimore, MD

In reply to Hollander's writing Frye (22 January 1981), at the suggestion of Richard Macksey of Johns Hopkins University, to ask his opinion of Thomas Pynchon.

Dear Mr. Hollander,

Thank you for your letter. My reaction to Pynchon is very mixed. I don't know the short stories and I never managed to finish *V.*, but I did read *Gravity's Rainbow* through, and was immensely impressed by it.[620] *The Crying of Lot 49* I have read twice, and think it an extraordinary example of what I think of as the "conspiracy novel." The sense of some kind of plot in the background, which never becomes clearly defined at any point but seems to be of overwhelming reality to the people involved in it, has never to my mind been more successfully sustained. I am rather confused by your reference to O. Henry: surely his mousetrap gimmicks couldn't be a "model" for any serious writer.[621]

With best wishes, and my very best also to Dick Macksey if you see him.

Jan Ulrik Dyrkjøb   4 February 1981
Birkerød, Denmark

In response to Dyrkjøb's having sent Frye a copy of his book, Northrop Fryes litteratur-teori *(Copenhagen: Berlingske Verlag, 1979).*

Dear Professor Dyrkjøb,

Thank you very much for sending me your book on my critical theory. I shall have to read it in bits and pieces, because my Danish is very far from fluent, but I shall be particularly interested to look at the final chapter on Utopias, as the Utopia has been an interest of mine from the beginning as a literary genre.

Richard Ellmann   16 February 1981
New College, Oxford, England

In response to Ellmann's letter of 25 January 1981 with news of his recent teaching and writing projects. Ellmann's letter was motivated by his coming across the description of Frye at Kenyon College in Maureen Howard's Facts of Life.[622]

Dear Dick:

Helen and I were delighted to get your letter. The main news with us is that I have reached retiring age, and that my junior administrative superiors go through the motions of deciding every year whether I shall be retiring or not. I have been made Chancellor of Victoria, which is largely an honorary post, as in British universities, but it does involve presiding at Convocations and Senate meetings.

I have just finished the first and introductory volume of what I think will be a two-volume work on the Bible, its narrative and imagery, and its influence on literature. That is, it is an attempt to disentangle the imaginative aspect of the Bible from the issues of faith, reason and scholarly knowledge. I have never had so much stage fright with a book before, and sometimes almost wish it could be a posthumous publication.

Both of us remember your parents with great pleasure[623] and of how fascinating it was to hear about the New York that they knew, with so much activity centered at the Cooper Union. I have seen relatively little of Indiana since then, but the Press publishes four or five of my books.

I am just considering an invitation to Japan for a couple of weeks this summer: I have been there before, and the impact of the various kinds of Japanese drama was an unforgettable experience. The Japanese are convinced that No plays bore the hell out of Westerners, and we only had an hour there, and I'd like to spend a longer time with it. Helen has also been talking about going to England, and though we have made no specific plans, it is perhaps time we did: we haven't been there for six years.[624] Perhaps if we do go I could get Maud to explain post-structuralism to me.[625]

I hope that your book on Wilde will be out before long.[626] I am sending a very small book of mine which will help explain about why I should very much like to see it.[627]

Love to Mary and yourself from both of us.

Fr. Walter J. Ong   2 March 1981
St. Louis University, St. Louis, MO

Fr. Ong gave the 1981 Alexander Lectures at the University of Toronto, published as Hopkins, the Self and God *(Toronto: University of Toronto Press, 1986).*

Dear Walter,

As Polyphemus would say, I rage, I burn; but like him it does me no good. The three days that you are giving the Alexander Lectures here, are exactly the three days that I have been committed, months ago, to give a series of lectures at Western Ontario on the problem comedies. I nevertheless hope to see you in passing.

Donna Gogan   **6 April 1981**
Amherst, Nova Scotia

On 13 March 1981 Frye lectured at Mt. Allison University in Sackville, NB, where he also visited an English class. Donna Grogan, a member of the class wrote to Frye (20 March 1981) to ask some questions about his reading. She also asked whether there was a transcript of his lecture.

Dear Donna Gogan,

Thank you very much for your letter. It is rather difficult to say how many books I read in a year, because I do a great deal of my reading along the lines of whatever I happen to be writing about. That means that I consult a good many books that I don't read through. It is not easy to say either how I find time to read at all, as the process gets increasingly furtive, like a squirrel burying nuts. I make no effort to try to keep up with literature on all fronts: the books that come up for my particular attention do so mainly because of their connexion with my teaching and lecturing.

I don't know if a transcript was made of my lecture: I'd a notion, as the lecture was being sponsored by a magazine, that the lecture would appear eventually in that.[628] But I may be entirely wrong.

Shirley Fairlinger   **14 July 1981**
Toronto, ON

In reply to Fairlinger's question about children's sermons.

Dear Mrs. Fairlinger:

Thank you for your letter, but I am afraid I have no quick answer to the problem. Preaching to adults is one highly specialized kind of activity, and teaching children is another. It is extremely rare that they are combined in the same person, and I should think that if children had proper teachers they would be rather better off than upstairs listening to a sermon for adults. What you say about ministers taking very little interest in children I have no answer to.

I shall discuss your problem with other people, as it is obviously a serious and central problem. I do not have the power to make the changes which you speak of, but I cannot agree more than I do with your sense of the necessity of getting younger people involved in all the church issues, including the theological ones, as soon as possible.

R.H. Martin   **14 July 1981**
Lindsay, ON

In reply to an inquiry about a book by Andrew James Bell (1856–1932), a long-time professor of Latin at Victoria College and of comparative philology at the University of Toronto. The book in question is apparently The Latin Dual and Poetic Diction: Studies in Numbers and Figures *(Oxford University Press, 1923).*

Dear Mr. Martin,

Thank you very much for your letter, which I was very interested to receive. I can assure you that there are at least two copies of Dr. Bell's book in the Victoria Library, because I have seen them there, but your anecdote makes it clear that classical scholars do not pay much attention to it. I never knew Dr. Bell myself, as he had retired just before I came to college. But of course the wash from his reputation was still splashing around.

B. Raymond Fink   16 September 1981
School of Medicine, University of Washington, Seattle, WA
In response to Fink's letter of 19 August 1981 requesting an offprint of Frye's article "The Bridge of Language." Fink, who had recently returned from Japan, wondered why Frye omitted Shinto from his list of major mythologies, and he asks where he might find Wallace Steven's "Description without Place," a poem Frye had referred to in his article.

Dear Professor Fink:

Thank you very much for your most friendly letter. There was no real reason for omitting Shinto, except that it has not had the publicity in this part of the world that, say, Zen Buddhism has had. And I have always admired the way that Shinto and Buddhism have managed to co-exist in Japanese culture: something no western religion was ever able to do.

Wallace Stevens' *Collected Poems* were published by Alfred A. Knopf in 1954, and the poem "Description Without Place" is in it.

I am sending the reprint as requested.

Harold Pagliaro   16 September 1981
Department of English Literature, Swarthmore College, Swarthmore, PA
In reply to Pagliaro's having sent Frye a copy of a recently published article, "Blake's 'Self-Annihilation': Aspects of Its Function in the Songs, with a Glance at Its History," English: The Journal of the English Association 30, no. 137 (July 1981): 117–46.

Dear Mr. Pagliaro,

Thank you very much for your offprint on Blake, which I have read with great interest. I think that Blake felt that one who had achieved the annihilation of the Selfhood would be a kind of epiphany, if not an actual incarnation, of the prophetic spirit. This, I take it, is not your main theme, which is rather that of the triumph over death, but it seems to me to account in part for Blake's willingness to remain relatively unknown in his time.

Barker and Nan Fairley   23 November 1981
Toronto, ON
A note of thanks for Fairley's sending Frye a copy of his book, Barker Fairley: Portraits (Toronto: Methuen, 1981). Fairley's portrait of Frye (p. 49) was painted in 1969.

Dear Barker and Nan,

Just a note to say how delighted Helen and I were with the book, which is extremely handsome, and is a real landmark on all counts. The notes by Barker[629] are very lucid and charming, and I have certainly never seen a book like it. Neither, I imagine, has anyone else.

If you get to a second edition, which I imagine there is no question of, I hope room will be possible for the portrait of Jay Macpherson that was bought by Carleton University. It also seems to me to be one of the very special ones.

Love to you both from us both.

Thomas M. Paikeday   **9 December 1981**
Mississauga, ON

In response to Paikeday's letter (22 November 1981), advising Frye that the troubles he has had with the computer manuscript of The Great Code, *which had been noted in the press, were the result of being connected to a large mainframe computer system.*

Dear Mr. Paikeday,

I am greatly obliged to you for your most friendly and helpful letter. I am very shortly going to be talking with the experts in this field, and will find your letter very useful. It was really a chapter of accidents that hit us, rather than simply computer breakdown or overload, but nevertheless your comment, that the key to the troubles is being hooked up to a large mainframe computer system, seems to me to be really the central factor involved. As there will be other books, I hope, published in the same way, there will be a good deal of exploration along the lines you suggest.

Michele Riel   **10 December 1981**
St. Martin's High School, Mississauga, ON

In reply to Reil's letter of 9 October 1981, asking if Frye could send a brief comment on his "perception of 'the Canadian identity' as expressed in our writing" for a permanent display in the library at her school.

Dear Michele,

Thank you for your letter. I think I may say that I feel that the Canadian identity as expressed in its literature is very much what it is in other aspects of Canadian life. The recent constitutional issue, for example, showed a good deal of regional disagreement, but eventually a common spirit emerged, which also, despite the barrier of language, includes a great deal more of Quebec than the P.Q. party imagines. It seems to me that Canadian literature is strongly regional, and rooted in the provinces, even in the smaller communities within the provinces, yet, in the aggregate, Canadian literature preserves a very strong feeling of a distinctive identity which has historically gone its own way, in a different direction from either Great Britain or the United States.

Nada Conić   **27 January 1982**
Massey College, University of Toronto

Conić, a graduate student in ancient Greek, had sent Frye a copy of her paper on Aristophanes, the seeds of which derived from Frye's course in the Mythology of Western Civilization, which she had taken as an undergraduate.

Dear Ms. Conić:

Thank you very much for the essay on Aristophanes which I have read with interest. One of the things that always fascinated me about *The Birds* was the way in which the hero is glorified in the regular ritual way at the end even though what he does would be regarded as nonsense by the audience. That seems to me a very important breakthrough in the structure of comedy.

Robert Sandler   **28 January 1982**
Toronto, ON

In reaction to a film about King Lear *that Sandler was working on with Frye.*

Dear Bob:

When you first broached the *King Lear* project to me, I was puzzled, but said I thought

I could trust your instinct in such matters. But I was very disturbed by your phone call on Sunday, and what Jane now tells me makes it clear that I have to say certain things that I was assuming you understood and had already allowed for.

There is only one thing in the world that really matters to me, and that is to get on with my major writing. That was what I was put into the world for; to allow anything to come between me and it would be betraying a whole set of values I hardly dare think about. My frantically crowded schedule makes it difficult to take on anything more, and the time I require for my work has to be unstructured time: that is, there must be peace and quietness of mind. Anything that is threat or obstacle to that peace of mind must be resisted, no matter what disguise it comes in and no matter what I may have said about it. I am now seventy: I have very little time left and very little of anything else, and I feel increasingly accountable for that time.

I am not an actor and never was, and never can be now at my age; I can never be a Lear physical type. Your remark that you were more interested in the process than the product I found reassuring: I don't mind making a fool of myself if there are other reasons for it. But such suggestions as growing a beard for a performance puts an emphasis on the product that to me is utterly terrifying, and would amount to altering my whole life-style. The way this is going is all wrong for me: it is not a creative variation on my own work but a major disturbance of it, and must be resisted by every means in my power. I have no alternative.

Wayne Booth   22 April 1982
Department of English, University of Chicago, Chicago, IL

In reply to Booth's apology (8 April 1982) for referring to Frye's Anatomy of Criticism *as* The Anatomy of Criticism *in the bibliography for* The Rhetoric of Fiction. *Booth says that the small error will be corrected in the reprinted edition.*

Dear Wayne,

Well, I don't suppose it did any harm to either book to have mine listed as "*The*" *Anatomy* for a brief time. Most people when speaking to me about it say "your Anatomy," which is much more disconcerting.

In the meantime, I am very pleased that "The" *Rhetoric of Fiction* continues to do so well.[630]

Hazel Merrett   22 April 1982
Senneville, QC

In reply to Merrett's letter of 8 April 1982, congratulating Frye on all the acclaim he was receiving in connection with the publication of The Great Code. *Merrett was Frye's first cousin. See headnote to letter of 21 August 1978.*

Dear Hazel,

Thank you very much for your letter. But surely, as we are old friends as well as cousins, it wouldn't be out of place for me to send you a copy of the book [*The Great Code*] myself.[631]

I don't know how much truth there is in the word "frail," as applied to me.[632] Some years ago I went to Guyana, after getting out of a ferociously concentrated schedule that they had planned for me, and explaining that I was getting to be an elderly and fragile object. When my host met me at the plane, he gave me a horse laugh, so clearly he didn't agree. But that, of course, was some time ago.

Alex Comfort   **29 April 1982**
Santa Barbara, CA

*In response to Comfort's writing (2 April 1982) to thank Frye for the insights he has pro-
vided into Blake's thought and art. Comfort's letter was accompanied by two of his books — I
and That and Tetrarch — and an article on David Bohm ("The Implications of an Implicate,"
Journal of Social Biological Structure 4 (1981): 363–74.*

Dear Dr. Comfort:

Thank you very much for your most friendly letter and for the books and the offprint.
I have read the tour through Blake country with great pleasure,[633] and have only just started
I and That.[634] I like its direct and condensed style very much.

Some time ago, a British Columbia writer, Crawford Kilian, sent me a novel called *The
Empire of Time*, which is about parallel worlds in different time dimensions, with such
names as Beulah and Vala and Orc (where the inhabitants read the New Orc Times).[635]
Also, of course, there are any number of allusions and references to Blake in the area so
vaguely called science fiction or fantasy. If I didn't know Blake I'd feel there was something
uncanny in his generating this kind of activity so long after his death. But nothing about
Blake surprises me any more.

Fr. Peter Du Brul, SJ   **10 June 1982**
Boston, MA

*In response to Du Brul's letter (12 May 1982), recommending three books he thinks Frye
might find useful for his second book on the Bible: Paul Beauchamp's L'Un et l'Autre Testament, René Girard's Les choses cachées depuis la fondation du monde, and Robert Caserio's
Plot, Story, and the Novel from Dickens and Poe to the Modern Period. Du Brul also records
his debts to Frye's Anatomy of Criticism and Fearful Symmetry.*

Dear Father Du Brul:

Thank you very much for your most friendly and thoughtful letter. I do know something about René Girard's work, but the Beauchamp one I have not read. There were so
many books that I was postponing reading until I got into my second volume and your
suggestions can save an immense amount of time for me by arranging priorities.

I have just got back from a three weeks visit to Israel, where the Six Days War and
the Exodus from Egypt both took place practically last Tuesday. So I know what you
mean about the intensity of the historical and political element in the Bible. Part of the
trouble is linguistic. Myth to me means *continuing* history, history not as a record of
the past but as a continuing process that involves the reader of it. But it is difficult to get
across this meaning of myth to most readers, and I don't know what other words I can
use.

With renewed thanks for the very well informed interest you have taken in my work.

Donald G. Ray, Peter G. White, and Albion Wright   **10 June 1982**
Office of the General Council, United Church of Canada, Toronto, ON

*In reply to three officials of the United Church of Canada who had written (3 May 1982)
to say they had just read The Great Code and that from their vantage point the United Church
"has a great sense of pride" in Frye's ministry.*

Dear Mr. Ray, Mr. White and Mr. Wright,

I was most pleased and gratified to get such a warm welcoming letter from my friends
in the General Council Office. I had rather hoped that it would be taken seriously as a con-

tribution to scholarship within the Church in which I serve, and I am more pleased than I can say to have your assurance that this is true.

Clara Thomas   10 June 1982
Toronto, ON

Dear Clara,

I have been reading your book on Deacon[636] with great pleasure and admiration. It was an extraordinary flash of insight that made you realize that Deacon would be the natural focus for a history of Canadian letters over a period of half a century, and he himself emerges as a figure of very genuine integrity. The only thing which still remains out of focus for me is his view of Pelham Edgar, which is so different from my experience of Pelham.

Once again, my warmest congratulations and best wishes to you both.

Rev. Peter D. Fraser   14 June 1982
United Church of Canada, Balcarres, SK

In reply to Fraser's request for advice about his idea of organizing his preaching around a one- or two-year study of the Bible, in lieu of readings from the lexionary. Fraser's plan, spurred by his reading of Frye's The Great Code, *would be to have his congregation read a book of the Bible every two weeks and to have his preaching center on the week's book.*

Dear Mr. Fraser:

Thank you very much for your letter. I certainly recognize the difficulty of making the kind of detailed reading of the Bible functional in the secularized calendar of today. The Anglican Prayer Book has its programme for getting through the Bible in a year, but needs conditions very different from those that face you. Granted some good will on the part of your congregation it seems to me that your experiment should have very good success. I sense in many students a very considerable increase of interest in the specific content of the Bible, and if that is true of students it should be even more true of the more committed church-going public. It is perhaps a matter of peripheral interest that the government of the Soviet Union, as I understand it, does not prohibit church services as such but does prohibit a continuous educational programme from being included in them, which would be negative evidence of the importance of what you were doing. In any case, my very best wishes and hopes for you.

Cyril Blackman   23 June 1982
Cambridge, England

In reply to Blackman's letter (28 April 1982), expressing admiration for Frye's The Great Code *but bafflement by the refusal of the book to deal with the content and meaning of the Bible. Blackman was a Congregational minister and biblical scholar who taught at Emmanuel College in the 1960s.*

Dear Cyril:

Thank you very much for your most careful and thoughtful letter about my book. I was particularly pleased to have it because I have profited a good deal from your book on hermeneutics.[637] It is true that my book rather neglects the content and meaning of the Bible, but, as I attempted to explain in the introduction, I felt that there were such immense quantities of material on that aspect of the Bible, and so little about its imaginative unity, its value to poets, and its significance as a literary influence, that it might be worth confining at least one book to that area. It is also true that the conclusion is tentative, even an anticlimax. This is connected in my own mind with the feeling that took possession of me while writing it that it was only an introduction to a much larger and more complex theme, some of which I might be able to deal with myself.

May I say again how very pleased I was to have your letter. The very best to you both from both of us.

Francesca Valente   23 June 1982

Via Facchinetti 18, Vicenza, Italy

In reply to Valente's request (3 June 1982) for a letter of recommendation in support of her application for graduate study in Italian literature at the University of California, Berkeley. Valente, who previously worked for the Italian consulate in Toronto, had orchestrated Frye's Italian trip in 1979.

Dear Francesca,

It seems to me very reasonable that you should want to do more work specifically on Italian culture, especially if you were not planning to return to Canada for a while. I should be very pleased to write to Professor Perella[638] on your behalf. But how are you? How are Carla[639] and her husband and her wonderful family? How is your mother? And how is Branko?[640] As you were writing from Vicenza please give our love to your mother and Carla's family at least.

We are still dizzy from having had three weeks in Israel,[641] although luckily the Lebanon War did not break out until after we had returned. It was a strenuous but very exhilarating time, as Israel is not remotely like any other place in the world that I know of.

All our love from Helen, Jane and myself.

Mrs. Samuel D. Scott   29 June 1982

Russell, KY

In response to Scott's inquiry (18 June 1982) about the meaning of the word "sexual" in Frye's account of the creation myths in The Great Code.

Dear Mrs. Scott,

Thank you very much for your letter. By the word "sexual" as applied to creation I meant only the creation myths which explain creation as having taken place in the same way that sexual reproduction does now. The artificial creation myth is not necessarily asexual, but it does represent a reaction to cyclical mythologies centred on the earth mother, and although there are people who speak of creation as being "begotten" by the Father rather than simply made by him, that has always been a minority view. I am surprised to hear that I believe that sexual intercourse began only after the fall: I have no beliefs in such matters, but would tend to sympathize with Milton when he takes the opposite view. The only interpretations of the type you mention[642] which I have considered in detail are those of Milton and of Blake, both of whom are extremely anti–Thomist.

James J. O'Donnell   27 July 1982

University of Pennsylvania, Philadelphia, PA

In reply to O'Donnell's query (9 July 1982) about why The Great Code *was so noncommittal a book and why it avoided specialist background commentary. O'Donnell enclosed some pages from a work in progress.*

Dear Professor O'Donnell,

Thank you for your letter. I have tried to explain in the Introduction why the book was as it was. I felt that it had to be non-committal, because it was addressing an uncommitted audience and trying to get them to take an interest in a subject about which, as I know from experience, many people are profoundly suspicious.

I was also trying to say that because the book was concerned with the imaginative and literary impact of the Bible, I not only was unable to draw on specialists in medieval typology, but had deliberately to keep away from any scholarly discipline that would throw my own book out of proportion. If any reader of my book should become more interested in what the specialists on the subject have to say, I should be delighted, and in fact I think there might be a chance of that.

Thank you for the Propositions, which I found consistently stimulating. I have very little difficulty with most of them, and feel particularly attracted to the ones on page 5.

Iris Selma Rozencwajg   27 July 1982
Rumson, NJ

Rozencwajg had written Frye on 22 June, praising The Great Code, *wishing she could find a copy of* Creation and Recreation, *and asking, "Mr. Buckminster Fuller? What kind of snooty remark is that?"*

Dear Mrs. Rozencwajg,

Thank you very much for your letter. As a matter of fact I seem to be totally out of copies of *Creation and Recreation* myself: the University of Toronto Press didn't seem to be very interested in that book.

I acquired the notion, back in my undergraduate days, that personal references to somebody still alive should be prefaced by "Mr.," or whatever was proper. There was no intention of being snooty, but I have never met him personally, so I cannot call him Bucky as Hugh Kenner does.

I greatly appreciated your friendly letter.

Daniel Cappon   3 August 1982
Physician in Psychological Medicine, Willowdale, Ontario

In connection with a book he was writing on religion, Cappon inquired of Frye (21 July 1982) whether or not the phases of language outlined in The Great Code *constituted "a retrospective or rearview mirror typology."*

Dear Dr. Cappon:

Thank you for your letter. To come at once to your direct question, whether the phases of language described in my book are a "rear view mirror" "typology," the answer to that is certainly yes. For a person living in the twentieth century A.D. nothing else is possible, and I do say, I think, that Homer's metaphors were not necessarily metaphors to him. It seems to me that the central point of what you are concerned with is the separation of experience into subject and object, so that you get some experiences that are "inside" and others that are "outside." For the last 2500 years at least we have been ascribing the centre of gravity in reality to the outside vision, and feeling that language that means anything has to point to the objective world. The revelatory visions at the origin of so much religion have to be, therefore, associated with the "inside" and so are regarded as only partly reachable by language. If somebody had an encounter with a god face to face, and if this experience was just as real to him as eating his dinner, it is clearly no good trying to tell *him* that his experience was only the poetic or metaphorical formulation that we can salvage from it. To understand the reality of his language would take us, insensibly but inexorably, into understanding the validity of his experience. His experience may have been pathological from our point of view, but it is just as possible that ours is from any point of view.

I am simply saying this for what it may be worth to you: I don't know if it meets your central concerns or not.

Michael Fischer   3 August 1982
Department of English, University of New Mexico, Albuquerque, New Mexico

Dear Professor Fischer,

Thank you very much for your offprint on Marxism and Romanticism,[643] which I have read with interest. I think it is true that the same social dissatisfactions that are behind Romanticism are also behind Marxism, and that one can see the connexion in Georg Lukacs. But there is not, of course, an effort on the part of contemporary Marxists to get beyond the simple-minded "social realism" of the thirties and to try to come abreast of the post-structuralists.

Jack Risk   3 August 1982
Parish of the Good Shepherd, Avonlea, SK

In response to Risk's letter of 5 March 1982 in which he raises questions about two words in Frye's lecture at Luther College, University of Regina on 4 March 1982 ("The Reformation in Mythology: The Christian Tradition and the Romantic Movement")— "historicism" and "structuralism." Risk thinks that the worldviews implied by both argue against the kind of continuity presupposed by Frye's lecture.

Dear Reverend Risk,

Thank you very much for your letter. Your questions are certainly of very direct relevance to what I was saying. First, it seems to me that there is both continuity and discontinuity in our view of history. I came to this from my study of literature, and my realization that Shakespeare, for instance, wrote plays understood by his own time which are nevertheless understood today for reasons that the original audience, perhaps including Shakespeare himself, would find unintelligible. What happens is a dissolving and reforming process in which certain structural outlines remain permanent. The same thing is true of discontinuity in space: I recently read a Japanese novel about a geisha girl which was totally remote from all my cultural assumptions, yet made complete sense as a human document. I think the same principle would apply to the structuralist view of language: there are both diachronic and synchronic approaches to language possible. If we exaggerate historicism, works of the past lose all other relevance to us; if we exaggerate continuity we kidnap everything in a past into our own cultural orbit.

R.H. Martin   16 August 1982
Lindsay, ON

In reply to Martin's letter of 15 July 1982, which included six anecdotes from his student days about Victoria College professors. Martin had graduated in classics from Victoria College in 1931.

Dear Mr. Martin,

Thank you very much for your letter: such reminiscences as yours get increasingly precious with the advance of time. The story about the car parked in the middle of the street is very commonly attributed to Ned,[644] because he had a reputation for both absentmindedness and difficulty with cars. I am glad to have it correctly attributed.

I still see Rhena Kendrick occasionally, and the next time I see her I shall convey your appreciation for her lectures.[645]

Incidentally, you will find the suggestion in *The Great Code* that the Bible might have been simpler if it had started with Exodus instead.[646]

Anne Innis Dagg   12 October 1982
Department of Physics, University of Queensland, Brisbane, Queensland, Australia

In reply to Dagg's letter of 19 September 1986 complaining that Frye's use of masculine pronouns excluded women from the university community. Dagg was the daughter of Harold Innis, pioneering Canadian communications theorist.

Dear Ms. Dagg,

Thank you very much for your letter: it was very pleasant to hear from you. I should not have thought that anyone would take "men producing flood myths" as meaning to exclude women, any more than the phrase "lions are found in Africa" would be taken to exclude lionesses. It is unfortunate that English does not have the German distinction between man and Mann.[647]

I am still occupied with advising the CRTC on its project of editing and publishing your father's uncompleted manuscript on the history of communications. There are many difficulties in the way, as you can imagine, but I think we shall eventually carry it through.[648]

With renewed thanks and best wishes.

Nancy Villarroel   2 November 1982
Bear River, Nova Scotia

In reply to Villarroel's letter of 30 September 1982 to her "Aunt Helen and Uncle Norrie," who were actually her godparents. Her mother, Edna Robinson (later, Edna Fulford), had rented the attic of the Fryes' Clifton Road home in the early 1940s.

Dear Nancy,

Thank you very much for your letter: you did tell us that you had gone to Nova Scotia, but I am delighted to know that you are settling in. We keep well: Helen's immediate family has all gone now, but her niece Susan,[649] married to an Englishman working for the United Nations, has just produced a daughter. As for me, I produce lectures. Not nearly so interesting a production line.

Love to you both from both of us as always. We were very sorry to see that George had gone too, though that happened when we were away and it took some time to learn about it.

Michael Steven Marx   11 November 1982
Department of English, University of Michigan, Ann Arbor, MI

In response to Marx's letter of 31 October 1982, which asked Frye how to resolve the paradox the comes from the Bible's having both literary and religious qualities: if its literary qualities are foregrounded, does it not lose its power as a religious text? Marx also wonder whether Frye's remark in The Great Code *about parallelism not adding anything to the sense of the passage where it is used might not lead to misunderstanding.*

Dear Mr. Marx,

Thank you very much for your letter. To come directly to your two questions, the paradox you speak of is, for me, the paradox of treating the Bible as not a work of literature when it is so full of literary characteristics. I rejected the "Bible as literature" approach because it meant destroying the form in which the Bible presents itself. But no literary critic can deny the literary qualities, even if they do not categorize the Bible as literature. I agree in general with C.S. Lewis' comment, but those who do not see the literary qualities of the Bible do not read it either.[650]

To say that the second half of a parallelism couplet often adds nothing to the sense is not to say that it has no function. In the same chapter I make the point that sometimes, as in music and oral literature, we demand that a rhythmical period be filled out regardless of the repetition. Consequently I am saying, or at least am trying to say, what Kugel says.[651]

I much appreciate your interest.

Herbert Lindenberger   25 November 1982
Department of English, Stanford University, Stanford, CA

Dear Herbert,

Thanks very much for your offprint.[652] I don't have the context very clear in my mind, so I find the section on "Puzzles" most rewarding.

I understand you have been very generous in replying to my biographer, John Ayre. It is very good of you, and you will understand that I feel a trifle uneasy about the whole operation.

The very best from us both.

Terence Moore   25 November 1982
Cambridge University Press, Cambridge, England

In reply to Moore's seeking Frye's judgement about a proposed seven-volume history of literary criticism.

Dear Mr. Moore:

I am sorry not to have replied to your June letter about the *Cambridge History of Literary Criticism*. It seems to me that your outline is on the whole a very good one, though I suspect that the last seven volumes, the ones starting with Saussure, would probably reduce in practice to three, or four at the most. It seems to me it would be better to try to illustrate the unifying tendencies in twentieth century criticism rather than the dissonant chorus that seven volumes would suggest. It is even possible that the Neo-classic and Enlightenment periods would fold up into one volume, and other compressions could be made which would be more the spirit of Wellek's broad and comprehensive approach. I would hope too that the volume on higher criticism would not start with nineteenth-century Biblical criticism, but with the earlier mythological commentaries (e.g. Henry Reynolds in the English tradition). Other than that, I have no suggestions, as I am somewhat out of touch with the market.[653]

Wayne R. Rood   26 November 1982
Berea College, Berea, KY

In reply to Rood's indicating (15 November 1982) that he planned to use Frye's framework of the seven phases of revelation from The Great Code *in a course he would be teaching at the Pacific School of Religion, adding that he might insert an eighth phase between Frye's "Law" and "Wisdom."*

Dear Professor Rood,

Thank you very much for your letter, which I was extremely pleased to receive. My book is intended to be helpful, but nothing in it is a patented invention, and if you find that the sequence of phases works better with the conception of kingdom inserted, please insert it. I can see many advantages in such a conception myself. I suppose I was unconsciously influenced by the prestige of the number seven in the Apocalypse, but consciously the number seven is pure accident.

Novica Milić   18 January 1983
Belgrade, Yugoslavia
Milić, a professor of literary theory at the University of Belgrade, had sent Frye a copy of his book, Antinomije kritike *(Novi Sad: Matica srpska, 1982). Earlier he had written an essay on Frye, "Antinomije kritike,"* Književnost *71 (March 1981): 565–77.*

Dear Mr. Milić,

Thank you very much for your letter and for the copy of your book. I am sorry that my reading knowledge of Serbo-Croatian is not sufficient to enable me to decipher it, but I can get the general sense of the orbit you revolve in. I should be very glad to see you in Toronto if it can be managed practically. In any case, I am very grateful to you for your interest in my work.

Robert D. Tarleck   20 January 1983
Faculty of Education, University of Lethbridge, Lethbridge, AB
In reply to Tarleck's suggestion (10 January 1983) that the reading process, according to psycholinguistic research, is more complicated than Frye's model of sequential reading implies.

Dear Professor Tarleck,

Thank you very much for your letter. My remarks about the sequential nature of reading were intended to make the point that sequential reading is the first and preliminary stage of the reading process, but only that. Once the sequential operation is completed, the whole verbal structure turns into a simultaneous pattern, and everything that goes on afterwards is a filling in of that pattern. This is naturally oversimplified, because some readers start sooner than others to build up this simultaneous apprehension. But I would never say that reading is a sequential process, only that it begins with one.

Frederick G. Brack   27 January 1983
North Massapequa, NY
In reply to Brack's five-word inquiry, dated "12/82": "What is God's last name?"

Dear Mr. Brack:

You may recall that when Tom Sawyer explains to Huckleberry Finn that kings had only a given name, Huck Finn said that he wouldn't want to have only a given name, like a nigger. God has no surname because he is (a) royal and (b) has more in common with "niggers," that is, the dispossessed and wretched of the earth. If he had a surname he would be a gentleman, and as *King Lear* says, the Prince of Darkness is that.

Trusting that this clears up the matter for you.

Zeph Stewart   10 February 1983
Department of Classics, Harvard University, Cambridge, MA
In reply to Stewart's follow-up on a visiting committee meeting at Princeton, 17–19 December 1982, to evaluate the School of Historical Studies, a wing of the Institute for Advanced Study. The committee had a second meeting in Boston, 18–20 March 1983.

Dear Zeph,

I am sorry that a mass of deadlines, a teaching routine, and a low grade 'flu made it impossible to report my impressions to you earlier. I think that I shall be most useful at a second meeting, as I discover that I have taken a great many notes and that they don't add up to a great deal. My general feeling is that the scheme set out by Elliott is the one to aim at. And with regard to Homer Thompson's letter, I can certainly understand his concern, and it is true that once one's place has become famous for a certain line of scholarship, others expect it to continue to be so. On the other hand, if first rate work has been done over a period of time at one place, it can be carried on elsewhere. I have a colleague here in Victoria, for example, a man named Traill,[654] who is continuing along the lines that Homer and others laid down. I feel that the effort of the Institute, in looking for new appointments, should be to try to see where the cutting edge of scholarship is likely to be. It is possible, for example, that work on Athens is no longer pioneering work, and that the pioneering centre of archaeology may have moved to the Near East, or Rome, or even the New World.

I feel the same way about, for example, an appointment in literature. I entirely agree, or at least sympathize, with Setton (I think it was) when he said he didn't feel much interested in somebody who had just written the thousandth book on Dante. But there is a cutting edge in humanities scholarship: I mentioned Curtius and Auerbach from a previous generation, and there is Frances Yates among those still alive. Naturally it requires pretty comprehensive knowledge to know where the pioneer fields are, but that's what they get their big salaries for.

There seemed to be general agreement that strong emphasis on seminars and symposia are a waste of time and diversion of energy. The Institute seems to be partly a place for post-doctoral supervision and partly a think tank for senior scholars. I doubt very much that any recommendations of ours will alter the presumptive system of appointing members, but there have to be precautions, of the kind Harry Woolf[655] mentioned, to prevent the school from disintegrating into discrete groups.

In spite of the prestige of Einstein,[656] there seems to be no place for the off-beat genius in such a place, except as a special appointment by the Director, of the kind Oppenheimer[657] was so good at.

I am afraid that my other reflections are pretty woolly to me at the moment, and I shall leave my colleagues on the Committee to clarify them.

Looking forward to seeing you again.

John I. Ades   **19 April 1983**
Department of English, Southern Illinois University, Edwardsville, IL

In response to Ades's letter (4 April 1983), recording his praise for The Great Code *and recalling that he and Frye had met in 1957 in Cincinnati. He recalls as well that Frye had accepted his paper on Charles Lamb for a 1958 MLA session chaired by Frye, and he describes a course on the Bible he teaches at Southern Illinois University, instituted after his proposal to establish a department of religious studies had been rejected.*

Dear Mr. Ades:

Thank you very much for your letter: it was most pleasant to hear from you again. I remember the Cincinnati visit — one of the cruder efforts on my part to get some shape into my notions about the Bible — I also remember the MLA meeting and your Lamb paper.

I was most interested to hear about your course on the Bible, and am very glad you got so far in spite of the Philistines. I was on a committee considering the setting up of a

Department of Religion here many years ago, and I said that to refuse to teach religion for fear of indoctrination was like refusing to teach political science for fear of influencing a student's vote. In any case we now have a religion department.

Michael Dolzani   3 May 1983

In response to Dolzani's contribution to Frye's Festschrift, *"The Infernal Method: Northrop Frye and Contemporary Criticism," in* Centre and Labyrinth, *59–68. Dolzani was Frye's research assistant.*

Dear Michael:

This is just to thank you, full orchestra and fortissimo, for your contribution to my *Festschrift*. Aside from anything else, it was a great boost to my morale — because in spite of all the nice things that have happened to me recently I still have fits of depression about some of the reactions to me, especially in connection with the *Great Code* book. You are quite right, and very lucid, about the priority of satire in my interests: the reason for my interest in romance is mainly the way that it preserves what I call its "proletarian" quality, of escaping every time it gets taken over by some class ideology and forming another context somewhere. Usually I just go blank whenever I read about myself, but you not only have so very clear a style but emphasize the things that make sense to me, such as the fact that the "system" in the *Anatomy* is there for the Blakean purpose of delivering people from systems.* I'm immensely grateful as well as honoured.

*You see the connection, for instance, between my declared affection for the anatomy form in the *Great Code* and the slight undercurrent of satire in it on what passes for historical Biblical scholarship in the academic fortresses.

Patricia Parker   3 May 1983

In response to Parker's contribution to Frye's Festschrift, *"Anagogic Metaphor: Breaking Down the Wall of Partition," in* Centre and Labyrinth, *38–58. Parker was Frye's colleague at Victoria College.*

Dear Pat:

This is to thank you, first, for your work in editing my birthday book, and, second, for contributing your essay to it. You spread a kind of echo net over those plays[658] (my memories of *Wuthering Heights* are vaguer) that starts one's mind fizzing like an alka-seltzer (you don't need to examine the metaphorical constructs of that one). I remember discussing one of the O.T. prototypes of the walls-falling-down with you, the Jericho story, and I suppose Samson's carrying off the gates of Gaza is a distant reverberation in the Herbert poem you quote. Your defence of the Folio "morall downe" reading in *A Midsummer Night's Dream* is brilliant, and of course the Quartos have "moon used," which may be nonsense but recalls the Jericho-moon associations, to say nothing of the moon-partition rhetoric of the lay itself — Helena speaks of the moon breaking through to the antipodes, and of course it spaces out the whole time sequence of the play. However, you've thought of all these things yourself: this is only to say what a fascinating piece of reading it was for me, and how honoured I am to have this kind of relationship to it.

On the general principle that it's always the most obvious insights that come last, it wasn't until I read you on anagogic metaphor that I really grasped what Donne meant by "We die and rise the same."

(He meant exactly that, of course: that was what was so difficult.)

Julian Patrick 3 May 1983

In response to Patrick's contribution to Frye's Festschrift, *"The Tempest* as Supplement," *in* Centre and Labyrinth, *160–80. Patrick was Frye's colleague at Victoria College.*

Dear Julian:

This is just to thank you, first, for your part in getting that magnificent *Festschrift* together, and, second, for your contribution to it. I don't know what I was expecting, but one of the things I should hardly have suspected would be the appearance of an article on *The Tempest*, of all things, that would start me rethinking that play again. You have certainly made an admirable use of Derrida's conception of the supplement (one of the things this *Festschrift* is doing for me is showing me some of the practical applications of contemporary theorists I've read without too much understanding), and it's fascinating to find the phrase *esse in futuro* attached to the word symbol by Peirce, whatever the context there. I am very grateful and honoured to have your essay.

I don't itemize all the things I liked, such as the "beating" repetition, because you've thought of them all yourself. (At least I don't know of any theory of criticism that would deny that inference.)

Harold Bloom 4 May 1983

In response to Bloom's contribution to Frye's Festschrift, *"Reading Freud: Transference, Taboo, and Truth," in* Centre and Labyrinth, *309–28. Bloom taught literature at Yale University. His theory of poetic influence was well known by this time.*

Dear Harold:

This note is primarily to thank you for contributing your splendid essay on Freud's conception of transference to my *Festschrift*. It made me think of a great number of things which perhaps have only a peripheral interest for you: the grotesque resemblance of Freud's "rather desperate myth," as I once called it, of killing the primal father to Vico's parable of giants terrified by the voice of the father in the thunderclap and dragging their women off to caves, thus starting private property. The way in which, in the Book of Revelation at the end of the New Testament, the Messiah figure is so violently called the "Lamb," as though the paternal wrath exemplified by the Last Judgment were being deflected by a symbolic totemic figure, who defines the body of his own society. The way in which the effectiveness of Karl Kraus's remark depends on the introduction of the word "cure." Surely all cures are homeopathic in the sense that they are themselves the disease: religion becomes the disease whenever it professes to "cure" anything or anybody, that is, negate or annihilate the condition it tackles. You seem to be moving toward a conception of the transference as the crisis in Freud's conception of Eros, and clearly there's a lot more to come. In the meantime, I can only express my gratitude and say what an honour it is to have your essay in a book presented to me.

Angus Fletcher 5 March 1983

In response to Fletcher's contribution to Frye's Festschrift, *"The Image of Lost Direction," in* Centre and Labyrinth, *160–80. Fletcher taught literature at the Graduate Center, City University of New York.*

Dear Angus:

This letter is to thank your, first, for your telegram, and second, for that marvellous essay, which not only provided my *Festschrift* with a title but ended it with exactly the right paradox: the image of lost direction showing the way to any number of new explorations.

I first got fascinated by labyrinths because of a book of essays on Biblical symbolism called *The Labyrinth* and edited by S.H. Hooke, who used to be at Victoria here. The title essay wasn't all that good, but its illustrations did provide me with some dim notion of your distinction between what you call the *intrico* and the one where you can't get lost. Then I realized, after staring at a map in the back of a Bible depicting the Israelites through the wilderness, that I was looking at another labyrinth, one where you do get lost, and linked with the guts of leviathan as well as a demonic one, the "mystical dance" of the stars and the angels that Raphael tells Adam about—Daedalus is a choreographer in Jonson's *Pleasure Reconciled to Virtue*. There are all kinds of wonderful things in your essay, including parenthetical remarks (Borges is more cheerful than Kafka because he's more elegiac), and your suggestion that the real way out is not through remembrance but through creative repetition in a new dimension, as in that little book of Kierkegaard's that's always fascinated me so much. I am profoundly grateful and honoured to have both your essay and the friendship it embodies.

Eli Mandel   4 May 1983

In response to Mandel's contribution to Frye's Festschrift, *"Northrop Frye and the Canadian Literary Tradition," in* Centre and Labyrinth, *284–98. Mandel taught literature at York University.*

Dear Eli:

This is primarily to thank you for your invaluable contribution to my birthday book. As you can see, there is no other essay on a Canadian topic. It helps me a great deal to have so sympathetic a discussion of what I, as well as you, can see to be an uneasy and tentative area of formulation, raising puzzling or paradoxical questions that contain tensions, and so could be quite fairly called inconsistencies as well. That is, as you indicate, very largely because the Canadian scene itself has changed so much, and even more because, as a critic who thinks metaphorically, I'm really a semi-participant in the process I discuss, as I'm not in the *Anatomy* area (for the most part). What I find most helpful of all, I think, is your demonstration that my very temporary regional-place identification is far too crude and won't do, which points to an exciting process of discovering, if I can, how this operation gets sublimated and transformed into language and states of mind. It's quite probable too that I should think more carefully about the myth-theme business—I've tended to think of "theme" as potential *mythos*, the kind of thing you find in poets who talk about what they feel instead of presenting it, and that gets shaped into myth by poets whose work has become articulate in form. However, this is speculation: what I really want to say is that I'm immensely grateful and honoured to have your essay in my book.

James Reaney   4 May 1983

In response to Reaney's contribution to Frye's Festschrift, *"Some Critics Are Music Teachers," in* Centre and Labyrinth, *298–308. Reaney taught literature at the University of Western Ontario.*

Dear Jamie:

This letter is primarily to thank you for that astonishingly lively and original contribution to my birthday book. The book as a whole is pretty impressive, and rather overwhelming as a gift to me, but there is nothing else in the category of your essay, which certainly ought to be a landmark in the history of dramatic production, in Canada at least.

I'm immensely hounoured and grateful. Incidentally, the issue devoted to you in the *Essays on Canadian Writing* is pretty damn impressive too.[659]

The very best to Colleen and yourself from us both, as always.

David Staines   4 May 1983

In response to Staines's contribution to Frye's Festschrift, *"The Holistic Vision of Hugh of St. Victor," in* Centre and Labyrinth, *147–61. Staines taught literature at the University of Ottawa.*

Dear David:

This letter is primarily to thank you for your contribution to my *Festschrift*. Your choice of Hugh of St. Victor was an inspired one, and, as you can see, no other contributor mentions that kind of influence on me. It was after I'd finished an essay on St. Augustine in Emmanuel I realized that what I'd started out by calling a philosophy of history was actually a structure of typology in *The City of God*. I had also realized the typological bent of Luther, and was looking for intermediate links: the Aristotelians, including St. Thomas, weren't of much help, and one couldn't hang a tradition that central on so peripheral a figure as Joachim of Floris. Somebody — quite possibly somebody in the Pontifical Institute — mentioned the Victorines. Knox library had Migne,[660] and my Latin was a lot better in those days, but as I remember there was just about no secondary material available in any language. But the dialectic emerging between the Gospel narrative and the liturgical year fascinated me, and I'm a long way from exploring it even yet in any real depth. In the meantime, I'm delighted and very greatly honoured to have your essay in my birthday book.

Jane and Deryck [Widdicombe] seem to have had a wonderful time visiting you, and I hope the terrific pressure of work on you has let up a little. Two-year leave my foot. Our love from us all here, and my gratitude again for your essay.

Thomas Willard   4 May 1983

In response to Willard's contribution to Frye's Festschrift, *"Alchemy and the Bible," in* Centre and Labyrinth, *115–27. Willard, a former student of Frye's, taught literature at the University of Arizona.*

Dear Tom:

Just a note to thank you with the greatest gratitude for contributing your fine essay on alchemy and Biblical symbolism to my birthday book. You write on some frantically complicated, often muddled, subjects with the greatest lucidity and objectivity, and once you get a larger survey on the market you'll have a real winner on your hands. Not many people would have much notion of the amount of work that made your simple sentences possible, but there are a lot of people who want to know something about what alchemy was really about without being bullied or teased in the process. It is a great honour to have your essay in a book presented to me, as a relatively early specimen of what will be a lot of very distinguished writing.

James Nohrnberg   5 May 1983

In response to Nohrnberg's contribution to Frye's Festschrift, *"Paradise Regained by One Greater Man: Milton's Wisdom Epic as a 'Fable of Identity,'" in* Centre and Labyrinth, *83–114. Nohrnberg, a former Ph.D. student of Frye's, taught literature at the University of Virginia.*

Dear Jim:

This letter is primarily to thank you for contributing your splendid essay on *Paradise*

Regained to my birthday book. I read it with the mounting excitement that one reads any dazzling tour de force: interpretation of the poem fitted beautifully into a psychological framework, including the main outline of Milton's own life. (You didn't get it all from Kerrigan, either, as I remember being so impressed with your use of similar material as early as your Spenser thesis.) Then there were the bits of Biblical typology, the fine Shakespeare parallels to Hamlet and Lear, and, of course, the Oedipus parallel. I'd realized, as you know, that the reference to Oedipus in the poem was pretty important, and in my last Bible book I suggested an Oedipus-Christ parallel much closer to yours than to Yeats', but the detail you give, plus the reference to the Telegonia, was in another dimension altogether. I'm enormously honoured and pleased to have this kind of relationship to the essay.

I should also pay tribute to your style, which has a crystallizing and epigrammatic quality that would be distracting if it ever called attention to itself, but, because it doesn't, consistently illuminates its context.

James Carscallen   9 May 1983

In response to Carscallen's contribution to Frye's Festschrift, *"Three Jokers: The Shape of Alice Munro's Stories," in* Centre and Labyrinth, *128–46. Carscallen was Frye's colleague at Victoria College.*

Dear Jim:

This is just to say how grateful and honoured I am to have your Alice Munro essay in my birthday book, as Jamie [Reaney] calls it. It takes a good deal of courage to write in this structural and archetypal way about a writer whose superficial texture is "realistic," or seems so, because there are so many aw-nuts trigger responses that make a point of ignoring the significance of titles like "Baptizing." I hope you will go on to expand your analysis, especially in regard to *Lives of Girls and Women*: if you do, I imagine that all kinds of other patterns will take shape around the central ones. I was reminded of Lacan's *stade du miroir*, for instance, in your discussion of body-identities and ego-identities. And, or course, what you glance at in passing: the curious sense of a growing power of language, as a child or young girl gradually finds out what words mean and the sense of stability that comes from knowing a name. In other words the word and the flesh interact as they grow up together. Your footnote I found very moving, as in fact I do the entire book.

Jennifer Levine   9 May 1983

In response to Levine's contribution to Frye's Festschrift, *"Reading* Ulysses," *in* Centre and Labyrinth, *264–83. Levine was Frye's colleague at Victoria College.*

Dear Jennifer:

This is just to thank you sincerely for contributing your fine essay on *Ulysses* to my birthday book. The links with Barthes and Merleau-Ponty are very illuminating, and so is your discussion of multivalent ironies. I always thought that Joyce took Stuart Gilbert for a bit of a ride (not impossibly himself too) over that chapter of parodies. The Oxen of the Sun episode in the *Odyssey* is a crucial and central disaster, not the birth or rebirth of anything. And if an embryo goes on developing and complicating until it reaches a climactic moment of birth, the history of language is clearly a miscarriage: it starts in bumble and goes through a set of mutations and finally disintegrates into a cluster of American colloquialisms that sound as though they'd come out of an old copy of *Punch*. History is a nightmare from which one awakes, the history of language and literature included. I never realized this ironic maladjustment in the chapter until I read your essay, which I am most honoured and grateful to have in "my" collection.

David Shaw   **5 June 1983**
In response to Shaw's contribution to Frye's Festschrift, *"Poetic Truth in a Scientific Age: The Victorian Perspective," in* Centre and Labyrinth, *245–63. Shaw was Frye's colleague at Victoria College.*

Dear David:

This is just to thank you with the greatest gratitude and appreciation for your contribution to my birthday book. The Victorian period is so full of unexpectedly good things: it makes one very impatient to see how people who would think anything said in Mill or Tyndall was old hat regard the same statements as profound and with-it when they find them in Mallarmé or Wittgenstein. It's fascinating too to see Bradley considered in his own proper Victorian context, instead of being attached to Eliot as he so often is. What used to be called the history of ideas approach isn't that any more: it's given place to realization that every age has a broad and rough but genuine consistency of outlook, manifest equally in poetry, science and philosophy. I like very much the comments on Tennyson, and you do a great deal to make clear why he wrote that tin-horn conclusion to "De Profundis," which begins by echoing the line about Arthur coming from and going to the great deep, and clearly should have ended, if it was going to end in a human cry, with ow-oo rather than hooray. I hadn't realized how anti–Hegelian the intellectual atmosphere of Victorian England was, and it explains why the same attitude washed over Canada: as an undergraduate taking philosophy lectures from Brett I was still being taught that Kant was the coping-stone of philosophy and Hegel was an expendable Prussian chauvinist. I am very honoured to have this sort of connection with your essay.

Helen Vendler   **5 June 1983**
In response to Vendler's contribution to Frye's Festschrift, *"The Golden Theme: Keats's Ode* To Autumn,*" in* Centre and Labyrinth, *181–96. Vendler taught literature at Boston and Harvard Universities.*

Dear Helen:

I wanted to thank you, first, for your delightful postcard. The reception of the *Festschrift* itself was a bit overwhelming: I'm something of a veteran of such books, having contributed to a good many, but I've never seen anything like a volume of this scale and scope before. I also wanted to thank you for the fine and eloquent essay on Keats's *Autumn* that you contributed to it. You make me see how the presence of the autumn-goddess depends on the absence of a sun *presence*, as distinct from the sun itself, and how the poem, like the Grecian urn ode in so different a way, describes a moment of time that suggests something on the other side of time, along with the possibility of collapsing back into the time cycle (by bursting and spoiling). It is secularized, as you say, but there are a few faint traces of the older wind-in-the-garden Biblical *ver perpetuum*, especially the gnats rising and falling "as the light wind lives or dies." This is the kind of insight that keeps one reading and rereading poetry, and I am most honoured and grateful to have your essay in my birthday book.

Milton Wilson   **5 June 1983**
In response to Wilson's contribution to Frye's Festschrift, *"Bodies in Motion: Wordsworth's Myths of Natural Philosophy," in* Centre and Labyrinth, *197–209. Wilson taught literature at Trinity College, University of Toronto.*

Dear Milton:

This is just to thank you very gratefully for the fine essay you contributed to my birthday book. Now that the history of science people are firmly ensconced in Victoria's upper story, I hope there'll be wider recognition of the fact that every era of history presents a roughly consistent world-outlook, extending over both literature and science. You are very illuminating on the way this shows up in Wordsworth, even though Wordsworth doesn't confine himself to echoes from contemporary science and aesthetics, but has some odd foreshadowings of yoga techniques. I am greatly honoured to have this kind of relationship to the essay, and I hope there will be a lot more to come, to remind me of such things as Burke's comment about beauty acting by relaxing solids— something I'd totally forgotten.

Only I'm still not very clear about the pre-transverse method of stopping skating by going back on the heels: if I tried that I'd stop all right, but in a much less dignified and more painful way.

Lucy Dougall   14 July 1983
Woodinville, WA

In reply to Dougall's having sent Frye a copy of War and Peace in Literature: Prose, Drama and Poetry which Illuminate the Problem of War *(Chicago: World without War Publications, 1982).*

Dear Ms. Dougall:

Thank you very much for your letter and for the book. I have looked through the book with great interest, but I don't know that I have many criticisms to offer. You mention William James on the moral equivalent of war, and perhaps greater emphasis on what Blake calls "mental fight" or "intellectual war," might be in order, as suggesting that the world we want is not a milk sop world but one of far greater strength and heroism than one gets in what Blake calls the "energy enslaved" of physical war.

Margaret Atwood   28 July 1983
Toronto, ON

A response to Atwood's having sent Frye a copy of Murder in the Dark: Short Fictions and Prose Poems *(Toronto: Coach House Press, 1983), her seventh work of fiction and tenth book of poems, along with* Bluebeard's Egg *(Toronto: McClelland & Stewart, 1983).*

Dear Peggy,

Thank you very much for the two books, which I was delighted to receive. I think *Murder in the Dark* is astonishingly haunting and resonant. I look at such things rather wistfully, because if I had taken to fiction that would be the kind of genre that would most attract me.

Much love to the three of you.

Ellen Karp   10 August 1983
Amnesty International, Toronto, ON

Dear Ms. Karp:

I am pleased to lend what support I can to *Amnesty International*, who are undertaking humanistic work that ought to have top priority with every civilized person. It has never been a political pressure group, but has always been consistently against cruelty, torture and injustice, and has constantly tried to help the victims of oppression everywhere, ranging from world famous scientists to children who are totally innocent victims of terror. I urge support for their work on every possible human ground.

Stephen Morrissey   18 August 1983
Huntingdon, QC

In response to Frye's having received a copy of Morrisey's second volume of poetry, Divisions *(Toronto: Coach House Press, 1983).*

Dear Mr. Morrissey,

Thank you for sending me a copy of your latest volume, *Divisions*, which I found extremely powerful, at once visionary and movingly personal. The title poem in particular achieves an extraordinary degree of eloquence about experiences which because of their very painfulness remain in most people suppressed and inarticulate—feelings of grief, loneliness and helpless abandonment which the poem by sheer intensity of language raises from the subjective to the universal. Good luck in all your further undertakings.

Arthur Holmberg   29 August 1983
Cambridge, MA

In reply to Holmberg's asking Frye (19 August 1983) whether "any actual productions you have seen have illuminated a new aspect of Shakespeare for you."

Dear Mr. Holmberg,

Thank you very much for your letter and the various offprints. I don't know that I can trace a definite influence from a Shakespeare production on my criticism. Most of my theatrical experience of Shakespeare has been acquired at Stratford, Ontario, and in the days of Tyrone Guthrie and Michael Langham people used to remark on how close my lectures there were to the productions, even though I had not seen them at the time of giving the lecture. Later, my reactions were chiefly negative ones.

There has recently been a *festschrift* for me, called *Centre and Labyrinth*, which is published by the University of Toronto Press. The essay in that by James Reaney has some very interesting things to say on how my criticism could influence productions of Shakespeare, and would if he were doing them.

John Freccero   26 September 1983

In response to Freccero's contribution to Frye's Festschrift, *"Manfred's Wounds and the Poetics of the* Purgatorio," *in* Centre and Labyrinth, *69–82. Freccero was professor of Italian at Stanford University.*

Dear John Freccero,

This is a very belated, but I trust not the less sincere, expression of the great pleasure and honour it was to have your essay in my *Festschrift*. For one thing, Dante is a very central figure in all my critical thinking, and I feel I know too little about Dante scholarship to write about him in any detail myself. For another, your essay is full of suggestive and haunting comments about the role of the written word in the creative process, and this is precisely what is preoccupying me now, as I attempt to write a more coherent sequel to *The Great Code*. I am struggling with the problem of isolating the identity of "Word of God" as Bible with "Word of God" as presence of Christ, without suggesting either Bible-worship or a new theological doctrine: it's a critical principle only. In wrestling with this I shall find some of your fine phrases, such as "the soul of the foetus or the spirit of the text," and "sins that are at once wounds and letters" constantly fertilizing my thinking. Thank you very much again.

Karleen Middleton Murphy   1 November 1983
Toledo, OH

In reply to Murphy's having sent Frye on 14 January 1983 a copy of her paper "The Vala Cycle" for comment. She inquired on 10 October 1983 whether the paper had safely arrived. Jane Widdicombe replied that it had indeed arrived but that it might be some time before Frye could respond. After reading the critique of the paper by his research associate Michael Dolzani, Frye replied three weeks later.

Dear Mrs. Murphy,

Thank you for your letter. I think that your sharpest observation is the associating of Vala with the phoenix, which is suggested by the "ashes" of *The Four Zoas* and the "fire on the hearth" in *The Mental Traveller*. It is of course important to remember at all times that there are no men or women in eternity: the female nature of emanation, as well as the male nature of the Zoas have to do with something like a Chinese yang and yin system. The "Female Will" is a runaway or over-objectified nature, which is called female because the mythology of experience speaks of Mother Nature, and because the elusiveness of the objective world is associated with females in some literary conventions, such as Courtly Love poetry. But this, because it belongs to the state of experience, is a muddled and confused analogy of the genuine thing. The Emanations oscillate between submissiveness and feminine wiles not because they are female, but because they are fallen. This is an often neglected point about the Emanations, and you almost put your finger on it. I don't think Blake ever thought of Vala as a central character of *The Four Zoas*, but rather as its singer or narrator: the same role that Vola has in the Elder Edda. If female figures like Ololon and Jerusalem are better behaved than Vala or Enitharmon, it is not because they are women behaving acceptably according to male standards, but because nature behaves better when it is loved rather than exploited.

I suppose you know most of this, and your analysis of Kala's role in *The Four Zoas* is very good. But it is as well to keep one's eye on *Visions of the Daughters of Albion* for Blake's view of human women, and on the first two poems of the *Songs of Experience* for the cosmic role of a female Earth, who in eternity is a part of the unfallen "Soul."

Julian Patrick   1 November 1983
Department of English, Victoria College, University of Toronto

Dear Julian,

I understand the Wendy Gunn wants you to read a Psalm at her mother's approaching funeral and that I am supposed to suggest which Psalm to read. The standard one is Psalm 90, but in view of Wendy's desire to make it a more positive service, perhaps the 139th Psalm would be better, either the first twelve verses or the first eighteen, whichever you would prefer. As long as we leave out the slaughter of the wicked at the end it can't miss.

Northrop Fox   23 November 1983
San Francisco, CA

Fox's letter is not extant. Fox seems to have written about his classmates making fun of his given name.

Dear Northrop Fox:

Thank you very much for your letter: it was lost by a freak accident, and I didn't copy your address, so I am sending this in the dark in the hope it will arrive.

In my view your classmates are a lot dumber than your name. It used to be very common to give family surnames as given names, though it may have gone out of fashion for a few years. I was named after Miss Sarah Ann Northrop of Lowell, Massachusetts, who eventually became my grandmother. It is quite a common name in New England, and there was a quite famous scholar in Yale of that name.[661]

So hold on to your name, and don't be ashamed of it.

Jonathan Bishop   1 December 1983
Department of English, Cornell University, Ithaca, NY

Dear Professor Bishop:

I am sorry that it has taken so long to thank you for sending me a copy of *The Covenant*[662]: since the publication of *The Great Code*, my backlog of prior commitments has begun to look a little like the Toronto telephone directory. I find your reading of the sacrifice and ritual aspects of the Old Testament in the light of the Catholic sacramental attitude to be quite intriguing. It is refreshing to be told that what is sometimes dismissed as idolatrous and pagan-derivative might also be looked upon as a positive creative activity, one that provided a balance to the prohibitive tendencies of law and the iconoclastic fervors of prophecy. In the area of the New Testament, I too of course am extremely interested in Paul's distinction between a soul and a spiritual body. The last and more personal section of the book I found quietly moving.

Ross V. Dobson   5 December 1983
Winnipeg, MB

In reply to Dobson's request (1 November 1983) for suggestions about how to approach a study of the relationship among vision, language, and meaning, a topic he intends to pursue in his study for the M.A. degree.

Dear Mr. Dobson:

Thank you for your letter. I don't know that I have much that is helpful to say about language and vision beyond what I have suggested in the *Anatomy* and elsewhere, namely that literature seems to be intermediate between the aural and the visual, and runs from the extremes of pure noise to verbalized pictures or diagrams. Naturally, having been brought up on Blake, with his pictorial interests, I have always felt that language and vision have much more than a metaphorical connection. The thing I am doubtful about is how far abstraction in any role gets "beyond" vision. Some sort of diagrammatic pattern always seems to me to underlie argumentative or metaphysical writing.

Your suggestion about the "unipeds" is very interesting,[663] and may well be the right answer.

Gilbert Reid   5 December 1983
Canadian Cultural Institute, Rome, Italy

Reid had written Frye on 24 August 1983 inviting him to tour Italy and offering to organize a conference centered on his work. He indicates, among other things, that he has recently had dinner with Irving Layton, who was lecturing in Urbino, and Adrienne Clarkson, who was representing Ontario in Paris.

Dear Gilbert Reid,

I am sorry to have left your very pleasant and friendly letter of August 24th unanswered for so long. I am not sure what to say about a tour of Italy. My difficulty is that it would be a seductively pleasant engagement, but that the second volume of my Bible study is still to be written and that I am still engaged in full time teaching. After 1984/85 my teaching will begin to taper off, but the major preoccupation of my writing commitments will still remain.

I was very interested in what you told me of Irving Layton and Adrienne Clarkson. Irving has just sent me his latest book of poems and a newspaper interview with him. Every interview with him these days mentions the possibility of his getting the Nobel Prize, which I think unlikely, for reasons which have less to do with him than with the mysterious movings of that committee, and to keep advertising it makes him more vulnerable than he should be. I have told him that while I would be delighted to see him get the prize, I certainly don't think it has the prestige of the science awards.

Returning to your main question, could we leave the matter of a visit to Italy until some of my pressing preoccupations have grown a little less opaque? I am very sorry to keep stalling in this way, but I simply don't know what else to do.[664]

The very best to you and Sofia and yourself from us both.

Francesca Valente   5 December 1983
Italian Cultural Institute, San Francisco, CA

In reply to Valente's invitation for Frye to present a paper at a conference she was organizing.

Francesca, my dear, I have been thinking very carefully over your proposal, and I don't think the reading week of February is going to be possible for me. I have a string of other commitments for the spring: I have two or three projects to get off my desk at the moment, and there is just no way of getting enough Vico and Bruno and Joyce read for a decent paper by that time.[665] The subject still fascinates me — it is about the only thing on Joyce that still does — and it would be a way of keeping in touch with Italian themes. But when I look at my present schedule and think of having to squeeze an extra paper in for my one free week it just seems beyond possibility. I find your proposals so attractive that I usually go further in trying to meet them than I should do, and I am very sorry that the sober second thought is so sober.

Anyway, much love to you and Branko[666] from the three of us here.

Paul Wilson   9 January 1984
Toronto, ON

In reply to Wilson's letter (5 January 1984) asking about Frye's attitudes to composing on a computer. Wilson, a former student, was writing an article for Books in Canada *on the use of micro-computers in writing and publishing.*

Dear Mr. Wilson,

I'm afraid I am still a Luddite in regard to computers. I start all my writing in longhand, eventually graduate to the typewriter and after a series of revisions on typed copies I get what I am after. What bothers me about composing on the typewriter, and would continue to bother me on a word processor, is seeing what I have written facing me. I write so slowly that early drafts look like a kind of accusation, and I even have to force myself to reread what I have actually completed and published. This may be why I repeat myself so much, though I should naturally prefer to think that I am always right and that repetition is consequently restricted.

None of this would of course apply if I were fifty or sixty years younger. I would then get adjusted to computers at a malleable age. I feel nervous in planes, but not in trains, for the same reason: something in me doesn't believe the plane has been invented yet. As for the long-term result of computer education, that, as always, depends on the kind of person involved. Good writers will find it easier to write; bad writers will find it easier to blither.

Trusting this answers your questions and knowing it doesn't.

Tzvetan Todorov   16 January 1984

Paris, France

In reply to Todorov, who had sent Frye a copy of the preface to the French edition of The Great Code, *published later in the year as* Le Grand Code: La Bible et la literature, *trans. Catherine Malamoud (Paris: Éditions du Seuil, 1984). Frye had earlier agreed to have Todorov's preface published with the translation.*

Dear M. Todorov,

Thank you very much for the copy of your introduction to *The Great Code*. I have only one negative comment. There seems to be nothing which forms an introduction to *The Great Code* itself as distinct from the critical views I have expressed elsewhere. Hence there is no indication about the later book's relation to the earlier work, and the reader faces a gap which he is given no help in bridging over. This is a suggestion only: I am, of course, as always, very grateful for your interest.[667]

Hazard Adams   30 January 1984

Department of English, University of Washington, Seattle WA

In response to Adams's having sent Frye a copy of his articles "Thinking Cassirer," in Criticism *25, no. 3 (Summer 1983): 181–95, and "How Departments Commit Suicide," in* ADE Bulletin *76 (1983): 7–13.*

Dear Hazard,

Thank you for the xeroxes of Cassirer and on English Departments. Fortunately I get the *ADE Bulletin*: I am sure the University of Washington can afford a better xeroxing machine. But what I really wanted to say was with how much pleasure I am reading the *Philosophy of [the] Literary Symbolic*.[668] It is beautifully lucid, and sets out straight and narrow way that runs through Vico and Humboldt and Blake and Yeats to Jerusalem's wall, and avoids all the deviant paths, especially the broad highway that leadeth to deconstruction.

P.S. Also it is particularly delightful to see a book on critical theory that omits Roland Barthes and Nietzsche from its bibliography.

John Paul Fullerton   30 January 1984

Texas A & M University, College Station, TX

In reply to Fullerton's undated letter, asking about Frye's views on Blake, Nietzsche, and deconstruction.

Dear Mr. Fullerton:

Thank you for your letter. I think the major difference between Blake and Nietzsche revolves around the fact that Blake is a strong Protestant Christian and would have no use for Nietzsche's master morality. He would have found less use for a doctrine of eternal recurrence, and would think of Nietzsche's "will of power" as something to be subdued by the creative imagination, as the Spectre of Urthona is by Los.

I am still trying to read Derrida and others of his school, so that when I finally do express an opinion of them it will be better informed one than I can make now. My work on the Bible has convinced me that in it, at any rate, the text *is* the presence, not an absence referring to a presence. I think Derrida's emphasis on "difference" describes the understanding of words in the original context of time and space. I feel it is the function of metaphor, which is counter-logical, and of myth, which is counter-historical, to reverse this perspective.

I find very little in my previous work that I want to repudiate or set aside. Once I have got something into print, it is for other people to say whether it is useful or not. Books, like children, have to be allowed to grow up and lead their own lives.

Pauline McGibbon   7 February 1984
Toronto, ON

McGibbon served as lieutenant-governor for Ontario from 1974–80.

Dear Pauline,

You've probably heard a good many variations of this story, but this version happens to be true, so I'm retelling it. My bibliographer Bob Denham was recently up from Virginia to dig in Jane's [Jane Widdicombe's] files for the revised edition of my bibliography he's preparing, and started asking Jane about my student days and who my classmates were. Jane said, "Well, there was Pauline McGibbon: she was the Lieutenant-Governor." Denham said "You know, that's a phrase I keep hearing in this country and don't understand. What is a left-handed governor?"[669] After all, he comes from a country of lootenants.[670]

Richard Brand   6 March 1984
Raleigh, NC

Dear Mr. Brand:

I am afraid your letter got mislaid in our office, and this is a reply based on memory only. As I remember, you were enquiring about the argument of the first chapter of *The Great Code*. I laid out a sequence of three modes of thought, and then said that the Bible wouldn't fit any one of them because if it did it would be a simply literary, simply doctrinal, or simply historical. As it is none of these things, the solution seems to be that it is written in a rhetorical style which adopts all these modes but is motivated by a hortatory interest. This seems to me to be true to the facts of the situation, and is also in accordance with traditional attitudes, as the Bible has always been regarded as divine rhetoric accommodated to human mentality.

I hope that this is what you are asking about and I am sorry about the accident to your letter.

Dinnah Pladott   6 March 1984
Department of English, Tel-Aviv University, Tel-Aviv, Israel

In reply to Pladott's letter (14 February 1984), asking Frye's advice about adding a chapter on the religious background of the South to the manuscript of her book, Faulkner's Tragic Vision, *which addition had been recommended by a reader of her manuscript.*

Dear Dr. Pladott:

It seems to me that there are arguments both for and against an introductory chapter on the social context of what Faulkner is writing about. You could hardly have written your book without learning enough about Faulkner's southern background to write such a chapter without too much difficulty, and adding it might make your book more marketable generally, and easier to recommend to undergraduate readers. It would enable you to make broader reference to novels of Faulkner that are not so fully treated, such as *Light in August*, and would suggest to your reviewers that they need not spend all their time quarreling with your views of tragedy. I should agree that the chapter is not essential to the book, and would lie somewhat outside the general argument you make. But I don't feel strongly enough to put my views in an open letter,[671] because I am in favour of anything that might make a book sell better.

William O. Fennell   19 March 1984
Etobicoke, ON

In reply to Fennell's having sent Frye a copy of his paper "Theology and Frye: Some Implications of The Great Code," *presented at the Canadian Theological Society's annual meeting in 1984. It was later published in the* Toronto Journal of Theology *1, no. 1 (Spring 1985): 113–21.*

Dear Bill:

Thanks very much for the article: I greatly appreciate the good will and good faith that impelled you to write it and send it to me. As you say, there is no point I trying to "reply" to all of it now, and I also hope that there will be many chances to discuss it further. I doubt if we are really so far apart: I have no difficulty in answering "yes" to all your final questions, and if those answers are not in my book, the reason is either unrealized writing or the limitations of its position.

That is, the book was primarily addressed to students of literature, with or without religious affinities, trying to alert them to the importance and relevance of the Bible in their own study. You would hardly believe how ignorant and prejudiced some of them are on such subjects. So on the question of whether the book should revolve around the orbit of faith or culture, I really had no choice.

I think of the Bible as a kind of gigantic parable of Jesus which ends: "Well, there's the story, now what are you going to do about it?" Most of the issues you raise concern what comes after. But of course it would be wholly "after" only if the initial reading were ideally complete, which it can't be. So I brought out what I thought was a neglected aspect of it, the imaginative aspect, in the hope of making some religious people more charitable and some non-religious people more sensitive.

Sandra Djwa   20 March 1984
Department of English, Simon Fraser University, Burnaby, BC

In reply to Djwa's questions about E.J. (Ned) Pratt for a research project she was working on.

Dear Sandra:

Thank you for your letter. The confrontation between the human being supported by the martyrdom of Christ and the "Panjandrum" who bullies him is of course very central to Blake, but it is central to other poets too, notably Shelley, whom Ned knew much better than he did Blake. What struck me with particular force was the way in which the

Panjandrum emerged as a negative or demonic creation of the human figure himself.[672] And then there was also the unmistakable identification of the Panjandrum with the kind of mystique that lay behind Nazism. I think in any comment I have ever made about this poem I have reiterated how important it was for a liberal in those days to find a poet he respected who is looking squarely at the evil of Nazism instead of running to God about it.

Regarding the Woodsworth business,[673] Ned was always ready to support any liberal cause as long as other people organized it and it didn't get him involved to the point of threatening his writing schedule. I know that he sympathized with the general liberal stance at Victoria at that time, but it seems to me that his religious difficulties were more cosmological than social. More of an Oedipal relation to Hardy, as you say. By all means send me the introduction. I expect to be getting the first volume of Pitt before long.[674]

Janet Conklin   1 June 1984
Grimsby, ON
In reply to an inquiry about the difference between an archetype and a stereotype.

Dear Ms. Conklin:

Archetype is a repeating unit of literary construction. An author may use an archetype in a fresh and original way, or he may use it in a conventional way, doing only what has been done before. The word stereotype, like the word cliché, is not a critical term at all. It is a metaphorical value judgment indicating that the reader is bored by the archetype in front of him. Your students who say that [Morley] Callaghan's woman is a stereotype are simply saying that they don't like the story. Similarly, people who don't like me say that I don't know the difference between an archetype and a stereotype.

Walter J. Peterson   12 June 1984
Walpole, MA

Dear Mr. Peterson,

I am extremely grateful to you for taking the time and trouble to point out to me that mistaken reference on page 40 of *The Great Code*. It is indeed a scribal error—I Kings doesn't even *have* twenty-nine chapters, and you are right in guessing that I actually meant I Kings 20. The scribe at fault was possibly electronic: thanks to a word processor with a creative sensibility, which apparently decided to do some redacting on its own, there were over fifty errors in the book's first printing. Again, thank you for drawing my attention to one that had still escaped notice.

John Paul Fullerton   27 June 1984
Texas A & M University, College Station, Texas
In response to Fullerton's letter of 24 May 1984 asking Frye about the visionary experience in his early study of Blake, Oscar Wilde, and the ahistorical view of the Bible.

Dear Mr. Fullerton:

What you referred to as a visionary experience in my earlier study of Blake was perhaps not really such at all: there were two occasions on which the shape of what I was doing and had yet to do seemed to clear up suddenly for me.

When Oscar Wilde speaks of "lying" he means that it is impossible to tell more than a very approximate truth by means of words because words are involved in their own fictions, and anyone handling words has to respect the nature of words and what they do best. I would never think it justifiable to make a deliberately untrue statement about anything, except in very complex circumstances.

I have never been worried about the historical integrity of the Bible, because I have never felt that it was possible to write history except by standing outside history. When a book stands as far outside history as the Bible does, there is no question of anything except what I call myth, which uses historical material but twists it around in a different dimension of time.

Jeffrey Elie   **17 July 1984**
Bethune College, York University, Downsview, ON
In reply to Elie's request for Frye to send inscribed copies of Fearful Symmetry, Anatomy of Criticism, *and* The Return of Eden *to Professor Nui Kangsheng at the Institute of Foreign Languages, Sichuan, People's Republic of China. Nui had asked Elie, who would shortly be taking up a position in Nui's department, to see if he could get copies of the three books.*

Dear Professor Elie:
Thank you very much for your letter: I am returning the copies herewith. I am very sorry to say — and perhaps you would explain this to Professor Niu — that *The Return of Eden* is out of print and I have only one copy. That is what comes of publishing books with the University of Toronto Press, which I do as seldom as possible.

With the best of luck for your work in China.

Herbert Deinert   **19 July 1984**
Cornell University, Ithaca, NY
In reply to Deinert's undated letter indicating that he wishes Frye had said that Jacob Boehme was a precursor of Marxism. In The Great Code *Frye had written that Hegel was Marx's "spiritual father" and Luther his "spiritual grandfather" (xx). Deinert enclosed several op-ed pieces he had written for the* Cornell Daily Sun.

Dear Professor Deinert:
Thank you very much for your letter and the enclosures. One of them revives a feeling I have often had myself, that the Nobel Prize Committee in not giving a prize to Nabokov [*sic*].[675] But then the Nobel people have missed a whole fleet of boats.

I was aware of Hegel's interest in Boehme, but had thought of him as a more fruitful influence on Schelling, and consequently has given birth to a rather different tradition. But then I am very unsure of myself with Boehme. I read a good deal of him when I was working on Blake, and am now trying to read him again, mainly because of the fire and light symbolism he had. I expect to find a good deal of profit in reading your article. In any case I wanted Luther because of the shock value.

Judith Fitzgerald   **24 July 1984**
Toronto, ON

Dear Ms. Fitzgerald:
Further to our telephone conversation, enclosed as promised is the statement by Dr. Frye for possible inclusion in your article. He hopes this will be useful to you.

Yours sincerely,
Jane Widdicombe (Mrs.)
Secretary to Dr. Northrop Frye

STATEMENT FOR JUDITH FITZGERALD FOR *QUILL AND QUIRE* ARTICLE

I've been on the Governor-General's Committee myself, and I know what a difficult and usually thankless job they have. As one of my committee said, if the job's hard somebody's being done an injustice; if it's easy it doesn't say much for the country's culture. As a rule a committee finds itself stuck with a short list of highly eligible books which is totally impossible to compare with each other.

As for the award this year, I was hoping that Christina McCall's *Grits* would get the award — I didn't know the Louisburg book. But they may have felt that her book, like mine, had already found its public, and that they could give some recognition to a book that was worthy of it but might be more helped by the recognition. They did the best they could in the circumstances. But perhaps there's too much really good stuff coming out each year in Canada now for any kind of "best book of the year" award to mean very much: possibly something more along the lines of the Nobel Committee, recognizing a whole body of work, might be more appropriate. Though heaven knows the Nobel committee have missed a lot of boats, and the Literature Prize doesn't have the prestige of the scientific ones. In the nature of things it couldn't have — how, for example, do you compare a poet with a novelist?

One thing that seems to be very important is that all the sub-committees, both English and French, should get together to discuss the short list. When Douglas Grant, Guy Sylvestre and I set up the original committee, somewhere around 1960, I found the comments of the French sub-committees invaluable, and it seems to me that that kind of cooperation is one that makes sense if we're going to have awards and committees for both languages.

Paul Ricoeur   1 August 1984

University of Chicago Press, Chicago, IL

In response to Ricoeur's contribution to Frye's Festschrift, "Anatomy of Criticism *and the Order of Paradigms," in* Centre and Labyrinth, *1–13.*

Dear Professor Ricoeur,

Your publishers have just sent me the translation of volume one of *Time and Narrative*. I have been able so far only to glance at it, but it seems to me extremely readable and lucid, and I am going to look forward to reading it.

My real reason for writing, however, is that I am being reminded that I omitted to thank you for your contribution to my *festschrift*. It was a signal honour to me for you to contribute to it, apart altogether from the inherent interest of the article itself. I have never felt that I was going in quite the same direction as the French structuralists, and I am all the more pleased to have the fact noted and clarified.

I am also pleased to see so much attention given in this new book to William Dray,[676] who at one time was a student of mine.

With my very best wishes.

Robertson Davies   20 August 1984

Massey College, University of Toronto

In reply to Davies's having written on 24 July 1984, "I have read with horror the furious exposure of yourself and your ideas about Marxism contained in a letter from Sandra Beattie. You may rely on me to stand by you if she should attempt physical violence anywhere within Massey College." The exposure in question was an open letter, dated July 1984 from Montreal, in which Beattie took Frye to task for his views on Marx, saying, among other things, "I presume that like most of our academics and intellectuals you speak with a feigned, or dishonest, sort of wisdom about the works of Karl Marx without ever having read them.... On the other hand, you may be one of the privileged few with a refuge in the Caribbean."

Dear Rob:

Many thanks for your declaration of solidarity and sympathy. I certainly got enough crank letters in response to that book [*The Great Code*], most of them predictable, but an attack from an anti–Leninist-Marxist was something I did not expect.[677]

Hazel Merrett   20 August 1984
Senneville, QC

In reply to Merrett's letter of 13 August 1984, saying that she had tried to call Frye but found that his telephone number was unlisted. She wanted to discuss with him establishing a memorial fund at McGill for her sister Alma Howard Rolleston Ebert, the renowned biologist, who had died on 1 April 1984. Hazel Merrett was Frye's first cousin. See headnote to letter of 21 August 1978.

Dear Hazel,

Our telephone number is 416-489-3654. I am very sorry: I thought you already had it. We got an unlisted number, not to keep off our friends, but to stop the flow of unwanted calls. I had eaten too many cold suppers through listening to high school students quoting practically the whole of one of my books and then asking what I meant by it. And after I had produced a book on the Bible, I thought life would be really too much. As it was, I got enough crank letters, including a letter from an anti–Leninist-Marxist informing me that she was sending copies to an enormous list of people and "1,000 others."[678]

Bill Solomon's address is: #1108, 400 Waterloo Avenue, Guelph, Ontario N1H 7H9. I haven't heard from him for some time, and gather that his health is not very good. But when he writes to me he usually calls himself Bill Solomon.[679] Izzy Halperin's address is: 39 Elm Ridge Drive, Toronto, Ontario M6B 1A2.[680] I wrote to him about Alma, and got a reply from his wife (present, Mary), which implied that they had been much closer to Alma than I realized. Unfortunately I have no clue to the ex-wife's address.

There was an exhibition here recently of research done in the arts and sciences, and a reception for those featured in it. There I met Francis Rolleston[681] and sat beside him at dinner.

Much love to you from us both.

Kathleen Coburn   28 August 1984
St. John's Hospital, Willowdale, ON

Coburn, the distinguished Coleridge scholar, was Frye's long-time colleague at Victoria College.

Dear Kay:

Helen and I were terribly sorry to hear of your recent set-back, and we both hope you will be out of that place before long. When Helen was there for her hysterectomy some years ago, one of the nuns asked her about her religion and Helen said that she was born an Anglican, and was married into the United Church. The nun said "and did you go all the way?" I have no doubt that you will keep floating at ease somewhere in the middle.

Much love from us both.

Robert Denham   12 September 1984
Department of English, Emory & Henry College, Emory, VA

In response to a request for Frye to review the primary entries in the bibliography Den-

ham was compiling. It was eventually published as Northrop Frye: An Annotated Bibliography of Primary and Secondary Sources *(Toronto: University of Toronto Press, 1987).*

Dear Bob,

I have gone through the first volume of the bibliography, and am lost in admiration at the size and comprehension of your project. To speak of my personal gratitude and to what it means to me is very difficult.

It seems to me that if you are really attempting a definitive bibliography, I should not get in your way and consequently I do not object to your including juvenilia and other trifles. Anyone sufficiently interested in me to consult the book has a right to know that I have produced an immense amount of hack work and joe-jobs, mainly for the College here (Victoria), that my work extends over several decades and consequently is bound to contain things that are inconsistent or immature or simply silly. I have no wish to whitewash myself for posterity. So if your instinct is to include them, I should want to go along with your instinct.

Best wishes as always.

Hazel Merrett   26 September 1984
Senneville, QC

In response to Merrett's letter of 16 September 1984, following up on their previous correspondence about establishing a memorial fund for her sister Alma (see letter of 20 August 1984). Merrett notes that in his letter of 20 August 1984 Frye did not say anything about the memorial fund, so she wonders if he approves of her plan. Merrett was Frye's first cousin. See letter of 21 August 1978.

Dear Hazel,

Thank you for your letter. I am very sorry not to have made any comment on setting up the scholarship in Alma's name. I am afraid I just took it for granted that you would know that I approved and would do my best to help out in any way.

I am glad to have the business about Izzy Halperin's wife straightened out: I was pretty sure there had been no divorce.[682]

All our love from us both to you both.

Rev. Robert K. Leland   30 October 1984
Toronto Area Presbytery, Toronto, ON

In reply to Leland's letter of 25 October 1984 requesting information from all those United Church ministers without a pastoral charge. The church manual required that all such ministers submit an annual statement that would guide the presbytery in determining whether or not they should be retained on the rolls. Frye's request to be transferred from the Chignecto to the Toronto Presbytery had been approved five years earlier.

Dear Bob Leland,

I have not put this on your application form, but thought it might be appropriate to send it to you under separate cover. After my graduation from Emmanuel, I was very hesitant about ordination because I knew by that time that I was unlikely to be engaged in conventional pastoral work and my belief in the priesthood of believers seemed to make it unnecessary. I consulted various friends: the general consensus was that I should take ordination, and having taken it, I regard it as permanent and wish to retain it.[683]

Helen J. Stewart   1 November 1984
St. Catharines, ON

In reply to Stewart's questions (26 October 1984): Who invited Jerome Bruner to Toronto in the early 1960s? Did Frye use the phrase "spiral curriculum" before his encounter with Bruner? And did Bert Case Diltz of the Ontario College of Education have more than a casual contact?

Dear Ms. Stewart,

The person who had the idea of inviting Jerome Bruner was Roy Sharp, at that time a member of the Board of Education who had been very active in getting the Joint Committee underway. He was rather disappointed in the actual lecture, as I remember, except for Bruner's suggestion that we form a Curriculum Institute, which was the next thing we did. I think that I took the phrase "spiral curriculum" from Bruner's book, and referred to the book. I don't remember having used it myself before.

No, Bert Diltz was not much of a hand for discussing questions of theory, and he distrusted people from the university on principle. He was a Barthian in theology and I once found myself addressing a group of Barthian preachers and laymen on the subject of the arts as religion analogy. Diltz was there, and seemed to like the paper, but that is the best I can do.

Robin Harris   12 December 1984
Faculty of Education, University of Toronto.

In reply to Harris's query (6 December 1984) on whether E.J. Pratt's fourth-year honour course in modern poetry and drama was open to students in the three-year pass course. The question was in connection with Harris's research for his English Studies at Toronto: A History (Toronto: Governing Council, University of Toronto, 1988), to which Frye wrote the foreword.

Dear Robin,

I don't actually know that Ned's course was open to the Pass Course students, but everything I do know about Ned suggests that the statement is probably true. Both Pratt and Robins greatly preferred teaching the Pass Course to the Honour Course, and while Robins had his special field in Philology and Old English, Ned always was aware of his role as a converted psychologist with his degrees in other disciplines. However, that was a minor element in the situation: he always chose Pass Courses, and his house was about the only one that Pass Course students got inside of.

I don't know if I ever told you that at the last meeting of the graduate department in 1953, which was also his last connexion with the graduate department, he had an item under "Other Business," which consisted of a bottle of rye in an otherwise empty briefcase.[684] So we adjourned to celebrate Ned's retirement from something he had totally lost interest in.

Joan Preston   12 December 1984
Department of Psychology, Brock University, St. Catharines, ON

In reply to Preston's letter (3 December 1984) which thanked Frye for the analysis of metaphor he provided in his talk at Brock University on 29 November, requested a copy of the paper, and offered some of her own ideas about metaphoric painting.

Dear Dr. Preston,

Thank you very much for your letter. I think that metaphor not only generates energies but juxtaposes them in a way that presents them as a unity to the viewer, or hearer. This juxtaposition is not possible except by accident and in very different patterns in normal experience. In my sense, therefore, all painting would be metaphorical painting, because the viewer's attention is thrown on the uniting of the images in the picture and not on the various objects they may or may not represent.

I am sending you a copy of the lecture I gave at Brock in a slightly revised form.[685]

Hon. Walter McLean   19 December 1984
The Secretary of State, Government of Canada, Ottawa, ON

Dear Sir:

I am writing to express my strong support of the brief submitted recently to you by CIHM (Canadian Institute for Historical Microreproductions).[686] The chemical combination of modern paper and ink has faced libraries and archives with a formidable pollution problem. The pollution does not directly attack the supply of air or water, but it does attack the cultural memory of the nation. The amount of work being done on Canadian history and culture is a burgeoning industry, not merely in Canada itself but in the great number of countries that have set up institutes of Canadian Studies, a number that now extends over most of the civilized world. It would be a calamity of major proportions if Canadian and foreign scholars were to find the physical facilities for research into Canada's past and present so gravely impaired that they would not be able to complete their research with any sense of satisfaction or of making a worthwhile contribution to the subject. I therefore urge that the brief of the CIHM should be carefully examined and its recommendations immediately implemented.

Robert Fisher   28 February 1985
Toronto, ON

In response to Fisher's letter of 18 February 1985 offering etymological confirmation, by way of Émile Benveniste, of Frye's claim in The Great Code *that the function of the king is to represent social unity in an individual form. Fisher provides a list of Indo-European words that illustrate such a meaning. He also suggests, drawing on his knowledge of Indo-European languages, that the Greek word for "zephyr" has some connection with wind, fertility, and creation. Fisher had received his Ph.D. in Indo-European Studies from ULCA in 1973.*

Dear Mr. Fisher:

Thank you very much indeed for a most interesting and informative letter. The things I know about Benveniste have never brought me into contact with his more technical works on etymology, so I simply assumed that the etymology of "king" would never be anything but a can of worms. What he says sounds most authoritative, and I am naturally delighted by the confirmation of my own suggestion it seems to represent.

The note on "zephyr" is very interesting too, because of the number of Renaissance poets who are so sold on the impregnating qualities of the west wind. I suppose the metaphor is still there, however concealed, in Shelley's Ode.

Aubrey Rosenberg   21 March 1985
Department of French, Victoria College, University of Toronto

*In response to Rosenberg's having sent Frye a copy of an interview, "Les lecteurs doivent manger le livre," *Liberation *21 November 1984: 29. Frye answered questions posed by Mathieu Lindon on the relation between the Bible, history, and literature in Western culture and on Marxism as a religion, among other things.*

Dear Aubrey,

Thanks very much for the copy of the piece in *Liberation.* I remember the two young people who came in to interview me. One of them didn't speak English and the other didn't understand it, so there may have been a communication gap.

Thank you also for your most lucid survey of contemporary critical theory in a recent *ACTA.*[687]

Paul Shullenberger   **10 April 1985**

John D. and Catherine T. MacArthur Foundation, Chicago, IL

In response to Schullenberger's request for Frye's assessment of two nominees for MacArthur Fellowships, known popularly as "genius grants." Harold Bloom received a fellowship in 1985.

Dear Mr. Shullenberger,

In regard to your enquiry about Harold Bloom and Geoffrey Hartman, I may say that I know both men well but can say little about them that would not simply be an echo of the nominations themselves. Both of them are at an eminence in their field which ought to enable them to practically write their own tickets, to receive without question whatever they need in the way of assistance. They are two of the chief reasons why Yale is the best known centre of literary and comparative studies on the continent. Harold Bloom has written books on critical theory, in which he has always taken a highly original line but has never isolated himself from the mainstream; he has opened up a great many new approaches to criticism, drawing even on the Kabbala. Such central conceptions of his as "anxiety of influence" and "misreading," have become practically household words in contemporary criticism.

Geoffrey Hartman wrote when still very young one of the classics of critical theory, *The Unmediated Vision,* and has simply gone ahead directly from there. His main field of interest has been the Romantic poets, and in English literature his work on Wordsworth is of particular importance. But his erudition and mastery of so many languages has enabled him to put the study of comparative literature on a quite new level of insight and broad vision.

Perhaps neither man is called a creative genius of the greatest of the French critical theorists, such as Derrida, Foucault, Lacan, and Levi-Strauss. But they are very close to these names, and an increasing body of American scholarship is grouping itself around their standards. Needless to say, I recommend them both without reservation.

Robin Harris   **23 April 1985**

Faculty of Education, University of Toronto

In connection with his research for his English Studies at Toronto: A History *(Toronto: Governing Council, University of Toronto, 1988), Harris had asked Frye what he remembered about Clementine Wien, a graduate student at Toronto in the early 1940s.*

Dear Robin,

Clementine Wien came to the Graduate School at a time when St. Michael's was turning out a flock of Ph.D.'s, all based on the same elementary text book. The text book said that St. Thomas Aquinas was the only philosopher anybody needed to know anything about, and everything from Descartes on was really idealism, which was self-refuting because it ended in solipsism. So we got a raft of people picking some modern writer as a clay pigeon of pure subjectivity, and contrasting him with St. Thomas and his grasp of reality. I supervised the thesis and realized at the time that it was something of a Catholic con-game, but there wasn't much I could do. I liked Clem well enough, but don't quite remember what happened to her afterwards—I had assumed that she went back to Marquette. One person who knew her quite well at the time and did a good deal of reading for her was Rosemarie Wolfe, whose husband is in geography at either York or the Province,[688] I forget which. Clem also talked about marrying, so she may gave retired into civil life.[689]

David Toolan   **1 May 1985**

Book Editor, *Commonweal,* New York, NY

Toolan had sent Frye (24 April 1985) an editorial he had written for Commonweal, *"The*

Natural Font of Authority," *which took a great deal of inspiration from* The Great Code: *"I have read it again and again, and with each reading, it grows on/in me with increasing pleasure and understanding."*

Dear Mr. Toolan,

Thank you very much for your kindly letter and for the copy of your editorial. I certainly agree that the clash between the liberty at the heart of every genuine religion and the authoritarianism at the heart of most social religious institutions is perhaps the central crisis of our time. I am delighted if I helped in the making of your statement about it.

Robin Harris   15 May 1985
Faculty of Education, University of Toronto

In reply to Harris's asking Frye (letter of 8 May 1985) what he recalled about the graduate English Club. The question was in connection with Harris's research for his English Studies at Toronto: A History *(Toronto: Governing Council, University of Toronto, 1988), to which Frye wrote the foreword. Harris also tells Frye about what happened to Clementine Wien (see Frye's letter of 23 April 1985).*

Dear Robin,

Thanks very much for the information on Clem Wien which I was very glad to have, though I don't suppose "glad" is really the word.[690]

The Graduate English Club was meeting at Hoskin Avenue during the years before the war, but I doubt if I attended much earlier than 1935. I was at Oxford in 1936/37, and came back to fill in for Roy Daniells, who went to Winnipeg, at Victoria during 37/38. In the fall I read a long paper on Chaucer which had been the product of my first tutorials with Edmund Blunden.[691] I also remember a paper by Kathleen Coburn on Coleridge, a paper by Francess Halpenny on Stephen Crane, and a mad paper by Wilson Knight on Nietzsche, with J.F. Macdonald squirming on a hard chair and saying "Fool!" at intervals. I remember too that Douglas Le Pan, Earle Birney, Woodhouse, Priestley, and others were regular attenders. Also, those were the good old days when women knew their place, which was in the kitchen to make coffee. Oh yes, Roy Daniells read a paper on Milton and Baroque, and I remember his being quite prepared for the steady rain of flak he got from Woodhouse.

The average attendance was as Priestley says,[692] but it drew from a fairly large segment of students and younger staff. For example, Mary Winspear would come with her younger sister, now Marjorie McEnaney of the CBC.

Barb Ryz   15 May 1985
Dauphin, MB

Ryz, a student at Dauphin Regional Comprehensive Secondary School, had written Frye (the letter is undated), saying that she had to write a research paper on mythology and asking his opinion on the influence of myths: do myths explain or do they teach?

Dear Barb,

I don't know how far I can help you with your paper, but myths to me are a certain kind of story. They are usually stories about gods, and they are designed to explain to the society where they occur something of what that society believes about its past. That is, they deal with stories of gods, of traditional history, of the origin of customs, and other things that seem important. As time goes on, literature develops as we know it, and the stories told in myths become adapted to epic poems, or, later, novels. I think you are right when you suggest that myths, in their origin, explain both social facts and rules to live by to their original societies. But later they become just story patterns. Writers, especially writers of the early twentieth century, realized the immense potential of mythology for storytelling, and used the earlier mythical stories as much as they could. Also, in modern times people are well aware that stories from the Bible and from the Classical literatures show a great many family resemblances. But of course earlier writers realized that too, right back to Chaucer's time at least.

Sometimes people use the term myth to mean, not so much a story, as a way of holding a view of history together. The fascists, the communists, and people in the democracies also, have historical myths that provide their vision of life. They cannot all be good examples, but they are very important as historical forces.

James R. English   19 June 1985
Edmonton, AB
In response to several questions from English (2 June 1985), apparently a high school student.

Dear Mr. English,

Thank you very much for your letter. I am afraid I cannot say very much about what Canadian authors have been a major influence on me, because I did not start reading Canadian literature in much depth or breadth until I was too old to be influenced. I was influenced by the teachers I had here at Victoria College, but with the exception of E.J. Pratt I cannot say that their writing particularly influenced me.

I think Canadian identity is consistently regional and is likely to remain so. This doesn't prevent Canadian literature from having people who live outside the country, like Mavis Gallant, nor would it prevent any Canadian writer from writing about any part of the world he or she likes. But in general the more serious writers, in any country, do come out of specific locales and write about them, even though their books may be marketed elsewhere.

C.M. Chadwick   10 July 1985
The British Council, British High Commission, Ottawa, ON
In reply to Chadwick's letter (2 July 1985) expressing appreciation for the encouragement and inspiration Frye's work had provided him over the years as a student of literature and as a diplomat. As an undergraduate at Trinity College, Chadwick had attended Frye's lectures in nineteenth-century thought. Before returning to the British High Commission in Ottawa in 1981, Chadwick had worked for the British Council in Africa, Brazil, and London.

Dear Mr. Chadwick:

It was a large boost to my morale to get your letter with the xerox of the letter in the *Times*. I have had some very friendly reviews in England, but I have also had some bewilderingly hostile ones, and I sometimes wonder if the country isn't being intellectually polarized between Margaret Thatcher and Arthur Scargill, and simply cannot deal with someone who wants to get rid of dogmas and ideologies.

I remember very well your coming over with the other Trinity students in the fifties, and I am delighted to hear of your career since then.

My very best wishes and renewed thanks.

Margaret C. Evans   17 July 1985
Woodstock, Vermont
In reply to Frye's inquiries about Rosamond Tuve, pioneering Renaissance scholar about

whom Evans was writing a biography. The book appeared as Rosamond Tuve: A Life of the Mind *(Portsmouth, NH: Peter E. Randall, Publisher, 2004).*

Dear Mrs. Evans:

It was very pleasant to hear from you and be reminded of our all too brief friendship with Rosemond. I can still see her bustling into the room she was occupying at Radcliffe with her hair full of pencils and carrying four ice cubes on the back of her wrist, about to fix drinks for my wife and myself. We went to visit her in New London, and I think it was after that that she made the visit to Toronto that you referred to. It was certainly Professor Woodhouse who arranged the visit, but he died even before she did. In any case she stayed with us, and drove us around (we don't have a car) the suburbs of Toronto. We showed her nineteenth-century houses full of gingerbread, which she loved, and of course being in a car with Rosemond was something to write epic poems about afterwards. I remember her getting pinched for turning up Columbus Avenue in New York the wrong way, but she charmed the cop out of his ticket.

I am afraid this all sounds very trivial, and no help to your book at all. But she was the kind of person with whom one could simply relax and talk intelligently. I remember too an alleged seminar which was actually a long dialogue between herself and Woodhouse about Milton. He had started out as an eighteenth-century scholar, she as a medievalist, and the curiously different assumptions from which they collided in the middle was quite an education in itself.

I remember her Lutheran background, her fondness for her brother, who was in physics (they sent each other mutually unintelligible offprints), and the profound religious feeling that kept bubbling up inside her.

I remember explaining to her something that she had never heard: that the War of 1812 had been fought mainly in Canada, including the Toronto area, and that the shelling of Washington was a reprisal for burning York, as Toronto was called then. But I am afraid that if I continue I shall simply go on adding trivia.

Edith Baguinho   29 July 1985
Toronto, ON

In response to Baguinho's letter (20 July 1985) asking Frye what he means by the word "literature" and whether the reading of literature, as Frye addresses the issue in The Educated Imagination, *is not related to the reader's wider experience of life.*

Dear Ms. Baguinho:

Thank you for your letter. I see the study of English literature as something that has a centre in the kind of poetry and prose that we normally think of as literature, and as extending out from there into everything else in words. Literature is the centre only because it is my centre: if I were a philosopher or historian I would have a different centre. The centre is an area, and there is no circumference with a boundary line. Books originally intended to be histories or works of philosophy may become literary in the course of time, and everything written in words has a literary aspect.

Whenever I speak to teachers of literature, I always remind them that they are in contact with the entire verbal experience of their students. This verbal experience is picked up from casual conversations, news media, etcetera, and only about one or two percent of it comprises what is usually called literature. In *The Educated Imagination*, which you referred to, I have tried to set out the perspective from which I operate.

Deanne Bogdan   **12 August 1985**

Ontario Institute for Studies in Education, Toronto, ON

Both Frye and Bogdan had been at the Shakespeare Festival in Stratford, Ontario, in late July, but had missed seeing each other. Frye had delivered a lecture at Stratford, "The Stage is All the World," on 28 July.

Dear Deanne,

Thank you very much for a most welcome letter. I am very sorry to have missed you at Stratford, but of course didn't realize you would be there, and I was in the hands of the Literary Director, Michael Schonberg, who wanted to take me off for photographs.

I am sorry that you have to spend so much of your time and energy in the front line, but I cannot think of anyone I would rather have in that position. It seems silly that there should be so many medals for producing culture, but none for courage in defending it.

All the best from all at this end.

Douglas Alley   **27 August 1985**

Auburn University, AL

In response to Alley's having sent Frye an account of the first of three summer institutes in literary criticism he had organized under a grant from the National Endowment for the Humanities. Alley's letter is not extant, but the Frye correspondence files do contain an earlier letter (3 February 1984) from Alley in which he outlines his plans for the institutes and invites Frye to participate in the first one.

Dear Professor Alley:

Thank you for your letter. It seems to me that an Institute in English Literature which tries to bring together the practical teaching process and critical theory is not merely useful but quite indispensable. Teachers in English who are not acquainted with the main structures of contemporary theory are rather like the old-fashioned bush pilots who used to "fly by the seat of their pants." The whole subject is far too technical and far too well organized to be approached any longer by purely subjective or intuitive means.

It is true that the various "schools" of criticism are not really separate from one another, and not many critics would appreciate being locked up within the category of a single school. I, for example, would adopt any critical method that I thought was valid or useful. Still, such a division as the one you suggest is probably essential for giving student teachers a map of the territory. The experience I have had myself in trying to expound my critical theories to secondary school teachers has convinced me that teachers are hungry for this kind of material and very grateful for it. I should recommend the funding of your Institute without reservation.

Prashant Kumar Misra   **27 August 1985**

Ranighat, Patna (Bihar), India

In reply to Misra's letter of 12 August 1985, asking Frye a series of questions about E.M. Forster.

Dear Mr. Misra,

I am sorry but I find your questions are difficult to deal with as the assumptions in them are somewhat elusive and many of them would require very extended treatment to answer seriously. F.R. Leavis for example, would have to speak for himself about his views on Forster. I suggest that if it is available in your library you might consult E.K. Brown,

Rhythm in the Novel, published by the University of Toronto Press. It picks up and develops Forster's views on rhythm, and the last chapter deals with *A Passage to India*.

Robin Harris   12 September 1985
Faculty of Education, University of Toronto
In reply to Harris's letter of 7 September 1985, inquiring about the details of Frances Smith's appointment at Victoria and her subsequent career. The question was in connection with Harris's research for his English Studies at Toronto: A History *(Toronto: Governing Council, University of Toronto, 1988), to which Frye wrote the foreword.*

Dear Robin,

I think that your Frances Smith was actually a Florence Smith. She came on the staff to teach courses in the Renaissance that were supposed to be taught by C.E. Auger,[693] who was registrar but was ill a great part of the time. I was under the impression that she had her Ph.D., and this would be somewhere between 1930 and 1932. I don't think she was ever a full time appointment, but picked up the notion somehow that she felt she had been led on by false promises. Some time later, when I was a graduate student, Knox[694] told me that she had applied for a specialist certificate for high school teaching.

It is possible that we are talking about two different people, but I don't remember any Frances Smith. Florence Smith, as I remember her, was conscientious, nervous, irritable, and pedantic.

Peter Hughes   12 September 1985
Universität Zürich, Zürich, Switzerland
In reply to Hughes's letter (20 June 1985), saying that that the paper he read for Frye at the International Symposium on Vico and Joyce in Venice was "a great success" and "a delight to read." The paper was "Vico, Bruno, and the Wake," later published as "Cycle and Apocalypse in Finnegans Wake," *in* Vico and Joyce, *ed. Donald Phillip Verene (Albany: State University Press of New York, 1987), 3–19, and reprinted in* MM, *356–74. Hughes had taught English and comparative literature at the University of Toronto before going to Zürich.*

Dear Peter,

Sorry to have left your letter and article[695] for so long: I spent the summer writing a book I didn't want to write,[696] and that's always exhausting. It was a most generous act of friendship on your part to read my paper in Venice, and I am deeply grateful.

Your Joyce paper is very interesting and exciting, and your conception of "implosion" interests me a great deal. One reason for the interest is my preoccupation with the Bible, which seems to me to throw out the centripetal fallacy along with the centrifugal one. Your suggestions about the influence of Quinet and Michelet on Joyce are quite fascinating. Michelet seems to me to follow the typical Romantic movement from political to internalized revolution, somewhat as Joyce moves from intense realism to anti-realism.

I am not sure that Joyce actually does use the term "psychopomp," but the idea is in his conversations with Georges Borach.[697] An English translation of these conversations appeared in, of all places, *College English* about thirty years ago.[698]

Very best wishes to you both, and with renewed thanks.

Lionel Pilkington   23 September 1985
Massey College, University of Toronto
In response to Pilkington's request (15 September 1985) for Frye to help formulate a short

statement for the student newspaper in support of nuclear disarmament and an October demonstration for ending the arms race.

Dear Mr. Pilkington:

Thank you for your letter. I wish very much that I could help by formulating a statement for your advertisement, but the trouble is that I do not know enough specific details to do so, although I do support the general policy. Sorry not to be more cooperative.

David Cook   17 October 1985

This is a response to Cook's having sent Frye a copy of his book, Northrop Frye: A Vision of the New World *(New York: St. Martin's, 1985), accompanied by a letter (7 October 1985). At the time, Cook was a vice-provost at the University of Toronto. He later served as principal of Victoria College.*

Dear David Cook,

Thank you very much for the book on me, which I have read with far more pleasure than I normally read discussions of myself. It takes its own line: it avoids the ready-made agreements and disagreements that I find so wearying, and it extracts an aspect of me which I certainly am as committed to as any other. Thank you very much for it and for the very hard work that must have gone into it. I particularly like the association with other people, especially Canadians, so that I am not treated in isolation.

Incidentally, I was most interested in your reference to Josef Pieper's book on leisure and culture. Thirty years ago an American journal sent me that book to review and I did review it, but then they decided that it wasn't the kind of book they wanted discussed in their columns.[699] But his translation of *scholasate* as "have leisure" always stuck in my mind. It made its way into a speech I gave at Claude Bissell's inaugural, also in the fifties.[700]

Jaroslav Pelikan   29 October 1985
Hamden, CT

Dear Professor Pelikan:

I am delighted to have *Jesus Through the Centuries*,[701] and am reading it with the greatest interest. You bring out some things I am aware of but don't often see so lucidly expressed: the way that every age creates its own Jesus and feels utterly certain that they've got at last the right one. It is because of these ideological costumings that one has to keep going back to the total body of what I call the *mythos* or story.

Imre Salusinszky   8 November 1985
New Haven, CT

In response to questions Salusinszky posed (1 November 1985) about his interview with Frye on 16 September 1985: Is criticism a mediator between society and the arts? Have Stevens's long poems, written late in his career, had "any additional resonance for you as you have entered that period of your own life?"

Dear Imre Salusinszky,

Thanks very much for the transcript of the interview,[702] which makes considerably more sense than I thought it was going to. I have made a few corrections in the interests of easier reading and avoiding repetition: they don't affect the sense.

On page 5 I think I'd say: yes, criticism has to be a mediator between literature and society, because its essential job is to examine first the literary and then the social context of whatever it's studying. But, as I keep saying, the mediation has to take account of the difference between the ideological and the mythological. For one thing, that's the only way to account for the fact that so many great writers have been ideological fatheads: Yeats, Pound, Lawrence — you name them.

On page 10 I'd say: yes, the conception of the "supreme fiction" in Stevens has acquired a good deal of resonance for me, though I get this resonance less from the long meditative poems than from shorter ones: Prologues to what is Possible, Forms of the Rock in a Night Hymn, the paramour soliloquy, the last poem, the Palm at the End of the Mind.

Claude de Mestral   6 December 1985

Montreal, QC

Mestral was a minister of the United Church of Canada, interested in missionary activities.

Dear Claude:

I was very sorry to have missed you on your last visit, but influenza at this time of year seems to strike without warning — at any rate it does me. And thanks very much for the Chouraqui translation of the New Testament, which I have been reading with great interest. I like its anti–Hellenizing tendency very much, as well as the reminders that everything in the New Testament grows out of the Old. I have been telling this to my students for forty years, but every generation seems to have to hear it again.

With my very best wishes. Please let my secretary know if you would like the book back.

Robin Harris   12 December 1985

Faculty of Education, University of Toronto

In response to Harris's query (undated letter) about the supervisor of Sister Mary Jerome's Ph.D. thesis on Sir John Davies. The question was in connection with Harris's research for his English Studies at Toronto: A History (Toronto: Governing Council, University of Toronto, 1988), to which Frye wrote the foreword. Sister Mary Jerome (Anna T. McHale) completed her Ph.D. in 1943, having written a thesis on Sir John Davies, after which she taught at Carlow College.

Dear Robin,

In those days a considerable latitude prevailed in consulting any member of one's Ph.D. committee. But Sister Jerome's real supervisor was Endicott. She phoned him around midnight on Christmas Eve to discuss her thesis with him at a time when he was decorating the tree and tying up presents for his two children (Elizabeth and Claire) who at that time were just baby things. The incident was typical of her exquisite tact. She was another of those Catholics I told you about: had read nothing except an introduction to St. Thomas, and then looked around for some figure in English literature to stick it on to. The reason why her examination in October 1942 was decreed possible was that we knew that she would simply sit there until the building fell down or she got her degree.

Crawford Kilian   18 December 1985

North Vancouver, BC

Kilian was a novelist, college professor, and public education columnist for the Vancouver Province. *He had sent Frye a copy of his book* School Wars: The Assault on B.C. Education *(New Star Books, 1985).*

Dear Mr. Kilian,

Thank you very much for your book on British Columbia education. I didn't expect that things would be much better than that, but even so it's depressing to see how bad they are. As I am quite fond of the man who has just taken up the Presidency of UBC,[703] I hope that university education at least may be capable of some improvement.

John Beckwith   23 January 1986

In reply to John Beckwith, Faculty of Music, University of Toronto, who had sent Frye a brochure on hymnody and who reported that he had included in his anthology a tune entitled "Moncton" by George Ross, Frye's music teacher during his early years.

Dear John,

Thank you for the brochure about the conference on Canadian hymnody. I am delighted that you included the "Moncton" tune. I wish some student would dig out his doctoral exercise which he submitted to the Faculty of Music some time around 1931. Unfortunately it was based on a text by Mrs. Hemans, but the fugue at the end was very interesting to me. I just saw the score: I have never heard it performed, nor did he.

Michael Smith   28 January 1986

Michael Smith, editor of Books in Canada, *had written Frye on 24 January 1986, asking it he might write a couple of sentences endorsing the review.*

Dear Mr. Smith,

It seems to me that *Books in Canada* does a heroic job of trying to keep up with its subject on all fronts, and anyone who cares about the fate of books in the country should care about the fate of the magazine. There is far too little of such resources available to anyone interested, and we cannot afford to lose or weaken what we have.

Helen Stewart   30 January 1986
St. Catharines, ON

Dear Ms. Stewart,

Thank you for the copy of your dissertation.[704] I read it with great interest, as I was never quite sure just what my relation to Diltz was. A large part of his energy was expended in getting university graduates down to size, and there were not many students who seemed to be equally fond of both of us. He was a strong Barthian in religion and I was interested and gratified by how sympathetic and understanding he was when I gave a paper to a small religious group about literature as an analogy of religion.

I have often said that I would have no confidence in my own views if I didn't believe that could be adapted to high school, or even elementary school teaching. But I have certainly been aware of the educational chaos that prevents teachers from making use of the teaching aids that are available to them. At all events, I am most impressed by your discussion, and grateful for your interest in my work.

John Ayre   18 February 1986
Guelph, ON

Ayre, Frye's biographer, had given a talk on his research at Brock University.

Dear John,

Your paper at the Brock conference gave me some indication of the amount and quality of research you have been doing. I had no idea that mother had summarized that pre-posterous essay of mine in her letters to Donald.[705] Nor did I know that you had actually made a pilgrimage to Stone Pile.[706] All of which makes me all the more eager to see the book.

All the best to all of you. A note to Evelyn[707] is enclosed.

Erika von Contra Bruce   24 February 1986
Social Science and Humanities Research Council, Ottawa, ON

Dear Dr. Contra Bruce,

I have received a copy of the Site Visit Committee's report on the project of The Collected Works of Erasmus. I have read both the report and the reaction of the Committee to it, and it is difficult for me not to feel that the Site Visit Committee approached this report with its mind already made up.

The size of the budget cut recommended seems to me a response to panic, much on the level of the column by Douglas Fisher in the *Sun* recommending that we "give Erasmus back to the Dutch." The Erasmus project, which has been going on for nearly twenty years, has attracted the respect and attention of the whole scholarly world, and has done a great deal to establish Toronto as one of the outstanding centres of humanist scholarship. If the S.V.C.'s report is accepted and implemented, it will be an act of the greatest irresponsibility on the part of the SSHRCC. The amount of money available depends on a sense of priorities, and the priorities as suggested cutting the Erasmus budget by 30% are as wrong as they can possibly be. Academic life in Canada has enough problems without being made to look ridiculous throughout the world as well.

Dennis Reid   25 March 1986
Art Gallery of Ontario, , Toronto, ON

Dear Dennis Reid,

Thank you very much for the book on Lawren Harris.[708] You were very kind about my 1948 article,[709] and I appreciate the reference very much. When Pete Colgrove and Bess [Harris] put that Macmillan book together,[710] they wanted me to stress his theosophical "thought" mainly, and as I didn't have the opinion of Harris as a thinker that I have of him as a painter the result was appropriately vague. But the book is, like the Lismer book,[711] a very useful and concise study.

Tong-choon Shin   25 April 1986
College of Humanities, Hanyang University, Sungdong, Korea

In reply to Shin's inquiry (29 March 1986) about Frye's knowledge of Indian philosophy and Buddhism. He also seeks advice on his research into Yeats and Buddhism.

Dear Mr. Shin,

Thank you very much for your letter: I greatly appreciated your writing to me and expressing your interest in my work. I have read a certain amount about Zen Buddhism, mostly Suzuki, and have read both the Lankavatara and the Avatamsaka Sutras. I know less about Hinduism, though I have struggled with the Vedic hymns and some of the Upanishads.

I should have thought that Yeats was more interested in Hinduism than in Buddhist sources, apart from his very obvious interest in Japanese drama. Eliot, on the other hand, seems to have been equally interested in both Hindu and Buddhist writings.

Robert Denham   **23 May 1986**
Department of English, Emory & Henry College, Emory, VA
In response to Denham's proposal to edit a collection of interviews with Frye. The collection was published as A World in a Grain of Sand: Twenty-Two Interviews with Northrop Frye *(New York: Peter Lang, 1991).*

Dear Bob,

Thank you very much for the collection of interviews, which I have gone through. I think they should make a presentable enough book, though there is naturally some repetition, and when the transcriber isn't you they sometimes make curious mistakes. Otherwise, there seems to be a good deal of variety of subject matter. I have not done any editing of the programs, as it seems to me that you are an eminently trustworthy editor in such matters. Sometimes there is no way to overcome the woolgathering interviewer's musings.

There are two other interviews you might be interested in: an early one with Roby Kidd for the CBC, which is in your bibliography (G6), and a recent one with Imre Salusinszky, which was in a series including Derrida, Bloom and Hartman. There was also the television interview done by the National Film Board and shown at the MLA in Washington.[712]

I'd be glad to write an introductory statement, perhaps with a brief comment on the interview as a contemporary literary genre.

I am delighted that the ADE job is coming in your direction[713]: that seems to me a very interesting and exciting job.

All the best from all of us here.

Irving Feldman   **10 June 1986**
Department of English, State University of New York, Buffalo, NY

Dear Irving Feldman,

I don't know whether it was you or your publisher that sent me the copy of *All of Us Here*,[714] but in either case I am delighted to have it. It's a very fine book. I have been following your work from quite early times, and continuing to get a bigger kick out of each book as it comes. Also, it's clear that you are still in mid-career, as there's no sign of self-repetition.

Alan Bishop   **18 August 1986**
Hamilton, ON
In response to several queries by Bishop, who was writing the authorized biography of Joyce Cary. *Bishop wrote on 10 June 1986, wanting to know the circumstances surrounding the copy of* Fearful Symmetry *in Cary's library, inscribed "With the compliments of the author, Northrop Frye," as well as any reminiscences or anecdotes he could provide about Cary.*

Dear Mr. Bishop,

I am sorry to have to return so blank and negative an answer to your enquiry about Joyce Cary. But I really have no recollection of having sent him my Blake book, nor do I recall any answer from him. I met him only once, in Oxford, where he was the guest of my old teacher Herbert Davis. He impressed me at the time as quite a lonely man, but unfortunately I cannot recall the details of the conversation with him. Naturally I was aware of his use of Blake in *The Horse's Mouth,* and I have read the trilogy that it belongs to. The rest of his work I know little about apart from what I have read in Hazard Adams.[715]

Again, I am very sorry to have to make so unrewarding a response.

Christopher C. Curtis   **19 August 1986**
Sullivan and Worcester, Boston, MA

In response to an attorney who was handling the estate of Kathryn Gabriella. Gabriella, who had written to Frye frequently from 1970 to 1978 (more than twenty letters survive), had, at her death, left her library to Frye.

Dear Mr. Curtis,

Thank you for your letter: I knew that Kathryn [Gabriella] had been ill for some time, but I was unable to answer her last communication to me, as I could not find an address for her, nor could the church she worked for supply one.

I am sorry to have delayed the response to this letter but I have been in Australia since June. It was very good of Kathryn to think of me in connection with her books, but the trouble is that I have reached an age level beyond what would make them of any use to me now, and I therefore feel that I ought in all conscience to decline the bequest. If you are able to make a charitable disposition of them, I should be greatly obliged, for the sake of Kathryn's memory, and also because it would undoubtedly serve a more useful purpose.

John Perry   **19 August 1986**
Seminole Road, Middlefield, CT

In response to Perry's letter of 5 August 1986, asking Frye's opinion of Van Wyck Brooks as a literary critic and whether or not Brooks's criticism might be considered on its artistic merits.

Dear Mr. Perry,

Thank you for your letter. It is a long time since I read Van Wyck Brooks, but I remember being greatly stimulated by his powers of synthesis and his sense of perspective. I heard various people disparage him, including Perry Miller, on the ground that he worked entirely with secondary sources. But a great deal of essential criticism does, and I feel that he had great strengths in narrative construction, wherever his research activities stopped. In short, I think your instinct is very sound in regarding his work as a type of creative criticism very close in this genre to the literature he worked with.

Fr. Walter J. Ong   **10 September 1986**
Jesuit Hall, Saint Louis University, Saint Louis, MO

Father Ong had written Frye (9 August 1986) about his enthusiasm for Walter Kasper's Jesus the Christ *(1974; trans. 1976), which he had used as "food for prayer" at his annual Jesuit retreat.*

Dear Walter,

Thank you very much for your letter: as soon as I got it I moved the Kasper book from the to-be-read-some-time category and read it. It is a wonderful book, very judicious in its assessment of contemporary scholarship, and it hits a bull's eye on practically every page. It was also a very consoling book, because it has been a rather distressing time for me.

I took a trip to Australia this summer, to speak at universities there, and took Helen along with me, as I have invariably done for some time. (She had an Alzheimer condition, not bad enough to cripple her socially, but she could not be left by herself.) In the final week of the visit she was hit by a lung embolism and died after ten days in the hospital.

I have greatly enjoyed reading the Hopkins book,[716] and will be sending a note about that soon as well.

Frank Ellis   **10 October 1986**

Department of English, Smith College, Northampton, MA

In reply to Ellis's having sent Frye a copy of his paper, "Northrop Frye's Theory of Comedy," presented at the annual meeting of the Northeast American Society for Eighteenth Century Studies, Philadelphia.

Dear Frank Ellis,

Thank you very much for your article on my theory of comedy, which is delightfully written and would be a great pleasure to read whatever its subject. The essay has the rare quality of conveying an enjoyment of the thing it talks about, namely comedy. Volpone always seemed to me the opposite of an *alazon* at the beginning of the play: he knows just what he is doing and why he is doing it. At that particular point towards the end that I mentioned he turns obsessive, and loses all the advantages of his self-knowledge. That makes him a kind of parody of a tragic hero, like Falstaff in a very different way.

I don't know if you know yet that Helen died on the return trip from Australia. She constantly spoke of our visit with you, and of Connie's kindness in giving her the ironstone piece. She constantly spoke of her intention to write her and thank you properly for it, but, as you may perhaps have noted, she already had an Alzheimer condition and that greatly weakened her will power. But the visit was one of the happiest of her recent memories.[717]

Mervin Nicholson   **10 October 1986**

Department of English, University of British Columbia, Vancouver

Dear Mervin,

By now you know what has delayed my response to your fascinating letter and poems. I like the poems very much: they are genuine incantations, not rhetorical exercises talking about being incantations. I like the first one in particular and the way it expresses one aspect of what you mean by "time-crystals."

I am naturally very pleased my work continues to be of use to you. I think myself that I have insisted on some overlooked aspects of the imagination, and visualizing would naturally be one with such a subject as Blake. It is obvious that you have a productive and distinguished career ahead of you.

Dennis Duffy   **16 October 1986**

Innis College, University of Toronto

In response to Duffy's thanking Frye for granting him an interview and asking about his connections with Harold Innis (10 October 1986). Duffy was at the time professor of English, Innis College, University of Toronto.

Dear Dennis,

Thanks very much for your note. I never had much contact with Innis while he was here, but got involved with his posthumous notes after the CRTC [Canadian Radio-Television Commission] decided to try to edit and publish them. I took a fairly active role with the editing of these notes, and wrote a preface to the proposed volume. This was turned down by the University of Toronto Press, and still is not published. But I am sending you a copy of my preface, which represents the only tangible link I have.[718]

Ian Balfour   **21 October 1986**

Princeton University, Princeton, NJ

Written in reply of Balfour's letter of 15 October 1986. Balfour enclosed a biographical

sketch, asking for confirmation of certain biographical details for the book on Frye he was writing for the Twayne series and for answers to several other queries.

Dear Ian Balfour,

Thank you for your letter. Naturally I am very interested in the Twayne book. After my ordination I went up to Merton College in Oxford in the fall of 1936, to read the undergraduate school in English. After three years of theology I had got a bit rusty in English, which I now realized that I wanted to teach. I returned to Victoria College for the year 1937/8, to fill in a space suddenly vacant there, and returned to Oxford for the year 1938/9. I am not certain about the date of my M.A., but it was some time around 1940.[719] I was writing the first drafts of my book on Blake while I was there, but on my own time, so to speak. I did not do a thesis on Burton or anyone else. At that time Toronto was still sufficiently anglophile not to require a Ph.D., and Oxford wasn't really equipped to teach anything except the undergraduate school. So, like Kathleen Coburn, Woodhouse, and Brett, I have only an M.A. from Oxford as an earned degree.

I suppose it could be added to my biography that I became President of the M.L.A. [Modern Language Association] in 1976, and that my wife died in August of 1986. The Shakespeare book is out now, and is distributed in the United States by Yale University Press. Its correct title is *Northrop Frye on Shakespeare*, as it is only a collection of undergraduate lecture notes, but Yale may have altered the title.

The very best to Deborah and yourself.

Xiong Hui-bing   11 November 1986
Foreign Language Department, Hubei University, China.

In reply to Hui-bing's letter of 11 September 1986, outlining his interest in Frye's work and wondering about his thesis in The Educated Imagination *that literature is made out of other literature.*

Dear Xiong Hui-bing,

Thank you very much for your letter. *The Educated Imagination* was a series of radio talks designed to try to explain the importance of literature, and of humanistic studies generally, to an audience without any special knowledge of them. It has done quite well in this country, and has been prescribed in many places as a high school textbook. But of course it was never designed to be a complete manual of critical procedure.

You ask about my conception of literature as being established out of earlier works of literature. The basis of my view resides in the question: if two people have had much the same kind of experience, why is it that one may become a novelist and another may have no interest in fiction? The difference between them comes from the fact that one has an interest in literature, and in how stories begin and develop and end. North America is full of bad novels by people who think they had the right kind of experience for a novel but had no interest in story-telling. That is, the writer's experience affects at most only his content: his form, where his technical skill resides, comes from his knowledge of literature and of how such things are handled in literature.

With all best wishes, and much appreciation for your interest in my work.

Hugh Maclean   15 December 1986
Delmar, NY

In response to Maclean's request to quote Frye's remark about an earlier paper on T.E. Lawrence, about which Frye wrote that "Lawrence's is essentially the Hamlet combination, surely: heroism, largely a matter, for leaders, of catching the rhythm of fortune, buggered up by a clairvoyant irony that can't make the uncritical surrender to that rhythm." Maclean says that he will delete "buggered up."

Dear Hugh,

Very nice to hear from you again. You are quite free to make whatever use you like of the remark about T.E. Lawrence, whether expurgated or not. I suppose convention requires Sunday clothes in all such quasi-academic quotations. Love to Janet and yourself as always.

William Taylor   **16 December 1986**
Social Sciences and Humanities Research Council of Canada, Ottawa, ON

Dear Dr. Taylor,

I am writing to you in connexion with the REED project, which for some years has been gathering together the records of early English drama.[720] It seems to me that the support of these very central humanistic projects should not depend on the whim, or, more politely, the judgment of the Committee of Award. Anyone who knows anything about the field knows that this is an invaluable project, and it was given very high praise by the assessors' reports. It greatly weakens the confidence of scholars and academics to have such uncertain support and mistaken guidance, and I can only urge that this matter should be looked into and rectified as soon as possible. I understand that the scholars on the project cannot appeal the decision, but it still remains true that your decision is simply wrong, and disastrous for the future of scholarship in this field in Canada.

Maurice Podbrey   **16 January 1987**
Montreal, QC

In response to Podbrey's inquiry (9 January 1986) about recommendations for texts that could be dramatized — texts that should be heard rather than read and studied. Podbrey was artistic director of the Centaur Theatre Company in Montreal.

Dear Mr. Podbrey,

Thank you for your very interesting letter. You have already shown so much originality and initiative in what you have done that I hardly know what to add. The Book of Job is an obvious choice, although you have undoubtedly already considered it, and if you could dramatize a Platonic dialogue, there are certainly others that lend themselves to dramatization such as the *Phaedo*. And actually the plays themselves could be read through, as they often are in such groups. One would need a play like *Prometheus Bound*, which is not as often acted as, say *The Trojan Women*, or *Philoctetes*. I should think that Boethius' *Consolation of Philosophy* would have some very good material, though it would require a skillful editing job.

You mention *Paradise Lost*: the students here got their English Department to read the whole twelve books of it, and the attendance kept up for the twelve weeks. They got me to read the first book, because they said I was the only one who sounded like the Devil.

Graham Forst   **21 January 1987**
Capilano College, North Vancouver, BC

In response to Forst's account (7 January 1987) of seeing a performance of Wagner's Ring *and his comment that the whole production was an exercise in displacement. Forst also offers to get Frye tickets for a 1988 Toronto performance of* Don Giovanni, *in which his wife would be playing Donna Elvira.*

Dear Graham,

Thank you very much for your letter: the history of what has been done to Wagner's *Ring* over the years would be quite a horrendous document. However, this sounds more imaginative than most. Your account of it reminded me a bit of that earlier play of Ibsen's which is a spoof on Viking mythology. Not really a spoof; just another case of displacement.

It is very kind and thoughtful of you to ask about tickets for *Don Giovanni* in the fall. I think I should like very much to have tickets if it is not inconvenient. I am all alone these days, but could still find a friend to go with me.

Walter Miale   11 February 1987
Philipsburg, QC

In response to Miale's letter of 17 January 1987, wondering if it would be possible to meet Frye if he ever came to Quebec and wanting to ask him about his experience in "dialoguing with evangelicals and fundamentalists." He enclosed an article he had written on Shakespeare.

Thank you for your letter and for the take-off of the alleged Shakespeare discovery. You live in the town that my father and mother married in in 1896. I don't get away from Toronto a great deal now as I am still teaching one course.

In regard to your question about "dialoguing" with fundamentalists, I can only say that I avoid them as much as possible. The conception of dialogue is unknown to them for the most part.

Mervin Nicholson   11 February 1987
Department of English, University of British Columbia, Vancouver, BC

In reply to Nicholson's inquiry as to whether Frye had ever contemplated writing a book of pensées.

Dear Mervin,

Thank you very much for your letter. I was very pleased to get the news from you, and I find the poems genuinely impressive.

I have always wanted to write the kind of book you mention, but some spiritual octopus seems to lie in wait every time and assimilates all my notes into some big structure. I am constantly writing notes in aphoristic form, and most of the labour in writing my books consists in giving them continuity. A book of reflections where I didn't need to worry too much about sequence or larger structure would attract me a great deal, but I don't think I can do it until at least the book I am struggling with now relaxes its grip.

Robert Denham   6 March 1987
Modern Language Association, New York, NY

In response to Denham's proposal to organize two sessions devoted to Frye's work at the annual convention of the Modern Language Association in San Francisco. Hazard Adams, David Staines, and Imre Salusinszky were asked to speak on the contexts of Frye's criticism, and Hayden White, Paul Hernadi, and Patricia Parker were asked to reflect on Anatomy of Criticism *thirty years after. These papers, along with essays by Denham and Thomas Willard and a talk by Frye himself, were published as* Visionary Poetics: Essays on Northrop Frye's Criticism *(New York: Peter Lang, 1991).*

Dear Bob,

Thank you very much for your letter. As Jane [Widdicombe] has told you, I will start to make plans for attending the M.L.A. at the end of the year. It is true that years ending in 7 seem to have some important for me: my marriage was in 1937 and 67 was the Canadian Centenary, for which I wrote *The Modern Century*. The people you have sent letters to are all admirable, and I hope that by that time the conception of the present book[721] will be clear enough in my mind for me to give some kind of coherent account of it. I hope very much that your other projects, the bibliography revision[722] and the interview book,[723] will go off without & hitch. As I remember from Elizabeth Cowan and others, your present job[724] is an extremely demanding and responsible one, and I certainly wish you all the best success.

Dorothy Bishop   10 March 1987
Ottawa, ON
In reply to Bishop's having enclosed with her letter of 28 February 1987 a copy of a review of Northrop Frye on Shakespeare *by Charles Haines, "Shakespeare Was a Hippy: The Bard's Motto Could Have Been 'Make Love, Not War.'" Ottawa Citizen 23 April 1997: A15. Haines had adopted the pose of a teacher marking a student's essay, and he had give Frye a B+ for his effort. Bishop, who graduated from Victoria College in 1932, had been a friend of Frye's since their student days.*

Dear Dorothy,

Thank you for your letter and the review. Naturally I wouldn't have any more confidence in his marks than I would have in my own. In fifty years of marking essays I doubt if I have ever given a mark that I felt completely confident about, and the whole operation of transforming literary compositions into marks strikes me as absurd. I suppose this was really his point.

Love as always.

Greg Gatenby   10 March 1987
Harbourfront Reading Series, Toronto, ON
In reply to Gatenby question about Frye's encounter with Wallace Stevens.

Dear Greg,

The story as I remember it is roughly this: the English Institute in those days met at Columbia University at the end of August. I think the year was 1943. Wallace Stevens was an evening speaker, on one hell of a hot night with all the windows open (no air conditioning in Columbia). He mumbled his paper (it was reprinted in *The Necessary Angel*)[725] while the Amsterdam Avenue traffic kept roaring up and down outside. At the reception afterwards, I was brought up to meet him and racked my brains for something to say about a paper of which I had not heard one complete sentence. He saw something of my difficulty, and attempted to put me at my ease, on hearing that I was from Toronto, on whether I knew various insurance people and stockbrokers whom he had met in Toronto the last time he was there, which was in 1908. This is what I remember of what happened, though with the noise and embarrassment and heat I may easily have got some of the details wrong.[726]

Olive Macklin   10 March 1987
Toronto, ON
In response to a neighbor's request that the noise from Frye's heat pump was disturbing her sleep.

Dear Miss Macklin,

I am very sorry that you have been exposed to noise at night. Aside from turning the furnace down when I go to bed, I don't know what I can do to help. I don't have a heat pump, only a gas furnace, which is practically inaudible to me. I have discussed the matter with the man who installed the furnace and looks after it each year, and he tells me that he thinks what is bothering you is another neighbour with an energy efficient furnace, several feet above the ground, which does make a noise when the heat goes on. I am turning down the heat as far as is practical without the danger of bursting pipes, but I doubt very much that you will notice any difference.

Hazel Merrett   8 April 1987
Senneville, QC

Merrett was Frye's first cousin. See headnote to letter of 21 August 1978. In response to Merrett's having written (31 March 1986) to say that she was enjoying reading his book on Shakespeare and that she had heard his interview with Peter Gzowski.

Dear Hazel:

How very nice to hear from you. I'm glad you like the Shakespeare book. The design was the idea of the editor at Fitzhenry and Whiteside, Helen Heller. She comes from England, and we've become good friends: I'm spending Passover/Easter with her and her husband. I didn't like the Gzowski interview either[727]: that "intimidating" line drives me up the wall, and I simply can't deal with it. Why anyone in his position should need to resort to it I don't know.[728]

I was amused at your reference to your father's full and earnest explanations, because it reminded me so much of mother—clearly it's a Howard characteristic.[729] Her scope wouldn't have been as extensive, but what she did know she was certainly ready to communicate. It would be well worthwhile to put together some of the memorabilia of the family, and you're in the right place to do it. I hope the sheet of vital statistics enclosed will help, and that the memoir I wrote of Helen (read at her memorial service here)[730] will be of interest.

I'm gradually settling into a more routine frame of mind: the shadow never goes away, but it moves out of the direct line of vision in time. I thought I was all set when a cheerful Newfoundland woman came in as part-time housekeeper, but she's been knocked out by a hysterectomy. I now have a pretty and charming black girl who wants to be an actress. Of course it's a big help having some sort of function still at the College—I'm Chancellor for another three years, and will be teaching one course again next year. Our new president comes from McGill—Eva Kushner, in the comparative literature department.

I've had occasional impulses to novel-writing at various times, but one has to keep in practice for such things, and if I chose a contemporary subject there'd be a generation gap.[731] However, once the book I'm working on now is out of the way I don't know what will turn up next: it could fiction, or autobiography.

At the end of May I'll be going to Rome for a three-day conference on me,[732] and later to Oxford for an honorary degree there.[733] The Department of External Affairs wants me to take in Scandinavia and the Soviet Union as well, but if they want a cultural ambassador on that scale and of my age, they should give more notice.

James Reaney   16 April 1987
London, ON

Reaney, a former student of Frye's and longtime friend, had recently been hospitalized for depression.

Dear Jamie,

I am very sorry to hear of the setback to your health, and of course your friends are very concerned to learn that emotional depression is part of it. The achievement of your life is unique in Canada, in poetry, drama, and criticism, and you have brought a whole new imaginative dimension into Canadian consciousness. Before you, southern Ontario was largely deaf and dumb, and it found its reality through you. But of course it takes a lot of courage to work on the front line all one's life in this way—courage, because you keep forming your own dragon all the time, the sense of the utterly meaningless that's the opposite of what you're creating.

All your friends are deeply concerned about you, anxious to close ranks around you, and yet confident that anyone with so much courage and energy will finally be all right. And some of your friends have gone through the same dark valley, and they know that hell is empty: there's nothing really there except the shadow of what makes you so uniquely Jamie. God bless and keep you, as he will.[734]

Walter Miale   8 May 1987
Philipsburg, QC

Miale replied to Frye's earlier letter (11 February 1987), saying, as regards fundamentalism, that he thought The Great Code *was a "wonderful antidote" to conservative ideology and that he would like to videotape Frye in conversation with a "more thoughtful" Christian conservative, and mentioning several groups and individuals where such views could be found. He also wonders if Frye has heard Van Morrison's musical settings of Blake's poems.*

Dear Mr. Miale,

Thank you for your letter. I was recently in the South, where I caught a few glimpses of the nature of the collision between fundamentalists and more liberal minded people. I got the impression that there is a higher proportion of genuine sincerity among fundamentalists, especially in the pentecostal groups, and not nearly as much malignancy as there used to be. I did hear however of one preacher who was trying to force everyone out of his church who did not publicly proclaim a belief in a literal hell — nothing said about heaven, naturally. But the recent discrediting of television evangelists may get rid of some of the charlatans at least.

Your interests seem to be very wide, and I am afraid I cannot claim much knowledge of the things you refer to, except that I have heard some of Morrison's settings of Blake.[735]

Ryan Stern   8 May 1987
Holyoke, CT

In reply to Stern's undated letter in which he asked Frye whether all Utopian fiction was not satiric and whether there were any significant Utopias written by women. Stern, a high school student, was doing research for his senior writing project.

Dear Mr. Stern,

I don't think that one can assume that all Utopian vision is satiric, except negatively and by implication. That is, a writer may be setting up a social model that he actually believes will work, and is quite serious about it. There would be no satire except in the contrast with the state of affairs around him. At the same time few people would want to live in anyone else's Utopia. Edward Bellamy's *Looking Backward* was a vision of Boston in 2000 published in 1889, and many people hailed it as the book that started them thinking seriously about social problems. On the other hand, many people would regard it as a quite intolerable social vision including William Morris, whose *News from Nowhere* was written as a counterblast to it.

I think there are very few women writers of Utopias because until quite recently women were more preoccupied with the discriminations and unfair treatment of them in existing society. Mary Wollstonecraft's *Rights of Women* would be an example.

Michael Dolzani   **19 May 1987**
Buffalo, NY
    Frye writes his research assistant on advice for a collection of essays, Northrop Frye on Education.

Dear Michael,
    This may distress you, and infuriate Helen Heller.[736] But I've been looking over the essays that are to go into the education book and the book seems to me quite intolerably skimpy, certain to be a comedown after the Shakespeare one. That's my fault for turning over so much of my stuff in that field to Jim Polk, but it's no good regretting that now.[737]
    I wonder whether at least two other papers wouldn't beef it up enough to be at least presentable? One is the "bridge" paper I did for Tuzo Wilson's science conference[738]: I haven't reread that paper, so I don't know if it's presentable or not. The other, the one on Ontario 1784–1984,[739] I do feel more confident about.
    Neither of these papers, I think, would damage the unity of the book as a book about education. On the contrary, they'd extend its borders to the point of giving a much better idea of the shape of my own interest in the subject. My preface to *Design for Learning*,[740] which is one of the best things I've done in this field, but which of course we can't reprint because of its dependence on the reports, covers education in science as well as the arts. And all my interest and writing on education has been very closely linked to my watching Canadian literature grow, an activity that's gone on for just about the same time, and is the practical application of all the Convocation speeches.
    After that, I'd like to put together a book of twelve essays— this will have to be delayed by the bumbling and often futile efforts to get them published by other people first. The twelve essays will be in three groups of four. The first group will be two Renaissance and two Victorian writers who combined Utopian and educational writing. More's *Utopia*, which I've just written a paper on; Castiglione; the Morris paper, and a paper on Samuel Butler I haven't written yet but feel I have to sooner or later. The second group will be the papers on Ruth, Blake (not the Art Gallery one but this one I'm writing now), Joyce-Vico-Bruno, and Parsifal. The third group will be theoretical essays. Three of them will be the Wiegand lecture, the Smith paper on convention, and the Royal Society paper on symbolism. What the fourth will be, whether one I've written or have still to write, I don't at this stage know.[741]
    But of course this is down the road: I'm anxious to make this education book one that you, Jane, Helen, and I won't be embarrassed about. If it had a bit more spaciousness and didn't look so much like emptying hampers, I could write a preface to it that I really believed in. Do let me know what you think of this.
    P.S. Sorry to bother you, but at my age you get rather worried about getting things put in order.

Michael Dolzani   **8 June 1987**
Buffalo, NY
    In reply to Dolzani's response to the previous letter.

Dear Michael,

Thank you very much for your letter, though there is certainly no occasion for blaming yourself. I'd like Gordon to have "By Liberal Things" and would welcome its publication alone with the sermon.[742] But I have just done what I usually put off doing: I have just reread my introduction to *Design for Learning*.[743] I had assumed that it couldn't stand on its own, but I think I was totally wrong: cut out the parenthetical page references and it will be O.K. I regard that Introduction as the spine so to speak of my work on education outside the university, and anything difficult for the reader to pick up can be explained in the introduction to the book.

So my reservations about the book are considerably less than they were, and, as you say, I am more or less committed to publishing the book anyhow. But unless you're strongly opposed to having this essay in, I think it will make all the difference to it.

Gerald E. and Beth Bentley   6 July 1987
Merton College, Oxford, England.

In response to the Bentleys' having delivered a copy of the Oxford ceremony in which Frye was awarded an honorary degree.

Dear Jerry and Beth,

I cannot tell you how pleased I was to see you in Oxford: it brightened my visit very considerably. Thank you too for your thoughtfulness in leaving the programme.

I was pleased to discover that the D.Litt. gown, which I am buying, is exactly the same as yours. I am particularly pleased about this because it legitimizes the degree, and puts it in the same class as the earned degree. As Shakespeare would say, fine word, legitimate.[744]

Blessings on you both.

Douglas LePan   8 July 1987
Massey College, University of Toronto

In reply to LaPan's congratulating Frye for the honorary degree he had received from Oxford. LePan has studied at Oxford 1935–37, overlapping Frye's first year at Merton College.

Dear Douglas,

Thank you very much for your most kindly and gracious note. I was particularly pleased about the degree from Oxford, as a degree from one's alma mater means more than usual. It was a bright sunny day, even though it rained cats and dogs every other day of the week I was there.

It was very nice to see old friends there, including Toronto friends: Gerry and Beth Bentley were there, and Jay Macpherson has a flat there. But what was particularly pleasant was going back to Merton College. The last time I was there — ten years ago — almost all the Senior Common Room seemed to be in fields like the philosophy of mathematics, and I felt a bit out of it. But now it seems to be a more humanistic college again, and a very warm and friendly place.

Renewed thanks and best wishes.

Donald McGibbon   18 July 1987
Toronto, ON

Dear Don,

Thanks for your note about the Heritage Fund. I am making just a one-shot contribution of $5000 at this time, because, being fairly close to the scene at Victoria, I can do more with occasional contributions to things as they arise. An example was the Erasmus New Testament that you may have heard Germaine Warkentin talking about in her report.[745]

Love to you both as always.

Greg Gatenby 11 August 1987
Harbourfront Corporation, Toronto, ON

In reply to Gatenby's request (19 July 1987) for Frye to verify several stories about Vachel Lindsay told at Pelham Edgar's house.

Dear Greg,

The story about Vachel Lindsay was told by Pelham at one of Ned's dinner parties. It was at a time when I was quite young, and I doubt very much if a single person present at that dinner would be alive now. I do not know of any written source for the story, or any other source whatever. When I edited the very chaotic manuscript of *Across My Path*, there was not a trace of a reference to it in the manuscript. So I am afraid I cannot be of very much help. Pelham was living at 286 St. George Street at the time, but the place where I heard it was certainly Ned's: I think the Courtleigh Boulevard house. Thanks very much for the xeroxes of the Lindsay visit: there would certainly be very little attention paid to such a visit now.

F.E.L. Priestley 12 August 1987
Richmond Hill, ON

Dear FELP,

Thanks very much for the xeroxes on John Robins, which I was delighted to receive. Your account of the Beowulf lecture reminded me of the time when Peter Fisher[746] and George Johnston were taking a mandatory Anglo-Saxon course from him. His classroom was next door to my office, and they used to drop in at the beginning to complain about having to take this mandatory course. Very shortly after they had taken it Peter was publishing articles on Beowulf and George had definitely gone into Old Norse as his chosen field.

Looking forward to seeing you both soon. I understand that Phyllis will be picking me up.

Ronald Bates 15 September 1987
London, ON

In reply to Bate's letter congratulating him for receiving the Governor General's Award for Northrop Frye on Shakespeare.

Dear Ronald,

Thank you very much for your letter. It was a strange occasion, and speaking very selfishly I was quite glad to be forced to be absent.[747] I got a very friendly letter from the man who got the award in the year that *The Great Code* was shortlisted.[748] He had a little case of guilt feelings.

The proceedings in Rome are supposed to be published, and in English.[749] There were about thirty papers, roughly twenty of them in Italian. My listening powers in Italian go up as far as andante, but not as far as the allegro which was the more normal speed.

Much love to you both.

Arthur Gelber   9 October 1987
Toronto, ON

In response to Gelber's proposal to organize a conference on Technology and the Humanities. Frye, Gelber, and five others (Norman Best, Mavor Moore, Jim Peterson, Calvin Gotlieb, and Douglas Wright) had met on 12 September 1987 to discuss the possibilities for such a conference. Gelber was a philanthropist and well-known patron of the arts. At the moment he was serving as the chair of the Ontario Bicentennial Advisory Commission.

Dear Arthur,

Thank you for a most pleasant afternoon. The subject I have been hammering at for the last thirty years is the contrast in direction between political and economic movements, which tend to centralize, and cultural movements which decentralize. Economically, Canada is appended to the United States: culturally, it is a lively and distinctive community in its own right. As soon as one has said that, it of course begins to look simplistic. A great deal of culture, including the mass media and the whole marketing operation, follows economic movements; many political and economic movements also tend to decentralize, even if they don't go all the way into separatism.

It seems to me that this is the central theme for the kind of programme you have in mind. Meech Lake[750] and the free trade deal will perhaps not be front page news for very long, but something else that raises the same kind of questions will be.

Herbert Lindenberger   9 October 1987
Stanford, CA

In reply to Lindenberger's letter of 26 September 1987 in which he expresses his sadness about Helen Frye's death.

Dear Herbert,

Thank you very much for your most kind letter. Helen and I were very close, and the loss is still very keen, but the support of one's friends does all that can be done.

Naturally I remember the seminar very vividly, and your presence in it.[751] It was as pleasant a teaching assignment as I ever remember having done.

John Hartman   13 October 1987
Penetanguishene, ON

In reply to letter from Hartman (2 September 1987) in which he pointed out similarities between the biblical Job and the native American story of Job Bearskin and the loss of his land to the James Bay Power Project. Hartman also thanked Frye for "providing an understanding of the cultural traditions within which I am working."

Dear Mr. Hartman,

Thank you very much for your letter. I would certainly agree that there could be remarkable imaginative and mythical parallels between the story of Job and the stories of people in native North American cultures. I quite understand the difficulty about doing imaginative work outside the range of fashionable conventions, but that seems to be one of the penalties of getting original ideas, and it was probably something that the original author of the Book of Job had to contend with as well.

With best wishes and thanks for your expression of interest in my own work. Naturally I am delighted if it has been of any help to you.

Joanne Bright Autrey   **24 February 1988**
Shreveport, Louisiana

Autrey had written Frye on 6 February 1988, saying that when her parents were renting the Fryes' home in 1950-51, she took a small, "delicately designed pin with oriental characters on it" from among items stored upstairs in the home. Thirty-eight years later she discovered the pin during a move, and so she returned the pin with her letter, apologizing for having stolen it, mentioning the neighbors she remembers (the Haddows who lived next door, and Turners across the street), and remarking about her discovery while living in the home that her father was having an affair with secretary, whom he later married..

Dear Mrs. Autrey,

Thank you very much for your letter and the pin, which arrived safely. I too remember that year very vividly. Things have naturally changed a great deal in nearly forty years: my wife died in Australia in 1986, just as we were coming back from a trip there. She had acquired an Alzheimer condition, and I am at least glad that she didn't have to go through the whole cycle of that. I continue to live in the house by myself. Jean Haddow also died some years ago, and Will, who is verging on ninety is also living by himself next door. The Turners have gone, and their daughter, who remarried after her first husband's death, has moved to Leaside.

I realized at the time that your parents' marriage was breaking up, but extremely pleased that your own has been so happy. I gather from your last phrase that your mother has also remarried.

M.F. Walker   **2 March 1988**
Camosun College, Victoria, BC

In reply to a letter (26 January 1988) from Walker, who was troubled by Frye's use of the language of slavery and war in an essay reprinted in the Toronto Star and by his use of language that is gender biased.

Dear Mr. Walker,

Thank you for your letter. The article In the *Star*[752] you referred to was concocted out of an interview with me, and therefore is not quite the way I would have written it. You are quite right in thinking that my use of militant language derives from Blake's "mental fight," and so far it seems better to me to sublimate such language than to avoid it. If one avoids it one leaves a vacuum that undesirable people are only too anxious to fill.

As for the use of he, his, and him to represent human beings and not males I think your feeling that it tends to perpetuate gender bias rather underestimates the capacity of language to fossilize conventional meanings. For example, the Society of Friends are often called Quakers, but that word no longer implies any hostility or imputation of hysteria. These are simply present and tentative feelings on my part, not principles or dogma.

Jon Pierce   **18 March 1988**
Preparatory School, Upper Canada College, Toronto, ON

In response to Pierce's having written Frye about George Steiner's review of The Literary Guide to the Bible, *ed. Robert Alter and Frank Kermode, which appeared in the New Yorker, 11 January 1988: 94–8. Steiner argues that literary criticism of the Bible, for all its merits, remains relatively trivial because it fails to account for the mysterium tremendum of theophany, prophecy, and passion narrative.*

Dear Jon,

Thank you for the Steiner review, which I have read, though like you I feel I have got to the end of Steiner. He tries hard, but I feel that the Bible is a bit beyond him, and I find all the panting to keep up with contemporary literary theory, as well as biblical scholarship, somewhat exhausting. I doubt very much that I am what he means by a believer, though my own conception of that word would be very different.

Thomas Willard   24 May 1988
Department of English, University of Arizona, Tucson, AZ

In reply to Willard's several questions (4 May 1988): where did Frye get the word "canon"? where could one find the reading lists for the old honour course at Toronto? and what does the phrase "rhetorical criticism" imply?

Dear Tom,

Thanks very much for your letter. I think your analysis of the word "canon" is correct. It seemed obvious to me that anything Blake took the trouble to engrave belonged in the canon of some kind; Bloom took the word from me, and then proceeded to apply it in a context which I had explicitly condemned. Apart from a remark or two in *The Great Code*, I don't think I have discussed the question elsewhere.

The University of Toronto calendars for the years 1930 to 1935 or so list the texts in English and describe the subjects and options available in the honour Courses. The Philosophy (English or History) course, which I took, was invented by the philosopher G.S. Brett. The Pratt Library would have the calendars—I don't know where we got the word "calendar"; American universities seem to use the word catalogue.

I certainly approve of the introduction of the study of rhetoric into English courses, but the separation of departments of English and Rhetoric was to my mind an unqualified mistake, and the result of straight empire-building. I think I derived the term "rhetorical" from what is called "new" criticism mainly from my reading and reviewing of R.S. Crane of Chicago.[753] Some time in the early fifties he did the Alexander lectures with a very long title: it would be in Robin Harris's book.[754]

Daryl Hine   27 May 1988
Evanston, IL

In reply to Hine (undated letter), who thanked Frye for the influence he had on his own life and work over the years. He mentions particularly the importance of Fearful Symmetry, *the essays on Dickinson and Shakespeare's sonnets in* Fables of Identity, *the ideas of anagogy and the archetype (which "have I do believe governed not only my work but my inner life"). "The thing you said to me that most influenced my life and often saved me from despair, is 'that only the soul can kill the soul,' when I asked if hack writing ... would prove fatal to that vital organ." Hine also announces that he has just completed his long poem* In and Out.

Dear Daryl,

I was very touched and moved by your letter, as well as being rather startled by the length of time our friendship goes back in the past. In particular, I was most interested to hear that you are completing a long poem, which I am naturally very anxious to see. I passed on your message to Jay,[755] whose life, as the only daughter of aging parents, naturally gets more complicated in proportion as they age.

With best wishes and, of course, assurance of my constant interest in you.

Sandra Djwa   **28 June 1988**

Department of English, Simon Fraser University, Burnaby, BC

In response to Djwa's letter (26 April 1988), asking for an audience with Frye in May and bringing him up to date on her research on the origins of the Literary History of Canada, *edited by Carl Klinck: Djwa had recorded her conversations with him. She also enclosed a draft version of her introduction to E.J. Pratt's* Collected Poems *and an essay she had written on Henry James.*

Dear Sandra,

Sorry we seem to have missed connections in May: I don't know whether I was out of town of not. In the meantime I have been reading through the Klinck material, the Pratt introduction and the article on Henry James. I haven't read *The Portrait of a Lady* for a long time, but your links with Pater and other such elements seem convincing enough. I think the Pratt essay is, if I may say so, immensely improved from earlier versions I have seen. It now seems very comprehensive and balanced in scope and to give the reader everything he would want in the way of an introduction. The Klinck recordings are utterly charming: Carl is the most lovable scholar I know, and that quality comes through very clearly. His memory seems very clear and accurate, so far as I can judge, though he omitted a remark that I will always cherish. After a long interview with Roy Daniells and myself, in which he submitted a great many things for our approval which he had decided to do anyway and of which we of course approved, he said he felt like a curate reporting to a couple of overworked bishops. Carl was so modest that it was almost impossible not sometimes to take the episcopal tone with him. I assume, by the way, that Douglas Creighton is Donald Creighton.

Barry Callaghan   **3 August 1988**

Toronto, ON

Dear Barry,

Thank you very much for the copy of *Stone Blind Love*,[756] which I find even more impressive on rereading. I was most pleased to see that Margaret Avison had spoken up for the book, as she doesn't give tongue very often.

Thanks very much for the clown-nose snapshot, although I don't think either you or I were really intended by nature to be clowns.[757]

Much love to you both.

Incidentally, I have just had a letter from Francesca asking for an updated copy of my presentation at the Italian Connection Congress to [sic] you.[758] This puts me in quite a quandary because I simply spoke from headings, which I have probably lost, as nothing was ever said to my remembrance about publishing the proceedings. If they were taped, I might work out something, but otherwise I hardly know what to do. I usually try to avoid assignments that involve manuscripts, because of the very limited number that I can produce, and I'd be glad to have your advice on the matter.

Hazel Merrett   **9 August 1988**

Senneville, QC

Merrett was Frye's first cousin. See letter of 21 August 1978.

Dear Hazel,

Thank you very much for your birthday note: this is a very belated acknowledgment but you will probably have realized by now that other things have happened. My remarriage has thrown things into a bit of confusion, but my wife, Elizabeth Brown, a classmate of Victoria 3T3 and the widow of an M.P. and judge in Brantford, is with me now after a very private wedding.

I was very glad to have the report about Alma's scholarship fund,[759] and certainly was not surprised that the Endowed Chair was out of reach. Victoria is opening what they call a Northrop Frye Centre, but they certainly cannot manage the Endowed Chair either.

I have not actually written anything biographical, but naturally I would take the keenest interest in anything you do, and of course would love to see you both whenever possible. In the meantime thanks again for your most kindly note.

Gordon McLennan   31 August 1988
Toronto, ON

In reply to McLennan's lengthy letter of 15 August 1988, will a full account of his grade 13 class's reaction to the news of Frye's marriage to Elizabeth Eedy Brown, various reports related to the publication of Frye's No Uncertain Sounds, *and his planned trip to Italy.*

Dear Gordon,

Thank you very much for your letter with its news of the effect of my marriage on your class.[760] It was a very sudden, even explosive decision on our part, but it seemed so utterly right when we made the decision that everything seemed to fall into place very quickly. Your remark that my life two years ago was a nightmare is quite simply true, and I am glad that that part of it is over.

Certainly I should like *No Uncertain Sounds*[761] to appear in Italian, though the Italians have been very long suffering about my work, and might find the allusions a trifle local. But I certainly hope you manage to get to Italy. I think Assisi would be more exhilarating than Florence, not only because of the way Florence has become filled up with traffic, noise, and stench. A friend of mine recently came back with a new translation of "Ruant coeli, fiat justitia"[762] as "if you think the sky is falling, it's all those Fiats."

I am delighted to hear of your success with the Francis book,[763] and was interested to hear about Katherine Hepburn.[764] I have written to your students and told the more perplexed ones that you would be much better explaining the archetype essay than I would.[765] It must be difficult for them to take in the notion that it was written long before they were born.

Barrington Nevitt   20 September 1988
Toronto, ON

In response to Nevitt's inquiry about what Frye learned from Marshall McLuhan and what anecdotes from Frye's experience demonstrated McLuhan's humanity. Nevitt, along with McLuhan's brother Maurice, was planning a book on McLuhan's influence. Nevitt collaborated with McLuhan through the 1960s and 1970s, producing articles and books, particularly the important Take Today: The Executive as Dropout, *which they co-wrote.*

Dear Mr. Nevitt,

This is in connection with your letter about your proposed book on Marshall McLuhan. I am sorry if I am unhelpful on this subject, but I doubt that I have anything very distinctive to say on the subject. What I could say I said at the teacher's awards meeting you referred to,[766] but unfortunately I had no text for that talk. I think I remember saying that Marshall was an extraordinary improviser in conversation, that he could take fire instantly from a chance remark, and that I have never known anyone to equal him on that score. I also feel, whether I said it or not, that he was celebrated for the wrong reasons in the sixties, and then neglected for the wrong reasons later, so that a reassessment of his work and its value is badly needed. I think what I chiefly learned from him, as an influence on me, was the role of discontinuity in communication, which he was one of the first people to understand the significance of. Beyond that, I am afraid I am not much use.

George Johnston   20 September 1988
Athelstan, QC

In reply to Johnston's letter containing good wishes to Frye following his marriage to Elizabeth Eedy Brown on 27 July 1987 and giving an account of his trip to Iceland.

Dear George,

Thanks very much for your letter and good wishes: we are much happier than I could have believed I ever would be again a year or so ago. Our reception came off very well, with about 250 people there.

I am glad you enjoyed Iceland: it was one of Helen's favourite spots though we never got to Shetland or the Orkneys.[767] The Orkneys in particular I should love to see, but what is turning up right now is a trip to the Soviet Union, which will take most of October.[768]

Love to you both as always.

James J. Yoch   14 October 1988
Department of English, University of Oklahoma, Norman, OK

In reply to Yoch's letter of 14 October 1988: "In 1982 I invoked your name in a seminar on Shakespeare and the Green World at the national meeting of the Shakespeare Association of America. As a gift for colleagues in the seminar, I delivered a garden plan expressing the issues raised in their papers, and you can see on the entry pavilion the 'mask of N. Frye.' Enjoyed the task and wanted to share it with you."

Dear Professor Yoch,

Thanks very much for putting my mask on your garden plan: I think this is the first time I have appeared in the role of a garden god. I only hope that I can be a sufficiently beneficial spirit.

Jon Pierce   16 November 1988
Preparatory School, Upper Canada College, Toronto, ON

Pierce had written Frye (20 October 1988), sending him a copy of Bruce Chatwin's Songlines *and an interview. He mentions that he has heard about Frye's trip to Russian and warns him about "engaging in arguments with hard-headed Marxist intellectuals."*

Dear Jon,

Thank you very much for the books and the interview, which I have read with great interest. We are just back from Russia now, and are trying to sort ourselves out. As for arguments on the Bible with Marxist intellectuals, the people I talked to were very anxious to hear about the Bible, and Marxist intellectuals in Russia, I gather, are rather like mammoths in Siberia: very impressive once, but more or less overlaid by more recent phenomena. More simply, Russian humanists have been stuffed to the gills with Marxism and hate the sound and stink of it.

Bert States   **2 December 1988**
Department of Dramatic Art, University of California, Santa Barbara, CA

Dear Bert States,

Thank you very much for the *Hudson Review* article.[769] It is a great relief to read something about myself by someone who thinks I am fun to read, instead of the usual lugubrious animadversions on my phenomenological assumptions.

With best wishes.

Amy Mickleburgh   **20 January 1989**
Watten Estate Condominium, Singapore

Dear Amy,

I am afraid our letters have been crossing, as seems natural enough with the distance. We are very well, and I am gradually adjusting to having a big family, for the first time in my experience. I don't know if you remember that we were in the Soviet Union for three weeks in October, where I was lecturing in Moscow, Kiev and Leningrad. In many respects it was the same old bureaucratic swamp it always was, but the people I talked to seemed to feel that within the last two years at last they had definitely turned a corner and were now embarking on the real Russian revolution.

We are going to Italy at the end of April, where I get a degree from the University of Bologna and speak at its convocation. (At least I think I do: there has been no official word as yet.)[770] Otherwise we are keeping fairly quiet, and are buying a small condominium in St. Marys, Ontario, just west of Stratford where Elizabeth was brought up, and where formerly her father and now her brother ran the town paper.

I am sorry if Singapore is turning into a branch-plant culture, but I suppose that is inevitable with a small unit, and that the same will become increasingly true of Canada with its free trade pact. There would be many things however to compensate for it, such as more freedom than the surrounding countries seem to have.

Much love to all of you from us both.

Gabriel Mario Gomez   **30 January 1989**
Buenos Aires, Argentina

In reply to Gomez's letter (4 January 1989) asking Frye why he considers that there is no historical confirmation of Jesus' life outside the New Testament.

Dear Mr. Gomez,

Thank you for your letter. My point was not that there are no references to Christianity as a new religion outside the New Testament. There is quite a body of them, not only in Suetonius but in Tacitus, Pliny and elsewhere. It was the references to the historical Jesus which are lacking, or at least so oblique that no one would pay any attention to them if it were not for the New Testament. My point in saying this, as you say, is that I think the New Testament writers wanted it in that way.

Leonard W.J. Chapman   **16 February 1989**
Toronto, ON

In response to Chapman's inquiry about whether Frye would read "my extraordinary book on the Apocalypse of John" (letter dated 10 February 1898).

Dear Mr. Chapman,

Thank you for your letter. I was most interested to hear that you had done so remarkable a piece of scholarship, but it does seem to me that someone with better scholarly equipment in the field would be a better person to ask, simply because it would do more justice to you. Naturally I should be most interested to see the book, but to pass judgment on it would I am afraid be beyond my ability.

George Ford   21 February 1989
English Department, University of Rochester, Rochester, NY

In reply to a letter from Ford pointing out that that, in his essay "Dickens and the Comedy of Humours," Frye had mistakenly referred to a character in Bleak House *as a major and that in a television interview he had referred to President Gerald Ford as George Ford.*

Dear George,

Thank you very much for your letter. Sorry about the Dickens blooper: I had been asked to write that paper by Gordon Ray, who wanted someone who knew nothing at all about Dickens. The result was that I read most of Dickens in airports and mistakes were bound to crop up. In any case I have never been like the woman in Jane Austen who was so sensitive to the difference between a knight and baronet.

I suppose the slip about Gerald Ford was a Freudian one after all: my point was that he had not made much of a dint on American history, so it was natural to forget his first name and substitute that of someone I knew considerably better. Sorry if it embarrassed you.

Ron Dart   28 February 1989
Vancouver, BC

In response to Dart's several inquiries (22 February 1989) about questions raised by The Great Code: *how can kerygma be taught in the universities in a detached way? and what is the relationship between kerygma and typology.*

Dear Mr. Dart,

Thank you for your letter. It does not do the Christian or any other religion any harm if it makes sense. I have taught a course on the typology of the Bible for forty years, and have practically never had a student who failed to grasp the central point: that what I was saying makes sense in terms of its own assumptions: whether he accepted those assumptions or not was his own business. The same thing is true of the relation between typology and kerygma. Any proclamation which is worth anything at all has to come from within a structure that is logical and coherent. Chaotic kerygma, or kerygma that merely asserts, soon becomes bigotry. I would even say that all bigotry is blasphemy, even if the Ayatollah doesn't know it yet.

Ron Dart   9 May 1989
Vancouver, BC

In response to Dart's several inquiries (20 March 1989) about typology and about Allen Ginsberg and Kathleen Raine on Blake.

Dear Mr. Dart,

Thank you for your letter. I think typology is in itself capable of totally revolutionising Christianity, but nothing works mechanically, and one can batter peoples' ears for a long time without making much impression. But it seems to me the most fruitful line of pursuit for it.

I think the Ginsberg people make their own use of Blake, and that is one of the things that Blake is for. Ms. Raine, on the other hand, is making a scholarly study of Blake, and most of it is wrong, at least in emphasis. Her thesis assumes that Blake was an eager and omnivorous reader, and he wasn't: he simple sniffed at books and took off. All except the Bible.

Ian Balfour   28 June 1989
Toronto, ON

Written in reply to Balfour's having delivered a copy of his book, Northrop Frye *(Boston: Twayne, 1988), to Frye, accompanied by a letter, dated 21 June 1985.*

Dear Professor Balfour,

Thank you very much for the copy of your book on me. I was very sorry to have been away when you brought it in, but my health has not been up to par recently.

It seems to me that your book does everything that such a book reasonably can do in counteracting the effect, not of the critics who honestly disagree with me, but of the pseudo-critics who assert that I have boxed myself in to some obviously indefensible position. For that, in particular, I am especially grateful, to say nothing of my sense of honour of having so carefully thought out a book written about me.

Amy Mickleburgh   12 July 1989
North York, ON

Dear Amy,

Thanks very much for your birthday card and your good wishes. I think I am perhaps getting the better of this disease, though it is a long and tedious process.[771]

Much love to you and all of yours.

Deanne Bogdan   3 August 1989
Ontario Institute for Studies in Education, University of Toronto

Deanne Bogdan and Stanley B. Straw, the editors of Beyond Communication: Reading Comprehension and Criticism, *had asked Frye to write a preface to their book, which he did. The editors, however, rejected the preface and returned it to him, saying that for all that it did to clarify their own view of humanist and post-humanist positions in reading comprehension and criticism, it did "not speak to the positive contributions of our authors" and thus bypassed the significance of the collection (letter of 21 July 1989). Rejecting Frye's preface was distressful for Bogdan, who wrote Frye another letter on 1 August 1989, saying that the editors saw the preface as something different from the beginning of a dialectic and that she was very grieved by the whole matter. Frye himself, rather than his secretary, typed the present letter. The preface was eventually published in volume 7 of Frye's Collected Works — WE, 611–15. The present letter is Frye's response to the rejection of his preface.*

Dear Deanne,

Thank you very much for your second letter. I was of course utterly bewildered by the reception of my preface, and despite your two letters I still am. However, I don't want to discuss the subject any further, and the incident gave me the shock I needed to confirm a decision I should have made years ago. A man of seventy-seven who still has so much that he wants to write, and has so little time left to write it in, can't afford to take any more chances with his writing schedule. So all preface-writing and similar peripheral activities have to come off my writing agenda permanently. I say this because there was a suggestion in the first letter about involving myself with the book in some other way. If I decline to do this I know you will understand that it's not sulking but simple self-preservation.

I was glad to hear about your student, who I hope and expect will be the first of a long and distinguished line.[772] I am looking forward somewhat apprehensively to an over-busy fall, which includes among many other things the PEN conference, the opening of the NF centre at Victoria College, the appearance of a biography, of an interview by Harry Rasky, and the processing of my second Bible book, which is complete so far as I can see except for footnotes, though that's a big enough exception. I feel as over-exposed as a model in *Penthouse*, though doubtless when the events turn up I shall get through them in a placid daze.

John Ayre   9 August 1989
Guelph, ON

John Ayre, Frye's biographer, had written Frye on 29 June 1989, asking him to identify some photos to be used in his biography, shortly to be released. The photos in question can be found between pp. 216 and 217 of Northrop Frye: A Biography *(Toronto: Random House, 1989).*

Dear John,

I am sorry to sound like such an idiot. The photograph of Helen and myself with the woman in the music library doesn't ring any sort of bell in my memory. I have no idea who she was or where the picture was taken, or why. I am pretty sure that the shot of Helen and me getting into a plane dates from a casual news photograph taken at the time of our 1962 trip. That year was our silver wedding anniversary, and I thought it appropriate to take Helen to a town with some silver in it.[773] Also, I am afraid I have nothing of my own in the way of Chancellor's picture, with or without clothes, as I assume that the College will be looking after such things themselves.

I haven't seen a copy of the cover yet, but I am pleased if there is interest in the book and in particular that you have been asked to appear on the Harbourfront programme.[774] I was also very pleased to hear that Evelyn got safely out of Kansas in French.[775]

Keath Fraser   11 December 1989
Vancouver, BC

Fraser had written Frye (17 November 1989) asking if he would contribute a marked up page of a manuscript for a benefit for Canadian Book Week. The funds were to go to the Vancouver chapter of P.E.N. Frye sent several pages from one of his drafts for Words with Power. *Fraser later reported (23 May 1990) that Frye's pages had sold for $190.*

Dear Mr. Fraser,

Thank you for your letter. I happen to be someone with an all-inspiring collection of junk paper, and I am sending you a page or two at random for you to choose.

1990s

Victor H. Fiddes   8 January 1990
Niagara Falls, ON

In reply to Fiddes' letter (29 December 1990) congratulating Frye on the urbane manner in which he answered Harry Rasky's questions on a CBC interview broadcast on Christmas day. Fiddes wondered why there was "no place in the disconnected exchange where the singularity of the Christmas event could be pursued." Fiddes was the author of Science and the Gospel.

Dear Dr. Fiddes,

Thank you very much for your most kind letter. When one is interviewed on such a programme, one is of course totally dependent on the quality and kind of questions one is asked. Also one has no idea when if ever the interview will be broadcast. I had no indication of any kind when this interview would go on the air, except a hint two weeks beforehand that it might be on Boxing Day. Had I known that it would be on Christmas Night, I should have insisted on a very different series of questions.

Ken Hertz   8 January 1990
Montreal, QC

In response to Hertz's letter of 30 December 1987: "Is there any way you can help me to have the operation? This is my last chance. I have raised two-thirds of the funds. The operation is scheduled for this February. Can you help?" The letter was signed by Jane Widdicombe, Frye's secretary.

Dear Mr. Hertz,

Enclosed please find Dr. Frye's check in the amount of $25.00. He hopes this will help with your operation.

Mark Richardson   11 January 1990
Halifax, Nova Scotia

In reply to Richardson's query (26 December 1989) about the nature of Jesus, triggered by his having read The Great Code *and seen the television presentation of Harry Rasky's* Northrop Frye: The Great Teacher. *Richardson tells Frye that he is the son-in-law of an Emmanuel College classmate, Newman Truax.*

Dear Mr. Richardson,

Thank you for your letter, and please remember me to Mr. Truax, whom I remember well at Emmanuel. I think there are two dimensions of the gospel: one is the specific set of events around which the New Testament revolves and the other is the message of the spirit which has lasted as long as the human race has done and transcends all distinctions of culture and creed. The latter is sometimes called "The Everlasting Gospel," from a phrase in the Book of Revelation.

Jean Little   24 January 1990
Guelph, ON

Jean Little, Victoria College, class of 1935, was a long-time friend of the Fryes and well-known author of children's books.

Dear Jean,

Thank you very much for your book and letter, as well as for your "Once Upon a Golden Apple."[776] I remarked many years ago in an article that the stability of nursery rhyme texts was produced by the conservatism of children.[777] A similar conservatism in an adult helps to preserve the difference between central and deviant myths. So if your book sells a million copies it will help to publicize my views. Therefore, with that noble generosity of which I am so famous, I am willing to waive my cut on your royalties.

It is true that I feel very squirmy on having a biography appear on me and being discussed in such length: with fifteen men on a dead man's chest and no rum in sight all one can do is split oneself in two and withdraw from the whole operation.

E.A. Mabee   24 January 1990
Cananoque, ON

On 11 January 1989 Philip Marchand, columnist for the Toronto Star, *forwarded to Frye a letter that had been sent him by E.A. Mabee. The latter recounted his breakfast-table encounters with Frye at Victoria College during the fall of 1929: "we tolerated each other & respected the other's viewpoint & were civil to each other, but we had nothing in common & argued over most everything—however we seem to have been civilized by our parents so that we both believed in democracy and its tenets." Because Marchand knew Frye, Mabee asked him if he might forward his letter, which also contains the information that he is the father of Stephen Mabee, minister of the Bloordale United Church.*

Dear Mr. Mabee,

Thank you for your letter to Philip Marchand which he has forwarded to me. I am not sure how clearly I remember arguing with you on various topics, because at that time of my life I argued with everybody about everything. Since then, I have rather lost my belief in the virtue of argument. In any case I remember Stephen Mabee, and please pass on to him my very best regards. You don't say whether Kay Mabee was connected with your family or not, but she was a classmate of mine and I remember her very well.[778]

Charles Dougherty   27 March 1990
Sarasota, FL

In response to Dougherty's letter (2 March 1990), praising Harry Rasky's film, Northrop Frye: The Great Teacher, *which he saw at a showing in Florida attended by 200 people, and asking whether Frye had ever published a remark about the Easter candle being a phallic symbol. Dougherty had been a doctoral student at Toronto, receiving his Ph.D. under the direction of A.S.P. Woodhouse in 1953. He later taught at the universities of St. Louis and Missouri.*

Dear Charles,

Thank you very much for your letter. I had no idea that the Rasky film was circulating that widely. The general reaction to it has been very mixed, and my own feelings about it are equally so.

The Easter candle as a phallic image is a very familiar one to me, but so far as I know it does not turn up anywhere in my own work. I rather suspect that it comes somewhere from Jung, although I am not sure: Jung was so jittery about Freud that he tended to ignore even such things as phallic symbols. Joseph Campbell might be another source although I have read very little of him.

It was very pleasant to hear from you and I was most interested in the news in your letter.

Helen Hogg Priestley   27 March 1990
Richmond Hill, ON

Helen Priestley had written Frye (28 February 1990) to thank him for delivering the F.E.L. Priestley lecture two years earlier at the University of Lethbridge on 17 February 1988 — a lecture named for her late husband — and for recent kindnesses. She mentions that her mother had come from Lowell, Massachusetts. Frye's lecture was published as "Reflections on Life and Habit" in the Northrop Frye Newsletter 1 (Spring 1990): 1-9, and reprinted in MM, 141–54, and in ENC, 341–53.

Dear Helen,

Thank you very much for your kindly and gracious letter. It was most interesting to hear that you had come from Lowell. My grandmother, Sarah Ann Northrop, was a Lowell factory girl at a time when Lowell was a model thriving town. Her enthusiasm for the place dragged my father across the border to start in the hardware business there, and it was there that my older brother, killed in the First World War, and my sister were born around 1900. But my mother, who was intensely anglophile, and whose people were all in Montreal, wanted to return to Canada, so I was born there. So my sister Vera, who died in 1966, would have been in Lowell just a few years before you. I think it was at Varney Street.

Artem Lozynsky   23 April 1990
Heilongjiang University, Harbin, Peoples Republic of China

In reply to Lozynsky's letter of 27 March 1990 in which he recounted his efforts to disabuse Chinese students of their crude moralistic readings of literature.

Dear Mr. Lozynsky,

I was most pleased to get your letter, and I feel that your remarks about my "two step shuffle" are very well taken.[779] I am presently engaged with a book[780] in which I attempt to show that this two-stage view of criticism is useful only in the context of criticism as a structure of knowledge. But as experience, the act of reading and the act of reflection of what one has read should both be repeated to the point at which they become the same thing.

Brian Spikes   23 April 1990
Scarborough, ON

In reply to Spikes's inquiry (21 March 1990) about the nature of wisdom in Ecclesiastes and about a pyramidal diagram on the hierarchy of intelligence he enclosed, which moved through these stages: sensation, perception, meaning, emotion, belief, knowledge, discernment, judgement, and wisdom.

Dear Mr. Spikes,

Thank you very much for your letter. The only thing that gives me pause about your hierarchy of intelligence is that it suggests a series of levels to be gone through one after the other. It seems to me rather more complex a process; knowledge, for example, can always accept both knowledge and belief. In short, I think that wisdom emerges from a conflict of force[s], which without it would exhaust each other [sic] in inner combats, like a hockey game without a referee.

In addition to the two books you mention,[781] I have written a book on the relation of the Bible to the imaginative use of words called *The Great Code* (1983) [1982]. In the section devoted to wisdom in the book I suggest a more positive view of Ecclesiastes than the one you suggest in your letter.

John Nicol   6 June 1990
Calgary, AB

In reply to Nicol's letter (10 May 1990), which uses John Ayre's biography as an occasion to reestablish contact after forty years. Nicol, a 1948 graduate of Victoria College, had been a member of the board of the Canadian Forum, *after having published a series of articles on the subarctic region.*

Dear John,

I was extremely pleased to get your letter: I knew that you had moved to Calgary, but wasn't sure that you were still there. I certainly remember very well our association with the *Forum*, and how much I enjoyed your articles on your visit to the far north. I am glad you liked John Ayre's book: it has been rather roughly handled by some people who felt that he had not covered the ideas in my work properly. But that would have been a different kind of book, and I think he did an excellent research job on my early life, about which he knows much more than I do.

Steven Helmling   21 June 1990
Department of English, University of Delaware, Newark, DE

In response to Helmling's having sent Frye a copy of his book, The Esoteric Comedies of Carlyle, Newman and Yeats *(Cambridge: Cambridge University Press, 1988), saying that the book owed much to Frye's work.*

Dear Mr. Helmling,

I have read your delightful book with the greatest pleasure and profit and feel that you have struck a vein that you can keep mining almost indefinitely. I have always been fascinated by that mysterious area way down there in the unconscious where the oracular keeps turning into the witty and back again, the world of *Finnegans Wake* and *Aurelia* and in a different way of Mallarmé. You have hooked this area on to the Menippean satire tradition, and the result is wonderfully fresh reading of three works that very badly need it.

A.D. Tushingham   21 June 1990
Toronto, ON

Tushingham, who had read about Frye's having competed in a typing competition in 1927, had written (14 June 1990) to ask Frye whether he had any information on champion typists he could share and whether he remembered Fred Jarrett and Irma Wright.

Dear Doug Tushingham,

Thank you for your most interesting letter. I am afraid however that I cannot be of very much help to you. Whatever memorabilia I collected at the time went to my parents in Moncton, New Brunswick, and disappeared in the course of clearing up after their deaths. I think a better source of information would probably be my biographer John Ayre, who did some research on that episode, in fact considerably more than the published version suggests.

The name Fred Jarrett does ring a faint bell, and Irma Wright and I do remember meeting and talking to. I don't know if you realize what a very humble role in that contest mine was. There were three categories: the professionals, who typed around 140 words per minute; the "amateurs" who were about 110, and "novice" who averaged between 80 and 90 and had to sign a statement that they had never operated a typewriter six months earlier than the contest. Needless to say, I was a novice. Your mother, on the other hand, sounds terrific.[782]

Betty Rizzo   **12 July 1990**
New Rochelle, NY

In reply to Rizzo's inquiry (4 July 1990) about the Frye genealogy. One of Rizzo's ancestors on her mother's side married Charlotte Frye from Andover, Massachusetts, and she is interested in seeing if she and Frye are related. She writes again on 22 September 1990 with more details about the Frye ancestry and wanting to know his connection with John Frye. But Frye is clearly not interested in her research and replies perfunctorily on 10 October 1990, referring her again to Ayre's biography. A final letter from Rizzo, written on 21 January 1991, two days before Frye's death, informs him they are eighth cousins and encloses a two-page genealogy.

Dear Ms. Rizzo,

Thank you for your letter. There is a lot of work on my ancestry in a biography of me written by John Ayre (1989), but I am afraid there is not an American edition of that book as yet. I certainly remember the Barker genealogy,[783] and I resisted a temptation to buy it in 1950 when I didn't have the price of such books available.

As I understand it, the original Frye was a seventeenth century Puritan who settled at Andover, having come from Andover in Hampshire. My branch of the family pushed across into the Canadian border in the early nineteenth century, presumably because land was cheaper. I understand that all the Fryes except those who were originally Frey, came from the Andover family. They gave their name to Fryeburg in Maine and one of them, Roland Frye, a professor at the University of Pennsylvania, even came from Georgia. We had breakfast together once at Princeton with my wife, who remarked what a weird experience it was to hear a southern accent coming out of a Frye face.

Greg Gatenby   **20 August 1990**
Harbourfront Reading Series, Toronto, ON

Dear Greg,

It sounds very ungracious to turn down the request to read in aid of a cause that I am profoundly sympathetic with, but my fall schedule is filling up at such a rate and my energies are declining in proportion, that I am really compelled to decline all engagements that are not absolutely habeas corpus— produce the body or else. As Chancellor here I have a good many of those. Needless to say, I hope very much that the evening will be a success, even though it sounds a bit like tearing down the walls of Jericho with trumpets.

Jay Macpherson   **20 August 1990**
Oxford, England

Dear Jay,

Thank you very much for the offprint, which looks very exhaustive, though no doubt there is a great deal more to come. I have just returned from a two week tour in Ireland with Elizabeth, her daughter (you may remember Cathy Brown as a student) and son-in-law Ian Morrison. Cathy is now head of the Cystic Fibrosis Foundation and Ian has Roby Kidd's old job.

I shall continue to teach my course next year, but be away most of September in Palmero and various centres in Yugoslavia. My book *Words with Power* is to come out in November, and I have just been finishing a series of lectures I did for the Emmanuel Alumni Reunion in May,[784] which I hope will serve as a popularization of that and *The Great Code*.

I shall be glad to hear from you at any time.

Evelyn MacLure   14 November 1990
Toronto, ON

Millar MacLure was a professor of English at Victoria College, Toronto, for thirty years. Born in 1917 at Albion Cross, Prince Edward Island, he received degrees at Acadia University (Hon. B.A. 1939), Queen's University, Kingston (M.A. 1944), and the University of Toronto (Ph.D. 1949). When his graduate studies in English literature at Johns Hopkins University were interrupted by the war in 1940, he taught at his former high school, Prince of Wales College in Charlottetown, during 1941–1943 and 1944–1945. After receiving his doctorate, he served as Professor of English and Chairman of the Department at United College, Winnipeg, 1949–1953. He returned to Toronto to teach at Victoria College until his retirement in 1983. During his tenure at Victoria and the University of Toronto Graduate Department of English, MacLure served as department chairman and edited the Tamarack Review *(1956–60) as well as the* University of Toronto Quarterly *(1960–65). His field of research was the English Renaissance, particularly Christopher Marlowe and George Chapman*

Dear Evelyn,

Elizabeth and I were very saddened to hear of Millar's passing. I am also sorry that I was attached to a radio therapy machine in Hamilton and was unable to attend the service. I remember Miller so clearly in Graduate School, partly because I have had so few students to whom I have taken so instant a liking. After he left for the University of Winnipeg I was determined to get him back to Victoria as soon as I possibly could, and I still regard having done so as one of the best things I ever did. I am sorry that we drifted away after both of us had physical setbacks that made it harder to meet, but my memory of him is as vivid as ever.

David Staines   8 January 1991
Department of English, University of Ottawa, Ottawa, ON

In reply to Staines's having sent Frye a copy of his edition of The Complete Romances of Chrétien de Troyes.

Dear David,

Thank you very much for your letter. David Jarraway is certainly a first-rate man on all counts and he would lend a good deal of distinction to your department.

The book is a delightful object to look at and handle, the printing and the paper being first class. It is a remarkable job altogether, as you probably don't need telling, and I was particularly pleased to see how you had rendered what you had talked to me about, the touches of dry humour in the tone.

I know that every close relationship, like yours with your mother, is a kind of symbiotic one, and its termination is a terrible shock all round.[785] For months after Helen's death

I dreamed every night that she was alive and still with me, or else that I was searching through empty buildings looking for her. Such things do not get duller or blunter with time, but the sense of proportion and perspective does change as they get more and more absorbed into the continuity of one's life.

Love as always.

John Borovilos   **16 January 1991**
Head of English, Danforth Technical School, Toronto, ON

In response to Borovilos's having sent Frye a copy of the anthology he edited, Breaking Through: A Canadian Literary Mosaic *(Scarborough, ON: Prentice-Hall, 1989). Frye's reply was written a week before his death.*

Dear John Borovilos,

Thanks for the copy of *Breaking Through*, which I've paged through finding old friends and making new discoveries— altogether an enjoyable reading experience. The "mosaic" theme is clearly one whose time has come, and I'm glad to see it incarnated in an anthology put together with such taste and intelligence, not to mention enthusiasm. Hoping that you remain basking in the warm glow of accomplishment, I wish you the best for the future.

Notes

Preface

1. *The Correspondence of Northrop Frye and Helen Kemp, 1932–1939*, ed. Robert D. Denham. 2 vols. (Toronto: University of Toronto Press, 1996).

2. Jane Widdicombe's typescripts are identified by the initials "jw" following Frye's signature. Judy White was Frye's secretary when he was principal of Victoria College (1959–1967). The letters preserved from this time identify her as the secretary (also "jw"). Pam Hillier served as Frye's secretary when he was appointed University Professor (1967). Letters typed by her are identified with "ph." The initials "cb" identify the typist Carol Bailey, who occasionally assisted Pam Hillier and her successor in 1968, Jane Widdicombe. The identity of the typists whose identifying initials are "k" (from the 1960s) and "jj" is unknown.

The Correspondence

1930s

3. Uncle Rate was Eratus Edwin Howard, brother of Frye's mother, Catharine (Cassie) Howard. A gold medal winner in math and physics from McGill, and later a gold medal winner in law, he established a law firm and later became a judge.

4. *William Blake* (London: Cape, 1933).

5. The Co-operative Commonwealth Federation (CCF) was a democratic socialist party, organized by farm and labor groups in Calgary in 1932. It sought "a commonwealth in which the basic principle regulating production, distribution, and exchange [would] be the supplying of human needs instead of the making of profits." The CCF was the forerunner of the New Democratic Party.

6. The eponymous personification of Canada.

7. R. B. Bennett, prime minister from 1930 to 1935.

8. One of Frye's C.C.F. parishioners was elected, but the liberals won in a landslide, which, Frye wrote to Helen Kemp, "was a big disappointment to this community, who had hoped for a better C.C.F. opposition. Too much nervous fear of a new idea. The largest single factor to be reckoned with in politics would be, I should think, the sheer dead weight of conservatism. The Stonepile poll was mainly Conservative, Stone C.C.F., and Carnagh mixed" (*NFHK*, 1:286). Stonepile, Stone, and Carnagh were the three small communities Frye was serving.

9. Frye's burlesque of T.S. Eliot's lines in part V of "The Hollow Men."

10. *Becky Sharp*, the movie of William Makepeace Thackeray's *Vanity Fair*, had been released on 28 June 1935. Miriam Hopkins was nominated for an Oscar in 1936 for her role as Becky Sharp. It won the award for the best color film at the 1935 Venice Film Festival.

11. Jerry Riddell, senior tutor at Victoria College.

12. In a letter to Helen Kemp, Frye says the same thing, adding that Glover had written "a (rather bad) book on the Jesus of history (T.R. Glover, *The Jesus of History* [New York: Association Press, 1917]. *NFHK*, 1:480. S.C.M. = Student Christian Movement.

13. This was the third edition of well-traveled *Representative Poetry*, a two-volume anthology, designed specifically for students in the three-year pass course in English at the University of Toronto.

14. Herbert J. Davis, a member of the English faculty of University College, University of Toronto, from 1922 to 1937. He was a well-known Jonathan Swift scholar. Frye took a course in Blake from Davis. Davis resigned his University of Toronto appointment in 1938 and accepted a position at Cornell, and later he was appointed as a reader at Oxford. Still later he became president of Smith College.

15. Norman J. Endicott, a member of the English faculty at University College, University of Toronto, from 1929 to 1970. One of the editors of *Representative Poetry*, he had enlisted Frye to be what amounted to an assistant editor. See *NFHK*, 1:495–6

16. James R. MacGillivray, a member of the English faculty at University College, University of Toronto, from 1930 to 1971.

17. Helen Kemp was spending the year studying art at the Courtauld Institute in London.

18. Kemp wrote to Frye on 20 June 1935 that she had told Daniells that she "was looking for someone to walk or cycle or get to Vienna with — I want to see the Brueghels there. And his face lit up and he said: 'Why I'm looking for someone to cycle to Vienna with! Let's go together!' I pondered a moment and said I'd go, and was full of plans in an instant. But he said no, it just wouldn't do, not for a member of the Victoria College staff. I'm sorry about that, it would have been such fun. There is some consolation in being regarded a menace by Mrs Grundy" (*NFHK*, 1:454).

19. Frye was writing his graduate seminar paper on Blake for Herbert J. Davis.

20. Frye is referring to the four-year honour course.

21. In Notebook 5, which dates from about this time, Frye sketched on the flyleaf, "Quiet Consummation / A Novel in Sonata Form / Eratus Howard / Part One, Exposition"; on the second leaf is an "Analysis" of the novel, outlined as the exposition, de-

velopment, and recapitulation. Eratus Howard is the name of both his grandfather (Eratus Edwin Howard) and his brother (Eratus Howard Frye). For more about Frye's novel, see *FMW*, 86–140.

22. Bert Arnold, a member of the German department at Victoria College

23. Margaret Roseborough.

24. Margaret (Peggy) Roseborough and Mary Winspear, both members of Herbert J. Davis's seminar in Blake.

25. Roy Kemp was Helen's younger brother.

26. For Frye's more detailed account of the week at the Muskoka cottage, see his letter to Kemp of 28 June 1935 (*NFHK*, 1:461–2). Both Helen's father and Roy Kemp had somewhat different views of the week: "Before the boys went to G.B. [Gordon Bay] for that week I asked Norrie both times he was here if I could help him in the way of a 5 or 10 dollar bill & he refused both times. Roy got a special rate for the two of them through the Camp Franklin office, & Norrie was supposed to pay him afterwards. So with Norrie neglecting to get his cash ready, Roy had 35¢ left when he got started on the train & beyond my reach & Norrie had one thin dime, to face a week at Gordon Bay.... Norrie says he got some money Thursday (I don't know how he did it, as my response to Roy's appeal did not reach him till Friday, though I hoped it would go north to Parry Sd. [Sound] & back to him at G.B. on Thursday.) Norrie was over here again on the Sunday after returning, and he did not seem particularly penitent. They had to live on oatmeal and eggs for several days" (S.H.F. Kemp to Helen Kemp, 28 June 1935, Helen Frye Fonds, 1992 accession, box 2, file 3). "The whole situation in which we found ourselves last week had its origin I really believe in the indifference or unpreparedness or carelessness of one H.N. Frye. I am not in the least perturbed at the man, but after living with him for a week I find that the ordinary tasks and necessities of life do not seem to cross his consciousness until the actual moment of their performance. And so he slept in Monday morning last, missed his breakfast, and did not get any money out of the bank. He is a good lad and I like him, but how woefully does he need to do a little shifting for himself! He is so utterly useless when it becomes a question of doing anything practical that he shies from it and leaves somebody else to worry about it. So it has always been with him, so it will always be. He is destined to live the academic life absolutely out of touch with the actual mechanics of our civilization. He is not much concerned with 'what makes the wheels go round.' All he has is a highly developed critical sense of the finished product, be it in art, music or literature. In a sense his whole relation to this society of ours is parasitical. And I say that quite dispassionately without envy, malice, jealousy or all the other motives which cause words of invective to be spoken. It is too bad, but I think Helen and he are going to have a good bit of adjusting to get used to each other's mode of existence. But to speak of our actual visit at Gordon Bay, the first two days Nature came to our assistance and we had no appetite for food. Found jar of jelly in sawdust. Also three jelly powders (not in sawdust). Consumed two dozen eggs. Also much oatmeal porridge" (Roy Kemp to his parents, Helen Frye Fonds, 1992 accession, box 2, file 3).

27. Alfred J. Johnston, Frye's homiletics instructor at Emmanuel College.

28. Arthur Richard Cragg, Frye's friend and Victoria and Emmanuel College classmate.

29. Cragg's girlfriend (and later wife) was Florence Clare. In early July Frye spent a week with her and her family in Brechin, Ontario. See Frye's letter to Helen Kemp of 24 July 1935 (*NFHK*, 1:476–8).

30. Sir Thomas Browne's meditative and mystical treatise, *Urn Burial* (1658).

31. Frye sailed to England on the *Alaunia*, a Cunard White Star liner.

32. A shadowy man named Pavitt.

33. The black and white striped poles with the flashing yellow balls on top found at pedestrian crossings, devised by Leslie Hore-Belisha in the 1930s.

34. The boarding house was at 90–92 Guilford St.

35. One of the two was Don Stuart (see *NFHK*, 2:567).

36. The shipboard acquaintance was a woman from Montreal who knew two of Frye's maternal twin aunts, Hazel and Evelyn Howard.

37. G. Wilson Knight was professor of English at Trinity College, University of Toronto. A Shakespearean, he later taught at Stowe School and then at the University of Leeds (1946–62). His brother was W.F. Jackson Knight.

38. Jackson Knight's book was published later in the year: *Cumaean Gates: A Reference of the Sixth Aeneid to the Initiation Pattern* (Oxford: Basil Blackwell, 1936).

39. At the time Berry had published two books of poems: *Gospel of Fire*, with an introduction by G. Wilson Knight (London: Mathews & Marrot, 1933), and *Snake in the Moon* (London: Williams & Norgate, 1936).

40. Maurice Ridgion (see *NFHK*, 2:567–8).

41. In 1926 Toller had begun writing an experimental play based on the events leading to the murder of Liebknecht and Luxemburg. He later named the play *Berlin 1919*, but he never completed it, and only fragments survive.

42. Barbara Sturgis, a friend of Helen Kemp's.

43. Sir Ralph Wedgwood, a railway administrator.

44. Edmund Blunden was Frye's tutor and English supervisor. On 17 December 1936 Frye had written to Helen Kemp, "I don't think Blunden liked my thesis much — he said something vague about all the sentences being the same length — what I think he really resents is the irrefutable proof that Blake had a brain. I am afraid I shall have to ignore him and just go ahead" (*NFHK*, 2:659).

45. That is, honors examinations which were held by all faculties at Oxford in June of each year. To receive a first on any "school" or subject was a notable distinction, and the colleges at Oxford prided themselves on the number of firsts their students received. The issue that confronts Frye later is whether he will take his B.A. degree by writing his Blake thesis or whether he will stand for school examinations, as his tutor Edmund Blunden would prefer. He chose the later: during the second week of June, 1938, Frye wrote his examinations and sat for his viva voce, earning a first, the only Merton student for the year to achieve such a mark in English literature. One of his examiners was C.S. Lewis.

46. Frye's tutor, the poet and critic Edmund Blunden. Frye's relationship with Blunden is presented in some detail in *NFHK*, vol. 2.

47. Frye is referring to S. Foster Damon's *William Blake: His Philosophy and Symbols* (1924).

48. Joseph Johnson, the first publisher to commission Blake as a copy-engraver.

49. Elizabeth Fraser, a Canadian graphic artist living a bohemian life in London, befriended Frye when he was at Oxford. Her not altogether Platonic relationship with Frye can be traced by following the index entries in *NFHK*, 951–2.

50. See n. 42, above.

51. That is, a scholarship from the Imperial Order Daughters of the Empire. On 28 April Frye wrote to his fiancée Helen Kemp, asking if she would look into the I.O.D.E. for him — to "find out who I have to write to, and so on" (*NFHK*, 2:739).

52. This was a somewhat overconfident projection: Frye's book on Blake was not published until ten years later.

53. Helen Kemp's parents owned a summer cottage at Muskoka. For the extending of the invitation, see her letter to Frye of 14 December 1936 (*NFHK*, 2:657).

54. Brown replied to Frye on 29 April 1937, saying that Victoria College was eager for Frye to have two years of study at Oxford and advising him to stay in London. He offered little encouragement about a scholarship, though he had gotten an agreement from Dr. Charles T. Currelly that Frye could get a $600 scholarship offered by Currelly on Brown's recommendation. He also said that Victoria had no loan fund to assist Frye, and he wondered if Oxford might not be able to provide some assistance.

55. These friends would have been Helen Kemp's parents, S.H.F. and Gertrude Kemp, who had a summer cottage in Muskoka.

56. Frye sailed from Southampton on 24 June on the *Empress of Australia*, arriving in Quebec on 1 July. A day or so before he returned to Canada Frye sent the first two chapters of his manuscript, which he had called *The Blake Prophecies*, to R.E. Stoneman at Faber & Faber. He took chapters three and four, which were twice as long as the first two, back to Canada with him, where he intended to make a final revision. His friend Elizabeth Fraser served as his intermediary, the correspondence with Faber & Faber being directed through her. On 6 July Stoneman rejected the manuscript because he "cannot foresee a wide enough sale" (R.E. Stoneman to Frye, 6 July 1937, Helen Frye Fonds, 1991 accession, box 3, file 1). Fraser mailed the rejection letter to Frye at Gordon Bay, but held on to the manuscript so it could be sent out again, asking him to forward to her "a series of fresh & inspired letters to all the publishers." Frye obliged in late July with a letter to Cambridge University Press.

57. Helen Kemp's parents owned a cottage at Gordon Bay, which was at the north end of Lake Joseph in the Muskoka Lakes area of Ontario.

58. A fantasy never realized, though for portions of a novel that Frye did write and other fictional experiments, see *FMW*, pt. 2.

59. Daniells had received an offer to teach summer school from 20 June to 29 July at Western Reserve University in Cleveland, Ohio. In July he would accept an offer to become chair of the English department at the University of Manitoba.

60. Herbert J. Davis, who had just announced that he was leaving Toronto for a position at Cornell.

61. Wallace had proposed that Frye canoe from Gordon Bay to Wallace's summer cottage at Go Home Bay (Ayre, 143), a trek of more than twenty miles by the waterways.

62. The original typing has a strike-over here.

63. For a fuller account of Frye's meeting with Chancellor Wallace, see his letter to Helen Kemp of 21 July 1937 (*NFHK*, 2:766–7).

64. John and Sallee Creighton. Sallee, a reader in the English department at Victoria College, had recently accepted a position at Bennington College.

65. A.S.P. Woodhouse was a member of the English department at University College. Kenneth Cousland had been Frye's church history teacher at Emmanuel College, the member of the faculty there he seemed most to admire.

66. M. St. A. (Moff) Woodside was a member of the classics department at Victoria College.

67. Roy and Harold Kemp.

68. That is, Frye has typed to the very end of the page. The last paragraph of the letter is a holograph addition, written on the verso.

69. In his letter of 14 July Daniells had written, "I'm frightfully jealous of your scholastic powers and your ability to write and your youth."

70. This was Elizabeth Fraser, a Canadian graphic artist with whom Frye and Helen Kemp had had a passing acquaintance in Toronto. A bohemian, pipe-smoking free spirit, she was trying to survive in Oxford by illustrating books. Fraser and Frye shared each other's company on a number of occasions during the 1937–38 year at Oxford, including time spent together in London. They feed off each other's loneliness and creative interests. Fraser's letters to Frye strongly suggest a romantic attachment as well.

71. The honor course in Milton.

72. Robert Burton, *The Anatomy of Melancholy* (1621).

73. Margaret Ray, associate librarian at Victoria College.

74. Helen — now Helen Frye — was working on educational and other projects for the Art Gallery of Toronto.

75. Jerry and Kay Riddell. Jerry was senior tutor at Victoria College.

76. The next page includes holograph examples of what Frye had apparently encountered in his students' papers: "The 14th century, in which Chaucer lived," "*This fact could* ‖ *but*," and "This fact (*which could* ...) is" [with an arrow drawn from "fact" to "could"].

77. That is, Frye has begun typing his letter halfway down the page.

78. Ernie Gould was Frye's classmate at Victoria College. His brother, also a Victoria College graduate (1929), taught classics at Victoria.

79. John Whitney Pickersgill taught history at Wesley College at the University of Manitoba in Winnipeg from 1929 to 1937, when he joined the Department of External Affairs.

80. Frye's friend and classmate from Victoria and Emmanuel Colleges. He became a United Church of Canada minister.

81. Bert Arnold, professor of German at Victoria College.

82. Frye and Helen Kemp were married on 24 August 1937. Art Cragg performed the ceremony.

83. Jerry Riddell, senior tutor at Victoria College.

He later joined the Canadian department of external affairs.

84. Stuart Gilbert, *James Joyce's "Ulysses"* (London: Faber and Faber, 1930).

85. The reference is Desmond Pacey's satire of Frye at some unknown event. "Bobbed" is a back-formation from the Victoria College Bob, an annual satiric and musical review, formally baptizing freshmen into the life of the college. It was begun in 1872 — when Victoria College was in Cobourg — as a "Bob party" for the benefit of the college janitor, Robert Beare, from whom the show took its name. See Frye's comment on the 1931 Bob in *Acta Victoriana*, 56 (October-November 1931): 30.

86. Margaret Roseborough was a member of the graduate seminar on Blake given by Herbert J. Davis that Frye had enrolled in during his first year at Emmanuel College; she later became a member of the English department at the University of Manitoba.

87. Douglas LePan was a 1935 graduate of University College, University of Toronto. He became a poet, novelist, university teacher, governmental bureaucrat, and principal of University College.

88. That is, the accounts that Frye owed at Merton College.

89. All of the papers that Frye wrote for his tutor Edmund Blunden, except for one on Chaucer, were not preserved. He apparently never retrieved his first-year papers from Pelham Edgar — or from Daniells. In *NFHK* Frye refers to at least fifteen papers he wrote for his tutorials at Oxford.

90. Norman J. Endicott and Florence Smith were members of the English staff at Victoria College. The other people in the Victoria College community mentioned in the letter: Margaret (Peggy) Roseborough was graduate student at the University of Toronto studying Anglo-Saxon; she had been a member of Herbert J. Davis's Blake seminar two years earlier. Bill Stobie was Peggy Roseborough's friend and later husband. Kenneth Maclean joined the English department at Victoria in 1938 as Pelham Edgar's replacement. Joseph Fisher was chair of the English department at Victoria. Herbert J. Davis taught at University College, University of Toronto from 1922 to 1937, when he left for an appointment at Cornell. Barker and Margaret Fairley: he was a distinguished member of the German department at Victoria College; she, a well-known activist and one of the founders of the Labour Progressive Party. Magda and Bert Arnold: she was a student of psychology who later wrote a number of books on emotion, personality, and motivation; he, a member of the German department at Victoria. Jessie Macpherson was dean of women at Victoria.

91. Frye had turned twenty-six the week before. The summer course he was teaching was for teachers rather than undergraduates (Ayre, 147).

92. See n. 57, above.

93. Several months later Frye would no doubt incorporate this talk into "Men as Trees Walking," which traces the development of surrealistic painting from the chaos of early Dadaism through the influences of Freud and Jung. See the headnote to his letter to Roy Daniells of September 1938.

94. That is, serving as a don in the women's residences.

95. Edward W. Wallace, Jr., the Wallace's only child, who graduated from Victoria College in 1938. He enlisted in the Air Force shortly thereafter and was killed in World War II.

96. After the term was over in Oxford — on 3 December — Frye went to London where he stayed with his friend Mike Joseph. He shortly set out for Paris, by way of Rouen, with Joseph and another friend, Rodney Baine.

97. For Frye's fuller account of his time in France, see his letters to his wife Helen of December 1938 and January 1939 in *NFHK*, 827 ff.

98. Frye may have lost interest, but he did receive a first from his examiners, one of whom was C.S. Lewis.

99. Henry Noyes, who had received his M.A. from the University of Toronto in 1936 and his Ph.D. from the University of London in 1938, taught at Victoria College during the 1938-39 academic year. His wife, Gertrude, had contracted tuberculosis; at the time, Canadian regulations required a five-year waiting period for people with tuberculosis to enter the country. Knowing of this regulation, she had no plans to leave England in 1939. After Britain entered the war, however, the Canadian regulations were altered, and in September she was given permission by the Canadian embassy to travel to Canada (Henry Noyes to Robert D. Denham, 20 December 1993).

100. Joseph Fisher was a member of the English department at Victoria College, having been appointed in 1937. He then served in World War II, returned to Victoria, and was appointed chair of the department in 1945.

101. Helen Frye was holding down two jobs, serving as staff lecturer at the Art Gallery of Toronto and as a don in the women's residences

102. Frye would write his examinations four months later and sit for his viva voce. He did earn a first, the only Merton student for the year to achieve such a mark in English literature.

103. The New Zealander was Mike Joseph, who is featured prominently in Frye's letters to Helen Frye, where a much more detailed account of Frye's vacation in Paris can also be found. See *NFHK*, 2:835–8.

104. Frye had completed his exams in mid–June, earning a first.

105. See n. 103, above.

1940s

106. Carol Coates Cassidy and Eugene Cassidy were close friends of Daniells. Both were born in Japan of missionary parents, and both attended the University of British Columbia. They returned to Japan in 1930 and in 1938 came to Toronto, where Carol, a poet, became involved with the educational theories of Rudolf Steiner and where Eugene began work as a photographer. They later separated: Eugene went to New York where he became a successful contract photographer for Condé Nast.

107. Joseph Fisher was chair of the department of English at Victoria, before volunteering for military duty. Archie Hare was registrar at Victoria.

108. Henry Noyes (see n. 99, above) had accepted a position at the University of Missouri.

109. Margaret Roseborough Stobie (see n. 86 above) and Bill Stobie, also a professor of English.

110. The Rhodes scholar was Rodney Baine.

111. Herbert J. Davis (see n. 60, above).

112. Mary Winspear, a classmate of Frye's in Herbert Davis's Blake seminar, ended up doing her Ph.D. at the University of Toronto, writing a thesis under the direction of A.S.P. Woodhouse on "The English Man of Feeling." She came to Canada from England in 1910. After receiving her Ph.D. she was dean of women at the University of Alberta and later headmistress of the Weston School in Montreal. In 1971 she retired to Sidney, BC, where she died in 1999 at the age of 99.

113. Daniells began broadcasting nationally on CBC Radio in 1940.

114. Frye is replying to Daniells' letter of 24 May.

115. The neighbor was Robert J. Cormier, whom Frye first met on a train trip to Moncton in August 1936. For another account of Cormier see *NFHK*, 2:521–2, 532, and 547.

116. The Scotsman John Mackinnon Robertson (1856–1933) was a rationalist critic of religion to the core; he published over one hundred books and thousands of articles in fields as diverse as sociology, economics, history, anthropology, Biblical criticism, and literary criticism.

117. A.S.P. Woodhouse was chair of the English department at University College. He had a wide and important influence on English studies, especially in Canada, having helped to direct the careers of many university teachers of English. Norman Endicott was his colleague at University College. See n. 15, above.

118. As Frye never learned to drive, he apparently accompanied his father on his hardware-selling trips.

119. On Eugene Cassidy and his wife Carol, see n. 106, above. In his letter of 24 May 1940, Daniells had written to Frye: "If you really know the Cassidys quite well, I would like, in the *strictest* confidence, to ask your advice about something. I lent him $200 some time ago, to which I have just had to add another $100. I cannot quite make out the situation. On one hand, he has two children to look after and he doubtless needs the money badly; I'm bound to him and more especially to Carol, by old ties of friendship. But on the other hand he seems to regard repayment as an airy contingency of the remote future and he lives in a house (I on the third floor of someone else's), he drives a good car (I none), he normally manages all sorts of extras, holidays, etc, which my people here would regard as great luxuries, their scale being far below his. In the circumstances I hardly know what to do and feel less and less inclined to regard the loan as a gift. What I have to do is offer still another $100 as a cushion against unexpected difficulties, if he will make small regular payments ($5 a month to begin with) into my account. I hate to be mean, but Eugene is not easy to deal with. If you have any information or suggestions to offer, I shall be grateful, as you are closer to them than I."

120. The Nazis saw Oswald Spengler as their intellectual precursor.

121. Eleanor Godfrey, editor of the *Canadian Forum.*

122. All three were poets who later made names for themselves.

123. Earle Birney, known for his experimental verse, taught at University College, University of Toronto, beginning in 1936. He served as a personnel officer in the Canadian Army from 1942 to 1945. Ernest Sirluck entered the Canadian Army in 1942 and served

until VE Day, 8 May 1945. He returned to Toronto in 1946, after which he became a member of the English faculty at University College, University of Toronto.

124. Eleanor Godfrey, editor of the *Canadian Forum.*

125. Managing editor of the *Canadian Forum.*

126. Frye is referring to James Laughlin's New Directions publishing venture in Norfolk, CT.

127. The reference is to Smith's anthology *A Book of Canadian Poetry,* which would be published in 1943.

128. More than twenty years later Frye wrote: "[D]uring the war, at an evening in Earle Birney's apartment in Toronto, I heard Ned read *The Truant,* and felt, not simply that I had heard the greatest of all Canadian poems, but that the voice of humanity had spoken once more, with the kind of authority it reserves for such moments as the bombing of London, when the powers of darkness test the soul and find once more that 'The stuff is not amenable to fire'" [l. 31] ("Ned Pratt: The Personal Legend," *Canadian Literature* 21 [Summer 1964]: 9).

129. Letter to Robert Denham, 22 September 1994.

130. Along with Emil Brunner and Karl Barth, Karl Heim is often called a crisis theologian, because they saw humanity as under the judgment of God, and the beginning of religion as when God presents himself to human beings in the crisis situation. The reference is to chapter 1 of *God Transcendent,* where Heim argues that the ideas of above and beyond usually assumed for God are no longer tenable. Moorhouse may also be referring to a footnote in which Heim quotes David Friedrich Strauss: "The housing-problem has now arisen in the case of God" (trans. Edward Dickie, [New York: Scribner's; London: Nisbet and Co., 1935], p. 31).

131. The "revelations" Daniells had sent Frye are uncertain.

132. A year after arriving at the University of Manitoba, Daniells began a series of radio programs on literature for the general public. See Sandra Djwa, *Professing English: A Life of Roy Daniells* (Toronto: University of Toronto Press, 2002), 175.

133. *Unit of Five,* edited by Ronald Hambleton, was a collection of poems by five young Canadians: Louis Dudek, Ronald Hambleton, P.K. Page, Raymond Souster, and James Wreford. Frye reviewed the collection in *Canadian Forum,* 25 (May 1945): 48, praising especially the work of Dudek. He discovered a certain derivative mannerism in Hambleton, self-consciousness of technique in Page, epigrammatic self-expression in Souster, and romanticism in Wreford, but he recommends that all five are worthy of "exhaustive critical analysis," as the small volume is "full of the real thing." The review was rpt. as "Unit of Five" in *NFCanada,* 44–6.

134. John D. Robins was chair of the English department at Victoria College; Walter T. Brown was president of Victoria.

135. Eleanor Godfrey, the previous editor of the *Canadian Forum*

136. G.M.A. Grube, professor of classics at the University of Toronto. He had been book review editor before taking over as managing editor of the *Canadian Forum.*

137. Alan Creighton, corresponding editor and, later, business manager of the *Canadian Forum.*

138. Daniells had told Frye in his letter of 26 July

1946 that he had lent his copy of *Fearful Symmetry* to Garnett Sedgewick (see n. 142, below), who in turn had lent it to Arthur Smith. When Smith returned the copy, Daniells then gave it to Ira Dilworth, who also taught English at the University of British Columbia. Daniells reports that he had ordered another copy of the book.

139. By this time *Fearful Symmetry* had received four reviews in the Canadian press: anonymously in the *Toronto Star* 17 May 1947: 9; William Arthur Deacon in the *Globe and Mail* 17 May 1947: 12; John Garrett in the *Canadian Forum* 27 (July 1947): 90; and B.K. Sandwell in *Saturday Night* 62 (19 July 1947): 17.

140. "Too kind, too kind"—Nightingale's response to King Edward on receiving the Order of Merit in 1907.

141. Lloyd Frankenberg, "Forms of Freedom," *Saturday Review of Literature* 30 (19 July 1947): 19. Frankenberg regards Frye's approach as unsystematic and piecemeal and says that he frequently fails in being able to organize and explain Blake's ideas.

142. Garnett Sedgewick (1882–1949), who served as head of the English department at the University of British Columbia from 1920 to 1948. He had given the Alexander Lectures at the University of Toronto, which were published as *Of Irony Especially in Drama* (Toronto: University of Toronto Press, 1934; 2nd ed., 1948).

143. Apparently a reference to the photograph of Frye that appeared with a review of *Fearful Symmetry*.

144. For Sedgewick, see n. 142, above.

145. John Douglas Grant, who had just completed a dissertation on Samuel Butler under the supervision of A.S.P. Woodhouse and had accepted an appointment at the University of British Columbia.

146. UBC President Norman had appointed Geoffrey Andrew, his personal assistant, to the English department. Andrew, whose B.A. degree was in history, later became dean.

147. "William Blake," *Spectator* 179 (10 October 1947): 466. Sitwell had written, "To say [*Fearful Symmetry*] is a magnificent, extraordinary book is to praise it as it should be praised, but in doing so one gives little idea of the huge scope of the book and of its fiery understanding."

148. Frye had written a brief review of *The Shadow of Cain* in the *Canadian Forum* 27 (January 1948): 238, remarking that Sitwell "is now a major poet, a necessary part of one's literary education and current reading alike, and this poem is a beautiful and erudite proof of the fact."

149. Sitwell had obviously mentioned C.M. Bowra and Pavel Tchelitchew in a previous (nonextant) letter. In replying to the present letter on 29 April 1948 Sitwell told Frye she had been in touch with C.M. Bowra to see if he could "put any pressure on" Oxford University Press to bring out *Fearful Symmetry* in England. She indicated that Pavel Tchelitchew, the Russian surrealist painter (1898–1957), might be writing Frye because *Fearful Symmetry* "has helped him solve certain very difficult problems of his own." Sitwell had fallen in love with Tchelitchew twenty years earlier.

150. Frye is referring to three reviews of *Fearful Symmetry* that had appeared in England: Sitwell's own review: "William Blake," *Spectator* 10 (October 1947): 466; Geoffrey Keynes, "The Poetic Vision," *Time and Tide* 28 (27 December 1947): 1394; and "Elucidation of Blake" by an anonymous reviewer in *TLS*, 10 January 1948: 25.

151. No records exist for a selection of Blake's poems edited by Sitwell and published by John Lehman in the Chiltern Library series.

152. In her letter of 29 April 1948 Sitwell repaid the compliment: "This is an inordinately long letter [6 pp.]. But it is profoundly exciting to me to write to so great a critic."

153. This paragraph is omitted in *Across My Path*. In his letter of 2 August, Edgar had told Frye of the thrombosis in his left leg.

154. Frye deleted "and authority" in the version of the letter in *Across My Path*.

155. This sentence is omitted in *Across My Path*.

156. In the version in *Across My Path*, this reads: "and for the summer had a small job." F. Louis Barber was the bursar and librarian at Victoria College.

157. In *Across My Path* this reads: "remark about Blake in a lecture."

158. In *Across My Path* this reads: eighteenth-century course."

159. In *Across My Path* this passage reads: " hooked. After graduation I snatched."

160. In *Across My Path*, this reads: "was giving, and was assigned."

161. The material from the beginning of the paragraph to this point is omitted in *Across My Path*.

162. The version in *Across My Path* reads: "went to two publishers."

163. In *Across My Path* this reads: "sent it to some more publishers, but I had lost interest."

164. In *Across My Path*, "manuscript."

165. The reference is to Frye's time as a student minister in and around Stone, Saskatchewan, during the summer of 1934.

166. This sentence is omitted from *Across My Path*.

167. Edgar's wife and daughter, respectively.

168. That is, Douglas Bush and E.K. Brown, both of whom had attended the University of Toronto. Bush, a teaching fellow at Victoria College in 1920-21, spent most of his career as a professor of English at Harvard. Brown taught English at University College, Toronto (1929–35; 1937–41), the University of Manitoba (1935–37), Cornell University (1941–44), and the University of Chicago (1944–51).

169. Charles N. Cochrane, "The Mind of Edward Gibbon," *University of Toronto Quarterly* 12 (December 1942): 1–17, and 12 (January 1943): 146–66.

1950s

170. "The Aesthetic Moment in Landscape Poetry," in Alan Downer, ed., *English Institute Essays* (New York: Columbia University Press, 1952), 168–81; rpt. in *The Interior Landscape: The Literary Criticism of Marshall McLuhan 1943–1962*, ed. Eugene McNamara (New York: McGraw-Hill, 1969), 91–7.

171. Margaret Roseborough Stobie had been, along with Frye, a member of H.J. Davis's Blake seminar in 1934-35.

172. Heilman had been trying to get Frye to accept a position at the University of Washington.

173. Johnston had sent Frye a copy of Jay Macpherson's *Nineteen Poems* (Mallorca, Spain: Seizin Press, 1952), which Frye did review in the *University of*

Toronto Quarterly 22 (April 1953): 269–80; rpt. in *BG*, 10–22 [19], and in *NFCanada*, 102–14 [110].

174. Alex Colville (1920–) and Miller Brittain (1919–68), two New Brunswick artists. Johnston had given a lecture on Colville, Brittain, and other New Brunswick artists two years earlier at the Hart House gallery, University of Toronto (see *Diaries*, 232).

175. Frye had recently been appointed chair of the English department at Victoria College.

176. George and Jeanne Johnston had four children. A fifth was born in 1959, and they would adopt a sixth in 1964.

177. Jay Macpherson would be arriving shortly from McGill, where she was earning a library degree, to study with Frye at Toronto. She had gotten to know Johnston as an undergraduate at Carleton and through summer and weekend visits to his home.

178. Johnston had begun a Ph.D. on Blake and Yeats under Frye's supervision, but eventually abandoned it.

179. The reference is to Ned (E.J.) Pratt and to John D. Robins, who was chair of the English department at Victoria College at the time of his death on 18 December 1952.

180. The Johnstons' oldest daughter.

181. See headnote to letter of 8 December 1952 to George Johnston. Macpherson was in library school at McGill, but had been spending summers and weekends back in Ottawa, working for Hans Jonas and visiting the Johnstons. According to her account, "When the library school arranged a class trip to introduce us to the great Toronto public library system, George said I must visit his friend Norrie Frye at Victoria, and wrote a note to introduce me.... I emerged from the interview with Frye—held mainly in Murray's [a restaurant], as he was escaping a meeting—with the offer ringing in my head that if I could get myself to Toronto he would 'teach me Blake'—by myself, as he wasn't otherwise giving a course." After being privately tutored by Johnston in Old English, Macpherson enrolled the next year in the graduate English program at Toronto (Jay Macpherson, "Smoothing the Way," in *The Old Enchanter: A Portrait of George Johnston*, ed. M.I. Cameron, et al. [Toronto: Penumbra Press, 1999], 37–8).

182. Frye had been invited to present a new series of lectures, financed by the Princeton class of 1932. The lectures turned out to form the backbone of *Anatomy of Criticism*.

183. Macpherson did follow Frye to Princeton, where she attended his lectures.

184. A reference apparently to Johnston's poems having been accepted by *The Spectator*. His *Hero's Kitchen* appeared in 190 (3 April 1953): 312; *In the Pond* in 193 (13 August 1954): 194; and *Pool* in 193 (22 October 1954): 499.

185. At the very end of his article, Friedman concludes his account of archetypal criticism by saying, "A measure of the use and validity of this method is to be found in the work of such men as Northrop Frye, W.H. Auden, or Gaston Bachelard, who bring to poetry a brilliant and wide-ranging insight, a deftness of touch, and a tact and subtlety of manner worthy of the highest ideals of scholarship and criticism" ("Imagery: From Sensation to Symbol," *Journal of Aesthetics and Art Criticism* 12, no. 1 [September 1953]: 37).

186. As Friedman's letter to Frye is not extant, the context of the remark here is uncertain, but the reference is to a line in George Meredith's *Modern Love*: "My feet were nourished on her breasts all night" (pt. 23, l. 16).

187. "Forming Fours," *Hudson Review* 6 (Winter 1954): 611–19, a review of C.G. Jung's *Two Essays in Analytical Psychology* and *Psychology and Alchemy*.

188. Apparently Charles A. Owen, Jr., a Chaucer scholar.

189. The Fryes had bought their Clifton Road home from Reid McCallum, a member of the philosophy department at the University of Toronto.

190. Macpherson had visited Graves in Mallorca. He had published he first book, *Nineteen Poems* (Mallorca: Seizin Press, 1952).

191. Frye's lectures Frye eventually presented at Princeton were entitled "The Critic and His Public," "Symbols of Fact and Fiction," "The Language of Poetry," and Myth and Society."

192. In 1950 Frye had broken his right arm and injured his forehead in a car accident on the New Jersey Turnpike, having had subsequently to spend a week in the hospital. When the accident occurred, he was being driven by Philip Wheelwright from Cambridge, MA, to Princeton, where they were headed to see a production of Eliot's *The Family Reunion* (Ayre, 226)

193. Wood had served in the army after graduating from Victoria College.

194. Wood had been in the hospital for a suspected ulcer.

195. A large mansion donated in 1925 to Victoria College by Mrs. E.R. Wood to be used as a centre for women students. Located west of the present campus across Avenue Road, it is now called Falconer Hall—a part of the University of Toronto Law School. It was named after Wood's two children, Wyman and Mildred Wood.

196. "Yes I know the young American by letters I think. He has the American passion for ideas, combined, I judge, with the American intellectual indolence and physical energy" (Letter to Robert Bridges, 4 January 1923, in *The Letters of W.B. Yeats*, ed. Allan Wade [New York: Macmillan, 1955], 696).

197. William J. Baumol, who taught at Princeton until 1972, when he accepted a position at New York University. He became a prolific scholar and a distinguished economist.

198. Both Dorothy Burr Thompson and Homer A. Thompson had held appointments in the department of classical archaeology at the University of Toronto. In 1947 they moved to Princeton, where Homer held a position in the Institute for Advanced Study.

199. Frye's four lectures were "The Critic and His Public," "Symbols of Fact and Fiction," "The Language of Poetry," and "Myth and Society." In his preface to *Anatomy of Criticism*, Frye wrote," I am also grateful to the Class of 1932 of Princeton University and to the Committee of the Special Program in the Humanities at Princeton, for providing me with a most stimulating term of work, in the course of which a good deal of the present book took its final shape. The book contains the substance of the four public lectures delivered at Princeton in March 1954" (vii).

200. George Johnston, a friend of Frye and Wood's colleague in English at Carleton University.

201. The conditions of Frye lectureship at Princeton required the teaching of a seminar, in addition to his public lectures.

202. On the Fryes' trip to England, see Ayre, 245–6.

203. In 1954 Joseph McCarthy was parodied by the radio comedy team Bob and Ray in their soap opera spoof *Mary Backstayge, Noble Wife*.

204. *The Story of Stories: The Book of Job*, with an introduction by Lawrence Montague Lande (Montreal: n.p., 1946).

205. The reference is to the idea of poetic form developed by R.S. Crane in *The Languages of Criticism and the Structure of Poetry* (Toronto: University of Toronto Press, 1953), and elsewhere.

206. For Gordon Wood's illness, see n. 194, above. For a similar account of the New Year's party, see *Diaries*, 593.

207. "Carl Schaefer—Artist and Man," *Queen's Quarterly* 61, no. 3 (Autumn 1954): 345–52.

208. As it turned out Gordon Wood, who received his M.A. from Toronto in 1947 and began teaching at Carleton College (later University) in 1951, never did complete his Ph.D. thesis.

209. The reference is to a TV program on Blake that Frye presented. On 15 February 1955 he went to the studio to view what he calls in his *Diaries* a "retake" of the program (607). The *Varsity* was the student newspaper at Victoria College.

210. This letter, which is not extant, was in reply to Friedman's letter of 6 December 1954, in which he asked Frye about the definition of certain of his terms ("convention," "genre," "morphology," "form," "content," "structural principles," and "pure archetype," and about the relation of the general to the particular, especially in R.S. Crane's view of the matter.

211. Frye reviewed Layton's book in his annual survey of Canadian poetry: "Letters in Canada," *University of Toronto Quarterly* 25 (April 1956): 290–304; rpt. in *BG*, 45–59 [53–4], and in *NFCanada*, 137–51 [144–5]. Two decades later Frye would write an introduction to the Italian translation of Irving's book, "Introduzione," *Il freddo verde elemento* by Irving Layton, trans. Amleto Lorenzini (Turin: Einaudi 1974), v–viii.

212. Frye reviewed *The Blue Propeller* in the annual survey recorded in the previous note. See *BG*, 54; *NF-Canada*, 144–5.

213. Layton's selected poems, *Improved Binoculars* (Highlands, NC: Jargon), with an introduction by William Carlos Williams, appeared in 1956. Frye reviewed the book, along with *The Bull Calf*, in his annual survey of Canadian poetry: "Letters in Canada," *University of Toronto Quarterly* 26 (April 1957): 296–311; rpt. in *BG*, 59–71 [69–70], and in *NFCanada*, 151–67 [166–7].

214. Frye's paper, "Preface to an Uncollected Anthology," was published in *Studia Varia: Royal Society of Canada: Literary and Scientific Papers*, ed. E.G.D. Murray (Toronto: University of Toronto Press, 1957), 21–36; rpt. in *BG*, 163–79, and in *NFCanada*, 255–71. Frye had mentioned Waddington's poems in his paper.

215. Frye apparently responded to Thorpe's initial request (10 December 1956), but lodged some reservations (that letter is lacking in the Thorpe papers). Thorpe's next letter (15 January 1957), expresses concern that Frye not be pressured into a project "he isn't going to relish," and Thorpe assures Frye that the editors will have "full responsibility for planning, assembling, and publishing" the volume. Frye's reply is to this second letter.

216. The paper in question was almost certainly the one Frye gave on 18 June 1957 at the meeting of the Association of Canadian Teachers of English in Ottawa. According to Roy Daniells's diary he spoke from notes on "critical method as applied to English."

217. Victor G. Hopwood, who had been a student of Frye's at the University of Toronto. He completed a Ph.D. thesis at Toronto in 1950—*A Critique of Objective Standards in Poetic Judgment*. For their various encounters, see *Diaries*, 211–12. Hopwood was hired by the English department at the University of British Columbia, along with six other new instructors. See Sandra Djwa, *Professing English: A Life of Roy Daniells* (Toronto: University of Toronto Press, 2002), 291.

218. The reference is to Johnston's *Music on the Water*, which later appeared in *The Cruising Auk* (Toronto: Oxford University Press, 1959), 36–7; rpt. in *Endeared by Dark: Collected Poems* (Erin, ON: The Porcupine's Quill, 1990), 45.

219. The allusion is to a line from Yeats's *Among School Children*: "the children's eyes / In momentary wonder stare upon /A sixty-year-old smiling public man."

220. All three poets mentioned here—Dudek, Souster, and Layton—were founders of Contact Press, a Montreal publisher of poetry in the 1950s and 1960s.

221. Frye has apparently returned from a recent trip to Ottawa, as both Wood and Beattie, who has been Frye's classmate at Victoria College, taught at Carleton University.

222. Frye's sister Vera taught public school in Chicago. Frye's father was living with her at the time.

223. This information ended up being included in Frye's preface.

224. Child was Chancellor's Professor of English at Trinity College, University of Toronto.

225. Kreisel, a member of the English department at the University of Alberta, had received his M.A. from the University of Toronto and his Ph.D. from the University of London. He was also a novelist, short story writer, and playwright. Sawyer had received his Ph.D. from the University of Toronto, having written his dissertation on Joseph Conrad. As it turned out, Gray was unsuccessful in his effort to publish a new edition of Conrad's *Victory*.

226. For the Frye-Fisher sessions see *Diaries*, 12, 23, 30 (Buddhist wisdom), 43 (the Rajas-Tamas opposition), 58, 73, 86–7, 97, 98 (Agni Yoga), 108, 109, 114, 117–8 (bardo), 124, 133–5 (Tibetan Buddhism's fear of Bön, Parabrahman, Japanese No drama), 143, 144, 149, 153, 157, 172 (Pratyekabuddha), 177, 183, 187, 198, 203–4, 206–7 (Isa Upanishad), 209, 212, 345, and 388.

227. Riddell had been a senior tutor when Frye was a student at Victoria College, and he later became the permanent Canadian delegate to the United Nations. He died suddenly in 1951 while representing Canada at the UN.

228. Frye is referring to his review of Jay Macpherson's *The Boatman* (Toronto: Oxford University Press, 1957), which had won the Governor General's Award for poetry for 1958. The review appeared in the *University of Toronto Quarterly* 27 (July 1958): 434–50, and was reprinted in *BG*, 72–7, and in *NFCanada*, 168–73.

229. Frye had recently returned from teaching in Columbia University's summer school.

230. This was the Second Congress of the Interna-

tional Comparative Literature Association at the University of North Carolina, where Frye gave a paper on Milton's *Lycidas*, which, by ironic coincidence, is an elegy on a drowned friend. Frye's paper was published in the *Proceedings of the Congress* 23 (1959): 44–55, and rpt. in *FI*, 119–26, and in *MB*, 24–34.

231. Bourinot's trademark was a very short line, ordinarily ranging from a single syllable to three or four beats.

232. Frank Davies, who was the designer for Pratt's *Collected Poems*. Davies was one of the founding members of the Society of Typographic Designers of Canada.

233. E.J. Pratt, *Collected Poems* (Toronto: Macmillan, 1944).

234. The reference is to Frank Davies's article, "Typescript into Book," *Tamarack Review* 9 (Autumn 1958): 48–55. The article includes a discussion of his design for *The Collected Poems of E.J. Pratt*, which was to set the poetry flush left on a slim page with wide center margins. Davies says that Frye "approved his [formatting] decision with enthusiasm" (49), but it is clear Frye still had reservations about this format for his introduction. See his letter to George Johnston of 28 October 1958.

235. Frye is referring to the lecture he gave on the occasion of the inauguration of Clause Bissell as president of the University of Toronto. Frye, representing the humanities, gave one of three talks, presented simultaneously in the three large lecture halls on the University of Toronto campus. Clyde Kluckhohn of Harvard spoke of behalf of the social sciences, and V.B. Wigglesworth of Cambridge spoke for the natural sciences. More than sixteen hundred people attended the lectures, and twelve hundred more were turned away because of lack of space. Frye's lecture was published as "Humanities in a New World," *3 Lectures: University of Toronto Installation Lectures, 1958* (Toronto: University of Toronto Press, [1959]), 9–23; rpt. in *Four Essays* (Toronto: University of Toronto Press, 1960), 15–29; in *DG*, 102–17, and in *WE*, 69–85.

236. The reference is to Johnston's poem *The Bulge*, which he enclosed with his letter of 29 September 1958 and which would be appearing soon in his new book, *The Cruising Auk* (1959). The poem's final quatrain: "Something enormous is bulging in Bridget—/ A milkman, a postman, a sugar-stick, a slop, / And old maid, a bad maid, a doughhead, a fidget, / Multiple sweet Bridget, what will she drop?" (George Johnston, *Endeared by Dark: Collected Poems* [Erin, ON: The Porcupine's Quill, 1990], 52).

237. See Frye's letters to Frank Upjohn of 15 September 1958 and 25 September 1958.

238. The allusions are to Johnston's forthcoming *The Cruising Auk* (Toronto: Oxford University Press, 1959), and to Jay Macpherson's *The Boatman* (Toronto: Oxford University Press, 1957).

239. "Poetry," in *The Arts in Canada: A Stocktaking at Mid-Century*, ed. Malcolm Ross (Toronto: Macmillan, 1958), 84–90. Rpt. in *NFCanada*, 280–92.

240. Pierce had announced his decision to retire as editor of Ryerson Press in 1960. He approached Frye with an offer to succeed him as editor, but Frye declined.

241. Frye is referring to two Ryerson books he edited—Pelham Edgar's *Across My Path* (1952) and Charles Trick Currelly's *I Brought the Ages Home*

(1956)—and two Ryerson volumes in which he had essays—"Trends in Modern Culture," in *The Heritage of Western Culture: Essays on the Origin and Development of Modern Culture*, ed. Randolph C. Chalmers (1952), 102–17, and "Religion and Modern Poetry" in *Challenge and Response: Modern Ideas and Religion*, ed. Randolph C. Chalmers and John A. Irving (1959), 23–36.

242. Frye had become principal of Victoria College in 1959.

243. Claude Bissell, president of the University of Toronto.

244. Johnston has gone to a reading by Ralph Gustafson in Toronto and had dropped by the Fryes' house following that.

245. That is, Frye's installation as the principal of Victoria College on 21 October 1959. In his letter of 25 October 1959 Johnston apologizes for not having attended the ceremony.

246. Here Frye has a marginal holograph annotation: "maybe the Judge had an s: I forget." Frye has spelled Judge Jeffrey (of the *Edinburgh Review*) correctly.

247. *Blackwood's Magazine* was widely known as "Maga."

248. The reference is to Erdman's *William Blake: Prophet against Empire* (1954). Although the manuscript he sent Frye never became a book, his work on Coleridge eventually became a part of his three-volume edition of Coleridge's *Essays on His Times* (1978).

1960s

249. Pierce was retiring as editor of Ryerson Press.

250. The *New Outlook* resulted from the merging in 1925 of the denominational newspapers of the Methodists, Presbyterians, and Congregationalists. It was the forerunner of the *United Church Observer*, which began publication in a magazine format in 1939.

251. In his annual survey of Canadian poetry Frye began his lengthy review by saying, "George Johnston's *The Cruising Auk* (Oxford) should appeal to a wider audience than most books of poems surveyed in these reviews. Even the envious reader should be disarmed by the simplicity, which may make him feel that he could do as well if he set his mind to it, or that here at last is a 'light' verse which 'doesn't take itself too seriously,' the favourite cliché of the culturally submerged. The critic, however, has to explain that the substance of Mr. Johnston's poetry is not at all the image of the ordinary reader that is reflected from its polished surface. He must explain that seriousness is not the opposite of lightness, but of portentousness, and that genuine simplicity is always a technical tour de force. In short, he must insist that Mr. Johnston's most pellucid lyrics have to be read as carefully as the most baffling paper chase of e. e. cummings" ("Letters in Canada," *University of Toronto Quarterly* 29 [July 1960]; rpt. in *BG*, 110–15, and in *NFCanada*, 209–13).

252. The footnote mentioned in the headnote to this letter was not deleted in subsequent editions of *Fearful Symmetry*.

253. The reference is to a poem, *Multitude*, that Johnston had sent Frye. Sadie is a character who appears in a number of Johnston's poems. *Multitude* was collected in *Home Free* (Toronto: Oxford University Press, 1966) and in *Endeared by Dark: The*

Collected Poems (Erin, ON: The Porcupine's Quill, 1990), 114.

254. Johnston's *Beside the Sea* was collected in *Home Free* and in *Endeared by Dark: The Collected Poems*, 84–6.

255. In his letter to Frye of 26 January 1960 Johnston wrote that *Beside the Sea* was written in "the anything goes spirit" of Irving Layton.

256. The line is from A.E. Housman's *Terrence, This Is Stupid Stuff*: "They put arsenic in his meat / And stared aghast to watch him eat; / They poured strychnine in his cup / And shook to see him drink it up: / They shook, they stared as white's their shirt: / Them it was their poison hurt. / — I tell the tale that I heard told. / Mithridates, he died old" (ll. 69–76). Mithridates, the king of Pontus (d. 63 B.C.E.), managed to survive the efforts to poison him by concocting an antidote of fifty-four ingredients.

257. Frye attended the conference and contributed a "Comment" on the paper delivered by Fr. Walter Ong. See *Approaches to the Study of Twentieth-Century Literature* (Proceedings of the Conference in the Study of Twentieth-Century Literature, First Session) (East Lansing: Michigan State University Press, 1961), 79–83. For Frye's contribution to the discussion of other symposium papers, see pp. 95–6, 100, 101, 122, 133, 143, 161–2, and 164–5.

258. Although Kenner spent his entire teaching career in the United States, he was born in Peterborough, ON, and attended the University of Toronto, where he came under the influence of Marshall McLuhan. At the time, he was teaching at the University of California at Santa Barbara. He later taught at Johns Hopkins University and the University of Georgia.

259. By 1960 Kenner already had a half-dozen books to his credit.

260. Barroll ended up teaching at Vanderbilt University, the University of South Carolina, and the University of Maryland.

261. *Eight Poems* (Toronto: Tortoise Press, 1959), Richard Outram's first book.

262. *Winter Sun* (London: Routledge, Kegan Paul, 1960).

263. Mandel's *Fuseli Poems* did appear in 1960 (Toronto: Contact Press).

264. Avison's *Winter Sun* did win the Governor General's Award for poetry for 1960.

265. Bloom was not awarded a Hodder Fellowship. Whether he applied for one is uncertain.

266. "The Realistic Oriole: A Study of Wallace Stevens," *Hudson Review* 10 (Autumn 1957): 353–70; rpt. in *FI*, 238–55.

267. The reference is to Van Ghent's edition of the novel (New York: Holt, Rinehart and Winston, 1961).

268. Bruner had been invited to come to Toronto by Roy Sharp, a member of the Toronto Board of Education.

269. Frye attended a symposium at Harvard on "Myth Today," 23–24 April 1960, sponsored by the American Academy of Arts and Sciences. His presentation was published as "Myth, Fiction, and Displacement," *Daedalus* 90 (Summer 1961): 587–605; rpt. in *FI*, 21–38, and in *EIOW*, 401–19.

270. Under the auspices of the National Academy of Sciences and the National Science Foundation, Brunner chaired an influential ten-day meeting of scholars and educators at Woods Hole on Cape Cod in 1959.

One result was his now-classic book *The Process of Education* (1960).

271. In 1961 the Canadian Conference on the Arts had organized the first major national arts conference, the O'Keefe Conference on Arts in Society, calling for increased funding and support for the arts.

272. Wilkinson (1910–61) was a Canadian writer who had published two volumes of poetry at the time of her death, *Counterpoint to Sleep* (1951) and *The Hangman Ties the Holly* (1955), both of which Frye had reviewed in his annual surveys of poetry for the *University of Toronto Quarterly*.

273. Frye's citation, "John George Diefenbaker," was presented on the occasion of the awarding of an honorary degree to Diefenbaker by Victoria University, 21 September 1961. It was first published in *NFCanada*, 313–15.

274. *The Rhetoric of Religion* (1961).

275. On 16 October Frye wrote to Morgan, "I regret very much to have to say at the last minute that I am not going to make the October 20 deadline. The book however is a very interesting one, and, as one would expect with Burke, thoroughly original, and when my review does get finished I think it will be useful to you." If Frye did in fact complete the review, it was never published.

276. Fiedler's *An End to Innocence: Essays on Culture and Politics* had been published by Beacon Press in 1955.

277. Johnston had sent Frye a copy of his "long story about nitro-glycerine" and asked that he pass it along to Jay Macpherson (Johnston's letter of 23 January 1962).

278. Frye means to say "Sadie and her sisters."

279. Mr. Murple is a character who makes repeated appearances in Johnston's *The Cruising Auk* (1959) and in a later poem entitled *Beside the Sea*.

280. Johnston had joined the Society of Friends, but he reports to Frye that this decision "had been premature," adding "I have since withdrawn as gracefully as I could, which is to say, not very gracefully, and followed my family into the Anglican Church" (Johnston's letter of 23 February 1962).

281. The Johnstons' son.

282. The reference is to a witty little sestet, *Annabelle*, in Johnston's *The Cruising Auk*.

283. Frye addressed the American Psychiatric Association, which met in Toronto, 7–11 May 1962. His talk, "The Imaginative and the Imaginary," was published in *The American Journal of Psychiatry* 119 (October 1962): 289–98; rpt. in *FI*, 151–67, and in *EIOW*, 420–35.

284. Bonamy Dobrée, *English Literature of the Eighteenth Century*, which Frye reviewed in *The Griffin* 9 (August 1960): 2–11; rpt. in *NFCL*, 147–55, and in *ENC*, 16–23.

285. *Prism* was founded in 1959 by a group of Vancouver writers, teachers, and others with literary interests, including several members of the University of British Columbia's Department of English. In 1963 it became affiliated with the Department of Creative Writing at UBC. *Canadian Literature* was founded at UBC in 1958, when Roy Daniells and others asked George Woodcock to edit a journal devoted solely to Canadian writing. Its first issue appeared in the autumn of 1959.

286. Macpherson was dean of women at Victoria College.

287. Johnston reported that Gordon Wood, one of Frye's former students and Johnston's colleague at Carleton University, was suffering from an ulcer.

288. A.B.B. Moore, president of Victoria University.

289. This is evidently a reference to Matthew 6:27: "Which of you by taking thought can add one cubit unto his stature?"

290. The reference here is to Matthew 6:25: "Therefore I say unto you, Take no thought for your life, what ye shall eat, or what ye shall drink; nor yet for your body, what ye shall put on. Is not the life more than meat, and the body than raiment?"

291. "The Road of Excess," originally published in *Myth and Symbol: Critical Approaches and Applications*, ed. Beatrice Slote (Lincoln: University of Nebraska Press, 1963), 3–20; rpt. in *StS*, 160–74, and in *MB*, 316–29.

292. *Blake's Apocalypse: A Study in Poetic Argument* (New York: Doubleday, 1963).

293. *Design for Learning: Reports Submitted to the Joint Committee of the Toronto Board of Education and the University of Toronto*, ed. with an introduction by Northrop Frye (Toronto: University of Toronto Press, 1962).

294. Pursewarden, the British intelligence agent in Lawrence Durrell's *Alexandria Quartet*, serves as a spokesman for Durrell.

295. *The Plough and the Pen: Writings from Hungary, 1930–1956*, ed. Ilona Duczynska and Karl Polanyi (Toronto: McClelland & Stewart, 1963).

296. Jean Erdman, *The Coach with Six Insides*, an adaptation of *Finnegans Wake* into a musical play.

297. Frye had regularly lunched with Fred Johnston when he taught summer school at Columbia in 1958.

298. The Board of Regents and the principal of Victoria did grant Frye a sabbatical for 1964–65, and in appreciation Frye dedicated his Bampton Lectures, *A Natural Perspective: The Development of Shakespearean Comedy and Romance* (1965), to them.

299. Williamson was the founder of the Boston Camerata, for many years the performing extension of the Collection of Musical Instruments at the Museum of Fine Arts, Boston.

300. Frye's sabbatical was actually not approved by the board of Victoria College until March 1964.

301. Frye was never able to complete this "third book" on the external relations of literary criticism. For a complete account of the "third book" see Michael Dolzani, "Introduction" to *TBN*.

302. The Fryes did spend the fall of 1965 in Britain, where he had a speaking tour of five universities.

303. Judy White, Frye's secretary.

304. MacLean was head of the English department at Victoria College; Trethewey, of French.

305. Squire did agree to postpone Frye's appointment to the commission, and on 25 June 1964 Frye wrote to Squire, "It is very good of you to overlook my sabbatical, and under the conditions you suggest I should be delighted to join the Commission on Literature."

306. In his 3500-word review, Smith had said, "It is the completeness and assuredness with which the whole field of communication and expression as prose, verse, or speech is here organized and 'dealt with' that makes this essay a unified work of art. Frye has seen the critic's task as one of analysis and synthesis, an im-

mense intellectual effort that must nevertheless be informed by love and illuminated by imagination. Satire, a sense of social responsibility, and a sort of controlled indignation set the tone of the first chapter; the second is largely intellectual, with here and there a metaphorical or aphoristic *tour de force*; and the third, as tightly organized as either of its predecessors, moves to a climax that is metaphysical if not mystical. The closing pages of the book are intensified by the organizational intellectual control, and this comes about because the substance, the ideas themselves, are so rich and so passionately, though unostentatiously, held."

307. E.J. Pratt Room of Contemporary Poetry at the Victoria University Library was opened in October 1964. It housed a collection of Pratt manuscripts, printed books, and records, and a collection of contemporary poetry, much of which had been donated by Frye. Shortly after the library was renamed the E.J. Pratt Library in 1967, the Pratt Room was closed.

308. Frye delivered the Alexander Lectures at the University of Toronto on 15–17 March 1966. They were published as *Fools of Time: Studies in Shakespearean Tragedy* (Toronto: University of Toronto Press, 1967).

309. This was a series of lectures on Romanticism Frye had committed to give at the Graduate School of Western Reserve University in May 1966. These lectures eventuated in the book *SER*.

310. A.S.P. Woodhouse. See n. 117, above. Woodhouse had died on 31 October 1964.

311. Douglas LePan (see n. 87, above) and Claude Bissell, a member of the English department at University College, 1941–56, and president of the University of Toronto, 1958–71.

312. For Layton's various comments on Frye over the years, see *Engagements: The Prose of Irving Layton*, ed. Seymour Mayne (Toronto: McClelland and Stewart, 1972), xiii, 58, 59, 109, 157, 159, 165–70, 172–4. Layton remarks at one point that Frye can be "safely ignored by poets and novelists," claiming that Frye separates literature from life and that his science of criticism is abstract and outdated. In a CBC Radio interview from 1972, Layton speaks of his early criticism of Frye and his present admiration of him, saying that in many ways he "mythologized" Frye, making him a sinister figure. He then adds, but "all along I had a huge suspicion of the overwhelming intellectual integrity and worth of Frye. But precisely because he was such a tremendous intellect and such a tremendous influence I had to fight him" ("This Is Robert Fulford" series, broadcast of 28 October 1972, audiotape in the CBC Archives, no. 721028-1).

313. Frye's sister Vera was suffering from a rare spinal cord ailment. Frye tried unsuccessfully to persuade her to return to Canada. She ended up in a convalescent hotel. See Ayre, 304.

314. Richard P. Blackmur, distinguished critic and founder of the Christian Gauss Seminars in Criticism at Princeton, had died on 2 February 1965.

315. *Arrows of Intellect: A Study in William Blake's Gospel of the Imagination* (Aligarh, India: Naya Kitabghar, 1965).

316. *Orion and Other Poems* was published by C.G.D. Roberts in 1880, when he was twenty years old.

317. Within a few years Frye would find himself involved in a project with Harcourt Brace Jovanovich to produce a series of readers for elementary and high school students. It eventually developed into a series

of twelve volumes, under the general title *Literature: Uses of the Imagination*, for which Frye was supervisory editor.

318. The sentence in question: "One early Orc rebellion was the Exodus from Egypt, where Orc is represented by a pillar of fire (the 'fiery joy') and Urizen by a pillar of cloud, or what *Finnegans Wake* calls 'Delude of Isreal.'"

319. In addition to these texts, Frye's preface also mentions selections from Gower, Mallet, and Freud.

320. Sharp was one of the co-chairs of the joint committee of the Toronto Board of Education and the University of Toronto. Morgan was the director of the Ontario Curriculum Institute, and Jackson was head of its program committee.

321. A. Owen Aldridge, editor of *Comparative Literature Studies*, had just left the University of Maryland for a position at Illinois, and Jost had begun negotiations with the university to take over support of the journal.

322. *Comparative Literature*, a journal founded in 1949.

323. In addition to John Stuart Mill, the reading list for the course included Newman, Burke, James Mill, Carlyle, Ruskin, Huxley, Arnold, Morris, and Butler.

324. "The Problem of Spiritual Authority in the Nineteenth Century," in *Literary Views: Critical and Historical Essays*, ed. Carroll Camden (Chicago: University of Chicago Press, 1964), 145–58; rpt. in *StS*, 241–56, and in *ENC*, 271–86.

325. In an undated letter to "Miss Barker," assistant librarian at Victoria University, Frye wrote: "I have carefully thought over your kind invitation to preach on January 25, and regret very much that I have to decline. For a variety of reasons preaching is more of a nervous and emotional strain on me than it perhaps should be, and at a time when I have lost so many colleagues and have been so anxious about others, it seems to me that I am not well enough equipped for it. This is not the manufactured excuse that it may well seem to be—I only wish it were."

326. That is, *The Cruising Auk* (Toronto: Oxford University Press, 1959), Johnston's first collection.

327. *Under the Tree* and *Love in High Places*.

328. "Elementary Teaching and Elemental Scholarship," *PMLA* 79 (May 1964): 11–18; "Criticism, Visible and Invisible," *College English* 26 (October 1964): 3–12; "Introduction," *Design for Learning: Reports Submitted to the Joint Committee of the Toronto Board of Education and the University of Toronto* (Toronto: University of Toronto Press, 1962).

329. Alvin A. Lee was appointed as dean of graduate studies in 1971, a position he held until 1973. He later served as president and vice-chancellor of McMaster (1980–90).

330. Dufferin Roblin, a Red Tory politician. He was premier of Manitoba from 1958 to 1967, when he resigned to run for the leadership of the federal Progressive Conservative Party at its 1967 leadership convention. He placed second to Nova Scotia Premier Robert Stanfield.

331. Kermode had written, "[T]his remarkable book ... seems to prove that Frye's systems are mnemotechnical in character, a way of making fruitful connections between disparate activities of an extraordinary mind."

332. Smith reported that Lionel Tardif, a junior English major, got a B- in the course Smith was teaching, organized around Frye's four *mythoi*.

333. In the two autobiographical novels that Frye mentions Frederick Philip Grove claimed to be of Anglo-Swedish origin. In 1971 Spettigue himself discovered that Grove had spent his first thirty years in Germany as Felix Paul Greve. To remove himself from the German scene, he staged a suicide in 1909.

334. The University of Western Ontario.

335. Laszlo struggles to understand Frye's position on the social function of literature, which he finds to be generally weak, but he does find Frye's argument about archetypes stimulating, even though it squeezes "the living reality of literature" into arbitrary categories. He worries that Frye pays too little attention to modern literature and that he avoids the issue of the development of new archetypes. Still, Laszlo observes that, for Marxists, Frye does not lose sight of the social content of literature.

336. "James Bond, Culture Hero," *New Republic* 150 (30 May 1964): 17–20.

337. *A Natural Perspective: The Development of Shakespearean Comedy and Romance* (New York: Harcourt, Brace and World, 1965), 45.

338. Butson never became a university teacher. His career took him down numerous other paths—those of an electrician's assistant, a pharmacy courier, a newspaper reporter, a tobacco primer, a mail carrier, a construction worker, a soldier, a high school teacher, and a widely published poet.

339. "The Revelation of the Grand Inquisitor," *Southern Review* 2 (1967): 240–60.

340. Grant had received an ACLS fellowship to study Blake's illustrations for Edward Young's *Night Thoughts*.

341. *The Modern Century* (1967).

342. The reference is to a paper Frye gave at the Midwest Modern Language Association on 2 November 1967 at Purdue University, where he had been invited to address the general theme of the conference, "The Revival of Romance." Frye's paper, entitled "One Bare Circumstance: The Quest of Endymion," became the heart of the chapter on Keats in *SER*, published the following year. The paper grew out of one of the lectures Frye gave at Western Reserve University in May 1966.

343. The reference here is to a paper on Keats's *Endymion* referred to in the previous note.

344. Sabri-Tabrizi proposed that Blake may have taken the word "Indra" from Sir William Jones's translation of the *Sakuntala*, published in 1789 and widely read in Britain.

345. Sabri-Tabrizi had written that the department of English at the University of Edinburgh considered Blake to be an "odd and diabolical writer."

346. Davis, who had been a student of Maynard Mack at Yale, reports that on a recent visit Mack told him that his Alexander Lectures at the University of Toronto would soon be published. They appeared as *The Garden & the City: Retirement & Politics in the Later Poetry of Pope, 1731–1743* (Toronto: University of Toronto Press, 1969).

347. "False Themes and Gentle Minds," *Philological Quarterly* 47, no. 1 (January 1968): 55–68, and "'The Nymph Complaining for the Death of Her Fawn': A Brief Allegory," *Essays in Criticism* 18, no. 2 (April 1968): 113–35.

348. The allusion is to Andrew Marvell's *An Horatian Ode upon Cromwell's Return from Ireland*.

349. The daughter of Viola and E.J. Pratt.

350. "Proteus Unbound: Some Versions of the Sea God in the Renaissance," in Peter Demetz, ed., *The Disciplines of Criticism* (New Haven: Yale University Press, 1968), 431–75.

351. This was a lecture Frye gave while visiting the Society for Humanities at Cornell. It developed into part 3 of *CP*.

352. A paper Frye presented at Sligo, Ireland. It was published as "The Top of the Tower: A Study of the Imagery of Yeats," *Southern Review* 5 (Summer 1969): 850–71; reprinted in *StS*, 257–77.

353. The essay, as Bloom acknowledges in his letter of 27 January 1969, was "The Ethics of Change: The Role of the University," in *A Symposium: The Ethics of Change* (Toronto: Canadian Broadcasting Corp., 1969), 44–55; rpt. *DG*, 156–66, and in *WE*, 345–59.

354. Bloom's book appeared four years later—*The Anxiety of Influence: A Theory of Poetry* (New York: Oxford University Press, 1973).

355. Abrams was almost certainly remembering some remark of Frye that took this form in *Anatomy of Criticism*: "Flaubert, Rilke, Mallarmé, Proust, were all in their very different ways 'pure' artists. Hence the central episodic theme is the theme of the pure but transient vision, the aesthetic or timeless moment, Rimbaud's *illumination*, Joyce's epiphany, the *Augenblick* of modern German thought, and the kind of non-didactic revelation implied in such terms as *symbolisme* and imagism" (61).

356. "I am not wholly unaware that at every step of this argument there are extremely complicated philosophical problems which I am incompetent to solve as such. I am aware also, however, of something else. That something else is the confused swirl of new intellectual activities today associated with such words as communication, symbolism, semantics, linguistics, metalinguistics, pragmatics, cybernetics, and the ideas generated by and around Cassirer, Korzybsky, and dozens of others in fields as remote (as they seemed until recently) as prehistory and mathematics, logic and engineering, sociology and physics. Many of these movements were instigated by a desire to free the modern mind from the tyranny of emotional rhetoric, from the advertising and propaganda that try to pervert thought by a misuse of irony into conditioned reflex. Many of them have also moved in the direction of conceptual rhetoric, reducing the content of many arguments to their ambiguous or diagrammatic structures. My knowledge of most of the books dealing with this new material is largely confined, like Moses' knowledge of God in the mount, to gazing at their spines, but it is clear to me that literary criticism has a central place in all this activity, and from the point of view of literary criticism I offer an admittedly very speculative suggestion" (*AC*, 350).

357. These were doubtless the following two presentation copies in Frye's library: *The Martian Chronicles*, with a new introduction by Fred Hoyle (New York: Time, 1963), and *The Vintage Bradbury: Ray Bradbury's Own Selection of His Best Stories*, with an introduction by Gilbert Highet (New York: Vintage Books, 1965).

358. In a 1950 review of *The Martian Chronicles*,

Christopher Isherwood observed, "Mr. Bradbury is a very great and unusual talent."

359. Hartman had enclosed an offprint, identifiable by Frye's remarks as "Adam on the Grass with Balsamum," *ELH* 36, no. 1 (March 1969):168–92.

360. See *WTC*, 80–1, 99.

361. The report of the Keiller Mackay Committee on religious education in the schools—*Religious Information and Moral Development* (1969)—recommended that religious education be removed from schools because it did not reflect the principles of modern education.

362. It is true that except for the table of apocalyptic categories in the Third Essay (141) the *Anatomy* contains no diagrams or summarizing charts. Frye did, however include two diagrams and one table in the manuscript he originally submitted to Princeton University Press. His notebooks for the *Anatomy* contain fourteen diagrams and ten charts or tables, and his other notebooks contain scores of such diagrammatic constructs. In his later work Frye was not at all averse to including spatial schema: *The Great Code* has eleven charts, diagrams, and tables, and there are five more in *Words with Power*.

363. Frye had attended the Eleventh Triennial Congress of the Fédération Internationale des Langues et Littératures Modernes in Islamabad, Pakistan, in September 1969.

364. Hendry had recommended that Frye read *The Practical Theorist: The Life and Work of Kurt Lewin*.

365. "The Rival Churches of St. Asaph and St. Osoff," in Stephen Leacock's comic masterpiece *Arcadian Adventures with the Idle Rich*.

366. In the review of *The Blasted Pine* in his annual survey of Canadian poetry, Frye had asked, "Where is Pamela Vining Yule, that engaging discovery of the first edition of Mr. Smith's anthology?" ("Letters in Canada: 1957, Poetry," *University of Toronto Quarterly* 27 (July 1958): 434–50; rpt. in *NFCanada*, 167–86 [183], and in *BG*, 70–87 [85].

367. The reference is to Premier W.A.C. Bennett's statement that he won the British Columbia elections because he was "plugged in to God." Bennett served as premier of British Columbia from 1952 to 1972.

368. William Aberhart was premier of Alberta's first Social Credit Government, 1935–43.

369. "We have Marvell, and Pope—why read Horace?"

370. Jacques Roos, *Aspects littéraires du mysticisme philosophique et l'influence de Boehme et de Swedenborg au début du romanticisme: William Blake, Novalis, Ballanche*, éd. P.-H. Heitz (Strasbourg, 1951).

371. Kizer asked Frye whether she had quoted correctly from the opening address he gave in Islamabad.

372. In his notebooks for *Anatomy of Criticism* and other books Frye drew scores of diagrams, including several for the six phases of the four mythoi. See n. 362, above.

373. The two papers were "Mythos and Logos," *The School of Letters, Indiana University: Twentieth Anniversary, 1968* (Bloomington, IN: N.p., 1968), 27–40, and "The University and Personal Life: Student Anarchism and the Educational Contract" in *Higher Education: Demand and Response* (The Quail Roost Seminar), ed. W.R. Niblett (London: Tavistock Publications, 1969), 35–59.

374. An essay by Robert Funk and a set of materi-

als that Noel was using in an introductory New Testament course at Lafayette College.

1970s

375. Frye never typed out his notes, but his lectures were taped and have been published as "Lectures on the Bible," in *RT*, 413–607, and as "Symbolism in the Bible," in *BCM*, 1–250.

376. That is, the student protest movement of the late 1960s.

377. The reference is to a sculpture of the Gandhara, which Anderson had brought back from Pakistan and had mounted on a block of wood.

378. That is, a meeting of the Modern Language Association in Denver, where Anderson had seen a number of the attendees of the FILLM conference.

379. "Problems of Reason, Feeling and Habitat," *Architectural Association Quarterly* 1, no. 3 (July 1969): 5–10, and "Five Ages of Urbanity," *Landscape* 17, no. 3 (Spring 1968): 7–10.

380. "*Jerusalem*: A Synoptic Poem," *Comparative Literature* 22 (Summer 1970): 265–78, which argues for a gospel form for Blake's narrative.

381. Webb wrote that he had served a small summer parish in North Hatley, QC.

382. All five were Blake scholars.

383. *AC*, 132–4.

384. The reference is to what Frye's colleague John Irving had told Frye about Pratt's interest in Wundt's theory of perception. See letter of 25 September 1970, above.

385. For Reich, Consciousness I, the "pioneer mentality," values independence, self-reliance, and self-satisfaction. Consciousness II, the grey-flannel suit or corporation mentality, values playing by the rules.

386. Reich's Consciousness III was the mentality of enlightened independence — a kind of hippie nirvana. As Frye suggests, Reich's prediction that Consciousness III would dominate after the 1970s did not come true, as hippie culture essentially faded into oblivion in the 1980s.

387. In September 1969 Frye had attended the congress of the Fédération Internationale des Langues et Littératures Modernes in Islamabad.

388. That is, at the meeting of the International Association of University Professors of English in Istanbul, which Frye attended in late August 1971.

389. Frye is referring to Hartman's first two essays, "Structuralism: The Anglo-American Adventure" and "Ghostlier Demarcations: The Sweet Science of Northrop Frye."

390. John Grierson, one of the pioneers of the documentary film and the first film commissioner of Canada's National Film Board. He spent much of his career in Paris, London, and Scotland, but had retuned to Canada in 1968 to lecture at McGill and to write.

391. The McGibbons, Don and Pauline, were long-time friends of the Fryes, their friendship going back to their student days at Victoria College.

392. Montreal: Delta Canada, 1970.

393. In 1971 the House of Anansi Press suffered a fire that destroyed about half of its stock.

394. That is, Dennis Lee, one of the founders of the House of Anansi Press, had delivered to Frye a copy of *BG*, which had just been published.

395. Don McGibbon, Pauline's husband, was a 1932 graduate of Victoria College.

396. Claire Pratt, an artist, poet, and editor, was the daughter of Viola and E.J. Pratt. The occasion in question was doubtless an exhibition of her graphic art.

397. The reference is to Frederick Crews, "Anaesthetic Criticism," *New York Review of Books* 14 (26 February 1970) and 14 (12 March 1970). Crews's polemic was directed against the prevalent tendency to renounce "methods that would plainly reveal literary determinants," and he sees Frye as on of the chief promulgators of the notion that critics should not stray outside of literature in developing their fundamental principles. He then establishes his own Freudian framework in opposition to Frye's.

398. Frye had received an honorary degree from Acadia University in 1969. Dryden had planned to attend the ceremonies, but the trip did not materialize.

399. Dryden had asked whether Frye knew Professor E.A. Dryden of the literature faculty at the State University of New York at Buffalo.

400. Jane Widdicombe, Frye's secretary.

401. The reference is to ll. 60–2 of *Samson Agonistes*: "But peace, I must not quarrel with the will / Of highest dispensation, which herein / Happ'ly had ends above my reach to know."

402. Frye had apparently run into Purdy a one of the meetings of the Canadian Radio-Television Commission he attended in Ottawa — on 9–11 June and again on 29–30 June.

403. Purdy had sent along two unidentified books, which he asked to be returned.

404. Thomas was director of and surgeon for the Grenfell Association and a strong supporter of the people of Labrador and Newfoundland.

405. In late August 1971 Frye would be attending a meeting of the International Association of University Professors of English in Istanbul.

406. Apparently Michael Collie, a nineteenth-century British fiction scholar at the University of Toronto.

407. The people mentioned here: Bissell served as president of the University of Toronto from 1958 to 1971; early in his career, he had been a lecturer in English at University College, University of Toronto; Sirluck was dean of graduate studies at the University of Toronto from 1964 to 1968 and vice-president and graduate dean from 1968 to 1970; LePan, who was a Merton College during Frye's years there, was a professor of English at Toronto, presently serving as principal of University College; MacKinnon was dean of the college of arts and sciences at Guelph University; and MacLure taught English Renaissance literature at Victoria College and was the former editor of the *University of Toronto Quarterly*.

408. Sister Ruth Ellen wonders whether Frye has any plans to visit South Africa.

409. Frye's "The Keys to the Gates" had been anthologized in Harold Bloom's *Romanticism and Consciousness: Essays in Criticism* (New York: Norton, 1970), 233–54.

410. Shattuck's essay was published as "Contract and Credentials: The Humanities in Higher Education," in Carl Kaysen, ed., *Content and Context: Essays on College Education: A Report Prepared for the Carnegie Commission on Higher Education* (New York: McGraw-Hill, 1973).

411. Shattuck had written, "I cannot for the life of me remember what occasion allowed us to meet many years ago—in a hotel, during a meeting, comparative literature I believe, and we had things to say about Hart Crane. Or am I inventing?"

412. *Banquet Years* (New York: Harcourt Brace, 1958) was Shattuck's study of the cultural avant-garde in Paris during the period 1880 to 1915 as seen in the lives of Alfred Jarry, Henri Rousseau, Erik Satie, and Guillaume Apollinaire

413. Frye is referring to the University of Toronto campuses in Scarborough and Mississauga.

414. Amis had asked for Frye's advice on the procedures for applying for a fellowship or scholarship.

415. Weinfield had sent Frye a copy of *The Dolorous Wood*, which eventually appeared in his collection *In the Sweetness of Time* (Atlanta: House of Keys, 1980), 37–8, with the dedication "to Northrop Frye."

416. The series was published as *Literature: Uses of the Imagination*, 12 vols. (New York: Harcourt Brace Jovanovich, 1972–3).

417. Frye served as a part-time commissioner for the Canadian Radio-Television Commission (later renamed the Canadian Radio-television and Telecommunications Commission) from 1968 until 3 April 1976. He first met with the research department of the commission in December 1968 and again in July 1969, having lengthy discussion with two members of the department, Rodrigue Chiasson and André Martin, about the media, technology, Canadian identity, censorship, Canadian art, and a host of other topics. Part of their discussion was motivated by the archetypes of Frye's "Logos Diagram," with its Adonis, Eros, Prometheus, and Hermes quadrants. Frye's role on the commission, outside of being the resident intellectual, was not well defined, but in late 1970 he met with the commission again, and from that meeting emerged the two brief papers, one on "Canadian Identity and Cultural Regionalism" and the other on "Icons and Iconoclasm" (both are published in *LS*). Frye eventually assumed the responsibility of viewing television programs and writing reports on them for the research department. He went to Ottawa on 5 November 1971 to screen with members of the research staff (Martin, Chiasson, and Patrick Gossage) a wide range of television shows, including news stories, "talking heads," musical programs, and documentaries. Following the screenings Frye wrote his reviews of eight programs, entitled "Reflections on November 5th." Back in Toronto he continued to view programs through March 1972, sending the research department more reflections, twelve of which have been preserved in the CRTC archives. The staff prepared program notes for the viewings, referred to as "the Frye diet," and often issued memos in response to Frye's written reports. The twenty reflections, "Reviews of Television Programs," are also published in *LS*. A transcript of the interview with Frye by Chiasson and Martin has been published in *I*, 88–144.

418. Bates had taken his chapter titles from *Finnegans Wake*.

419. Bates's wife, whose name was actually Kirsti.

420. An anthology of Pakistani poetry in English that Ashraf had edited.

421. Cherry, dean of arts and sciences at the University of Saskatchewan, had shown an interest in bringing Ashraf to Canada.

422. Eleanor Godfrey.

423. "William Blake," *The English Romantic Poets and Essayists: A Review of Research and Criticism,* ed. Carol W. and Lawrence H. Houtchens (New York: Modern Language Association of America, 1957), 1–31; rpt. in *MB*, 266–89.

424. René Wellek, "Romanticism Re-examined," in *Romanticism Reconsidered: Selected Papers from the English Institute,* ed. Northrop Frye (New York: Columbia University Press, 1963), 107–33. On Peckham, see pp. 109–11.

425. Four years later Frye was elected president of the Modern Language Association.

426. "To Define True Madness," *Canadian Forum* 29 (September 1949): 125. An unsigned editorial; rpt. in *RW*, 394–5.

427. "Idols of the Marketplace," *Canadian Forum* 26 (September 1946): 124–5.

428. "Anaesthetic Criticism," *New York Review of Books* 14 (26 February 1970) and 14 (12 March 1970).

429. Walter Jackson Bate, *Criticism: The Major Texts* (New York: Harcourt Brace Jovanovich, 1970); Hazard Adams, *Critical Theory since Plato* (New York: Harcourt Brace Jovanovich, 1971).

430. *Modern Literary Criticism: 1900–1970,* ed. Lawrence I. Lipking and A. Walton Litz (New York: Atheneum, 1972).

431. *Northrop Frye* (Toronto: McClelland and Stewart, 1971).

432. The reference is to Frye's statement at the beginning of his "Towards Defining the Age of Sensibility: "The period of English literature which covers roughly the second half of the eighteenth century is one which has always suffered from not having a clear historical or functional label applied to it.... What we do is to set up, as the logical expression of Augustanism, some impossibly pedantic view of following rules and repressing feelings, which nobody could ever have held, and then treat any symptom of freedom or emotion as a departure from this. Our students are thus graduated with a vague notion that the age of sensibility was the time when poetry moved from a reptilian Classicism, all cold and dry reason, to a mammalian Romanticism, all warm and wet feeling" (*FI*, 130; rpt. in *ENC*, 7).

433. McPherson had gone to McGill in 1970 to direct the program in communications there.

434. *Journal of Canadian Fiction* 1 (Winter 1972): 47–56.

435. At the ACUTE conference at McGill, 31 May–2 June 1972, Frye presented a talk on "The Critic and the Writer."

436. Frye had visited the Serpent Mound, east of Cincinnati atop a ridge that over looks the Ohio Brush Creek. Apparently an effigy mound, it is thought to have been constructed by the Adena Indians.

437. A reference to Frye's having been made a Companion of the Order of Canada. Daniells had written Frye a note on 26 June offering his congratulations.

438. Frye is alluding to the pamphlet issued three years earlier: Pauline Kogan (pseud.), *Northrop Frye: The High Priest of Clerical Obscurantism* (Montreal: Progressive Books and Periodicals, 1969).

439. Frye presented the Birks Lectures, entitled "Revelation and Response," at McGill University, 4–7 October 1971.

440. That is, the introductions to the various writers included in the projected anthology. Fletcher indicates that he has received copies of some of Frye's introductions: "You seem to be able to concentrate the character of a writer's career in such a way that one believes your account of the writer and his work completely." Although Frye's general editor's introduction survived (and has been published in *LS*, 3–130), his introductions to individual writers did not.

441. "Littérature et mythe" in *Poétique: revue de théorie et d'analyse littéraires*, no. 8 (1971), 489–514, a translation by Jacques Ponthoreau of Frye's "Literature and Myth," in *Relations of Literary Study: Essays on Interdisciplinary Contributions*, ed. James Thorpe (New York: Modern Language Association, 1967), 22–54.

442. "Introduction," *Shakespeare's Tempest*, gen. ed., Alfred Harbage (Baltimore: Penguin, 1959), 14–26; rev. ed., 1970; "Dickens and the Comedy of Humours" in *Experience in the Novel*, ed. Roy Harvey Pearce (New York: Columbia University Press, 1968), 49–81; reprinted in *StS*, 218–4, and in *ENC*, 287–308.

443. "The Idea of a Critical Approach," in *Essays on European Literature* (St. Louis: Washington University Press, 1972), 237–54.

444. The three other "major critics" in part 1 of the anthology were Ezra Pound, T.S. Eliot, and I.A. Richards.

445. Josephine Miles, "The Language of William Blake," *English Institute Essays 1950*, ed. Alan S. Downer (New York: Columbia University Press, 1951), 141–69.

446. Jon Pearce and Bruce M. Littlejohn, ed., *Marked by the Wild: An Anthology of Literature Shaped by the Canadian Wilderness* (Toronto: McClelland and Stewart, 1972).

447. Stephen Graubard, the editor of *Dædalus*.

448. In his preface to *The Bush Garden*, Frye wrote that "the Canadian conception of Canadian poetry has been largely formed by Mr. Smith, and in fact it is hardly too much to say that he brought that conception into being" (vii).

449. *Natural Supernaturalism: Tradition and Revolution in Romantic Literature* (New York: Norton, 1971).

450. Abrams, drawing on Frye's essay "The Critical Path," had written, "Schelling was one of the philosophers who helped establish the present views, of which Northrop Frye is a distinguished representative, that human needs inevitably impel the creation of a mythology to live by, in civilized no less than in primitive societies" ("Coleridge's 'A Light in Sound': Science, Metascience, and the Poetic Imagination," *Proceedings of the American Philosophical Society* 16, no. 6 [21 December 1972]: 473).

451. *AC*, 122.

452. Doob announced in a postscript that an article of hers on Ezra Pound and the critics was forthcoming in the *Chicago Review*.

453. Richard P. Adams, "'The Comedian of the Letter C': A Somewhat Literal Reading," *Tulane Studies in English* 18 (1970); and "Wallace Stevens and Schopenhauer's *The World as Will and Idea*," *Tulane Studies in English* 20 (1972): 135–68.

454. "Ideology and Literary Studies: A Dilemma," *PMLA* 88 (1973): 321–3. Baker's piece, in the Forum section of *PMLA*, was a critique of an earlier article by Frederick Crews, "Objectivity in Scholarship," *PMLA* 86, no. 2 (March 1971): 280–1.

455. "Anaesthetic Criticism I" and "Anaesthetic Criticism II," *New York Review of Books* 14 (26 February and 12 March 1970); rpt. in Crews's *Psychoanalysis and Literary Process* (Cambridge, Mass.: Winthrop Press, 1970), 1–24.

456. *A Pictorial Key to the Tarot* (London: Rider and Sons, 1911).

457. S. Foster Damon, *Blake's Job: William Blake's Illustrations of the Book of Job* (Providence, RI: Brown University Press, 1966).

458. In her final paragraph Lowinsky thanks Frye for being "one of the critical highlights" of her undergraduate years.

459. "There's no such thing as a morally bad novel: its moral effect depends entirely on the moral quality of its reader, and nobody can predict what that will be" (*EI*, 94).

460. "We notice in passing that the creative and the neurotic minds have a lot in common. They're both dissatisfied with what they see; they both believe that something else ought to be there; and they try to pretend it is there or to make it be there" (*EI*, 29).

461. Kogan's attack also appeared in *Ideological Forum*, nos. 3, 4, and 5 (Montreal: The Internationalists, n.d.) and with minor changes in *Alive Magazine: Literature and Ideology*, no. 43 (1975): 22–31.

462. Daniells had had a rather serious fall. He reported to Frye that he had pulled a couple of ribs. On 2 October 1973 he wrote again, saying that he had "completely recovered from injury to ribs."

463. *StS*, 34.

464. "I bless my self and am thankful ... that I never saw Christ nor His Disciples" (*Religio Medici*, ed. W.A. Greenhill [London: Macmillan, 1950], 18 [pt. 1, sec. 9]).

465. Frye had been made a Companion of the Order of Canada in 1972. Daniells had received the honor the previous year. In a footnote to his letter, Daniells wrote, "As you know, our being in the Order gives me immense satisfaction. I feel I have been drawn up from the level I belong on, quite undeservedly, while you on your level grace the Order and give it meaning, but somehow the Canadian national sensibility, like the grace of God (if I may still use the term), wraps round us both."

466. *The Saga of Gisli the Outlaw*, trans. George Johnston (Toronto: University of Toronto Press, 1963).

467. C.L. Barber, *Shakespeare's Festive Comedy* (Princeton, NJ: Princeton University Press, 1972).

468. "Wallace Stevens and the Variation Form," in *Literary Theory and Structure: Essays in Honor of William K. Wimsatt*, ed. Frank Brady, John Palmer, and Martin Price (New Haven, CT: Yale University Press, 1973), 395–414; rpt. in *SM*, 275–94.

469. Frye's first article on Stevens was 'The Realistic Oriole: A Study of Wallace Stevens," *Hudson Review* 10 (Autumn 1957): 353–70; rpt in *FI*, 238–55.

470. As a student Frye had read Fridell's *A Cultural History of the Modern Age*, 3 vols. (New York: Knopf, 1932). See *SE*, 475 n. 23.

471. All of Johnston's letters to Frye, along with the poems he copied, were in calligraphy.

472. "Some will say, Is not God alone the Prolific? I answer, God / only Acts & Is, in existing beings or Men" (*The Marriage of Heaven and Hell*, plate 16).

473. "Babylon Revisited or the Story of Luvah and Vala," in *Blake's Sublime Allegory: Essays on the "Four Zoas," "Milton," and "Jerusalem,"* ed. Stuart Curran and Joseph A. Wittreich (Madison: University of Wisconsin Press, 1973), and "Christ's Body," in *William Blake: Essays in Honour of Sir Geoffrey Keynes*, ed. Morton D. Paley and Michael Phillips (London: Oxford University Press, 1973).

474. *Post-historic Man* (New York: Viking, 1950). Seidenberg argued that the human race was being trapped into moral immobility by rational mechanisms aimed at organizing and thus controlling the natural and human worlds.

475. Ehrenfeld believes that Seidenberg "has posed a plausible and direct challenge to Spengler's view of history."

476. Stevenson had emigrated from Scotland to Vancouver Island in 1907. He graduated from the University of British Columbia, received his M.A. from the University of Toronto and his Ph.D. from the University of California (at 22). He taught at Arizona State, Duke, and Southern California and was visiting Distinguished Professor at the University of British Columbia when he died December 1973.

477. Published as "Dickens and the Comedy of Humours," in *Experience in the Novel*, ed. Roy Harvey Pearce (New York: Columbia University Press, 1968), 49–81; rpt. in *StS*, 218–40, and in *ENC*, 287–308.

478. In a telegram from the Franklin Mint 2 October 1973, one of several urgent messages imploring Frye to join the project, he was told that Willard Thorp of Princeton (who had recommended Frye to the advisory board), Alan Heimert of Harvard, Albert Guerard of Stanford, Frank Kermode of Cambridge, and Richard Ellmann of Oxford had already signed on. The Mint even sent a representative, Darby Perry, to visit Frye in his office at Victoria College. Nine scholars altogether eventually submitted their recommendations for the one hundred great books. Frye's recommendations were accompanied by this note of 23 October 1973 to Ron Wallace of the Franklin Mint: "I am sending with this the form sent me, marked up according to instructions. As I considered the list, however, I found myself drafting a more analytical table of what I would consider the hundred essential books of Western culture, following your own categories closely. I hope it will be more helpful than confusing."

Frye's List
Category 1: Novels outside the English-speaking World.

1. Apuleius, *Metamorphoses* (substituted for Petronius, on list).
2. Murasaki, *The Tale of Genji* (on list).
3. Selected *Arabian Nights* (on list, transferred).
4. Rabelais, *Gargantua and Pantagruel* (on list).
5. Cervantes, *Don Quixote* (on list).
6. Balzac, *Cousine Bette* (substituted for *Père Goriot*, on list).
7. Flaubert, *Madame Bovary* (on list).
8. Stendhal, *Charterhouse of Parma* (substituted for *The Red and the Black*, on list).
9. Hugo, *The Hunchback of Notre Dame* (on list).
10. Proust, *Swann's Way* (substituted for *Cities of the Plain*, on list).
11. Camus, *The Plague* and *The Stranger* (on list separately).
12. Tolstoy, *War and Peace* (on list).

13. Tolstoy, *Anna Karenina* (added).
14. Dostoevsky, *The Brothers Karamazov* (substituted for *Crime and Punishment*, on list).
15. Dostoevsky, *The Idiot* (on list).

Possible alternates: Kafka, *The Trial* (on list); Musil, *The Man without Qualities*; Mann, *The Magic Mountain* (on list); Marquez, *One Hundred Years of Solitude* (there isn't any Latin-American title on the list).

Notes:

1. I think Apuleius has more general appeal than Petronius, apart from the fact that the latter is exasperatingly fragmentary.
3. I transferred the *Arabian Nights* from children's books: you mention the Burton translation, which would need pretty careful editing if children were to read it.
9. I'd prefer *Les Miserables* for a lifetime library, but it's too long.
10. *Swann's Way* is the first novel of the Proust series, and the obvious choice: *Sodome et Gomorrhe* is very difficult to follow unless one knows something of what preceded it.

Category 2: British Novels.

1 (16). Bunyan, *The Pilgrim's Progress* (on list transferred).
2 (17). Swift, *Gulliver's Travels* (on list, transferred).
3 (18). Defoe, *Robinson Crusoe* (on list, transferred).
4 (19). Defoe, *Moll Flanders* (on list).
5 (20). Fielding, *Tom Jones* (on list).
6 (21). Sterne, *Tristram Shandy* (on list).
7 (22). Austen, *Pride and Prejudice* (on list).
8 (23). Emily Brontë, *Wuthering Heights* (on list).
9 (24). Dickens, *Great Expectations* (substituted for David Copperfield, on list).
10 (25). Thackeray, *Vanity Fair* (on list).
11 (26). George Eliot, *Middlemarch* (substituted for *The Mill on the Floss*, on list).
12 (27). Conrad, *Lord Jim* (on list).
13 (28). Hardy, *The Return of the Native* (on list).
14 (29). Lawrence, *Sons and Lovers* (on list).
15 (30). Joyce, *Ulysses* (on list, transferred).

Possible Alternates: Meredith, *The Egoist*; Trollope, *Last Chronicle of Barset*; Woolf, *To the Lighthouse* (on list); Patrick White, *Voss*; Forster, *A Passage to India* (on list).

Notes:

1, 2, 3. I've transferred these books from other categories: *Robinson Crusoe* is not a child's book, unless abridged and edited in a way I shouldn't care for.

Category 3: American Novels

1 (31). Hawthorne, *The Scarlet Letter* (on list).
2 (32). Melville, *Moby Dick* (on list).
3 (33). Mark Twain, *Tom Sawyer* AND *Huckleberry Finn* (on list separately).
4 (34). Howells, *The Rise of Silas Lapham* (added).
5 (35). James, *The Ambassadors* (substituted for *The American*, on list).
6 (36). Lewis, *Babbitt* (substituted for *Main Street*, on list).
7 (37). Dreiser, *Sister Carrie* (substituted for *An American Tragedy*, on list).
8 (38). Fitzgerald, *The Great Gatsby* (on list).
9 (39). Hemingway, *A Farewell to Arms* (substituted for *For Whom the Bell Tolls*, on list).
10 (40). Faulkner, *The Sound and the Fury* (on list).

Category 4: Short Stories and Novellas.

1 (41). Boccaccio, *Decameron* (on list).

2 (42). Poe, *Selected Stories* (on list).

3 (43). Melville, *Billy Budd* (on list; see note).

4 (44). Henry James, *The Turn of the Screw* (on list; see note).

Notes:

3. This book should contain *Benito Cereno* and *Bartleby*, or, perhaps, instead of them, *The Confidence Man*, which is really a novella.

4. This should also be combined with one or two other James stories of comparative length, such as *The Beast in the Jungle* or *The Pupil*. Another possibility, and one I like better, would be a book of three short novels by different authors: James, *The Turn of the Screw*; Conrad, *Heart of Darkness*; D. H. Lawrence, *The Man Who Died*.

Category 5: Children's Stories.

5 (45). *Grimm's Fairy Tales* (on list).

6 (46). *Andersen's Fairy Tales* (on list).

7 (47). Carroll, *Alice in Wonderland* AND *Through the Looking Glass* (on list separately).

8 (48). Dickens, *Christmas Carol* (on list; see note).

9 (49). Stevenson, *Treasure Island* (on list).

10 (50). Kipling, *The Jungle Book* (substituted for *Just-So-Stories*, on list).

Notes:

8. Again, *Christmas Carol* might look a bit skimpy unless combined with *The Chimes* or *The Cricket on the Hearth*. Another possibility would be to collect three Victorian stories for younger readers under a common title: *Christmas Carol*, Kingsley's *Water Babies*, and George MacDonald's *At the Back of the North Wind*.

Category 6: Poetry.

1 (51). Homer, *The Iliad* (on list).

2 (52). Homer, *The Odyssey* (on list).

3 (53). Virgil, *The Aeneid* (on list).

4 (54). Ovid, *Metamorphoses* (on list).

5 (55). Dante, *Divine Comedy* (on list).

6 (56). Chaucer, *The Canterbury Tales* (on list).

7 (57). Milton, *Paradise Lost* (on list).

8 (58). Goethe, *Faust* (on list, transferred).

9 and 10 (59–60). *Two Anthologies* (added; see note).

Notes:

It seems to me that, apart from epic, poetry is impossible to add to a series like this without making special anthologies. There's room for two collections of British and American poetry in my scheme, say one on British Poetry 1550–1880, running from Shakespeare's age down to the first-generation Romantics (Blake, Wordsworth, Coleridge), and one on British and American Poetry 1800–1950, running form the second-generation Romantics (Byron, Shelley, Keats) to our own day. Owing to the difficulty of translating poetry, I don't include translations of shorter poems by non–English poets, important as they are.

Category 7: Drama.

1 (61). Classical Tragedies (selected from Aeschylus, Sophocles, Euripides, on list).

2 (62). Classical Comedies (selected from Aristophanes, Terence, Plautus, on list).

3, 4, 5 (63, 64, 65). Shakespeare (on list)

6 (66). Plays Selected from Shakespeare's Contemporaries (Jonson, Webster, Marlowe, etc.; added).

7 (67). English Comedies, selected from Wycherley, Congreve, Sheridan, Goldsmith, Wilde, Synge, O'Casey (added).

8 (68). Shaw, *Arms and the Man*, *Major Barbara*, *Heartbreak House* (substituted for the Puritan plays, on list).

9 (69). Plays selected from Ibsen (on list) Chekhov (on list), Strindberg (added).

10 (70). Plays selected from O'Neill (on list), Pirandello (on list), Sartre (added) and Beckett (added).

Note:

Drama, like poetry, is difficult to represent except in collections.

Category 8: Biography and Essays.

1 (71). Plutarch, *Selected Lives* (on list).

2 (72). Boethius, *Consolation of Philosophy* (added).

3 (73). Erasmus, *The Praise of Folly* (on list).

4 (74). Castiglione, *The Courtier* (added).

5 (75). Montaigne, *Selected Essays* (on list).

6 (76). Bacon *Essays* and *Advancement of Learning*, Book I (first on list; second added).

7 (77). Boswell, *Life of Johnson* (on list).

8 (78). Voltaire, *Candide* (on list; see note).

9 (79). Carlyle, *Sartor Resartus* (added).

10 (80). Thoreau, *Walden* (on list).

Possible Alternates: Pascal, *Pensées* (on list).

Notes:

4. There doesn't seem to be on your list a book specifically on education, which is why I add what is in my opinion the world's best book on the subject.

8. Candide is reasonably short: I'd like to see *Zadig* or *Micromegas* added (or even, perhaps, Diderot's *Le neveau de Rameau*).

Category 9A: Discursive Prose to 1600.

1 (81). The Bible (on list; see note).

2 (82). Dictionary (on list; see note).

3 (83). Plato, *Republic* (on list).

4 (84). Plato, Shorter Dialogues (should include at least Apology, *Phaedo*, *Phaedrus*, *Symposium*, *Timaeus*, and *Critias*; added).

Notes:

1. There's no doubt that the Bible is one of the world's hundred great books, but whether it should be in a series like this I'm not sure. I could see an abridged or "essential" Bible as a possibility.

2. Again, there's no doubt that a good dictionary is essential to a good library, whether or not it should be one of the hundred books. Perhaps it should be left outside the numbering. I should have no objection to Webster, but others might want to exclude the famous Third.

8. You have both the *Bhagavadgita* and selections from the *Vedas* on your list: perhaps there should be a volume of "Hindu Wisdom," including these along with selections from the *Upanishads* and the Patanjali *Yoga Sutras*.

Category 9B: Discursive Prose from 1600.

11 (91). Descartes, *Discourse on Method*; Spinoza, *On the Improvement of the Understanding*; Leibnitz, *Monadology* (first two on list; third added; see note).

12 (92). Hegel, *The Philosophy of History* (added).

13 (93). Rousseau, *The Social Contract* (on list).

14 (94). Mill, *On Liberty* AND Locke, *Second Treatise on Government* (first on list; second added).

15 (95). Darwin, *Origin of Species* (on list).

16 (96). Kierkegaard, *Fear and Trembling* AND *The Concept of Dread* (first on list, second added).

17 (97). Marx, *Das Kapital*, Book I AND *The Communist Manifesto* (on list separately).

18 (98). Freud, *Basic Writings* (on list).

19 (99). *Nietzsche, Thus Spake Zarathustra* (on list).

20 (100). Whitehead, *Science and the Modern World* (added).

Notes:

11. These three works are all fairly short and the three together would give a good idea of the foundations of modern philosophy. I don't include Kant in the list, mainly because I doubt whether a subscriber to this series would actually want to read, say, *The Critique of Pure Reason*.

16. *Fear and Trembling* is quite short; *The Concept of Dread* is for the source of the whole "existentialist" movement concerned with anxiety and similar ideas, so it would be useful to include it.

20. It's difficult to pick classical scientific books: most such books belong to the history of science, and many of them are unreadable. A good example is Copernicus: Copernicus believed that the sun was motionless and that all heavenly bodies revolved at the same speed; consequently his book is impossibly muddled. There's only one translation into English, made around 1950 for the Chicago hundred-book scheme, and it's bloody awful. That's why I substitute Whitehead for Newton, Einstein, et al.

479. Member of the department of English at the University of Toronto, 1952–64; later, University historian.

480. Margaret Stobie was the first women appointed to the academic panel of the Canada Council. She and her husband Bill taught at the University of Manitoba.

481. Bertrand Russell, George Orwell, Somerset Maugham, and E.M. Forster.

482. Frye is referring to the Japanese translation of *The Educated Imagination* by Toro Egawa and Masahiko Maeda: *Kyôyô no tame no sôzôryoko* (Tokyo: Taiyosha, 1969). The English edition for Japanese students was edited by Hisaaki Yamanouchi (Tokyo: Tsurumi shoten, 1967).

483. *Yes, They Can: A Practical Guide for Teaching the Adolescent Slower Learner* (Toronto: Methuen, 1974).

484. David Holbrook, *English for the Rejected: Training Literacy in the Lower Streams of the Secondary School* (New York: Cambridge University Press, 1964).

485. Alex Colville (1920–), magical realist painter of international fame; William Kurelek (1927–77), painter, writer, and evangelist, known for his realistic and symbolic paintings of prairie farm scenes and religious subjects; E.J. Hughes (1913–2007), printmaker, muralist, Canadian war artist, and prolific painter of British Columbia landscapes; David Blackwood (1941–), popular graphic artist and painter, whose works are often inspired by his Newfoundland roots.

486. Jean Paul Lemieux (1904–90), somber painter of landscapes and everyday life.

487. Albert J. Franck (1899–1973), the founder of a school of Toronto urban art.

488. Jean-Paul Riopelle (1923–2002), painter, graphic artist, and sculptor.

489. *Le Refus Global* was the anti-establishment manifesto of 1948, issued by a group of sixteen Québécois artists and intellectuals, including the painters Paul-Émile Borduas and Jean-Paul Riopelle. The manifesto, which proclaimed total freedom of expression, was seen by many as one of the basic causes of the Quiet Revolution in French Canada in the 1960s.

490. "We have just enough Religion to make us hate, but not enough to make us love one another" ("Thoughts on Various Subjects" (1711) in *Prose Works of Jonathan Swift*, ed. Herbert Davis [Oxford: Blackwell, 1957], 1:241).

491. In the Ethiopic text of the Apocalypse of Peter, the Lord says to Peter, "but thou must not tell that which thou hearest [that sinners will be saved by the prayers of the righteous] unto the sinners lest they transgress the more."

492. Cheney's essay was eventually published as "Moll Cutpurse as Hermaphrodite in Dekker and Middleton's *The Roaring Girl*," *Renaissance and Reformation*, n.s. 7, no. 2 (May 1983): 120–34.

493. John Milton, *The Kingdom of Kings and Magistrates* in *Complete Poems and Major Prose*, ed. Merritt Y. Hughes (New York: Odyssey Press, 1957), 758–9. See also *Paradise Regained*, bk. 1, ll. 460–4.

494. What Frye attached is uncertain but the most likely candidate seems to be pages from part 5 of *CP* and would doubtless have included the material on pp. 113 ff.

495. Singh had written on his twenty-sixth birthday.

496. Eugene Korkowski, "Donne's *Ignatius* and Menippean Satire," *Studies in Philology* 72, no. 4 (1975): 419–38.

497. Robert D. Denham, *Northrop Frye: An Enumerative Bibliography* (Metuchen, NJ: Scarecrow Press, 1974).

498. This turned out to be *Spiritus Mundi: Essays on Literature and Society* (Bloomington: Indiana University Press, 1976).

499. "The Fate of Blake's Sunflower: A Forecast and Some Conclusions," *Blake Studies* 5 (1974): 7–64.

500. *Day of the Leopards: Essays in Defense of Poems* (New Haven: Yale University Press, 1976). "Northrop Frye: Criticism as Myth" had first appeared in *Northrop Frye in Modern Criticism*, ed. Murray Krieger (New York: Columbia University Press, 1966), 75–107.

501. Daniells had quoted a passage from Gilbert Murray on the different views of punishment in Aeschylus and St. Paul.

502. Desmond Pacey (1917–1975), the author of numerous studies in Canadian literature, spent most of his teaching career at the University of New Brunswick. He was a 1938 graduate of Victoria College.

503. Alfred Bailey had been a colleague of Pacey's at the University of New Brunswick and was a well-known historian and critic.

504. *AC*, 122.

505. From 1910 to 1925 Sapir directed the Anthropological Division in the Geological Survey of Canada in Ottawa. It was during this time that his important book *Language* was published, as well as a number of monographs on Nootka and other languages.

506. Most notably in *EI* and *CP*.

507. The references are to Morris W. Croll, *Attic and Baroque Prose Style: The Anti-Ciceronian Movement* (Princeton, NJ: Princeton University Press, 1969) and George Williamson, *The Senecan Amble: A Study*

in Prose Form from Bacon to Collier (Chicago: University of Chicago Press, 1966).

508. Kostelanetz had written that "the only time an ex-student ever saw Frye panic-stricken occurred at a government function, when an officially bilingual civil servant addressed him in French!" (*Three Canadian Geniuses: Glenn Gould, Marshall McLuhan, Northrop Frye* (Toronto: Colombo and Co., 2001), 128.

509. What Kostelanetz ended up saying is that Frye and McLuhan "keep a sporadic friendship" (*Three Canadian* Geniuses, 121).

510. John Robert Colombo had said that "McLuhan and Frye are Canada's Aristotle and Plato. McLuhan is the scientist, and Frye the mystical theorist, with the eternal paradigms and everlasting forms" (qtd. by Kostelanetz, *Three Canadian Geniuses*, 131).

511. Singh reports that Harry Levin had told him that Frye was writing a book of the theory of romance and he wonders if Frye plans to write anything on the Book of Job, a text that Singh has recently taught.

512. Elizabeth Cowan, director of the Association of Departments of English at the Modern Language Association.

513. William D. Schaefer, executive director of the Modern Language Association, 1972–78.

514. Breé had referred to a letter-signing operation that consumed too much of the MLA president's time; the letter apparently was to be sent out to some MLA membership group.

515. "The Limits of Dialogue," later published in *WGS*, 5–22; rpt. in *I*, 174–89.

516. Mandel replied on 16 March 1976: "My own notes, no doubt even more disorganized and less trustworthy than the CBC's, show March 1969 as the time of that interview." The interview was in fact recorded on 19 March 1969.

517. The visit was with Jay Macpherson, who, according to Mandel's reply of 16 March 1976, involved her reading "the whole of her *Welcoming Disaster* to a graduate seminar (plus visitors) here, a most impressive (and disturbing) poem."

518. Kemp indicated that he would send color prints of Frye later.

519. Vincent Tovell would be sending the New York office of CBC a video-cassette of Frye's television program, "Journey without Arrival." Kemp reports that he and his children, Peter and Susan, would have a special showing of the film.

520. Evelyn Rogers was Frye's girlfriend during his high school years.

521. Frye is referring to Kenneth Walker's *A Study of Gurdjieff's Teaching* (London: Jonathan Cape, 1967), an annotated copy of which is in the NFL.

522. Daniells was honored in 1976 at the annual banquet of the Association of Canadian University Teachers of English held in Quebec City.

523. Frye, who was president of the Modern Language Association, had an executive council meeting in New York City, 19–22 May, and left from there to receive an honorary degree at Coe College in Cedar Rapids, Iowa, on 23 May.

524. Elizabeth Eedy Brown, who would become Mrs. Northrop Frye on 27 July 1988.

525. The Craggs were planning a trip to a cottage in Gravenhurst,

526. The flogging and blood-reciprocity idea does in fact appear in Lawrence's chapter devoted to Dana's

Two Years before the Mast (*Studies in Classic American Literature*, chap. 9).

527. The reference is to a book by John Nance, *The Gentle Tasaday: A Stone Age People in the Philippine Rain Forest* (New York: Harcourt Brace, 1975), which describes a primitive people living in a totally loving community without words for warfare and hatred.

528. Frye did take the trip to Japan, leaving Toronto on 11 May 1977 and returning on 19 May.

529. The passage in question: "For let the words of a country be in part unhandsome and offensive in themselves, in part debased by wear and wrongly uttered, and what do they declare but, by no light indication, that the inhabitants of that country are an indolent, idly yawning race, with minds already long prepared for any amount of servility? On the other hand, we have never heard that any empire, any state, did not flourish moderately at least as long as liking and care for its own language lasted" (qtd. in *CP*, 63).

530. That is, to Rowland McMaster as well, Juliet's husband who also was teaching at the University of Alberta. He has received his Ph.D. in English from the University of Toronto.

531. "One of the roots from which these chapters grew was an abandoned essay on the Waverley novels of Scott. The home I was brought up in possessed a good edition of the Waverley novels, and I had, I think, read them all in early life, with utter fascination. Some years later, at college, *Guy Mannering* was on a course and I reread it, but I had entered the age of intolerance by then, and *Guy Mannering* now seemed to me only a clumsy and faked narrative with wooden characters and an abominable style. I read Scott as little as possible through my earlier professional life, but about twenty years ago I was talking to a late friend whose name it is a pleasure to mention here, Richard Blackmur, about the amount of tedium in modern life caused by plane journeys and waiting in airports. He remarked that he had got through a long and exhausting trip himself with the aid of Scott. "I love Scott," he said. I tried the recipe. Richard was right, as he so often was: when one is travelling by jet plane it is deeply reassuring to have a stagecoach style for a travelling companion" (*SeS*, 5).

532. Fraser's book was published as *A Mingled Yarn: The Life of R.P. Blackmur* (New York: Harcourt Brace Jovanovich, 1981).

533. Eleanor Jess Atwood Gibson.

534. This "Memorandum" was a poem Daniells had written to and about Frye.

535. Singh had earlier forwarded several issues of *Commentary* to Frye.

536. "Comedy and Philosophy in *Man and Superman*," *Modern Drama* 19 (1976): 161–76.

537. "Toynbee and Spengler," *Canadian Forum* 27 (August 1947): 111–13.

538. "*The Decline of the West* by Oswald Spengler," *Dædalus* 103 (Winter 1974): 1–13.

539. "Nature Methodized," *The Griffin* 9 (August 1960): 2–11, a review of Bonamy Dobrée's *English Literature of the Early Eighteenth Century*.

540. Hain's grandfather was Charles Eric "Chick" Hendry, director of the University of Toronto's School of Social Work from 1950 to 1979. Hain reports that Hendry had expressed admiration for Frye's work.

541. Hain had only recently discovered that Frye was an Honourary Fellow of Merton College.

542. "This envelope has come to hand / And, unaware, I licked the band / Not seeing it addressed to you. / And now what shall, what shall I do? / Earth shows not anything more fair / Than Norrie rumpling up his hair / And with the wedge of wisdom's wit / Prepare some knotty log to split. / Good luck and angels' voices guide / Your keen researches far and wide / And, like that mighty moss called sphagnum, / May every opus be a magnum."

543. *Anatomia della critica: Quattro saggi,* trans. Paola Rosa-Clot and Sandro Stratta (Turin: Einaudi, 1969).

544. The revised translation was published in 1972 (Turin: Einaudi).

545. Frye did go on a lecture tour of Italy in 1979 (May 12–June 1), speaking at various venues on Castiglione and on *The Tempest* to capacity audiences in Milan, Vicenza, Padua, Venice, Florence, Urbino, and Rome. See William French, "Frye the Conqueror Wows Them in Italy," *Globe and Mail* 14 June 1979: 15.

546. The reference is to the title Culler's recent book, *Structural Poetics* (Ithaca, NY: Cornell University Press, 1975).

547. *WTC,* 133.

548. The reference is to David G. Pitt's biography of E.J. Pratt, which Pitt had had proposed to Pratt 1960. The first volume appeared in 1984; the second, in 1987.

549. Floss (Florence) Pratt was E.J. (Ned) Pratt's sister.

550. Parker later addressed the meaning of "dilation" in her "Dilation and Delay: Renaissance Matrices," *Poetics Today* 5, no. 3 (1984): 519–35 (for Rahab, see especially 524); in "Deferral, Dilation, Differance: Shakespeare, Cervantes, Jonson," in *Literary Theory/Renaissance Texts* (Baltimore: Johns Hopkins University Press, 1986); and in *Shakespeare from the Margins: Language, Culture, Context* (Chicago: University of Chicago Press, 1996), *passim.*

551. Struthers's inquiry was in connection with a paper he was giving at a meeting in Fredericton, NB, for which he would be leaving on 28 May; so Frye's response did arrive too late for it to benefit Struthers's presentation.

552. *Savage Fields: An Essay in Literature and Cosmology* (Toronto: Anansi, 1977). Lee appropriates Heidegger's notion of "dwelling" in his exploration of the interrelationship between "earth" (nature, instinct) and "world" (civilization, consciousness).

553. The reference is to Robert's *A Stranger and Afraid* (Toronto: McClelland and Stewart 1964), the story of a strange obsession of a young woman.

554. Regarding the contemporary French critics, Culler writes: "Taking as their model not the Jungian archetypes that guide Frye's *Anatomy,* but the concepts and analytical techniques of modern linguistics, these 'structuralists,' as they have generally been labeled, have begun to fill the need which Frye authoritatively described" ("Foreword," *The Poetics of Prose* [Ithaca, NY: Cornell University Press, 1977], 7).

555. Father Walter Ong had just assumed the presidency of the Modern Language Association.

556. Patrick Colm Hogan went on to teach at the University of Kentucky and later at the University of Connecticut as professor of English and Comparative Literature.

557. Norman referred to himself as a "spermologos," borrowing the word from Acts 17:18. The word

means literally a bird that picks up seeds from the field, or metaphorically an empty talker.

558. Frye traveled to Guyana 1–8 January, where he gave two lectures at the University of Guyana: "Why Study English Literature?" and "Literature and the Educated Imagination."

559. Frye's reservations notwithstanding, *Mosaic* did publish a special issue on "Liturgy and Literature" with a dozen articles on the topic (12, no. 2 [1979]).

560. Frye's "The University and Personal Life," *University of Toronto Graduate* 2 (Summer 1969): 36–52, had been reprinted as "The Utopian State of Mind" in the *New Statesman,* 77 (23 and 30 December 1977): 896–900.

561. The reference is to a series of lectures that Frye had been invited to give at Emory & Henry College. He presented the lectures, "Reconsidering Levels of Meaning," on 15–16 March 1979. The lectures were published under that title in *FMW,* 303–26.

562. "A Summary of the *Options* Conference," *University of Toronto Bulletin* 33 (24 October 1977): 6–7.

563. Charles Taylor, "Choice and Master Spirit: Fame Is Pursuing Northrop Frye," *Maclean's* 91 (6 March 1978): 36b–36d. An anecdotal portrait of Frye, written on the occasion of a projected (though never produced) television series featuring Frye on the great heroes of literature. Taylor writes about Frye's life as a student, teacher, and writer, his influence on Canadian writers, his commitment to Canada, his political sympathies, and his personal shyness.

564. John Tuzo Wilson. Fraser had suggested that Frye contact Wilson, who had some unfortunate experiences with a television series on science (see previous note), so as to avoid potential problems. Wilson, Fraser's wife's cousin, was a distinguished geophysicist at the University of Toronto from 1946 until 1974, when he retired from teaching and became the Director of the Ontario Science Centre. He made major contributions to the development of the plate-tectonics theory in the 1960s.

565. Fraser, former music and dance critic for the Toronto *Globe and Mail,* served as the newspaper's Beijing correspondent from 1977 to 1979. He later became columnist (1979–81), national editor (1981–84), and European correspondent (1984–1987) for the *Globe and Mail,* editor of *Saturday Night,* and Master of Massey College.

566. "Northrop Frye and Speech Criticism: An Introduction," *Quarterly Journal of Speech* 56 (December 1970): 417–25.

567. Following one of Frye's sessions at the University of Tennessee, Conville had asked a question about Lévi-Strauss, and Frye replied, according to Conville's letter, by saying that he "had trouble seeing anything from Lévi-Strauss as *useful* (provocative maybe, but not useful)."

568. Douglas had compared and contrasted Frye, a Calvinist Odysseus, and Tillich, a Lutheran Achilles, in his first chapter.

569. "Lutheranism begins with a Catholic monk and ends with a great humanist like Tillich, while Calvinism begins with a Senecan humanist and ends with a poet like Blake who is writing his own parody of the biblical journey from garden to apocalypse" (pp. 7–8 of Douglas's manuscript).

570. Douglas's chapter on Frye was ultimately incorporated in a revised form in his *Positive Negatives:*

A Motif in Christian Tradition (New York: Peter Lang, 1992).

571. The congratulations were for Frye's having received the Royal Bank Award.

572. In one of the commercial systems of the Erewhonians "all mercantile transactions were accompanied with music, so that they were called Musical Banks. The currency in such banks had no commercial value in the outside world" (Samuel Butler, *Erewhon*, ed. Peter Mudford [London: Penguin, 1985], 137–9 [chap. 15]). Butler's point is to parody the idea of spiritual riches one cannot spend. As for the "more physical form," the Royal Bank Award was accompanied by a check for $50,000.

573. The conclusion of an allegory which Daniells wrote in his later years and which was eventually published as *The Current of Time*. See Sandra Djwa's account of the Bunyan imitation in *Professing English*, 393–5.

574. Walter Map (ca.1140–ca.1210), English author of *De nugis curialium* [Courtiers' Trifles], a Latin prose collection of legends, tales, gossip, and anecdotes. A favorite of Henry II, he traveled with the king and became archdeacon of Oxford.

575. Alma Howard, Hazel Merrett's sister and Frye's first cousin, the youngest daughter of his Uncle Eratus Edwin (Rate) and Evelyn Howard. A member of the department of genetics at McGill; she became a distinguished biochemist and made an important discovery about the timing of DNA synthesis.

576. Olive Howard, the wife of Frye's first-cousin Wilbert Howard. Her father-in-law, Daniel Hersey Howard, was the brother of Frye's mother.

577. Merrett had inquired whether Frye's interest in music came from his father's side of the family

578. Hazel Merrett's sons: Timothy was a professor of computer science at McGill; Brian, a photographer.

579. El Saffar has been asked to participate in a special session at the 1978 annual meeting of the Modern Language Association, "Northrop Frye and Hispanic Studies," organized by Luis F. Fernández Sosa. Other participants in the session, held on 29 December 1978, were James A. Parr, Alfred J. MacAdam, and Frye himself.

580. Johnston had written: "It says black tie. I have worn my black tie once since the war & had developed a sort of thing against wearing it, but Jeanne & I got out my old dinner jacket and trousers, which were made for me in 1932 or 3, & with a little letting out, which Jeanne reckons she can do, they will fit. But I'm still not sure about wearing them because I have no black shoes, & I'll not likely get a pair to fit my outsize feet without buying them" (20 August 1978).

581. Forrest Scott, professor of English at the University of Auckland, had a long-standing interest in *Eyrbyggja Saga*, and published an edition of the poem. Scott, incidentally, later wrote an obituary for Frye's Merton College friend, Mike Joseph (*Zelandia*, 22 November 1981).

582. *The Oxford Companion to Canadian History and Literature* (Toronto: Oxford University Press, 1967).

583. That is, the various reference books produced by John Robert Colombo: *Colombo's Book of Canada* (1978), *Colombo's Canadian Quotations* (1974), *Colombo's Canadian References* (1976), *et al.*

584. The Royal Society of Canada, founded in 1882, is a national academy dedicated to promoting exceptional learning, research, and accomplishments in the arts, humanities, and sciences. Its fellows are selected by their peers.

585. Frye presented a paper at this meeting, later published as "The Times of the Signs: An Essay on Science and Mythology," in *On A Disquieting Earth Five Hundred Years after Copernicus* (Ottawa: Royal Society of Canada, 1974), 59–84; rpt. in *SM*, 66–96.

586. Robert D. Denham, *Northrop Frye and Critical Method* (University Park: Pennsylvania State University Press, 1978).

587. This is apparently a copy of El Saffar's paper, "Authority and Subversion in Cervantes and Calderón," which she would present at Columbia University in September 1980.

588. The honorary degree was not offered to Frye at a later date.

589. Johnston has been asked by Elizabeth Cowan, editor of the *CEA Critic*, to contribute to one of the two special issues of the magazine paying tribute to Frye's achievement. He wrote the essay in England and Scotland, the first leg of his European trip, and it was eventually published as "Northrop Frye: Some Recollections and Observations," *CEA Critic* 42, no. 2 (January 1980): 21–5. For Frye's response to Johnston's recollections, see his letter of 24 January 1980, below.

590. Johnston would be awarded a D.Litt. from Carleton University in June 1979.

591. Daniells, their mutual friend, had died from a heart attack on 13 April 1979 (Good Friday).

592. David Knight, *Farquharson's Physique and What It Did to His Mind* (New York: Stein and Day, 1971).

593. Garrett was a Canadian Rhodes Scholar who taught English at Trinity College, University of Toronto, before accepting a position at the University of Canterbury, New Zealand.

594. Joe Clark, of the Progressive Conservative party, replaced Pierre Trudeau as Prime Minister of Canada in June 1979.

595. John Paul II's papal pilgrimage to Poland in 1979 was widely viewed as a crucial moment in Poland's Solidarity trade union movement.

596. Joseph's wife.

597. A number of Kilian's place names in *The Empire of Time* derive from Blake's mythology: Beulah, Los, Eden, Ahania, Albion, Urthona, Vala, Thel, Tharmas, and so on.

598. Ottawa: The Golden Dog Press, 1978.

599. *Taking a Grip* contained several occasional poems, and Johnston reports in his letter that he has recently composed five more.

600. The Johnstons' youngest daughter, who was transferring from Carleton University to Victoria College.

601. Forrest Scott. See n. 581, above.

602. "Further Education Study—NWT 1978."

603. "Fifties Vic," *CEA Critic* 42 (November 1979): 19–22, a reflection on life at Victoria College in the 1950s, on the undergraduates' attitudes toward Frye, and on his influence on her own work.

604. "Northrop Frye and Structuralism: Identity and Difference," *University of Toronto Quarterly* 49 (Fall 1979): 33–47.

605. The reference is to a biography of Roberts by Gwen R.P. Norman, Howard Norman's wife and

Roberts's daughter, which was rejected by Ryerson Press and declared by another reader to be "too personal." Gwen Norman's book was eventually published as *Grace Unfailing: The Radical Mind and the Beloved Community of Richard Roberts* (Etobicoke, ON: The United Church Publishing House, 1998).

606. Norman had proposed having the Fryes come to dinner at his home, along with Nancy and Bill Whitla (Norman's daughter and son-in-law) and Wai Lan and Earle Birney.

607. See letter to Don Thompson and Jim Handley of 3 May 1978, above.

608. Robert Sandler.

1980s

609. Sturges's daughter.

610. Jay Macpherson, Frye's former student and colleague (she taught at Victoria College from 1957 to 1996). Her book, *The Spirit of Solitude: Conventions and Continuities in Late Romance*, was published in 1982 by Yale University Press.

611. "Northrop Frye: Some Recollections and Observations," *CEA Critic* 42 (January 1980): 21–5.

612. Frye had said in *The Educated Imagination* that "the differences [between the creative and the neurotic minds] are more important, but we're not ready for them yet."

613. MacQuarrie was the first person to receive the Burritt/Thompson Award for his work in film.

614. On Frye's Italian trip, see William French, "Frye the Conqueror Wows Them in Italy," *Globe and Mail* 14 June 1979: 15.

615. Frye's colleague in English at Victoria College. MacQuarrie had asked to be remembered to Carscallen.

616. Johnston had written a long, untitled poem inscribed for "Norrie and Helen Frye." In his beautiful calligraphic hand, the poem begins, "MONCTON did you know /that your streets grew / Canada's famousest / speed typist, // and that his childish fare / included Samuel Butler / at your Maritime / bosom, // and Bernard Shaw? Two such / master wits would teach / his wit / to bite." The poem was later published as *A Celebration for Northrop Frye* in Johnston's *Endeared by Dark: The Collected Poems* (Erin, Ont.: Porcupine's Quill, 1990), 237–9.

617. On 9–13 March Frye gave three lectures in New Brunswick, speaking at the Universities of New Brunswick in Fredericton and St. John and then at Mount Allison University in Sackville.

618. Marian and Roy Kemp were Helen Frye's younger siblings. Roy and Mary Kemp's children were Susan and Richard.

619. Helen Frye had lived at 205 Fulton Ave. in Toronto. Her parents were Gertrude and S.H.F. Kemp. The Danforth was a Toronto neighborhood located on Danforth Avenue, between Chester Avenue and Dewhurst Boulevard in east Toronto; the area was known for its architecture and its Greek restaurants and stores.

620. Frye occasionally wrote about the distinction between destructive and creative paranoia in Pynchon. See *DG*, 17–18, and *DV*, 25–6, *RT*, 328, 332, 344, 523, and *NFR*, 185–6.

621. Hollander had written that he was working on a monograph on Pynchon's short stories, which he found "to be at odds with the standard O. Henry model short story."

622. The passage Ellmann had encountered from the section of Howard's autobiography entitled "Dining Out": "I remember a lunch served up in the back bedroom of a second-story faculty flat in Ohio to Northrop Frye, the literary critic, our visiting dignitary at Kenyon College.... I sat at the head of the table, a veritable Madame de Sévigné of central Ohio, exhausted by my labors. I cannot remember one word the great man said, yet getting up from the table I knew that I would dine out on having had him for lunch. I will not bore you with the menu which I do remember down to the last braised turnip in the grande marmite. I was charming too, always that, and knew what to ask, had 'read up on,' if not read his book on Blake. Myopic and proper, bending into his soup, he talked as though we wanted really to say something. I got the impression of a generous man, so committed to his work that he could not fathom my triviality" (*Facts of Life* [Boston: Little, Brown, 1978], 78).

623. Frye and his wife had met Ellmann's parents earlier in Bloomington, Indiana. Ellmann had reported that both of his parents were now dead.

624. Ellmann had asked for Frye to let him know if he and Helen planned to be in England for a visit.

625. Maud was Richard and Mary Ellmann's daughter, identified by Ellmann as "a post-structuralist" teaching at the University of Southampton.

626. Ellmann had indicated that his biography of Wilde existed in manuscript but needed "a lot more work."

627. The book was *Creation and Recreation* (1980), which takes its point of departure from several of Wilde's essays.

628. Frye's lecture, "The Human and the Humane," was never published, at least under that title.

629. That is, the commentaries provided by Fairley for each of the portraits.

630. Booth remarked that he was now embarrassed by the article "The" in the title of his book.

631. Merrett had asked whether Frye would send her an autographed copy of *The Great Code* if she would pay for it.

632. Merrett had written, "I do hope that you are well and all this about your getting frail isn't true." She was referring to a cover story in a news magazine in which the author reported that Frye was becoming "increasingly frail" (Mark Czarnecki, "The Gospel According to Frye," *Maclean's*, 5 April 1982: 40).

633. Comfort's *Tetrarch* (1981) was a fantasy novel set in the lands of Blake's mythology.

634. *I and That: Notes on the Biology of Religion* (New York: Crown, 1979).

635. See Frye's letter to Kilian of 11 June 1979, above.

636. *William Arthur Deacon: A Canadian Literary Life* (Toronto: University of Toronto Press, 1982). Deacon was literary critic for the *Mail and Empire* (1928–36) (later the *Globe and Mail*, 1936–61) and *Saturday Night* magazine (1922–28). A literary nationalist, he participated in and helped to stir up the literary ferment of the 1920s.

637. *Biblical Interpretation: The Old Difficulties and the New Opportunity* (London: Independent Press, 1957).

638. Nicholas J. Perella, Italianist; widely published literary historian.

639. Carla Plevano Pezzini, Valente's friend; they had collaborated in translating Frye's *Fearful Symmetry* (1976).

640. Branko Gorjup, Valente's husband.

641. Frye and his wife Helen has been in Israel from 12 May to 2 June. He had lectured at Bar Ilan University in Ramat Gan and the Van Leer Institute in Jerusalem.

642. Scott had asked Frye whether he was familiar with any biblical interpretations of "the relationship between men and women, and the relationship between mankind and work and childbirth, as being both satisfactory and complete before the fall."

643. "Marxism and English Romanticism: The Persistence of the Romantic Movement," *Romanticism Past and Present* 6, no. 1 (1982): 27–46.

644. Martin had related the story of the absent-minded Pelham Edgar, professor of English, who had left his car running outside a bookstore and, after buying a book he was to review, returned home by public transportation, whereupon he asked his wife where their car was. This story, doubtless apocryphal, was attributed to others, including N.W. DeWitt, professor of Latin and, as Frye says, E.J. (Ned) Pratt.

645. Martin reported that as a student he "probably derived more sheer delight from Rhena Kendrick's lectures on Aristophanes than from any other source."

646. Martin wrote that he once remarked to a clergyman that he thought Genesis could be excised from the Bible with no great loss.

647. Dagg objected to Frye's illustration, writing him on 8 November 1982 to say that "one cannot really compare lions and people.... If one sees 3 lionesses in the Serengeti one often says 'Look at the lions!' If one sees 3 women there, one never says 'Look at the men.'"

648. The difficulties of publishing Innis's papers became insurmountable, and the project fell through, although Frye's essay on Innis, intended to serve as the introduction to one of the volumes, was published in *LS*, 302–6.

649. Susan Kemp Sydenham, the daughter of Helen Frye's brother Roy.

650. Marx had referred to C.S. Lewis's comment that those who read the Bible as literature do not read the Bible.

651. Marx had referred Frye to James L. Kugel, *The Idea of Biblical Poetry: Parallelism and Its History* (New Haven: Yale University Press, 1981).

652. "Postlogue, Postlude, Postscript," Lindenberger's discussion of the articles in an issue of *New Literary History* devoted to "Parodies, Puzzles, Paradigms" (13, no. 3 [Spring 1982]: 33–42).

653. As it turned out, *Cambridge* published nine titles (eleven volumes) in its *History of Literary Criticism.*

654. John Traill, professor of Greek history and epigraphy at the University of Toronto. Traill directed the on-line *Athenians* project, which recorded the names of people who lived in ancient Athens.

655. Harry Woolf was the present director of the Institute, having assumed that post in 1976.

656. Albert Einstein was a member of the Institute faculty from 1933 to 1955.

657. J. Robert Oppenheimer was director of the Institute from 1947 to 1966.

658. Shakespeare's *Comedy of Errors* and *A Midsummer Night's Dream.*

659. *Essays on Canadian Writing* 24–25 (Winter-Spring 1982-83); also published as *Approaches to the Work of James Reaney*, ed. Stan Dragland (Downsview, ON: ECW Press, 1983).

660. Jacques Paul Migne, the French priest who published three great series.(471 volumes) of the writings of the Church Fathers. Frye had access to the volumes at Knox College, the Presbyterian theological school affiliated with the Toronto School of Theology, a federation of seven colleges within the University of Toronto.

661. F.S.C. Northrop.

662. Springfield, IL: Templegate Publishers, 1983.

663. The reference is to Frye's interpretation of "unipeds" in the Icelandic sagas as meaning "people who had only one foot" (*The Great Code*, 43). Dobson thinks "uniped" might be a mistranslation of "einfoetinger," meaning "first-footer" (pioneer or settler).

664. Reid replied on 10 January 1984 indicating that he would wait until the time was ripe for a tour of Italy. The conference on Frye's work, Ritratto di Northrop Frye, eventually took place in May 1987.

665. Two years later Frye did produce a lecture "Vico, Bruno and the Wake," presented at the University of California at Berkeley, the University of Santa Clara, and UCLA (February 1985), and published in Italian in *Mito Metafora Simbolo*, trans. Carla Pezzini Plevano and Francesca Valente Gorjup (Rome: Editori Riuniti, 1989), 163–81. The talk was published in English as "Cycle and Apocalypse in Finnegans Wake" in *Vico and Joyce*, ed. Donald Philip Verene (New York: State University of New York Press, 1987), 5–19; reprinted in *MM*, 356–74.

666. Branko Gorjup, Valente's husband.

667. Todorov replied in his letter of 30 January 1984 that he felt a general overview would be more useful for French readers, who knew little of Frye's work, "*The Great Code* being, on the other hand, a perfectly clear and self-sufficient work."

668. Adams's book had appeared the previous year (Tallahassee: University Presses of Florida)

669. Frye hasn't got the story quite right. Frye's bibliographer actually heard what he thought was "left-handed governor" on CBC Radio.

670. McGibbon replied on 15 February 1984, saying "I still don't understand how they hear left-handed."

671. Pladott had requested that Frye record his opinions in an open letter ("To Whom It May Concern").

672. In Pratt's *The Truant* the Panjandrum was the stupid personification of mechanical force and metaphysical conformity.

673. J.S. Woodsworth was the founder of the Cooperative Commonwealth Federation in 1932, the party having been formed by a number of socialistc, farm, cooperative and labor groups, and the League for Social Reconstruction.

674. The reference is to the first volume of David G. Pitt's biography of Pratt, *E.J. Pratt: The Truant Years*, which was published later in the year by the University of Toronto Press.

675. In one of his op-ed pieces, "The Write Right Rite," Deinert mentioned that Nabokov had never received the Nobel Prize (*The Cornell Daily Sun*, 13 November 1981).

676. A philosopher of history, who was interested in the narrative basis of history as a discipline. He taught at the University of Ottawa and was a Fellow of the Royal Society of Canada.

677. Beattie claimed that neither Engels nor Lenin understood Marx's main thesis about money.

678. This is a reference to the "open letter" of Sandra Beattie referred to in the previous letter, copies of which were sent to some eighty individuals and journals "and 1000 others."

679. Bill Solomon was Frye's first cousin, the son of his mother's sister Tessie Solomon. Merrett had asked Frye for his address.

680. Israel (Izzy) Halperin was in the class preceding Frye's at Victoria College, graduating in 1932. He became a well-known mathematician and taught at Queen's University and the University of Toronto. Merrett has asked Frye for his address.

681. Dr. Francis Rolleston held a number of administrative positions with the Medical Research Council of Canada. He was also Chairman of the Ottawa Research Ethics Board.

682. In her letter of 13 August 1984 Merrett had referred to Dr. Mary Halperin, whom Frye had taken to be Izzy Halperin's wife, rather than his daughter.

683. Thirteen years earlier Frye had written to the Reverend C.R. Moase, "It is thirty-five years since I debated in my mind whether to take ordination or not. In view of the United Church doctrine about the priesthood of believers, I was very dubious about taking orders when I knew that I would not be entering the active ministry. I considered the advice of some of my friends, including some who have since become quite prominent in the church, such as Hal Vaughan. Having made my decision, I do not wish to resign from the ministry, even though that might be the simplest solution" (letter of 15 April 1971). For still other versions of this decision, see Frye's accounts in WE, 522, and NFC, 66.

684. "At the end of the meeting yesterday Woodhouse said wearily, 'any more business?' The last man in the department one would expect to respond to such a challenge got up & said he had something to say. The dissolving department had to be peremptorily summoned back to hear Ned's 'further business.' Ned, beaming, produced a bottle of rye from his bag & we all adjourned for a drink" (Diaries, 307).

685. The talk Frye gave at Brock University was entitled "The Authority of Literature," but as no manuscript with that title is extant, the revised form of the lecture that Frye sent is almost certainly "The Expanding World of Metaphor," a talk he gave at the meeting of the American Academy of Religion Chicago on 8 December 1984.

686. The Canadian Institute for Historical Microreproductions was established in 1978 at the request of Canadian scholars and librarians, with the mandate to microfilm printed Canadian materials, thus preserving them and making them available to researchers.

687. "Academic Graffiti," Acta Victoriana 110, no. 2 (1985): 1, 4, 9, 14, 25, 26, 32.

688. Rosemarie Wolfe (née Schawlow) and her husband Roy has been friends of Frye from the early 1950s. Roy was a professor of geography at York University. He had previously worked for the Ontario Ministry of Highways ("the Province").

689. In his letter of 8 May 1985 Harris sends Frye the news, by way of the president of Marquette University where Wien (now Clementine Terry) had taught philosophy, that Wien had died tragically in a fire in 1984.

690. Because of death in a fire at age 69, as Harris had learned from the president of Marquette University, who sent him a newspaper clipping he enclosed with his letter.

691. The paper was published in SE, 432–67.

692. F.E.L. Priestley had reported to Harris that up to twenty people would attend the meetings of the club.

693. In addition to being registrar, Auger taught in the English department at Victoria College.

694. Robert S. Knox, member of the English Department at University College (1920–57).

695. Hughes had enclosed a copy of his paper, later published as "From Allusion to Implosion: Vico, Michelet, Joyce, Beckett," in Vico and Joyce, ed. Donald Phillip Verene (Albany: State University of New York Press, 1987), 83–99.

696. Northrop Frye on Shakespeare (New Haven: Yale University Press, 1986).

697. Hughes had asked Frye where Joyce speaks of himself as a psychopomp. Frye had written: "The merging of the individual dream with the total dream of mankind appears to be the central postulate on which Joyce's book [Finnegans Wake] is based. In one extraordinary interview, Joyce spoke of himself as a kind of psychopomp summoning the spirits of the dead." Although Joyce does not say this in the conversations jotted down by his student Borach, he does "summon" a number of the themes in the Odyssey which attracted him.

698. George Borach, "Conversations with Joyce," College English 15, no. 6 (March 1954): 325–7.

699. Frye's review of Joseph Pieper's Leisure: The Basis of Culture was later published in LS, 325–9.

700. "Humanities in a New World," in Three Lectures: University of Toronto Installation Lectures (Toronto: University of Toronto Press, 1959), 9–23; rpt. in WE, 69–85. Frye must be referring to the word "leisure," for neither Pieper nor scholasate is in the installation speech. About leisure he wrote, "The point of contact between the arts and the human mind is the moment of leisure, one of the most misunderstood words in the language. Leisure is not idleness, which is neurotic, and still less is it distraction, which is psychotic. Leisure begins in that moment of consciousness peculiar to a rational being, when we become aware of our own existence and can watch ourselves act, when we have time to think of the worth and purpose of what we are doing, to compare it with what we might or would rather be doing. It is the moment of the birth of human freedom, when we are able to subject what is actual to the standard of what is possible. William Blake calls it the moment in the day that Satan cannot find" (WE, 82).

701. Jesus through the Centuries: His Place in the History of Culture (New Haven, CT: Yale University Press, 1985).

702. The interview was published as "Northrop Frye," in Criticism in Society, ed. Imre Salusinszky (New York: Methuen, 1987), 26–42; rpt. as "Criticism in Society," I, 752–69.

703. David W. Strangway, who served as president of UBC until 1997. He had previously served as Chair

of the Geology Department at the University of Toronto and then as Vice-President and Provost of the University and Acting President.

704. *Northrop Frye's Theory of Imagination: A Study of the Theory in the Context of the Work of Bert Case Diltz and Ontario Secondary School English, 1952–1962.* Ph.D. thesis, University of Toronto, 1985. Stewart looks at Frye's theory of education in the context of secondary school English in Toronto during the 1950s. She argues that Frye's theory offers a better model for teaching English than those offered by the reigning educational philosophies in Ontario from the 1950s to the present, particularly the philosophy of Bert Case Diltz. She concludes that Frye's views, unlike those of Diltz, offer a way of looking at literature that is sequential, structured, and coherent.

705. In her letter of 28 December 1932 Frye's mother, Cassie, reported to her nephew Donald that Frye had written an essay on eccentricity during the summer. "He divided his subject into different phases.... Then he put writers, poets, musicians, that is, their works into these classes."

706. The remote outpost in Saskatchewan where Frye had served as a circuit-riding student preacher during the summer of 1934. The principal congregation was at Stone; the two other preaching places were Carnagh and Stonepile.

707. John Ayre's daughter.

708. Dennis Reid's exhibition catalogue, *Atma Buddhi Manas: The Later Work of Lawren Harris* (Toronto: Art Gallery of Ontario, 1985). Reid was curator of the Art Gallery of Ontario.

709. The reference is to Frye's article on an exhibition of Lawren Harris's paintings, "The Pursuit of Form," *Canadian Art* 6 (Christmas 1948): 54–7; rpt. in *RW*, 43–6, and in *NFCanada*, 85–7.

710. *Lawren Harris*, ed. Bess Harris and R.G.P. Colgrove (Toronto: Macmillan, 1969). Frye wrote the introduction to the volume, pp. ix–xii; rpt. in *BG*, 207–12, and in *NFCanada*, 398–402.

711. Dennis Reid, *Canadian Jungle: The Later Work of Arthur Lismer* (Toronto: Art Gallery of Ontario, 1985).

712. All three of these interviews were included in *WGS*.

713. Denham had just accepted a two-year appointment as Director of the Association of Departments of English and Director of English Programs for the Modern Language Association.

714. The fourth collection of Feldman's poems, which was a finalist for the National Book Critics Circle Award.

715. Hazard Adams, *Joyce Cary's Trilogies: Pursuit of the Particular Real* (Gainesville: University Press of Florida, 1986).

716. Walter Ong, *Hopkins: The Self and God* (Toronto: University of Toronto Press, 1986). Annotated copies of both the Kasper and Ong books are in the NFL.

717. Frye is referring to his visit to Smith College, Northampton, MA, 23–25 October 1985, where he presented a lecture, "Framework and Assumption."

718. This preface was later published as "Harold Innis: The Strategy of Culture" in *The Eternal Act of Creation*, 153–67; rpt. as "Introduction to *A History of Communications*" in *NFCanada*, 582–95.

719. Frye was awarded the M.A. in 1940.

720. REED was an international scholarly project devoted to examining the historical manuscripts that provide external evidence of drama, secular music, and other communal entertainment and ceremony from the Middle Ages until 1642, when the Puritans closed the London theatres. It was centered at Victoria College.

721. Frye's second book on the Bible, *Words with Power* (1990).

722. Robert D. Denham, *Northrop Frye: An Annotated Bibliography of Primary and Secondary Sources* (Toronto: University of Toronto Press, 1987). A copy was presented to Frye at the MLA convention.

723. This book, *WGS*, was published several years later (1991).

724. In 1986 Denham had taken a two-year leave of absence to serve as Director of English Programs and Director of the Association of Departments of English for the Modern Language Association. Elizabeth Cowan had held that position when Frye was president of the Modern Language Association.

725. Stevens's paper was "Imagination as Value," presented at the English Institute in 1948.

726. Frye gives a similar account of this encounter with Stevens in an interview published in *Scripsi* (University of Melbourne) 2, no. 4 (1984): 220–6; rpt. as "Making the Revolutionary Act New" in *WGS*, 249–57 (see p. 257); and in *I*, 685–92 (see p. 692).

727. Peter Gzowski interviewed Frye on the CBC program "Morningside," 30 March 1987, on the occasion of the publication of *Northrop Frye on Shakespeare*. Published in *I*, 813–20.

728. Gzowski began the interview by saying, "Now, I'm intimidated. I don't know how to deal with the fact of being intimidated in the presence of Northrop Frye. Are other people intimidated?"

729. Merrett had written that she was not intimidated by her father but that his explanations left her "breathless."

730. The "memoir" was a eulogy read on the occasion of a memorial service for Helen Frye, September 1986. It was published in *FMW*, 39–42. Frye enclosed the "vital statistics" for his mother, father, brother, sister, and wife, along with an explanation of the origin of his and his sister Vera's given names.

731. Merrett had written, "I want you to write a novel — or a play. I think you're old enough and shouldn't let it not be written any longer! Have you ever been tempted?"

732. "Ritratto di Northrop Frye," was held at the University of Rome, 25–27 May 1987.

733. Frye traveled to Oxford in late June 1987 to receive his thirty-fifth honorary degree — a D.Litt.

734. Reaney wrote to Frye on 30 June 1987 that he had been released from the hospital and expected to resume teaching in the fall.

735. Direct references to Blake appear in a number of Morrison's lyrics, including "You Don't Pull No Punches But You Don't Push the River," "Golden Autumn Day," "When Will I Ever Learn to Live in God?" "Ancient of Days," and "Let the Slave."

736. Frye's editor at Fitzhenry and Whiteside.

737. Frye is referring to the edition of his essays edited by James Polk, *Divisions on a Ground: Essays on Canadian Culture* (Toronto: Anansi, 1982).

738. "The Bridge of Language," *Science* 212 (10

April 1981): 127–32; rpt. in *OE*, 153–67, and in *NFMC*, 315–29

739. "Culture and Society in Ontario, 1784–1984," presented as an address at McMaster University, 7 September 1984, and first published in *OE*, 168–82; rpt. in *MythC*, 175–89, and in *NFCanada*, 614–28.

740. "Introduction," *Design for Learning: Reports Submitted to the Joint Committee of the Toronto Board of Education and the University of Toronto* (Toronto: University of Toronto Press, 1962), 3–17. This introduction was included in *OE*, 46–61, and rpt. in *WE*, 127–42.

741. Ten of the eleven papers Frye refers to eventually ended up in *MM*. The essay on Ruth was reprinted in *EAC*.

742. See n. 761, below.

743. See n. 740, above.

744. "Our father's love is to the bastard Edmund / As to the legitimate: fine word, — legitimate! / Well, my legitimate, if this letter speed, / And my invention thrive, Edmund the base / Shall top the legitimate" (*King Lear* 1.2.17–21).

745. That is, the annual report of Germaine Warkentin, Frye's colleague and director of the Centre for Reformation and Renaissance Studies at Victoria University. Frye had made an anonymous contribution of $10,000 to help purchase a 1516 New Testament edited by Erasmus, offered by a rare book dealer for $25,000. After Frye's death the book became known at the Centre as the "Frye Bible" (Germaine Warkentin to Robert Denham, 3 March 2008).

746. See headnote to letter of 5 September 1958 to George Johnston.

747. At the time of the awards ceremony Frye was attending a conference at the University of Rome devoted to his work.

748. The winner of the Governor General's Award for nonfiction in 1982 was Christopher Moore's *Louisbourg Portraits: Life in an Eighteenth-Century Garrison Town*.

749. The proceedings were published as *Ritratto di Northrop Frye*, ed. Agostino Lombardo (Rome: Bulzoni Editore, 1989).

750. The Meech Lake Accord was a set of constitutional reforms designed to induce Quebec to accept the Canada Act, the constitutional act of 1982 that made Canada a sovereign state. Among the Accord's basic principles was a guarantee of Quebec's special status as a "distinct society" and a commitment to Canada's linguistic duality. The Accord died when Newfoundland and Manitoba failed to approve it, leading many Quebeckers to reconsider independence.

751. Lindenberger, professor of English at Stanford, had been a member of the seminar that Frye offered at the University of Washington during the summer of 1951. Lindenberger wrote an account of his summer experience for John Ayre's biography (231–2), and Lindenberger tells Frye that Ayre has sent him this segment from the manuscript of his book.

752. "Now Don't You Think It's Time To Start Thinking," *Toronto Star*, 25 January 1988: M6, which was a reprinting of eight paragraphs from "Northrop Frye Talks about the Role of the Humanities," *Columns* (University of Toronto), Fall 1985: 6–7.

753. Frye reviewed Crane's *The Languages of Criticism and the Structure of Poetry* in the *University of Toronto Quarterly* 24 (October 1954): 92–7; rpt. in *RW*, 131–6, and in *EIOW*, 197–202.

754. Robin S. Harris, *English Studies at Toronto: A History* (Toronto: Governing Council, University of Toronto, 1988). Harris's book includes scattered references to Frye's role in the English department at the University of Toronto. See especially chapters 6 and 7. The Ph.D. theses supervised by Frye (and others) are listed in Appendix 2a of Harris's book.

755. Hine had asked Frye to pass on his love to Jay Macpherson, who had been friends with Hine since her student days at Toronto.

756. A collection of poems (Toronto: Exile Editions, 1989).

757. In his *Barrelhouse Kings* (Toronto: MacArthur and Co., 1998), Barry Callaghan records the anecdote of the clown-nose photo:

> The supper to launch *A Wild Old Man on the Road*—a story about two writers, a meditation on the nature of celebrity, youth and age, fathers and sons, betrayal and love — was given at George Guernon's Le Bistingo by General Publishing, his new house headed by my old friend and first publisher, Nelson Doucet. There were some seventy people there ... the one writer in the country that Morley truly admired and felt affection for — Alice Munro— and the premier, David Peterson, and Zachary flew in from Saratoga, and Peter Gzowski and Greg Gatenby, Robert Fulford and Northrop Frye all had a chair. In charge of chairs, I had mischievously put the actress Gale Garnett beside Frye on a banquette. The great scholar, whose public manner was often "shy reluctance" (masking an enthusiasm for the scatological), eyed her ample cleavage. People kept interrupting with "Good evening, Doctor Frye" and "Very pleased, Doctor Frye," until Gale — a forthright literate woman of gumption, beauty and wit, a trouper in the finest sense (schooled as a girl by John Huston, a star in *Hair*, a companion to Pierre Trudeau, a journalist for *The Village Voice*, novelist and a mature actress in fine movies, including *Mr. and Mrs. Bridge*), said, "Doesn't anyone ever talk to you like a human being?"
>
> "Not often," Frye said.
>
> "I've a cure for that," she said, taking two red sponge balls out of her purse. She squeezed one, it opened, and she clamped it on his nose. She clamped the other on her own nose and the two sat side-by-side beaming, clowns on a banquette.
>
> A film producer from Amsterdam cried, "Norrie, how are you?" Frye stood up and clasped his hands, saying, "Fine, fine." Gale handed out a half-dozen clown's noses and soon Greg Gatenby and Francesca Valente, director of the Istituto Italiano, and Premier Peterson were posing with Frye for snapshots, all clowning, happily wearing red noses.
>
> Frye, sporting a red nose, was strange, but Frye partying among us was more than strange [551–2].

758. Francesca Valente, director of the Instituto Italiano di Cultura, had written Frye on 18 July 1988, asking for an updated copy of his presentation at "The Italian Connection" congress held in Toronto in April 1988.

759. Alma Howard. See n. 575, above.

760. Frye and Elizabeth Eedy Brown, a Victoria College classmate, were married on 27 July 1988.

761. Gordon McLennan had been responsible for publishing *No Uncertain Sounds*, a reprinting of Frye's 1959 address on the occasion of his installation as principal of Victoria College ("By Liberal Things"), along with his sermon, "To Come to Light," delivered at Metropolitan Church commemorating Victoria University's first one hundred fifty years. The small book was privately published as "A Gordon Lawson McLennan Edition" under McLennan's imprint, Chartres Books (Toronto, 1988).

762. "Even though the heavens fall, let justice be done," William Watson's version of the famous maxim of Ferdinand I (1503–64), "*fiat iustitia et pereat mundus*" ("let justice be done though the world perish").

763. Another privately published volume — Robert Francis, *Gusto, Thy Name was Mrs. Hopkins: A Prose Rhapsody* (Toronto: Chartres Books, 1988).

764. On a trip to New England McLennan had given a copy of the book to Katherine Hepburn, the niece of the actress.

765. McLennan had enclosed letters written to Frye by his students, along with their names and addresses, and asked Frye if he would send them some acknowledgment.

1990s

766. The occasion was the Distinguished Teacher Awards, December 1987.

767. The Fryes had vacationed in Iceland the last two weeks of August 1973.

768. Frye and his wife Elizabeth left for the Soviet Union by way of London on 30 September, returning on 27 October after visits to Leningrad, Moscow, and Kiev.

769. Bert O. States, "Northrop Frye: The Anatomy of Wit," *Hudson Review* 40 (1988): 457–79.

770. Frye did give a convocation address on the occasion of his receiving an L.H.D. degree — his thirty-sixth honorary degree at the time — from the University of Bologna, 24 April 1989. It was published as "Convocation Address, University of Bologna" in *LS*, 340–6.

771. Frye had been diagnosed as having a rare form of skin cancer.

772. In her letter of 1 August Bogdan had told Frye about the senate oral of her first doctoral student, who had quoted from liberally from Frye's works.

773. In August 1962 the Fryes traveled to Copenhagen for their silver wedding anniversary.

774. A distinguished Toronto reading series, established in 1974. More that 4000 writers have read at Harbourfront Centre including more than a dozen Nobel laureates.

775. Ayre had told Frye that his daughter Evelyn had starred in a school performance of *The Wizard of Oz*— in French.

776. A children's book in which the narrator-father fractures a number of common fairy tales in telling the story to his two daughters. It was published in an illustrated edition by Viking Canada in 1991.

777. Frye made the point in his review of *The Oxford Dictionary of Nursery Rhymes*, ed. Iona and Peter Opie (Oxford: Clarendon Press, 1951), originally published in *Canadian Forum* 31 (February 1952): 258–60; rpt. in *RW*, 163–6, and in *EIOW*, 146–9.

778. In his 1942 diary, Frye records this encounter: "Met Kay Mabee at Feinsod's: Children's Aid on Isabella. Just through with taking five kids to court, packed in rumble seat, to charge parents with neglect & get custody. She noticed they seemed to be playing some sort of game, & she discovered it was seeing who could amass the biggest collection of fleas" (*Diaries*, 48).

779. Lozynsky explains this description as follows: "There is the act of reading with its tremors and sighs, followed by the act of criticism in which the personal response is set aside and the work examined in terms of various conventions."

780. *Words with Power*, which was published later in the year.

781. *Creation and Recreation* and *Anatomy of Criticism*.

782. Tushingham reported that his mother had considerable skills as a typist herself, producing at the rate of one hundred words a minute, which earned her the Canadian championship in 1923.

783. Ellen Frye Barker, *Frye Genealogy* (New York, 1920).

784. Published posthumously as *The Double Vision: Language and Meaning in Religion* (Toronto: United Church Publishing House, 1991).

785. Staines's mother, who had been speechless from a stroke for some time, had recently died.

Index